Praise for *Dimensions of Human Behavior: Person and Environment* and *The Changing Life Course*

"This is the most thorough and comprehensive text on human behavior that I have seen. It brings together the preeminent sociological, psychological, and anthropological theories on human behavior and the social environment. It covers every possible scenario related to the practice of social work one could imagine. Nothing is sacrificed. The case studies reflected the diversity of the range of consumers of social work services and were utilized well as instruments for understanding and applying concepts."

—Gretchen Heidemann, Whittier College, CA

"I like these books a great deal. I will continue to use the texts in my course. I like the way in which it exposes students to various theories. The dimensions for assessing human development and behavior are clear. Because I use both texts together, I feel that students gained an understanding on human development that is grounded in an environmental context."

—Glenda Dewberry, Augsbury College, MN

"Overall, I think the volume-set is excellent. I love the 'big idea' focus, and the attention to environmental contexts."

—Jim Vanderwoerd, Dordt College, IA

"The three greatest strengths of the book are the inclusion of item/topics of spirituality, case studies, and active learning tasks. The chapters dealing with the lifespan (mainly young adulthood and beyond) and the opening chapters of both books (are also great strengths)."

—Annalisa Enrile, University of Southern California

"I am greatly pleased with the text. It emphasizes diversity. There are good illustrations that bring the concepts to life throughout. It is well organized. I teach in an urban context where students tend to practice with the poor. I like the questions that encourage critical thinking."

—Kimberly Mann, Chicago State University

DIMENSIONS
of Third Edition
HUMAN
BEHAVIOR
The Changing Life Course

Elizabeth D. Hutchison
Virginia Commonwealth University

SAGE Publications
Los Angeles • London • New Delhi • Singapore

For information:

Sage Publications, Inc.
2455 Teller Road
Thousand Oaks, California 91320
E-mail: order@sagepub.com

Sage Publications Ltd.
1 Oliver's Yard
55 City Road
London EC1Y 1SP
United Kingdom

Sage Publications India Pvt. Ltd.
B 1/I 1 Mohan Cooperative Industrial Area
Mathura Road, New Delhi 110 044
India

Sage Publications Asia-Pacific Pte. Ltd.
33 Pekin Street #02-01
Far East Square
Singapore 048763

Printed in the United States of America.

Library of Congress Cataloging-in-Publication Data

Dimensions of human behavior : The changing life course / [edited by] Elizabeth D. Hutchison.
   p. cm.
Includes bibliographical references and index.
ISBN 978-1-4129-4126-6 (pbk.)
   1. Social psychology. 2. Human behavior. 3. Social structure. 4. Social service. I. Hutchison, Elizabeth D. II. Title: Changing life course.
HM1033.D553 2008
302—dc22

This book is printed on acid-free paper.

07 08 09 10 11   10 9 8 7 6 5 4 3 2 1

Acquisitions Editor:	Kassie Graves
Associate Editor:	Elise Smith
Editorial Assistant:	Veronica Novak
Production Editor:	Karen Wiley
Copy Editor:	Gretchen Treadwell
Typesetter:	C&M Digitals (P) Ltd.
Proofreader:	Charlotte J. Waisner
Indexer:	Naomi Linzer
Cover Designer:	Candice Harman
Marketing Manager:	Carmel Withers

BRIEF CONTENTS

Preface   xvii

Acknowledgments   xx

Chapter 1   A Life Course Perspective   1
   Elizabeth D. Hutchison, Virginia Commonwealth University

Chapter 2   Conception, Pregnancy, and Childbirth   39
   Marcia P. Harrigan, Virginia Commonwealth University
   Suzanne M. Baldwin, Virginia Beach, Virginia

Chapter 3   Infancy and Toddlerhood   95
   Debra J. Woody, University of Texas at Arlington

Chapter 4   Early Childhood   137
   Debra J. Woody, University of Texas at Arlington
   David Woody, III, Catholic Charities, Diocese of Fort Worth

Chapter 5   Middle Childhood   175
   Leanne Charlesworth, Nazareth College of Rochester
   Jim Wood, St. John Fisher College
   Pamela Viggiani, Nazareth College of Rochester

Chapter 6   Adolescence   227
   Susan Ainsley McCarter, Charlotte, North Carolina

Chapter 7   Young Adulthood   283
   Holly C. Matto, Virginia Commonwealth University

Chapter 8   Middle Adulthood   321
   Elizabeth D. Hutchison, Virginia Commonwealth University

Chapter 9   Late Adulthood   369
   Michael Melendez, Simmons College
   Peter Maramaldi, Simmons College
   Matthias J. Naleppa, Virginia Commonwealth University

Chapter 10 Very Late Adulthood   417
   Pamela J. Kovacs, Virginia Commonwealth University

References 453

Index/Glossary 543

About the Author 597

About the Contributors 599

Photo Credits 602

DETAILED CONTENTS

Chapter 1: A Life Course Perspective   1
    Elizabeth D. Hutchison
Key Ideas   3
Case Study 1.1: ■ David Sanchez's Search for Connections   4
Case Study 1.2: ■ Mahdi Mahdi's Shared Journey   5
Case Study 1.3: ■ The Suarez Family After September 11, 2001   8
A Definition of the Life Course Perspective   9
Theoretical Roots of the Life Course Perspective   11
Basic Concepts of the Life Course Perspective   11
    Cohorts   11
    Transitions   14
    Trajectories   15
    Life Events   15
    Turning Points   18
Major Themes of the Life Course Perspective   19
    Interplay of Human Lives and Historical Time   19
    Timing of Lives   20
        Dimensions of Age   21
        Standardization in the Timing of Lives   22
    Linked or Interdependent Lives   24
        Links Between Family Members   24
        Links With the Wider World   25
    Human Agency in Making Choices   26
    Diversity in Life Course Trajectories   27
    Developmental Risk and Protection   30
Strengths and Limitations of the Life Course Perspective   33
Integration With a Multidimensional, Multitheoretical Approach   34
Implications for Social Work Practice   36
Key Terms   36
Active Learning   36
Web Resources   37

Chapter 2: Conception, Pregnancy, and Childbirth   39
     Marcia P. Harrigan and Suzanne M. Baldwin
Key Ideas   41
Case Study 2.1: ■ A Change of Plans for Nicole Evans   42
Case Study 2.2: ■ The Thompsons' Premature Birth   43
Case Study 2.3: ■ The Gerekes' Late-Life Pregnancy   45
Sociocultural Organization of Childbearing   46
     Family Diversity   47
     Conception and Pregnancy in Context   48
     Childbirth in Context   49
       Place of Childbirth   50
       Childbirth Education   51
       Hospital Stay   53
Reproductive Genetics   54
     Genetic Mechanisms   54
     Genetic Counseling   56
Control Over Conception and Pregnancy   58
     Contraception   58
     Medical Abortion   61
     Infertility Treatment   63
Normal Fetal Development   67
     First Trimester   67
       Fertilization and the Embryonic Period   67
       The Fetal Period   69
     Second Trimester   70
     Third Trimester   70
     Labor and Delivery of the Neonate   70
Pregnancy and the Life Course   71
     Teen Pregnancy   72
     Early Adulthood Pregnancy   74
     Delayed Pregnancy   75
Risk and Protective Factors in Conception, Pregnancy, and Childbirth   76
Social Work and Challenges in Childbearing   77
     Problem Pregnancies   78
       Undesired Pregnancy   78
       Ectopic Pregnancy   78
       Miscarriage and Stillbirth   79
       Maternal Brain Death   79
     At-Risk Newborns   80
       Prematurity and Low Birth Weight   80
       Newborn Intensive Care   82
       Major Congenital Anomalies   83
     Special Parent Populations   86
       Pregnant Substance Abusers   86
       Mothers With Eating Disorders   88
       Lesbian Mothers   88

Mothers and Fathers With Disabilities   89
Incarcerated Pregnant Women   90
HIV-Infected Mothers   90
Implications for Social Work Practice   91
Key Terms   92
Active Learning   92
Web Resources   93

Chapter 3: Infancy and Toddlerhood   95
Debra J. Woody
Key Ideas   97
Case Study 3.1: ■ Holly's Early Arrival   98
Case Study 3.2: ■ Sarah's Teen Dad   99
Case Study 3.3: ■ Overprotecting Henry   99
Healthy Development in Infants and Toddlers   100
Physical Development   101
Self-Regulation   102
Sensory Abilities   103
Reflexes   104
Motor Skills   105
The Growing Brain   107
Childhood Immunizations   108
Cognitive Development   109
Piaget's Stages of Cognitive Development   110
Prelanguage Skills   113
Socioemotional Development   114
Erikson's Theory of Psychosocial Development   114
Emotional Control   115
Temperament   117
Bowlby's Theory of Attachment   118
Ainsworth's Theory of Attachment   119
Attachment and Brain Development   122
The Role of Play   122
Developmental Disruptions   124
Child Care Arrangements in Infancy and Toddlerhood   124
Family Leave   124
Paid Child Care   125
Infants and Toddlers in the Multigenerational Family   126
The Breastfeeding Versus Bottle Feeding Decision   127
Postpartum Depression   128
Risks to Healthy Infant and Toddler Development   129
Poverty   129
Inadequate Caregiving   131
Child Abuse   131
Protective Factors in Infancy and Toddlerhood   132
Education   132

Social Support	133
Easy Temperament	133
Implications for Social Work Practice	133
Key Terms	134
Active Learning	134
Web Resources	134

Chapter 4: Early Childhood 137

Debra J. Woody and David Woody, III

Key Ideas	139
Case Study 4.1: ■ Terri's Terrible Temper	140
Case Study 4.2: ■ Jack's Name Change	140
Case Study 4.3: ■ A New Role for Ron and Rosiland's Grandmother	141
Healthy Development in Early Childhood	142
Physical Development in Early Childhood	142
Cognitive and Language Development	143
Piaget's Stages of Cognitive Development	144
Language Skills	145
Moral Development	146
Understanding Moral Development	147
Helping Young Children to Develop Morally	148
Personality and Emotional Development	149
Erikson's Theory of Psychosocial Development	149
Emotions	149
Aggression	150
Attachment	150
Social Development	150
Peer Relations	151
Self-Concept	151
Gender Identity and Sexual Interests	152
Racial and Ethnic Identity	153
The Role of Play	154
Play as an Opportunity to Explore Reality	156
Play's Contribution to Cognitive Development	156
Play as an Opportunity to Gain Control	156
Play as a Shared Experience	156
Play as the Route to Attachment to Fathers	157
Developmental Disruptions	158
Early Childhood Education	159
Early Childhood in the Multigenerational Family	160
Risks to Healthy Development in Early Childhood	162
Poverty	162
Ineffective Discipline	163
Divorce	165
Violence	166

Community Violence 166
Domestic Violence 168
Child Maltreatment 170
Protective Factors in Early Childhood 170
Implications for Social Work Practice 171
Key Terms 172
Active Learning 172
Web Resources 172

Chapter 5: Middle Childhood 175
    Leanne Charlesworth, Jim Wood, and Pamela Viggiani
Key Ideas 177
Case Study 5.1: ■ Anthony Bryant's Impending Assessment 177
Case Study 5.2: ■ Brianna Shaw's New Self-Image 178
Case Study 5.3: ■ Manuel Vega's Difficult Transition 179
Historical Perspective on Middle Childhood 181
Middle Childhood in the Multigenerational Family 182
Development in Middle Childhood 183
    Physical Development 183
    Cognitive Development 186
    Cultural Identity Development 191
    Emotional Development 193
    Social Development 194
        The Peer Group 197
        Friendship and Intimacy 198
        Team Play 199
        Gender Identity and Gender Roles 199
Middle Childhood and Formal Schooling 201
    Formal Schooling and Cognitive Development 202
    Formal Schooling and Diversity 204
    Formal Schooling: Home and School 205
    Formal Schooling: Schools Mirror Community 206
Special Challenges in Middle Childhood 209
    Poverty 210
    Family and Community Violence 212
    Mental and Physical Challenges 215
        Attention Deficit Hyperactivity Disorder (ADHD) 215
        Autistic Spectrum Disorders 215
        Emotional/Behavioral Disorder 217
    Family Disruption 220
Risk Factors and Protective Factors in Middle Childhood 221
Implications for Practice 224
Key Terms 224
Active Learning 225
Web Resources 225

Chapter 6: Adolescence   227
    Susan Ainsley McCarter
Key Ideas   229
Case Study 6.1: ■ David's Coming-Out Process   230
Case Study 6.2: ■ Carl's Struggle for Identity   230
Case Study 6.3: ■ Monica's Quest for Mastery   231
The Social Construction of Adolescence Across Time and Space   232
The Transition From Childhood to Adulthood   232
Biological Aspects of Adolescence   233
    Nutrition, Exercise, and Sleep   233
    Puberty   236
    The Adolescent Brain   237
Psychological Aspects of Adolescence   238
    Psychological Reactions to Biological Changes   238
    Changes in Cognition   240
    Development of an Identity   241
        Theories of Self and Identity   242
        Identity Formation   245
        Gender Differences   246
Social Aspects of Adolescence   247
    Relationships With Family   247
    Relationships With Peers   248
    Relationships With Institutions   249
        School   249
        Work   251
        Leisure   251
        The Internet   253
    Relationships With Culture   255
Spiritual Aspects of Adolescence   256
Issues, Challenges, and Problems During Adolescence   258
    Sexuality   259
        Masturbation   259
        Sexual Orientation   259
        Sexual Decision Making   261
        Oral Sex   263
        Pregnancy and Childbearing   264
        Sexually Transmitted Diseases   265
    Substance Use and Abuse   268
        Decision Making About Substance Use   270
        Consequences of Substance Use and Abuse 271
    Juvenile Delinquency   271
    Other Threats to Physical and Mental Health   273
        Violence   273
        Dating Violence and Statutory Rape   274
        Poverty and Low Educational Attainment 275

Obesity and Eating Disorders 276
Depression and Suicide 278
Risk Factors and Protective Factors in Adolescence 278
Implications for Social Work Practice 279
Key Terms 280
Active Learning 280
Web Resources 280

Chapter 7: Young Adulthood 283
Holly C. Matto
Key Ideas 285
Case Study 7.1: ■ Jerome's Break from School 286
Case Study 7.2: ■ Ben's New Environment 286
Case Study 7.3: ■ Carla's Transition to Parenthood 287
A Definition of Young Adulthood 288
Theoretical Approaches to Young Adulthood 290
Erikson's Psychosocial Theory 290
Levinson's Theory of Life Structure 291
Arnett's "Emerging" Adulthood 292
Cultural Variations 294
Multigenerational Concerns 295
Physical Functioning in Young Adulthood 296
The Psychological Self 298
Cognitive Development 298
Spiritual Development 299
Identity Development 301
Social Development and Social Functioning 302
Relationship Development in Young Adulthood 305
Romantic Relationships 306
Parenthood 309
Mentoring 311
Work and the Labor Market 312
Immigration and Work 313
Role Changes and Work 314
Race, Ethnicity, and Work 314
Risk Factors and Protective Factors in Young Adulthood 316
Implications for Social Work Practice 317
Key Terms 318
Active Learning 318
Web Resources 318

Chapter 8: Middle Adulthood 321
Elizabeth D. Hutchison
Key Ideas 323
Case Study 8.1: ■ Viktor Spiro, Assuming New Responsibilities as He Turns 40 324
Case Study 8.2: ■ Helen Tyson, Struggling to Be a "Good Mother" at 42 326

Case Study 8.3: ■ Robert Johnson, Enjoying Fatherhood at 48   327
The Changing Social Construction of Middle Adulthood   328
    Changing Age Demographics   329
    A Definition of Middle Adulthood   330
    Culture and the Construction of Middle Adulthood   331
Theories of Middle Adulthood   332
    Erikson's Theory of Generativity   333
    Jung's and Levinson's Theories of Finding Balance   334
    Life-Span Theory and the Gain-Loss Balance   334
Biological Changes and Physical and Mental Health in Middle Adulthood   336
    Changes in Physical Appearance   336
    Changes in Mobility   337
    Changes in the Reproductive System and Sexuality   337
    Changes in Health Status   340
Intellectual Changes in Middle Adulthood   345
Personality Changes in Middle Adulthood   346
    The Argument for Personality Stability   347
    The Argument for Personality Change   347
    Evidence for Stability and Change in Midlife Personality   348
    Whitbourne's Identity Process Model   349
Spiritual Development in Middle Adulthood   350
Relationships in Middle Adulthood   353
    Middle Adulthood in the Context of the Multigenerational Family   355
       Relationships With Spouse or Partner   357
       Relationships With Children   358
       Relationships With Parents   359
       Other Family Relationships   360
    Relationships With Friends   361
    Community/Organizational Relationships   362
Work in Middle Adulthood   362
Risk Factors and Protective Factors in Middle Adulthood   365
Implications for Social Work Practice   367
Key Terms   367
Active Learning   367
Web Resources   368

Chapter 9: Late Adulthood   369
    Michael Melendez, Peter Maramaldi, and Matthias J. Naleppa
Key Ideas   371
Case Study 9.1: ■ The Smiths in Early Retirement   372
Case Study 9.2: ■ Ms. Ruby Johnson, Caretaker for Three Generations   373
Case Study 9.3: ■ The Moros' Increasing Needs for Care   374
Demographics of the Older Population   374
Cultural Construction of Late Adulthood   379
Psychosocial Theoretical Perspectives on Social Gerontology   382
Biological Changes in Late Adulthood   386

Health and Longevity 387
Age-Related Changes in Physiology 389
Psychological Changes in Late Adulthood 391
Personality Changes 391
Intellectual Changes, Learning, and Memory 392
Mental Health and Mental Disorders 394
Social Role Transitions and Life Events of Late Adulthood 396
Families in Later Life 396
Grandparenthood 399
Work and Retirement 401
Caregiving and Care Receiving 404
Widowhood 405
Institutionalization 405
The Search for Personal Meaning 407
Resources for Meeting the Needs of Elderly Persons 408
Informal Resources 408
Formal Resources 409
Risk Factors and Protective Factors in Late Adulthood 411
Implications for Social Work Practice 413
Key Terms 413
Active Learning 414
Web Resources 414

Chapter 10: Very Late Adulthood 417
Pamela J. Kovacs
Key Ideas 419
Case Study 10.1: ■ Carmen Ruiz Is Institutionalized 420
Case Study 10.2: ■ Bina Patel Outlives Her Son 421
Case Study 10.3: ■ Pete Mullin Loses His Sister's Support 421
Very Late Adulthood: Charting New Territory 422
Very Late Adulthood in Historical and Cultural Perspective 423
What We Can Learn From Centenarians 427
Functional Capacity in Very Late Adulthood 429
Relationships in Very Late Adulthood 431
Relationships With Family and Friends 431
Intimacy and Sexuality in Very Late Adulthood 433
Relationships With Organizations and Community 434
The Housing Continuum 434
Spirituality in Very Late Adulthood 435
The Dying Process 437
Advance Directives 439
Care of People Who Are Dying 440
End-of-Life Signs and Symptoms 441
Loss, Grief, and Bereavement 443
Theories and Models of Loss 445
Culture and Bereavement 448

The Life Course Completed   449
Implications for Social Work Practice   450
Key Terms   450
Active Learning   450
Web Resources   451

References   **453**

Index/Glossary   **543**

About the Author   **597**

About the Contributors   **599**

Photo Credits   **602**

PREFACE

Like many people, my life has been full of change since the first edition of this book was published in 1999. After a merger/acquisition, my husband took a new position in Washington, D.C., and we moved to the nation's capitol from Richmond, Virginia, where we had lived for 13 years. I changed my teaching affiliation from the Richmond campus of the Virginia Commonwealth University School of Social Work to the satellite program in Northern Virginia. While I worked on the second edition of the book in 2002, my mother-in-law, for whom my husband and I had served as primary caregivers, began a fast decline and died rather quickly. A year later, my mother had a stroke and my father died a month after that. Shortly after, my son relocated from Pennsylvania to North Carolina and my daughter entered graduate school. In 2005, we celebrated the marriage of my daughter. These events have all had an impact on my life course.

But, change has not been confined to change in my multigenerational family. Since the first edition of the book was published, we have had a presidential election for which the outcome stayed in limbo for weeks. The economy has peaked, declined, and revitalized. Terrorists hijacked airplanes and forced them to be flown into the twin towers of the World Trade Center in New York City and into the Pentagon near my school. The United States entered military conflicts in Afghanistan and Iraq that continue to be waged at this writing. Thirty-three students at Virginia Tech University died in a mass murder/suicide rampage that shook the campus on a beautiful spring day. Natural disasters have killed and traumatized millions around the world. New communication technologies have continued to be developed at a fast clip, increasing our global interdependence.

Since I was a child listening to my grandmother's stories about the challenges, joys, and dramatic as well as mundane events in her life, I have been captivated by people's stories. I have learned that a specific event can be understood only in the context of an ongoing life story. Social work has historically used the idea of person-in-environment to develop a multidimensional understanding of human behavior. This idea has become popular as well with most social and behavioral science disciplines. Recently, we have recognized the need to add the aspect of time to the person-environment construct, to capture the dynamic, changing nature of person-in-environment.

Organized around time, this book tries to help you understand the relationship between time and human behavior. The companion volume to this book, *Person and Environment*, analyzes relevant dimensions of person and environment and presents up-to-date reports on theory and research about each of these dimensions. The purpose of this volume is to show

how these multiple dimensions of person and environment work together with dimensions of time to produce patterns in unique life course journeys.

Life Course Perspective

As in the first edition, my colleagues and I have chosen a life course perspective to capture the dynamic, changing nature of person-environment transactions. In the life course perspective, human behavior is not a linear march through time, nor is it simply played out in recurring cycles. Rather, the life course journey is a moving spiral, with both continuity and change, marked by both predictable and unpredictable twists and turns. It is influenced by changes in the physical and social environment as well as by changes in the personal biological, psychological, and spiritual dimensions.

The life course perspective recognizes *patterns* in human behavior related to biological age, psychological age, and social age norms. In the first edition, we discussed theory and research about six age-graded periods of the life course, presenting both the continuity and the change in these patterns. Because mass longevity is leading to finer distinctions among life phases, nine age-graded periods were discussed in the second edition and continue to be discussed in this third edition. The life course perspective also recognizes *diversity* in the life course related to historical time, gender, race, ethnicity, social class, and so forth, and we emphasize group-based diversity in our discussion of age-graded periods. Finally, the life course perspective recognizes the *unique life stories* of individuals—the unique configuration of specific life events and person-environment transactions over time.

General Knowledge and Unique Situations

The purpose of the social and behavioral sciences is to help us to understand *general patterns* in person-environment transactions over time. The purpose of social work assessment is to understand *unique configurations* of person and environment dimensions at a given time. Those who practice social work must weave what they know about unique situations with general knowledge. To assist you in this process, as we did in the first two editions, we begin each chapter with stories, which we then intertwine with contemporary theory and research. Most of the stories are composite cases and do not correspond to actual people known to the authors. We also call attention to the successes and failures of theory and research to accommodate human diversity related to gender, race, ethnicity, culture, sexual orientation, and disability.

In this third edition, we continue to use some special features that we hope will aid your learning process. As in the first two editions, key terms are presented in bold type in the chapters and defined in the Glossary. As in the second edition, we present orienting questions at the beginning of each chapter to help the reader to begin to think about why the content of the chapter is important for social workers. Key ideas are summarized at the beginning of each chapter to give readers an overview of what is to come. Active learning exercises are presented at the end of each chapter.

The bulk of this third edition will be familiar to instructors who used the second edition of *Dimensions of Human Behavior: The Changing Life Course*. Many of the changes that do occur came at the suggestion of instructors who have been using the second edition. To respond to the rapidity of changes in complex societies, all chapters have been updated.

⊠ Also New in This Edition

The more substantial revisions for this edition include the following:

- The human life course is placed in global context.
- Advances in neuroscience have been incorporated throughout the chapters.
- More content has been added on the effects of gender, race, ethnicity, social class, sexual orientation, and disability on life course trajectories.
- Greater attention has been given to the role of fathers.
- New exhibits have been added and others updated.
- Some new case studies have been added to reflect contemporary issues.
- Web resources have been updated.

⊠ One Last Word

I hope that reading this book helps you to understand how people change from conception to death, and why different people react to the same stressful situations in different ways. I also hope that you will gain a greater appreciation for the ongoing life stories in which specific events are embedded. In addition, when you finish reading this book, I hope that you will have new ideas about how to reduce risk and increase protective factors during different age-graded periods and how to help clients find meaning and purpose in their own life stories.

You can help me in my learning process by letting me know what you liked or didn't like about the book.

—Elizabeth D. Hutchison
School of Social Work
Northern Virginia Program
Virginia Commonwealth University
6295 Edsall Road
Alexandria, VA 22312
ehutch@vcu.edu

ACKNOWLEDGMENTS

A project like this book is never completed without the support and assistance of many people. A third edition stands on the back of the first and second editions, and by now I have accumulated a large number of people to whom I am grateful.

Steve Rutter, former publisher and president of Pine Forge Press, shepherded every step of the first edition and provided ideas for many of the best features of the second edition that are carried forward in this book. Along with Paul O'Connell, Becky Smith, and Maria Zuniga, he helped to refine the outline for the second edition, and that outline continues to be used in this third edition.

The contributing authors and I are grateful for the assistance Dr. Maria E. Zuniga offered during the drafting of the second edition. She contributed the David Sanchez case study in Chapter 1 and provided many valuable suggestions of how to improve the coverage of cultural diversity in each chapter. Her suggestions improved the second edition immensely and have stayed with us as lasting lessons about human behavior in a multicultural society.

I am grateful once again to work with a fine group of contributing authors. They were gracious about tight timelines and incorporating feedback from reviewers. Most importantly, they were committed to providing a state-of-the-art knowledge base for understanding human behavior across the life course.

We were lucky to be working again with the folks at Sage. Art Pomponio got us started in envisioning what a third edition should look like. Kassie Graves came on board just in time to provide the cheerleading to help us keep the inspiration and focus necessary to accomplish the revisions on an ambitious timetable. In February 2006, I was lucky to have an invigorating day of meetings with Jerry Westby, Kassie Graves, Elise Smith, and a host of other folks at Sage who manage the various stages of turning ideas into books and getting them into the hands of students and faculty. Veronica Novak has managed the flow of work and graciously deescalated my moments of anxiety. Karen Wiley was the capable production editor, and Gretchen Treadwell provided further editorial refinement. Now in the third edition, I know enough to be grateful to a whole collection of people at Sage that I will most likely never meet.

I am grateful to Dean Frank Baskind and my faculty colleagues at Virginia Commonwealth University (VCU) who generously granted me a leave of absence to work on this and other projects. The leave allowed me to engage in intense study of globalization and its impact on human behavior in the United States and around the world. I am also grateful to Dr. Jeffrey Schwamm, Program Director, and my colleagues at the VCU School of Social Work Program in Northern Virginia. They picked up my slack while I was on leave and did so without complaining (at least to me). Danny Wilson and Janice Berry-Edwards competently taught the course sections that would have been assigned to me. Also, my conversations about the human behavior curriculum with colleague Holly Matto over the past seven years have stimulated much thinking and resulted in many ideas found in this book.

My students also deserve a special note of gratitude. They teach me all the time, and many things that I have learned interacting with them show up in the pages of this book. They also provide a great deal of joy to my life journey. Those moments when I encounter former students doing informed, creative, and humane social work are special moments indeed. I have also enjoyed e-mail conversations with students who are using the book, and have found their insights to be very helpful.

My deepest gratitude goes to my husband, Hutch. Since the first edition of this book was published, we have weathered several challenging years and experienced many celebratory moments. He is constantly patient and supportive, and often technically useful. But, more importantly, he makes sure that I don't forget that life can be great fun. Brad and Abby continue to add spice to my life journey; it is such a pleasure to synchronize my life with the transitions in theirs.

Finally, I am enormously grateful to a host of reviewers who thoughtfully evaluated the second edition and provided very useful feedback about how to improve upon it. Their ideas were very helpful in framing our work on this third edition:

Parris Baker
Department of Social Work
Gannon University, PA

Ann Dannerback Janku
School of Social Work
University of Missouri, MO

Glenda Dewberry
Department of Social Work
Augsbury College, MN

Annalisa Enrile
School of Social Work
University of Southern California, CA

Gretchen Heidemann
Department of Social Work
Whittier College, CA

Patti Ivry
Department of Social Work
Western Connecticut State University, CT

Kimberly Mann
Department of Social Work
Chicago State University, IL

Elisabeth Reichert
Department of Social Work
Southern Illinois University, IL

David Spruill
Educational Leadership, Research,
　and Counseling
Louisiana State University, LA

Jim Vanderwoerd
Director, Department of Social Work
Dordt College, IA

Elizabeth D. Hutchison

In memory of my grandmother, Louise Doran, who was such a central figure in the first two decades of my life journey. She gave me unconditional love, delighted me with poems and stories, and modeled integrity and community service.

CHAPTER

1

A LIFE COURSE PERSPECTIVE

Elizabeth D. Hutchison

Key Ideas	3
Case Study 1.1: ■ David Sanchez's Search for Connections	4
Case Study 1.2: ■ Mahdi Mahdi's Shared Journey	5
Case Study 1.3: ■ The Suarez Family After September 11, 2001	8
A Definition of the Life Course Perspective	9
Theoretical Roots of the Life Course Perspective	11
Basic Concepts of the Life Course Perspective	11
Cohorts	11
Transitions	14
Trajectories	15
Life Events	15
Turning Points	18
Major Themes of the Life Course Perspective	19
Interplay of Human Lives and Historical Time	19
Timing of Lives	20
Dimensions of Age	21
Standardization in the Timing of Lives	22
Linked or Interdependent Lives	24
Links Between Family Members	24
Links With the Wider World	25

Human Agency in Making Choices   26
Diversity in Life Course Trajectories   27
Developmental Risk and Protection   30
Strengths and Limitations of the Life Course Perspective   33
Integration With a Multidimensional, Multitheoretical Approach   34
Implications for Social Work Practice   36
Key Terms   36
Active Learning   36
Web Resources   37

❖ Why do social workers need to understand how people change from birth to death?

❖ What do social workers need to know about biological, psychological, social, and spiritual changes over the life course?

❖ Why do different people react to the same type of stressful life event in different ways?

KEY IDEAS

As you read this chapter, take note of these central ideas:

1. The life course perspective attempts to understand the continuities as well as the twists and turns in the paths of individual lives.

2. The life course perspective recognizes the influence of historical changes on human behavior.

3. The life course perspective recognizes the importance of timing of lives not just in terms of chronological age, but also in terms of biological age, psychological age, social age, and spiritual age.

4. The life course perspective emphasizes the ways in which humans are interdependent and gives special attention to the family as the primary arena for experiencing and interpreting the wider social world.

5. The life course perspective sees humans as capable of making choices and constructing their own life journeys, within systems of opportunities and constraints.

6. The life course perspective emphasizes diversity in life journeys and the many sources of that diversity.

7. The life course perspective recognizes the linkages between childhood and adolescent experiences and later experiences in adulthood.

David Sanchez's Search for Connections

David Sanchez has a Hispanic name, but he explains to his social worker, as he is readied for discharge from the hospital, that he is a member of the Navajo tribe. He has spent most of his life in New Mexico but came to Los Angeles to visit his son Marco, age 29, and his grandchildren. While he was visiting them, he was brought to the emergency room and then hospitalized for what has turned out to be a diabetic coma. He had been aware of losing weight during the past year, and felt ill at times, but thought these symptoms were just signs of getting older, or perhaps, the vestiges of his alcoholism from the ages of 20 to 43. Now in his 50s, although he has been sober for seven years, he is not surprised when his body reminds him how he abused it.

The social worker suggests to Mr. Sanchez that he will need to follow-up in the outpatient clinic, but he indicates that he needs to return to New Mexico. There he is eligible—because he is a Vietnam veteran—for health services at the local VA hospital outpatient clinic. He also receives a disability check for a partial disability from the war. He has not been to the VA since his rehabilitation from alcohol abuse, but he is committed to seeing someone there as soon as he gets home.

During recent visits with Marco and his family, David started to recognize how much his years of alcohol abuse hurt his son. After Mrs. Sanchez divorced David, he could never be relied on to visit Marco or to provide child support. Now that Marco has his own family, David hopes that by teaching his grandchildren the ways of the Navajo, he will pay Marco back a little for neglecting him. During the frequent visits of this past year, Marco has asked David to teach him and his son how to speak Navajo. This gesture has broken down some of the bad feelings between them.

David has talked about his own childhood during recent visits, and Marco now realizes how much his father suffered as a child. David was raised by his maternal grandmother after his father was killed in a car accident when David was 7. His mother had been very ill since his birth and was too overwhelmed by her husband's death to take care of David.

Just as David became attached to his grandmother, the Bureau of Indian Affairs (BIA) moved him to a boarding school. His hair was cut short with a tuft left at his forehead, which gave the teachers something to pull when he was being reprimanded. Like most Indian children, David suffered this harshness in silence. Now, he feels that it is important to break this silence. He has told his grandchildren about having his mouth washed out with soap for speaking Navajo. He jokes that he has been baptized in four different religions—Mormon, Catholic, Lutheran, and Episcopalian—because these were the religious groups running the boarding schools he attended. He also remembers the harsh beatings for not studying, or for committing other small infractions, before the BIA changed its policies for boarding homes and the harsh beatings diminished.

David often spent holidays at the school, because his grandmother had no money for transportation. He remembers feeling so alone. When David did visit his grandmother, he realized he was forgetting his Navajo and saw that she was aging quickly.

He joined the Marines when he was 18, like many high school graduates of that era, and his grandmother could not understand why he wanted to join the "white man's war." David now recognizes why his grandmother questioned his decision to go to war. During his alcohol treatments, especially during the use of the Native sweat lodge, he often relived the horrible memories of the bombings and killings in Vietnam;

these were the memories he spent his adult life trying to silence with his alcohol abuse. Like many veterans, he ended up on the streets, homeless, seeking only the numbness his alcoholism provided. But the memories were always there. Sometimes his memories of the children in the Vietnam villages reminded him of the children from the boarding schools who had been so scared; some of the Vietnamese children even looked like his Indian friends.

It was through the Indian medicine retreats during David's rehabilitation that he began to touch a softer reality. He began to believe in a higher order again. Although his father's funeral had been painful, David experienced his grandmother's funeral in a more spiritual way. It was as if she was there guiding him to enter his new role. David now realizes this was a turning point in his life.

At his grandmother's funeral, David's great-uncle, a medicine man, asked him to come and live with him because he was getting too old to cut or carry wood. He also wanted to teach David age-old cures that would enable him to help others struggling with alcohol dependency, from Navajo as well as other tribes. Although David is still learning, his work with other alcoholics has been inspirational, and he finds he can make special connections to Vietnam veterans.

Recently, David attended a conference where one of the First Nations speakers talked about the transgenerational trauma that families experienced because of the horrible beatings children encountered at the boarding schools. David is thankful that his son has broken the cycle of alcoholism and did not face the physical abuse to which he was subjected. But he is sad that his son was depressed for many years as a teen and young man. Now, both he and Marco are working to heal their relationship. They draw on the meaning and strength of their cultural and spiritual rituals. David's new role as spiritual and cultural teacher in his family has provided him with respect he never anticipated. Finally he is able to use his grandmother's wise teachings and his healing apprenticeship with his great-uncle to help his immediate family and his tribe.

A social worker working a situation like this—helping Mr. Sanchez with his discharge plans—must be aware that discharge planning involves one life transition that is a part of a larger life trajectory.

—*Maria E. Zuniga*

Case Study 1.2

Mahdi Mahdi's Shared Journey

Social workers involved in refugee resettlement work are eager to learn all they can about the refugee experience. Social workers in these scenarios are learning from their clients, but they will also find it helpful to talk with other resettlement workers who have made a successful adjustment after entering the United States as a refugee. In this particular case, the social worker has been particularly grateful for what she has learned from conversations with Mahdi Mahdi. Mahdi works as an immigration specialist at Catholic Social Services in Phoenix, providing the kind of services that he could have used when he came to Phoenix as a refugee in 1992.

(Continued)

(Continued)

Mahdi was born in Baghdad, Iraq, in 1957. His father was a teacher, and his mother stayed at home to raise Mahdi and his four brothers and two sisters. Mahdi remembers the Baghdad of his childhood as a mix of old and new architecture and traditional and modern ways of life. Life in Baghdad was "very good" for him until about 1974, when political unrest and military control changed the quality of life.

Mahdi and his wife were married after they graduated from Baghdad University with degrees in fine arts in 1982. Mahdi started teaching high school art when he graduated from college, but he was immediately drafted as an officer in the military to fight in the Iran-Iraq War. He was supposed to serve for only two years, but the war went on for eight years, and he was not able to leave the military until 1989. Mahdi recalls that many of his friends were killed in the war.

By the end of the war, Mahdi and his wife had two daughters, and after the war Mahdi went back to teaching. He began to think, however, of moving to the United States, where two of his brothers had already immigrated. He began saving money and was hoping to emigrate in November 1990.

But on August 2, 1990, Iraq invaded Kuwait, and war broke out once again. Mahdi was drafted again to fight in this war, but he refused to serve. According to the law in Iraq, anyone refusing the draft would be shot in front of his house. Mahdi had to go into hiding, and he remembers this as a very frightening time.

After a few months, Mahdi took his wife, two children, and brother in a car and escaped from Baghdad. He approached the American army on the border of Iraq and Kuwait. The Americans took Mahdi and his family to a camp at Rafha in northern Saudi Arabia and left them there with the Saudi Arabian soldiers. Mahdi's wife and children were very unhappy in the camp. The sun was hot, there was nothing green to be seen, and the wind storms were frightening. Mahdi also reports that the Saudi soldiers treated the Iraqi refugees like animals, beating them with sticks.

Mahdi and his family were in the refugee camp for about a year and a half. He was very frightened because he had heard that some members of the Saudi Arabian army had an unofficial agreement with the Iraqi army to drop any refugees that they wanted at the Iraq border. One day he asked a man who came into the camp to help him get a letter to one of his brothers. Mahdi also wrote to the U.S. Embassy. Mahdi's brother petitioned to have him removed from the camp, and Mahdi and his family were taken to the U.S. Embassy in Riyadh. Mahdi worked as a volunteer at the embassy for almost a month, and then he and his family flew to Switzerland, on to New York, and finally to Arizona. It was now September of 1992.

Mahdi and his family lived with one of his brothers for about a month and a half, and then they moved into their own apartment. Mahdi worked as a cashier in a convenience store and took English classes at night. He wanted to be able to help his daughters with their schoolwork. Mahdi reports that although the culture was very different from what he and his family were accustomed to, it did not all come as a surprise. Iraq was the first Middle Eastern country to get television, and Mahdi knew a lot about the United States from the programs he saw.

After a year and a half at the convenience store, Mahdi decided to open his own moving company, USA Moving Company. He also went to school half time to study physics and math. He kept the moving company for two years, but it was hard. Some customers didn't like his accent, and some of the people he hired didn't like to work for an Iraqi.

After he gave up the moving company, Mahdi taught seventh grade fine arts in a public school for a couple of years. He did not enjoy this job, because the students were not respectful to him.

For the past several years, Mahdi has worked as an immigration specialist for Catholic Social Services. He enjoys this work very much, and has assisted refugees and immigrants from many countries, including Somalia, Vietnam, and the Kosovo region of Yugoslavia. Mahdi has finished 20 credits toward a master's degree in art education, and he thinks he might go back to teaching someday.

Mahdi's father died in 1982 from a heart attack; Mahdi thinks that worrying about his sons' safety killed his father. Mahdi's mother immigrated to Arizona in 1996 and lives about a mile from Mahdi and his family, next door to one of Mahdi's brothers. (Three of Mahdi's brothers are in Phoenix and one is in Canada. One sister is in Norway and the other is in Ukraine.) Mahdi's mother loves being near the grandchildren, but she does not speak English and thus has a hard time meeting new people. In 1994, Mahdi and his wife had a third daughter. About 11 months ago, Mahdi's mother- and father-in-law immigrated to the United States and came to live with Mahdi and his family. His wife now stays home to take care of them. Mahdi is sensitive to how hard it is for them to move to a new culture at their age.

Mahdi and his family live in a neighborhood of Anglo Americans. His daughters' friends are mostly Anglo Americans and Hispanic Americans. Although Mahdi and his family are Muslim, Mahdi says that he is not a very religious person. They do not go to mosque, and his wife does not wear a veil—although his mother does. Mahdi says that his faith is a personal matter, and he does not like to draw attention to it. It is much better, he says, to keep it personal.

This part of the conversation brings Mahdi to mention the aftermath of September 11, 2001, and what it is like living in the United States as an Iraqi American since the terrorist attack. He says that, overall, people have been very good to him, although he has had some bad experiences on the street a few times, when people have stopped him and pointed their fingers angrily in his face. His neighbors and colleagues at work have offered their support.

Mahdi suggests that the social worker might want to talk with his daughter, Rusel, to get another view of the family's immigration experience. Rusel recently graduated from high school and is preparing to enroll at the University of Arizona to study civil engineering.

When Rusel thinks of Baghdad, it is mostly the war that she remembers. She remembers the trip in the car that took her family away from Baghdad, and she remembers being confused about what was happening. Her memories of the refugee camp in Rafha are not pleasant. The physical environment was strange and frightening to her: no trees, hot sand, flies everywhere, no water for a shower, no way to get cool, living in a tent with the sound of sandstorms.

When the Mahdi family left the camp, Rusel did not know where they were going, but she was glad to be leaving. Her memories of coming to the United States are very positive. She was happy to be living in a house instead of a tent and to be surrounded by uncles, aunts, and cousins. At first, it was very hard to communicate at school, but her teacher assigned another student, Nikki, to help Rusel adjust. Rusel is still grateful for the way that Nikki made her feel comfortable in her new surroundings. Rusel is also quick to add that she was in an English as a second language (ESL) program for three years, and she wants everybody to know how important ESL is for immigrant children. Certainly, she now speaks with remarkable English fluency. Rusel also is grateful that she had "Aunt Sue," an American woman married to one of her uncles, who helped her whole family adjust. She knows that many immigrant families come to the United States without that kind of built-in assistance, and she is proud of the work her father does at the Catholic Social Services.

Rusel is an exuberant young woman, full of excitement about her future. She turned somber, however, at the end of the conversation when she brought up the subject of September 11, 2001. She was very frightened then, and continues to be frightened, about how people in the United States view her and other Arabic people. She says, "I would not hurt a fly," but she fears that people will make other assumptions about her.

A social worker who will assist many refugee families has a lot to gain from learning stories like this—about Mahdi Mahdi's preimmigration experience, migration journey, and resettlement adjustments. We must realize, however, that each immigration journey is unique.

—*Story told June 2002*

The Suarez Family After September 11, 2001

Maria is a busy, active 7-year-old whose life was changed by the events of September 11, 2001. Her mother, Emma Suarez, worked at the World Trade Center and did not survive the attack.

Emma was born in Puerto Rico and came to the mainland to live in the South Bronx when she was 5, along with her parents, a younger brother, two sisters, and an older brother. Emma's father, Carlos, worked hard to make a living for his family, sometimes working as many as three jobs at once. After the children were all in school, Emma's mother, Rosa, began to work as a domestic worker in the homes of a few wealthy families in Manhattan.

Emma was a strong student from her first days in public school, and was often at the top of her class. Her younger brother, Juan, and the sister closest to her in age, Carmen, also were good students, but they were never the star pupils that Emma was. The elder brother, Jesus, and sister, Aida, struggled in school from the time they came to the South Bronx, and both dropped out before they finished high school. Jesus has returned to Puerto Rico to live on the farm with his grandparents.

During her summer vacations from high school, Emma often cared for the children of some of the families for whom her mother worked. One employer was particularly impressed with Emma's quickness and pleasant temperament and took a special interest in her. She encouraged Emma to apply to colleges during her senior year in high school. Emma was accepted at City College and was planning to begin as a full-time student after high school graduation.

A month before Emma was to start school, however, her father had a stroke and was unable to return to work. Rosa and Aida rearranged their work schedules so that they could share the care of Carlos. Carmen had a husband and two young children of her own. Emma realized that she was now needed as an income earner. She took a position doing data entry in an office in the World Trade Center and took evening courses on a part-time basis. She was studying to be a teacher, because she loved learning and wanted to pass on that love to other students.

And then Emma found herself pregnant. She knew that Alejandro Padilla, a young man in one of her classes at school, was the father. Alejandro said that he was not ready to marry, however. Emma returned to work a month after Maria was born, but she did not return to school. At first, Rosa and Aida were not happy that Emma was pregnant with no plans to marry, but once Maria was born, they fell hopelessly in love with her. They were happy to share the care of Maria, along with Carlos, while Emma worked. Emma cared for Maria and Carlos in the evenings so that Rosa and Aida could work.

Maria was, indeed, an engaging baby, and she was thriving with the adoration of Rosa, Carlos, Aida, Juan, and Emma. Emma missed school, but she held on to her dreams to be a teacher someday.

On the morning of September 11, 2001, Emma left early for work at her job on the 84th floor of the south tower of the World Trade Center, because she was nearing a deadline on a big project. Aida was bathing Carlos when Carmen called about a plane hitting the World Trade Center. Aida called Emma's number, but did not get through to her.

The next few days, even weeks, are a blur to the Suarez family. Juan, Carmen, and Aida took turns going to the Family Assistance Center, but there was no news about Emma. At one point, because Juan was worried about Rosa, he brought her to the Red Cross Disaster Counseling Center where they met with a social worker who was specially trained for working in disaster situations. Rosa seemed to be near collapse.

Juan, Rosa, and Aida all missed a lot of work for a number of weeks, and the cash flow sometimes became problematic. They have been blessed with the generosity of their Catholic parish, employers, neighbors, and a large extended family; however, financial worries are not their greatest concerns at the moment. They are relieved that Maria will have access to money for a college education. But they miss Emma terribly and struggle to understand the horrific thing that happened to her. They all still have nightmares about planes hitting tall buildings.

Maria is lucky to have such a close loving family, and she has quit asking for her mother. She seems keenly aware, however, that there is enormous sadness in her home, and her hugs don't seem to take away the pain.

A social worker doing disaster relief must be aware of the large impact that disasters have on the multigenerational family, both in the present and for years to come.

⊠ A Definition of the Life Course Perspective

One of the things that the stories of David Sanchez, Mahdi Mahdi, and the Suarez family have in common is that they unfolded over time, across multiple generations. We all have stories that unfold as we progress through life. A useful way to understand this relationship between time and human behavior is the **life course perspective,** which looks at how chronological age, relationships, common life transitions, and social change shape people's lives from birth to death. Of course, time is only one dimension of human behavior; characteristics of the person and the environment in which the person lives also play a part (see Exhibit 1.1). But it is common and sensible to try to understand a person by looking at the way that person has developed throughout different periods of life.

| Exhibit 1.1 | The Relationship of Person, Environment, and Time |

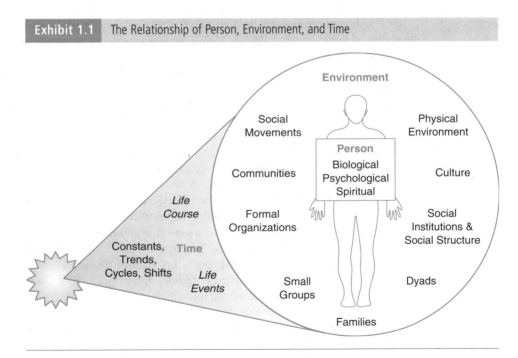

▲ **Photo 1.1**   The life course perspective emphasizes ways in which humans are interdependent and gives special emphasis to the family as the primary arena for experiencing the world.

You could think of the life course as a path. But note that it is not a straight path; it is a path with both continuities and twists and turns. Certainly, we see twists and turns in the life stories of David Sanchez, Mahdi Mahdi, and Emma Suarez. Think of your own life path. How straight has it been to date?

If you want to understand a person's life, you might begin with an **event history,** or the sequence of significant events, experiences, and transitions in a person's life from birth to death. An event history for David Sanchez might include suffering his father's death as a child, moving to live with his grandmother, being removed to a boarding school, fighting in the Vietnam War, getting married, becoming a father, divorcing, being treated for substance abuse, participating in Indian medicine retreats, attending his grandmother's funeral, moving to live with his great-uncle, and reconnecting with Marco. Mahdi Mahdi's event history would most likely include the date he was drafted, the end of the Iran-Iraq War, escape from Baghdad, and resettlement in the United States. For little Maria Suarez, the events of September 11, 2001 will become a permanent part of her life story.

You might also try to understand a person in terms of how that person's life has been synchronized with family members' lives across time. David Sanchez has begun to have a clearer understanding of his linkages to his great-uncle, father, son, and grandchildren. Mahdi Mahdi tells his story in terms of family connections, and Maria's story is thoroughly entwined with that of her multigenerational family.

Finally, you might view the life course in terms of how culture and social institutions shape the pattern of individual lives. David Sanchez's life course was shaped by cultural and institutional preferences for placing Indian children in boarding schools during middle childhood and adolescence and for recommending the military for youth and young adults.

Mahdi Mahdi's life course was also heavily influenced by cultural expectations about soldiering. The economic system is shaping Maria Suarez's life, through its influence on work opportunities for her family members.

◪ Theoretical Roots of the Life Course Perspective

The life course perspective is a theoretical model that has been emerging over the last 45 years, across several disciplines. Sociologists, anthropologists, social historians, demographers, and psychologists—working independently and, more recently, collaboratively—have all helped to give it shape.

Glen Elder Jr., a sociologist, was one of the early authors to write about a life course perspective, and he continues to be one of the driving forces behind its development. In the early 1960s, he began to analyze data from three pioneering longitudinal studies of children that had been undertaken by the University of California, Berkeley. As he examined several decades of data, he was struck with the enormous impact of the Great Depression of the 1930s on individual and family pathways (Elder, 1974). He began to call for developmental theory and research that looked at the influence of historical forces on family, education, and work roles.

At about the same time, social history emerged as a serious field. Social historians were particularly interested in retrieving the experiences of ordinary people, from their own vantage point, rather than telling the historical story from the vantage point of the wealthy and powerful. Tamara Hareven (1978, 1982b, 1996, 2000) has played a key role in developing the subdiscipline of the history of the family. She is particularly interested in how families change and adapt under changing historical conditions and how individuals and families synchronize their lives to accommodate to changing social conditions.

As will become clearer later in the chapter, the life course perspective also draws on traditional theories of developmental psychology, which look at the events that typically occur in people's lives during different stages. The life course perspective differs from these psychological theories in one very important way, however. Developmental psychology looks for universal, predictable events and pathways, but the life course perspective calls attention to how historical time, social location, and culture affect the individual experience of each life stage.

◪ Basic Concepts of the Life Course Perspective

Scholars who write from a life course perspective and social workers who apply the life course perspective in their work rely on a handful of staple concepts: cohorts, transitions, trajectories, life events, and turning points (see Exhibit 1.2 for concise definitions). As you read about each concept, imagine how it applies to the lives of David Sanchez, Mahdi Mahdi, and Maria Suarez, as well as to your own life.

Cohorts

With their attention to the historical context of developmental pathways, life course scholars have found the concept of cohort to be very useful. In the life course perspective, a **cohort** is a group of persons who were born at the same historical time and who experience particular social changes within a given culture in the same sequence and at the same age (Alwin & McCammon, 2003; Newman, 2006; Settersten, 2003a; Settersten & Mayer, 1997).

Exhibit 1.2	Basic Concepts of the Life Course Perspective

Cohort: Group of persons who were born at the same historical time and who experience particular social changes within a given culture in the same sequence and at the same age

Transition: Change in roles and statuses that represents a distinct departure from prior roles and statuses

Trajectory: Long-term pattern of stability and change, which usually involves multiple transitions

Life Event: Significant occurrence involving a relatively abrupt change that may produce serious and long-lasting effects

Turning Point: Life event that produces a lasting shift in the life course trajectory

Cohorts differ in size, and these differences affect opportunities for education, work, and family life. For example, the baby boom that followed World War II (born 1946 to 1964) in the United States produced a large cohort. When this large cohort entered the labor force, surplus labor drove wages down and unemployment up (Pearlin & Skaff, 1996; Uhlenberg, 1996). Similarly, the large "baby boom echo" cohort, sometimes called generation Y or the millennium generation (born 1980 to late 1990s), began competing for slots in prestigious universities at the beginning of the twenty-first century (Argetsinger, 2001).

Some observers suggest that cohorts develop strategies for the special circumstances they face (Easterlin, Schaeffer, & Macunovich, 1993). They suggest that "boomers" responded to the economic challenges of their demographic bubble by delaying or avoiding marriage, postponing childbearing, having fewer children, and increasing the presence of mothers in the labor force. However, one study found that large cohorts in affluent countries have higher rates of suicide than smaller cohorts, suggesting that not all members of large cohorts can find positive strategies for coping with competition for limited resources (Stockard & O'Brien, 2002).

One way to visualize the configuration of cohorts in a given society is through the use of a **population pyramid,** a chart that depicts the proportion of the population in each age group. As Exhibit 1.3 demonstrates, different regions of the world have significantly different population pyramids. In nonindustrial and recently industrializing countries (in Africa, Southeast Asia, Latin America, India, and the Middle East), fertility rates are high and life expectancies are low, leading to a situation in which the majority of people are young. In these countries, young people tend to overwhelm labor markets and education systems, and national standards of living decline. Some of these countries, such as the Philippines, have developed policies that encourage out-migration while other countries, such as China, have developed policies to limit fertility. In affluent, late industrial countries (Europe, North America, Japan), fertility rates are low and life expectancy is high, resulting in large numbers of older adults and a declining youthful population. These countries are becoming increasingly dependent on immigration (typically more attractive to young adults) for a work force to support the aging population. In the United States, migration of legal and illegal immigrants accounted for more than one-fourth of the population growth in the 1980s and for about one-third of the growth in the 1990s (McFalls, 1998). High rates of immigration are continuing in the early part of the twenty-first century, but despite the economic necessity of immigrants, in the United States, as in many other affluent countries, there are strong anti-immigrant sentiments and angry calls to close the borders.

▲ **Photo 1.2**   Marriage is a life transition, which is a significant occurrence with long-lasting effects.

Exhibit 1.3 also shows the ratio of males to females in each population. A cohort's **sex ratio** is the number of males per 100 females. Sex ratios affect a cohort's marriage rates, childbearing practices, crime rates, and family stability. Although there are many challenges to getting reliable sex ratio data, it is estimated that there are 101 males for every 100 females in the world (Clarke & Craven, 2005). In most parts of the world, 104–108 males are born for every 100 female births. However, in countries where there is a strong preference for male children, such as China, Taiwan, and South Korea, female abortion and female infanticide have led to sex ratios of 110 at birth (Clarke & Craven, 2005). As you can see in Exhibit 1.3, sex ratios decline across adulthood because males die at higher rates at every age. Again, there are exceptions to this trend in impoverished countries with strong male preference, where female children may be abandoned, neglected, given less food, or given up for foreign adoption (Newman, 2006). Sex ratios can be further unbalanced by war (which leads to greater male mortality) or high rates of either male or female out-migration or in-migration.

For some time, sex ratios at birth have been lower for blacks than for whites in the United States, meaning that fewer black boy babies are born per 100 girl babies than is the case in the white population (see Ulizzi & Zonta, 1994). This disparity holds up across the life course, with a sex ratio of 81 men to 100 women among black adults over age 18 compared to 94 men to 100 women among white adults. When this difference in sex ratios is juxtaposed with a growing disadvantage of black men in the labor market and their increasing rates of incarceration, it is not surprising that a greater percentage of black adults (39%) than white adults (21%) had never been married in 1999 (U.S. Bureau of the Census, 2000).

Exhibit 1.3	Population Pyramids in Less Developed and Developed Countries

SOURCE: Newman, 2006.

Transitions

A life course perspective is stage-like because it proposes that each person experiences a number of **transitions,** or changes in roles and statuses that represent a distinct departure from prior roles and statuses (Elder & Kirkpatrick Johnson, 2003; George, 1993; Hagestad, 2003). Life is full of such transitions: starting school, entering puberty, leaving school, getting a first job, leaving home, retiring, and so on. Leaving his grandmother's home for boarding school and enrolling in the military were important transitions for David Sanchez. Rusel Mahdi is excited about the transition from high school to college.

Many transitions relate to family life: marriages, births, divorces, remarriages, deaths (Carter & McGoldrick, 2005a; Hagestad, 2003). Each transition changes family statuses and roles and generally is accompanied by family members' exits and entrances. We can see the dramatic effects of birth and death on the Suarez family as Maria entered and Emma exited the family circle.

Transitions in collectivities other than the family, such as small groups, communities, and formal organizations, also involve exits and entrances of members, as well as changes in statuses and roles. In college, for example, students pass through in a steady stream. Some of them make the transition from undergraduate to graduate student, and in that new status they may take on the new role of teaching or research assistant.

Trajectories

The changes involved in transitions are discrete and bounded; when they happen, an old phase of life ends and a new phase begins. In contrast, **trajectories** involve a longer view of long-term patterns of stability and change in a person's life, involving multiple transitions (Elder & Kirkpatrick Johnson, 2003; George, 2003; Heinz, 2003). We do not necessarily expect trajectories to be a straight line, but we do expect them to have some continuity of direction. For example, we assume that once David Sanchez became addicted to alcohol, he set forth on a path of increased use of alcohol and deteriorating ability to uphold his responsibilities, with multiple transitions involving family disruption and job instability.

Because individuals and families live their lives in multiple spheres, their lives are made up of multiple, intersecting trajectories—such as educational trajectories, family life trajectories, health trajectories, and work trajectories (Cooksey, Menaghan,& Jekielek, 1997; George, 2003; Heinz, 2003; Settersten & Mayer, 1997; Shanahan, Miech, & Elder, 1998). These interlocking trajectories can be presented visually on separate lifeline charts or as a single lifeline. See Exhibit 1.4 for instructions on completing a lifeline of interlocking trajectories.

| Exhibit 1.4 | My Lifeline (Interlocking Trajectories) |

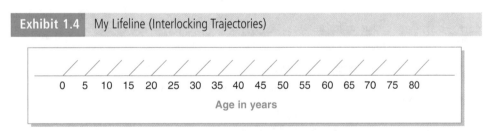

Assuming that you live until at least 80 years of age, chart how you think your life course trajectory will look. Write in major events and transitions at the appropriate ages. To get a picture of the interlocking trajectories of your lifeline, you may want to write family events and transitions in one color, educational events and transitions in another, occupational events and transitions in another, and health events and transitions in another.

Life Events

Specific events predominate in the stories of David Sanchez, Mahdi Mahdi, and Maria Suarez: death of a parent, escape from the homeland, terrorist attack. A **life event** is a significant occurrence involving a relatively abrupt change that may produce serious and long-lasting effects (Settersten, 2003a; Settersten & Mayer, 1997). The term refers to the happening itself and not to the transitions that will occur because of the happening. A transition is a more gradual change that occurs with a life event.

One common method for evaluating the effect of such stressful events is Thomas Holmes & Richard Rahe's Schedule of Recent Events, also called the Social Readjustment Rating Scale (Holmes, 1978; Holmes & Rahe, 1967). The Schedule of Recent Events, along with the rating of the stress associated with each event, appears in Exhibit 1.5. Holmes and Rahe constructed their schedule of events by asking respondents to rate the relative degree of adjustment required for different life events.

Exhibit 1.5	Life Change Events From the Holmes and Rahe Schedule of Recent Events

Life Event	Stress Rating
Death of a spouse	100
Divorce	73
Marital separation from mate	65
Detention in jail or other institutions	63
Death of a close family member	63
Major personal injury or illness	53
Marriage	50
Being fired at work	47
Marital reconciliation with mate	45
Retirement from work	45
Major change in the health or behavior of a family member	44
Pregnancy	40
Sexual difficulties	39
Gaining a new family member (e.g., through birth, adoption, elder moving in)	39
Major business readjustment (e.g., merger, reorganization, bankruptcy)	39
Major change in financial state (a lot worse off or a lot better off than usual)	38
Death of a close friend	37
Changing to a different line of work	36
Major change in the number of arguments with spouse (more or less)	35
Taking out a mortgage or loan for a major purchase	31
Foreclosure on a mortgage or loan	30
Major change in responsibilities at work (e.g., promotion, demotion, lateral transfer)	29
Son or daughter leaving home	29
Trouble with in-laws	29
Outstanding personal achievement	28
Wife beginning or ceasing work outside the home	26

Life Event	Stress Rating
Beginning or ceasing formal schooling	19
Major change in living conditions (e.g., building a new home, remodeling, deterioration of home or neighborhood)	19
Revision of personal habits (e.g., dress, manners, associations)	18
Trouble with the boss	17
Major change in working hours or conditions	16
Change in residence	15
Change to a new school	15
Major change in usual type and/or amount of recreation	13
Major change in church activities (e.g., a lot more or a lot less than usual)	12
Major change in social activities (e.g., clubs, dancing, movies, visiting)	11
Taking out a mortgage or loan for a lesser purchase (e.g., for a car, TV, freezer)	26
Major change in sleeping habits (a lot more or a lot less sleep, or change in part of day when asleep)	25
Major change in number of family get-togethers (e.g., a lot more or a lot less than usual)	24
Major change in eating habits (a lot less food intake or very different meal hours or surroundings	23
Vacation	20
Christmas	20
Minor violations of the law (e.g., traffic tickets, jaywalking, disturbing the peace)	20

SOURCE: Holmes, T. (1978). Life situations, emotions, and disease. *Psychosomatic Medicine, 19,* 747.

Inventories like the Schedule of Recent Events can remind us of some of the life events that affect human behavior and life course trajectories, but they also have limitations:

Life events inventories are not finely tuned. One suggestion is to classify life events along several dimensions: "major versus minor, anticipated versus unanticipated, controllable versus uncontrollable, typical versus atypical, desirable versus undesirable, acute versus chronic." (Settersten & Mayer, 1997, p. 246)

Existing inventories are biased toward undesirable, rather than desirable, events. Not all life events prompt harmful life changes (Pearlin & Skaff, 1996).

Specific life events have different meanings to various individuals and to various collectivities. Those distinctive meanings have not been measured in most research on life events (George, 1996; Hareven, 2000). One example of a study that has taken different meanings into account found that women report more vivid memories of life events in relationships than men report (Ross & Holmberg, 1992).

Life events' inventories are biased toward events more commonly experienced by certain groups of people: young adults, men, whites, and the middle-class (Settersten & Mayer, 1997, p. 246). In one small exploratory study that used a lifeline rather than an inventory of events in an attempt to correct for this bias, women reported a greater number of life events than men did (de Vries & Watt, 1996). Researchers have also developed a Children's Life Events Inventory, which has been used to study minority children and youth (Monaghan, Robinson, & Dodge, 1979) and an inventory to capture military events in the Chinese army (Hong-zheng, Zue-rong, & Mei-ying, 2004).

Turning Points

David Sanchez describes becoming an apprentice medicine man as a turning point in his life. For Mahdi Mahdi, the decision to refuse the draft was a turning point. Even though Maria Suarez was too young to think of September 11, 2001 as a turning point in her life, there is no doubt that the events of that day changed the course of her life. A **turning point** is a point in the life course that represents a substantial change or discontinuity in direction; it serves as a lasting change and not just a temporary detour (Rutter, 1996). As significant as they are to individuals' lives, turning points usually become obvious only as time passes (Wheaton & Gotlib, 1997). Yet in one survey, more than 85% of the respondents reported that there had been turning points in their lives (Clausen, 1990, cited in Wheaton & Gotlib, 1997). According to traditional developmental theory, the developmental trajectory is more or less continuous, proceeding steadily from one phase to another. But life course trajectories are seldom so smooth and predictable. They involve many discontinuities, or sudden breaks, and some special life events become turning points that produce a lasting shift in the life course trajectory. Inertia tends to keep us on a particular trajectory, but turning points add twists and turns or even reversals to the life course (Wheaton & Gotlib, 1997). For example, we expect someone who is addicted to alcohol to continue to organize his or her life around that substance unless some event becomes a turning point for recovery (Schulenberg, Maggs, & O'Malley, 2003).

Longitudinal research indicates that three types of life events can serve as turning points (Rutter, 1996):

1. Life events that either close or open opportunities

2. Life events that make a lasting change on the person's environment

3. Life events that change a person's self-concept, beliefs, or expectations

Some events, such as migration to a new country, are momentous because they qualify as all three types of events (Jasso, 2003). Migration, whether voluntary or involuntary, certainly makes a lasting change on the environment in which the person lives; it may also close and open opportunities and cause a change in self-concept and beliefs. Certainly, that seems to be the case with Mahdi Mahdi. Keep in mind, however, that individuals make subjective assessments of life events (George, 1996). The same type of life event may be a turning point for one individual, family, or other collectivity, but not for another. Less dramatic transitions may also become turning points, depending on the individual's assessment of its importance. An Australian study of women found a change in the nature of turning points in midlife—before midlife, turning points were likely to be related to role transitions; but after midlife, they were more likely to be related to personal growth (Leonard, 2006). A transition can become a turning point under five conditions (Hareven, 2000):

1. When the transition occurs simultaneously with a crisis or is followed by a crisis

2. When the transition involves family conflict over the needs and wants of individuals and the greater good of the family unit

3. When the transition is "off-time," meaning that it does not occur at the typical stage in life

4. When the transition is followed by unforeseen negative consequences

5. When the transition requires exceptional social adjustments

Loss of a parent is not always a turning point, but when such a loss occurs off-time, as it did with David Sanchez and Maria Suarez, it is often a turning point. Emma Suarez may not have thought of her decision to take a job in the World Trade Center as a turning point, because she could not foresee the events of September 11, 2001.

Most life course pathways include multiple turning points, some that send life trajectories off track and others that bring life trajectories back on track (Wheaton & Gotlib, 1997). David Sanchez's Vietnam experience seems to have gotten him off track, and his grandmother's death seems to have gotten him back on track. In fact, we could say that the intent of many social work interventions is to get life course trajectories back on track. We sometimes do this when we work with a family that has gotten off track and on a path to divorce. We also do this when we plan interventions to precipitate a turning point toward recovery for a client with an addiction. Or, we may plan an intervention to help a deteriorating community reclaim its lost sense of community and spirit of pride. It is interesting to note that many social service organizations have taken "Turning Point" for their name.

⊠ Major Themes of the Life Course Perspective

Over a decade ago, Glen Elder (1994) identified four dominant, and interrelated, themes in the life course approach: interplay of human lives and historical time, timing of lives, linked or interdependent lives, and human agency in making choices. The meaning of these themes is discussed below, along with the meaning of two other related themes that Elder (1998) and Michael Shanahan (2000) have recently identified as important: diversity in life course trajectories and developmental risk and protection. The meaning of these themes is summarized in Exhibit 1.6.

Interplay of Human Lives and Historical Time

As sociologists and social historians began to study individual and family life trajectories, they noted that persons born in different years face different historical worlds, with different options and constraints—especially in rapidly changing societies, such as the United States at the beginning of the twenty-first century. They suggested that historical time may produce

Exhibit 1.6	Major Themes of the Life Course Perspective

Interplay of human lives and historical time: Individual and family development must be understood in historical context.

Timing of lives: Particular roles and behaviors are associated with particular age groups, based on biological age, psychological age, social age, and spiritual age.

Linked or interdependent lives: Human lives are interdependent, and the family is the primary arena for experiencing and interpreting wider historical, cultural, and social phenomena.

Human agency in making choices: The individual life course is constructed by the choices and actions individuals take within the opportunities and constraints of history and social circumstances.

Diversity in life course trajectories: There is much diversity in life course pathways, due to cohort variations, social class, culture, gender, and individual agency.

Developmental risk and protection: Experiences with one life transition have an impact on subsequent transitions and events, and may either protect the life course trajectory or put it at risk.

cohort effects when distinctive formative experiences are shared at the same point in the life course and have a lasting impact on a birth cohort (Alwin & McCammon, 2003). The same historical events may affect different cohorts in different ways. For example, Elder's (1974) research on children and the Great Depression found that the life course trajectories of the cohort that were young children at the time of the economic downturn were more seriously affected by family hardship than the cohort that were in middle childhood and late adolescence at the time.

Analysis of large data sets by a number of researchers provides forceful evidence that changes in other social institutions impinge on family and individual life course trajectories (e.g., Cooksey et al., 1997; Elder, 1986; Rindfuss, Swicegood, & Rosenfeld, 1987; Shanahan et al., 1998). Tamara Hareven's historical analysis of family life (2000) documents the lag between social change and the development of public policy to respond to the new circumstances and the needs that arise with social change (see also Riley, 1996). One such lag today is the lag between trends in employment among mothers and public policy regarding child care during infancy and early childhood. Social work planners and administrators confront the results of such a lag in their work. Thus, they have some responsibility to keep the public informed about the impact of changing social conditions on individuals, families, communities, and formal organizations.

Timing of Lives

"How old are you?" You have probably been asked that question many times, and no doubt you find yourself curious about the age of new acquaintances. Every society appears to use age as an important variable, and many social institutions in advanced industrial societies are organized, in part, around age—the age for starting school, the age of majority, retirement age, and so on (Settersten, 2003b; Settersten & Mayer, 1997). In the United States, our speech abounds with expressions related to age: "terrible 2s," "sweet 16," "20-something," "life begins at 40," "senior discounts," and lately "60 is the new 40."

Age is also a prominent attribute in efforts by social scientists to bring order and predictability to our understanding of human behavior. Life course scholars are interested in the age at which specific life events and transitions occur, which they refer to as the timing of lives. They may classify entrances and exits from particular statuses and roles as "off-time" or "on-time," based on social norms or shared expectations about the timing of such transitions (George, 1993; Settersten, 2003b). For example, child labor and childbearing in adolescence are considered off-time in modern industrial countries, but in much of the world, such timing of roles is seen as a part of the natural order (Dannefer, 2003a, 2003b). Likewise, death in early or middle adulthood is considered off-time in modern industrial societies, but, due to the HIV/AIDS epidemic, has now become commonplace in much of Africa. Survivors' grief is probably deeper in cases of "premature loss" (Pearlin & Skaff, 1996), which is perhaps why Emma Suarez's family keeps saying, "She was so young; she had so much life left." Certainly, David Sanchez reacted differently to his father's and his grandmother's deaths.

Dimensions of Age

Chronological age itself is not the only factor involved in timing of lives. Age-graded differences in roles and behaviors are the result of biological, psychological, social, and spiritual processes. Thus, age is often considered from each of the perspectives that make up the biopsychosocial framework (e.g., Cavanaugh, 1996; Kimmel, 1990; Settersten & Mayer, 1997). Although life course scholars have not directly addressed the issue of spiritual age, it is an important perspective as well.

Biological age indicates a person's level of biological development and physical health, as measured by the functioning of the various organ systems. It is the present position of the biological person in relation to the potential life cycle. There is no simple, straightforward way to measure biological age. Any method for calculating it has been altered by changes in life expectancy (Shanahan, 2000) and by changes in the main causes of death (Bartley, Blane, & Montgomery, 1997). With the development of modern medicine, the causes of death have shifted from infectious diseases to chronic diseases (National Center for Health Statistics, 2001a). Life course researchers need to collaborate with geneticists to understand the effect on biological age of late-emerging genetic factors and with endocrinologists to understand how social processes are related to biological aging (Shanahan, 2000).

Psychological age has both behavioral and perceptual components. Behaviorally, psychological age refers to the capacities that people have and the skills they use to adapt to changing biological and environmental demands. Skills in memory, learning, intelligence, motivation, emotions, and so forth are all involved (Settersten & Mayer, 1997). Perceptually, psychological age is based on how old people perceive themselves to be. Life course researchers have explored the perceptual aspect of psychological age since the 1960s, sometimes with questions such as, "Do you feel that you are young, middle-aged, old, or very old?" (e.g., Barak & Stern, 1986; Markides & Boldt, 1983). Researchers have also used a more multifaceted way of exploring perceived age. Some have distinguished between "feel-age, look-age, do-age, and interests-age" (Henderson, Goldsmith, & Flynn, 1995). Anthropological examination of life transitions suggests that men and women attach different social meanings to age and use different guidelines for measuring how old they are (Hagestad, 1991), but empirical research on the role gender plays in self-perceived age is mixed. Culture is another factor in perceptions of age. In one study, the researchers found less discrepancy between chronological age and self-perceived age among a Finnish sample than among a U.S. sample, with the U.S. sample demonstrating a definite tendency to say they considered themselves more youthful than their chronological age (Uotinen, 1998).

Social age refers to the age-graded roles and behaviors expected by society—in other words, the socially constructed meaning of various ages. The concept of **age norm** is used to indicate the behaviors that are expected of people of a specific age in a given society at a particular point in time. Age norms may be informal expectations, or they may be encoded as formal rules and laws. For example, cultures have an informal age norm about the appropriate age to begin romantic dating, if romantic dating is the method used for mate selection. On the other hand, many countries have developed formal rules about the appropriate age for driving, drinking alcohol, and voting. Life course scholars suggest that age norms vary not only across historical time and across societies but also by gender, race, ethnicity, and social class within a given time and society (Chudacoff, 1989; Kertzer, 1989; Settersten, 2003b; Settersten & Mayer, 1997).

Although biological age and psychological age are recognized in the life course perspective, social age receives special emphasis. For instance, life course scholars use life phases such as middle childhood and middle adulthood, which are based in large part on social age, to conceptualize human lives from birth to death. In this book, we talk about nine phases, from conception to very late adulthood. Keep in mind, however, that the number and nature of these life phases are socially constructed and have changed over time, with modernization and mass longevity leading to finer gradations in life phases and consequently a greater number of them (Settersten & Mayer, 1997). Such fine gradations do not exist in most preindustrial and newly industrializing countries (Dannefer, 2003a, 2003b).

Spiritual age indicates the current position of a person in the ongoing search for "meaning and morally fulfilling relationships" (Canda, 1997, p. 302). David Sanchez is certainly at a different position in his search for life's meaning than he was when he came home from Vietnam. Although life course scholars have not paid much attention to spiritual age, it has been the subject of study by some developmental psychologists and other social scientists. In an exploration of the meaning of adulthood edited by Erik Erikson in 1978, several authors explored the markers of adulthood from the viewpoint of a number of spiritual and religious traditions, including Christianity, Hinduism, Islam, Buddhism, and Confucianism. Several themes emerged across the various traditions: contemplation, moral action, reason, self-discipline, character improvement, loving actions, and close community with others. All the authors noted that spirituality is typically seen as a process of growth, a process with no end.

James Fowler (1981) has presented a theory of faith development, based on 359 in-depth interviews, that strongly links it with chronological age. Ken Wilber's (1977, 1995) Full-Spectrum Model of Consciousness also proposes an association between age and spiritual development, but Wilbur does not suggest that spiritual development is strictly linear. He notes, as do the contributors to the Erikson book, that there can be regressions, temporary leaps, and turning points in a person's spiritual development.

Standardization in the Timing of Lives

Life course scholars debate whether the trend is toward greater standardization in age-graded social roles and statuses or toward greater diversification (Settersten, 2003b; Settersten & Lovegreen, 1998; Shanahan, 2000). Ironically, life patterns seem to be becoming, at the same time, more standardized and more diversified. The implication for social workers is that we must pay attention to the uniqueness of each person's life course trajectory, but we can use research about regularities in the timing of lives to develop social work interventions.

Many societies engage in **age structuring**, or standardizing of the ages at which social role transitions occur, by developing policies and laws that regulate the timing of these transitions. For example, in the United States there are laws and regulations about the ages for compulsory education, working (child labor), driving, drinking, being tried as an adult, marrying, holding public office, and receiving pensions and social insurance. However, countries vary considerably in the degree to which age norms are formalized (Settersten, 2003b; Settersten & Mayer, 1997; Shanahan, 2000). Some scholars suggest that formal age structuring becomes more prevalent as societies modernize (Buchmann, 1989; Meyer, 1986). European life course scholars suggest that U.S.-based life course scholars have underplayed the role of government in age structuring, suggesting that, in Europe, strong centralized governments play a larger role than in the United States in structuring the life course (Leisering, 2003; Marshall & Mueller, 2003).

Formalized age structuring has created a couple of difficulties that affect social workers. One is that cultural lags often lead to a mismatch between changing circumstances and the age structuring in society (Foner, 1996). Consider the trend for corporations to offer early retirement, before the age of 65, in a time when people are living longer and with better health. This mismatch has implications both for public budgets and for individual lives. Another problem with the institutionalization of age norms is increasing age segregation; people are spending more of their time in groups consisting entirely of people their own age. Social work services are increasingly organized around the settings of these age-segregated groups: schools, the workplace, long-term care, and so forth.

Some life course scholars argue, however, that modernization has allowed the life course to become more flexibly structured (Guillemard & van Gunsteren, 1991; Neugarten & Hagestad, 1976). Indeed, there is much diversity in the sequencing and timing of adult life course markers, such as completing an education, beginning work, leaving home, marrying, and becoming a parent (George & Gold, 1991). Trajectories in the family domain may be more flexible than work and educational trajectories (Elder, 1998; Settersten, 2003b; Settersten & Lovegreen, 1998). On the other hand, the landscape of work is changing, with less opportunity for continuous and stable employment, and this is creating greater diversity in work trajectories (Heinz, 2003). In addition, while educational trajectories remain standardized for the most well-off, who move smoothly from secondary to higher education, they are less structured for other members of society (Pallas, 2003). Life course trajectories also vary in significant ways by gender, race, ethnicity, and social class (Elder, 1998; Settersten & Lovegreen, 1998; Shanahan, 2000). This issue will be discussed further later in the chapter.

To gain a better understanding of regularities and irregularities in life course trajectories, researchers have studied the order in which life events and transitions occur (George, 1993). Most of the research has been on the entrance into adulthood, focusing specifically on the completion of school, first full-time job, and first marriage (Hogan, 1978, 1981; Modell, Furstenberg, & Hershberg, 1976; Settersten, 1998; Shanahan et al., 1998). Life course scholars also are interested in the length of time that an individual, family, or other collectivity spends in a particular state, without changes in status or roles. In general, the longer we experience specific environments and conditions, the more likely it is that our behavior will be affected by them (George, 1996). The duration of Mahdi Mahdi's stays in various settings and statuses—soldier, refugee, convenience store clerk, immigration specialist—is important. Finally, life course scholars are studying the pace of transitions. Transitions into adult roles in young adulthood (such as completing school, leaving home, getting the first job, getting married, having the first child) appear to be more rapidly timed than transitions in middle and late adulthood (such as launching children, retiring, losing parents) (Hareven, 1978, 2000).

Linked or Interdependent Lives

The life course perspective emphasizes the interdependence of human lives and the ways in which relationships both support and control an individual's behavior. **Social support**, which is defined as help rendered by others that benefits an individual or collectivity, is an obvious element of interdependent lives. Relationships also control behavior through expectations, rewards, and punishments.

In the United States, particular attention has been paid to the family as a source of support and control. In addition, the lives of family members are linked across generations, with both opportunity and misfortune having an intergenerational impact. The cases of David Sanchez, Mahdi Mahdi, and Maria Suarez are rich examples of lives linked across generations. But they are also rich examples of how people's lives are linked with those of people outside the family.

Links Between Family Members

Certainly, parents' and children's lives are linked. Elder's longitudinal research of children raised during the Great Depression found that as parents experienced greater economic pressures, they faced a greater risk of depressed feelings and marital discord. Consequently, their ability to nurture their children was compromised, and their children were more likely

▲ **Photo 1.3**   Parents' and children's lives are linked—When parents experience stress or joy, so do children.

to exhibit emotional distress, academic trouble, and problem behavior (Elder, 1974). The connection between family hardship, family nurturance, and child behaviors is now well established (e.g., Conger, Elder, Lorenz, Simons, & Whitbeck, 1992; Conger et al., 1993). In addition to the economic connection between parents and children, parents provide social capital for their children, in terms of role models and networks of social support (Cooksey et al., 1997).

It should also be noted that parents' lives are influenced by the trajectories of their children's lives. For example, parents may need to alter their work trajectories to respond to the needs of a terminally ill child. Or parents may forgo early retirement to assist their young adult children with education expenses. Parents may be negatively affected by stressful situations that their children face. For instance, Mahdi Mahdi says that his father died from worrying about his sons.

Older adults and their adult children are also interdependent. The pattern of mutual support between older adults and their adult children is formed by life events and transitions across the life course (Hareven, 1996). It is also fundamentally changed when families go through historical disruptions such as wars or major economic downturns. For example, the traditional pattern of intergenerational support—parents supporting children—is often disrupted when one generation migrates and another generation stays behind. It is also disrupted in immigrant families when the children pick up the new language and cultural norms faster than the adults in the family and take on the role of interpreter for their parents and grandparents (Hernandez & McGoldrick, 2005).

What complicates matters is that family roles must often be synchronized across three or more generations at once. Sometimes this synchronization does not go smoothly. Divorce, remarriage, and discontinuities in parents' work and educational trajectories may conflict with the needs of children (see, e.g., Ahrons, 2005; Cooksey et al., 1997). Similarly, the timing of adult children's educational, family, and work transitions often conflicts with the needs of aging parents (Hareven, 1996). The "generation in the middle" may have to make uncomfortable choices when allocating scarce economic and emotional resources. When a significant life event in one generation (such as death of a grandparent) is juxtaposed with a significant life event in another generation (such as birth of a child), families and individual family members are especially vulnerable (Carter & McGoldrick, 2005a).

Links With the Wider World

We know a lot more at this point about the ways that individuals and their multigenerational families are interdependent than about the interdependence between individuals and families and other groups and collectivities. However, we may at least note that work has a major effect on family transitions (George, 1993). In this vein, using data for 6- and 7-year-old children from the National Longitudinal Survey of Youth, researchers found that the children's depression and aggressive behavior were not associated with whether their mothers were employed but rather with the type of work those mothers did (Cooksey et al., 1997). Children whose mothers are in occupations requiring complex skills are less likely to be depressed and behave aggressively than children whose mothers are in less skilled work environments. Perhaps performing complex tasks at work enhances parenting skills. Or perhaps the mothers in more skilled occupations benefit emotionally from having greater control over their work environments. This finding would, of course, have meaning only in an advanced industrial society and would offer no insight about parenting skills in traditional societies.

The family seems to have much more influence on child and adolescent behaviors than the neighborhood does (Elder, 1998; Furstenberg, Cook, Eccles, Elder, & Sameroff, 1999; Klebanov, Brooks-Gunn, Gordon, & Chase-Lansdale, 1997). More differences in the behavior of children and adolescents have been found among families within a given neighborhood than have been found when comparing the families in one neighborhood with families in other neighborhoods. There is evidence, however, that the neighborhood effects may be greater for children living in high-poverty areas, which are often marked by violence and environmental health hazards, than for children living in low-poverty neighborhoods (Katz, Kling, & Liebman, 1999, cited in Shonkoff & Phillips, 2000; Rosenbaum, 1991).

It is important for social workers to remember that lives are also linked in systems of institutionalized privilege and oppression. The life trajectories of members of minority groups in the United States are marked by discrimination and lack of opportunity, which are experienced pervasively as daily insults and pressures. However, various cultural groups have devised unique systems of social support to cope with the "mundane extreme environments" in which they live (McAdoo, 1986). Examples include the extensive and intensive natural support systems of Hispanic families like the Suarez family (Falicov, 2005) and the special role of the church for African Americans (Billingsley, 1999). Others construct lives of desperation or resistance in response to limited opportunities.

Dale Dannefer (2003a, 2003b) reminds us that, in the global economy, lives are linked around the world. The lifestyles of people in affluent countries depend on cheap labor and cheap raw products in Africa, South America, the Caribbean, parts of Asia, and other places. Children and women in impoverished countries labor long hours to make an increasing share of low-cost products consumed in affluent countries. Women migrate from impoverished countries to become the domestic laborers in affluent countries, allowing women in affluent countries to leave the home to take advantage of career opportunities, and allowing the domestic workers to send the money they make back home to support their own families (Parrenas, 2001).

Human Agency in Making Choices

Mahdi Mahdi made a decision to refuse the draft, and this decision had a momentous impact on his own life course as well as the trajectory of members of his extended family. Like all of us, he made choices that fundamentally changed his life (Elder, 1998). In other words, he participated in constructing his life course through the exercise of **human agency**, or the use of personal power to achieve one's goals. The emphasis on human agency may be one of the most positive contributions of the life course perspective (Hareven, 2000).

A look at the discipline of social history might help to explain why considering human agency is so important to social workers. Social historians have attempted to correct the traditional focus on lives of elites by studying the lives of common people (Hareven, 2000). By doing so, they discovered that many groups once considered passive victims—for example, working-class people and slaves—actually took independent action to cope with the difficulties imposed by the rich and powerful. Historical research now shows that couples tried to limit the size of their families even in preindustrial societies (Wrigley, 1966), that slaves were often ingenious in their struggles to hold their families together (Gutman, 1976), and that factory workers used informal networks and kinship ties to manage, and sometimes resist, pressures for efficiency (Hareven, 1982a). These findings are consistent with social work approaches that focus on individual, family, and community strengths (Saleeby, 1996).

Clearly, however, human agency has limits. Individuals' choices are constrained by the structural and cultural arrangements of a given historical era. For example, Mahdi Mahdi's choices did not seem limitless to him; he faced the unfortunate choices of becoming a soldier again or refusing the draft. Unequal opportunities also give some members of society more options than others have. Elder (1998) notes that the emphasis on human agency in the life course perspective has been aided by Albert Bandura's (1986) work on the two concepts of *self-efficacy,* or sense of personal competence, and *efficacy expectation,* or expectation that one can personally accomplish a goal. It is important to remember, however, that Bandura (1986) makes specific note about how social inequalities can result in low self-efficacy and low efficacy expectations among members of oppressed groups. In his recent work, Bandura (2002) has suggested that there are three types of human agency: *personal agency* or use of personal power, *proxy agency* or actions of some on behalf of others, and *collective agency* accomplished through group action. The concepts of proxy agency and collective agency bring us back to linked and interdependent lives. These concepts add important dimensions to the discussion of human agency, and can serve to counter-balance the extreme individualism of U.S. society.

Diversity in Life Course Trajectories

Life course researchers have long had strong evidence of diversity in individuals' life patterns. Early research emphasized differences between cohorts, but increasing attention is being paid to variability within cohort groups. However, the life course research to date has been based on samples from affluent societies and fails to account for global diversity, particularly for the life course trajectories of the great majority of the world's people who live in nonindustrial or early industrializing countries (Dannefer, 2003a, 2003b). Consequently, the life course perspective has the potential to accommodate global diversity, but has not adequately done so to date.

We also want to interject a word here about terminology and human diversity. As we attempted to uncover what is known about human diversity in life course trajectories, we struggled with terminology to define identity groups. We searched for consistent language to describe different groups, and we were dedicated to using language that identity groups would use to describe themselves. However, we ran into challenges endemic to our time related to the language of diversity. First, it is not the case that all members of a given identity group at any given time embrace the same terminology for their group. Second, as we reviewed literature from different historical moments, we recognized the shifting nature of terminology. In addition, even within a given historical era, we found that different researchers used different terms and had different decision rules about who comprises the membership of identity groups. So, in the end, you will find that we have not settled on fixed terminology that is used consistently to describe identity groups. Rather, we use the language of individual researchers when reporting their studies, because we want to avoid distorting their work. We hope that you will recognize that the ever-changing language of diversity has both constructive potential to find creative ways to affirm diversity and destructive potential to dichotomize diversity into *the norm* and *the other.*

As we strive to provide a global context, we encounter current controversies about appropriate language to describe different sectors of the world. For a long time, many scholars have used the language of First World, Second World, and Third World to define global sectors. *First World* has been used to describe the nations that were the first to industrialize, urbanize, and modernize. *Second World* was used to describe nations that have industrialized but have not yet become central to the world economy. *Third World* has been used to refer to nonindustrialized nations that have few resources and are considered expendable in the global economy. This approach has lost favor in recent years (Leeder, 2004). Immanuel Wallerstein (1974, 1979) uses different language but makes a similar distinction; he refers to wealthy *core* countries, newly industrialized *semiperiphery* countries, and the poorest *periphery* countries. Other writers divide the world into *developed* and *developing* countries (McMichael, 2004), referring to the level of industrialization, urbanization, and modernization. Still others divide the world into the *Global North* and the *Global South*, calling attention to a history in which the Global North colonized and exploited the resources of the Global South. And, finally some writers talk about the *West* versus the *East*, where the distinctions are largely cultural. We recognize that such categories carry great symbolic meaning and can mask systems of power and exploitation. As with diversity, we attempted to find a respectful language that could be used consistently throughout the book. Again, we found that different researchers have used different language and different characteristics to describe categories of nations, and when reporting on their findings, we have used their own language to avoid misrepresenting their findings.

It seems, in any case, that Elder's four themes of the life course perspective can be used to more completely recognize diversity in its many forms:

1. *Interplay of human lives and historical time.* Cohorts tend to have different life trajectories because of the unique historical events each cohort encounters. Mahdi Mahdi wanted his daughter to tell her story because he knew that he and she had experienced the war, escape, and resettlement very differently. But, the same birth cohort in different parts of the world face very different historical events. For example, the post-World War II era was very different for young adults in Germany than it was in the United States. And, the children of Darfur in 2006 face very different historical events from the children in Australia.

2. *Timing of lives.* Age norms change with time and place and culture. The life course perspective, developed in late industrial affluent countries, has paid little attention to such age norms as childhood marriage in Bangladesh, but it can be extended to accommodate a more global perspective (Chowdhury, 2004). Age norms also vary by social location, or place in the social structure of a given society, most notably by gender, race, ethnicity, and social class (Settersten, 2003a; Settersten & Mayer, 1997). These variables create differences from one cohort to another as well as differences among the individuals within a cohort.

3. *Linked or independent lives.* The differing patterns of social networks in which persons are embedded produce differences in life course experiences. Likewise, the different locations in the global economy produce very different life course trajectories. The intersection of multiple trajectories—for example, the family lifeline, the educational lifeline, and the work lifeline—introduces new possibilities for diversity in life course patterns. Like many midlife adults, Mahdi Mahdi must find a way to balance his family lifeline, educational lifeline, and work lifeline.

4. *Human agency in making choices.* Human agency, particularly personal agency, allows for extensive individual differences in life course trajectories as individuals plan and make choices between options. It is not surprising, given these possibilities for unique experience, that the stories of individuals vary so much. It is also important to remember that proxy agency and collective agency can produce both individual and group-based differences in life course trajectories.

A good indication of the diversity of life course trajectories is found in an often cited study by Ronald Rindfuss and colleagues (Rindfuss et al., 1987). They examined the sequencing of five roles—work, education, homemaking, military, and other—among 6,700 U.S. men and 7,000 U.S. women for the eight years following their high school graduation in 1972. The researchers found 1,100 different sequences of these five roles among the men and 1,800 different sequences among the women. This and other research on sequencing of life course transitions has called increasing attention to the heterogeneity of life course trajectories (Settersten, 1998, 2003a; Settersten & Lovegreen, 1998; Shanahan et al., 1998).

These research results indicate that men's life course trajectories are more rigidly structured, with fewer discontinuities, than women's. One explanation for this gender difference is that women's lives have been more strongly interwoven with the family domain than men's, and the family domain operates on nonlinear time, with many irregularities (Settersten & Lovegreen, 1998). Men's lives are still more firmly rooted in domains outside the family, such as the paid work world, and these domains operate in linear time. Men's and women's life trajectories have started to become more similar, and it has been suggested that this convergence is primarily because women's schooling and employment patterns are moving closer to men's, and not because men have become more involved in the family domain (Settersten & Lovegreen, 1998). However, the recent decline in employment stability is also leading to greater discontinuity in the life course trajectories of men (Heinz, 2003).

Life course trajectories also vary by social class. In impoverished societies, and in neighborhoods in affluent societies that are characterized by concentrated poverty, large numbers of youth drop out of school by the ninth grade (Dannefer, 2003a, 2003b; Kliman & Madsen, 2005). This was the case for Jesus and Aida Suarez. In contrast, youth in upper middle-class and upper-class families expect an extended period of education with parental subsidies. These social class differences in educational trajectories are associated with differences in family and work trajectories. Affluent youth go to school and postpone their entry into adult roles of work and family. Less affluent youth, however, often enter earlier into marriage, parenting, and employment.

Research suggests that the family life trajectories in minority groups in the United States are different from the family life trajectories of whites. Minority youth tend to leave home to live independently later than white youth do, at least in part because of the high value put on "kinkeeping" in many minority cultures (Stack, 1974). However, in a random sample from a major urban U.S. city, minority respondents gave earlier deadlines for leaving home than white respondents when questioned about the appropriate age for leaving home—even though the minority respondents actually left home at a later age than the white respondents (Settersten, 1998). This finding may reflect the bicultural conflict that complicates the lives of young adults in ethnic minority groups. It also reflects differences in financial resources for leaving home.

Another source of diversity in a country with considerable immigration is the individual experience leading to the decision to immigrate, the journey itself, and the resettlement period (Devore & Schlesinger, 1999; Hernandez & McGoldrick, 2005). The individual's decision to immigrate may involve social, religious, or political persecution, and it increasingly involves a search for economic gain. Or, as in Mahdi Mahdi's case, it may involve war and a dangerous political environment. The transit experience is sometimes traumatic, and Mahdi Mahdi does not like to recall his escape in the middle of the night. The resettlement experience requires establishment of new social networks, may involve changes in socioeconomic status, and presents serious demands for acculturating to a new physical and social environment. Mahdi Mahdi speaks of the struggles in being a convenience store clerk with a college education. Gender, race, social class, and age all add layers of complexity to the migration experience. Family roles often have to be renegotiated as children outstrip older family members in learning the new language. Tensions can also develop over conflicting approaches to the acculturation process (Fabelo-Alcover, 2001). Just as they should investigate their clients' educational trajectories, work trajectories, and family trajectories, social workers should be interested in the migration trajectories of their immigrant clients.

Developmental Risk and Protection

As the life course perspective has continued to evolve, it has more clearly emphasized the links between the life events and transitions of childhood, adolescence, and adulthood (McLeod & Almazan, 2003; Shanahan, 2000). Studies indicate that childhood events sometimes shape people's lives 40 or 50 years later (George, 1996).

In fact, the long-term impact of developmental experiences was the subject of the earliest life course research, Glen Elder's (1974) examination of longitudinal data for children from the Great Depression. He compared a group of children (referred to as the Oakland children) who were born in 1920 and 1921 with a group of children (referred to as the Berkeley children) who were born in 1928 and 1929. The Oakland children experienced a relatively stable and secure childhood before they encountered the economic deprivations of the Great Depression during their adolescence. They also made the transition to adulthood after the worst of the economic downturn. The Berkeley children, on the other hand, experienced early childhood during the worst years of the Depression. When they reached adolescence, their parents were involved in World War II, with many fathers away in military roles and many mothers working long hours in "essential industry." Although both groups experienced economic hardship and later difficulties in life transitions, the Berkeley children were more negatively affected than the Oakland children. 20-21   28-29

Elder (1998) has recently, more clearly, enunciated the idea of developmental risk and protection as a major theme of the life course perspective this way, "[T]he developmental impact of a succession of life transitions or events is contingent on when they occur in a person's life" (p. 3). Other life course scholars have suggested that it is not simply the timing and sequencing of hardships but also their duration and spacing that provide risk for youth as they make the transition into adulthood. For instance, poverty alone is much less of a risk than extended poverty (Shanahan, 2000). Families are more vulnerable to getting off track when confronted simultaneously by multiple events and transitions (Carter & McGoldrick, 2005a). Life course scholars have borrowed the concepts of **cumulative advantage** and **cumulative disadvantage** from sociologist Robert Merton to explain inequality within cohorts across the life course (Bartley et al., 1997; O'Rand, 1996; Settersten, 2003a). Merton (1968) found that in scientific careers, large inequalities in productivity and recognition had accumulated. Scholarly productivity brings recognition, and recognition brings resources for further productivity, which of course brings further recognition and so on. Merton proposed that, in this way, scientists who are productive early in their careers accumulate advantage over time, whereas other scientists accumulate disadvantage. Sociologists propose that cumulative advantage and cumulative disadvantage are socially constructed; social institutions and societal structures develop mechanisms that ensure increasing advantage for those who succeed early in life and increasing disadvantage for those who struggle (Settersten & Lovegreen, 1998).

Consider the effect of advantages in schooling. Young children with affluent parents attend enriched early childhood programs and well-equipped primary and secondary schools, which position them for successful college careers, which position them for occupations that pay well, which provide opportunities for good health maintenance, which position them for healthy, secure old age. This trajectory of unearned advantage is sometimes referred to as **privilege** (McIntosh, 1988). Children who do not come from affluent families are more likely to attend underequipped schools, experience school failure or dropout, begin work in low-paying sectors of the labor market, experience unemployment, and arrive at old age with compromised health and limited economic resources.

Early deprivations and traumas do not inevitably lead to a trajectory of failure, but without intervention that reverses the trajectory, these early experiences are likely to lead to accumulation of disadvantage. Individual trajectories may be moderated not only by human agency but also by historical events and environmental supports. As one example of the positive impact of historical events, many children of the Great Depression were able to reverse disadvantages in their life trajectories through their military service in World War II (Elder, 1986). On the other hand, military service in wartime may involve traumatic stress, as we see with David Sanchez and Mahdi Mahdi. In terms of environmental support, governmental safety nets to support vulnerable families at key life transitions have been found to reduce the effects of deprivation and trauma on health (Bartley et al., 1997). For example, researchers have found that home nurse visitation during the first two years of a child's life can reduce the risk of child abuse and criminal behavior among low-income mothers (Olds et al., 1997).

The life course perspective and the concept of cumulative disadvantage are beginning to influence community epidemiology, which studies the prevalence of disease across communities (e.g., Brunner, 1997; Kellam & Van Horn, 1997; Kuh & Ben-Sholomo, 2004). Researchers in this tradition are interested in social and geographical inequalities in the distribution of chronic disease. They suggest that risk for chronic disease gradually accumulates over a life course through episodes of illness, exposure to unfavorable environments, and unsafe behaviors. They are also interested in how some experiences in the life course can break the chain of risk.

This approach to public health mirrors efforts in developmental psychology and other disciplines to understand developmental risk and protective factors (Fraser, 2004; Rutter, 1996; Werner & Smith, 2001). The study of risk and protection has led to an interest in the concept of **resilience**, which refers to the ability of some people to fare well in the face of risk factors. Researchers studying resilient children are examining the interplay of risk factors and protective factors in their lives. Although the study of protective factors lags behind the study of risk factors, researchers speculate that a cumulative effect will also be found for protective factors (Fraser, 2004; Luthar, 2003).

Many scholars now recommend that we think of risk and protection as processes over time, which is very much like the way that life course scholars write about life trajectories. Exhibit 1.7 shows how phases of life are interwoven with various risks and protective factors.

Exhibit 1.7	Risk and Protective Factors for Specific Life Course Phases	
Life Course Phase	*Risk Factors*	*Protective Factors*
Infancy	Poverty Child abuse/neglect Parental mental illness Teenage motherhood	Active, alert, high vigor Sociability Small family size
Infancy-Childhood	Poverty Child abuse/neglect Divorce Parental substance abuse	"Easy," engaging temperament
Infancy-Adolescence	Poverty Child abuse/neglect Parental mental illness Parental substance abuse Teenage motherhood Divorce	Maternal competence Close bond with primary caregiver (not necessarily biological parent) Supportive grandparents
Infancy-Adulthood	Poverty Child abuse/neglect Teenage motherhood	Low distress/low emotionality Mother's education
Early Childhood	Poverty	Advanced self-help skills
Preschool-Adulthood	Poverty Parental mental illness Parental substance abuse Divorce	Supportive teachers Successful school experiences
Childhood-Adolescence	Poverty Child abuse/neglect Parental mental illness Parental substance abuse Divorce	Internal locus of control Strong achievement motivation Special talents, hobbies Positive self-concept For girls: emphasis on autonomy with emotional support from primary caregiver For boys: structure and rules in household For both boys and girls: assigned chores Close, competent peer friends who are confidants
Childhood-Adulthood	Poverty Child abuse/neglect Parental mental illness Parental substance abuse Divorce Teenage parenthood	Average/above-average intelligence Ability to distance oneself Impulse control Strong religious faith Supportive siblings Mentors
Adolescence-Adulthood	Poverty	Planning, foresight

Source: Based on Werner, 2000, pp. 118–119.

⊠ Strengths and Limitations of the Life Course Perspective

As a framework for thinking about the aspect of time in human behavior, the life course perspective has several advantages over traditional theories of human development. It encourages greater attention to the impact of historical and social change on human behavior, which seems particularly important in a rapidly changing society such as ours. Because it attends to biological, psychological, and social processes in the timing of lives, it is a good fit with a biopsychosocial perspective. Its emphasis on linked lives shines a spotlight on intergenerational relationships and the interdependence of lives. At the same time, with its attention to human agency, the life course perspective is not as deterministic as some earlier theories, and acknowledges people's strengths and capacity for change. Life course researchers are also finding strong evidence for the malleability of risk factors and the possibilities for preventive interventions (Kellam & Van Horn, 1997). With attention to the diversity in life course trajectories, the life course perspective provides a good conceptual framework for culturally sensitive practice. And finally, the life course perspective lends itself well to research that looks at cumulative advantage and cumulative disadvantage, adding to our knowledge about the impact of power and privilege, and subsequently suggesting strategies for social justice.

To answer questions about how people change and how they stay the same across a life course is no simple task, however. Take, for example, the question of whether there is an increased sense of generativity, or concern for others, in middle adulthood. Should the researcher study different groups of people at different ages (perhaps a group of 20-year-olds, a group of 30-year-olds, a group of 40-year-olds, a group of 50-year-olds, and a group of 60-year-olds) and compare their responses, in what is known as a cross-sectional design? Or should the researcher study the same people over time (perhaps at 10-year intervals from age 20 to age 60) and observe whether their responses stay the same or change over time, in what is known as a longitudinal design? I hope you are already raising the question, what happens to the cohort effect in a cross-sectional study? This question is, indeed, always a problem with studying change over time with a cross-sectional design. Suppose we find that 50-year-olds report a greater sense of generativity than those in younger age groups. Can we then say that generativity does, indeed, increase in middle adulthood? Or do we have to wonder if there was something in the social and historical contexts of this particular cohort of 50-year-olds that encouraged a greater sense of generativity? Because of the possibility of cohort effects, it is important to know whether research was based on a cross-sectional or longitudinal design.

Although attention to diversity and heterogeneity may be the greatest strength of the life course perspective, heterogeneity may also be its biggest challenge. The life course perspective, like other behavioral science perspectives, searches for patterns of human behavior. But the current level of heterogeneity in countries such as the United States may well make discerning patterns impossible (George, 1993). Perhaps, instead of thinking in terms of patterns, we can think in terms of processes and mechanisms. Another challenge related to diversity—perhaps a larger challenge—is that the life course perspective has not been used to consider diversity of experiences on a global level. This failure has led some scholars to suggest that the life course perspective, as it currently stands, is a perspective that only applies to affluent, late industrial societies (Dannefer, 2003a, 2003b; Fry, 2003). I would suggest, however, that there is nothing inherent in either the basic conceptions or the major themes of the life course perspective that make it inappropriate for use to understand human behavior at a global level. This is particularly true if human agency is understood to include proxy agency and collective agency.

Another possible limitation of the life course perspective is a failure to adequately link the micro world of individual and family lives to the macro world of social institutions and formal organizations (Dannefer, 2003a, 2003b; George, 1993; Leisering, 2003). Social and behavioral sciences have, historically, divided the social world up into micro and macro and studied them in isolation. The life course perspective was developed by scholars like Glen Elder Jr. and Tamara Hareven, who were trying to bring those worlds together. Sometimes, however, this effort is more successful than at other times, and this remains a challenge for the future.

⬚ Integration With a Multidimensional, Multitheoretical Approach

A companion volume to this book, *Dimensions of Human Behavior: Person and Environment,* recommends a multidimensional, multitheoretical approach for understanding human behavior. This recommendation is completely compatible with the life course perspective presented in this volume. The life course perspective clearly recognizes the biological and psychological dimensions of the person and can accommodate the spiritual dimension. The life course emphasis on linked or interdependent lives is consistent with the idea of the unity of person and environment presented in Volume I of this book. It can also easily accommodate the multidimensional environment (physical environment, culture, social institutions and social structure, families, small groups, formal organizations, communities, and social movements) discussed in the companion volume.

Likewise, the life course perspective is consistent with the multitheoretical approach presented in Volume I. The life course perspective has been developed by scholars across several disciplines, and they have increasingly engaged in cross-fertilization of ideas from a variety of theoretical perspectives (see, e.g., George, 1993, 1996; Kellam & Van Horn, 1997; O'Rand, 1996; Pearlin & Skaff, 1996). Because the life course can be approached from the perspective of the individual, from the perspective of the family or other collectivities, or seen as a property of cultures and social institutions that shape the pattern of individual lives, it builds on both psychological and sociological theories. Exhibit 1.8 demonstrates the overlap between the life course perspective and the eight theoretical perspectives presented in Chapter 2, of *Dimensions of Human Behavior: Person and Environment.*

Exhibit 1.8	Overlap of the Life Course Perspective and Eight Theoretical Perspectives on Human Behavior Implications for Social Work Practice

Theoretical Perspective	*Life Course Themes and Concepts*
Systems Perspective: Human behavior is the outcome of reciprocal interactions of persons operating within organized and integrated social systems.	Themes: Timing of Lives; Linked or Interdependent Lives Concepts: Biological Age, Psychological Age, Social Age, Spiritual Age
Conflict Perspective: Human behavior is driven by conflict, dominance, and oppression in social life.	Theme: Developmental Risk and Protection Concepts: Cumulative Advantage; Cumulative Disadvantage
Rational Choice Perspective: Human behavior is based on self-interest and rational choices about effective ways to accomplish goals.	Theme: Human Agency in Making Choices Concepts: Choices; Opportunities; Constraints
Social Constructionist Perspective: Social reality is created when actors, in social interaction, develop a common understanding of their world.	Themes: Timing of Lives; Diversity in Life Course Trajectories; Developmental Risk and Protection Concepts: Making Meaning of Life Events; Social Age; Age Norms; Age Structuring; Acculturation; Cumulative Advantage and Disadvantage
Psychodynamic Perspective: Internal processes such as needs, drives, and emotions motivate human behavior; early childhood experiences are central to problems of living throughout life.	Themes: Timing of Lives; Developmental Risk and Protection Concepts: Psychological Age; Capacities; Skills
Developmental Perspective: Human behavior both changes and stays the same across the life cycle.	Themes: Interplay of Human Lives and Historical Times; Timing of Lives; Developmental Risk and Protection Concepts: Life Transitions; Biological Age, Psychological Age, Social Age, Spiritual Age; Sequencing
Social Behavioral Perspective: Human behavior is learned when individuals interact with the environment; human behavior is influenced by personal expectations and meanings.	Themes: Interplay of Human Lives and Historical Time; Human Agency in Making Choices; Diversity in Life Course Trajectories; Developmental Risk and Protection Concepts: Life Events; Human Agency
Humanistic Perspective: Human behavior can be understood only from the internal frame of reference of the individual; human behavior is driven by a desire for growth and competence.	Themes: Timing of Lives; Human Agency in Making Choices Concepts: Spiritual Age; Meaning of Life Events and Turning Points; Individual, Family, and Community Strengths

IMPLICATIONS FOR SOCIAL WORK PRACTICE

The life course perspective has many implications for social work practice, including the following:

- Help clients make sense of their unique life's journeys and to use that understanding to improve their current situations. Where appropriate, help them to construct a lifeline of interlocking trajectories.
- Try to understand the historical contexts of clients' lives and the ways that important historical events have influenced their behavior.
- Where appropriate, use life event inventories to get a sense of the level of stress in a client's life.
- Be aware of the potential to develop social work interventions that can serve as turning points that help individuals, families, communities, and organizations to get back on track.
- Work with the media to keep the public informed about the impact of changing social conditions on individuals, families, communities, and formal organizations.
- Recognize the ways that the lives of family members are linked across generations and the impact of circumstances in one generation on other generations.
- Recognize the ways lives are linked in the global economy.
- Use existing research on risk, protection, and resilience to develop prevention programs.
- When working with recent immigrant and refugee families, be aware of the age norms in their countries of origin.
- Be aware of the unique systems of support developed by members of various cultural groups, and encourage the use of those supports in times of crisis.
- Support and help to develop clients' sense of personal competence for making life choices.

KEY TERMS

age norm	event history	resilience
age structuring	human agency	sex ratio
biological age	life course perspective	social age
cohort	life event	social support
cohort effects	population pyramid	spiritual age
cumulative advantage	privilege	trajectories
cumulative disadvantage	psychological age	transitions
		turning point

Active Learning

1. Prepare your own lifeline of interlocking trajectories (see Exhibit 1.4 for instructions). What patterns do you see? What shifts? How important are the different sectors of your life—for example, family, education, work, health?

2. One researcher found that 85% of respondents to a survey on turning points reported that there had been turning points in their lives. Interview five adults and ask whether there have been turning points in their lives. If they answer no, ask about whether they see their life as a straight path or a path with twists and turns. If they answer yes, ask about the nature of the turning point(s). Compare the events of your interviewees as well as the events in the lives of David Sanchez, Mahdi Mahdi, and Emma Suarez, with Rutter's three types of life events that can serve as turning points and Hareven's five conditions under which a transition can become a turning point.

3. Think of someone whom you think of as resilient, someone who has been successful against the odds. This may be you, a friend, coworker, family member, or a character from a book or movie. If the person is someone you know and to whom you have access, ask them to what they owe their success. If it is you or someone to whom you do not have access, speculate about the reasons for the success. How do their life journeys compare to the common risk and protective factors summarized in Exhibit 1.7?

WEB RESOURCES

Each chapter of this textbook contains a list of Internet resources and Web sites that may be useful to readers in their search for further information. Each site listing includes the address and a brief description of the contents of the site. Readers should be aware that the information contained in Web sites may not be truthful or reliable and should be confirmed before being used as a reference. Readers should also be aware that Internet addresses, or URLs, are constantly changing; therefore, the addresses listed may no longer be active or accurate. Many of the Internet sites listed in each chapter contain links to other Internet sites containing more information on the topic. Readers may use these links for further investigation.

Information not included in the Web Resources sections of each chapter can be found by using one of the many Internet search engines provided free of charge on the Internet. These search engines enable you to search using keywords or phrases, or you can use the search engines' topical listings. You should use several search engines when researching a topic, as each will retrieve different Internet sites.

GOOGLE
www.google.com

ASK
www.ask.com

YAHOO
www.yahoo.com

EXCITE
www.excite.com

LYCOS
www.lycos.com

A number of Internet sites provide information on theory and research on the life course:

Bronfenbrenner Life Course Center (BLCC)
www.human.corness.edu/che/BLCC/

Site presented by the Bronfenbrenner Life Course Center at Cornell University contains information on the Center, current research, working papers, and links to work/family Web sites, demography Web sites, and gerontology Web sites.

The Finnish Twin Cohort Study
kate.pc.helsinki.fi/

Site presented by the Department of Public Health at the University of Helsinki contains information on an ongoing project begun in 1974 to study environmental and genetic factors in selected chronic diseases with links to other related resources.

Michigan Study of Adolescent and Adult Life Transitions (MSALT)
www.rcgd.isr.umich.edu/msalt/home.htm

Site presented by the Michigan Study of Adolescent and Adult Life Transitions project contains information about the longitudinal study begun in 1983, publications on the project, and family-oriented Web resources.

The German Life History Study (GLHS)
www.mpib-berlin.mpg.de/en/forschung/bag

Site presented by the Max Planck Institute for Human Development in Berlin, Germany, contains information on comprehensive research on social structure and the institutional contexts of the life course.

Life Course Project
lifecourse.anu.edu.au/

Site presented by the Life Course Project of the Australian National University contains information on a longitudinal study of gender roles.

Project Resilience
www.projectresilience.com

Site presented by Project Resilience, a private organization based in Washington, D.C., contains information on teaching materials, products, and training for professionals working in education, treatment, and prevention.

CONCEPTION, PREGNANCY, AND CHILDBIRTH

Marcia P. Harrigan and Suzanne M. Baldwin

Key Ideas 41

Case Study 2.1: ■ A Change of Plans for Nicole Evans 42

Case Study 2.2: ■ The Thompsons' Premature Birth 43

Case Study 2.3: ■ The Gerekes' Late-Life Pregnancy 45

Sociocultural Organization of Childbearing 46
    Family Diversity 47
    Conception and Pregnancy in Context 48
    Childbirth in Context 49
        Place of Childbirth 50
        Childbirth Education 51
        Hospital Stay 53
Reproductive Genetics 54
    Genetic Mechanisms 54
    Genetic Counseling 56
Control over Conception and Pregnancy 58
    Contraception 58
    Medical Abortion 61
    Infertility Treatment 63
Normal Fetal Development 67

First Trimester 67
 Fertilization and the Embryonic Period 67
 The Fetal Period 69
Second Trimester 70
Third Trimester 70
Labor and Delivery of the Neonate 70
Pregnancy and the Life Course 71
Teen Pregnancy 72
Early Adulthood Pregnancy 74
Delayed Pregnancy 75
Risk and Protective Factors in Conception, Pregnancy, and Childbirth 76
Social Work and Challenges in Childbearing 77
Problem Pregnancies 78
 Undesired Pregnancy 78
 Ectopic Pregnancy 78
 Miscarriage and Stillbirth 79
 Maternal Brain Death 79
At-Risk Newborns 80
 Prematurity and Low Birth Weight 80
 Newborn Intensive Care 82
 Major Congenital Anomalies 83
Special Parent Populations 86
 Pregnant Substance Abusers 86
 Mothers With Eating Disorders 88
 Lesbian Mothers 88
 Mothers and Fathers With Disabilities 88
 Incarcerated Pregnant Women 89
 HIV-Infected Mothers 90
Implications for Social Work Practice 91
Key Terms 92
Active Learning 92
Web Resources 93

❖ What biological, psychological, social, and spiritual factors influence the beginning of the life course?

❖ What recent technological advances related to conception, pregnancy, and childbirth are important to social work intervention?

❖ What unique knowledge do social workers bring to multidisciplinary teams working with issues of conception, pregnancy, and childbirth?

KEY IDEAS

As you read this chapter, take note of these central ideas:

1. Conception, pregnancy, and childbirth should be viewed as normative life transitions that require family or family-like supportive relationships to maximize favorable outcomes.

2. Conception, pregnancy, and childbirth are influenced by changing family structures and gender roles.

3. Variations in human behavior at this life stage related to social class, race and ethnicity, and religion—and their interplay—must be considered in assessment and intervention.

4. Women who are poor or lack social support—and therefore experience greater stress than other women—are most at risk for poor pregnancy outcomes.

5. Prenatal care, including childbirth education, ensures the most positive pregnancy outcome possible. Universal access to prenatal care, then, should be a social work priority.

6. Although we are increasingly learning about the role of genetics in human development, 80 to 90% of fertilized ova with a genetic anomaly will abort spontaneously, resulting in 94 to 96% of all births occurring without genetic anomaly.

7. The incidence of low birth weight infants continues to be high, particularly for neonates born to poor and minority women and those exposed to teratogens such as nicotine, illegal drugs, and alcohol.

A Change of Plans of Nicole Evans

For as long as 15-year-old African American Nicole Evans can remember, her mother has told her that she would be the first in the family to go to college. Nicole's mother had once planned to live out this dream herself, but the dream began to fade when Nicole was born. Her mother was 13-years-old at the time. Over and over, Nicole's mother has told her about the reality that displaced the dream: years of poverty and struggle, multiple pregnancies, spontaneous abortion, and four children ages 15, 14, 9, and 6—the last born with sickle-cell anemia. Diagnosed with Human Immunodeficiency Virus (HIV) four years ago, Nicole's mom now increasingly focuses on Nicole's future—as a college-educated woman and the family caretaker. "Don't play the fool, Nicole. Get an education, a steady pay job, one that makes the rent and the doctor . . . then have your babies."

Tonight Nicole lies in her own bed, listening to the sounds of her brothers who share the room next to hers. Outside, tires screech. She holds her breath and then quickly lets it out when she does not hear metal crashing. Then she hears the familiar "pop"—perhaps a gunshot. Nicole feels relieved that everyone is in bed and out of the line of any stray bullet.

Nicole closes her eyes, trying to recapture how she felt that night over a month ago. She wanted to say, "No, I don't do that," but it did not seem to fit the occasion. She had already declined the heroin that many of her friends used as a buffer against the strain of living in a violent neighborhood. But Nicole remembers saying yes to some wine, thinking a little would not hurt; maybe it would even offer some relief from her constant feelings of dread and anxious anticipation of more "bad news." But the wine only led to other things: "Come on, Nicole, you'll like it. Ain't nothing you ever felt. Don't deny me my manhood, girl. Heck, there's nothin' to worry for . . . this is God's gift." God. Comfort. Hope. But in the end what she felt was not the promise she had felt a few years ago, singing in the choir, listening to the preacher talk about the promised land and better times. "Is there any more wine?" Nicole remembers asking, while thinking it was not really her voice giving in to the moment. She had made a request. Or was it a choice? Are they the same? What "choice" did she have? Why did she think she was so different from her friends, who laughed and seemed to enjoy the moment?

Now, six weeks later, Nicole feels nauseous for the second morning in a row. A missed period: pregnant. What will her mother say? Nicole cringes to think that her life goals may have been sacrificed for an hour spent pursuing peace and pleasure—a high price for any 15-year-old girl. Yet, maybe her mother would be proud. Nicole recalls how her mother had responded to her aunt's first pregnancy: "You're no woman until you have that first one."

A few days later, Nicole drops by the community center—where, until two years ago, she was an active member of an after-school program run by a social worker who is still there with an attentive ear. Nicole shares her confusion.

The Thompsons' Premature Birth

The movement of her growing fetus drew Felicia into an entrancing world of hope and fantasy. Within days of discovering she was pregnant, her husband Will was suddenly deployed to a conflict zone. Through e-mails and occasional cellular phone calls, Felicia told Will details about the changes she experienced with the pregnancy but more and more, it seemed as if she and her baby were inhabiting a different world than that of her husband. His world was filled with smoke, dirt, bombs, and danger, punctuated with periods of boredom. Although she was only six months into the pregnancy, she had selected muted colors for the nursery and soft clothing in anticipation of the birth. Her changing figure was eliciting comments from her coworkers in the office where she worked part time as a secretary. With weeks of nausea and fatigue behind her, a general sense of well-being pervaded Felicia's mind and body. She avoided all news media as well as "war talk" at the office to protect her from worry and anxiety. Yet, even the sound of an unexpected car pulling into the front of her home produced chills of panic. Was this the time when the officers would come to tell her that Will had been killed or wounded in combat? Her best friend only recently had experienced what every military wife fears may happen. The growing life within her and the constant threat of death filled her waking and sleeping hours.

Then, with dawn hours away, Felicia woke to cramping and blood. With 14 more weeks before her delivery date, Felicia was seized with fear. Wishing that Will were there, Felicia fervently prayed for herself and her fetus. The ambulance ride to the hospital became a blur of pain mixed with feelings of unreality. When she arrived in the labor and delivery suite, masked individuals in scrubs took control of her body while demanding answers to a seemingly endless number of questions. Felicia knew everything would be fine if only she could feel her son kick. Why didn't he kick?

As the pediatrician spoke of the risks of early delivery, the torrent of words and images threatened to engulf her. Suddenly, the doctors were telling her to push her son into the world—her fragile son who was too small and vulnerable to come out of his cocoon so soon. Then the pain stopped. Oblivious to the relief, Felicia listened for her baby's cry. It didn't come. Just a few hours earlier, she had fallen asleep while the fetus danced inside her. Now there was only emptiness. Her arms ached for the weight of her infant, and her heart broke with what she believed was her failure as a mother.

In the newborn intensive care unit (NICU), a flurry of activity revolved around baby boy Thompson. Born weighing only 1 pound 3 ounces, this tiny red baby's immature systems were unprepared for the demands of the extrauterine world. He was immediately connected to a ventilator, intravenous lines were placed in his umbilicus and arm, and monitor leads were placed on all available surfaces. Nameless to his caregivers, the baby, whose parents had already named Paul, was now the recipient of some of the most advanced technological interventions available in modern medicine.

About an hour after giving birth, Felicia saw Paul for the first time. Lying on a stretcher, she counted 10 miniature toes and fingers. Through a film of tears, trying to find resemblance to Will, who is of Anglo heritage, or herself, a light-skinned Latina, in this tiny form, Felicia's breathing synchronized to Paul's as she willed him to keep fighting.

Alone in her room, she was flooded with fear, grief, and guilt. What had she done wrong? Could Paul's premature birth have been caused by paint fumes from decorating his room? From her anxiety and worry about Will?

(Continued)

(Continued)

The Red Cross sent the standard message to Will. Was he in the field? Was he at headquarters? It mattered because Paul may not even be alive by the time Will found out he was born. How would he receive the news? Who would be nearby to comfort him? Would the command allow him to come home on emergency leave? If he were granted permission for emergency leave, it could be days of arduous travel, waiting for space on any military plane, before he landed somewhere in the United States. Felicia knew that Will would be given priority on any plane available; even admirals and generals step aside for men and women returning home to meet a family crisis. But, then again, the command may consider his mission so essential that only official notification of Paul's death would allow him to return home. Although Felicia told herself she was being unreasonable, she was angry that Will was not here to comfort her. After all, she had supported his decision to join the military and had accepted that she would deliver her child alone. Then, why was this so overwhelming?

Thirteen days after his arrival, Paul took his first breath by himself. His hoarse, faint cry provoked both ecstasy and terror in his mother. A few days earlier Felicia had been notified by the Red Cross that her husband was on his way home but information was not available regarding his arrival date. Now that he was off the ventilator, she watched Paul periodically miss a breath, which would lead to a decreased heart rate, then monitors flashing and beeping. She longed for Will's physical presence and support.

Will arrived home two days later. He walked into the NICU 72 hours after riding in an armed convoy to the airport. Although Paul would spend the next 10 weeks in the hospital, Will had 14 days before starting the journey back to his job, a very different battlefield than the one on which Paul was fighting.

Paul's struggle to survive was the most exhilarating yet terrifying roller-coaster ride of his parents' lives. Shattered hopes were mended, only to be re-shattered with the next telephone call from the NICU. Now Felicia dreaded the phone as well as the sound of an unfamiliar car. For Felicia, each visit to Paul was followed by the long trip home to the empty nursery. For Will, stationed thousands of miles away, there was uncertainty, guilt, helplessness, and sometimes an overwhelming sense of inadequacy. Felicia feared the arrival of a car with officers in it, and Will dreaded a Red Cross message that his son had died.

Great joy and equally intense anxiety pervaded Paul's homecoming day. After spending 53 days in the NICU and still weighing only 4 pounds, 13 ounces, Paul was handed to his mother. She made sure that a video was made so that Will could share in this moment. How she wished he could participate, but she also knew that his heart and thoughts spanned the distance between war on the other side of the world and Paul's quiet victory at home. With more questions than answers about her son's future and her ability to take care of him, Felicia took their baby to his new home.

As the NICU social worker at a military hospital, the major goal must be to support the family as they face this challenging transition to parenthood. In the past 53 days, the social worker has helped Felicia answer her questions, understand the unfamiliar medical language of the health care providers, and understand and cope with the strong emotions she is experiencing. The social worker also helped during the transition of Will's arrival from war and his departure back to war. Understanding the dynamics of a neonatal intensive care unit, families in crisis, and the needs of the military family separated by an international conflict is critical to providing this family the level of support needed to manage the multifaceted role transitions.

The Gerekes' Late-Life Pregnancy

Thirty-one years ago, at age 44, Hazel Gereke gave birth to her fifth child, Terry. At the time of his birth, Terry's siblings ranged in age from 2 to 25, and his father was 48. The following interview tells the story of this German American family:

Q: It's been 31 years, but what do you remember about your pregnancy with Terry?

A: Well, I menstruated regularly and had long, heavy bleeding. It lasted two to three weeks every month, so I went to the doctor. He said I was 4–1/2 months pregnant! I cried . . . I was too far along to do anything. You see, back then you had to have three doctors go before the hospital board to say the pregnancy jeopardized the mother's health. Well, my doctor was Catholic, so I knew that would not happen.

Q: Do you remember how Mr. Gereke reacted to this pregnancy?

A: I can remember exactly what he said like it was yesterday: "Hazel, we'll love it!"

Q: What was the rest of the pregnancy like?

A: Horrible! Right after I found out, in October, Grandma and Grandpa moved in to live with us, and in November, Ann, our oldest child, got married! I wasn't feeling the best in the world. I would wake up at 3:00 A.M. with pains in my hand, elbows, and arm . . . I walked the floor. I had carpel tunnel, but at the time I thought it was the pregnancy. In December, I had false labor and was due in January. Terry was born on February 7, 1966.

Q: What was Terry's pregnancy like compared to the other four?

A: Ann's was normal; she was born in 1941 at home, with a doctor and a nurse who came with gas, oxygen, and a birthing table. John was more difficult; I had a prolapsed uterus and difficult delivery. He was premature and blue at birth. Gail, I carried breech, but she was turned in labor. You could tell by her black-and-blue nose, mouth, chin, and forehead! But everything was okay. Mike was normal. I had no morning sickness but a long delivery. Terry, I don't remember because I was put under when I went into the delivery room. They said the delivery was hard due to my age.

Q: What do you remember right after Terry's birth?

A: I bottle-fed him but had difficulty, so the nurse taught me how. The doctor said, "He might be a little slow."

Q: When and how did you find out that Terry had Down's syndrome?

A: I first heard "Down's" when I enrolled him in school and saw on the record "Down's child"! I went right away to the doctor, who said the test would cost $75. Well, I said, "there's no need for a test—it won't change what he is." He wasn't that bad. After his first birthday, he sat, began to walk, and said "Mama," "Daddy," "bye-bye," and "eat"—about 7 to 10 words. He was beginning to dress and potty train. At birth the nurses said, "You won't have any problem training this one; when he's wet, he screams!" But when he was 15 to 18 months old he had terrible seizures . . . all summer. He left the

(Continued)

(Continued)

table, walked into the living room, and we heard a terrible sound. He had fallen backwards and hit his head on the table. He was limp. They put him on dilantin and phenobarbital and kept increasing it. He became a vegetable. I gradually withdrew him from his medication . . . boy, was the doctor upset when he found that out, but Terry was doing better!

Q: What impact do you remember Terry's difficulties having on the rest of the family?

A: Gail and Mike were still at home. Gail said, "He doesn't look good—he looks funny." I took Terry to the mirror to teach him his eyes, ears, and mouth like I had the others. "Look at the pretty baby!" I said. He hung his head . . . he never looked in the mirror again. He was down about himself; he knew he was different. I worried that Mike was teased by the other kids when the bus came for Terry—they called it "the dummy bus." I always knew who had compassion, because if they did, Terry stayed around. Otherwise, he went to his room.

Five years ago, the Gerekes followed advice they had received and arranged for Terry to go to a group home, but no one in the family felt comfortable about this plan. The day he was to move into the group home, Hazel Gereke learned that Terry would be sharing a room with five other adult males, and she refused to let him live there. After two more years at home, at age 29, Terry moved to a different group home. Now, he visits his parents every Saturday and helps his father mow the grass, but he is always eager to return to the group home.

When asked if she thinks anything should have happened differently over the years, Hazel reluctantly but honestly replies that "the pregnancy should have been stopped." When asked "What has Terry contributed to your family?" she replies, "He has kept the family together and taught us not to take things for granted."

Although the Gerekes did not have contact with a social worker when they first encountered their late-life pregnancy, Hazel Gereke has reminded us about the ambivalences and ambiguities that social workers need to keep in mind when working with issues of problem pregnancies.

⊠ Sociocultural Organization of Childbearing

These three stories tell us that conception, pregnancy, and childbirth are experienced in different ways by different people. But they do not tell us about all the possible variations, which reflect the complex interplay of person, environment, and time. The biological processes vary little for the vast majority of women and their families, but researchers continue to study the psychological, social, and spiritual dimensions of childbearing. This chapter presents a multidimensional overview of current knowledge about conception, pregnancy, and childbirth gleaned from the literatures of anthropology, genetics, medicine, nursing, psychology, social work, and sociology.

In what other ways might culture affect the childbearing experience?

As you read, keep in mind that all elements of childbearing have deep meaning for a society. Procreation allows a culture to persist, as children are raised to follow the ways of their predecessors. Procreation may also allow a culture to expand if the birthrate exceeds the rate at which the society loses members. As

Valsiner (1989a) reminds us, "Human procreation is socially organized in all its aspects. In any cultural group around the world, society regulates the conditions under which a woman is to become pregnant, how she and her husband [family] should conduct themselves during the pregnancy, how labor and delivery take place, and how the newborn child is introduced into society" (p. 117). Pregnancy and childbearing practices are changing with ever-increasing globalization, demographic changes in immigration patterns to the United States, and refugees seeking asylum from war-torn countries. Unfortunately, health caregivers, including social workers, in the United States are often ill-prepared to provide culturally sensitive services (Davis, 2001; Gagnon et al., 2004; Ito & Sharts-Hopko, 2002; Yeo & Maeda, 2000).

In the United States, the social meaning of childbearing has changed rather dramatically over the past 30 years, in several ways (Carter & McGoldrick, 2005a; Chadiha & Danziger, 1995; Skolnick & Skolnick, 1996):

- Marriage and childbirth are more commonly delayed.
- People want smaller families.
- There are approximately 80 million involuntarily childless persons in the world (Bos, van Balan, & Visser, 2005).
- Various options for controlling reproduction are more available and accessible.
- Sexual freedom has increased.
- Single women of all ages get pregnant and keep the baby, but adolescents show a decline in birth rates.
- Family values and sexual mores vary more.
- Parents are less subject to gender role stereotyping—mom takes care of the baby while dad earns a paycheck, and so on.
- Fathers are considered more important in the baby's life, beyond their genetic contributions.
- Spouses return home unexpectedly from a war zone more often due to wives experiencing problematic pregnancies than to other family crises (Schumm, Bell, & Knott, 2000).
- Medical advances and cultural globalization are raising new ethical issues.

These trends have prompted considerable debate over how our society should define *family*. The family operates at the intersection of society and the individual. For most people it serves as a safe haven and a cradle of emotional relationships. It is both the stage and partial script for the unfolding of the individual life course.

Family Diversity

We continue to witness what family historians call **family pluralism,** or recognition of the many viable types of family structures. Such pluralism is nothing new, but our tolerance for all types of families has grown over the past few decades. The definition of family must reflect this pluralism. Yet, unresolved moral, political, and economic issues abound (Stacey, 1996). These debates influence which family research proposals are funded (Udry, 1993); how abortion and family policy is constructed (Figueira-McDonough, 1990), particularly at the national level; and who gets access to such family resources as infertility treatment, birth control pills methods, and prenatal care.

We know that many children are born into a family comprising a married couple and their offspring all living together. We are well aware that some children are born to single women with and without significant others, and others are relinquished at birth. In addition, recent global conflicts have also affected children who have lost a parent in war. Other infants come into the world in the midst of natural disasters, as evidenced during Hurricane Katrina where women gave birth in alleys while waiting for rescue (Buekens, Xiong, & Harville, 2006). Many neglected, abused, and abandoned children are placed in foster care. Yet, all these children live, formally or informally, for better or for worse, with a family of some type: foster, adoptive, extended, fictive kin, blended, and reunited are examples. Rarely does a child live without some type of family configuration, even those who live in arrangements such as group homes; thus, almost all children still experience the life course through a family lens.

The physical presence of "family" members is not the only factor influencing the experience of conception, pregnancy, and childbirth. When a child is born, a new role emerges for people other than the mother: grandma, uncle, second cousin, half sibling, and foster brother, to name a few. This new family role influences expectations both for the parents and the other caretakers. Furthermore, all families have a life cycle that includes a past, present, and hopes for the future (Carter & McGoldrick, 2005a). This family life cycle influences individual development in complex ways. For example, the timing and other circumstances of pregnancy are influenced by the family constellation. Consider your own family beliefs about favorable and unfavorable circumstances of conception, pregnancy, and childbirth. Perhaps these views vary across the generations, but the views of past generations can still create an expectation for certain circumstances and behaviors. Consider the story of Nicole Evans, who uses the words that her mother spoke to her aunt to help wrestle with the awareness of being pregnant: "You're no woman until you have that first one." Although Nicole's unplanned pregnancy may well alter her life course, this family belief buffers the negative impact.

In the absence of a biological family "history," individuals tend to seek a substitute history. The literature is replete with accounts of the quest to find one's birth family in order to discover the past and predict the future. Yet, other children who were separated from their birth parents decide to accept their surrogate parents and the accompanying family network as sufficient for support of the necessary tasks of parenthood and other family roles over the life course.

For families separated by major cultural differences and great geographical distances, as is the situation for most immigrant families, the response to multigenerational family expectations, rituals, and themes related to conception, pregnancy, and childbirth may be difficult or problematic. Such experiences pressure families to adapt and change. Still, responses to conception, pregnancy, and childbirth continue to resonate with the themes, myths, legacies, and secrets that bind families across many generations.

Conception and Pregnancy in Context

The three case studies at the beginning of this chapter remind us that the emotional reaction to conception may vary widely. The Thompsons' conception brought joy, in contrast to Nicole Evans's initial dismay followed by rising hopefulness; Mr. Gereke voiced confidence in contrast to his wife's apprehension. The conception experience is influenced by expectations the parents learned growing up in their own families of birth, as well as by many other factors: the parents' ages, health, marital status, social status, cultural expectations, peer expectations, school or employment circumstances, and prior experiences with conception and childbearing, as well as the interplay of these factors with those of other people significant to the mother and father.

The conception experience may also be influenced by organized religion. Church policies reflect different views about the purpose of human sexual expression: pleasure, procreation, or perhaps both. Many mainstream religions, in their denominational policy statements, specify acceptable sexual behaviors (Bullis & Harrigan, 1992). Unwanted conception may be seen as an act of carelessness, promiscuity, or merely God's will—perhaps even punishment for wrongdoing. These beliefs are usually strongly held and have become powerful fodder for numerous social, political, and religious debates related to conception.

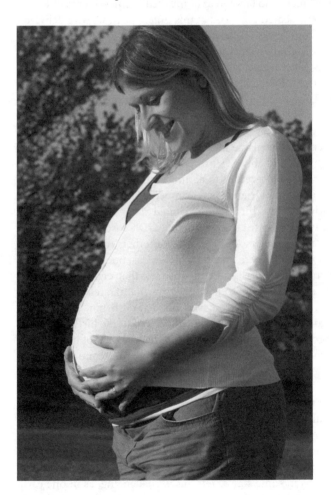

▲ **Photo 2.1**   Societal views of pregnancy in the United States have changed from simply waiting to being actively involved in nurturing the mother's and baby's health.

Even the mechanisms of conception are socially constructed. Some traditional cultures, such as the Telefomin of New Guinea, believe that repeated intercourse is necessary to conceive, but they forbid intercourse after conception so that multiple births will not occur. In contrast, the Dusan of Borneo believe that conception occurs when the body heat created between males and females causes the woman's blood to boil, forming the child drop by drop; consequently, intercourse must occur throughout pregnancy for the child to develop fully (Valsiner, 1989a). In the United States, conception is believed to be a complex biological event.

Just as the experience of conception has varied over time and across cultures, so has the experience of pregnancy. It too is influenced by religious orientations, social customs, changing values, economics, and even political ideologies. For example, societal expectations of pregnant women in the United States have changed, from simply waiting for birth to actively seeking to maintain the mother's—and hence the baby's—health, preparing for the birth process, and sometimes even trying to influence the baby's cognitive and emotional development while the baby is in the uterus.

Childbirth in Context

Throughout history, families—and particularly women—have passed on to young girls the traditions of childbirth practices. These traditions have been shaped by cultural and institutional changes. At the same time, the social function of childbirth has been institutionalized, changing the historical dynamics of pregnancy and childbirth dramatically.

Place of Childbirth

Until the early twentieth century, 95% of births in the United States occurred at home with a midwife (a trained birthing specialist). Most U.S. presidents were born at home; Jimmy Carter (the 39th president) was the first to be born in a hospital (Rothman, 1991). The family was intimately involved. During the "lying-in month" following birth, the mother was sheltered from outside influences, often lying in a darkened room while being taught by family members how to care for her newborn (Devitt, 1977). Yet, home births faced some danger: in 1900, 8 of every 1,000 women who labored at home died (Achievements in Public Health, 1999). Hospital births also presented great risk at this time: one in six who delivered in a hospital also died, primarily from sepsis (Vellery-Rodot, 1926). As formalized medical training developed, so did the medicalization of childbirth. By 1940, over 50% of deliveries occurred in hospitals (Campbell & MacFarlane, 1986), structuring the birthing process and ending the traditional lying-in month. Reflecting this trend, Hazel Gereke's first child was born at home, but her later children were born in a hospital. To further the trend away from home births, the American College of Obstetricians and Gynecologists (ACOG) issued a policy statement in 1975, affirmed in 1999, that protested out-of-hospital births and asserted that acceptable levels of safety were only available in the hospital. In fact, the former president of ACOG labeled home births as child abuse (Hosmer, 2001).

The feminist movement contributed to a return to natural birthing practices, as women advocated for less invasive deliveries in more friendly environments (Johanson, Newburn, & Macfarlane, 2002). By 1998, a study of 26,000 births in the United States found that only 1% occurred at home (Ventura et al., 1998), despite an approximately 75% cost savings for home births over hospital births (Anderson & Anderson, 1999). Most mothers who report participating in planned home births were over 30, were married, had at least one other child, lived in less populated areas (small town or rural area), and either had less than eight years of education or had college or graduate degrees; they also had lower mortality rates than hospital deliveries (Buitendijk, Offerhaus, van Dommelen, & van der Pal-de-Bruin, 2005; Scott, Berkowitz, & Klaus, 1999). A 2000 study ($n = 5418$) reviewed 98% of home births in North America attended by a certified professional midwife and found that the risks of home delivery were equal to those for low-risk infants delivered in the hospital. Approximately 12.1% of those women who intended to deliver at home were then transferred to the hospital (Johnson & Davis, 2005).

Today there are over 7,000 certified nurse-midwives practicing in all 50 states, mostly in hospitals (American College of Nurse-Midwives, 2006). A current debate centers on the use of midwives in home deliveries. ACOG's policy prohibits board-certified physicians from supervising noncertified nurse-midwives, thereby limiting midwives to practice primarily in hospitals and birthing centers. There is, however, a current legislative push to license certified midwives to attend home births in some states. Yet, this is challenging, as in one early decision, the South Dakota state legislature reaffirmed previous policy that disallowed midwives (both certified and unlicensed) to attend home births, therefore leaving some women to deliver at home without a qualified provider (Douglas, 2006).

Two other major developments have occurred during the last 30 years (Bain, Gau, & Reed, 1995; Hodnett, Downe, Edwards, & Walsh, 2005): the use of doulas (laywomen who are employed to stay with the woman through the entire labor, encouraging her and providing comfort measures), and the recent growth of *birthing centers* located close to a major hospital or within the hospital itself (Klaus, Kennel, & Klaus, 1993). Birthing centers offer an alternative to home delivery in a "home-like" freestanding facility with medical support. Recent research reveals that birthing centers reduce the number of medical interventions and increase maternal satisfaction (Hodnett et al., 2005; Oliver, 2005). Other studies have found that increased use of technology is linked to a decrease in the mother's satisfaction regarding the birthing process (Kornelsen, 2005; van der Hulst, van Teijlingen, & Bonsel, 2004). Birthing centers de-emphasize technology and model the dynamics of a home birth while allowing for rapid medical intervention if needed. Cultural perceptions regarding the use of technology must also be considered when working with diverse populations (Pollock, 2005).

A major change over time is the role of fathers in childbirth. During the 16th century, law and custom excluded men from observing deliveries, because labor was viewed as "something to be endured by women under the control of other experienced and knowledgeable women" (Johnson, 2002, p. 165). During the 1960s, when childbirth moved out of the home, hospitals still excluded fathers from participating in the labor process (Kayne, Greulich, & Albers, 2001). This became accepted practice but began to change in the 1970s. As more women were subjected to episiotomies (incisions to enlarge the opening for the baby during birth), enemas, and anesthesia in a male-dominated arena, often without their full knowledge or consent (Ashford, LeCroy, & Lortie, 2001), fathers were first invited in by physicians to serve as witnesses to avoid litigation (Odent, 1998, 1999). A 1995 survey in the United Kingdom found that fathers were present at 80% of all births, often serving as a "coach" (Woollett et al., 1995).

Whatever the original reason for encouraging the father's presence in the delivery room, father-supported childbirth appears to increase the mother's satisfaction in the birth process and decrease the amount of pain medication needed (Smith et al., 1991). Fathers who attend the birth of their child have increased paternal satisfaction, in spite of lack of role clarity (Dellmann, 2004; Odent, 1999), and increased empathetic and nurturing characteristics (Reed, 2005). Reflect on the Thompson's situation with Will in Iraq, unaware of the pending birth of his first child, and Felicia in premature labor without any family present. What role could a social worker play?

> **How does childbirth education support human agency in making choices?**

Childbirth Education

Childbirth education was not formalized until the early 1900s, when the Red Cross set up hygiene and health care classes for women as a public health initiative. In 1912, the U.S. Children's Bureau (created as a new federal agency to inform women about personal hygiene and birth) published a handbook titled *Prenatal Care*, emphasizing the need for medical supervision during pregnancy (Barker, 1998). When Dr. Grantley Dick-Read published *Childbirth Without Fear* in 1944, the medical establishment reacted negatively. The idea that women who were educated about childbirth would have less fear and therefore less need for pain medication was summarily rejected.

Not until the 1950s did the idea of childbirth education gain credibility. A French obstetrician, Dr. Fernand Lamaze, learned of Russian attempts to use hypnosis to reduce childbirth pain. His book *Painless Childbirth* (1958) has become the foundation for contemporary childbirth education. It instructs women, and more recently fathers and significant others, about female anatomy, the physiology of pregnancy, and relaxation techniques based on hypnosis (DeHart, Sroufe, & Cooper, 2000; Novak & Broom, 1995).

Childbirth education became a governmental priority during the 1980s as the gap widened between African Americans and other ethnic groups regarding the incidence of low birth weights and infant mortality (Armstrong, 2000). The need for childbirth classes cuts across demographic lines in theory, but, in many cases, not in practice. Studies show that better-educated women of higher socioeconomic status are more likely to participate in childbirth classes (Grossman, Fitzsimmons, Larsen-Alexander, Sachs, & Harter, 1990; Riedmann, 1996). Efforts have been made to improve access to childbirthing resources, as illustrated with the Maternity Care Access Act of 1989, which created a means-tested program called First Steps to provide parenting and childbirth classes to women who previously could not afford them (Rabkin, Balassone, & Bell, 1995). Healthy People 2000, the federal government's national health goals, also supported prenatal education as a way to alter individual women's behavior, thereby improving pregnancy outcomes (Armstrong, 2000; Magill-Cuerden, 2006). Some claim that childbirth classes acculturate the family to the hospital's protocols and expectations and thus facilitate medical management of labor and delivery (Armstrong, 2000).

Childbirth classes do seem to help. Some outcome studies have shown that childbirth classes result in decreased pain and anxiety (Dickason, Schult, & Silverman, 1990; Goldberg, Cohen, & Lieberman, 1999), shorter labor, decreased use of forceps, improved infant outcome, and an overall positive experience (Riedmann, 1996). Recent research has also shown that emotional support during labor can be more effective than childbirth classes (Waldenstrom, Hildingsson, Rubertsson, & Radestad, 2004). Meditation and psychological insight into the dynamics of labor and delivery may augment the traditional information offered in childbirth classes (Newman, 2005). Childbirth educators are also using the Internet to provide prenatal education and support (Bradley, 1995).

Childbirth classes must address the needs of all involved in this major life event. In one study, the researchers found that fathers who tended to avoid information were more dissatisfied with the childbirth experience after attending childbirth classes than fathers who had not attended. There was no relationship between fathers' attendance at childbirth classes and attachment to the infant six weeks after birth (Tiedje, 2001). Another study found that the level of coping response a father exhibited at the time of the birth of his child was predictive of his ability to adjust in one year and possibly the level of support he provided for his partner (Johnson & Baker, 2004). It is noteworthy that adolescent fathers are more involved during the prenatal period when they are employed, score high on measures of empathy, and when the mother does not have friends with children (Fagan, Barnett, Bernd, & Whiteman, 2003). While we do not know whether or not these factors apply to Nicole Evans, the findings point to potentially useful areas to explore if you are her social worker. Clearly, more information is needed to understand how prenatal education can meet the father's needs as well as the mother's needs—and not just the obstetrician's needs.

Hospital Stay

Pregnancy is one of the most common reasons for hospital admission. In 2004, there were 4.1 million deliveries in the United States, and most of these deliveries occurred in hospitals (Hamilton, Martin, Ventura, Sutton, & Menacker, 2006). In 2003, 71% of births were vaginal and 29% cesarean (Hoyert, Mathews, Menacker, Strobino, & Guyer, 2006)

Despite the frequent use of hospital delivery, we are in the midst of a changing philosophy. The view of pregnancy as an "illness" is giving way to the view that giving birth is a normal life transition. We are also living in an era that values cost-effective, innovative, comprehensive health services. Thus, policies regarding the length of the new mother's stay in the hospital are also changing.

> What historical trends are related to these changes in the view of childbirth?

Forty years ago, women remained hospitalized for 7 to 10 days following birth. By the early 1990s, the norm was 2 to 3 days. During the mid-1990s, however, controversial managed-care policies pushed for women with uncomplicated deliveries to be discharged within 24 hours, a savings of 2 hospital days. However, both mother and infant undergo rapid transitions during the period following delivery. The infant must adjust to a new environment, learn to nurse, and begin the process of bonding with parents. Life-threatening problems, such as heart problems, jaundice, or infections, may not be detected until the second or third day of life. As compensation for early discharge, some birthing facilities sent a nurse to visit the home for the first few days after discharge to assess the mother and the infant for any problems. These home visitors also provided education and emotional support.

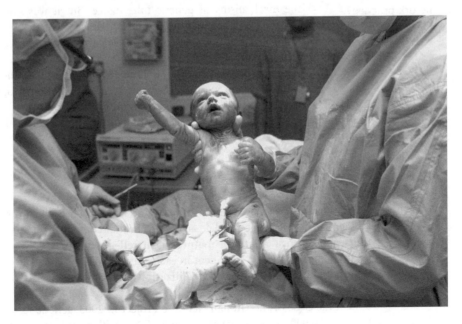

▲ **Photo 2.2**   A typical delivery—Here a newborn baby is delivered by medical professionals in a hospital delivery room.

However, the early discharge protocols were based on inadequate studies and created difficulties for many new mothers and infants. An outcry from patients and physicians led to congressional hearings about "drive-through deliveries" and the subsequent enactment of the Newborns' and Mothers' Health Protection Act of 1996. This federal legislation compelled insurers to provide a minimum stay of 2 days for mother and newborn following a vaginal delivery and 4 days following a cesarean section (Sitzer, 1998) but leaves the final decision to the pediatrician (American Academy of Pediatrics, 2004). It also has spurred studies focusing on the risks of premature discharge, with early results showing increased readmission rates of the newborn for jaundice, dehydration, and infection (Sacchetti, Gerardi, Sawchuck, & Bihl, 1997). Women over 32, African American women who have a cesarean delivery, and women who are giving birth for the first time are at greatest risk for readmission (Lydon-Rochelle, Holt, Martin, & Easterling, 2000).

⊠ Reproductive Genetics

Recognition of the need for genetics knowledge is not new to social work. In fact, Mary Richmond (1917) advocated that a social worker "get the facts of heredity" in the face of marriage between close relatives, miscarriage, tuberculosis, alcoholism, mental disorder, nervousness, epilepsy, cancer, deformities or abnormalities, or an exceptional ability.

> What are the implications of this knowledge explosion for social work practice?

Almost 50 years later, James Watson and Francis Crick (1953) first described the mechanisms of genetic inheritance. But it was not until 1970 that our knowledge of genetics began to explode. In 1990, the Human Genome Project (HGP) was funded by the U.S. Department of Energy and the National Institutes of Health as an international effort to map all the human genes by 2003. The goal was to treat, cure, and prevent disease. By June 2000, the first working draft of the human genome was completed and in 2003 this project ended. The knowledge that resulted from the HGP has altered social work practice in many areas, primarily in working with persons of reproductive age. Genetic research continues around the world with future findings that will impact social work practice.

Genetic Mechanisms

Chromosomes and genes are the essential components of the hereditary process. Genetic instructions are coded in **chromosomes** found in each cell; each chromosome carries **genes,** or segments of deoxyribonucleic acid (DNA), that contain the codes producing particular traits and dispositions. Each mature **germ cell**—ovum or sperm—contains 23 chromosomes, half of the set of 46 present in each parent's cells. As you can see in Exhibit 2.1, when the sperm penetrates the ovum (**fertilization**), the parents' chromosomes combine to make a total of 46 chromosomes arrayed in 23 pairs.

At the close of the Human Genome Project in 2003, genetic researchers estimated that there are 20,000 to 25,000 genes in human DNA, with an average of 3,000 to 5,000 genes per chromosome, slightly more than the number mice have (Human Genome Project, 2002). However, the debate about the total number of human genes continues, due—in part–to differences in the ways that genes are counted and estimated. And, the quest for increased

Exhibit 2.1 Germ Cell Division, Fertilization, and Chromosome Pairs

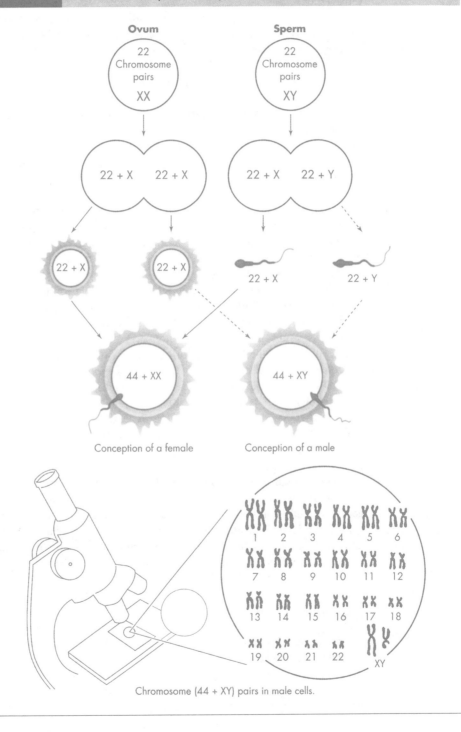

Conception of a female

Conception of a male

Chromosome (44 + XY) pairs in male cells.

knowledge continues through both publicly and privately funded projects and centers (Stein, 2004).

The genes constitute a "map" that guides the protein and enzyme reactions for every subsequent cell in the developing person and across the life span. Thus, every physical trait and many behavioral traits are influenced by the combined genes from the ovum and sperm.

Every person has a unique **genotype,** or array of genes, unless the person is an identical twin. Yet, the environment may influence how each gene pilots the growth of cells. The result is a **phenotype** (observable trait) that differs somewhat from the genotype. Thus, even a person who is an identical twin has some unique characteristics. On initial observation, you may not be able to distinguish between identical twins, but if you look closely enough, you will probably find some variation, such as differences in the size of an ear, hair thickness, or temperament.

A chromosome and its pair have the same types of genes at the same location. The exception is the last pair of chromosomes, the **sex chromosomes**, which, among other things, determine sex. The ovum can contribute only an X chromosome to the 23rd pair, but the sperm can contribute either an X or a Y and therefore determines the sex of the developing person. A person with XX sex chromosomes is female; a person with XY sex chromosomes is male (refer to Exhibit 2.1).

Genes on one sex chromosome that do not have a counterpart on the other sex chromosome create **sex-linked traits.** A gene for red/green color blindness, for example, is carried only on the X chromosome. When an X chromosome that carries this gene is paired with a Y chromosome, which could not carry the gene, red/green color blindness is manifested. So, almost all red/green color blindness is found in males. This gene for color blindness does not manifest if paired with an X chromosome unless the gene is inherited from both parents, which is rare. However, if a woman inherits the gene from either parent, she can unknowingly pass it on to her sons.

Whether genes express certain traits depends on their being either dominant or recessive. Traits governed by **recessive genes** (e.g., hemophilia, baldness, thin lips) will only be expressed if the responsible gene is present on each chromosome of the relevant pair. In contrast, traits governed by **dominant genes** (e.g., normal blood clotting, curly hair, thick lips) will be expressed if one or both paired chromosomes have the gene. When the genes on a chromosome pair give competing, yet controlling, messages, they are called **interactive genes**, meaning that both messages may be followed to varying degrees. Hair, eye, and skin color often depend on such interactivity. For example, a light-skinned person with red hair and hazel eyes may mate with a person having dark skin, brown hair, and blue eyes and produce a child with a dark complexion, red hair, and blue eyes.

Genetic Counseling

Although Mary Richmond noted in 1917 that many physical traits, medical problems, and mental health problems have a genetic basis, only recently has technology allowed us to identify the specific genes governing many of these traits. Now that the initial mapping of the human genome is complete, the next step is to further identify the complex interactions between the genes. The goal is to develop genetic interventions to prevent or cure various diseases or disorders as well as affect conception, pregnancy, and childbirth in other ways. At present, research is underway to genetically alter sperm, leading to male contraception (Herdiman, Nakash, & Beedham, 2006).

Our quickly increasing ability to read a person's genetic code and understand the impact it could have on the person's life has led to the relatively new discipline of *genetic counseling*, which provides information and advice to guide decisions for persons concerned about hereditary abnormalities. Social workers, with their biopsychosocial perspective, are well positioned to assess the need and in some circumstances provide such services (Bishop, 1993; Schild & Black, 1984; Takahashi & Turnbull, 1994). The interdisciplinary field of genetic counseling acknowledges social work as one of its essential disciplines, thereby making at least a rudimentary understanding of genetics and related bioethical issues essential for social work practice (Garver, 1995; Human Genome Project, 2002; Rauch, 1988; Reed, 1996). For example, researchers recently reported that a genetic variation has been identified that may explain why there is a higher rate of premature delivery for African American women compared with European American women. This is information that a social worker could use to encourage pregnant African American clients to seek medical consultation related to possible genetically based premature birth risks (Wang et al., 2006).

Social workers need to understand the rising bioethical concerns that genetic research fosters and use such knowledge to help clients faced with genetically related reproductive decisions. The U.S. government has the largest bioethics program in the world to address questions such as: Who should have access to genetic information? Do adoptive parents have the right to know the genetic background of an adoptee? Will genetic maps be used to make decisions about a pregnancy? Which genes should be selected for reproduction? Will persons who are poor be economically disadvantaged in the use of genetic information?

A major concern of genetic counseling is whether all genetic information should be shared with a client. Some information may only cause distress, because the technology for altering genes is in its infancy and applicable to only a few situations. But recent advances allow for earlier diagnosis, which reduces or prevents the effects of some rare diseases as well as gives some clients more decision options. Today, for example, a late-life pregnancy such as Hazel Gereke's could be evaluated genetically using amniocentesis or chorion villi testing. Such evaluation could lead to decisions ranging from abortion to preparation for parenting a child with a disability. However, these options typically are laced with economic, political, legal, ethical, moral, and religious considerations (Andrews, 1994; Chadwick, Levitt, & Shickle, 1997).

Ethical issues related to genetic engineering have an impact not only at the individual and family levels but also at the societal level. For example, when we are able to manipulate genes at will, we must be on guard against genetic elitism. It is one thing to use genetic engineering to eliminate such inherited diseases as sickle-cell anemia, but quite another to use it to select the sex, body type, or coloring of a child. We are living in a time of tremendous ethical complexity, involving the interplay of new reproductive technologies; changing family structures, values, and mores; political and religious debate; and economic considerations. This ethical complexity extends to issues of social justice; as increasing numbers of persons gain the ability to control conception, plan pregnancy, and control pregnancy outcomes, social workers need to protect the interests of those who lack the knowledge and other resources to do so.

◼ Control Over Conception and Pregnancy

The desire to plan the timing of childbearing is an ancient one, as is the desire to stimulate pregnancy in the event of infertility. Contraception and induced abortion have probably always existed in every culture. Effective solutions for infertility are more recent. But it is important to remember that not all methods of controlling conception and pregnancy are equally acceptable to all people. Cultural and religious beliefs, as well as personal circumstances, make some people more accepting of some methods than others.

How are decisions about timing of childbearing related to biological age, psychological age, social age, and spiritual age?

Contraception

The range of birth control options available today provides women and men with the ability to plan pregnancy and childbirth more than ever before. Four million women give birth in the United States each year. The overall birth rate in the United States in 2004 was 14.0 births for every 1,000 population and the fertility rate was 66.3 live births per 1,000 women ages 15 to 44. The highest fertility rates are among Hispanic women (97.7 births per 1,000 women ages 15 to 44) and the lowest are among non-Hispanic white women (58.5) (Hoyert et al., 2006). The rate of teen pregnancy continued to fall, dropping 1% between 2003 and 2004, and 33% since 1991. The pregnancy rate for younger adolescents (between 15 and 17) fell 43% in the past fifteen years. Slightly more than one-third of all infants were born to unmarried women in 2004 (Hamilton et al., 2006; Hoyert et al., 2006). At the same time, remarkable new methods of contraception have become available (Martin, Hamilton, Ventura, Menacker, & Park, 2002). Each birth control option needs to be considered in light of its cost, failure rate, potential health risks, and probability of use, given the user's sociocultural circumstances.

In 2000, the World Health Organization (WHO) increased medical restrictions on contraception, decreasing the number of women who are eligible for oral contraceptives and intrauterine device (IUD) insertion, citing health concerns. However, the risk of pregnancy is generally higher than the risk of adverse reactions to contraceptives (Best, 2002). Studies by the WHO have found that in developing countries, abortions (often performed in unsafe conditions) and dependency on sterilization to decrease family size can be moderated by the availability of contraceptive choices (World Health Organization, 2004). The world population is doubling every 30 to 40 years, but the use of contraceptives and delayed marriage have led to a slowdown in population growth. With an uneven overpopulation distribution, there is an urgent need to provide inexpensive, safe, convenient, and appropriate contraceptive devices to women and men worldwide (Goldenberg & Jobe, 2001).

Complete sexual abstinence is the only certain form of contraception. Without any contraception, an estimated 85% of heterosexual couples who engage in regular intercourse will conceive within one year (Dirubbo, 2006). Approximately 50% of pregnancies in the United States are unintended (Miller & Holman, 2006; Van der Wijden, Kleijnen & Van den Berk, 2003). The basis for this is uncertain, as contraceptive failure rate data vary across studies. Data from Fu and colleagues provide one estimate of possible failure rates for several types of contraception (Fu, Darroch, Haas, & Ranjit, 1999). Sexually active women have these options:

◆ *Breastfeeding.* Women who are breastfeeding are less likely than other women to conceive. Breastfeeding without the use of other contraceptives carries a pregnancy risk of between 1.2% and 6% a year (Van Der Wijden et al., 2003; ChildbirthSolutions, Inc., n.d.). For breastfeeding to be an effective contraceptive (e.g., less than 1% chance of pregnancy) during the first six months after delivery, a woman must nurse ten or more times per day and not introduce the infant to other foods, a practice known as the Lactational Amenorrhoea Method (LAM) (Van der Wijden et al., 2003).

◆ *Coitus interruptus.* Premature withdrawal of the penis from the vagina, before ejaculation, is probably the oldest form of birth control. However, the failure rate is approximately 19% a year (4% if used perfectly), and coitus interruptus offers no protection from STDs and HIV (ChildbirthSolutions, Inc., n.d.; Fu et al., 1999; Hatecher et al., 1994).

◆ *Periodic abstinence.* Natural family planning, or the rhythm method, involves daily tracking of changes in the woman's body associated with the menstrual cycle and an avoidance of intercourse during fertile periods. The effectiveness rate is 90% to 98% if used perfectly but is much less effective for women who are breastfeeding, have menstrual irregularity, or who do not abstain during periods of fertility (American Academy of Family Physicians, 2005).

◆ *Barrier methods.* The male condom (failure rate 3% when used correctly, 14% when used incorrectly or inconsistently over a 12-month period), the diaphragm (6% failure rate), and the cervical cap (20% to 36% failure rate) provide increased protection against STDs. But, except for the condom, protection against HIV is uncertain (Fu et al., 1999). Like male use condoms, the female condom protects against STDs, including HIV, and has approximately a 5% failure rate when used correctly, 21% when used incorrectly or inconsistently (Family Health International, 2006). The female condom costs between $2.50 and $5 per use, is visible after insertion (some women are requesting colored condoms), and may cause crackling or popping sounds. Originally thought to provide protection for low-income women internationally, it has not been well accepted (Severy & Spieler, 2000). Male condom usage among adolescents increased significantly between 1991 and 2003, from 21% in 1979 to 63% in 2003 (Anderson, Santelli, & Morrow, 2006). Spermicides, acting as chemical barriers, have a high failure rate (8% if used perfectly, 25% with typical use). Recent evidence shows that spermicides provide up to 25% protection against STDs including HIV (Severy & Spieler, 2000). Vaginal gels have also been found to have a wide variance in failure rates, many women are reluctant to use them, and often discontinue their use (Grimes et al., 2006).

◆ *Oral contraceptives.* The introduction of birth control pills in the United States in 1960 precipitated major changes in reproduction. With a failure rate of only about 0.3% to 8.0%, they revolutionized family planning (Alan Guttmacher Institute, 2005). The results of recent studies have raised concerns about long-term problems associated with "the pill," especially among women who smoke, but this method accounts for 30% of all utilized birth control (Alan Guttmacher Institute, 2005; Frye, 2006).

◆ *Intramuscular injections.* In 1992, the introduction in the United States of Depo-Medroxyprogestrone acetate (Depo-Provera), a drug used for many years in Europe, allowed women protection against pregnancy for three months. There are concerns that Depo-Provera may reduce absorption of calcium, leading to decreased bone density at the same time (during adolescence) that almost half of adult bone mass is being formed ("Providers examine," 2001). Depo-Provera also produces a significant increase in weight gain and fat redistribution with potential long-term effects (Clark, Dillon, Sowers, & Nichols, 2005). There is a 0.05% to 3.0% failure rate over 12 months (Alan Guttmacher Institute, 2005). Lunelle is a relatively new drug which is given by injection every month compared to the every three month injection by Depo-Provera (Freeman, 2004).

♦ *Intrauterine devices (IUDs).* The use of IUDs has been marked by controversy and legal disputes for a number of years. They were introduced in the early 1900s, but high rates of infection and tissue damage discouraged their use until the 1960s. Most manufacturers discontinued production in the 1980s following expensive legal settlements. However, newer IUDs are widely used and considered safe and reliable. Approximately 15% of women discontinue use of the IUD within one year because of complications, but they have a contraceptive failure rate over one year of only 0.1% to 1.0% (Fu et al., 1999). Although IUDs are chosen as a contraceptive by only 2% of women (Alan Guttmacher Institute, 2005), conception after discontinuing for the first three months is higher than after stopping the pill (71% to 80% for the IUD and 60% for women stopping the pill) (Kaplan et al., 2005). The IUD has been found to be the optimal contraceptive for women approaching menopause (Bhathena & Guillebaud, 2006).

♦ *Voluntary surgical sterilization.* Tubal ligation, surgical sterilization for women, is considered permanent and has an effectiveness rate of approximately 99.5% (Alan Guttmacher Institute, 2005). Vasectomy, or male sterilization, likewise is considered the most reliable method of contraception with a failure rate of 0.08% to 0.015% in the first year (Hepp & Meuleman, 2006). Both surgeries require expertise with appropriate preoperative counseling which may not be available in nonindustrial countries (Awsare et al., 2005). Recent advances in microsurgery have increased the success rates for reversal procedures for both tubal ligation and vasectomy. Fertility can be restored in up to 50% of men and 70% of women with reversal surgery (Riberio et al., 2004). Informed consent is required prior to surgical sterilization. Tubal ligations reduce the risk of pelvic inflammatory disease and ovarian cancer (Fu et al., 1999).

♦ *Emergency contraception (EC).* In July 2006, the FDA approved the "morning after pill," otherwise known as "Plan B," to be available to women without a prescription. It contains the same ingredients as oral contraceptives but higher doses are taken. There has been significant controversy about this medication and some pharmacists have refused to provide it to women (Karpa, 2006), but in one study 84% of women stated that talking to a pharmacist was helpful (Foster et al., 2006). Postcoital administration of hormones (estrogen and progesterone) given twice within 72 hours of unprotected intercourse, 12 hours apart, is estimated to reduce the risk of pregnancy by 75%. The U.S. Agency for International Development (USAID) has recommended EC for women who have been raped, whose partner's condom breaks, who run out of other forms of contraceptives, who have forgotten to take several consecutive oral contraceptives doses, and who did not expect to have sexual relations (Severy & Spieler, 2000). The American Academy of Pediatrics has also supported the over-the-counter availability of EC (American Academy of Pediatrics-Committee on Adolescence, 2005). However, concerns have been expressed that women may rely on EC as a routine method of contraception rather than as an emergency form, leading to increased risk behaviors, and it offers no protection from STDs (Harvey, Beckman, Sherman & Petitti, 1999). The cost is low but there may be side effects, including nausea, vomiting, and bleeding (American Medical Association, 2002).

◆ *New contraceptive methods.* Several new choices are recently available. On July 18, 2006, the United States government approved the use of Implanon, the only *long-term implantable* birth control product available in the United States and used by over 2.5 million women in over 30 countries. The single rod, the size of a matchstick, can remain implanted for up to three years (Miller & Holman, 2006; Wechselberger, Wolfram, Pulzl, Soelder, & Schoeller, 2006). The *vaginal ring* remains in place for three weeks and then is removed for one week. It provides protection by releasing hormones similar to oral contraceptives but with steadier levels in the blood. Recent studies have shown that women are more satisfied with the vaginal ring than oral contraceptives (Schafer, Osborne, Davis, & Westhoff, 2006), and they experience less bleeding than with the pill (Roumen, Op Ten Berg, & Hoomans, 2006). A recent study has shown that the vaginal ring can be used as emergency contraception because 87.5% of women who inserted the ring and maintained use for seven days after intercourse experienced either no ovulation or disrupted ovulation (Croxatto et al., 2005). A *contraceptive patch* is applied to the lower abdomen, buttocks, or upper body for three weeks and then discontinued for one week. It is ineffective 0.3% to 8.0% of the time (Alan Guttmacher Institute, 2005) but the FDA has issued a warning that women using the patch may be exposed to higher levels of estrogen than if they used oral contraceptives (U.S. Food and Drug Administration, 2005). In populations that are high risk for unintended pregnancies and abortions, the patch had lower continuation and effectiveness rates than oral contraceptives but in non high-risk populations, the women are more compliant using the patch than oral contraceptives (Bakhru & Stanwood, 2006; Miller & Holman, 2006). With obesity becoming a major international concern it is important to know that women over 198 pounds experienced a higher failure rate with the patch (Chatfield, 2002). Finally, in the spring of 2006, the FDA approved Seasonique, an oral contraceptive that allows a woman to experience menses only four times per year (U.S. Food and Drug Administration, 2006).

◆ *Male contraception.* It is expected that more contraceptive methods for males will soon become available. It will probably be a patch, topical gel, or a bi-monthly injection because oral contraceptives can have serious side effects in males (Herdiman et al., 2006). The suppression of sperm production has been studied in other countries and has been shown to be both effective and reversible (Liu, Swerdloff, Christenson, Handelsmen, & Wang, 2006; Wu, 2006).

Consider the circumstances of Nicole Evans, Felicia Thompson, and Hazel Gereke. What contraception options might they have today that they did not have at the time they became pregnant? What personal, familial, and cultural factors would possibly influence their use, or nonuse, of contraceptive options that are now available?

Medical Abortion

Abortion may be the most politicized, hotly debated social issue related to pregnancy today. But it was not always so controversial. Prior to the mid-1800s, abortion was practiced in the

United States but was not considered a crime if performed before the fetus quickened (or showed signs of life). After 1860, however, physicians advocated banning abortion because of maternal harm caused by the use of dangerous poisons and practices (Figueira-McDonough, 1990). Legislators also wanted to see growth in the U.S. population. By 1900, all states had legislation prohibiting abortion except in extreme circumstances, typically medically related. Over the years, moral issues increasingly became the basis for debate. Hazel Gereke recounted that as late as 1966, legal abortion had to be "medically related," which did not cover the difficulty of another child for older parents or the difficulty of raising a child with Down's syndrome, a condition that at that time could not be ascertained prenatally. Hazel's situation was also influenced by the moral or religious stance of the physician and perhaps the hospital.

Despite laws controlling abortion, it has remained an option for those with the economic means. Poor women have been the ones whose access to abortion services is limited. In 1973, in *Roe v. Wade,* the U.S. Supreme Court legalized abortion in the first trimester and left it to the discretion of the woman and her physician. However, the Supreme Court ruled in 1989, in *Webster v. Reproductive Health Services,* that Medicaid could no longer fund abortions and that much of the decision making related to abortion should return to the states. Today, states vary considerably in who has access to abortion, when, how, and at what cost. In some states, new rules are effectively decreasing access, particularly for poor and minority populations. Some poor African American women have no greater access to abortion now than they did more than 100 years ago (Ross, 1992). It is unlikely that Nicole Evans would have monetary access to a legal and safe abortion if she were interested in that option.

Today, approximately half of all pregnancies in the United States are unintended and half of these end in abortion (Finer & Henshaw, 2006). Globally, approximately 46 million abortions are performed annually, with only 26 million of these being legal. In 2000, there were an estimated 68,000 maternal deaths due to unsafe abortions world-wide (World Health Organization, 2004). During the first trimester and until **fetal viability** (the point at which the baby could survive outside the womb) in the second trimester, U.S. federal law allows for a pregnant woman to legally choose an abortion although states can narrow this option. Approximately 87% of abortions in the United States are performed during the first 12 weeks of pregnancy, 9.9% from 13 to 20 weeks, and 1.4% after 21 weeks (Strauss et al., 2002). Recent controversy regarding procedures for terminating a pregnancy after fetal viability have raised ethical and legal dilemmas that are being addressed in the legal system, by most religions, and in other parts of U.S. culture. Opinion polls continually reveal, however, that like Hazel Gereke, the vast majority of Americans favor abortion as an option under specified conditions (Cook, Jelen, & Wilcox, 1992; Figueira-McDonough, 1990). A January 2006 CBS News poll revealed that only 5% of respondents said that abortion should "never" be permitted (PollingReport. com, 2006).

The 16% decline in the rate of induced abortion in the United States between 1990 and 1996 is attributed to better education and increased use of birth control including abstinence (Centers for Disease Control and Prevention [CDC], 2000). But, economic disparities continue to increase with poorer women having a greater proportion of unwanted pregnancies compared to more affluent women. Between 1994 and 2001, the rate of unintended pregnancy among poor women increased by 29%, and the rate of unintended births increased by 44%. During this same period, the rate of unintended pregnancy among women at or above twice the poverty level declined by 20% and the rate of unintended births declined as well. The social class disparity in abortion rates increased during this period as well (Finer &

Henshaw, 2006). Due to these combined factors, poor women were five times as likely as their affluent age counterparts to have unintended births. This disparity may, in large part, be due to the fact that poor women are twice as likely as affluent women to have no health insurance (Finer & Henshaw, 2006; Sonfield, 2003).

Abortion procedures fall into three categories:

1. *Chemical abortion*, also known as medical or nonsurgical abortion, uses the drugs methotrexate or mnifepristone, followed by prostaglandin. This procedure is used in 10% of all U.S. and European abortions. This combined regimen has 92% efficacy if used within 49 days gestation. Prostaglandin can be used alone but has lower efficacy (Spitz, Bardin, Benton, & Robbins, 1998).

2. *Instrumental evacuation.* One of two types of instruments is used in 98.9% of all U.S. surgical abortions. The standard first-trimester vacuum curettage, also called Manual Vacuum Aspiration or MVA, is the one most frequently performed in an outpatient clinic. A suction device is threaded through the cervix to remove the contents of the uterus. It is fairly safe, but because it is invasive, it introduces greater risks than the use of prostaglandin. The second-trimester curettage abortion, accounting for 2.4% of U.S. abortions in 2002 (Strauss, et al., 2002), requires even greater dilatation of the cervix to allow passage of a surgical instrument to scrape the walls of the uterus. If cutterage abortion is performed on an out-patient basis, a second visit is required. With both types of instrumental evacuation, the woman faces risks of bleeding, infection, and subsequent infertility.

3. *Amnioinfusion.* In the second trimester, a saline solution can be infused into the uterus to end the pregnancy. Amnioinfusion is used in only 0.4% of abortions and requires the greatest medical expertise and follow-up care.

Regardless of the timing or type of abortion, all women should be carefully counseled before and after the procedure. Unplanned pregnancies typically create considerable psycho-logical stress, and social workers can help pregnant women consider all alternatives to an unwanted pregnancy—including abortion—consistent with the client's personal values and beliefs. Following an abortion, most women experience only mild feelings of guilt, sadness, or regret that abate fairly soon, followed by relief that the crisis is resolved (David, 1996). Nevertheless, some women have a more severe response and may require ongoing counseling, particularly those women who had faced pre-abortion trauma. Some researchers have found that as many as 40% of women undergoing abortion have prior unwanted sexual experiences (Rue, Coleman, Rue, & Reardon, 2004). Counseling is also particularly important from a pre-vention perspective, because women receiving counseling following a first abortion have been found to practice contraception with greater frequency and success (David, 1996). Social workers need to be mindful of their personal views about abortion in order to help a client make an informed decision that reflects the client's values, religious beliefs, and available options. In addition, it is important to assess for prior traumatic experiences.

Infertility Treatment

Children in many segments of today's society are taught that one of their major goals in life should be to become a parent. Thus, **infertility,** the inability to create a viable embryo after

How does infertility
affect the
multigenerational
family?

one year of intercourse without contraception (Jordon & Ferguson, 2006), is often a life crisis. There are over 80 million "childless persons" in the world (Bos et al., 2005), but not all by choice. Approximately 10% to 15% of couples in the United States experience infertility at some point in their reproductive lives with male infertility accounting for approximately 50% of this rate (Elster, 2006; Meng, Greene, & Turek, 2005).

The mind-body connection is clearly seen in the psychological consequences when infertility occurs. Studies have shown that women experiencing infertility have a 50% increase in depression, peaking at two to three years, compared to control groups (Cwikel, Gidron, & Sheiner, 2004). Women waiting for in vitro fertilization (IVF) experience four times the rate of depression as women without fertility problems, and if IVF is unsuccessful, the rate of depression increases (Cwikel, Gidron, & Sheiner, 2004). Anxiety, social stress, and marital dissatisfaction also have been shown to increase with infertility problems (Cwikel et al., 2004; Newton, Sherrard, & Glavac, 1999; Verhaak et al., 2005). However, social support, specifically a positive marital relationship, more than any other factor, modifies the psychological distress following failure of IVF (Verhaak et al., 2005). Women who have experienced childhood or adult sexual abuse and domestic violence have higher rates of gynecological problems, including Pelvic Inflammatory Disease (PID), that contribute to an increase in infertility (Champion, Piper, Holden, Korte, & Shaine, 2004; Champion et al., 2005; Cwikel et al., 2004).

The causes of infertility are many. Recent studies have shown that obesity in both men and women (Pasquali, 2006; Sallmen, Sandler, Hoppin, Blair, & Baird, 2006), Polycystic Ovary Syndrome (PCOS) with associated insulin resistance (Hahn et al., 2006; Pasquali, Gambineri, & Pagotto, 2006), high exposure to lead (Chang et al., 2005), ovulation disorders, blocked fallopian tubes, endometriosis, chromosomal abnormalities, and cervical and uterine congenital defects all affect fertility (Kelly-Weeder & O'Connor, 2006). One study of 1,500 infertility patients found that African American and Hispanic women were more likely to have a lower education level, lower household income, and more tubal problems than Caucasian women and also wait longer to receive care (Jain, 2006).

Defective sperm function is a leading cause of infertility (Altken, Wingate, De Iullis, Koppers, & McLaughlin, 2006) and recent research has focused on understanding this problem. Occupational factors that have been found to affect male fertility include exposure to leads, pesticides, estrogens, radiation, and heat (Giudice, 2006; Sheiner, Sheiner, Hammei, Potashnik, & Carel, 2003). Other factors have been implicated in male infertility including driving for extended periods of time (Figa-Talamanca et al., 1996) and advanced age (Sloter et al., 2006). About 10% to 15% of male infertility is due to genetic problems (an important issue when IVF is considered) (Ferlin, Arredi, & Foresta, 2006). Cigarette smoking reduces the volume of semen (Pasqualotto, Sobreiro, Hallak, Pasqualotto, & Lucon, 2006; Sepaniak et al., 2006) and affects circulation levels of estrogen in women (Grainger, Frazier, & Rowland, 2006; Kelly-Weeder & O'Connor, 2006), contributing to both male and female infertility. Caffeine has been shown to inhibit DNA repair in men, negatively affecting fertility (Papachristou Ornoy, 2006; Papachristou et al., 2006) and to be a risk factor for increased infertility and spontaneous abortions in women (Hassan & Killick, 2004; Tolstrup et al., 2003; Wen, Shu, Jacobs, & Brown, 2001). One study showed a 50% less chance of conception if the mother drank alcohol during her menstrual cycle (Hakin, Gray, & Zacur, 1998) and other studies have shown that alcohol decreases male fertility (Stefankiewicz, Kurzawa, & Drozdzik, 2006). In the past, infertile couples could keep trying and hope for the best, but medical technology has given today's couples a variety of options, summarized in Exhibit 2.2.

The primary treatment for male infertility, diagnosed by a sperm analysis, is artificial insemination, using fresh or frozen donor sperm. The success rate is typically 15% to 20% and costs approximately $250 per cycle. Ethical and legal questions have been raised, however, regarding the legal status of the sperm donor (what parental rights does he have?) and the psychosocial impact on the mother. Sperm donors are routinely screened for genetic defects and physical suitability, but psychological screening remains controversial—in large part because it is nonstandardized and thus easily misinterpreted.

The birth of the first "test tube baby" in 1978, demonstrating the first of many **assisted reproductive technologies (ART)**, initiated a new era in infertility management and research. The first test tube baby was conceived in the United States in 1983, and the number of such births has increased each year since that time. ART involves the recovery of eggs following hormonal treatment to induce ovulation. The eggs are surgically retrieved, inseminated in the laboratory, and, if fertilized, are transferred either into the cervix (in vitro fertilization) or into the fallopian tubes. Other procedures that only include manipulation of sperm are not considered ART (e.g., artificial insemination). Recent improvements have allowed more than 50% of infertile women to conceive using ART (Hart, 2002) and 35% resulted in a live birth (Wright, Chang, Jeng, & Masaluso, 2006).

By the time a couple considers the use of ART, they have often struggled with infertility for a long time, emotionally and physically, and may be desperate. But the high cost and limited success rates deter some prospective candidates. Some ART centers require a psychological

Exhibit 2.2	Causes and Cures for Infertility		
Male Infertility		**Female Infertility**	
Problem	*Treatment*	*Problem*	*Treatment*
Low sperm count	Change of environment; antibiotics; surgery; hormonal therapy; artificial insemination	Vaginal structural problem	Surgery
		Abnormal cervical mucus	Hormonal therapy
Physical defect affecting transport of sperm	Microsurgery	Abnormal absence of ovulation	Antibiotics for infection; hormonal therapy
Genetic disorder	Artificial insemination	Blocked or scarred fallopian tubes	Surgery; in vitro fertilization
Exposure to work environment substances	Early detection and changes in work environment	Uterine lining unfavorable to implantation	Hormone therapy; antibiotics; surgery
Alcohol and caffeine use and cigarette smoking	Reduction or abstinence pre-conception	Obesity	Weight reduction
Advancing age	Sperm banking at younger age; artificial insemination	Alcohol and caffeine use and cigarette smoking	Abstinence pre-conception (and post to maximize pregnancy outcome)

evaluation of the couple to assess competency to parent, often focusing on issues of stress, guilt, anxiety, depression, and isolation (Hart, 2002). Treatment focuses on decreasing psychological denial and disengagement (van den Akker, 2005), and when conception occurs, treatment centers on decreasing anxiety in order to increase self-esteem and parenting efficacy (Cox, Glazebrook, Sheard, Ndukwe, & Oates, 2006). Infertile women seeking ART have more education and are less likely to have a child than surrogate or adoptive parents (van den Akker, 2005). There is current controversy about the use of ART with women who have HIV, although the current rate of transfer of the virus to the fetus is less than 2% (Zutlevics, 2006).

The most common types of ART are the following:

- *In vitro fertilization* (IVF), where ova are surgically removed during ovulation and mixed with donor sperm, has a success rate of 74% when a woman's eggs are freshly fertilized but only 14% with thawed embryo (Wright et al., 2006). In the United States, one round of IVF costs approximately $21,661 to transfer one egg (embryo) and $39,212 to transfer five embryos, with a 13% cost increase for women over age 42 (Little, Radcliffe, & Caughey, 2006). Obviously, in impoverished countries where childlessness is a "crippling social taboo" this procedure is beyond the reach of most of the population (Cheap IVF needed, 2006).
- *Gamete intrafallopian tube transfer* (GIFT) represents 1% of ART procedures and has a pregnancy success rate of 50.9% and delivery rate of 35.7%. GIFT, used often in situations of advanced endometrioses (Lodhi et al., 2004), requires the same procedure as IVF, except that the fertilized ova are surgically returned to the woman's fallopian tubes. It also entails an increased risk for ectopic pregnancy, multiple births, and surgical complications (CDC, 1999). For both IVF and GIFT, the use of marijuana during fertility treatments reduces success rates (Klonoff-Cohen, Natarajan, & Chen, 2006).
- *Intrauterine insemination* (IUI) involves bypassing the cervix (usually altered by antibodies or infection) and surgically implanting the ovum and spermatozoa into the uterus. It is a costly procedure, often used during the early stages of endometriosis. Pregnancy success rates are less than with GIFT (Lodhi et al., 2004).
- *Preservation and gestational surrogacy* is the harvesting of embryos to preserve for future use. This procedure is often used when women face surgery due to cancer and will not be able to conceive in the future (Plante, 2000). Cervical cancer is the fourth most frequent cancer diagnosed in women between 15 and 39 years old, and it directly affects fertility. Recent surgical procedures that avoid hysterectomy have led to increased fertility but have a 33% rate of miscarriage in the first two trimesters (Plante, 2006).

All of these procedures except preservation and gestational surrogacy may use donated ova, but that practice has raised further legal and ethical questions, especially regarding parental rights and responsibilities. Psychological and emotional issues may also arise, related to the introduction of third-party genetic material, secrecy, and confidentiality.

Although ART was originally limited to married couples, unattached females in increasing numbers are using this method of conception. A growing population of older women is delaying childbirth for a number of reasons (e.g., not having a partner, 50%; wanting financial security, 32%; a career, 19%; being unaware of the impact of age on fertility, 18%; and only becoming interested in having children later in life, 26%) (Hammarberg & Clarke, 2005). Whatever the reason, when women try to conceive later in life, they often end up using ART. Surrogate mothers have increasingly volunteered to provide the opportunity for homosexual couples to bear children, also utilizing ART techniques (Ross, Steele, & Epstein, 2006). This trend has raised additional moral and ethical questions in some segments of society, such as whether or not a single mother, a lesbian mother, or an older mother can raise a child, as well as those in more traditional roles. These questions have led not only to hot debate but also to research seeking to provide evidence of successful parenting outcomes (Harris, 2005).

Adoption is one last alternative for the infertile couple. It is not much less daunting than infertility treatment, however. Infertility coupled with exposure to adoptive relationships is the primary motivator to consider adoption (Bausch, 2006). A time-consuming multiphase evaluation, which includes a home study, is required before finalization of custody. The idea of parenting an infant with an unknown genetic heritage may also be a challenge for some people, particularly because an increasing number of problems previously thought to be environmentally induced are being linked—at least in part—to genetics. On the positive side, however, some individuals and couples prefer adoption to the demands and uncertainties of ART, and some adoptive parents are also committed to giving a home to children in need of care.

▧ Normal Fetal Development

The 40 weeks of **gestation,** during which the fertilized ovum becomes a fully developed infant, are a remarkable time. **Gestational age** is calculated from the date of the beginning of the woman's last menstrual period, a fairly easy time for the woman to identify. In contrast, **fertilization age** is measured from the time of fertilization, approximately 14 days after the beginning of the last menstrual period. The average pregnancy lasts 280 days when calculated from gestational age and 266 days from the time of fertilization. Conventionally, the gestation period is organized by trimesters of about three months each. This is a convenient system, but note that these divisions are not supported by clearly demarcated events.

First Trimester

In some ways, the first 12 weeks of pregnancy are the most remarkable. In an amazingly short time, sperm and ovum unite and are transformed into a being with identifiable body parts. The mother's body also undergoes dramatic changes.

Fertilization and the Embryonic Period

Sexual intercourse results in the release of an average of 200 million to 300 million sperm. Their life span is relatively short, and their journey through the female reproductive tract is fraught with hazards. Thus, only about 1 or 2 in 1,000 of the original sperm reach the fallopian tubes, which lead from the ovaries to the uterus. Typically, only one sperm penetrates the ripened ovum, triggering a biochemical reaction that prevents entry of any other sperm. The **zygote** (fertilized egg) continues to divide and begins about a seven-day journey to the uterus.

Following implantation in the uterine wall, the zygote matures into an **embryo**. The placenta, which acts like a filter between the mother and the growing embryo, also forms. The umbilical cord connects the fetus to the placenta. Oxygen, water, and glucose, as well as many drugs, viruses, bacteria, vitamins, and hormones, pass through the placenta to the embryo. Amniotic fluid in the uterus protects the embryo throughout the pregnancy.

By the third week, tissue begins differentiating into organs. During this period, the embryo is vulnerable to **teratogens**—substances that may harm the developing organism— but most women do not know they are pregnant. Exhibit 2.3 shows how some relatively common drugs may have a teratogenic effect in the earliest stage of fetal development. Research is also showing that maternal diet has an influence on brain development. One study found that nutritional deficiency in the first trimester resulted in an increase in brain abnormalities including a potential risk for later development of schizophrenia (Rifas-Shiman et al., 2006). Research has also shown that thyroid hormones (e.g., iodine deficiency) play an important role in brain development and deficiencies during the first and third trimesters possibly leading to later learning disabilities (de Escobar, 2004; Rifas-Shiman et al., 2006; Sethi, 2004).

Exhibit 2.3 Potential Teratogens During the First Trimester	
Substance	*Effects on Fetal Development*
Acetaminophen (Tylenol)	None
Amphetamines	Cardiac defects, cleft palate
Antacids	Increase in anomalies
Antianxiety medications	Increase in anomalies
Antiepileptic medications	Neural tube defects, esp. facial
Antihistamines	None
Barbiturates	Increase in anomalies
Gentamycin (antibiotic)	Eight cranial nerve damage
Glucocorticoids (steroids)	Cleft palate, cardiac defects
Haloperidol	Limb malformations
Insulin	Skeletal malformations
Lithium	Goiter, eye anomalies, cleft palate
LSD	Chromosomal abnormalities
Penicillin	None
Phenobarbital	Multiple anomalies
Podophyllin (in laxatives)	Multiple anomalies
Tetracycline (antibiotic)	Inhibition of bone growth, discoloration of teeth
Tricyclic antidepressants	Central nervous system and limb malformations

The Fetal Period

After the 8th week, the embryo is mature enough to be called a **fetus** (meaning "young one") (Novak & Broom, 1995), and as we see in Nicole Evans' story, the mother is experiencing signs of her pregnancy. Usually the mother has now missed one menstrual period, but if her cycle was irregular, this may not be a reliable sign. Approximately 50% of women experience nausea and vomiting (morning sickness) during the first trimester. A few experience vomiting so severe that it causes dehydration and metabolic changes requiring hospitalization. **Multigravidas**, women who have had a previous pregnancy, often recognize the signs of excessive fatigue and soreness in their breasts as a sign of pregnancy.

Between the 8th and 12th week, the fetal heart rate can be heard using a Doppler device. At 12 weeks, the gender of the fetus can be detected, and the face is fully formed. The fetus is moving within the mother, but it is still too early for her to feel the movement.

Newly pregnant women often feel ambivalence. Because of hormonal changes, they may experience mood swings and become less outgoing. Concerns about the changes in their bodies, finances, the impact on their life goals, lifestyle adjustments, and other interpersonal interactions may cause anxiety. Often the father experiences similar ambivalence, and he may be distressed by his partner's mood swings. Parents who have previously miscarried may have a heightened concern for the well-being of this fetus.

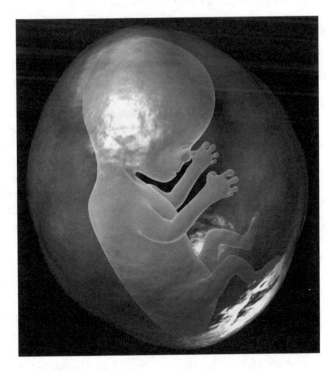

▲ **Photo 2.3**   After week 8, the embryo is mature enough to be called a fetus.

Second Trimester

By the 16th week, the fetus is approximately 19 centimeters (7.5 inches) long and weighs 100 grams (3.3 ounces). The most rapid period of brain development is during the second trimester (van de Beek, Thijssen, Cohen-Kettenis, van Goozen, & Buitelaar, 2004). Recent evidence cautions pregnant women to monitor the eating of fish with higher levels of mercury to avoid negative impact on the infant's cognitive skills (Oken et al., 2005). The second trimester is generally a period of contentment and planning for most women, as it seems to have been for Felicia Thompson. For problem pregnancies, or in troubled environments, quite the opposite may occur. However, the fatigue, nausea and vomiting, and mood swings that often accompany the first few weeks usually disappear in the second trimester.

Hearing the heartbeat and seeing the fetus via ultrasound often bring the reality of the pregnancy home. As seen in the story of the Thompsons, *quickening*—the experience of feeling fetal movement—usually occurs around this time, further validating the personhood of the fetus. *Fetal differentiation,* whereby the mother separates the individuality of the fetus from her own personhood, is usually completed by the end of this trimester. Many fathers too begin to relate to the fetus as a developing offspring.

Some fathers enjoy the changing shape of the woman's body, but others may struggle with the changes. Unless there are specific contraindications, sexual relations may continue throughout the pregnancy, and some men find the second trimester a period of great sexual satisfaction. Often during the second trimester the pregnant woman also experiences a return of her prepregnancy level of sexual desire.

Third Trimester

By 24 weeks, the fetus is considered viable in many hospitals. Today, neurosonography can visualize the fetal brain anatomy when central nervous system (CNS) anomalies are suspected (Malinger, Lev, & Lerman-Sagie, 2006). In spite of fetal viability, parents are not usually prepared for childbirth early in the third trimester. Felicia Thompson, for instance, was not prepared for the birth of her son, Paul, who at 26 weeks' gestation, struggled to survive. Not only are parents not prepared, but the risks to newborns are very great if birth occurs prior to the 26th week of pregnancy. Recent research indicates another caution for mothers during the third trimester: Smoking during this period can affect critical brain development and contribute to subsequent behavioral problems (Huang & Winzer-Serhan, 2006).

The tasks of the fetus during the third trimester are to gain weight and mature in preparation for delivery. As delivery nears, the increased weight of the fetus can cause discomfort for the mother, and often she looks forward to delivery with increasing anticipation. Completion of preparations for the new arrival consume much of her attention.

Labor and Delivery of the Neonate

Predicting when labor will begin is impossible. However, one indication of imminent labor is *lightening* (the descent of the fetus into the mother's pelvis). For a **primipara**—a first-time mother—lightening occurs approximately two weeks before delivery. For a **multipara** a mother who has previously given birth—lightening typically occurs at the beginning of labor. Often the mother experiences *Braxton-Hicks contractions,* brief contractions that prepare the mother and fetus for labor—what Hazel Gereke referred to as "false labor." Usually, true labor begins with a show or release of the mucous plug that covered the cervical opening.

Labor is divided into three stages:

1. In the first stage, the cervix thins and dilates. The amniotic fluid is usually released during this stage ("water breaking"), and the mother feels regular contractions that intensify in frequency and strength as labor progresses. Many factors determine the length of this stage, including the number of pregnancies the mother has experienced, the weight of the fetus, the anatomy of the mother, the strength of the contractions, and the relaxation of the mother in the process. Despite the stories that abound, most mothers have plenty of time to prepare for the upcoming birth. Near the end of this phase, "transition" occurs, marked by a significant increase in the intensity and frequency of the contractions and heightened emotionalism. The head crowns (is visible at the vulva) at the end of this stage.

2. The second stage is delivery, when the **neonate** (newborn) is expelled from the mother. If the newborn is born breech (feet or buttocks first) or is transverse (positioned horizontally in the birth canal) and cannot be turned prior to birth, the mother may require a cesarean section.

3. Typically, within one hour after delivery, the placenta, the remaining amniotic fluid, and the membrane that separated the fetus from the uterine wall are delivered with a few contractions. If the newborn breastfeeds immediately, the hormone oxytocin is released to stimulate these contractions.

Following birth, the neonate undergoes rapid physiological changes, particularly in its respiratory and cardiac systems. Prior to birth, oxygen is delivered to the fetus through the umbilical vein, and carbon dioxide is eliminated by the two umbilical arteries. Although the fetus begins to breathe prior to birth, breathing serves no purpose until after delivery. The neonate's first breath, typically in the form of a cry, creates tremendous pressure within the lungs, which clears amniotic fluid and triggers the opening and closing of several shunts and vessels in the heart. The blood flow is rerouted to the lungs.

Many factors, such as maternal exposure to narcotics during pregnancy or labor, can adversely affect the neonate's attempts to breathe—as can prematurity, congenital anomalies, and neonatal infections. Drugs and other interventions may be administered to maintain adequate respiration. To measure the neonate's adjustment to extrauterine life, *Apgar scores*—rather simple measurements of physiological health—are assessed at one, five, and ten minutes after birth. Apgar scores determine the need for resuscitation and indicate the effectiveness of resuscitation efforts and long-term problems that might arise. The other immediate challenge to the newborn is to establish a stable temperature. Inadequately maintained body temperature creates neonatal stress and thus increased respiratory and cardiac effort, which can result in respiratory failure. Close monitoring of the neonate during the first four hours after birth is critical to detect any such problems in adapting to extrauterine life.

⬛ Pregnancy and the Life Course

As the three case studies at the beginning of the chapter indicate, pregnancy is a period of transition. Each family member faces changes in role identification and prescribed tasks.

Regardless of the age of the parents or number of previous births, the pregnant woman, and the father when involved, must complete four different developmental tasks:

1. The parent(s) must provide for the mother's safety and that of the neonate throughout pregnancy, labor, and delivery.

2. The parent(s) must help people in her/their social support system to accept this event.

3. The parent(s) must bond with her/their unborn child.

4. The parent(s) must come to terms with the inequality inherent in a parent/neonate relationship. (based on Rubin, 1995)

> Under what conditions might the transition to parenthood become a turning point?

Although the tasks were the same for Nicole Evans, Felicia Thompson, and Hazel Gereke, and their partners, each had very different resources for negotiating the tasks. To some extent, those resources were specific to their position in the life course. Remember, however, that the tasks are the same regardless of maternal age.

Teen Pregnancy

Nicole Evans represents a well-known situation in the United States. Fifty percent of adolescents are sexually active, resulting in approximately 750,000–850,000 pregnancies per year in women ages 15 to 19. Between 74% and 95% of these pregnancies are unintended. Approximately half of these pregnancies result in a live birth, 28% end in abortion, and 14% in miscarriage or stillbirth.

The good news is that despite an 8% increase in overall birthrates between 1991 and 2004, teen birthrates declined by 25%, reaching the lowest level ever recorded with a birthrate of 22.1 per every 1,000 females. The most marked decline was among black, non-Hispanic, teenagers ages 15 to 19 (down 47%) and teens between the ages of 15 and 17 (down 57%). During this same time period, Hispanic births for teens ages 15 to 19 showed the least decline of 21%. For Asian or Pacific Islander teens ages 15 to 19, the birthrate dropped 36% and for American Indian teens there was a 38% birthrate decline (Hamilton et al., 2006). Although births to unmarried mothers as a percentage of all births rose from 34.6% to 35.7% in 2004, the number of births to unmarried teens continued to decline between 1991 and 2004 (down 33%) (Hamilton et al., 2006).

Nevertheless, adolescent pregnancy in the United States is among the highest in the industrialized world, with teen pregnancies accounting for 10% of babies born (Hamilton et al., 2006; Tomal, 1999). The social costs are high: an estimated $7 billion is spent each year on adolescent pregnancy, and only one third of the teens are able to earn a high school diploma (Kaplan et al., 2001; Koshar, 2001).

One study showed that teens who are coerced into sex, or raped, are twice as likely as their nonabused peers to experience teenage pregnancy (Kenney, Reinholtz, & Angelini, 1997). A boyfriend was identified as the perpetrator in almost 30% of these rapes. Approximately 5% of all rapes result in pregnancy regardless of age (Holmes, Resnick, Kilpatrick, & Best, 1996). In addition, one study found that 29% of pregnant teens between the ages of 12 and 19 were victims of violence during their pregnancy. The victims of physical and sexual violence were more likely to use cigarettes, alcohol, and illicit drugs than nonvictims (Martin, Clark, Lynch,

Kupper, & Cilenti, 1999). Social workers are often on the front line helping these teens as they struggle with emotional and physical suffering.

Teen pregnancy carries medical risks also. Pregnant teens have higher incidences of toxemia (pregnancy-induced high blood pressure) and anemia than adult women, and their neonates are at greater risk for low birth weight, prematurity, and infant mortality than neonates born to adult women. The rate of prematurity and low birth weight among African American adolescents is twice as high as the rate for Hispanic and European American adolescents. Although pregnancy-related complications are not limited to teen mothers, it is important for social workers to note that black women are three times as likely to die from such complications as Caucasian women are (a rate that has risen 33% in the past 100 years) (Population Council, Inc., 1999).

Limited financial resources, the inadequate and fragmented facilities often found in impoverished communities, and the normal adolescent avoidance of problems frequently contribute to a delayed diagnosis of pregnancy for disadvantaged young women. Of course, delayed diagnosis hampers timely prenatal care and limits pregnancy options, increasing the risks of both mortality and morbidity (sickness) for fetus, newborn, and mother.

The experience of pregnancy varies somewhat with stage of adolescence:

◆ *Young adolescents, ages 10 to 14.* Following years of increases, pregnancy rates for this group are dropping. Nine percent of 14-year-old sexually active women become pregnant each year, but they account for only 1.6% of all teen births (Kaplan et al., 2001; Tomal, 1999). The bulk of teen pregnancies are still occurring at later ages. One study found that the rate of pregnancy for this age group was significantly affected by the parents' marital status, indicating that family stability may be a more powerful influence in pregnancy prevention than socioeconomic status (Tomal, 1999). Some of the pregnancies in this age group can be attributed to increased rates of child sexual abuse (National Center for Child Abuse and Neglect, 1995). Long-standing incest can result in pregnancy as the teen becomes fertile. As the average age of first menstruation decreases, it is not uncommon for girls as young as 10 years old to ovulate. At the same time, the interval between the onset of menstruation and the completion of the educational process has lengthened, increasing the possibility of disrupting pregnant teens' education and thus predisposing them to a lifetime of poverty. Long-term commitment and financial support from the father of the pregnant teen's child are unusual, further contributing to the isolation and impoverishment of the young adolescent mother. Premature birth is 3.4 times more common for young adolescents than for nonadolescent women, possibly because of the difficulty of meeting the nutritional demands of both the growing fetus and the growing adolescent (DuPlessis, Bell, & Richards, 1997).

◆ *Middle adolescents, ages 15 to 17.* This age group comprises 32% of all births to mothers under 20 years of age. Young women at this age have completed most of their physical growth but are still emotionally immature. They may engage in sexual activity to demonstrate independence, maintain status in their peer group (which appears to be part of the story for Nicole Evans), explore self-identity, or experiment with new behaviors. The sense of invulnerability that permeates adolescence often provides a false sense of security.

◆ *Late adolescents, ages 18 to 19.* This group accounts for two-thirds, 67%, of all births to mothers under age 20. The relatively recent phenomenon of "adolescence" has redefined pregnancy for this age group. Until the twentieth century, marriage and childbearing were normative during this life stage. Late adolescents who become pregnant tend to be more mature than younger teens and often have a positive relationship with the infant's father. They are more focused on the future and may have more social supports. However, if the teen's education is disrupted, the pregnancy may be viewed as a major impediment to achieving career goals.

One significant feature of teen pregnancy is the extent to which the adolescent mother connects with other family members. From a family systems perspective, the pregnant teen may be repeating her mother's behaviors, as seen in Nicole Evans' story. Research also suggests that younger sisters of pregnant teens, compared to younger sisters without a pregnant older sister, show more acceptance of at-risk behaviors for pregnancy, engage in more problem behaviors, and have more interaction with the older sibling's social network (East, 1996; East & Shi, 1997). The family's response to the pregnancy and the teen mother's emotional stability will significantly influence her parenting behaviors. Positive role modeling of family dynamics and social support are especially important.

How important is the multigenerational family in social work practice with pregnant teens?

Many initiatives have focused on pregnancy prevention (Cowley & Farley, 2001). A metaanalysis of studies found that pregnancy prevention programs had no effect on reducing teen sexual activity but did lead to the increased use of condoms and a reduction in pregnancy rates (Franklin & Corcoran, 2000). While many teen females report that their first intercourse is involuntary, about 75% of females and 82% of teen males use some method of contraception at first intercourse. Communities are increasingly allocating resources to facilitate education programs, at times funded by local businesses (Koshar, 2001; National Campaign to End Teen Pregnancy, 2002). Effective prevention programs must also consider issues outside the pregnancy, such as violence and substance abuse.

The role and needs of the adolescent father have been woefully neglected in the research on adolescent pregnancy. One study of 84 teen mothers and 57 teen fathers revealed that romantic involvement, support of extended family, and presence of a mother's childless friends predicted prenatal father involvement (Fagan et al., 2003). Teen fathers who remain involved with the mother and infant provide a significant source of support for both (Osofsky, Hann, & Peebles, 1993). One study showed that the best predictor of an adolescent girl's attitude toward her pregnancy was her boyfriend's desire for a baby (Cowley & Farley, 2001). Pregnant adolescents who maintain a relationship with the baby's father seek prenatal care earlier than teens who terminate the relationship (Moss, 1987). For these reasons, many programs targeting teen mothers also provide services to engage teen fathers. What are the social work implications of this information in relation to Nicole Evans and the father of her baby?

Early Adulthood Pregnancy

Physiologically, a young woman in her 20s and 30s is at the optimal age for pregnancy. Psychologically, young adults are involved in establishing life goals, and these often involve parenthood. Thus, pregnancy during this period of the life course is a normative event in most cultures.

Research suggests that even during the prime childbearing years, women who have appropriate social support are healthier psychologically and physically during their pregnancies. Their infants are six times less likely to experience problems, and they have more positive developmental outcomes, compared to women who lack social support (Hogoel, Van-Raalte, Kalekin-Fishman, & Shlfroni, 1995; Oakley, Hickey, Rojan, & Rigby, 1996). Social support is an important protective factor for mother and child.

Delayed Pregnancy

An increasing number of women are delaying childbirth until their late 30s and 40s, even into their 50s and 60s. Many have been struggling with infertility for several years; others deliberately have chosen to wait until their careers are established. Other women are choosing to have children with a new partner. Some single women, driven by the ticking of the so-called biological clock, finally choose to go ahead and have a child on their own, often using artificial insemination (Hammarberg & Clarke, 2005).

> What cohort effects can you recognize in attitudes toward delayed pregnancy?

Waiting until later in the life cycle to reproduce increases pregnancy risks. While birthrates for women age 35 to 44 more than doubled between 1978 and 2000, one-third of women age 35 to 39 and two-thirds of women over age 40 experience fertility problems (March of Dimes, 2006a). The fertility rate for women age 40 to 47 is only between 5% and 7% (Berryman & Wendridge, 1991; Fleming, 2000). The rate of miscarriage for women over 45 is 75% (Fleming, 2000). The trend to delay childbearing increases the risk of maternal mortality rates for women over 35, especially those delivering their first child (Waterstone, Bewley, Wolfe, & Murphy, 2001). Most fertility clinics discourage women over 40 from using their own eggs for in vitro fertilization because the woman's eggs age as she does, with an increased risk of chromosomal abnormalities. Some infertility clinics are using the DNA from the older woman's egg and transferring it into the cytoplasm of a younger woman's donated egg. Research is being conducted on the efficacy of freezing a slice of ovarian tissue (containing thousands of immature eggs) for later implantation (Klotter, 2002).

Unlike Hazel Gereke, who 31 years ago unexpectedly became pregnant in later life, many women are purposely choosing to face the risks of delayed pregnancy and childbirth. They are often less traditional than their peers, have a more autonomous personality, and are more likely to have younger partners (Berryman & Wendridge, 1991). Social workers may work with families when infants are born to mothers of advanced maternal age (AMA) as well as provide guidance to older persons considering pregnancy.

Women who conceive after 35 may have more difficulty adjusting to the pregnancy during the first trimester than do their younger cohorts, but by the third trimester there is no difference in acceptance (Berryman & Wendridge, 1996). Preexisting medical conditions, such as diabetes or hypertension, may increase the risks of pregnancy, and older women, like Hazel Gereke, face the increased risk of giving birth to an infant with Down's syndrome. These women also have a two-fold risk of onset of high blood pressure and diabetes during pregnancy, three-fold for women over age 40, compared to women in their 20s (March of Dimes, 2006a). Older women have higher incidences of complications during labor and delivery and an increased rate of cesarean births. With appropriate physical care, however, most women can successfully negotiate most of the hazards of later-life pregnancy (Nabukera, Wingate, Alexander, & Salihu, 2006; Waterstone et al., 2001).

In some cases, *elderly gravidas*—the medical term for pregnant women over 35—may be concerned about care for the child as they age, leading to increased stress. Older children may also have difficulty accepting the mother's pregnancy and the arrival of a new sibling.

However, older women may be more financially stable and feel more self-confident in their mothering role (Pridham & Chang, 1992), and increasing numbers of women are choosing to have a child after age 35, despite the greater risks.

⊠ Risk and Protective Factors in Conception, Pregnancy, and Childbirth

Despite significant advances in the medical management of pregnancy and childbirth, the United States ranks 25th in the world in infant mortality and 21st in maternal mortality, worse than most industrialized nations (Homer, 2001). Thus, the understanding and prevention of **risk factors,** the characteristics that increase the likelihood of a problem, are of particular concern. Risk factors include biological, psychological, social, familial, environmental, and societal dimensions. Like risk factors, **protective factors,** which help reduce or protect against risk, also range from biological to societal dimensions. Exhibit 2.4 presents selected risk and protective factors for conception, pregnancy, and childbirth.

Exhibit 2.4	Selected Risk and Protective Factors for Conception, Pregnancy, and Birth	
	Risk Factors	*Protective Factors*
Conception	Low sperm count	Father drug abstinence (marijuana)
	Fallopian tubal factors	Gynecological care
	Genetic abnormality	Genetic counseling
	Adolescent promiscuity	Family life education; contraception; abstinence
	Endometriosis	Hormone therapy; surgery
	Inadequate nutrition for sexually active women of childbearing age	Folic acid supplement
Pregnancy	Obesity	Normal weight maintenance
	Sexually Transmitted Diseases (STDs)	Barrier birth control methods
	Female age (<18 or >35)	Family life education; birth control
	Delivery before 38 weeks	Prenatal care; WIC Program
	Gestation, toxemia, diabetes	Prenatal care
	Stress due to inadequate resources	Social and economic support
	Trauma	Accident prevention (falls, fire, car)
	Smoking	Prenatal care; smoking cessation programs
Birth	Venereal diseases such as gonorrhea and positive GBS	Prenatal care; antibiotic eye drops for neonate; maternal testing
	Meconium aspiration; anoxia	C-section delivery; drugs during pregnancy; well-managed labor and delivery
	Prolonged and painful labor	Birthing classes; social support; father presence at birth; adequate pain control

<table>
<tr><td>What do social workers need to know about the effects that different aspects of fetal development can have on subsequent development?</td></tr>
</table>

Social workers must be knowledgeable about the risk and protective factors that are associated with the most commonly occurring problems they address with individuals and families. It is also critical that social workers remember that the presence of a risk or protective factor cannot totally predict any one outcome. Even when a risk factor is present, it may not be sufficient to result in the related outcome, or the effect may have a rather broad range of impact. For example, pregnant women's prenatal heroin use is known as a risk factor for their children's intelligence, but children exposed to heroin in the womb have had IQ scores ranging from 50 to 124 (Wachs, 2000).

Another consideration is timing. One child with a defective gene may experience the onset of a genetic illness much earlier or later than another child with the same gene.

And finally, most outcomes are determined by several factors. Seldom is one environmental, social, or biological risk factor solely responsible for an outcome (Epps & Jackson, 2000). We are unlikely to ever be able to predict all the developmental patterns that might result from a given set of risks (Vallacher & Nowak, 1998; Wachs, 2000).

One explanation for the great variability in individual outcomes when risk factors are present is the concept of resiliency, or the ability to cope and adapt (Garmezy, 1993; Werner, 2000). Both individuals and families are faced with stressful situations, chronic or crisis, over the life course (Walsh, 1998). And both the individual and family may possess characteristics that have been identified as the ability to bounce back, respond, adapt, or successfully cope with these life events. Certain family characteristics related to resiliency—such as good communication and problem-solving processes—can serve as protective factors for individual development (Hawley & DeHaan, 1996). Family risk factors with individual impact may include marital discord and inadequate parenting skills.

The Gereke family demonstrated characteristics of resiliency in how it responded to Terry's birth. The parents' life courses were dramatically altered, from anticipating the arrival of adulthood for their youngest child (empty nest) to becoming the parents of a newborn with a major disability. In fact, however, the lives of all family members were altered by this one event. Ultimately, they said that Terry's birth changed their family for the better, bringing them all emotionally closer and making them more responsive to others' needs. For each person, Terry's birth also set into motion multiple transitions, and in a like manner Terry's life course was affected by these family and individual transitions.

▧ Social Work and Challenges in Childbearing

The events related to childbearing are affected by economic, political, and social forces. Social workers, with their understanding of changing configurations of person and environment, are well equipped to address the needs of all persons of reproductive age that derive from these forces. Although most pregnancies result in favorable outcomes, for those that do not, social workers can play an important role. Moreover, many negative outcomes can be prevented through social work interventions, prenatal care, childbirth education, introduction to new medical technologies, and genetic counseling. The social worker who participates in these interventions requires knowledge of, and collaboration with, a range of other professionals.

Problem Pregnancies

In some sense, each of the pregnancies described at the beginning of this chapter is a problem pregnancy. Pregnancy can become problematic for a variety of reasons, but only four types of problem pregnancies are discussed here: undesired pregnancy, ectopic pregnancy, miscarriage and stillbirth, and maternal brain death.

Undesired Pregnancy

Pregnancies that are unplanned are a problem because they are associated with increased stress. They carry a higher risk for inadequate prenatal care, health problems late in the pregnancy and right after birth, and significant postnatal problems. Some data indicate that women who are unhappy about their pregnancy during the first trimester may experience up to two times greater neonatal mortality than women who are accepting of their pregnancy (Bustan, 1994; Wang & Lin, 1999). Of particular concern for social workers is the growing disparity of unwanted pregnancy related to income.

As noted in earlier discussion, Hispanic teens show the least decline in pregnancy rates compared to all other groups, and there may be some cultural factors involved: 46% of Hispanic teen females report that they would be very upset if they become pregnant, compared to 60% of all other teens (Ryan, Franzetta & Manlove, 2005). Social workers can use such knowledge to provide culturally sensitive service that presents essential information, links teens to reproductive resources, and assists in problem solving about other reproductive concerns.

Ectopic Pregnancy

An ectopic pregnancy occurs if the zygote implants outside the uterus, usually in the fallopian tubes. The rate of ectopic pregnancy rose six fold in the United States between 1970 and 1992 and continues to increase, but morbidity and mortality have substantially decreased (Kdous, 2006). Each year over 100,000 pregnancies are terminated due to ectopic implantation, and it accounts for over 9% of the maternal deaths in the first trimester (Walling, 2001). Although over 50% of women presented with an ectopic pregnancy have no known risk factors (Brown-Guttovz, 2006), women who have had previous ectopic pregnancies, tubal damage from surgeries or infection (especially Chlamydia trachomatis, a major cause of pelvic inflammatory disease), a history of infertility, in vitro fertilization, or a maternal age over 35 are at greater risk for an ectopic pregnancy (Ankum, 2000; Blandford & Gift, 2006).

The initial clinical symptoms, abdominal pain and vaginal bleeding, are nonspecific and only occur in 50% of the patients with an ectopic pregnancy (Brown-Guttovz, 2006), but if tubal rupture occurs, the situation is life threatening and requires a visit to the emergency clinic. Early diagnosis is critical to the outcome. Techniques such as imaging studies and measurement of pregnancy hormonal levels may help decrease maternal mortality (Guvendag, 2006; Splete, 2002). However, because the diagnosis of ectopic pregnancy cannot be made without sophisticated medical equipment, all sexually active women with lower abdominal pain and vaginal bleeding should be evaluated (Tay, Moore, & Walker, 2000).

When found within the first six weeks of pregnancy, ectopic pregnancy is typically treated with medication (methotrexate); otherwise, abdominal surgery is necessary (Api et al., 2006; Cooper, 2000). Only 30% of women with an ectopic pregnancy will have difficulty with subsequent conception (Brown-Guttovz, 2006).

Miscarriage and Stillbirth

Miscarriage is the naturally occurring loss of a fetus prior to 20 weeks' gestation—a **spontaneous abortion**. Approximately 10% to 20% of all clinically recognized pregnancies end in spontaneous abortion, often without a discernible cause and often unrecognized by the mother (Neugebauer et al., 2006). Recurrent miscarriage, three or more consecutive miscarriages, occur in 2% to 3% of women and are usually caused by chromosomal abnormalities, metabolic disorders, immune factors, problems with the woman's reproductive anatomy, or metabolic disorders (Horn & Alexander, 2005). Approximately 70% of these women ultimately are able to conceive (Kiwi, 2006; New concepts on the causes of recurrent miscarriage, 2006). Recent research focusing on the causes of miscarriage point to multiple potential factors, including fetal chromosomal anomalies (Christiansen, Nielsen, & Kolte, 2006), sickle cell trait (Taylor et al., 2006), uterine cancer (Critchley & Wallace, 2005), polycystic ovary syndrome (PCOS) (van der Spuy & Dyer, 2004), rubella (Edlich, Winters, Long, & Gubler, 2005), number of members in a household, coffee consumption, number of pregnancies, history of abortion (Nojomi, Akbarian, & Ashory-Moghadam 2006), stress (Nepomnaschy et al., 2006), and obesity (Yu, Teoh & Robinson, 2006). At greater risk are those women who are African American, have less education, and of lower socioeconomic status, especially with income below the poverty level (Price, 2006).

An estimated 20.9% of threatened spontaneous abortions become complete abortions (Buss et al., 2006). If the abortion is incomplete, any placenta or fetus that is not expelled must be surgically removed or the mother risks hemorrhage and infection. Counseling of women who struggle with miscarriages focuses on genetics and the biopsychological needs of the woman and her family (Laurino et al., 2005; Neugebauer et al., 2006).

In late pregnancy, at 24 or more weeks gestation, if the fetus does not breathe or exhibit a heartbeat, or if the umbilical cord stops pulsating, the birth is considered a *stillbirth* or *intrauterine fetal death* (IUFD) (Cartlidge & Stewart, 1995). Each year, over 4 million stillbirths occur annually, most in underdeveloped countries (McClure, Nalubamba-Phiri, & Goldenberg, 2006; Nhu et al., 2006). In the United States, stillbirths occur at the rate of 0.6 to 1.9 stillbirths per 1,000 live births until after 39 weeks of gestation when the rate increases to 2 fetal deaths per 1,000 living fetuses (Hankins, Clark, & Munn, 2006). In developing countries, the rate of stillbirth dramatically increases to 12.9 stillbirths per 1,000 births, primarily due to prolonged labor, home deliveries, inadequate treatment, and infections (McClure et al., 2006; Nhu et al., 2006). In cases of stillbirth, labor generally proceeds immediately and is allowed to occur naturally. But the pregnancy may continue for several days following cessation of movement, and in extreme cases surgery may be needed to end the pregnancy. Stillbirths are often unexpected, resulting in great stress and anguish for parents, who blame themselves and struggle with unresolved guilt. Social workers can help parents to understand and cope with the strong emotions they are experiencing (Pauw, 1991).

Maternal Brain Death

Until recently, if a pregnant woman suffered irreversible brain death, the death of the fetus was almost inevitable. Today recent technological advances can maintain the woman on life support for up to 107 days, allowing for the maturation of the fetus before delivery. Although the ability to support a woman who is brain dead physiologically until the fetus is more mature is relatively new, Julius Caesar was born by Cesarean section after his mother died

(Sperling, 2004). Factors that promote successful fetal outcomes include appropriate resuscitation, prompt diagnosis of brain death, and adequate maternal nutrition (Hussein, 2004; Mallampalli & Guy, 2005; Souza et al., 2006). Legal and ethical issues are also raised by supporting a mother until delivery of the fetus, including organ harvesting, the rights of the fetus and the mother, and consideration of family member's decisions (Hussein, 2004; Hussein, Govenden, Grant, & Said, 2006; Lane et al., 2004; Sperling, 2004). Social workers often participate as members of medical ethics teams where such issues are deliberated.

At-Risk Newborns

Not all pregnancies proceed smoothly and end in routine deliveries. In the United States more than 250,000 low-birth-weight babies are born each year and they are four times more likely to die than a full term newborn (National Committee for Quality Assurance, 2003). The newborn may face a variety of risks related to genetics, pregnancy complications, and birth complications.

Prematurity and Low Birth Weight

A radical shift has occurred in our culture over the past 20 years: at first glance the desire for a positive pregnancy outcome has been replaced by the assumption that the pregnancy will be flawless and the baby will be perfect; yet, there is parental anxiety about maternal health and that of the baby (Tiran & Chummun, 2004). The rates of premature birth are growing at an alarming pace, increasing 13% nationwide between 1992 and 2002 and leading to the first rise in infant mortality since 1958 (Mathews, Menacker, & MacDoman, 2004). In 2002, there were 480,812 **premature births** (births after less than 37 weeks' gestation) in the United States with one in eight newborns (12%) meeting the criteria for prematurity (Cockey, 2005; Nelson, 2004; Van Riper, 2001). Prematurity is the leading cause of death for infants (33% of all infant deaths), with 66% of these deaths involving infants at 24 weeks gestation or less. The highest rate of preterm birth is among blacks (17.7%) and the lowest among Asian or Pacific Islanders (10.4%). One theory regarding the racial disparity is that the chronic stress of racism may decrease a woman's ability to carry a pregnancy to full term.

The overall rate of **low birth weight (LBW)** infants—infants weighing less than 2,500 grams (5 pounds 8 ounces) at birth—has increased from 6.7% in 1984 to 8.1% in 2004. Part of this increase is due to an increase in multiple births over this period (accounting for 3.3% of all births in 2004) (Hoyert et al., 2006). It is postulated that the overall increase is due to advanced maternal age, increased treatments for infertility, and multiple births, rather than to a change in socioeconomic status (Ashton, 2006; March of Dimes, 2004).

The rate of **very low birth weight (VLBW)** infants—infants weighing less than 1,500 grams (3 pounds 3 ounces)—has increased from 1.15% of all births in 1980 to 1.47% in 2004 (Hoyert et al., 2006). Although mortality rates vary, between 10% and 15.7% of these infants die before hospital discharge (Aly, Massaro, & El-Mohandes, 2006; Kessenich, 2003; Kusuda et al., 2006; Roy et al., 2006). Infants born in rural areas have lower success rates than those born in urban areas, possibly due to access to NICUs (Abdel-Latif et al., 2006). There are significant racial differences in the number of VLBW infants born, with Caucasians accounting for 59.1%, African Americans 12.9%, Puerto Ricans 9.3%, Filipinos 8.3%, Mexicans 5.2%, and Chinese 5.2%. These statistics have remained relatively stable through the past decade despite advances in obstetrical and neonatal care (Hoybert, Friedman, Strobino, & Guyer, 2001).

Extremely low birth weight (ELBW) infants—infants weighing less than 1,000 grams (2.2 pounds)—experience approximately a 50% to 80% survival rate. Survival rates for EKBW infants weighing between 750 and 1,000 grams is 80%, but the survival rates for ELBW babies weighing less than 750 grams is 50%. At 1 pound 3 ounces (approximately 540 grams), Paul Thompson is considered an ELBW newborn, and at approximately 540 grams, he had a 50% chance of survival.

The United States ranks 183 out of 225 countries for infant mortality and LBW deliveries, with an infant mortality rate of 6.43 per 1,000 live births (CDC, 2006a). Among wealthy industrialized nations, the United States has the second highest rate of newborn deaths. Children born in the United States are three times more likely to die than children born in Japan with only Latvia having a higher death rate (Green, 2006). One-third of newborns that died in the first week died because they were preterm, making this the most frequent cause of early death (CDC, 2006a). Although African Americans have the highest rate of prematurity in the United States (17.5% compared to 11.1% for European Americans) (Illinois Maternal and Child Health Coalition, 2004; March of Dimes, 2004), the black preterm birthrate has decreased 6% between 1990 and 2002 while the rate for Caucasians increased over 30% (March of Dimes, 2004). Despite the high preterm delivery rate among blacks, the neonatal mortality rate for black premature infants is lower than that of whites or Hispanics (Alexander et al., 2003).

About 30% of LBW births can be attributed to natal environmental factors, such as maternal illness (e.g., stress and genital infections), some maternal working conditions, smoking, poor maternal weight gain during pregnancy along with being underweight before the pregnancy, intrauterine infections, and maternal short stature (Goldenberg, Hauth, & Andrews, 2000; Heck, Schoendorf, & Chavez, 2002; Spencer & Logan, 2002).

One of the greatest risk factors for the infant's decreased birth weight (LBW, VLBW, ELBW, or intrauterine growth retardation) is maternal smoking. Women who smoke have smaller babies, with female neonates more negatively affected than males (Volgt, Hermanussen, Wittwer-Backofen, Fusch, & Hesse, 2006). The death rate for newborns whose mothers smoked is 10.5 per 1,000 births, versus 6.6 deaths per 1,000 for the nonsmokers (National Vital Statistics Report, 2002). Because smoking reduces the amount of oxygen and the flow of nutrients to the fetus, smoking during the third trimester, a period of rapid fetal weight gain, is especially harmful (Huang & Winzer-Serhan, 2006).

Other risk factors for prematurity and LBW include alcohol use and other drug use (especially polydrug and cocaine users) (Bada et al., 2005). Also, advanced maternal age (greater than 30), high blood pressure, and a nontechnical/nonprofessional paternal occupation (perhaps a measure of socioeconomic status) were associated with repetitive premature deliveries (Sclowitz & Santos, 2006). The mother's adequate nutrition prior to conception, as well as during pregnancy, is another important factor in fetal health. It is normal to gain between 20 and 35 pounds with a singleton pregnancy. Overweight mothers may have larger babies and are at a higher risk for diabetes, whereas women who are 10% below average weight run the risk of premature delivery, preeclampsia, and bleeding (Cooper, 2000).

Babies born to women who receive no prenatal care are three times more likely to have low birth weight babies and five times more likely to die than mothers who receive prenatal care (National Committee for Quality Assurance, 2003). Unmarried mothers had an infant death rate of 10.2 per 1,000 compared to 5.5 per 1,000 for married mothers (National Vital Statistics Report, 2002). Clearly, there is a need for social workers to help impoverished, poorly educated, young, and unmarried mothers access and use the appropriate services. Otherwise babies die.

Children born prematurely are at risk for lower IQ scores, more impairments in language and visual motor skills, higher attentional problems and self-regulatory problems, and more learning disabilities than full-term controls (Kessenich, 2003). Less than 5% of infants of normal birth weight are affected by cerebral palsy, hydrocephalus and microcephaly (disorders of the cranium), blindness, deafness, and seizures. However, neonates weighing less than 1,000 grams (2.2 pounds) have a 49% chance for abnormal neurodevelopment and sensory assessments; 17% have cerebral palsy, 23% have long-term disabilities, and 33% require frequent hospitalizations during their first years of life (Jones, Guildea, Stewart, & Cartlidge, 2002; Koeske & Koeske, 1992; Vohr et al., 2000). Infants who are born at less than 30 weeks have a 10% overall risk for cerebral palsy, 17% risk for severe cognitive delay, 11% risk for neurosensory difficulties, and 10% risk for severe psychomotor delay (Woodward, Anderson, Austin, Howard, & Inder, 2006). Thus, the Thompsons have reason to wonder what the future holds for their baby.

Although the mortality and morbidity of VLBW and ELBW neonates is significant (Roy et al., 2006; Sehgal, Telang, Passah, & Jyothi, 2004), the first cohort of survivors is now reaching early adulthood and early studies are heartening because their high school graduation rates are equal to their normal birth weight peers (Nursing Standard, 2006). While the ongoing ethical debate about whether or not to withhold care of these fragile babies continues, withholding of care increases the mortality rate. One study found that 72% of infants in this weight category either had care withheld or withdrawn, but these decisions may be influenced in the future by new outcome studies (Barton & Hodgman, 2005).

The survival rates of premature infants have improved largely because of explosive growth in the field of neonatal medicine and the establishment of regional NICUs. Studying the long-term effects of prematurity is difficult because today's 5-year-old who was LBW received significantly less sophisticated care than the current patients in the NICU. It is proposed that the vulnerability of the premature brain during this critical period of fetal development is negatively affected by the stressful neonatal environmental conditions (Elley, 2001; Perlman, 2001). Therefore, neonatal environmental conditions may be as much of a risk factor for negative pregnancy outcomes as simple prematurity.

> What impact will these changes in health care for premature infants have on families and schools?

Newborn Intensive Care

As the Thompsons know all too well, parents' expectations for a healthy newborn are shattered when their child is admitted to a NICU. Their fear and anxiety often make it hard for them to form a strong emotional bond with their newborn. About 90% of mothers and 80% of fathers report that they develop an attachment to the infant during the third trimester of pregnancy. But when an infant is premature, the parents have not had the same opportunity. In addition, the fear that a sickly newborn may die inhibits some parents from risking attachment. Others are consumed with guilt at their baby's condition and believe that they will only harm the newborn by their presence. Felicia and Will Thompson had to work hard to contain their anxiety about Paul's frailties.

Early disruption in bonding may have a larger long-term impact on the child than the infant's actual medical condition (Wigert, Johannson, Berg, & Hellstrom, 2006). The response has been a movement toward family-centered NICU environments, which are structured to promote interaction between the infant and the parents, siblings, and others in the family's support system. Ample opportunity to interact with Paul facilitated Felicia and Will Thompson's attempts to bond with him.

Neuroscientists have recently called attention to the physical environment needs of prematurely born babies, noting the competing needs of these vulnerable babies and the medical staff that care for them in NICUs. The medical staff needs lights, noisy equipment, and alarms to signal physiological distress. The vulnerable baby needs a physical environment that more nearly approximates the uterus, without bright lights and stressful noise stimulation (Zeisel, 2006). With this discrepancy in mind, NICUs are being modified to accommodate the neurological needs of the vulnerable newborns.

Understanding the psychological stresses confronting the family with a baby in the NICU is the basis for social work interventions. As the Thompsons' story suggests, deciding whether to invest in the newborn and risk great loss, or to withdraw in an effort to protect oneself against pain, causes continuing tension. Witnessing the suffering and death of other neonates is traumatizing as well (Yu, Jamieson, & Asbury, 1981). Social workers can help parents understand and cope with this stress.

Neonatology, the care of critically ill newborns, has only recently been recognized as a medical specialty. It is a much-needed specialty, however. In 2003, NICU care was estimated to cost $224,400 for a newborn weighing between 500 and 700 grams, $4,300 for a newborn between 2,250 and 2,500 grams, and $1,000 for an infant greater than 3,000 grams (Gilbert, Nesbit, & Danielsen, 2003). Since the advent of the NICU in the 1970s, the survival rate of critically ill neonates has continued to increase. It is highly unlikely that Paul Thompson would have survived in 1970.

Social workers in an NICU must negotiate a complex technological environment requiring specialized skill and knowledge while attempting to respond with compassion, understanding, and appropriate advocacy. It helps to remember that the effort could affect a neonate's life course.

Major Congenital Anomalies

Overall, only 2% to 4% of all surviving newborns have a birth defect. However, the number of neonates born with anomalies due to genetics and exposure to teratogens, or nonhereditary factors that affect development of the fetus, does not reflect the number of abnormal embryos. Fewer than half of all fertilized ova result in a live birth; the rest are spontaneously aborted. The probability that a fertilized ovum with a genetic anomaly will abort spontaneously ranges from 80% to 90% (Opitz, 1996). Social workers need to be mindful of the low probability that a child will be born with a genetic disorder or congenital anomaly when responding to parental fears. The American College of Medical Genetics with the March of Dimes has established a recommended list of 28 metabolic, endocrine, and hemoglobin disorders for which newborns should be screened because early intervention for these hereditary yet rare diseases is essential. As of March 2006, only five U.S. states met all of these recommendations. Each state health department or the National Newborn Screening and Genetics Resource Center (http://www.nccrcg.org/about.asp) provides the list of mandatory screenings by a specific state.

Preventing, diagnosing, and predicting the outcome of genetic disorders is very difficult because of the complexities of genetic processes:

◆ *Variable expressivity.* Genes manifest differently in different people. For example, persons with cystic fibrosis, caused by a recessive gene, display wide variability in the severity of symptoms. The expression of the disorder appears to be influenced by the interplay of psychological, social, political, economic, and other environmental factors. The effects can be exacerbated by maternal substance abuse, inadequate maternal nutrition, and birth trauma. Children with cystic fibrosis born into poverty may not have benefited from early diagnosis, may live in an inner city that exposes them to increased levels of pollution, or may lack adequate home medical care because the primary caregiver is also responsible for meeting the family's economic needs.

◆ *Genetic heterogeneity.* The same characteristic may be a consequence of one of a number of genetic anomalies. For example, neural tube defects may result either from gene mutations or from exposure to specific teratogens (Motamedi & Meador, 2006; Ornoy, 2006).

◆ *Pleiotropy principle.* The same gene may influence seemingly unrelated systems (Rauch, 1988). Hair color, for example, is typically linked to a particular skin color (such as blonde hair with light complexion, black hair with olive complexion).

◆ *Epigenetics.* More recently, researchers have focused on another dimension of heritability that points to environmental factors which influence gene expression (phenotype) without changing the genetic makeup of a person (genotype). These factors influence the chemicals that trigger (methyl groups) or inhibit (acetyl groups) genetic expression. Furthermore, these chemicals appear to have a generational influence without genetic alterations. Examples of these epigenetic environmental influences include nutrition, trauma such as childhood abuse, and teratogens (Lederberg, 2001). The epigenetic influences in many cases are preventable and treatable, especially if identified early in development. Based on the knowledge of epigenetics that is expanding rapidly, social workers have the potential to influence and intervene when environmental conditions are known to impact the human condition.

Genetic anomalies fall into four categories, summarized in Exhibit 2.5 (Opitz, 1996; Rauch, 1988; Reed, 1996; Vekemans, 1996):

1. *Inheritance of a single abnormal gene.* An inherited anomaly in a single gene may lead to a serious disorder. The gene may be recessive, meaning that both parents must pass it along, or it may be dominant, in which case only one parent needs to have the gene in order for it to be expressed in the child. A third possibility is that the disorder is sex-linked, meaning that it is passed along by either the father or the mother.

2. *Multifactorial inheritance.* Some genetic traits, such as height and intelligence, are influenced by environmental factors such as nutrition. Their expression varies because of **multifactorial inheritance**, meaning that they are controlled by multiple genes. Multifactorial inheritance is implicated in traits that predispose a person to mental illnesses, such as depression. However, these traits are merely predisposing factors, creating what is called **genetic liability**. Siblings born with the same genetic traits may thus vary in the likelihood of developing a specific genetically based disorder, such as alcoholism or mental illness (Rauch, 1988; Takahashi & Turnbull, 1994).

3. *Chromosomal aberration.* Some genetic abnormalities are not hereditary but rather are caused by a genetic mishap during development of the ovum or sperm cells. Sometimes the cells end up missing chromosomes or having too many. When the ovum or sperm cell has fewer than 23 chromosomes, the probability of conception and survival is minimal. But in the presence of too many chromosomes in the ovum or the sperm, various anomalies occur. Down's syndrome,

Exhibit 2.5	Four Categories of Genetic Anomalies

Inheritance of Single Abnormal Gene

Recessive	Dominant	Sex-Linked
Sickle-cell anemia	Neurofibromatosis	Hemophilia
Tay-Sachs disease	Huntington's disease	Duchenne's muscular dystrophy
Cystic fibrosis		

Multifactorial Inheritance

Possible mental illness	Alcoholism	

Chromosomal Aberration

Down's syndrome (additional 21st chromosome)	Turner's syndrome (X)	Klinefelter's syndrome (XXY)

Exposure to Teratogens

Radiation	Infections	Maternal Metabolic Imbalance	Drugs and Environmental Chemicals
Neural tube defects	Rubella: deafness, glaucoma	Diabetes: neural tube defects	Alcohol: mental retardation
	Syphilis: neurological, ocular, and skeletal defects	Folic acid deficiency: brain and neural tube defects	Heroin: attention deficit disorder
		Hyperthermia (at 14–28 days): neural tube defects	Amphetamines: urogenital defects

or trisomy 21, the most common chromosomal aberration, is the presence of 47 chromosomes—specifically, an extra chromosome in the 21st pair. Its prevalence is 1 in 600 to 1,000 live births overall, but as seen in the Hazel Gereke's story, it increases to 1 in 350 for women over age 35 (Vekemans, 1996). Other chromosome anomalies include Turner's syndrome (a single sex chromosome, X) and Klinefelter's syndrome (an extra sex chromosome, XXY).

4. *Exposure to teratogens.* Teratogens can be divided into four categories: radiation, infections, maternal metabolic imbalance, and drugs and environmental chemicals. In the Thompson story, Felicia wondered if Paul's premature birth was a result of prenatal exposure to paint fumes. It may have been, depending on what specific chemicals were involved when exposure occurred, and to what degree. Parents who, like the Thompsons, are experiencing considerable guilt over their possible responsibility for their baby's problems may take comfort from the knowledge that the impact of exposure to teratogens can vary greatly. Much depends on the timing of exposure. The various organ systems have different critical or **sensitive periods**, summarized in Exhibit 2.6.

Parents who have reason to fear these congenital anomalies often opt for diagnosis during pregnancy. *Amniocentesis* is the extraction of amniotic fluid for chromosomal analysis; it involves inserting a hollow needle through the abdominal wall during the second trimester.

Chorion villi testing (CVT) involves the insertion of a catheter through the cervix into the uterus to obtain a sample of the developing placenta; it can be done as early as eight weeks but carries a slightly higher risk of causing spontaneous abortion (miscarriage). A more frequent procedure is *ultrasonography* (ultrasound), which produces a visual image of the developing fetus.

If an anomaly is detected, the decisions that need to be made are not easy ones. The possibility of false readings on these tests makes the decisions even more complicated. Should the fetus be aborted? Should fetal surgery—a surgical specialty still in the early stages of development—be undertaken? Could *gene replacement therapy,* implantation of genetic material to alter the genotype—still a costly experimental procedure—prevent an anomaly or limit its manifestation? Do the parents have the financial and psychological means to care for a neonate with a disability? This was a question that the Gerekes asked of themselves. What is the potential impact on the marriage and extended family system? Nonurgent decisions should be postponed until parents have an opportunity to adjust to the crisis and acquire the necessary information (Fost, 1981). The multidimensional perspective of social workers can contribute to a more holistic understanding of a client's situation, leading to appropriate and effective interventions when genetic anomalies are likely to, or do, occur.

> How might culture, social class, and religious orientation affect these decisions?

Special Parent Populations

Social workers should recognize the risks involved in the configurations of person and environment for some special parent populations. Six of these special populations are discussed here.

Pregnant Substance Abusers

Our knowledge of the developmental impact of maternal use of illegal and legal substances is rapidly increasing. The good news is that health care professionals are increasingly able to avoid prescribing legal drugs that might harm the developing fetus, once pregnancy is confirmed. The bad news is that too many pregnant women are still harming their babies through use of illegal drugs or abuse of legal substances. And, unfortunately, many women do not know they are pregnant during the first trimester, a period when the fetus is very vulnerable to teratogens.

Although it is difficult to obtain reliable statistics, an estimated 22% of females of childbearing age abuse substances. Moreover, approximately 25% of pregnant women use two or more teratogenic substances. Among pregnant substance abusers, 91% use heroin, methadone, or other opiates, 35% use stimulants, 25% cannabis, 22% benzodiazepines, and 7% hallucinogens—with 38% injecting their main drug (McElhatton, 2000).

Possible effects of commonly abused legal and illegal substances are presented in Exhibit 2.7. Cocaine and crack use is connected with increased chances of the placenta separating from the uterine wall, which can lead to maternal and fetal death, intracranial hemorrhage for both mother and newborn, urinary and genital defects in the neonate, and increased risk of SIDS as well as neonatal withdrawal that can last for several weeks. Amphetamines are associated with increased rates of spontaneous abortions and possible heart defects. Ecstasy seems to increase the likelihood of cardiovascular and musculoskeletal anomalies in the fetus (McElhatton, 2000). *Fetal alcohol syndrome* (FAS), a complex of anomalies, is the leading cause of mental retardation worldwide (Abel & Sokol, 1987; Beckman & Brent, 1994; LaDue,

Exhibit 2.6	Sensitive Periods in Prenatal Development

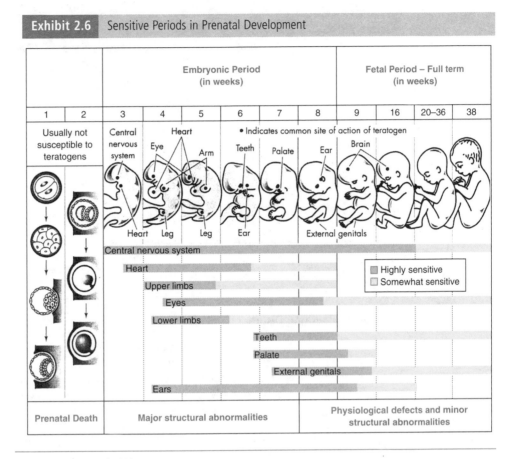

SOURCE: Moore & Persend, 1993.

2001; Light, Irvine, & Kjerulf, 1996). Pregnant substance abusers in general have a higher incidence of miscarriages, prematurity, and LBW, as well as STDs, tuberculosis, and AIDS, than other pregnant women (Kesmodel, Wisborg, Olsen, Henriksen, & Secher, 2002; March of Dimes, 2006b). Furthermore, the neonate who was exposed prenatally to substances like alcohol, tobacco, and illegal drugs is 46 times more likely than normal to die in the first month of life (Larson, 1995).

Interestingly, some individuals appear to be "resistant" to teratogens like alcohol, and no teratogen causes defects all the time (Opitz, 1996). In fact, about 60% of babies born to alcoholic mothers show no signs of being affected by their mother's drinking (Opitz, 1996).

Still, teratogenic substances should be avoided during pregnancy to increase the chances of a healthy outcome. Social workers are collaborating with other professionals to provide public education to women in the childbearing years about the teratogenic effects of alcohol, tobacco, and other drugs. Because fathers are known to influence the substance use by mothers, and there is increasing evidence that paternal use impacts sperm, fathers increasingly are included in preventive efforts (Bertrand, Floyd, & Weber, 2005; Chang, McNamara, Orav, & Wilkins-Haug, 2006).

Exhibit 2.7	Commonly Abused Drugs and Fetal Effects				
	Alcohol	Cocaine	Amphetamines	Cigarettes	Heroin
Abortion	X	X	X		X
Stillbirth	X	X	X		X
Prematurity	X	X	X	X	X
Intrauterine growth retardation	X	X	X	X	X
Respiratory distress	X	X			X
Withdrawal	X	X	X		X
Fine motor problems	X				X
Malformations	X	X	X		X
Developmental delays	X	X	X		X

Mothers With Eating Disorders

There was an increase in eating disorders, primarily anorexia nervosa (self-imposed starvation) and bulimia (binging and purging), among U.S. teenagers and women in the United States during the past century, but the rate has stabilized in recent years (Hoek, 2006). Because eating disorders frequently result in menstrual disorders, reduced sex drive, and infertility, pregnancy is frequently overlooked in this population (Bonne, Rubinoff, & Berry, 1996). Apparently, however, some women first develop eating disorders during pregnancy, perhaps in response to their weight gain and change in shape (Fahy, 1991).

An eating disorder is likely to result in poor pregnancy outcomes, such as fetuses **small for gestational age (SGA)**, LBW infants, and increased neonatal mortality (National Eating Disorders Association, 2005). Premature delivery occurs at twice the expected rate, and perinatal mortality is six times the expected rate. The length of time the mother is able to breast-feed her infant has not been found to be affected by eating disorders, however (Brinch, Isager, & Tolstrup, 1988). Social workers who work regularly with women with eating disorders or with pregnant women need to be knowledgeable about the possibilities for poor pregnancy outcomes in pregnant women with eating disorders.

Lesbian Mothers

In recent years, the number of lesbians who are or who desire to be mothers has increased, but these women continue to face many obstacles and dilemmas (Gartrell et al., 1996). More than one third of lesbians are estimated to be mothers, and it is reasonable to assume that more would choose motherhood if the larger society offered greater support.

Perhaps one of the major risk factors for lesbian mothers is the potential for rejection or disapproval by the members of a society with negative views of homosexuality (King, 2001; Laird & Green, 1996). Conception, pregnancy, and childbirth demand role realignments for heterosexual couples and create stress. These same dynamics occur in lesbian couples, but they often face a greater challenge due to society's reluctance to recognize lesbian relationships.

Lesbian mothers face other challenges. Despite increased availability of alternative fertilization methods, many health care providers remain insensitive to issues that lesbian women may face when using them. Lesbian women who become pregnant may lack the support of family and friends, and birthing facilities may not allow female partners to be involved with the birth process. In addition, employers may limit access to, or reluctantly provide, resources such as medical benefits for pregnancy and childbirth (Laird & Green, 1996). The lesbian partner of a child-bearing or adopting lesbian mother may not be recognized as the child's parent in many states.

Yet, lesbian mothers have advantages that some other special parent populations do not have. A study of 27 lesbian mothers indicated that these family households are strong, individual functioning is good, and a variety of parenting skills are common (Dundas & Kaufman, 2000). Other studies of lesbian mothers report that all respondents sought prenatal care and that 89% to 100% attended childbirth education classes (Gartrell et al., 1996; Harvey, Carr, & Bernheime, 1989). Social workers can help health care providers recognize both the strengths of and the special challenges facing lesbian mothers.

Mothers and Fathers With Disabilities

One in five persons reports a physical or mental disability, and over half of these people are female (Jans & Stoddard, 1999). People with physical or mental disabilities may be perceived as "asexual," and thus conception, pregnancy, and childbirth frequently are not considered relevant issues for them (Cole & Cole, 1993; Sawin, 1998). This is not the case. For one thing, not all disabilities negatively affect reproduction. For example, 75% of women with rheumatoid arthritis experience remission of disease during pregnancy (Connie, 1988; Corbin, 1987). Other interesting data come from a 4-year national study funded by the National Institutes of Health (NIH), which compared 506 women with physical disabilities to 444 women without a disability (Nosek, 1995).

The NIH study found a remarkable difference between the two populations in the use of contraception, because women with disabilities have more limited options. For example, the use of barrier methods may be compromised by limited use of hands. Overall, women with disabilities were less likely to use oral contraception, possibly because their access to it was limited. Disabled and nondisabled women did not differ in their rates of tubal ligation and partner vasectomy, but women with disabilities were much more likely to have had a hysterectomy (22% versus 12%), the most invasive and risky surgical sterilization option (Nosek, 1995).

Perhaps one of the most striking findings of the NIH study was that 10% of women with disabilities reported abuse—such as coerced sterilization—by health care providers, compared to only 3% of nondisabled women. In addition, for the women who had access to medical care, 37% of women with disabilities perceived their physician as uninformed about the effect of their disability on reproductive health (Nosek, 1995).

Women with disabilities who do decide to become pregnant must be monitored more closely than nondisabled women to offset the increased risks associated with the disability. Although women with disabilities have higher rates of complications during pregnancy (Nosek, Howland, Rintal, Young, & Chanpong, 1997), with careful planning they can make the adaptations needed to care for newborns. For a summary of the effects of selected disabilities on conception, pregnancy, and childbirth, see Sawin (1998).

Despite public distaste for the practice, some persons with disabilities continue to be targets of involuntary sterilization (Rock, 1996; Smith & Polloway, 1993; Waxman, 1994). Professionals do not agree about how to handle the reproductive rights of individuals with severe inheritable disorders or with limited capacity to care for a child (Brantlinger, 1992). Many do agree, however, that physical, environmental, interpersonal, informational, and policy barriers leave people with disabilities disenfranchised from both the reproductive health system and other reproductive options.

Not surprisingly, a 1997 study identified reproductive health as one of the four top research priorities for disabled persons (Berkeley Planning Associates, 1996). As society slowly begins to recognize persons with disabilities as full members of society, some of the negative implications of conception, pregnancy, and childbirth with this population may be dispelled. Meanwhile, however, social workers—who have traditionally been a voice for this population—must not let that voice be lost at this stage of the life course.

Incarcerated Pregnant Women

An estimated one out of four women inmates are pregnant when they are incarcerated or have delivered a baby within the preceding year (Wooldredge & Masters, 1993). These women and their babies are at particular risk because most of the mothers are poor, many abuse drugs both prior to and after incarceration, many have severe physical and mental health problems, and most lack education and skills related to pregnancy, childbirth, and prenatal care (Kaplan & Sasser, 1996). A recent analysis of research findings from 10 studies, all that reported a comparison group, revealed that prematurity and low birth weight occurred more frequently for imprisoned women if the comparison group was not disadvantaged. Otherwise, birth outcomes were more favorable for imprisoned women (Knight & Plugge, 2005).

With the rise in the proportion of women who are incarcerated, services for pregnant inmates have increased some, considerably improving the odds of good pregnancy outcomes (U.S. Federal Bureau of Prisons, 1998). In fact, one study found that the birth weights of children of incarcerated mothers were no different from those of nonincarcerated women; rather, longer incarceration was related to higher birth weights (Martin et al., 1997). However, good prenatal care is typically found only in larger prisons associated with academic medical centers (Cordero et al., 1992; Gabel & Johnston, 1995). Pregnant women in other types of facilities are at greater risk and this risk may be greater if these women have a disadvantaged background.

Regardless of the type of facility, prison life is stressful (Young, 1996). Alternative living environments that provide adequate services are a possible means of improving pregnancy outcomes for this group of women (Blinn, 1997; Bloom & Steinhart, 1993; Siefert & Pimlott, 2001; Stevens & Patton, 1998).

HIV-Infected Mothers

The United Nations program on HIV and AIDS (UNAIDS) estimates that over 600,000 mother-to-newborn HIV transmissions occur each year, with the numbers increasing rapidly, especially in Africa and Southeast Asia (UNAIDS, 2006). Transmission from mother to infant is estimated at 20% to 45% if the mother takes no preventive drugs and breastfeeds (Kanabus, 2006). However, 2005 data revealed that with the use of antiretroviral drugs for treatment and prophylaxis, no breastfeeding and elected caesarian birth when appropriate, the risk of transmission is reduced to less than 2% (Mofenson, 2006).

Elective cesarean sections reduce the risk of mother-to-infant transmission by 50%, and the use of Antiretroviral therapy (AZT, also known as zidovudine or ZDV) has reduced the rate of transmission to less than 5% (Kanabus, 2006; McIntyre & Gray, 2002). Recent studies are suggesting that AZT is a teratogen, causing mutations of the DNA if taken in the first trimester, but the risks must be weighed against the transmission of a potentially fatal viral infection (Kanabus, 2006). However, the cost of either treatment is prohibitive to women in impoverished countries and it is not widely available to them.

Breastfeeding is an area of special concern. HIV can be transmitted through breast milk and is significant in the high rates of this disease in Africa, but accurate data regarding the rate of transmission are difficult to obtain. To further complicate the issue, infant mortality rates have increased in poor countries where formula feeding has been implemented—partially due to contaminated water supplies used to make the formula. The United Nations suggests that in poorer countries, breastfeeding is a better option because it does help prevent infectious disease and malnutrition (Guay & Ruff, 2001; Kanabus, 2006; Kent, 2002). However, it also recommends that women be informed about their choices for infant feeding.

The standard protocol for neonates born to HIV-positive mothers is to treat them with the drug zidovudine (ZDV) for 6 weeks (Cotter & O'Sullivan, 2004). However, this medication is not widely available in poorer countries, increasing the number of children who will die from AIDS.

The news is encouraging in other ways. In 1994, the American Society for Reproductive Medicine discouraged women who were HIV-positive from having children because transmission of the virus could not be prevented. In 2002, the same group said that the recent advances in therapies greatly reduce the rate of transmission, and withdrew their recommendations to avoid childbearing. The Society (2002) suggested cesarean sections, bottle feeding, special sperm washing and testing if the father is HIV-positive, and counseling if both mother and father are HIV-positive, due to the possibility of orphaning the baby (ASRM, 2002).

The social worker must be aware of the complexities of this issue as well as societal prejudices against women with HIV infections. Working to increase HIV awareness and promote clear notification of HIV status will continue to be important social work roles in the next decade.

IMPLICATIONS FOR SOCIAL WORK PRACTICE

Social workers practicing with persons at the stage of life concerned with conception, pregnancy, and childbirth should follow these principles:

- ◆ Respond to the complex interplay of biopsychosocial and spiritual factors related to conception, pregnancy, and childbirth.
- ◆ When working with clients, both females and males, of childbearing age, always consider the possibility of conception, pregnancy, and childbirth; their potential outcomes; and their impact on the changing person/environment configuration.
- ◆ Identify the needs of vulnerable or at-risk groups, and work to provide services for them. For example, structure birth education classes to include not only family but family-like persons, and provide interpreters for the hearing impaired.

◆ Actively pursue information about particular disabilities and their impact on conception, pregnancy, and childbirth.

◆ Acquire and apply skills in advocacy, education about reproductive options, consumer guidance in accessing services, and case management.

◆ Assume a proactive stance when working with at-risk populations to limit undesirable reproductive outcomes and to help meet their reproductive needs. At-risk groups include adolescents, low-income women, women involved with substance abuse, women with eating disorders, and women with disabilities who lack access to financial, physical, psychological, and social services.

◆ Assist parents faced with a potential genetic anomaly to gain access to genetic screenings, prenatal diagnosis, postnatal diagnosis, treatment, and genetic counseling.

◆ Involve parents in decision making to the greatest extent possible by delaying nonurgent decisions until parents have had a chance to adjust to any crisis and acquire the necessary information to make an informed decision.

◆ Establish collaborative relationships with other professionals to enhance and guide assessment and intervention.

◆ Identify and use existing programs that provide education and prenatal services to women, particularly for those most at risk of undesirable outcomes.

KEY TERMS

assisted reproductive
  technologies (ART)
chromosomes
dominant genes
embryo
epigenetics
family pluralism
fertilization
fertilization age
fetal viability
fetus
genes
genetic heterogeneity
genetic liability
genotype

germ cell
gestation
gestational age
infertility
interactive genes
low birth weight (LBW)
miscarriage
multifactorial inheritance
multigravida
multipara
neonate
phenotype
pleiotropy principle
premature birth
primipara

protective factors
recessive genes
risk factors
sensitive period
sex chromosome
sex-linked trait
small for gestational
  age (SGA)
spontaneous
  abortion
teratogen
variable expressivity
very low birth
  weight (VLBW)
zygote

Active Learning

1. Select one topic from the chapter outline. Identify a community service setting that addresses the chosen topic. Interview a professional from that setting, preferably a social worker, to solicit the following information:

   * Services provided
   * The role of the social worker
   * The roles of the other disciplines
   * The mechanisms used to acquire new knowledge on the topic
   * The challenges and rewards of social work practice in that setting

2. Locate the National Association of Social Workers Code of Ethics on the organization's Web site at www.naswdc.org. Choose an ethical issue from the list below. Using the Code of Ethics as a guide, what values and principles can you identify to guide decision making related to the issue you have chosen?

   ✳ Should all women and men, regardless of marital status or income, be provided with the most current technologies to conceive when they are unable to do so?

   ✳ What are the potential issues of preservation and gestational surrogacy in terms of social justice and diversity?

   ✳ Should pregnant women who abuse substances be incarcerated to protect the developing fetus?

   ✳ Do adoptive parents have the right to know the genetic background of an adoptee?

   ✳ Which genes should be selected for reproduction?

   ✳ Will persons who are poor be economically disadvantaged in the use of genetic information?

3. Select one of the three life journeys that introduced this chapter: Nicole Evans's, the Thompsons', or the Gerekes'. Identify the risk and protective factors related to their conception, pregnancy, and childbirth experience. Then change one factor in the story; for example, assume Nicole was age 20 when she became pregnant. How might that alter her life course and that of her child? Then try changing another factor; for example, assume Nicole had completed three years of college. How does that change the trajectory of her story? Try again; for example, assume Nicole was being treated for depression when she became pregnant. Again, how does that factor alter her life course and that of her child?

WEB RESOURCES

Information About Pregnancy
www.thebabiesplanet.com/bbpregna.htm

Site presented by The Last Planet Internet Services contains links to various sites concerning pregnancy and childbirth.

Childbirth.org
www.childbirth.org

Award-winning site maintained by Robin Elise Weiss contains information on birth plans, cesareans, complications, episiotomies, feeding, fertility, health, and labor, and a FAQ section.

Family and Social Demographic Data
www.census.gov

Site presented by the U.S. Census Bureau provides current census data related to the family and social context of conception, pregnancy, and childbirth.

Genetic Alliance
www.geneticalliance.org/

Celebrating its 20th birth date in 2006, this information and advocacy organization brings together the government, other organizations, private industry, and others concerned with genetic conditions to assist individuals and their families who are responding to a genetic condition.

Infertility Center
www.womens-health.com/InfertilityCenter

Site presented by Women's Health Interactive and the National Council on Women's Health contains information on human reproduction, assessment of pregnancy factors, infertility evaluations and treatments, emotional aspects of infertility, and a FAQ section.

Planned Parenthood
www.plannedparenthood.org

Official site of the Planned Parenthood Federation of America Inc. contains information about Planned Parenthood, health and pregnancy, birth control, abortion, STDs, prochoice advocacy, and a guide for parents.

Human Genome Project
www.ornl.gov/hgmis

Site of the Human Genome Program of the U.S. Department of Energy that has sequenced the genes present in human DNA.

Center for Research on Women with Disabilities (CROWD)
www.bcm.tmc.edu/crowd

Site presented by the Center for Research on Women with Disabilities contains reports on women with disabilities, educational materials, and links to other research on women with disabilities.

3

INFANCY AND TODDLERHOOD

Debra J. Woody

Key Ideas	97
Case Study 3.1: ■ Holly's Early Arrival	98
Case Study 3.2: ■ Sarah's Teen Dad	99
Case Study 3.3: ■ Overprotecting Henry	99
Healthy Development in Infants and Toddlers	100
Physical Development	101
Self-Regulation	102
Sensory Abilities	103
Reflexes	104
Motor Skills	105
The Growing Brain	107
Childhood Immunizations	108
Cognitive Development	109
Piaget's Stages of Cognitive Development	110
Prelanguage Skills	113
Socioemotional Development	114
Erikson's Theory of Psychosocial Development	114
Emotional Control	115
Temperament	117

Bowlby's Theory of Attachment 118
Ainsworth's Theory of Attachment 119
Attachment and Brain Development 122
The Role of Play 122
Developmental Disruptions 124
Child Care Arrangements in Infancy and Toddlerhood 124
Family Leave 124
Paid Child Care 125
Infants and Toddlers in the Multigenerational Family 126
The Breastfeeding Versus Bottle Feeding Decision 127
Postpartum Depression 128
Risks to Healthy Infant and Toddler Development 129
Poverty 129
Inadequate Caregiving 131
Child Abuse 131
Protective Factors in Infancy and Toddlerhood 132
Education 132
Social Support 133
Easy Temperament 133
Implications for Social Work Practice 133
Key Terms 134
Active Learning 134
Web Resources 134

❖ Why is it important for social workers to know about brain development?

❖ Why is it important for social workers to understand attachment issues between infants and parents?

❖ How do child care provisions in the United States compare to those in other countries?

KEY IDEAS

As you read this chapter, take note of these central ideas:

1. Although growth and development in young children have some predictability and logic, the timing and expression of many developmental skills vary from child to child and depend in part on the environment and culture in which the child is raised.

2. Physical growth, brain development, and the development of sensory abilities and motor skills are all important aspects of physical development in infants and toddlers.

3. According to Piaget, infants and toddlers are in the sensorimotor stage of cognitive development, responding to what they hear, see, taste, touch, smell, and feel.

4. Erikson describes two stages of psychosocial development relevant to infants and toddlers, each with its own central task: trust versus mistrust (birth to age 1½) and autonomy versus shame and doubt (1½ to 3 years).

5. The attachment relationship between infants and toddlers and their caregivers can affect brain development.

6. Researchers have found that children who live in poor economic conditions face serious risks to development in all dimensions.

7. Prenatal care, diet, parental education, and social support are thought to influence infant mortality rates in the United States.

ACKNOWLEDGMENT: The author wishes to thank Suzanne Baldwin, Ph.D. for her contributions to the discussion of breastfeeding.

Holly's Early Arrival

Although Marilyn Hicks had been very careful with her diet, exercise, and prenatal care during pregnancy, Holly arrived at 23 weeks' gestation, around 6 months into the pregnancy. Initially she weighed 3 pounds, 11 ounces, but she quickly lost the 11 ounces. Immediately after birth, Holly was whisked away to the neonatal unit in the hospital, and her parents had just a quick peek at her. The assigned social worker's first contact with Marilyn and Martin Hicks, an Anglo couple, was in the neonatal unit. Although Marilyn Hicks began to cry when the social worker first spoke with her, overall both parents seemed to be coping well and had all their basic needs met at that time. The social worker left his business card with them and instructed them to call if they needed anything.

Despite her early arrival, Holly did not show any signs of medical problems, and after 6 weeks in the neonatal unit, her parents were able to take her home. The social worker wisely allowed the newly formed Hicks family time to adjust, and in keeping with the policy of the neonatal program, scheduled a follow-up home visit within a few weeks.

When the social worker arrives at the house, Marilyn Hicks is at the door in tears. She states that taking care of Holly is much more than she imagined. Holly cries "constantly" and does not seem to respond to Mrs. Hicks's attempts to comfort her. In fact, Mrs. Hicks thinks that Holly cries even louder when her mother picks her up or tries to cuddle with her. Mrs. Hicks is very disappointed, because she considers herself to be a nurturing person. She is unsure how to respond to Holly's "rejection of her." The only time Holly seems to respond positively is when Mrs. Hicks breastfeeds her.

Mrs. Hicks has taken Holly to the pediatrician on several occasions and has discussed her concerns. The doctor told her that nothing is physically wrong with Holly and that Mrs. Hicks has to be more patient.

Mrs. Hicks confides during this meeting that she read some horrifying material on the Internet about premature infants. According to the information she read, premature infants often have difficulty bonding with their caretaker, which in some children may ultimately result in mental health and emotional problems. Mrs. Hicks is concerned that this is the case with Holly.

This social worker must take into consideration that in addition to her fears, Mrs. Hicks must be exhausted. Her husband returned to work shortly after the baby came home, and Mrs. Hicks has not left the house since then. She tried taking a break once when her aunt came for a visit, but Holly cried so intensely during this time that her aunt refused to be left alone with Holly again. The social worker must now help Mrs. Hicks cope with the powerful feelings that have been aroused by Holly's premature birth, get any needed clarification on Holly's medical condition, and find ways to get Mrs. Hicks a break from caregiving. He will also want to help her to begin to feel more confident about her ability to parent Holly.

Sarah's Teen Dad

Chris Johnson is the only dad in the teen fathers group, facilitated by the social worker at a local high school, who has sole custody of his infant daughter. Initially Sarah, Chris's daughter, lived with her mom and maternal grandparents. Chris was contacted by the social worker from Child Protective Services (CPS) who informed him that Sarah was removed from the mom's care due to physical neglect. The referral to CPS was made when Sarah was seen in a pediatric clinic and the medical staff noticed that she had not gained weight since the last visit, and was generally unresponsive in the examination. Further investigation by the CPS worker revealed that Sarah was left in her crib for most of the day, and few of Sarah's basic daily care needs were being fulfilled. Although Chris's contact with Sarah had been sporadic since her birth, he did not hesitate to pursue custody, especially given that the only other alternative was Sarah's placement in foster care. Chris's parents were also supportive of Chris's desire to have Sarah live with all of them. However, although they were willing to help, they were adamant that the responsibility for Sarah's care belonged to Chris, not them. They were unwilling to raise Sarah themselves and in fact required Chris to sign a written statement indicating that he, not them, would assume primary responsibility for Sarah's care. Chris's parents also insisted that he remain in school and earn his high school diploma.

Thus far the situation seems to be working well. At the last medical appointment, Sarah's weight had increased significantly and she responded to the nurse's attempts to play and communicate with her. Chris is continuing his education at the alternative high school, which also has a day care for Sarah. Chris admits that it is much more difficult than he anticipated. He attends school for half the day, works a part-time job the other half, and then has to care for Sarah in the evenings. Chris has shared several times in the group that it is a lot for him to juggle. He still mourns the loss of his freedom and "carefree" lifestyle. Like most of the other teen dads in the group, whether they physically live with the child or not, Chris is concerned about doing the best he can for Sarah; he states that he just wants to be a good dad.

Overprotecting Henry

Irma Velasquez is still mourning the death of her little girl Angel, age 2, who was killed when a stray bullet came into their home through the living room window. Although it has been about a year since the incident, no one has been arrested. The police do know, however, that neither Ms. Velasquez's daughter nor her family was the intended victim. The stray bullet was the result of a shoot-out between two rival drug dealers in the family's neighborhood.

Ms. Velasquez is just glad, now, that 14-month-old Henry was in his crib in the back of the house instead of in the living room on that horrible evening. He had fallen asleep in her lap a few minutes before but she had just returned from laying him in his crib when the shooting occurred. Irma Velasquez confides in her

(Continued)

(Continued)

social worker at Victim Services that her family has not been the same since the incident. For one, she and her husband barely speak. His method of dealing with the tragedy is to stay away from home. She admits that she is angry with her husband because he does not make enough money for them to live in a safer neighborhood. She thinks that he blames her because she did not protect Angel in some way.

Ms. Velasquez admits that she is afraid that something bad will also happen to Henry. She has limited their area in the home to the back bedroom, and they seldom leave the house. She does not allow anyone, even her sister, to take care of him, and confesses that she has not left his side since the shooting. Even with these restrictions, Ms. Velasquez worries. She is concerned that Henry will choke on a toy or food, or become ill. She still does not allow him to feed himself, even dry cereal. He has just begun walking, and she severely limits his space for movement. Ms. Velasquez looks worn and exhausted. Although she knows these behaviors are somewhat irrational she states that she is determined to protect Henry. She further states that she just could not live through losing another child.

Healthy Development in Infants and Toddlers

What happens during the prenatal period and the earliest months and years of a child's life has lasting impact on the life course journey. In the earliest moments, months, and years, interactions with parents, family members, and other adults and children influence the way the brain develops, as do such factors as nutrition and environmental safety. Although it is never too late to improve health and well-being, what happens during infancy and toddlerhood sets the stage for the journey through childhood, adolescence, and adulthood. We were all infants and toddlers once, but sometimes, in our work as social workers, we may find it hard to understand the experience of someone 2 years old or younger. (Young children are typically referred to as **infants** in the first year, but as they enter the second year of life and become more mobile, they are usually called **toddlers,** from about 12 to 36 months of age.) As adults, we have become accustomed to communicating with words, and we are not always sure how to read the behaviors of the very young child. And we are not always sure how we are to behave with them. The best way to overcome these limitations, of course, is to learn what we can about the lives of infants and toddlers.

What must social workers know about biological age, psychological age, and social age to understand whether an infant's or toddler's behavior is healthy or problematic?

In all three of the case studies at the beginning of this chapter, factors can be identified that may adversely affect the children's development. However, we must begin by understanding what is traditionally referred to as "normal" development. But because *normal* is a relative term with some judgmental overtones, we will use the term *healthy* instead.

Social workers employed in schools, hospitals, community mental health centers, and other public health settings are often approached by parents and teachers with questions about development in young children. To assess whether any of the children they bring to your attention require intervention, you must be able to distinguish between healthy and problematic development in three areas: physical, cognitive, and socioemotional development. As you will see, young children go through a multitude of changes in all three areas simultaneously. Inadequate development in any one of them—or in multiple areas—may have long-lasting consequences for the individual.

▲ **Photo 3.1**   Babies depend on others for basic physical and emotional needs. Family support and affection are important factors in healthy development.

Keep in mind, however, that what is considered to be healthy is relative to environment and culture. Every newborn enters a world with distinctive features structured by the social setting that he or she encounters (Rogoff, 2003; Valsiner, 2000). Therefore, all aspects of development must be considered in a cultural context.

To make the presentation of ideas about early childhood manageable, this chapter follows a traditional method of organizing the discussion by type of development: physical development, cognitive development, emotional development, and social development. In this chapter, emotional development and social development are combined under the heading Socioemotional Development. Of course, all these types of development and behavior are interdependent, and often the distinctions blur.

Physical Development

Newborns depend on others for basic physical needs. They must be fed, cleaned, and kept safe and comfortable until they develop the ability to do these things for themselves. At the same time, however, newborns have an amazing set of physical abilities and potentials right from the beginning.

In Case Study 3.2, the pediatrician and CPS social worker were concerned that Sarah Johnson was not gaining weight. With adequate nourishment and care, the physical growth of the infant is quite predictable. Infants grow very rapidly throughout the first two years of life, but the pace of growth slows a bit in toddlerhood. The World Health Organization (WHO) undertook a project, called the Multicentre Growth Reference Study (MGRS), to construct standards for evaluating children from birth through 5 years of age. One part of that project was to construct growth standards to propose how children *should* grow in *all* countries, of interest because of WHO's commitment to eliminate global health disparities. MGRS collected growth data from 8,440 affluent children from diverse geographical and cultural settings, including Brazil, Ghana, India, Norway, Oman, and the United States. To be eligible for the study, mothers needed to be breastfeeding and not smoking, and the environment needed to be adequate to support unconstrained growth.

The researchers found that there were no differences in growth patterns across sites, even though there were some differences in parental stature. Given the striking similarity in growth patterns across sites, they concluded that the data could be used to develop an international standard. Across sites, the average length at birth was 19.5 inches (49.5 cm), 26.3 inches (66.7 cm) at 6 months, 29.5 inches (75.0 cm) at 12 months, and 34.4 inches (87.4 cm) at 24 months (WHO Multicentre Growth Reference Study Group, 2006a). By 1 year of age, infant height was about 1.5 times birth height, and by 2 years, the toddler had nearly doubled the birth height.

In terms of weight, most newborns weigh between 5 and 10 pounds at birth. Infants triple their weight in the first year, and by age 2 most infants are quadruple their original weight. Thus, the average 2-year-old weighs between 20 and 40 pounds. Evidently, the size of individual infants and toddlers can vary quite a bit. Some of the difference is due to nutrition, exposure to disease, and other environmental factors; much of it is due to genetics. Some ethnic differences in physical development have also been observed. For example, Asian American children tend to be smaller than average, and African American children tend to be larger than average (Tate, Dezateux, Cole, and the Millennium Cohort Study Child Health Group, 2006). In recent years, there has been a great deal of concern about rapid weight gain during the first 6 months, which has been connected to overweight by age 4 and to several chronic diseases in adulthood. Researchers have found Hispanic American infants to be twice as likely as other infants in the United States to have this pattern of early rapid weight gain (Dennison, Edmunds, & Stratton, 2006). The WHO child weight growth standards, calculated by different methods, can be found at www.who.int/childgrowth.

Self-Regulation

Before birth, the bodily functions of the fetus are regulated by the mother's body. After birth, the infant must develop the capacity to engage in self-regulation (Davies, 2004; Shonkoff & Phillips, 2000). At first, the challenge is to regulate bodily functions, such as temperature control, sleeping, eating, and eliminating. That challenge is heightened for the premature or medically fragile infant, as Holly's mother is finding.

As any new parent will attest, infants are not born with regular patterns of sleeping, eating, and eliminating. With maturation of the central nervous system in the first 3 months, and with lots of help from parents or other caregivers, the infant's rhythms of sleeping, eating, and eliminating become much more regular (Davies, 2004). A newborn usually sleeps about 16 hours a day, dividing that time evenly between day and night. Of course, this is not a good fit with the way adults organize their sleep lives. At the end of 3 months, most infants are sleeping 14 to 15 hours per day, primarily at night, with some well-defined nap times during the day. Parents also gradually shape infants' eating schedules so that they are eating mainly during the day.

What have you observed about how culture influences the parenting of infants and toddlers?

There are cultural variations in, and controversies about, the way caregivers shape the sleeping and eating behaviors of infants. In some cultures, infants sleep with parents, and in other cultures, infants are put to sleep in their own beds and often in their own rooms. In some cultures, putting an infant to sleep alone in a room is considered to be neglectful (Korbin, 1981). There are also cultural variations and controversies about breastfeeding versus bottle feeding. It is interesting to note that both breastfeeding and sleeping with parents induce shorter bouts of sleep and less sound sleep than the alternatives (Shonkoff & Phillips, 2000). Some researchers have speculated that the infant's lighter and shorter sleep pattern may protect against sudden infant death syndrome (SIDS). Of course, parents sleeping with infants must be aware of the hazard of rolling over and suffocating the infant. Luckily, parents have also been found to sleep less soundly when they sleep with infants (Shonkoff & Phillips, 2000).

Parents become less anxious as the infant's rhythms become more regular and predictable. At the same time, if the caregiver is responsive and dependable, the infant becomes less anxious and begins to develop the ability to wait to have needs met.

There are cultural variations in beliefs about how to respond when infants cry and fuss, whether to soothe them, or leave them to learn to soothe themselves. When parents do attempt to soothe infants, interestingly, they seem to use the same methods across cultures: "They say something, touch, pick up, search for sources of discomfort, and then feed" (Shonkoff & Phillips, 2000, p. 100). Infants who have been consistently soothed usually begin to develop the ability to soothe themselves after 3 or 4 months. This ability is the precursor to struggles for self-control and mastery over powerful emotions that occur in toddlerhood.

Sensory Abilities

Full-term infants are born with a functioning **sensory system**—the senses of hearing, sight, taste, smell, touch, and sensitivity to pain—and these abilities continue to develop rapidly in the first few months. Indeed, in the early months the sensory system seems to function at a higher level than the motor system, which allows movement. The sensory system allows infants, from the time of birth, to participate in and adapt to their environments. A lot of their learning happens through listening and watching (Newman & Newman, 2006; Novak & Pelaez, 2004). The sensory system is an interconnected system, with various sensory abilities working together to give the infant multiple sources of information about the world.

Hearing is the earliest link to the environment; in the uterus the fetus is sensitive to auditory stimulation. Newborns show a preference for their mother's voice over other female voices (De Casper & Fifer, 1980). Young infants can also distinguish changes in loudness, pitch, and location of sounds (Kuhl, 1987), and they appear to be particularly sensitive to language sounds.

The newborn's *vision* improves rapidly during the first 4 months. By about the age of 4 months, the infant sees objects the same way that an adult would. Of course, infants do not have the same cognitive associations with objects that adults have. Infants respond to a number of visual dimensions, including depth, brightness, movement, color, and distance. Human faces have particular appeal for newborns. One to two days after birth, infants are able to discriminate among—and even imitate—happy, sad, and surprised expressions, but this ability wanes after a few weeks (Field, Woodson, Greenberg, & Cohen, 1982). By 3 months, most infants are able to distinguish a parent's face from the face of a stranger (Zucker, 1985).

Some researchers have found that infants are distressed by a lack of facial movement in the people they look at, showing that they prefer caregivers to have expressive faces (Muir & Lee, 2003).

Taste and *smell* begin to function in the uterus, and newborns can differentiate sweet, bitter, sour, and salty tastes. Sweet tastes seem to have a calming effect on newborns (Blass & Ciaramitaro, 1994). Breastfed babies are particularly sensitive to their mother's body odors.

Both animal and human research tells us that *touch* plays a very important role in infant development. In many cultures, swaddling, or wrapping a baby snugly in a blanket, is used to soothe a fussy newborn. We also know that gentle handling, rocking, stroking, and cuddling are all soothing to an infant. Regular gentle rocking and stroking have been very effective in soothing low birth weight (LBW) babies, who may have underdeveloped central nervous systems. Infants also use touch to learn about their world and their own bodies. Young infants use their mouths for exploring their worlds, but by 6 months of age, infants can make controlled use of their hands to explore objects in their environment (Blass & Ciaramitaro, 1994).

There is clear evidence that from the first days of life, babies feel pain. Recently, pediatric researchers have been studying newborn reactions to medical procedures such as heel sticks, the sticks used to draw blood for lab analysis. One researcher found that newborns who undergo repeated heel sticks learn to anticipate pain and develop a stronger reaction to pain than other infants (Taddio, Shah, Gilbert-Macleod, & Katz, 2002). These findings are leading pediatricians to reconsider their stance on the use of pain medications with newborns.

Reflexes

Although dependent on others, newborns are equipped from the start with tools for survival that are involuntary responses to simple stimuli, called **reflexes**. Reflexes aid the infant in adapting to the environment outside the womb.

Newborns have two critical reflexes:

1. *Rooting reflex.* When infants' cheeks or the corners of their mouths are gently stroked with a finger, they will turn their head in the direction of the touch and open their mouths in an attempt to suck the finger. This reflex aids in feeding, because it guides the infants to the nipple.

2. *Sucking reflex.* When a nipple or some other suckable object is presented to the infant, the infant sucks it. This reflex is another important tool for feeding.

Many infants would probably perish without the rooting and sucking reflexes. Imagine the time and effort it would require for one feeding if they did not have them. Instead, infants are born with the ability to take in nutriment.

Reflexes disappear at identified times during infancy (see Exhibit 3.1). Both the rooting reflex and sucking reflex disappear between 2 and 4 months (Newman & Newman, 2006). By this time, the infant has mastered the voluntary act of sucking and is therefore no longer in need of the reflexive response. Several other infant reflexes appear to have little use now, but probably had some specific survival purposes in earlier times.

Reflexes are important in the evaluation of neurological functioning. The absence of reflexes can indicate a serious developmental disorder. Given Holly Hicks's early arrival, her reflex responses were thoroughly evaluated.

Exhibit 3.1	Infant Reflexes	
Reflex	*Description*	*Visible*
Sucking	The infant instinctively sucks any object of appropriate size that is presented to it.	First 2 to 4 months
Rooting	The head turns in the direction of a stimulus when the cheek is touched. The infant's mouth opens in an attempt to suck.	First 3 months
Moro/Startle	The arms thrust outward when the infant is released in midair, as if attempting to regain support.	First 5 months
Swimming	When placed face down in water, the infant makes paddling, swimlike motions.	First 3 months
Stepping	When the infant is held in an upright position with the feet placed on a firm surface, the infant moves the feet in a walking motion.	First 3 months
Blinking	The eyes blink in response to light, air, and other stimuli.	Lifetime
Grasping	The infant grasps objects placed in its hand.	First 4 months
Babinski	The toes spread when the soles of the feet are stroked.	First year

Motor Skills

The infant gradually advances from reflex functioning to motor functioning. The development of **motor skills**—the ability to move and manipulate—occurs in a more or less orderly, logical sequence. It begins with simple actions such as lifting the chin and progresses to more complex acts such as walking, running, and throwing. Infants usually crawl before they walk.

> How do these motor skills help to promote a sense of human agency in making choices?

Motor development is somewhat predictable, in that children tend to reach milestones at about the same age and in the same sequence. As a part of the MGRS, WHO undertook a project to construct standards for evaluating the motor development of children from birth through 5 years of age. MGRS collected longitudinal data on six gross motor milestones of children ages 4 to 24 months in Ghana, India, Norway, Oman, and the United States. The milestones studied were sitting without support, standing with assistance, hands-and-knees crawling, walking with assistance, standing alone, and walking alone. Because WHO was trying to establish standards for evaluating child development, healthy children were studied in all five study sites. The researchers found that 90% of the children achieved five of the six milestones in the same sequence, but 4.3% of the sample never engaged in hands-and-knees crawling (WHO Multicentre Growth Reference Study Group, 2006b).

Based on the data collected, MGRS developed "windows of milestone achievement" for each of the six motor skills, with achievement at the 1st and 99th percentiles as the window boundaries. All motor achievement within the windows is considered normal variation in ages of achievement for healthy children. The windows of achievement for the six motor skills studied are reported in Exhibit 3.2. The results reveal that the windows vary from 5.4 months for sitting without support to 10.0 months for standing alone. This is quite a wide range for normal development and should be reassuring to parents who become anxious if their child is not at the low end of the window. Many parents, for example, become

▲ **Photo 3.2** Fine motor skills, the ability to move and manipulate objects, develop in a logical sequence.

concerned if their child has not attempted to walk unassisted by age 1. However, some children walk alone at age 9 months; others do not even attempt to walk until almost 18 months.

Exhibit 3.2	Windows of Milestone Achievement in Months
Motor Milestone	*Window of Milestone Achievement*
Sitting without support	3.8–9.2 months
Standing with assistance	4.8–11.4 months
Hands-and-knees crawling	5.2–13.5 months
Walking with assistance	5.9–13.7 months
Standing alone	6.9–16.9 months
Walking alone	8.2–17.6 months

SOURCE: Taken from WHO Multicentre Growth Reference Study Group, 2006b.

Culture and ethnicity appear to have some influence on motor development in infants and toddlers. MGRS found that girls were slightly ahead of boys in gross motor development but the differences were not statistically significant. They did find small, but statistically significant, difference between sites of the study, however. The researchers speculate that these differences probably reflect culture-based child care behaviors, but the cause cannot be determined from the data, and a genetic component is possible. The earliest mean age of achievement for four of the six milestones occurred in the Ghanaian sample, and the latest mean age of achievement for all six milestones occurred in the Norwegian sample (WHO Multicentre Growth Reference Study Group, 2006c). The U.S. sample mean was in the middle range on all milestones except for hands-and-knees crawling, where it had the lowest mean achievement.

The development of motor skills (and most other types of skills, for that matter) is a continuous process. Children progress from broad capacities to more specific refined abilities. For example, toddlers progress from eating cereal with their fingers to eating with a spoon.

Parents are usually quite patient with their child's motor development. However, toilet training (potty training) is often a source of stress and uncertainty for new parents. Every human culture has mechanisms for disposing of human waste and socializes infants and toddlers to that method. One of the basic issues in this socialization is whether it should be in the hands of the child or the caregiver (Valsiner, 2000). In the United States until recently, many child development experts recommended that babies be potty trained during the first year of life. Consequently, many parents exercised strong measures, including scolding and punishment, to ensure timely toilet training. Even now, many grandparents proudly report that they tied their infants to the potty chair at times of predicted elimination (after eating, for example) until the child was able to master the skill. T. Berry Brazelton (1983), one of the best known pediatricians in the United States, endeavored to change this negative perspective. He advocated that parents begin potty training during the second year of life, during the lull time after standing and walking have been accomplished. Only then, he says, is the infant physiologically and psychologically ready to master this skill. That is the current position of the American Academy of Pediatrics (1999) who recommends waiting until the child is ready and guiding toilet training in a systematic way, beginning with bowel training. By age 3, most children have mastered toilet training, but even 5-year-olds are still prone to soiling accidents. It should be noted, however, that in some parts of the world there is a perception of readiness at a much earlier age (Valsiner, 2000).

The Growing Brain

Like the brains of other primates, human brains contain neurons, or nerve cells that store and transmit information (Huttenlocher & Kabholkar, 1997). Between these neurons are **synapses,** or neural connections, through which information is transported. During the prenatal period, the brain overproduces neurons in massive numbers. In fact, the human newborn has more synapses than the human adult. During infancy and toddlerhood, each neuron joins with thousands of other neurons to form a colossal number of synapses or connections. The period of overproduction of synapses, or **blooming,** is followed by a period of **pruning,** or reduction, of the synapses to improve the efficiency of brain functioning. It is through this process of creating elaborate communication systems between the connecting neurons that more and more complex skills and abilities become possible. Thus, during these early years of life, children are capable of rapid new learning. The blooming and pruning of synapses process continues well into childhood and adolescence at different timetables in different regions of the brain. For example, overproduction of synapses in the visual cortex of the brain peaks in the fourth month after birth, and pruning in that region continues until sometime toward the end of the early childhood period (Huttenlocher & Kabholkar, 1997). By contrast, in the medial prefrontal cortex part of the brain, where higher-level cognition and self-regulation take place, synaptic blooming peaks at about 1 year of age, and pruning continues until middle to late adolescence.

The available evidence suggests that both genetic processes and early experiences with the environment influence the timing of brain development (Thompson & Nelson, 2001). For example, exposure to speech in the first year expedites the discrimination of speech sounds; exposure to patterned visual information in the first few years of life is necessary for normal development of some aspects of vision. Some suggest that the entire infancy period is a crucial and sensitive time for brain development, given the quantity and speed at which the neurons develop and connect (Zigler, Finn-Stevenson, & Hall, 2002). Positive physical experiences (feeding, safety, etc.) and positive psychological experiences (touching, cooing, and playing) activate and simulate brain activity (Shonkoff & Phillips, 2000). So good nutrition and infant stimulation are essential for brain development, and exposure to environmental toxins, abuse, emotional trauma, and deprivation is hazardous (Shonkoff & Phillips, 2000; Teicher, 2002; Zigler et al., 2002).

> What role can social workers play in informing the public about the impact of the environment on brain development?

There are risks to brain development associated with prematurity. Premature infants born at 24 to 28 weeks gestation have high rates of serious intracranial hemorrhage, which can lead to problems in cognitive and motor development, including cerebral palsy and mental retardation. Less serious intracranial hemorrhage can lead to later behavioral, attentional, and memory problems (Shonkoff & Phillips, 2000). Also, the premature infant faces the challenging environment of the neonatal intensive care unit (NICU) at a time when the brain is developing rapidly. With this in mind, architects and neonatalists have been working together in recent years to make the NICU a more nurturing environment for this rapid brain development (Zeisel, 2006). It is not yet clear whether Holly Hicks suffered any type of brain hemorrhage and what impact it will have on her future development if she did.

Recent research has focused on the relationship between infant/parent attachment and brain development. One of the most popular perspectives on this issue is presented in a book entitled, *Why Love Matters, How Affection Shapes a Baby's Brain,* by Sue Gerhardt (2004). The premise here is that without affection and bonding, the frontal cortex of the brain cannot develop. The connection between attachment and brain development is discussed in more detail in the attachment section of this chapter.

Childhood Immunizations

Immunization, also called vaccination or inoculation, is a method of administering microorganisms, bacteria, or viruses that have been modified or killed to protect humans from disease. Most vaccinations are administered by injection. The purpose of immunization is to stimulate the body's immune system to build a defense against a specific disease.

Important breakthroughs in vaccine development have led to eradication or near eradication of such life-threatening diseases as smallpox, poliomyelitis, diphtheria, and tetanus, and this has been a boon to health during infancy, toddlerhood, and early childhood (Betts, 2002). Since the early 1980s, the development of vaccines has proliferated, and vaccines have now been developed for much less serious childhood illnesses such as mumps, measles, rubella, and chickenpox. The development of these new vaccines has resulted in an increase in the total number of vaccinations administered to young children. The National Vaccine Information Center (NVIC) reports that currently 34 doses of 10 different vaccines are administered before the child's fifth birthday.

Since the 1980s, some child advocates have challenged both the quality and quantity of vaccinations being administered. They suggest that the increased use of immunization has become harmful to many children, both because of the quantity of vaccines being taken and because of inadequate vaccine safety research. One supporter is Congressman Dan Burton, from Indiana, who joined with these advocacy groups to argue for vaccine reform by the federal government. His interest in the issue of vaccines developed when a granddaughter became seriously ill after receiving a hepatitis B shot and a grandson became autistic at age 14 months after receiving nine vaccines on one day (Betts, 2002).

Three vaccines have been targeted by child advocates as most questionable: the hepatitis B vaccine; the measles, mumps, rubella (MMR) vaccine; and the pertussis (whooping cough) portion of the diphtheria, pertussis, tetanus (DPT) vaccine. The hepatitis B vaccine has been linked to a number of serious health problems, and in 1998, France became the first country to discontinue requirement of hepatitis B vaccination for school-age children. Some researchers have linked the pertussis portion of the DPT to SIDS. The MMR vaccine is suspected as playing a role in the rapid increase of autism since the 1980s, an increase from 1 in 2,500 children before 1980 to 1 in 150 children currently (NVIC, n.d.). The practice of adding thimerosol as a preservative in multidose vaccines has been a particular concern of the child advocacy groups. Thimerosol is 49% mercury, and mercury is known to cause neurological damage. Mercury in vaccines was banned in the United Kingdom, Finland, and Sweden by 1995 and in the United States in 1999.

Most parents are unaware of the immunization controversy, but the debate over immunization safety creates hard decisions for those parents who are aware. They want to protect their children from the harmful effects of disease, but they do not welcome potential harms from vaccines. Some researchers argue that the benefits of immunizations outweigh the hazards, and many health care workers fear the public health consequences if parents begin to avoid immunizing their young children (Trifiletti, 2001). Additionally, many public school systems do not allow children to be admitted without up-to-date vaccinations. Luckily, both scientists and government reformers are currently investigating the issue of vaccine safety as this book is being written. On the basis of the above discussion about early brain development, vaccine safety is an important issue in infancy and toddlerhood. Some infants and toddlers will be more vulnerable than others to multiple doses of multiple vaccines.

Cognitive Development

As the brain develops, so does its ability to process and store information and to solve problems. These abilities are known as **cognition**. When we talk about how fast a child is learning, we are talking about cognitive development. Researchers now describe the infant as "wired to learn," and agree that infants have an intrinsic drive to learn and to be in interaction with their environments (Shonkoff & Phillips, 2000). A central element of cognition is language, which facilitates both thinking and communicating. Exhibit 3.3 lists some milestones in cognitive development.

How do the drives to learn and be in interaction with the environment promote interdependence?

Exhibit 3.3	Selected Milestones in Cognitive Development

Milestone	Age of Onset
Coos responsively	Birth to 3 months
Smiles responsively	3 to 4 months
Smiles at self in mirror	3 to 4 months
Laughs out loud	3 to 4 months
Plays peek-a-boo	3 to 4 months
Shows displeasure	5 to 6 months
Babbles	6 to 8 months
Understands simple commands	12 months
Follows directions	2 years
Puts two to three words together	2 years
Uses sentences	2 to 3 years

Piaget's Stages of Cognitive Development

To assess children's cognitive progress, many people use the concepts developed by the best-known cognitive development theorist, Jean Piaget (1952). Piaget believed that cognitive development occurs in successive stages, determined by the age of the child. His overall contention was that as a child grows and develops, cognition changes not only in quantity but also in quality.

Piaget used the metaphor of a slow-motion movie to explain his theory, which is summarized in Exhibit 3.4 as follows:

1. **Sensorimotor stage** (ages birth to 2 years). Infants at this stage of development can look at only one frame of the movie at a time. When the next picture appears on the screen, infants focus on it and cannot go back to the previous frame.

2. **Preoperational stage** (ages 2 to 7). Preschool children and children in early grades can remember (recall) the sequence of the pictures in the movie. They also develop **symbolic functioning**—the ability to use symbols to represent what is not present. However, they do not necessarily understand what has happened in the movie or how the pictures fit together.

3. **Concrete operations stage** (ages 7 to 11). Not until this stage can children run the pictures in the movie backward and forward to better understand how they blend to form a specific meaning.

4. **Formal operations stage** (ages 11 and beyond). Children gain the capacity to apply logic to various situations and to use symbols to solve problems. Adding to Piaget's metaphor, one cognitive scientist describes formal operations as the ability of the adolescent not only to understand the observed movie but also to add or change characters and create an additional plot or staging plan (Edwards, 1992).

▲ **Photo 3.3** The most important thing that adults can do to assist with language development is to provide high-quality interactions.

The first of Piaget's stages applies to infants and toddlers. During the sensorimotor period, they respond to immediate stimuli—what they see, hear, taste, touch, and smell—and learning takes place through the senses and motor activities. Piaget suggests that infant and toddler cognitive development occurs in six substages during the sensorimotor period.

Substage 1: *Reflex Activity (birth to 1 month)*. Because reflexes are what the infant can "do," they become the foundation to future learning. Reflexes are what infants build on.

Substage 2: *Primary Circular Reactions (1 to 4 months)*. During this stage, infants repeat (thus the term circular) behaviors that bring them a positive response and pleasure. The infant's body is the focus of the response, thus the term primary. If, for example, infants by chance hold their head erect or lift their chest, they will continue to repeat these acts because they are pleasurable. Infants also have limited anticipation abilities.

Substage 3: *Secondary Circular Reactions (4 to 8 months)*. As in the second substage, the focus is on performing acts and behaviors that bring about a response. In this stage, however, the infant reacts to responses from the environment. If, for example, 5-month-old infants cause the rattle to sound inadvertently as their arms move, they will continue attempts to repeat this occurrence.

Substage 4: *Coordination of Secondary Circular Reactions (8 to 12 months)*. The mastery of **object permanence** is a significant task during this stage. Piaget contended that around 9 months of age, infants develop the ability to understand that an object or a person exists even when they don't see it. Piaget demonstrated this ability by hiding a favored toy under a blanket. Infants are able to move the blanket and retrieve the toy. Object permanence is related to the rapid development of memory abilities during this period (Rovee-Collier, 1999). Two other phenomena are related to this advance in memory. **Stranger anxiety**, in which the infant reacts with fear and withdrawal to unfamiliar persons, has been found to occur at about 9 months across cultures. Many first-time parents comment, "I don't know what has gotten into her; she has always been so outgoing." Babies vary in how intensely they react to the strange situation and in how they express their anxiety (Rieser-Danner, 2003). **Separation anxiety** also becomes prominent in this period. The infant is able to remember previous separations

Exhibit 3.4	Piaget's Stages of Cognitive Development
Stage	*Characteristics*
Sensorimotor (birth to 2 years)	Infant is egocentric; he or she gradually learns to coordinate sensory and motor activities and develops a beginning sense of objects existing apart from the self.
Preoperational (2 to 7 years)	The child remains primarily egocentric but discovers rules (regularities) that can be applied to new incoming information. The child tends to overgeneralize rules, however, and thus makes many cognitive errors.
Concrete operations (7 to 11 years)	The child can solve concrete problems through the application of logical problem-solving strategies.
Formal operations (11 years and beyond)	The person becomes able to solve real and hypothetical problems using abstract concepts.

and becomes anxious at the signs of an impending separation from parents. With time, the infant also learns that the parent always returns.

Substage 5: *Tertiary Circular Reactions (12 to 18 months)*. During this stage, toddlers become more creative in eliciting responses and are better problem solvers. For example, if the first button on the talking telephone does not make it talk, they will continue to press other buttons on the phone until they find the correct one.

Substage 6: *Mental Representation (18 months to 2 years)*. Piaget described toddlers in this stage as actually able to use thinking skills in that they retain mental images of what is not immediately in front of them. For example, the toddler will look in a toy box for a desired toy and move other toys aside that prohibit recovery of the desired toy. Toddlers can also remember and imitate observed behavior. For example, toddlers roll their toy lawn mower over the lawn, imitating their parents' lawn mowing.

As much as Piaget's work has been praised, it has also been questioned and criticized. Piaget constructed his theory based on his observations of his own three children. Thus, one question has been how objective he was and whether the concepts can really be generalized to all children. Also, Piaget suggested that his developmental model describes the "average" child, but he did not define or describe what he meant by average. Finally, Piaget also did not address the influence of environmental factors—such as culture, family, and significant relationships and friendships—on cognitive development.

Research findings have also called into question some aspects of Piaget's theory. For example, Piaget described young children as being incapable of object permanence until at least 9 months of age. However, infants as young as 3½ and 4½ months of age have been observed who are already proficient at object permanence (Baillargeon, 1987). Other researchers (Munakata, McClelland, Johnson, & Siegler, 1997) have found that although infants seem aware of hidden objects at 3½ months, they fail to retrieve those objects until about 8 months of age. These researchers suggest that cognitive skills such as object permanence may be multifaceted and gradually developed (Baillargeon, 2004). Findings like these suggest using Piaget's model with caution. It remains, however, our most useful view of how cognition develops.

Prelanguage Skills

Some of the developmental milestones for language development are listed in Exhibit 3.3. Although infants communicate with their caretakers from the beginning (primarily by crying), language development truly begins around 2 months of age. The first sounds, cooing, are pleasing to most parents. By age 4 months, infants babble. Initially, these babbles are unrecognizable. Eventually, between 8 and 12 months, infants make gestures to indicate their desires. The babble sounds and gestures together, along with caretakers' growing familiarity with the infant's "vocabulary," make it easier for infants to communicate their desires. For example, 12-month-old infants may point to their bottle located on the kitchen cabinet and babble "baba." The caretaker soon learns that "baba" means "bottle."

By the age of 18 to 24 months, the toddler can speak between 50 and 200 words. Piaget asserts that children develop language in direct correlation to their cognitive skills. Thus, most of the words spoken at this age relate to people and significant objects in the toddler's environment. These include words such as "mama," "dada," "cat," and "sissy" (sister), for example. Toddlers' first words also include situational words such as "hot," "no," and "bye." Between 20 and 26 months, toddlers begin to combine two words together, also in tandem with growing cognitive abilities. For example, children can say "all gone" as they develop an understanding of object permanence (Berk, 2005).

Even with these skills, toddlers may be difficult to understand on occasion. Cindy, the mom of 24-month-old Steven, describes collecting her son from day care. During the trip home, Steven initiated conversation with Cindy by calling out "Mama." He began to "tell" her about something that Cindy assumes must have occurred during the day. Steven continued to babble to his mother with animation and laughs and giggles during the story. Although Cindy laughed at the appropriate moments, she was unable to understand most of what Steven was sharing with her.

The most important thing that adults can do to assist with language development is to provide opportunity for interactions. Adults can answer questions, provide information, explain plans and actions, and offer feedback about behavior. Adults can also read to infants and toddlers and play language games. The opportunity for interaction is important for deaf children as well as hearing children, but deaf children need interaction that involves hand and eye, as with sign language (Shonkoff & Phillips, 2000). Researchers have found that when talking with infants and toddlers, adults and even older children will engage in behaviors that facilitate language development; they tend to speak in a high pitch, use shorter sentences, and speak slowly (Singh, Morgan, & Best, 2002). However, there appear to be cultural differences in how adults communicate with infants and toddlers, and it is not clear how these differences affect language acquisition (Sabbagh & Baldwin, 2001).

Children who are bilingual, or multilingual, from birth seem to develop language ability at the same pace as children who are monolingual (Shonkoff & Phillips, 2000). Of course, language ability in any language is not retained unless the environment provides an opportunity for using the language.

Socioemotional Development

Infants and toddlers face vital developmental tasks in the emotional arena (some of which are listed in Exhibit 3.5), as well as in the social arena. Development during these early ages may set the stage for socioemotional development during all other developmental ages. This section addresses these tasks.

Erikson's Theory of Psychosocial Development

Erik Erikson's (1950) theory explains socioemotional development in terms of eight consecutive, age-defined stages of emotional development. Each stage requires the mastery of a developmental task. Mastery at each stage depends on mastery in the previous stages. If the "task facilitating factors" for a stage are absent, the individual will become stuck in that stage of development.

Each of Erikson's stages is overviewed in Exhibit 3.6 and discussed in the chapter about the part of the life course to which it applies. The following two stages are relevant to infants and toddlers:

Exhibit 3.5	Selected Milestones in Emotional Development
Milestone	*Age*
Emotional life centered on physical states. Exhibits distress, fear, and rage.	Newborn
Emotional life begins to be centered on relationships. Exhibits pleasure and delight.	3 months
Emotional life continues to be relational, but distinctions are made between those relationships, as in stranger anxiety and separation anxiety. Exhibits joy, fear, anxiety, and anger.	9 months
Emotional life becomes sensitive to emotional cues from other people. Exhibits a range of emotion from joy to rage.	End of first year
Emotional life becomes centered on regulation of emotional states.	Second and third year

SOURCE: Based on Davies, 2004, and Shonkoff & Phillips, 2000.

1. *Trust versus mistrust* (ages birth to 1½). The overall task of this stage is for infants to develop a sense that their needs will be met by the outside world and that the outside world is an okay place to be. In addition, the infant develops an emotional bond with an adult, which Erikson believes becomes the foundation for being able to form intimate, loving relationships in the future. Erikson argues the need for one consistent mother figure. The most important factor facilitating growth in this stage is consistency in having physical and emotional needs met: being fed when hungry, being kept warm and dry, and being allowed undisturbed sleep. In addition, the infant has to be protected from injury, disease, and so on, and receive adequate stimulation. Infants who develop mistrust at this stage become

How does the development of trust during infancy affect future relationships?

suspicious of the world and withdraw, react with rage, and have deep-seated feelings of dependency. These infants lack drive, hope, and motivation for continued growth. They cannot trust their environment and are unable to form intimate relationships with others. Given Ms. Velasquez's view that the outside world is not a safe place, described at the beginning of the chapter, her young son, Henry, is at risk of developing feelings of mistrust.

2. *Autonomy versus shame and doubt* (ages 1½ to 3). A child with autonomy has a growing sense of self-awareness and begins to strive for independence and self-control. These children feel proud that they can perform tasks and exercise control over bodily functions. They relate well with close people in the environment and begin to exercise self-control in response to parental limits. To develop autonomy, children need firm limits for controlling impulses and managing anxieties, but at the same time still need the freedom to explore their environment. Exhibit 3.7 summarizes possible sources of anxiety for toddlers (Davies, 2004). Toddlers also need an environment rich with stimulating and interesting objects and with opportunities for freedom of choice. Adults must accept the child's bodily functions as normal and good and offer praise and encouragement to enhance the child's mastery of self-control. At the other end of the spectrum are children who doubt themselves. They fear a loss of love and are overly concerned about their parents' approval. These children are ashamed of their abilities and develop an unhealthy kind of self-consciousness.

> How does the toddler's experience with autonomy contribute to the capacity for human agency?

Erikson does not address whether tasks that should be mastered in one stage can be mastered later if the facilitating factors—such as a dependable, nurturing caregiver—are introduced. For example, we know that Sarah suffered some neglect until Chris Johnson and his parents provided a dependable, nurturing environment for her. At what point is it too late to undo psychosocial damage? Critics also question Erikson's emphasis on the process of individualization, through which children develop a strong identity separate from that of their family. Many believe this to be a North American, Western value and therefore not applicable to collectivistic societies such as many African, Latin, and Asian societies or to collectivistic subcultures in the United States.

Emotional Control

Researchers have paid a lot of attention to the strategies infants develop to cope with intense emotions, both positive and negative ones. They have found that by the middle of the second year, toddlers have built a repertoire of ways to manage strong emotions. They make active efforts to avoid or disregard situations that arouse strong emotions. They engage in reassuring self-talk. And they develop substitute goals if they become thwarted in goal-directed behavior (Shonkoff & Phillips, 2000).

You may not be surprised to learn that researchers have found that one of the most important elements in how an infant learns to manage strong emotions is the assistance provided by the caregiver for emotion management (Siegel, 1999). The child's temperament also makes a difference, as you will see in the next section.

Finally, there are cultural differences in expectations for management of emotions in infants. For example, Japanese parents try to shield their infants from the frustrations that would invite anger. In other words, some emotions are regulated by protecting the child from

Exhibit 3.6	Erikson's Stages of Psychosocial Development	
Life Stage	*Psychosocial Challenge*	*Characteristic*
Infancy (birth to about 1 year)	Basic trust versus basic mistrust	Infants must form trusting relationships with caregivers or they will learn to distrust the world.
Toddlerhood (about 1 to 3 years)	Autonomy versus shame and doubt	Toddlers must develop self-confidence and a sense of mastery over themselves and their worlds and they use newly developed motor skills or they will develop shame and doubt about their inability to develop control.
Early childhood (3 to 5 years)	Initiative versus guilt	Young children must develop a growing capacity to plan and initiate actions or they may feel guilt about their taking initiative.
Middle childhood (6 to 11 years)	Industry versus inferiority	School-aged children must develop a sense of competence to master and complete tasks or they learn to feel inferior or incompetent.
Adolescence (11 to 20 years)	Identity versus role diffusion	Adolescents must develop a sense of who they are and where they are going in life or they become confused about their identity.
Young adulthood (21 to 40 years)	Intimacy versus isolation	Young adults must develop the capacity to commit to deep associations with others or they feel a sense of isolation.
Middle adulthood (40 to 65 years)	Generativity versus stagnation	Midlife adults must develop the capacity to transcend self-interest to guide the next generation or they feel stagnated.
Late adulthood (over 65 years)	Ego integrity versus despair	Older adults must find integrity and contentment in their final years by accepting their life as it has been or they feel a sense of despair.

SOURCE: Based on Erikson, 1950, 1978.

Exhibit 3.7	Some Possible Sources of Anxiety for Toddlers

Difficulty understanding what is happening

Difficulty communicating

Frustration over not being able to do what others can do or what they imagine others can do

Conflicts between wanting to be independent and wanting their parents' help

Separation or threat of separation from caregivers

Fears of losing parental approval and love

Reactions to losing self-control

Anxieties about the body

SOURCE: Adapted from Davies, 2004.

situations that would arouse them (Miyake, Campos, Kagan, & Bradsi
also cultural differences in how much independence infants and todc
exercise in managing emotions. In one study comparing Anglo and Pu
Harwood (1992) found that Anglo mothers expected their infants to ma
anxiety and separation anxiety without clinging to the mother. The Puei
on the other hand, expected their infants to rely on the mother for solace.

Temperament

Another way to look at emotional development is by evaluating **temperament**—the individual's innate disposition. The best-known study of temperament in infants and young
children was conducted by Alexander Thomas, Stella Chess, and Herbert Birch (1968, 1970).
They studied nine components of temperament: activity level, regularity of biological functions, initial reaction to any new stimulus, adaptability, intensity of reaction, level of stimulation needed to evoke a discernible response, quality of mood, distractibility, and attention
span or persistence. From their observations, the researchers identified three types of temperament: easy, slow to warm up, and difficult.

For an idea of the differences in infant temperament, consider the range of reactions you
might see at a baptism service. One infant might scream when passed from one person to
the other and when water is placed on his or her forehead. The mother might have difficulty
calming the infant for the remainder of the baptism service. At the other extreme, one infant
might make cooing noises throughout the entire service and seem unbothered by the rituals. The slow-to-warm-up infant might cautiously check out the clergy administering the
baptism and begin to relax by the time the ritual is completed.

Thomas and his colleagues believed that a child's temperament appears shortly after
birth and is set, or remains unchanged, throughout life. Recent research indicates, however,
that a stable pattern of temperament is not evident until about 4 months, when the central
nervous system is further developed (Shonkoff & Phillips, 2000). Whether temperament
is permanent or not is still unresolved. There is growing agreement, however, about two
aspects of temperament: 1) there is some stability to a child's positive or negative reactions
to environmental events, and 2) this stability of reaction leads to patterned reactions from
others (Vaughn & Bost, 1999).

Thomas, Chess, and Birch cautioned that a difficult temperament does not necessarily
indicate future childhood behavior problems, as one might logically assume. More significant than an infant's temperament type is the "goodness of fit" between the infant and
the expectations, temperament, and needs of those in the child's environment (Thomas &
Chess, 1986). In other words, how well the infant's temperament matches with that
of parents, caregivers, and siblings is crucial to the infant's emotional development. For
example, there appears to be a "problematic fit" between Holly Hicks and her mother.
Although Mrs. Hicks is able to meet Holly's basic needs, she feels rejected and overwhelmed
by Holly's "difficult" temperament. Holly seems to get irritated with Mrs. Hicks's nurturing
style. Thomas and Chess suggest that regardless of a child's temperament, caregivers and
others in the child's environment can learn to work with a child's temperament. Thus, helping Mrs. Hicks develop a better fit between herself and Holly will help Holly develop toward
healthy functioning.

Research investigating temperament as a predictor of preschool behavior problems
yielded a surprising result (Oberklaid, Sanson, Pedlow, & Prior, 1993). Investigators found

that the parent's perception of the preschool child's temperament had more influence on the development of behavior problems than did the child's actual temperament. Children who were perceived by their caregivers as having a "difficult" temperament were twice as likely to develop a behavior problem during the preschool years, regardless of their empirically measured temperament type.

Studies like these call into question whether temperament is genetically determined or environmentally induced. In a study of temperament among twins and among adopted siblings, investigators found that genetics contributed more than environment to temperament development (Braungart, Plomin, DeFries, & Fulker, 1992). The twins' temperaments were more alike than were those of the adopted siblings. The researchers concluded that environment contributes very little to temperament. However, another team of researchers (deVries & Sameroff, 1984) studied temperament among infants from three distinct East African societies and concluded that factors in the infants' environment—such as child-rearing practices, level of social change or modernization, maternal attitudes, ecological setting, and specific early life events—have more influence on temperament development than genetics. We could infer from this study that temperament is "neutral" and then molded and shaped by parental characteristics and expectations (Oberklaid et al., 1993). As with other aspects of personality, however, perhaps children are born with a genetic predisposition to a temperament type that is then significantly influenced by environmental factors.

Bowlby's Theory of Attachment

Another key component of emotional development is **attachment**—the ability to form emotional bonds with other people. Many child development scholars have suggested that attachment is one of the most important issues in infant development, mainly because attachment is the foundation for emotional development and a predictor of later functioning. Note that this view of attachment is similar to Erikson's first stage of psychosocial development. This perspective is similar to the one Mrs. Hicks found on the Internet, which raised issues of concern for her.

How important is the early attachment relationship for the quality of future relationships?

The two most popular theories of attachment were developed by John Bowlby (1969) and Mary Ainsworth and colleagues (Ainsworth, Blehar, Waters, & Wall, 1978). Bowlby, who initially studied attachment in animals, concluded that attachment is natural, a result of the infant's instinct for survival and consequent need to be protected. Attachment between infant and mother ensures that the infant will be adequately nurtured and protected from attack or, in the case of human infants, from a harsh environment. The infant is innately programmed to emit stimuli (smiling, clinging, etc.) to which the mother responds. This exchange between infant and mother creates a bond of attachment. The infant initiates the attachment process, but later the mother's behavior is what strengthens the bond.

Bowlby hypothesized that attachment advances through four stages: preattachment, attachment in the making, clear-cut attachment, and goal-corrected attachment. This process begins in the first month of life, with the infant's ability to discriminate the mother's voice. Attachment becomes fully developed during the second year of life, when the mother and toddler develop a partnership. During this later phase of attachment, the child is able to manipulate the mother into desired outcomes, but the child also has the capacity to understand the mother's point of view. The mother and the child reach a mutually acceptable compromise.

Bowlby contends that infants can demonstrate attachment behavior to others; however, attachment to the mother occurs earlier than attachment to others and is stronger and more consistent. It is thought that the earliest attachment becomes the child's **working model** for subsequent relationships (Bowlby, 1982).

Attachment explains the child's anxiety when the parents leave. However, children eventually learn to cope with separation. Toddlers often make use of **transitional objects**, or comfort objects, to help them cope with separations from parents and to handle other stressful situations. During such times, they may cuddle with a blanket, teddy bear, or other stuffed animal. The transitional object is seen as a symbol of the relationship with the caregiver, but toddlers also see it as having magic powers to soothe and protect them (Davies, 2004).

Ainsworth's Theory of Attachment

One of the most widely used methods to investigate infant attachment, known as the strange situation procedure, was developed by Ainsworth and colleagues (Ainsworth et al., 1978). The Ainsworth group believed that the level of infant attachment to the mother could be assessed through the infant's response to a series of "strange" episodes. Basically, the child is exposed over a period of 25 minutes to eight constructed episodes involving separation and reunion with the mother. The amount of child attachment to the mother is measured by how the child responds to the mother following the "distressing" separation.

Ainsworth and her colleagues identified three types of attachment:

1. Secure attachment. The child uses the mother as a home base and feels comfortable leaving this base to explore the playroom. The child returns to the mother every so often to ensure that she is still present. When the mother leaves the room (act of separation), the securely attached child will cry and seek comfort from the mother when she returns. But this child is easily reassured and soothed by the mother's return.

2. Anxious attachment. The child is reluctant to explore the playroom and clings to the mother. When the mother leaves the room, the child cries for a long time. When the mother returns, this child seeks solace from the mother but continues to cry and may swat at or pull away from the mother. Ainsworth and colleagues described these infants as somewhat insecure and doubted that their mothers would ever be able to provide the security and safety they need.

3. Avoidant attachment. Some infants seem indifferent to the presence of their mother. Whether the mother is present or absent from the room, these children's responses are the same.

More recent scholars have added a fourth response, known as the *insecure disorganized/ disoriented* response (Belsky, Campbell, Cohn, & Moore, 1996; Main & Hesse, 1990). These children display contradictory behavior: they attempt physical closeness, but retreat with acts of avoidance. These infants typically have mothers who either have a history of abusive behavior or continue to struggle with a traumatic experience in their own lives. As a result, the infants become confused in the "strange" situation. They fear the unknown figure and seek solace from the mother, but retreat because they are also fearful of the mother. Some authors have suggested that the behavior associated with the disorganized style is actually an adaptive response to harsh caregiving (Stovall & Dozier, 1998).

According to Ainsworth's attachment theory, children whose mothers are consistently present and responsive to their needs and whose mothers exhibit a warm, caring relationship develop an appropriate attachment. Findings from studies indicate that this is true, even when there are negative family issues such as alcoholism by the father (Edwards, Eiden, & Leonard, 2006). However, the implication is that only mother-infant attachment exists or is relevant to healthy infant development. This assumption probably seemed unquestionable when these theories were constructed. Today, however, many fathers have prominent, equal, and/or primary responsibilities in childrearing and childcare, sometimes by choice, and other times because of necessity. Sarah Johnson's dad for example became the primary caretaker for Sarah out of necessity. The gender of the parent is irrelevant in the development of secure infant attachment. Rather, it is the behavior of the primary caregiver, regardless of whether it is mother or father, which has the most influence on infant attachment (Geiger, 1996). When fathers who are the primary caregivers are able to provide infants with the warmth and affection they need, the infants develop secure attachments to their fathers. In fact, under stress, the fathers become a greater source of comfort to their infants than the mothers who are the secondary caregivers (Geiger, 1996). Perhaps the best scenario is when infants develop secure attachments to both parents. In one study, infants with secure attachments to both parents demonstrated less behavioral difficulties as toddlers, even less problems than toddlers with only secure mother infant attachment (Volling, Blandon, & Kolak, 2006).

In addition to a more prominent role by fathers over the past 20 to 30 years, more women have entered the workforce, and many more children experience alternative forms of childcare, including day care. The effect day care has on the development of attachment in young children continues to be a hotly debated topic. Some argue that day care has a negative effect on infant attachment and increases the risk of the infant's developing insecure and avoidant forms of attachment (see, e.g., Belsky, 1987; Belsky & Braungart, 1991). The risks are especially high if the infant attends day care during the first year of life. Others argue that day care does not have a negative effect on infant and early childhood attachment (Griffith, 1996; Shonkoff & Phillips, 2000). In fact, in one study, day care was found to mitigate the adverse effects of insecure mother-infant attachment (Spieker, Nelson, & Petras, 2003).

The question of how day care attendance affects attachment is probably not as simplistic as either side contends. Many factors appear to be associated with the development of attachment for children in day care. The overriding factor is the quality of the relationship between the infant and parents, regardless of the child's care arrangements. For example, mothers who have a positive attitude toward their infant, are emotionally available to their infant, and encourage age-appropriate levels of independence produce infants with secure attachment (Clarke-Stewart, 1988; Shonkoff & Phillips, 2000). Also, infants whose parents have a stable and loving marriage and whose father is significantly involved in their nurturing and care tend to develop secure attachment, even if they spend a significant portion of the day in child care (Schachere, 1990).

Recently, researchers have begun to study attachment among children in foster care. Over a half million children are in foster care in the United States (Children's Defense Fund, 2001). Most of these children come into foster care without secure attachments. Once in foster care, many children are subjected to frequent changes in their foster homes (Smith, Stormshak, Chamberlain, & Whaley, 2001). Problems with attachment may contribute to foster home disruptions, but foster home disruptions also contribute to attachment problems. Others conclude that institutional care can also have the same devastating effects on attachment (Johnson, Browne, & Hamilton-Giachritsis, 2006). Regardless, the child welfare system has paid too little attention to issues of attachment.

Let's look at one other issue concerning attachment. The manner in which infant attachment is measured raises some concerns. Most studies of attachment have used the Ainsworth group's strange situation method. However, this measure may not yield valid results with some groups or under certain conditions. For example, the avoidant pattern of attachment some investigators have noted among children in day care may not indicate lack of attachment, as some have concluded (Clarke-Stewart, 1989). These children may be securely attached but seem indifferent to the exit and return of the mother simply because they have become accustomed to routine separations and reunions with their mother.

The appropriateness of using the strange situation method with certain ethnic groups has also been questioned. Researchers evaluating attachment in Puerto Rican and Dominican infants (Fracasso, Busch-Rossnagel, & Fisher, 1994) have concluded that the pattern of attachment in these ethnic groups is different from that identified in studies of European American infants and is thus often mislabeled. For instance, multiple caregiving is traditional in the African American community (Jackson, 1993); many extended-family members (both blood and nonblood relations) participate in the rearing of children—for a number of reasons, including accommodation of parents' unconventional work schedules. This multiple caregiving arrangement encourages African American infants to befriend "strangers" introduced to them by their mothers. As a result, African American children often are more independent and do not experience the same level of anxiety that European American children experience when left by their mother. The "apathy" of African American children toward the mother may not be apathy at all, but rather an indication that they have adapted to the multiple caregiver arrangement. Interestingly, this tradition of shared child rearing echoes the African proverb "It takes a village to raise a child," which has become a popular adage in the United States. Also, it should be noted that the extended kinship network has been found to be a strength of African American families (Hill, 1972; Logan, Freeman, & McRoy, 1990).

> In what other ways does culture affect infant and toddler development?

At the other end of the continuum, Asian mothers traditionally have rarely left their infants in the care of others. One researcher found that Japanese mothers leave their babies in the care of others an average of 2.2 times in a given month, and only in the care of an immediate family relative such as the father or grandmother. They also keep their infants in close proximity; they often sleep in the same room and infants are carried on the mother's back (Takahashi, 1990). As a result, Japanese infants tend to be highly anxious when their mothers leave the room. The response to the mother leaving is so intense that these infants are not easily comforted when the mother returns. Some might label the response by these infants as a sign of insecure attachment, although the response is consistent with the environment they have experienced. Quite likely, the infants in fact have a secure and appropriate attachment to their mother (Takahashi, 1990).

Attachment and Brain Development

Attachment directly affects brain development (Gerhardt, 2004; Zigler et al., 2002; Perry, 2002). The suggestion is that the brain is physically affected by the presence or absence of attachment. Gerhardt concludes that without emotional bonding with an adult, the orbitofrontal cortex in the brain of infants (the part of the brain that allows social relationships to develop) cannot develop well. This process has been called the social brain. Supporters of this perspective cite several studies to support these conclusions, including a recent investigation of infants reared in orphanages in Romania conducted by Chugani et al. (2001). The infants had little contact with an adult, were left in their cots for most of the day, fed with propped-up bottles, and were never smiled at or hugged. Research with these infants found that their brain development was severely impaired.

One question of concern is whether these deficiencies in brain development are permanent. Some suggest that the brain impairments can be reversed if changes in care and attachment occur early enough (Zigler et al., 2002). They highlight the strides in brain development made by the Romanian orphans who were adopted into caring homes before they were 6 months of age. Perhaps Sarah Johnson's improvement was due to early intervention and moving her quickly to live with her dad. Others suggest that the brain impairments caused by lack of attachment with a primary caregiver are permanent (Perry, 2002). Regardless, the implication is that future brain growth is seriously jeopardized if brain development is not adequately nurtured in the first two to three years. Gerhardt concludes that the best advice we can offer parents of newborns is to forget about holding flashcards in front of the baby, but, instead, hold and cuddle the infants and simply enjoy them.

The Role of Play

Historically, play was thought to be insignificant to development, especially for infants and toddlers. However, we now know that play allows infants and toddlers to enhance motor, cognitive, emotional, and social development.

Because of their differences in development in all areas, infants and toddlers play in different ways. Exhibit 3.8 describes four types of infant play and three types of play observed in very young children. These later types of play begin in toddlerhood, and develop in union with cognitive and motor development. For example, young toddlers will play with a mound of clay by hitting and perhaps squishing it. More developed toddlers will mold the clay into a ball, and older toddlers will try to roll or throw the molded ball.

One zealous mother describes joining the "Toy of the Month Club" in which she received developmental toys through the mail each month for the first two years of her child's life. This mother wanted to be sure that her child had every opportunity to advance in terms of motor and cognitive skills. Although this mother's efforts are to be applauded, she admits that these toys were very costly and that perhaps she could have achieved the same outcome with other less costly objects. For example, there is no evidence that a store-bought infant mobile is any more effective than a homemade paper one hung on a clothes hanger. The objective is to provide stimulation and opportunities for play.

Exhibit 3.8	Types of Play in Infancy and Toddlerhood
Types of Infant Play	
Vocal play	Playful vocalizing with grunts, squeals, trills, vowels, etc. to experiment with sound and have fun with it
Interactive play	Initiating interactions with caregivers (at about 4–5 months), by smiling and vocalizing, to communicate and make connection
Exploratory play with objects	Exploring objects with eyes, mouth, and hands to learn about their shape, color, texture, movement, and sounds and to experience pleasure
Baby games	Participating in parent-initiated ritualized, repetitive games, such as peek-a-boo, that contain humor, suspense, and excitement and build an emotional bond
Types of Toddler Play	
Functional play	Engaging in simple, repetitive motor movements
Constructive play	Creating and constructing objects
Make-believe play	Acting out everyday functions and tasks and playing with an imaginary friend

SOURCES: Types of Infant Play based on Davies, 2004; Types of Toddler Play based on Rubin, Fein, & Vandenberg, 1983.

Another important aspect of play is parent/child interaction. Parent/infant play may increase the likelihood of secure attachment between the parent and child (Call, 1995; Davies, 2004; Scarlett, Naudeau, Salonius-Pasternak, Ponte, 2005). The act of play at least provides the opportunity for infants and parents to feel good about themselves by enjoying each other and by being enjoyed (Call, 1995; McCluskey & Duerden, 1993). Even before infants can speak or understand language spoken to them, play provides a mechanism of communication between the parent and infants. Infants receive messages about themselves through play, which promotes their sense of self (McCluskey & Duerden, 1993; Scarlett et al., 2005).

Play also is a vehicle for developing peer relations. A few decades ago, it was thought that babies really aren't interested in each other and cannot form relationships with each other. Recent research challenges this view (Shonkoff & Phillips, 2000). The peer group becomes more important at earlier ages as family size decreases and siblings are no longer available for daily social interaction. Researchers have found that very young infants get excited by the sight of other infants; by 6 to 9 months, infants appear to try to get the attention of other infants; and by 9 to 12 months infants imitate each other. Although toddlers are capable of establishing relationships, their social play is a struggle, and a toddler play session is quite a fragile experience. Toddlers need help in structuring their play with each other. And yet, researchers have found that groups of toddlers in preschool settings develop play routines that they return to again and again over periods of months (Corsaro, 2005). These toddler play routines are primarily nonverbal, with a set of ritualized actions. For example, Corsaro notes a play routine in one Italian preschool in which a group of toddlers would rearrange the chairs in the room and work together to move them around in patterns. They returned to this routine fairly regularly over the course of a year, modifying it slightly over time. Peer relations are being built by "doing things together."

Developmental Disruptions

Providing interventions to infants and toddlers with disabilities is mandated by the Developmental Disabilities Assistance and Bill of Rights Act. However, accurately assessing **developmental delays** in young children is difficult (Zipper & Simeonsson, 2004). One reason is that although we have loose guidelines for healthy development in infants and toddlers, development varies by individual child. Young children walk, master potty training, and develop language skills on different time tables. It is therefore difficult to assess whether a particular child has a case of delayed development—and if so, which faculties are delayed. Premature infants like Holly Hicks, for example, often need time to catch up in terms of physical, cognitive, and emotional development. At what point does Holly's social worker decide that she is not developing fast enough, and label her developmentally delayed?

The other reason that accurate assessment of developmental difficulties in infants and toddlers is hard is that although many physical and cognitive disabilities have been found to be genetic and others to be associated with environmental factors, the cause of most disabilities is unknown. For example, mental retardation has 350 known causes, yet the cause of most identified cases of mental retardation is unknown (Zipper & Simeonsson, 1997). Anticipating what the risk factors might be for a particular child and how they might influence developmental delays is therefore difficult. Assessment should be multidimensional, including the child, the family, and the broader environment (Zipper & Simeonsson, 2004).

Regardless, early intervention services for infants and toddlers who truly are delayed appear to be effective, especially in enhancing cognitive development (Shonkoff, Hauser-Cram, Krauss, & Upshur, 1992). The earlier the intervention begins, the better. Parent involvement is also crucial to the child's progress (Simeonsson, Edmondson, Smith, Carnahan, & Bucy, 1995).

Child Care Arrangements in Infancy and Toddlerhood

Human infants start life in a remarkably dependent state, in need of constant care and protection. On their own, they would die. Toddlers are full of life and are making great strides in development in all areas, but they are also "not ready to set out for life alone in the big city" (Newman & Newman, 2006, p, 182). Societal health is dependent on finding good solutions to the question, who will care for infants and toddlers?

With large numbers of mothers of infants and toddlers in the paid work force, and not at home, this question becomes a challenging one. The United States seems to be responding to this challenge more reluctantly than other highly industrialized countries are. This difference becomes clear in comparative analysis of two solutions for early child care: family leave and paid child care.

Family Leave

What impact might this trend have over time on the current cohort of infants and toddlers?

Because of changes in the economic institution in the United States between 1975 and 1999, the proportion of infants with mothers in paid employment increased from 24% to 54% (Shonkoff & Phillips, 2000). A similar trend is occurring around the world.

In response, most industrialized countries have instituted social policies that provide for job-protected leaves for parents to allow them to take off from work to care for their young children. Sweden was the first country to develop such a policy in 1974. The Swedish policy guaranteed paid leave.

By the early 1990s, the United States was the only industrialized country without a family leave policy (Kamerman, 1996). But in 1993, the U.S. Congress passed the Family and Medical Leave Act (FMLA) of 1993 (P.L. 103-3). FMLA requires businesses with 50 or more employees to provide up to 12 weeks of unpaid, job-protected leave during a 12-month period for workers to manage childbirth, adoption, or personal or family illness. Eligible workers are entitled to continued health insurance coverage during the leave period, if such coverage is a part of their compensation package.

Exhibit 3.9 highlights the family leave policies in selected countries. In 2002, the United States and Australia were the only affluent countries of the world that did not offer some *paid* parental leave at the time of birth and adoption. Australia does, however, provide families with a universal, flat rate maternity grant of $4,000 for each new child to assist with the costs of birth or adoption. The grant is scheduled to increase to $5,000 in July 2008 (Australian Government: Department of Family and Community Services: Office for Women, 2006). European countries also provide birth or maternity grants and family allowances. This is an area for social work advocacy in the United States.

Paid Child Care

Historically in the United States, mothers were expected to provide full-time care for infants and toddlers at home. If mothers were not available, it was expected that children would be cared for by domestic help or a close relative but still in their home setting (Kamerman & Kahn, 1995). Even in the 1960s, with the development of Head Start programs, the focus was

Exhibit 3.9	Family Leave Policies in Selected Countries, 1999–2002	
Country	*Duration of Leave*	*Percentage of Wage Replaced*
Afghanistan	3 months	100%
Australia	1 year	Unpaid
Belgium	15 weeks	75% to 80%
Canada	1 year	55%
Denmark	1 year	60%
Greece	2 weeks paternity	60%
Italy	16 weeks	50%
Mexico	5 months	80%
Norway	12 weeks	100%
Peru	52 weeks (or 42 weeks at 100%)	80%
Sweden	First 3 months	100%
	Subsequent 1 year	80%
United States	12 weeks	Unpaid

SOURCE: Based on Clearinghouse on International Developments in Child, Youth and Family Policies at Columbia University, 2002.

on preschool age children; infants and toddlers were still expected to be cared for at home (Kamerman & Kahn, 1995). Thus, historically there was very little provision of alternative child care for most children below school age.

This phenomenon has changed dramatically, however, over the last 20 years. In 1999, about 61% of women in the United States with children age 6 and under worked outside the home, and 54% of women with children age 1 year and younger worked outside the home (Shonkoff & Phillips, 2000). Therefore, alternative child care has become a necessity in the United States.

Many advocates for day care refer to the European model as an ideal for the United States. Countries in Europe provide "universal" child care for all children, regardless of the parents' income, employment status, race, age, and so forth. These programs are supported through national policy and funded through public funds. If they pay at all, parents pay no more than a quarter of the monies needed. Parents in Europe thus pay far less than parents in the United States typically pay.

Currently, there are some innovative programs in Europe in which the focus is on providing alternative group care for toddlers in group settings outside the home (Kamerman & Kahn, 1995). The thought is that the cognitive and social skills of children age 2 and older can be enhanced in a group setting. This care is also funded and regulated through public funds. Workers who provide this care are well trained in child development and are paid well (by United States' standards) for their services. Most important, this care is available to all families and children.

Research results indicate that day care in general is not harmful to infants and toddlers (Shonkoff & Phillips, 2000). The primary concern is the quality of the day care provided. Researchers conclude that quality day care can even enhance cognitive development among 9-month-old infants (Schuetze, Lewis, & DiMartino, 1999). The National Research Council (1990) has identified three factors essential to quality day care, described in Exhibit 3.10. Others propose that quality day care must include a well-defined curriculum and be based on child development theory (Bredekamp, 1992; Dodge, 1995).

Exhibit 3.10	Identified Factors of Quality Day Care
Staff/child ratio	1:3 for infants, 1:4 for toddlers, and 1:8 for preschoolers
Group size	no larger than 6 for infant, 8 for toddlers, and 16 for preschoolers
Staff training	on child development and age-appropriate child care

SOURCE: National Research Council, 1990.

⬚ Infants and Toddlers in the Multigenerational Family

What have you observed about how family relationships change when a baby is born?

Maria, a new mom, describes the first visit her mother and father made to her home after the birth of Maria's new infant. "Mom and Dad walked right past me as if I was not there, even though we had not seen each other for six months. I quickly realized that my status as their 'princess' was now replaced with a new little princess. During their visit, my husband and I had to fight to see our own child. When she cried, they immediately ran to her. And my mother criticized everything I did—she didn't like the brand of diapers I used, she thought the color of the room was too dreary for an infant—and she even scolded my husband at one point for waking the baby when he went to check on her. I appreciated their visit, but I must admit that I was glad when it was time for them to leave." Maria's description is not unique. The involvement of grandparents and other extended family members in the care of infants and toddlers may be experienced either as a great source of support or as interference and intrusion (and sometimes as a little of each). And, of course, cultures of the world have different norms about who is involved, and in what ways, in the care of infants and toddlers.

Yet, the specific roles of grandparents and other extended family members is rarely discussed within the family, which is why conflicts often occur (Hines, Preto, McGoldrick, Almeida, & Weltman, 2005). When these roles are clearly articulated and agreed upon, extended family members can provide support that enhances infant and toddler development (Hines et al., 2005). Family involvement as a form of social support is further discussed as a "protective factor" later in this chapter.

The birth of a child, especially of a first child, brings about a major transition not only for parents but also for the entire kin network. Partners become parents; sons and daughters become fathers and mothers; fathers and mothers become grandfathers and grandmothers; and brothers and sisters become aunts and uncles. The social status of the extended family serves as the basis of the social status of the child, and the values and beliefs of the extended family will shape the way they care for and socialize the child (Carter & McGoldrick, 2005b; Newman & Newman, 2006). In addition, many children's names and child-rearing rituals, decisions, and behaviors are passed from past generations to the next.

To illustrate this point, there is an old joke about a mother who prepared a roast beef for most Sunday family dinners. She would always cut the roast in half and place it in two pans before cooking it in the oven. Observing this behavior, her young daughter asked her why she cut the roast in half. After some thought she told her daughter that she did not know for sure; she remembered that her mother had always cut her roast in half. Later the mother asked her mother why she had cut her roast in half before cooking it. The senior mother explained that she did not have a pan large enough for the size roast she needed to feed her family. Thus, she would cut the roast in half in order to fit it into the two pans that she did own.

Similar behavior affects decisions regarding infants and toddlers. One mother reports giving her infant daughter herb tea in addition to an ointment provided by her physician for a skin rash. It seems that this skin rash was common among infant girls in each generation in this family. A specific herb tea was traditionally used to treat the rash. This mother confesses that she did not tell her mother or grandmother that she used the ointment prescribed by her doctor. It is interesting for us to note that although the mother did not have complete faith in the tea, she also did not have complete faith in the ointment. The mother states that she is not sure which one actually cured the rash. Violation of family and cultural rituals and norms can be a source of conflict between new parents and other family members (Hines et al., 1999). For example, differences of opinion about baptism, male circumcision, and even child care arrangements can create family disharmony. One decision that often involves the multigenerational family is the decision whether to breastfeed or bottle feed the infant.

The Breastfeeding Versus Bottle Feeding Decision

Throughout history, most infants have been breastfed. However, alternatives to breastfeeding by the mother have always existed, sometimes in the form of a wet nurse (a woman employed to breastfeed someone else's infant) or in the form of animal milks. Following

World War II, breastfeeding ceased to be the primary nutritional source for infants because of the promotion of manufactured formula in industrialized and nonindustrialized countries. Since the 1980s, cultural attitudes have shifted again in favor of breastfeeding. However, in the United States, only 39% of infants are breastfed at 6 months, 40% less than the Healthy People 2010 goal (Centers for Disease Control and Prevention, 2006b). Employer support, including on-site day care centers, is needed to expand breastfeeding among working mothers, especially for women at risk of discontinuing breastfeeding early (Pascoe, Pletta, Beasley, & Schellpfeffer, 2002). It is important to note that in many impoverished countries, it is hazardous to use formula because of the lack of access to a safe water supply for mixing with the formula.

In European American and Mexican American families, the mother often seeks the opinion of the baby's father and maternal and paternal grandparents, whereas in African American families, the maternal grandmother and peers tend to be most influential in the decision to breastfeed (Baranowski, 1983). Korean mothers-in-law care for the new mother and are a powerful influence in choices about breastfeeding. In Saudi Arabia, a woman may breastfeed her infant openly and receive no notice, although otherwise she is fully veiled. In France, topless swimming is culturally acceptable, but breastfeeding in public is not (Riordan & Auerbach, 1999).

Most women decide to nurse primarily for infant health benefits. One benefit is increased immunity—which begins in the third trimester of pregnancy—to viruses such as mumps, chicken pox, and influenza (Jackson & Nazar, 2006). Breastfeeding has also been demonstrated to decrease the risk of obesity during childhood and adolescence, especially if infants are exclusively breastfed for six months (Weyermann, Beermann, Brenner, & Rothenbacher, 2006). Contraindications to breastfeeding are few, but they include maternal medical conditions such as untreated tuberculosis, leukemia, breast cancer diagnosed during lactation, drug abuse, and sexually transmitted diseases (Dickason, Silverman, & Kaplan, 1998). Mothers who are positive for human immunodeficiency virus (HIV) are often advised to avoid breastfeeding because breastfeeding is a risk factor for mother-to-infant transmission (Mbori-Ngacha et al., 2001). However, in poor countries the contaminated water supply may pose more risk than breastfeeding (Piwoz, Ross, & Humphrey, 2004).

Postpartum Depression

Family dynamics are often altered when mothers are depressed following childbirth. There is evidence that, around the world, between 10% and 15% of mothers will have postpartum depression in the first year of the infant's life (Posmontier & Horowitz, 2004; Wisner, Chambers, & Sit, 2006). Although social factors no doubt contribute to postpartum depression, it is generally accepted that the precipitous hormonal changes at birth, to which some women seem especially sensitive, play a large role. Postpartum depression often goes undiagnosed and untreated across cultural groups (Dennis & Chung-Lee, 2006), but it is more likely to receive attention in societies that have regular postpartum visits from midwives or nurses. For example, in the United Kingdom, new parents receive seven visits from midwives in the first two weeks postpartum (Posmontier & Horowitz, 2004). Postpartum depression can be very disruptive to the early mother-infant relationship and, as discussed below, increases risk of impaired cognitive, emotional, and motor development (Wisner et al., 2006). Both social support and pharmacological interventions have been found to be helpful (Sword, Watt, & Krueger, 2006). Different cultures have different expectations for maternal adaptation, and it is important for health providers to recognize these cultural influences (Posmontier & Horowitz, 2004).

There is very little research on psychosocial and mental health issues for new fathers, but the Australian First Time Fathers Study has attempted to address this gap in knowledge (Condon, 2006). This study finds no evidence of male postnatal depression, but it does find that male partners of women with postpartum depression are at risk of depression, anxiety, and abusing alcohol. At first, most men are confused by their wives' depression, but supportive. If the depression lasts for months, which it often does, support is usually gradually withdrawn. Men report that they find their wives' irritability and lack of physical affection more troubling than the sadness and tearfulness. This study also found that male partners and other family members of depressed mothers often take on more and more of the care of the infant over time, which reinforces the mother's sense of incompetence. Communication breakdowns are very common in these situations.

▨ Risks to Healthy Infant and Toddler Development

Unfortunately, not all infants and toddlers get the start they need in life. Millions of infants and toddlers around the world are impoverished, abandoned, neglected, and endangered. Collectively, the adults of the world have not ensured that every child has the opportunity for a good start in life. You have probably already surmised what some of the environmental factors are that inhibit healthy growth and development in infants and toddlers. This section addresses a few of those factors that social workers are especially likely to encounter: poverty, inadequate caregiving, and child abuse.

Poverty

When a family is impoverished, the youngest are the most vulnerable, and, indeed, children birth to age 3 have the highest rates of impoverishment around the world (UNICEF, 2005).

Bellamy (2004) reports that one billion children across the world live in poverty, representing one in two children. Although children living in the poorest countries are much more likely than children living in wealthy countries to be poor (UNICEF, 2005), the proportion of children living in poverty in 17 of the 24 wealthiest nations has been rising (UNICEF Innocenti Research Centre, 2005). Using a relative measure of poverty as income below 50% of the national median income, the UNICEF researchers found that the percent of children living in poverty in 26 industrialized countries ranged from 2.4% in Denmark to 27.7% in Mexico. The United States had the second highest rate, 21.9%. All of the Scandanavian countries had child poverty rates less than 5%. Most European countries had rates between 5% and 10%.

> In what ways does social class affect the development of infants and toddlers?

In the United States, the National Center for Children in Poverty (NCCP) (2006a) estimates that families need an income about two times the U.S. federal poverty level to meet basic needs, and they refer to families below this level as low income. NCCP reports that of the 12 million infants and toddlers in the United States, 5.2 million (43%) live in low-income families, and 2.6 million (21%) live in families below the poverty level. There are racial and ethnic differences in the rates: 63% of Latino infants and toddlers live in low-income families, compared to 66% of black infants and toddlers, 26% of Asian infant and toddlers, and 30% of white infants and toddlers. Infants and toddlers with immigrant parents are more likely than infants and toddlers with native-born parents to live in low-income families, 61% compared to 40%. Half (51%) of infants and toddlers living in low-income families have at least one parent who works full-time, year-round.

Although some young children who live in poverty flourish, poverty presents considerable risks to children's growth and development. (That risk continues into preschool and middle childhood, as Chapters 4 and 5 explain.) Children living in poverty often suffer the consequences of poor nutrition and inadequate health care. Many of these children do not receive proper immunizations, and many minor illnesses go untreated, increasing the potential for serious health problems. This phenomenon is particularly disturbing because many of these minor illnesses are easily treated. Most childhood ear infections, for example, are easily treated with antibiotics; left untreated, they can result in hearing loss.

In addition to inadequate health care and nutrition, children living in poverty often experience overcrowded living conditions. Overcrowding restricts opportunities for play, and thus, because most learning and development in young children takes place in the context of play, restricts healthy development. A study of development among 12-month-old Haitian American children found that the poorer children experienced more overcrowded conditions than those not living in poverty and consequently had less play time, fewer toys, a smaller number of safe areas to play, and less private time with parents (Widmayer, Peterson, & Larner, 1990). The living conditions of the children who were poor were associated with delayed motor development and lower cognitive functioning.

Children are affected not only by the direct consequences of poverty but also by indirect factors such as family stress, parental depression, and inadequate or nonsupportive parenting (UNICEF, 2005). Irma Velasquez's depression and anxiety will affect her relationship with Henry. Poor children are also more likely to be exposed to environmental toxins (Song & Lu, 2002).

Most disturbing is the link between poverty and **infant mortality**—the death of a child before his or her first birthday. In general, infant mortality rates are the highest in the poorest countries (United Nations Development Program, 2005). Infant mortality rates in the United States are high compared to other industrialized nations (UNICEF, 2005), but Malaysia, a country with one-quarter the average income of the United States, has achieved the same infant mortality rate as the United States (United Nations Development Program, 2005). Within the United States, mortality rates for infants are higher among the poor, and the rate among African Americans is twice that of European Americans (United Nations Development Program, 2005). As discussed in Chapter 2, low birth weight (LBW) as a result of inadequate prenatal care is the primary factor that contributes to the high infant mortality rate (United Nations Development Program, 2005).

Interestingly, the infant mortality rate for Hispanic women is lower than that of European American women (Hessol & Fuentes-Afflick, 2005), even though inadequate prenatal care is prominent among Hispanic women. This fact suggests that differences in prenatal care explain only part of the disparity in infant mortality rates. The mother's diet and social support network have been suggested as other factors that may affect birth weight and infant mortality rates (Gonzalez-Quintero et al., 2006; McGlade, Saha, & Dahlstrom, 2004). One comparative study found lower rates of alcohol and tobacco use among Hispanic women than among women of other racial/ethnic groups and the presence of stronger family, cultural, and social ties (McGlade et al., 2004). These findings suggest that social support may offset the consequences of inadequate prenatal care.

Inadequate Caregiving

The most pervasive response to inadequate caregiving is nonorganic failure to thrive (NOFTT). This diagnosis is used to describe infants, usually between ages 3 to 12 months, who show poor development, primarily in terms of weight gain. These infants weigh less than 80% of the ideal weight for their age. The "nonorganic" feature refers to the lack of medical causes for the poor development, and is thought to be a consequence of environmental neglect (lack of food) and stimulus deprivation (Bassali & Benjamin, 2002). Overall, NOFTT is a consequence of the infant's basic needs going unmet, primarily the needs for feeding and nurturing.

A review of the literature identified several parental factors that appear to increase the likelihood of the development of NOFTT (Bassali & Benjamin, 2002; Marino, Weinman, & Soudelier, 2001). These include maternal depression, maternal malnutrition during pregnancy, marital problems between parents, and mental illness and/or substance abuse in the primary caretaker.

Parental mental illness and depression are associated with other problems among infants and toddlers as well. For example, infants of depressed mothers demonstrate less positive expressions of mood and personality and are less attentive in play (Gomez, 2001). Overall, they demonstrate less joy, even when they were securely attached to the mother. One analysis of the literature on parental mental illness and infant development concluded the following (Seifer & Dickstein, 2000):

- Parental mental illness increases the likelihood of mental health problems among their children.
- Mothers who are depressed are more negative in interaction with their infants.
- Similarly, infants with depressed mothers are more negative in their exchange with their mothers.
- There is an association between parental mental illness and insecure attachment between parents and infants.
- Depressed mothers view their infant's behavior as more negative than nondepressed mothers.

Child Abuse

Almost all parents in the United States use some type of physical punishment, and hitting children usually begins in infancy (McGoldrick, Broken Nose, & Potenza, 1999). Apparently, many parents are simply not aware of how dangerous it can be to use physical punishment with such young children. Infants and toddlers who are abused demonstrate delayed cognitive and language development (Veltman & Browne, 2001). As abuse and neglect continue, the infant's cognitive skills continue to decline and reach levels of "intellectual disability" (Strathearn, Gary, & O'Callaghan, 2001). Interestingly, these infants also have smaller than average head sizes. Also, according to reports from the U.S. Department of Health and Human Services (1995), most children who die from child abuse or neglect are under age 5, and the majority of these children are less than 1 year of age.

> How might child abuse or neglect experienced as an infant or toddler affect later development?

Several factors are thought to contribute to the abuse of infants and toddlers. Consistently, poverty is reported as a factor that contributes to abuse and neglect (Lee &

George, 1999). Factors that interact with poverty and increase the likelihood of abuse are young motherhood and single parenthood.

An association also has been found between infant temperament and abuse (Thomlison, 2004). Infants who have "difficult" temperament are more likely to be abused and neglected. Others suggest that the combination of difficult temperament and environmental stress interact (Thomlison, 2004). Similarly, infants and toddlers with mental, physical, or behavioral abnormalities are also at a higher risk for abuse (Guterman & Embry, 2004).

Parental characteristics such as lack of education, poor self-esteem, lack of family support, and parental depression also contribute to child abuse and neglect (Coohey, 1998; Levine & Sallee, 1999; Thomlison, 2004). Of course, parents who abuse their children were often abused themselves as children (Zuravin & Di Blasio, 1996).

The number of infants removed from their home due to parental substance abuse has increased (Chasnoff, 1998), and thus the relationship between substance abuse and child abuse has become a focus of research. The abuse of alcohol and other substances is reported to contribute to child abuse (Sun, Shillington, Hohman, & Jones, 2001). Some suggest that parental substance abuse is present in at least half of all families in Child Protective Service caseloads (Murphy et al., 1991); others predict that this number may be as high as 80% (Barth, 1994). Many advocate for substance abuse treatment programs that include mothers and their infants and toddlers (Clark, 2001).

Regardless of cause, contrary to what most of us believe, most abusive parents feel terrible afterward and express feelings of guilt and remorse (Kempe & Kempe, 1976).

⧊ Protective Factors in Infancy and Toddlerhood

Many young children experience healthy growth and development despite the presence of risk factors. They are said to have *resilience*. Several factors have been identified as mediating between the risks children experience and their growth and development (Fraser, Kirby, & Smokowski, 2004; Werner, 2000). These factors are "protective" in the sense that they shield the child from the consequences of potential hazards (Fraser et al., 2004). Following are some protective factors that help diminish the potential risks to infants and toddlers.

Education

Research indicates that the education of the mother directly affects the outcome for infants and toddlers. This effect was found even in the devastating poverty that exists in Nicaragua (Pena & Wall, 2000). The infant mortality rate is predictably high in this country. However, investigators found that the higher the mother's level of formal education, the lower the infant mortality rate. Investigators hypothesize that mothers with higher levels of formal education provide better quality of care to their infants by feeding them more conscientiously, using available health care, keeping the household cleaner, and generally satisfying the overall needs of the infant. These mothers simply possessed better coping skills.

Similar results were found in a study of mothers and infants with two strikes against them—they are living in poverty and the infants were born premature (Bradley et al., 1994). Infants whose mothers had higher intellectual abilities demonstrated higher levels of cognitive and social development and were more likely to be in the normal range of physical development.

Social Support

Social support is often found in informal networks, such as friends and extended family members, or in formal support systems, such as the church, community agencies, day care centers, social workers, and other professions. The availability of social support seems to buffer many risk factors, such as stress experienced by parents (Werner & Smith, 2001). For example, Mrs. Hicks could truly benefit from having the opportunity to take a break from the stresses of caring for Holly. Both formal and informal social support can fill this gap for her. Even child abuse is reduced in the presence of positive social support networks (Coohey, 1996).

Extended family members often serve as alternative caregivers when parents cannot provide care because of physical or mental illness or job demands. Reliance on an extended family is particularly important in some cultural and socioeconomic groups. Sarah's dad, Chris Johnson, probably would not have been able to care for her without the support of his family. And, it is through the support of his family that he has been able to continue his education.

Easy Temperament

Infants with a positive temperament are less likely to be affected by risk factors (Fraser et al., 2004). The association between easy temperament and "protection" is both direct and indirect. Infants with a positive temperament may simply perceive their world more positively. Infants with a positive temperament may also induce more constructive and affirming responses from those in their environment.

IMPLICATIONS FOR SOCIAL WORK PRACTICE

In summary, knowledge about infants and toddlers has several implications for social work practice:

- ◆ Become well acquainted with theories and empirical research about growth and development among infants and toddlers.
- ◆ Assess infants and toddlers in the context of their environment, culture included.
- ◆ Promote continued use of formal and informal social support networks for parents with infants and toddlers.
- ◆ Continue to promote the elimination of poverty and the advancement of social justice.
- ◆ Advocate for compulsory health insurance and quality health care.
- ◆ Advocate for more affordable, quality child care.
- ◆ Collaborate with news media and other organizations to educate the public about the impact of poverty and inequality on early child development.
- ◆ Learn intervention methods to prevent and reduce substance abuse.
- ◆ Help parents understand the potential effects of inadequate caregiving on their infants, including the effects on brain development.
- ◆ Provide support and appropriate intervention to parents to facilitate effective caregiving for infants and toddlers.

KEY TERMS

attachment	infant mortality	sensory system
blooming	motor skills	separation anxiety
cognition	object permanence	stranger anxiety
concrete operations stage	plasticity (brain)	symbolic functioning
developmental delay	preoperational stage	synapses
formal operations stage	pruning	temperament
immunization	reflex	toddler
infant	sensorimotor stage	transitional object

Active Learning

1. Spend some time at a mall or other public place where parents and infants frequent. List behaviors that you observe that indicate attachment between the infant and caretaker. Note any evidence you observe that may indicate a lack of attachment.

2. Ask to tour a day care facility. Describe the things you observe that may have a positive influence on cognitive development for the infants and toddlers who are placed there. List those things that you think are missing from that setting that are needed to create a more stimulating environment.

3. Social support is considered to be a protective factor for individuals throughout the life course. List the forms of social support that are available to Marilyn Hicks, Chris Johnson, and Irma Velasquez. How do they help them with their parenting? In what ways could they be more helpful? How do they add to the level of stress?

WEB RESOURCES

The Jean Piaget Society
www.piaget.org/index.html

Site presented by The Jean Piaget Society, an international interdisciplinary society of scholars, teachers, and researchers, contains information on the society, a student page, a brief biography of Piaget, and Internet links.

National Center for Children in Poverty (NCCP)
www.nccp.org

Site presented by the NCC of the Mailman School of Public Health of Columbia University contains media resources, child poverty facts, as well as information on child care and early education, family support, and welfare reform.

Zero to Three
www.zerotothree.org

Site presented by Zero to Three: National Center for Infants, Toddlers & Families, a national nonprofit charitable organization with the aim to strengthen and support families, contains Parents' Tip of the Week, Parenting A–Z, BrainWonders, a glossary, and links to the Erikson Institute and other Internet sites.

National Network for Child Care
www.nncc.org

Site presented by the Cooperative Extension System's National Network for Child Care contains a list of over 1,000 publications and resources related to child care, an e-mail listserve, and a newsletter.

The Clearinghouse on International
Developments on Child, Youth and Family Policies
www.childpolicyintl.org

Site maintained at Columbia University contains international comparisons of child and family policies.

EARLY CHILDHOOD

Debra J. Woody and David Woody, III

Key Ideas	139
Case Study 4.1: ■ Terri's Terrible Temper	140
Case Study 4.2: ■ Jack's Name Change	140
Case Study 4.3: ■ A New Role for Ron and Rosiland's Grandmother	141
Healthy Development in Early Childhood	142
Physical Development in Early Childhood	142
Cognitive and Language Development	143
Piaget's Stages of Cognitive Development	144
Language Skills	145
Moral Development	146
Understanding Moral Development	147
Helping Young Children to Develop Morally	148
Personality and Emotional Development	149
Erikson's Theory of Psychosocial Development	149
Emotions	149
Aggression	150
Attachment	150
Social Development	150
Peer Relations	151
Self-Concept	151
Gender Identity and Sexual Interests	152
Racial and Ethnic Identity	153

The Role of Play 154
    Play as an Opportunity to Explore Reality 156
    Play's Contribution to Cognitive Development 156
    Play as an Opportunity to Gain Control 156
    Play as a Shared Experience 156
    Play as the Route to Attachment to Fathers 157
Developmental Disruptions 158
Early Childhood Education 159
Early Childhood in the Multigenerational Family 160
Risks to Healthy Development in Early Childhood 162
    Poverty 162
    Ineffective Discipline 163
    Divorce 165
    Violence 166
        Community Violence 166
        Domestic Violence 168
        Child Maltreatment 170
Protective Factors in Early Childhood 170
Implications for Social Work Practice 171
Key Terms 172
Active Learning 172
Web Resources 172

❖ Why do social workers need to know about the ability of young children (ages 3 to 6) to express emotions and feelings?

❖ What is the process of gender and ethnic recognition and development among young children?

❖ What do social workers need to know about play among young children?

KEY IDEAS

As you read this chapter, take note of these central ideas:

1. Healthy development is in many ways defined by the environment and culture in which the child is raised. In addition, although growth and development in young children have some predictability and logic, the timing and expression of many developmental skills vary from child to child.

2. According to Piaget, preschoolers are in the preoperational stage of cognitive development and become capable of cognitive recall and symbolic functioning.

3. Erikson describes the task of children ages 3 to 6 as being the development of initiative versus guilt.

4. As young children struggle to discover stability and regularity in the environment, they are often rigid in their use of rules and stereotypes.

5. Regardless of country of residence or culture, all children ages 3 to 6 engage in spontaneous play.

6. Three types of parenting styles have been described: authoritarian, authoritative, and permissive. Parenting styles are prescribed to some extent by the community and culture in which the parent resides. However, authoritarian and permissive styles have the potential to lead to emotional and behavioral problems.

7. Poverty, ineffective discipline, divorce, and exposure to violence all pose special challenges for early childhood development.

Terri's Terrible Temper

Terri's mother and father, Mr. and Mrs. Smith, really seem at a loss about what to do. They adopted Terri, age 3, when she was an infant. They describe to their social worker how happy they were to finally have a child. They had tried for many years, spent a lot of money on fertility procedures, and had almost given up on the adoption process when Terri seemed to be "sent from heaven." Their lives were going well until a year ago, when Terri turned 2. Mrs. Smith describes an overnight change in Terri's behavior. Terri has become a total terror at home and at preschool. In fact, the preschool has threatened to dismiss Terri if her behavior does not improve soon. Terri hits and takes toys from other children, she refuses to cooperate with the teacher, and does "what she wants to do."

Mr. and Mrs. Smith admit that Terri runs their household. They spend most evenings after work coaxing Terri into eating her dinner, taking a bath, and going to bed. Any attempt at a routine is nonexistent. When the Smiths try to discipline Terri, she screams, hits them, and throws things. They have not been able to use time-outs to discipline her because Terri refuses to stay in the bathroom, the designated time-out place. She runs out of the bathroom and hides. When they attempt to hold her in the bathroom, she screams until Mr. Smith gets too tired to continue to hold her or until she falls asleep. Mr. and Mrs. Smith admit that they frequently let Terri have her way because it is easier than saying no or trying to discipline her.

The "straw that broke the camel's back" came during a family vacation. Mrs. Smith's sister and family joined the Smiths at the beach. Mr. Smith describes the vacation as a total disaster. Terri refused to cooperate the "entire" vacation. They were unable to eat at restaurants because of her tantrums, and they were unable to participate in family activities because Terri would not let them get her ready to go. They tried allowing her to choose the activities for the day, which worked until other family members tired of doing only the things that Terri wanted to do. Terri would scream and throw objects if the family refused to eat when and where she wanted or go to the park or the beach when she wanted. Mrs. Smith's sister became so frustrated with the situation that she vowed never to vacation with them again. In fact, it was the sister who insisted that they get professional help for Terri.

Jack's Name Change

Until last month, Jack Lewis, age 4, lived with his mother, Joyce Lewis, and father, Charles Jackson Lewis, in what Joyce describes as a happy home. She was shocked when she discovered that her husband was having an affair with a woman at work. She immediately asked him to leave and has filed for divorce. Charles moved in with his girlfriend and has not contacted Joyce or Jack at this point. Joyce just can't believe that this is happening to her. Her mother had the same experience with Joyce's father but had kept the marriage going for the sake of Joyce and her siblings. Joyce, on the other hand, is determined to live a different life from the life her mother chose. She saw how depressed her mother was until her death at age 54. Joyce states that her mother died of a broken heart.

Although Joyce is determined to live without Charles, she is concerned about how she and Jack will live on her income alone. They had a comfortable life before the separation, but it took both incomes. Although she plans to seek child support, she knows she will need to move, because she cannot afford the mortgage on her own.

Joyce would prefer for Jack not to have contact with his father. In fact, she is seriously considering changing Jack's name because he was named after his father. Joyce has tried to explain the situation to Jack as best she can. However, in the social worker's presence, she told Jack that she hopes he does not grow up to be like his father. She also told Jack that his father is the devil and is now living with a witch.

Joyce also shares that Jack has had difficulty sleeping and continues to ask when his father is coming home. Joyce simply responds to Jack by telling him that they probably will never see Charles again.

Case Study 4.3

A New Role for Ron and Rosiland's Grandmother

Ron, age 3, and Rosiland, age 5, have lived with Ms. Johnson, their grandmother, for the last year. Their mother, Shirley, was sent to prison a year ago after conviction of drug trafficking. Shirley's boyfriend is a known drug dealer and had asked Shirley to make a "delivery" for him. Shirley was arrested as she stepped off the bus in another state where she had taken the drugs for delivery. Ron and Rosiland were with her when she was arrested, because she had taken them with her. Her boyfriend thought that a woman traveling with two young children would never be suspected of delivering drugs.

Ron and Rosiland were put into foster care by Child Protective Services until Ms. Johnson arrived to pick them up. It had taken her two weeks to save enough money to get to the children and fly them all home. Ms. Johnson shares with the social worker how angry she was that Shirley's boyfriend refused to help her get the children home. Shirley calls the children when she can, but because her crime was a federal offense, she has been sent to a prison far away from home. The children ask about her often and miss her terribly. Ms. Johnson has told the children that their mom is away but has not told them that she will be away for some time. She is also unsure how much they understand about what happened, even though they were present when their mom was arrested.

Ms. Johnson shares that she has no choice but to care for the children, although this is definitely not the life she has planned. She was looking forward to living alone; her husband died several years ago. With her small savings, she was planning to visit her sister in another state for an extended visit. But that money is gone now, because these funds were used to get the children home. She seems to love both of the children but confides that the children "drive her crazy." She is not accustomed to all the noise, and they seem to need so much attention from her. Getting into the habit of having a scheduled day is also difficult for Ms. Johnson. Both children attend preschool, an arrangement Shirley made before her incarceration. Ms. Johnson describes the fact that the children attend preschool as a blessing, because it gives her some relief. Her social worker suspects that preschool is a blessing for the children as well.

▧ Healthy Development in Early Childhood

As children like Terri Smith, Jack Lewis, and Ron and Rosiland Johnson emerge from toddlerhood, they turn their attention more and more to the external environment. Just as in infancy and toddlerhood they worked at developing some regularity in their body rhythms, attachment relationships, and emotional states, they now work to discover some stability and regularity in the external world. That is not always an easy task, given their limitations in cognitive and language development. Much happens in all interrelated dimensions of development between ages 3 and 6, however, and children emerge from early childhood with a much more sophisticated ability to understand the world and their relationships to it. They work out this understanding in an increasingly wider world, with major influences coming from family, school, peer groups, neighborhood, and the media.

> What historical trends are influencing our understanding of social age in early childhood?

Some child development scholars still refer to the period between ages 3 and 6 as the preschool age, but others have recently begun to refer to this period as early school age, reflecting the fact that most children are enrolled in some form of group-based experience during this period. We will simply refer to this period between 3 and 6 years of age as early childhood. Remember as you read that the various types of development discussed in this chapter under separate headings actually are interdependent, and sometimes the distinctions between the dimensions blur.

Physical Development in Early Childhood

As Chapter 3 explained, infants and toddlers grow rapidly. From ages 3 to 6, physical growth slows significantly. On average, height during this stage increases about two to three inches per year, and the young child adds about five pounds of weight per year. As a result, young children look leaner and better proportioned than they did as toddlers (Bright Futures, n.d.). There is great variation in the height and weight of young children, and racial and ethnic differences in height and weight are still evident in the early childhood years. For example, in the United States, African American children in early childhood on average are taller than white and Hispanic children of the same age, and there is some evidence that Hispanic American children weigh more on average than other young children (Dennison et al., 2006; Overpeck et al., 2000). Children of low economic status are more likely than other children to be overweight during early childhood (Wang & Zhang, 2006).

One of the main arenas for physical development at this age is the brain. By age 5, the child's brain is 90% of its adult size. Motor and cognitive abilities increase by leaps and bounds because of increased interconnections between brain cells, which allow for more complex cognitive and motor capability. In addition, through a process called **lateralization**, the two hemispheres of the brain begin to operate slightly differently, allowing for a wider range of activity. Simply stated, brain functioning becomes more specialized. The left hemisphere is activated during tasks that require analytical skills, including speaking and reading. Tasks that involve emotional expression and spatial skills, such as visual imagery, require

▲ **Photo 4.1** During early childhood, young children make advancement in the development of fine motor skills, including the ability to draw.

response from the right hemisphere. With the development of the right hemisphere and the social-emotional components there, young children develop the ability to reflect on the feelings and thoughts of others (Beatson & Taryan, 2003). Note that this reflective function is a critical component of attachment.

Due to other developments in the brain, children also obtain and refine some advanced motor skills during this time, such as running, jumping, and hopping. A 3-year-old can pedal a tricycle, a 4-year-old can gallop, and a 5-year-old can jump rope and walk on a balance beam. In addition to these **gross motor skills**—skills that require use of the large muscle groups—young children develop **fine motor skills**, including the ability to scribble and draw, cut with scissors, and by age 5, print their name.

Increases in fine motor skills also allow young children to become more self-sufficient. At age 3, children can manage toilet needs without supervision; by age 4, they can dress and undress themselves and pour water into a glass. Most young children enjoy the independence that performing these skills allows. However, allowing the extra time needed for young children to perform these tasks can be frustrating to adults. Ms. Johnson, for example, has lived alone for some time now and may need to readjust to allowing extra time for the children to "do it themselves." Spills and messes, which are a part of this developmental process, are also often difficult for adults to tolerate.

Cognitive and Language Development

Recently, the first author of this chapter was at a doctor's office when a mother walked into the waiting area with her son, about age 3. The waiting area was very quiet, and the young child's voice seemed loud in the silence. The mother immediately began to "shh" her son. He responded by saying, "I don't want to shh, I want to talk." Of course, everyone laughed, which made the child talk even louder. The mother moved immediately to some chairs in the corner and attempted to get her son to sit. He refused, stating that he wanted to stand on one foot. The mother at once attempted to engage him with the toys she had with her. They played with an electronic game in which the child selects pieces to add to a face to make a complete face. This game kept the child's attention for a while until he became bored. The mother told him to "make the game stop." The child responded by yelling at the game, demanding that it stop making the face. The mother, understanding that her son had taken a literal interpretation of her comments, rephrased her directions and showed her son how to push the stop button on the game.

Next, the two decided to read a book about the Lion King. The child became very confused, because in the book, different from his memory of the movie, the main character, Simba, was already an adult at the beginning of the book. The child, looking at the pictures, argued that the adult lion was not Simba but instead was Simba's father. The mother attempted to explain that this book begins with Simba as an adult. She stated that just as her son will grow, Simba grew from a cub to an adult lion. The son looked at his mother bewildered, responding with, "I am not a cub, I am a little boy." The mother then tried to make the connection that just like the son's daddy was once a boy, Simba grew up to be a lion. The boy responded by saying that men and lions are not the same. Needless to say, the mother seemed relieved when her name was called to see the doctor.

This scene encapsulates many of the themes of cognitive and moral development in early childhood. As memory improves, and the store of information expands, young children begin to think much more in terms of categories, as the little boy in the doctor's office was doing (Davies, 2004). He was now thinking in terms of cubs, boys, lions, and men. They also begin to recognize some surprising connections between things. No doubt, in a short time, the little boy will recognize a connection between boys and cubs, men and lions, boys and men, as well as cubs and lions. Young children are full of big questions such as where do babies come from, what happens to people when they die, where does the night come from, etc. They make great strides in language development and the ability to communicate. And they make gradual progress in the ability to judge right and wrong and to regulate behavior in relation to that reasoning.

Piaget's Stages of Cognitive Development

In early childhood, children fit into the second stage of cognitive development described by Piaget, the preoperational stage. This stage is in turn divided into two substages:

Substage 1: Preconceptual stage (ages 2 to 3). The most important aspect of the preoperational stage is the development of symbolic representation, which occurs in the preconceptual stage. Through play, children learn to use symbols and actively engage in what Piaget labeled deferred imitation. Deferred imitation refers to the child's ability to view an image and then, significantly later, recall and imitate the image. For example, 3-year-old Ella, who watches the *Dora the Explorer* cartoon on TV, fills her backpack with a pretend map and other items she might need, such as a blanket and a flashlight, puts it on, creates a pretend monkey companion named Boots, and sets off on an adventure, using the kitchen as a barn, the space under the dining table as the woods, and keeping her eyes open all the while for the "mean" Swiper the Fox. Ella's cousin, Zachery, who is enthralled with the *Bob the Builder* cartoon, often pretends that he is Bob the Builder when he is playing with his toy trucks and tractors. Whenever Zachery encounters a problem, he will sing Bob's theme song, which is "Bob the Builder, can we fix it, yes we can!!"

Substage 2: Intuitive stage (ages 4 to 7). During the second part of the preoperational stage, children use language to represent objects. During the preconceptual stage, any object with long ears may be called "bunny." However, during the intuitive stage, children begin to understand that the term bunny represents the entire animal, not just a property of it. However, although young children are able to classify objects, their classifications are based on only one attribute at a time. For example, given a set of stuffed animals with various sizes and colors, the young child will group the animals either by color or by size. In contrast, an older child who has reached the intuitive stage may sort them by both size and color.

In early childhood, children also engage in what Piaget termed **transductive reasoning**, or a way of thinking about two or more experiences without using abstract logic. This can be explained best with an illustration. Imagine that 5-year-old Sam immediately smells chicken when he enters his grandmother's home. He comments that she must be having a party and asks who is coming over for dinner. When the grandmother replies that no one is coming over and that a party is not planned, Sam shakes his head in disbelief and states that he will just wait to see when the guests arrive. Sam recalls that the last time his grandmother cooked chicken was for a party. Because grandmother is cooking chicken again, Sam thinks another party is going to occur. This type of reasoning is also evident in the example of the mother and child in the doctor's office. Because the child saw Simba as a cub in the movie version of the *Lion King,* he reasons that the adult lion in the picture at the beginning of the book cannot possibly be Simba.

One last related preoperational concept described by Piaget is **egocentrism**. According to Piaget, in early childhood, children perceive reality only from their own experience and believe themselves to be at the center of existence. They are unable to recognize the possibility of other perspectives on a situation. For example, a 3-year-old girl who stands between her sister and the television to watch a program believes that her sister can see the television because she can. This aspect of cognitive reasoning could be problematic for most of the children described in the case examples. Jack may believe that it is his fault that his father left the family. Likewise, Ron and Rosiland may attribute their mother's absence to their behavior, especially given that they were present when she was arrested.

Language Skills

Language development is included under cognitive development because it is the mechanism by which cognitive interpretations are communicated to others. Note that for language to exist, children must be able to "organize" their experiences.

At the end of toddlerhood, young children have a vocabulary of about 1,000 words, and they are increasing that store by about 50 words per month (Davies, 2004). They can speak in two-word sentences, and they have learned the question form of language. They are asking "why" questions, persistently and often assertively, to learn about the world. Three-year-old speech is generally clear and easy to understand.

How does language development in early childhood promote human agency in making choices?

By the fourth year of life, language development is remarkably sophisticated. The vocabulary is becoming more and more adequate for communicating ideas, and 4-year-olds are usually speaking in sentences of 8 to 10 words. They have mastered language well enough to tell a story mostly in words, rather than relying heavily on gestures, as toddlers must do. But perhaps the most remarkable aspect of language development in early childhood is the understanding of grammar rules. By age 4, young children in all cultures understand the basic grammar rules of their language (Newman & Newman, 2006). They accomplish this mostly by a figuring out process. As they figure out new grammar rules, as with other aspects of their learning, they are overly regular in using those rules, because they have not yet learned the exceptions. So we often hear young children make statements such as "she goed to the store," or perhaps "she wented to the store."

There has been a long-standing debate about how language is acquired. How much of language ability is a result of genetic processes, and how much of it is learned? B. F. Skinner (1957) argued that children learn language by imitating what they hear in the environment and then being reinforced for correct usage. When children utter sounds heard in their environment, Skinner contended, parents respond in a manner (smiling, laughing, clapping) that encourages young children to repeat the sounds. As children grow older, they are often corrected by caregivers and preschool teachers in the misuse of words or phrases. At the other end of the spectrum, Noam Chomsky (1968) contended that language ability is primarily a function of genetics. Although somewhat influenced by the environment, children develop language skills as long as the appropriate genetic material is in place.

There is increasing consensus that both perspectives have merit. Although the physiology of language development is still poorly understood, it is thought that humans inherit, to a much higher degree than other organisms, a genetic capacity for flexible communication skills including language and speech (Novak & Pelaez, 2004). But, many scholars also argue that language is "inherently social because it has to be learned from other persons" (Bloom, 1998, p. 332). Children learn language by listening to others speak and by asking questions. Past toddlerhood, children increasingly take charge of their own language acquisition by asking questions and initiating dialogues (Bloom, 1998). Parents can assist children by asking questions, eliciting details, and encouraging children to reflect on their experiences (Haden, Hayne, & Fivush, 1997). One longitudinal study found that the size of vocabulary among 3-year-olds is correlated with the size of the vocabulary spoken to them from the age of 9 months and the amount of positive feedback provided for language development (Hart & Risley, 1995).

> How do social class, culture, and gender affect the "developmental niche" during early childhood?

Developmental niche is another environmental factor considered important in the development of language skills (Harkness, 1990). From observation of their environment—physical and social surroundings, child-rearing customs, and caregiver personality—children learn a set of regulations, or rules for communication, that shape their developing language skills. Children have an innate capacity for language, but the structuring of the environment through culture is what allows language development to occur.

Moral Development

During early childhood, children move from a moral sense that is based on outside approval to a more internalized moral sense, with a rudimentary moral code. They engage in a process of taking society's values and standards as their own. They begin to integrate these values and standards into both their worldview and their self-concept. There are three components of moral development during early childhood (Newman & Newman, 2006):

1. *Knowledge* of the moral code of the community and how to use that knowledge to make moral judgments

2. *Emotions* that produce both the capacity to care about others and the capacity to feel guilt and remorse

3. *Actions* to inhibit negative impulses as well as to behave in a **prosocial**, or helpful and empathic manner

Understanding Moral Development

Moral development has been explored from several different theoretical perspectives that have been found to have merit. Three of these approaches to moral development are explored here:

1. *Psychodynamic approach.* Sigmund Freud's psychoanalytic theory proposed that there are three distinct structures of the personality: id, ego, and superego. According to Freud, the superego is the personality structure that guides moral development. There are two aspects to the superego: the *conscience*, which is the basis of a moral code, and the *ego ideal*, which is a set of ideals expected in a moral person. Freud (1927) thought that the superego is formed between the ages of 4 and 7, but more recent psychodynamic formulations suggest that infancy is the critical time for the beginning of moral development (Kohut, 1971). Freud thought that children would have more highly developed superegos when their parents used strict methods to inhibit the children's impulses. Contemporary research indicates the opposite, however, finding that moral behavior is associated with parental warmth, democratic decision making, and modeling of temptation resistance (Maccoby, 1992). New psychodynamic models emphasize a close, affectionate bond with the caregiver as the cornerstone of moral development (Emde, Biringen, Clyman, & Oppenheim, 1991). Freud also believed that males would develop stronger superegos than females, but research has not supported this idea.

2. *Social learning approach.* From the perspective of social learning theory, moral behavior is shaped by environmental reinforcements and punishments. Children are likely to repeat behaviors that are rewarded, and they are also likely to feel tension when they think about doing something that they have been punished for in the past. From this perspective, parental consistency in response to their children's behavior is important. Social learning theory also suggests that children learn moral conduct by observing models. Albert Bandura (1977) found that children are likely to engage in behaviors for which they see a model rewarded and to avoid behaviors that they see punished.

3. *Cognitive developmental approach.* Piaget's theory of cognitive development has been the basis for stage models of moral reasoning, which assume that children's moral judgments change as their cognitive development allows them to examine the logical and abstract aspects of moral dilemmas. Moral development is assisted by opportunities to encounter new situations and different perspectives. The most frequently researched stage model is the one presented by Lawrence Kohlberg (1969, 1976) and summarized in Exhibit 4.1. Kohlberg described three levels of moral reasoning, with two stages in each level. It was expected that in early childhood, children will operate at the **preconventional level**, with their reasoning about moral issues based, first, on what gets them rewarded or punished. This type of moral reasoning is thought to be common among toddlers. In the second stage, moral reasoning is

based on what benefits either the child or someone the child cares about. This is consistent with the child's growing capacity for attachments. There is some empirical evidence that children between the ages of 3 and 6 do, indeed, begin to use the type of moral reasoning described in Stage 2 (Walker, 1989). The idea of a hierarchical sequence of stages of moral development has been challenged as being based on a western cultural orientation, but longitudinal studies in a variety of countries have produced support for the idea of evolution of moral reasoning (Gielen & Markoulis, 2001).

Exhibit 4.1	Kohlberg's Stages of Moral Development
Level I:	Preconventional
	Stage 1: Moral reasoning is based on whether behavior is rewarded or punished.
	Stage 2: Moral reasoning is based on what will benefit the self or loved others.
Level II:	Conventional
	Stage 3: Moral reasoning is based on the approval of authorities.
	Stage 4: Moral reasoning is based on upholding societal standards.
Level III:	Postconventional
	Stage 5: Moral reasoning is based on social contracts and cooperation.
	Stage 6: Moral reasoning is based on universal ethical principles.

SOURCE: Based on Kohlberg, 1969, 1976.

All of the above approaches to moral development in early childhood have been criticized for leaving out two key ingredients for moral development: **empathy**, or the ability to understand another person's emotional condition, and **perspective taking**, or the ability to see a situation from another person's point of view (Eisenberg, 2000). There is growing agreement that empathy begins in infancy and grows throughout early childhood. By age 3 or 4, children across cultures have been found to be able to recognize the type of emotional reaction that other children might have to different situations (Borke, 1973). Perspective taking has been found to grow gradually, beginning at about the age of 4 or 5 (Iannotti, 1985). Longitudinal research has found that children who show empathy and perspective taking at 4 and 5 years of age are more likely to exhibit prosocial behavior and sympathy during adolescence and early adulthood (Eisenberg et al., 1999).

> Why is the development of empathy important for future capacity for relationships?

Helping Young Children to Develop Morally

There is growing evidence that some methods work better than others for helping children develop moral reasoning and conduct. Activities that are particularly helpful are those that help children control their own behavior, help them understand how their behavior affects others, show them models of positive behavior, and get them to discuss moral issues (Walker & Taylor, 1991). It is important, however, to consider a child's temperament when undertaking disciplinary actions. Some children are more sensitive to messages of disapproval than others; sensitive children require a small dose of criticism and less sensitive children usually require more focused and directive discipline (Kochanska, 1997).

Although religious beliefs play a central role in most societies in clarifying moral behavior, little research has been done to explore the role of religion in moral development in young children. Research (Roof, 1999) has indicated that adults often become affiliated with a religious organization when their children are in early childhood, even if the parents become "religious dropouts" after the children are out of the home. Religious rituals link young children to specific actions and images of the world as well as to a community that can support and facilitate their moral development. The major world religions also teach parents about how to be parents. Young children, with their comfortable embrace of magic, easily absorb religious stories on topics that may be difficult for adults to explain. Religion that emphasizes love, concern, and social justice can enrich the young child's moral development. On the other hand, religion that is harsh and judgmental may produce guilt and a sense of worthlessness, which do not facilitate higher levels of moral reasoning.

Personality and Emotional Development

The key concern for Jack Lewis and for Ms. Johnson's grandchildren—Ron and Rosiland—is their emotional development. Specifically, will they grow into happy, loving, well-adjusted people despite the disruptions in their lives? Young children do face important developmental tasks in the emotional arena. This section addresses these tasks, drawing on Erikson's theory of psychosocial development.

Erikson's Theory of Psychosocial Development

Erikson labeled the stage of emotional development that takes place during the early childhood years as *initiative versus guilt* (ages 3 to 6). (Refer back to Exhibit 3.6 for the complete list of Erikson's stages.) Children who pass successfully through this stage learn to get satisfaction from completing tasks. They develop imagination and fantasies, and learn to handle guilt about their fantasies.

At the beginning of this stage, children's focus is on family relationships. They learn what roles are appropriate for various family members, and they learn to accept parental limits. In addition, they develop gender identity through identification with the parent of the same sex. Age and sex boundaries must be appropriately defined at this stage, and parents must be secure enough to set limits and resist the child's possessiveness.

By the end of this stage, the child's focus turns to friendships outside the family. Children engage in cooperative play and enjoy both sharing and competing with peers. Children must also have the opportunity to establish peer relationships outside the family. This is one of the functions the preschool program serves for Ms. Johnson's grandchildren.

Children who become stuck in this stage are plagued with guilt about their goals and fantasies. They become confused about their gender identity and about family roles. These children are overly anxious and self-centered.

Emotions

Growing cognitive and language skills give young children the ability to understand and express their feelings and emotions. They are able to label their own emotions—"I feel sad;

What are our societal expectations for regulation of emotions during early childhood?

I feel happy." However, they attribute most of their feelings to external causes— "I am sad because Mommy took my toy; I feel happy because Daddy is home from work" (Fabes, Eisenberg, Nyman, & Michealieu, 1991).

Children in early childhood can also identify feelings expressed by others and use creative ways to comfort others when they are upset. A friend describes the response of her 5-year-old son Marcus when he saw her crying about the sudden death of her brother in a car accident. Marcus hugged his mom and told her not to cry, because, although she was sad about Uncle Johnny, she still had Marcus. Marcus promised his mother to never drive a car so she would not have to worry about the same thing happening to him. This attempt to reduce his mother's sadness is a typical response from a child of this age (Findlay, Girardi, & Coplan, 2006).

The ability to understand emotion continues to develop as young children have more opportunity to practice these skills. Children reared in homes in which emotions and feelings are openly discussed are better able to understand and express feelings (Bradley, 2000).

Aggression

One behavior that increases during the early childhood years is aggression. Two types of aggression are observed in young children: **instrumental aggression,** which occurs while fighting over toys and space, and **hostile aggression,** which is an attack meant to hurt another individual. Recently, researchers have studied another typology of aggression: physical aggression and relational aggression. **Physical aggression**, as the name suggests, involves using physical force against another person. **Relational aggression** involves behaviors that damage relationships without physical force, behaviors such as threatening to leave a relationship unless a friend complies with demands, or using social exclusion or the silent treatment to get one's way. Researchers are finding that boys make greater use of physical aggression than girls and girls make greater use of relational aggression (Ostrov, Crick, & Stauffacher, 2006).

Although some children continue high levels of aggression into middle childhood, usually physical aggression peaks early in the early childhood years (Alink, Mesmon, & van Zeijl, 2006). By the end of the early childhood years, children learn better negotiation skills and become better at asking for what they want and using words to express feelings. Terri Smith, in the first case study in this chapter, obviously has not developed these moderating skills.

Attachment

In early childhood, children still depend on their attachment relationships for feelings of security. In particularly stressful times, the attachment behavior of the young child may look very much like the clinging behavior of the 2-year-old. For the most part, however, securely attached children will handle their anxieties by verbalizing their needs. For example, at bedtime, the 4-year-old child may say, "I would like you to read one more story before you go." This increased ability to verbalize wants is a source of security. In addition, many young children continue to use transitional objects, such as blankets or a favorite teddy bear, to soothe themselves when they are anxious (Davies, 2004).

Social Development

In early childhood, children become more socially adept than they were as toddlers, but they are still learning how to be social and how to understand the perspectives of other people.

The many young children who enter group care face increasing demands for social competence.

Peer Relations

In early childhood, children form friendships with other children of the same age and gender; boys gravitate toward male playmates and girls choose girls. When asked about the definition of a friend, most children in this age group think of a friend as someone with whom you play (Corsaro, 2005). Our neighbor children, for example, made their initial approach to our young son by saying, "Let's be friends; let's play" and "I'll be your friend if you will be mine." They do not view friendship as a trusting, lasting relationship. Even this limited view of friendship is important for this age group, however. For example, children who enter kindergarten with identified friends adjust better to school (Johnson, Ironsmith, Snow, & Poteat, 2000).

Research indicates that young children are at a higher risk of being rejected by their peers if they are aggressive and comparatively more active, demonstrate a difficult temperament, are easily distracted, and demonstrate lower perseverance (Campbell, 2002; Johnson et al., 2000; Walker, Berthelsen, & Irving, 2001). One would wonder, then, how young peers respond to Terri Smith. The rejection of some children is long lasting. Even when they change their behavior and fit better with the norm, often they continue to be rejected (Walker et al., 2001).

Self-Concept

In early childhood, the child seems to vacillate between grandiose and realistic views of the self (Davies, 2004). On the one hand, children are aware of their growing competence, but at the same time, they have normal doubts about the self, based on realistic comparisons of their competence with the competence of adults.

Some investigators have suggested that during early childhood, the child's ever increasing understanding of the self in relation to the world begins to become organized into a **self-theory** (Epstein, 1973, 1991, 1998; Epstein, Lipson, Holstein, & Huh, 1993). As children develop the cognitive ability to categorize, they use categorization to think about the self. By age 2 or 3, children can identify their gender and race (discussed in greater detail shortly) as a factor in understanding who they are. Between the ages of 4 and 6, young children become more aware that different people have different perspectives on situations. This helps them to begin to understand cultural expectations and sensitizes them to the expectations that others have for them.

This growing capacity to understand the self in relation to others leads to self-evaluation, or **self-esteem**. Very early interpersonal experiences provide information that becomes incorporated into self-esteem. Messages of love, admiration, and approval lead to a positive view of the self (Brown, Dutton, & Cook, 2001). Messages of rejection or scorn lead to a negative view of the self (Heimpel, Wood, Marshall, & Brown, 2002). In addition to these interpersonal messages, young children observe their own competencies and attributes, and compare them with the competencies of other children as well as adults. And they are very aware of being evaluated by others, their peers as well as important adults (Newman & Newman, 2006).

Of course, a young child may develop a positive view of the self in one dimension, such as cognitive abilities, and a negative view of the self in another dimension, such as physical abilities (Harter, 1998). Children also learn that some abilities are more valued than others in the various environments in which they operate. For example, in individualistic-oriented societies, individual success is valued while seniority and group solidarity are valued in most collectivistic-oriented societies. Self-esteem is based on different values in these different types of cultures (Brown, 2003; Sedikides, Gaertner, & Toguchi, 2003).

Gender Identity and Sexual Interests

How does gender influence early childhood development?

During early childhood, gender becomes an important dimension of how children understand themselves and others. There are four components to gender identity during early childhood (Newman & Newman, 2006):

1. *Making correct use of the gender label.* By age 2, children can usually accurately identify others as either male or female, based on appearance.

2. *Understanding gender as stable.* Later, children understand that gender is stable, that boys grow up to be men and girls to be women.

3. *Understanding gender constancy.* Even with this understanding of gender stability, young children, with their imaginative thinking, continue to think that girls can turn into boys and boys into girls by changing appearance. For example, a 3-year-old given a picture of a girl is able to identify the person as a girl. But if the same girl is shown in another picture dressed as a boy, the 3-year-old will label the girl a boy. It is not until sometime between age 4 and 7 that children understand *gender constancy,* the understanding that one's gender does not change, that the girl dressed as a boy is still a girl.

4. *Understanding the genital basis of gender.* Gender constancy has been found to be associated with an understanding of the relationship between gender and genitals (Bem, 1998).

Before going further, it is important to differentiate among four concepts: sex, gender, gender identity, and sexual orientation. *Sex* refers to biologically linked distinctions that are determined by chromosomal information. An infant's external genitalia are usually used as the determinant of sex. In most humans, chromosomes, hormones, and genitalia are consistent and determining sex is considered unambiguous. However, this is not always the case. Chromosomal, genetic, anatomical, and hormonal aspects of sex are sometimes not aligned (Rudacille, 2005). *Gender* is the cognitive, emotional, and social schemes that are associated with being female or male. *Gender identity* refers to one's sense of being male or female. *Sexual orientation* refers to one's preference for sexually intimate partners.

Human societies use gender as an important category for organizing social life. There are some rather large cultural and subcultural variations in gender role definitions, however. Existing cultural standards about gender are pervasively built into adult interactions with young children and into the reward systems that are developed for shaping child behavior. There is much research evidence that parents begin to use gender stereotypes to respond to their children from the time of birth (O'Brien, 1992). They cuddle more with infant girls and play more actively with infant boys. Later, they talk more with young girls and expect young boys to be more independent. Recent studies have found that the nature of parental influence on children's gender role development is more complex than this. Parents may hold to stereotypical gender expectations in some domains but not in others. For example, parents may have similar expectations for boys and girls in terms of sharing or being polite (McHale, Crouter, & Whiteman, 2003).

Once toddlers understand their gender, they begin to imitate and identify with the same-sex parent, if he or she is available. Once young children begin to understand gender role standards, they become quite rigid in their playing out of gender roles—only girls cook, only men drive trucks, only girls wear pink flowers, only boys wear shirts with footballs. This gender understanding also accounts for the preference of same-sex playmates and sex-typed toys (Davies, 2004). Remember, though, that the exaggeration of gender stereotypes in early childhood is in keeping with the struggle during this period to discover stability and regularity in the environment.

A few researchers have found, with longitudinal research, that young boys who engage in unusual amounts of play with girls and female-identified activities are more likely than boys who engage in gender stereotypical play to have a bisexual or homosexual orientation in adolescence and young adulthood. This finding is usually interpreted to indicate an early biological factor in sexual orientation (Bailey & Zucker, 1995).

During early childhood, children become increasingly interested in their genitals. They are interested, in general, in how their bodies work, but the genitals seem to hold a special interest as the young child learns through experimentation that the genitals can be a source of pleasure. Between 3 and 5, children may have some worries and questions about genital difference; little girls may think they once had a penis and wonder what happened to it. Little boys may fear that their penises will disappear, like their sister's did. During early childhood, masturbation is used both as a method of self-soothing and for pleasure. Young children also "play doctor" with each other, and often want to see and touch their parents' genitals. Many parents and other caregivers are confused about how to handle this behavior, particularly in our era of heightened awareness of childhood sexual abuse. In general, parents should not worry about genital curiosity or about children experimenting with touching their own genitals. They should remember, however, that at this age children may be overstimulated by seeing their parents' genitals. And we should always be concerned when children want to engage in more explicit adult-like sexual play that involves stimulation of each others genitals (Davies, 2004; Newman & Newman, 2006).

Racial and Ethnic Identity

Findings from research suggest that children first learn their own racial identity before they are able to identify the race of others (Kowalski, 1996). However, identification of others by race is limited to skin color. Young children may label a Hispanic individual, for example, as either African American or white, depending on the individual's skin color. Young children also show a preference for members of their own race over another (Katz, 1976). Perhaps this choice is similar to the preference for same-sex playmates, a result of young children attempting to learn their own identity.

How important is racial and ethnic identity in early childhood?

Social scientists concerned about the development of self-esteem in children of color have investigated racial bias and preference using children in early childhood as subjects. The most famous of these studies was conducted by Kenneth Clark and Mamie Clark in 1939. They presented African American children with black dolls and white dolls and concluded that African American

▲ **Photo 4.2** Play is one of the few elements in the development of children that is universal—regardless of culture.

children responded more favorably to the white dolls and had more negative reactions to the black dolls. A similar study 40 years later, observing young African American children in New York and Trinidad, reported similar results (Gopaul-McNicol, 1988). The young children from both New York and Trinidad preferred and identified with the white dolls. Interestingly, the same results have been reported more recently in studies of Taiwanese young children (Chang, 2001). Most of the Taiwanese children in the study indicated a preference for the white dolls and demonstrated a "pro-white attitude."

It is questionable, however, whether these preferences and biases are equated with self-concept and low self-esteem for children of color. Most argue that they are not. For example, racial bias and self-concept were not related among the young Taiwanese children (Chang, 2001). Likewise, findings from studies about young African American children indicate high levels of self-concept despite the children's bias in favor of the white culture and values (Crain, 1996; Spencer, 1985). Spencer concludes, "Racial stereotyping in black children should be viewed as objectively held information about the environment and not as a manifestation of personal identity" (p. 220).

The Role of Play

The young child loves to play, and play is essential to all aspects of early child development. We think of the play of young children as fun-filled and lively. And yet it serves a serious purpose. Through play, children develop the motor skills essential for physical development, learn the problem-solving skills and communication skills fundamental to cognitive

▲ **Photo 4.3**   During early childhood, children engage in cooperative play and enjoy sharing and competing with peers.

development, and express the feelings and gain the self-confidence needed for emotional growth. Essentially, play is what young children are all about; it is their work.

Play may be one of the few elements in the development of young children that is universal, regardless of culture. Comparing children from six different countries with significantly different cultures, one study found that all children in early childhood constructed spontaneous play activities (Whiting & Whiting, 1975). Even children in cultures that require young children to work or complete chores included play in their work activities. Some suggest that the act of play is almost automatic, driven by physiological functions (Gandelman, 1992; Panksepp, 1986).

The predominant type of play in early childhood, beginning around the age of 2, is **symbolic play**, otherwise known as fantasy play, pretend play, or imaginary play (Pelligrini & Galda, 2000). Children continue to use vivid imaginations in their play, as they did as toddlers, but they also begin to put more structure into their play. Thus, their play is intermediate between the fantasy play of toddlers and the structured, rules-oriented play of middle childhood. Although toddler play is primarily nonverbal, the play of young children often involves highly sophisticated verbal productions. There is some indication that this preference for symbolic play during early childhood exists across cultures, but the themes of the play reflect the culture in which it is enacted (Roopnarine, Shin, Donovan, & Suppal, 2000).

Symbolic play during early childhood has four primary functions: providing an opportunity to explore reality, contributing to cognitive development, allowing young children to gain control over their lives, and serving as a shared experience and opportunity for development of peer culture. These functions are explained in more detail below.

Play as an Opportunity to Explore Reality

Young children imitate adult behavior and try out social roles in their play (Davies, 2004). They play house, school, doctor, police, firefighter, and so on. As they "dress up" in various guises of adult roles, or even as spiders and rabbits, they are using fantasy to explore what they might become. Their riding toys allow them to play with the experience of having greater mobility in the world.

Play's Contribution to Cognitive Development

The young child uses play to think about the world, to understand cause and effect (Roskos & Christie, 2000). Throughout early childhood, young children show increasing sophistication in using words in their dramatic play.

Some researchers have asked the question, does symbolic play facilitate cognitive development, or does symbolic play require mature cognitive abilities? The question is unresolved; the available evidence indicates only that cognitive development is connected with play in early childhood (Roopnarine et al., 2000). Childhood sociologists have found that children create sophisticated language games for group play that facilitate the development of language and logical thinking (Corsaro, 2005). A number of researchers have studied how young children build literacy skills through play, particularly play with books (Roskos & Christie, 2000). Play that is focused on language and thinking skills has been described as **learning play** (Meek, 2000).

Play as an Opportunity to Gain Control

In his cross-cultural study of play, William Corsaro (2005), a childhood sociologist, demonstrates that young children typically use dramatic play to cope with fears. They incorporate their fears into their group play and thus develop some mastery over stress and anxiety. This perspective on young children's play is the cornerstone of play therapy (Chethik, 2000).

Anyone who has spent much time in a child care center has probably seen a group of 4-year-olds engaged in superhero play, their flowing capes improvised with towels pinned on their shirts. Such play helps the child compensate for inadequacy and fear that comes from recognizing that one is a small person in a big world (Davies, 2004). Corsaro (2005) suggests that the love for climbing toys that bring small children high over the heads of others serves the same purpose.

> How does play develop skills for human agency in making choices?

Children in preschool settings have also been observed trying to get control over their lives by subverting some of the control of adults. Corsaro (2005) describes a preschool where the children had been told that they could not bring any play items from home. The preschool teachers were trying to avoid the kinds of conflicts that can occur over toys brought from home. The children in this preschool found a way to subvert this rule, however: they began to bring in very small toys, such as matchbox cars, that would fit in their pockets out of sight when teachers were nearby. Corsaro provides a number of other examples from his cross-cultural research of ways that young children use play to take some control of their lives away from adults.

Play as a Shared Experience

There is increasing emphasis on the way that play in early childhood contributes to the development of peer culture. Many researchers who study the play of young children suggest that **sociodramatic play**, or group fantasy play in which children coordinate their fantasy, is the most important form of play during this time. Indeed, one researcher has reported that two-thirds of the play among North American young children is sociodramatic play (Rubin, 1986). Young children are able to develop more elaborate fantasy play and sustain it by forming friendship groups, which in turn gives them experience with group conflict and group problem solving that carries over into the adult world (Corsaro, 2005).

As young children play in groups, they attempt to protect the opportunity to keep the play going by restricting who may enter the play field (Corsaro, 2005). Young children can often be heard making such comments as, "We're friends; we're playing, right?" Or perhaps, "You're not our friend, you can't play with us." The other side of the coin is that young children must learn how to gain access to play in progress (Garvey, 1984). An important social skill is being able to demonstrate that they can play without messing the game up. Young children learn a set of do's and don'ts to accomplish that goal (see Exhibit 4.2) and develop complex strategies for gaining access to play.

Exhibit 4.2	Do's and Don'ts of Getting Access to Play in Progress

Do's

Watch what's going on.

Figure out the play theme.

Enter the area.

Plug into the action.

Hold off making suggestions about how to change the action.

Don'ts

Don't ask questions for information (if you can't tell what's going on, you'll mess it up).

Don't mention yourself or your reactions to what is going on.

Don't disagree or criticize what is happening.

Source: Based on Garvey, 1984.

Conflict often occurs in young children's play groups, and researchers have found gender and cultural variations in how these conflicts get resolved. Young girls have been found to prefer dyadic (two-person) play interactions, and young boys enjoy larger groups (Benenson, 1993). These preferences may not hold across cultures, however. For example, white middle-class young girls in the United States are less direct and assertive in challenging each other in play situations than either African American girls in the United States or young girls in an Italian preschool (Corsaro, 2005). Greater assertiveness may allow for more comfortable play in larger groups.

Play as the Route to Attachment to Fathers

Most of the efforts to understand attachment focus on the link between mothers and children, and the effect of the maternal relationship. More recently, though, there has been growing concern about and interest in the importance of fathers in the development of attachment for young children. Some suggest that father-child attachment may be promoted mainly through play, much like mother-child relationship may be the result of caregiving activities (Laflamme, Pomerleau & Malcuit, 2002; Roggman, 2004). Differences in play style noted for mothers versus that seen in fathers is of particular interest. Investigators conclude that more physical play is seen between fathers and young children compared to more object play and conventional play interaction between mothers and children (Goldberg, Clarke-Stewart, Rice, & Dellis, 2002). Both forms of play can involve the display of affection by the parent. Thus, both forms of play contribute to the development of parent-child attachment. This research broadens the notion that only certain kinds of play have the potential to effect positive attachment, and affirms the notion that there is developmental value for children in father child physical play. In fact, physical play stimulates, arouses, and takes children out of their comfort zone. Roggman (2004) further notes that the style of play often ascribed to fathers provides opportunity for young children to overcome their limits and to experience taking chances in a context where there is some degree of confidence that they will be protected.

Developmental Disruptions

Most developmental problems in infants and young children are more accurately described as **developmental delays**, offering the hope that early intervention, or even natural processes, will mitigate the long-term effects. In contrast, developmental problems in school-age children are typically labeled disabilities and classified into groups, such as mental retardation, learning disabilities, and motor impairment (Zipper & Simeonsson, 2004).

Many young children with developmental difficulties, including emotional and behavioral concerns, are inaccurately assessed and misdiagnosed—often because young children are assessed independently of their environment (Freeman & Dyer, 1993; Sameroff, Bartko, Baldwin, Baldwin, & Seifer, 1998). After interviewing professionals who work with children age 6 and under, one research team compiled a list of traits observed in young children that indicate emotional and behavioral problems: extreme aggressive behavior, difficulty with change, invasion of others' personal space, compulsive or impulsive behavior, low ability to trust others, lack of empathy or remorse, and cruelty to animals (Schmitz & Hilton, 1996). Parents and teachers often handle these behaviors with firmer limits and more discipline. However, environmental risk factors, such as emotional abuse or neglect and domestic violence, may be the actual cause.

Given the difficulty of accurate assessment, assessment in young children should include many disciplines, to gain as broad an understanding as possible (Zipper & Simeonsson, 2004). Assessment and service delivery should also be culturally relevant (Parette, 1995). In other words, culture and other related issues—such as family interaction patterns and stress, the social environment, ethnicity, acculturation, social influences, and developmental expectations—should all be considered when evaluating a child's developmental abilities.

For those children who have been labeled developmentally delayed, the main remedy has been social skill development. In one such program, two types of preschool classrooms were evaluated (Roberts, Burchinal, & Bailey, 1994). In one classroom, young developmentally delayed children were matched with nondelayed children of the same age; in another classroom, some of the "normal" children were the same age as the developmentally delayed children and some were older. Social exchange between the children with disabilities and those without disabilities was greater in the mixed-aged classroom. Another study evaluated the usefulness of providing social skills training to children with mild developmental disabilities (Lewis, 1994). In a preschool setting, developmentally delayed children were put in situations requiring social interaction and were praised for successful interaction. This method increased social interaction between the young children.

It is also important to recognize the parental stress that often accompanies care of children with developmental disabilities. Researchers have found that an educational intervention with parents that teaches behavioral management and how to plan activities that minimize disruptive behavior results in improved child behavior, improved parent-child relationship, and less parental stress (Clare, Mazzucchelli, Studman, & Sanders, 2006).

Early Childhood Education

Universal early childhood enrollment, defined as a 90% enrollment rate, begins later in the United States than in several other countries: age 5 in the United States, compared to age 3 in France and Italy, and age 4 in Japan and the United Kingdom. In France, a large number of children below the age of 3 are enrolled in formal education (Sen, Partelow, & Miller, 2005).

There is much evidence that low-income and racial minority students in the United States have less access to quality early childhood education than their age peers (Education Trust, 2006). Many poorer school districts do not provide pre-kindergarten programs, and recent budget cuts to Head Start have resulted in many low-income children being placed on a waiting list. With tightening budgets, some low-to-middle-income districts are canceling full-day kindergarten, and some public school districts have begun to provide for-pay preschool and full-day kindergarten, a practice that clearly disadvantages low-income children. Wealthy families are competing for slots for their young children in expensive preschool programs, called the "baby ivies," that provide highly enriched early learning environments, further advancing opportunities for children in privileged families (Kozol, 2005). Middle-class families, as well as impoverished families, are increasingly unable to access quality early childhood education; 78% of families who earned over $100,000 per year in 2004 sent their young children to early childhood educational programs compared to less than half of families earning less than $50,000 per year (Calman & Tarr-Whelan, 2005).

In recent years, a coalition of business leaders, economists, and child development scholars has called for universal quality early childhood education in the United States, arguing that it is a wise investment (see Calman & Tarr-Whelan, 2005). Empirical evidence is mounting to support this argument. One longitudinal study has followed a group of children who attended the High/Scope Perry Preschool Program in Ypsilanti, Michigan until they reached the age of 40 (Schweinhart et al., 2005). Between 1962 and 1967, the researchers identified a sample of 123 low-income African American children who had been assessed to be at high risk of school failure. They randomly assigned 58 of these children to attend a high quality two-year preschool program for 2- and 3-year-olds, while the other 65 attended no preschool program. The program met for two and half hours per day, five days a week, and teachers made home visits every two weeks. The teachers in the preschool program had bachelor's degrees and education certification. No more than eight children were assigned to a teacher, and the curriculum emphasized giving children the opportunity to plan and carry out their own activities. By age 40, the preschool participants, on average, were doing better than the nonparticipants in several important ways:

- They were more likely to have graduated from high school (65 % vs. 45%).
- They were more likely to be employed (76% vs. 62%).

- They had higher median annual earnings ($20,800 vs. $15, 300).
- They were more likely to own their own home (37% vs. 28%).
- They were more likely to have a savings account (76% vs. 50%).
- They had fewer lifetime arrests (36% vs. 55% arrested five or more times).
- They were less likely to have spent time in prison or jail (28% vs. 52% never sentenced).

The researchers report that the preschool program cost $15,166 per child and the public gained $12.90 for every dollar spent on the program by the time the participants were 40 years old. The savings came from reduced special education costs, increased taxes derived from higher earnings, reduced public assistance costs, and reduced costs to the criminal justice system.

Another longitudinal study began in North Carolina in 1972, when 112 low-income infants were randomly assigned to either a quality preschool program, or to no program (Masse & Barnett, 2002). The group assigned to the preschool program was enrolled in the program for five years, instead of the two years in the High/Scope Perry study. The participants in this study were followed to the age of 21. The children who participated in the preschool program were less likely to repeat grades, less likely to be placed in special education classes, and more likely to complete high school. It is important to note that the researchers in this study also investigated the impact of the preschool program on the mothers. They found that the preschool program mothers earned $3,750 more per year than the mothers whose children did not attend the program, for a total of $78, 750 more over 21 years.

The above two longitudinal studies investigated the impact of quality preschool education on low-income children, but there is also preliminary evidence of the benefit of early childhood education on all children. A study conducted at Georgetown University has examined the effect of pre-Kindergarten programs in Tulsa, Oklahoma (Gromley, Gayer, Phillips, & Dawson, 2004). These programs are considered high quality because teachers are required to have a bachelor's degree, there are no more than 10 children per teacher, and teachers are paid on the same scale as public school teachers. The researchers found that children who attended pre-K scored better on letter-word identification, spelling, and applied problems than children of the same age who had not attended pre-K. This was true regardless of race or socio-economic status.

These studies suggest that early childhood education programs are good for children, for families, for communities, and for the society. With such evidence in hand, social workers can join with other child advocates to build broad coalitions to educate the public about the multilevel benefits and to push for public policy that guarantees universal quality early childhood education

▨ Early Childhood in the Multigenerational Family

Curiosity and experimentation are the hallmarks of early childhood. Young children are sponges, soaking up information about themselves, their worlds, and their relationships. They use their families as primary sources of information and as models for relationships. Where there are older siblings, they serve as important figures of identification and imitation. Aunts, uncles, cousins, and grandparents may also serve this role, but parents are, in most families, the most important sources of information, support, and modeling for young children.

Parents play two very important roles for their age-3-to-6 child: educator and advocate (Newman & Newman, 2006). As educators, they answer children's big and little questions, ask questions to stimulate thinking and growth in communication skills, provide explanations, and help children figure things out. They teach children about morality and human connectedness by modeling honest, kind, thoughtful behavior, and by reading to their children about moral dilemmas and moral action. They help children develop emotional intelligence by modeling how to handle strong feelings, and by talking with children about the children's strong feelings. They take young children on excursions in their real physical worlds as well as in the fantasy worlds found in books. They give children opportunities to perform tasks that develop a sense of mastery.

Not all parents have the same resources for the educator role or the same beliefs about how children learn. And some parents take their role as educators too seriously, pushing their young children into more and more structured time with higher and higher expectations of performance (Elkind, 1981). Many of these parents are pushing their own frustrated dreams onto their young children. The concern is that these children are deprived of time for exploration, experimentation, and fantasy.

In the contemporary era, children are moving into organized child care settings at earlier ages. As they do so, parents become more important as advocates who understand their children's needs. The advocate role is particularly important for parents of young children with disabilities. These parents may need to advocate to ensure that all aspects of early childhood education programs are accessible to their children.

▲ **Photo 4.4** A positive relationship with at least one parent or teacher is said to promote resilience in early childhood.

For some children, like Ron and Rosiland Johnson, it is the grandparent and not the parent who serves as the central figure. Estimates are that 5.4 million children live in homes headed by a grandparent or other relative (Children's Defense Fund, 2001). In about 50% of these families, no biological parent is present in the home. Substance abuse, divorce, teen pregnancy, the AIDS epidemic, and imprisoned mothers like Shirley account for the large number of children living in grandparent-headed homes (Jendrek, 1993). Some custodial grandparents describe an increased purpose for living (Roe & Minkler, 1998/99), but others describe increased isolation, worry, physical and emotional exhaustion, and financial concerns (Roe & Minkler, 1998/99). These are some of the same concerns expressed by Ms. Johnson. In addition, grandparents caring for children with psychological and physical problems experience high levels of stress (Sands & Goldberg, 2000).

The literature indicates that young children often do better under the care of grandparents than in other types of homes (Jendrek, 1993). However, children parented by their grandparents must often overcome many difficult emotions (Smith, Dannison, & Vach-Hasse, 1998). These children struggle with issues of grief and loss related to loss of their parent(s) and feelings of guilt, fear, embarrassment, and anger. These feelings may be especially strong for young children who feel they are somehow responsible for the loss of their parent(s).

Although children in this age group are capable of labeling their feelings, their ability to discuss these feelings with any amount of depth is very limited. In addition, grandparents may feel unsure about how to talk about the situation with their young grandchildren.

Professional intervention for the children is often recommended (Smith et al., 1998). Some mental health practitioners have had success providing group sessions that help grandparents gain control over their grandchildren's behavior, resolve clashes in values between themselves and their grandchildren, and help grandparents avoid overindulgence and set firm limits (Stokes & Greenstone, 1981).

⌧ Risks to Healthy Development in Early Childhood

This section addresses a few risk factors that social workers are likely to encounter in work with young children and their families: poverty, ineffective discipline, divorce, and violence (including child abuse). In addition, the section outlines the protective factors that ameliorate the risks.

> Why is it important to recognize risk factors and protective factors in early childhood?

Poverty

As reported in Chapter 3, there are one billion children around the world living in poverty. Over 11 million children live in poverty in the United States—including 17% of children age 6 and younger. About 40% of U.S. children between the ages of 3 and 6 live in low-income families, with incomes below 200% of the poverty level. Over 60% of African American and Latino children under age 6 live in low-income families (National Center for Children in Poverty, 2006b). Poverty—in the form of poor nutrition, inadequate health care, and overcrowded living conditions—presents considerable risks to children's growth and development. Estimates are that thousands of young children, especially those from poor African American communities, are not being immunized, threatening their long-term health (Copeland, 1996). Overcrowding is particularly problematic to young children in that it restricts opportunities for play, the means through which most development occurs. Research indicates that young children reared in poverty are significantly delayed in language and other cognitive skills (Locke, Ginsborg, & Peers, 2002). The effects of poverty on children in early childhood appear to be long lasting. Children who experience poverty during their early years are less likely to complete school than children whose initial exposure to poverty occurred in the middle childhood years or during adolescence (Brooks-Gunn & Duncan, 1997). Researchers have also found that children who live in poverty are at high risk for low self-esteem, peer conflict, depression, and childhood psychological disorders (McLoyd & Wilson, 1991; McWhirter, & McWhirter, 1993). These problems are primarily the outcome of living in a violent setting or in deteriorated housing and of the instability that results from frequent changes in residence and schools (McLoyd & Wilson, 1991). Overall, children who live in poverty, regardless of other adversities, suffer the worst consequences (Brooks-Gunn & Duncan, 1997).

Ineffective Discipline

A popular guidebook for parents declares, "Under no circumstances should you ever punish your child!!" (Moyer, 1974, p. 40). Punishment implies an attempt to get even with the child, whereas **discipline** involves helping the child overcome a problem. Physical discipline can take many forms, as can the notion of punishment. Many parents struggle with defining and differentiating between discipline and punishment. For some, discipline and punishment are synonymous and seen as precursors to violence.

Parents often struggle with how forceful to be in response to undesired behavior. The Smiths are a good example of this struggle. Because parents are not formally trained in parenting skills in the United States, the type of discipline they use, and the circumstances in which they use it, is often molded by how they were disciplined as children and by cultural and societal norms. However, parenting styles are not permanent (Hemenway, Solnick, & Carter, 1994). Even adults who experienced the most punitive type of correction as children have the potential to escape the "transgenerational cycle" of punitive child-rearing practices. Diane, the mother of a 3- and 5-year-old, declares that she does not use any type of physical punishment with her children. She states that her parents ruled by fear, and she admits that her relationship with them, even to this day, is based on fear, not affection or respect. She is insistent that she will have a different relationship with her children.

How can social workers help parents with parenting young children? Following extensive research, Diana Baumrind (1971) described three parenting styles: authoritarian, authoritative, and permissive (see Exhibit 4.3). The **authoritarian parenting** style uses low warmth and high control. These parents favor punishment and negative reinforcement, and children are treated as submissive. Children reared under an authoritarian parenting style become hostile and moody and have difficulty managing stress. Discipline that is punitive, especially spanking, is associated with increased levels of aggression in children (Carey, 1994; Welsh, 1985). The **authoritative parenting** style, in which parents consider the child's viewpoints but remain in control, is considered the most desirable approach to discipline and behavior management. Baumrind suggests that children reared from the authoritative perspective are energetic, competent, and more socially adept than others. The **permissive parenting** style accepts children's behavior without attempting to modify it. Children reared from the permissive parenting orientation are said to be cheerful but demonstrate little if any impulse control. In addition, these children are overly dependent and have low levels of self-reliance. The Smiths' style of parenting probably fits here. Certainly, Terri Smith's behavior mirrors behavior exhibited by children reared with the permissive style. Some researchers have presented a fourth parenting style, **disengaged parenting**, parents who are aloof, withdrawn, and unresponsive (Novak & Pelaez, 2004).

Exhibit 4.3	Three Parenting Styles	
Parenting Style	*Description*	*Type of Discipline*
Authoritarian	Parents who use this type of parenting are rigid and controlling. Rules are narrow and specific, with little room for negotiation, and children are expected to follow the rules without explanation.	Cold and harsh Physical force No explanation of rules provided
Authoritative	These parents are more flexible than authoritarian parents. Their rules are more reasonable, and they leave opportunities for compromises and negotiation.	Warm and nurturing Positive reinforcement Set firm limits and provide rationale behind rules and decisions
Permissive	The parents' rules are unclear, and children are left to make their own decisions.	Warm and friendly toward their children No direction given

Source: Adapted from Baumrind, 1971.

Parenting styles are prescribed in part by the community and the culture. For example, West Indian and Puerto Rican communities typically use physical punishment as a discipline technique (Canino & Spurlock, 1994).

Also, some differences in parenting styles are a product of the socioeconomic environment in which they occur. Low-income parents are often more authoritarian than other parents, exercising rigid, controlling techniques (Maccoby, 1980). This practice, however, may seem more legitimate in context. Parents usually respond with discipline to three types of situations: physical danger, their children's expression of psychobiological drives such as sex and aggression, and their children's socializing inside and outside of the family (Epstein, Bishop, Ruan, Miller, & Keitner, 1993). Logically, dangerous situations require more rigid and uncompromising forms of discipline. A middle-income mother who professes to be radically opposed to physical punishment may admit that she spanked her child once for running out of a store into a busy parking lot. Low-income parents are likely to be confronted with many dangerous situations involving their children. In neighborhoods where violence is a part of everyday life, rules become a matter of protection, and adherence to the rules is a survival tactic. However, physical punishment for disobeying the rules is not necessarily the best or only solution.

In addition, findings from studies about punishment and young children indicate that punishment is also problematic because parents often use it in response to early childhood behavior that is age appropriate. So rather than encouraging the independence which is otherwise expected for a child, such age appropriate behavior is discouraged (Culp, McDonald Culp, Dengler, & Maisano, 1999). In addition, recent evidence indicates that brain development can be affected by the stress created by punishment or physical discipline (Glaser, 2000). Harsh punishment and physical discipline interfere with the neural connection process that begins in infancy and continues throughout early childhood. But for many low-income parents, harsh punishment may be less an issue of control or "bad parenting" than an effort to cope with a desperate situation.

Divorce

How are young children affected by this historical trend toward high rates of divorce?

The divorce rate has quadrupled over the past 20 years, and in 1997, over one third of all U.S. families were families where children were being raised by one parent, usually the mother (Children's Defense Fund, 1997). It is estimated that over half of the children born in the 1990s spent some of their childhood in a single-parent household (Anderson, 2005). These single-parent families often live in poverty, and as we have already mentioned, poverty can have a negative effect on children's development.

Regardless of family income level, many children suffer when their parents divorce. It has been suggested, however, that the negative effects children experience may actually be the result of parents' responses to divorce rather than of the divorce itself (Hetherington & Kelly, 2002). In fact, parental coping and adjustment may be solely responsible for the negative adjustment of children after a divorce (Kurtz, 1995).

One significant parental issue is the relationship that the parents maintain during and after the divorce. With minimal conflict between the parents about custody, visitation, and child-rearing issues, and with parents' positive attitude toward each other, children experience fewer negative consequences (Hetherington & Kelly, 2002). Unfortunately, many children, like Jack Lewis in the case study, end up as noncombatants in the middle of a war, trying to avoid or defuse raging anger and disagreement between the two parents.

Many divorced parents have difficulty maintaining effective levels of parenting. Consequently, children often experience inconsistent discipline and a decrease in attention and nurturing. For example, divorced mothers of young children provide less stimulation and support to their children, a consequence of the mothers' dissatisfaction with and concern about their own lives (Poehlmann & Fiese, 1994). This lack of stimulation and support has a negative effect on the children's cognitive development.

In early childhood, children are more vulnerable than older children to the emotional and psychological consequences of separation and divorce (Wallerstein & Blakeslee, 1989; Wallerstein & Corbin, 1991; Wallerstein, Corbin, & Lewis, 1988). One reason may be that young children have difficulty understanding divorce and often believe that the absent parent is no longer a member of the family and will never be seen again. In addition, because of young children's egocentrism, they often feel that the divorce is a result of their behavior and experience the absent parent's leaving as a rejection of them. One wonders if Jack Lewis thinks he not only caused his father to leave but also caused him to become the devil.

The good news/bad news is that children's adaptation to divorce is not necessarily permanent. One study found that many children who initially were negatively affected by their parents' divorce were well adjusted when evaluated 10 years later (Wallerstein & Blakeslee, 1989). Conversely, however, many children who initially seemed to adjust well to their parents' divorce were not as well adjusted 10 years later.

To successfully adjust to their parents' divorce, children must accomplish six tasks (Wallerstein, 1983):

1. Come to accept that their parents are divorced and that their access to at least one parent will change
2. Disengage from their parents' conflict and get on with their own "work" (school, play, friends, etc.)
3. Cope with losses such as moving, losing income, and losing a parent
4. Acknowledge and resolve their feelings of anger at themselves or at one or both parents
5. Accept that the divorce is permanent
6. Realize that just because their parents' marriage failed does not mean they are incapable of healthy relationships with others—in other words, that their parents' divorce does not preclude a successful marriage for them

Task 6 is the most important, and the child's ability to accomplish it depends on successful resolution of the other five tasks. Most young children are not capable of resolving all these tasks, but they can begin working toward resolution during the early childhood years.

Violence

Many parents complain that keeping violence away from children requires tremendous work even in the best of circumstances. Children witness violence on television and through video and computer games and hear about it through many other sources. In the worst of circumstances, young children not only are exposed to violence but become victims of it as well. This section discusses three types of violence experienced by many young children: community violence, domestic violence, and child abuse.

Community Violence

In some neighborhoods, acts of violence are so common that the communities are labeled "war zones." However, most residents prefer not to be combatants. When surveyed, mothers in a Chicago housing project ranked neighborhood violence as their number one concern and as the condition that most negatively affects the quality of their life and the lives of their children (Dubrow & Garbarino, 1989). Unfortunately, neighborhood violence has become a major health issue for children (Krug, Dahlberg, Mercy, Zwi, & Lozano, 2002; Pennekamp, 1995).

A few years ago, the first author (Debra) had the opportunity to observe the effects of community violence up close when she took her daughter to get her hair braided by someone who lived in a housing project, an acquaintance of a friend. Because the hair-braiding procedure takes several hours, she and her daughter were in the home for an extended period. While they were there, the news was released that Tupac Shakur (a popular rap singer) had died from gunshot injuries received earlier. An impromptu gathering of friends and relatives of the woman who was doing the braiding ensued. Ten men and women in their early 20s, along with their young children, gathered to discuss the shooting and to pay tribute to Tupac, who had been one of their favorite artists. As Tupac's music played in the background, Debra was struck by several themes:

- Many in the room told of a close relative who had died as a result of neighborhood violence. Debra noticed on the wall of the apartment three framed programs from funerals of young men. She later learned that these dead men were a brother and two cousins of the woman who lived in the apartment. All three had been killed in separate violent incidents in their neighborhood.
- A sense of hopelessness permeated the conversation. The men especially had little hope of a future, and most thought they would be dead by age 40. Clinicians who work with young children living in neighborhoods in which violence is prevalent relate similar comments from children (National Center for Clinical Infant Programs, 1992). When asked if he had decided what he wanted to be when he grew up, one child is quoted as saying, "Why should I? I might not grow up" (p. 25).
- Perhaps related to the sense of hopelessness was an embracing of violence. Debra observed that during lighter moments in the conversation, the guests would chuckle about physical confrontations between common acquaintances.

Ironically, as Debra and her daughter were about to leave, gunshots sounded and the evening get-together was temporarily interrupted. Everyone, including the children, ran out of the apartment to see what had happened. For Debra, the significance of the evening was summarized in one of the last comments she heard before leaving. One of the men stated, "If all that money didn't save Tupac, what chance do we have?" It is interesting to note that Tupac's music and poetry continue to be idolized. Many still identify with his descriptions of hopelessness.

These sorts of conditions are not favorable for adequate child development (Dubrow & Garbarino, 1989; Krug et al., 2002). Investigations into the effects of living in violent neighborhoods support this claim. Children who grow up in a violent environment are reported to demonstrate low self-esteem, deficient social skills, and difficulty coping with and managing conflict (MacLennan, 1994). When Debra and her daughter visited the housing project, for example, they witnessed a 3-year-old telling her mother to "shut up." The mother and child then began hitting each other. Yes, some of this behavior is a result of parenting style, but one cannot help wondering about the influence of living in a violent community.

For many children living in violent neighborhoods, the death of a close friend or family member is commonplace. When the second author (David) was employed at a community child guidance center, he found that appointments were often canceled so the parents could attend funerals.

Living so intimately with death has grave effects on young children. In one study of young children whose older siblings had been victims of homicide, the surviving siblings showed symptoms of depression, anxiety, psychosocial impairment, and post-traumatic stress disorder (Freeman, Shaffer, & Smith, 1996). These symptoms are similar to those observed in young children in situations of political and military violence—for example, in Palestinian children in the occupied West Bank (Baker, 1990) and in children in South African townships during apartheid (Magwaza, Kilian, Peterson, & Pillay, 1993). Perhaps the label "war zone" is an appropriate one for violent communities. However, positive, affectionate, caregiving relationships—whether by parents or other family members or individuals in the community—can play an important mediating role in how violence is managed by very young children (Glaser, 2000).

Domestic Violence

Domestic violence may take the form of verbal, psychological, or physical abuse, although physical abuse is the form most often implied. An estimated 3 million to 10 million children per year witness their mothers being assaulted by their fathers (Silvern & Kaersvang, 1989; Vissing, Straus, Gelles, & Harrop, 1991). The number of children who witness domestic violence is even higher when instances of abuse by stepfathers, boyfriends, and other male liaisons—as well as abuses perpetrated by women—are included.

> How does psychological age affect children's responses to domestic violence?

In early childhood, children respond in a number of ways during violent episodes (Smith, O'Connor, & Berthelsen, 1996). Some children display fright—that is, they cry and scream. Others attempt to stop the violence by ordering the abuser to stop, by physically placing themselves between the mother and the abuser, or by hitting the abuser. Many children attempt to flee by retreating to a different room, turning up the volume on the TV, or trying to ignore the violence.

The effects of domestic violence on children's development are well-documented. Distress, problems with adjustment, characteristics of trauma, and increased behavior problems have all been observed in children exposed to domestic violence (Hughes, 1988; Perloff & Buckner, 1996; Shepard, 1992; Silvern & Kaersvang, 1989; Turner, Finkelhor, & Ormond, 2006). In addition, these children develop either aggressive behaviors or passive responses, both of which make them potential targets for abuse as teens and adults (Suh & Abel, 1990; Tutty & Wagar, 1994). Unfortunately, researchers are finding that children who witness intimate partner violence at home are also more likely to be victimized in other ways, including being victims of child maltreatment and community violence. The accumulation of victimization produces great risk for a variety of mental health problems in children (Turner et al., 2006).

In early childhood, children are more vulnerable than older children to the effects of living with domestic violence (O'Keefe, 1994; Smith et al., 1996). Younger children simply have fewer internal resources to help them cope with the experience. In addition, older children have friendships outside the family for support, whereas younger children rely primarily on the family. Many parents who are victims of domestic violence become emotionally unavailable to their young children. Battered mothers, for example, often become depressed and preoccupied with the abuse and their personal safety, leaving little time and energy for the attention and nurturing needed by young children. Another reason that young children are more vulnerable to the effects of domestic violence is that children between the ages of 3 and 6 lack the skills to verbalize their feelings and thoughts. As a result, thoughts and feelings about the violence get trapped inside and continually infringe upon the child's thoughts and emotions. Finally, as in the case of divorce, because of their egocentrism, young children often blame themselves for the domestic abuse.

Domestic violence does not always affect children's long-term development, however. In one study, one third of the children seemed unaffected by the domestic violence they witnessed at home; these children were well adjusted and showed no signs of distress, anxiety, or behavior problems (Smith et al., 1996). Two factors may buffer the effect domestic violence has on children (O'Keefe, 1994):

1. *Amount of domestic violence witnessed by the child.* The more violent episodes children witness, the more likely they are to develop problematic behavior.

2. *Relationship between the child and the mother,* assuming the mother is the victim. If the mother-child relationship remains stable and secure, the probability of the child developing behavioral difficulties decreases significantly—even when the amount of violence witnessed by the child is relatively high.

Interestingly, the father-child relationship in cases of domestic abuse was not found to be related to the child's emotional or psychological development (O'Keefe, 1994). However, this finding should be reviewed with caution because it is often difficult to find fathers to include in this type of research, and then to accurately measure the quality of attachment a younger child in such a circumstance experiences with the father or father figure (Mackey, 2001).

Exhibit 4.4	Some Potential Effects of Child Abuse on Growth and Development	
Physical Impairments	*Cognitive Impairments*	*Emotional Impairments*
Physical Abuse and Neglect		
Burns, scars, fractures, broken bones, damage to vital organs and limbs	Delayed cognitive skills	Negative self-concept
	Delayed language skills	Increased aggressiveness
	Mental retardation	Poor peer relations
Malnourishment	Delayed reality testing	Poor impulse control
Physical exposure	Overall disruption of thought processes	Anxiety
Poor skin hygiene		Inattentiveness
Poor (if any) medical care		Avoidant behavior
Poor (if any) dental care		
Serious medical problems		
Serious dental problems		
Failure-to-thrive syndrome		
Death		
Sexual Abuse		
Trauma to mouth, anus, vaginal area	Hyperactivity	Overly adaptive behavior
Genital and rectal pain	Bizarre sexual behavior	Overly compliant behavior
Genital and rectal bleeding		Habit disorders (nail biting)
Genital and rectal tearing		Anxiety
Sexually transmitted disease		Depression
		Sleep disturbances
		Night terrors
		Self-mutilation
Psychological/Emotional Abuse		
	Pessimistic view of life	Alienation
	Anxiety and fear	Intimacy problems
	Distorted perception of world	Low self-esteem
	Deficits in moral development	Depression

Child Maltreatment

It is difficult to estimate the rate of **child maltreatment**, because many incidences are never reported and much that is reported is not determined to be child maltreatment. Here are a couple of ways that the rate child maltreatment is estimated. Every day in the United States, 7,942 children are reported abused or neglected (Children's Defense Fund, 2001). Child abuse may take the form of verbal, emotional, physical, or sexual abuse or child neglect. About three children die from maltreatment in the United States every day, and 86% of the children who die from child maltreatment are under 6 years of age (Thomlison, 2004). Girls are most likely to be victimized overall, but boys have a higher incidence of fatal injuries than girls (Sedlak & Broadhurst, 1996). National incidence data indicate no race or ethnicity differences in maltreatment incidence, but official reports of child maltreatment include an over-representation of African American and American Indian/Alaska Natives (Sedlak & Broadhurst, 1996). Poverty and the lack of economic resources are correlated with abuse, especially physical abuse and neglect (Sedlak & Broadhurst, 1996). In addition, family isolation and lack of a support system, parental drug and alcohol abuse, lack of knowledge regarding child rearing, and parental difficulty in expressing feelings are all related to child abuse (Gelles, 1989; Veltkamp & Miller, 1994; Wolfner & Gelles, 1993). An association has also been noted between abuse of young children and the overload of responsibilities that women often encounter. Mothers who work outside the home and are also responsible for most or all of the domestic responsibilities, and mothers with unemployed husbands, are more prone to abuse their young children than other groups of mothers are (Gelles & Hargreaves, 1981).

Child abuse creates risks to all aspects of growth and development, as shown in Exhibit 4.4, but children ages birth to 6 are at highest risk of having long lasting damage (Thomlison, 2004).

⬚ Protective Factors in Early Childhood

Many of the factors listed in Chapter 3 that promote resiliency during the infant and toddler years are equally relevant during the early childhood years. Other protective factors also come into play (Fraser et al., 2004):

◆ *Social support.* Social support mediates many potential risks to the development of young children. The presence of social support increases the likelihood of a positive outcome for children whose parents divorce (Garvin, Kalter, & Hansell, 1993), moderates the effects for children who experience violence (Nettles, Mucherah, & Jones, 2000), facilitates better outcomes for children of mothers with mental illness (Oyserman, Bybee, Mowbray, & MacFarlane, 2002), and is even thought to reduce the continuation of abuse for 2- and 3-year-olds who have experienced parental abuse during the first year of life (Kotch et al., 1997). Social support aids young children in several ways (Fraser et al., 2004). Having a consistent and supportive aunt or uncle or preschool teacher who can set firm but loving limits, for example, may buffer the effects of a parent with ineffective skills. At the community level, preschools, church programs, and the like may help to enhance physical and cognitive skills, self-esteem, and social development. Through social support from family and nonfamily relationships, young children can receive care and support, another identified protective factor.

◆ *Positive parent-child relationship.* A positive relationship with at least one parent helps children to feel secure and nurtured (Fraser et al., 2004). Remember from Chapter 3 that a sense of security is the foundation on which young children build initiative during the early childhood years. Even if Jack Lewis never has contact with his father, Charles, a positive relationship with Joyce, his mother, can mediate this loss.

◆ *Effective parenting.* In early childhood, children need the opportunity to take initiative but also need firm limits, whether they are established by parents or grandparents or someone else who adopts the parent role. Terri Smith, for example, has not been able to establish self-control because her boundaries are not well defined. Effective parenting promotes self-efficacy and self-esteem and provides young children with a model of how they can take initiative within boundaries (Fraser et al., 2004).

◆ *Self-esteem.* A high level of self-worth may allow young children to persist in mastery of skills despite adverse conditions. Perhaps a high level of self-esteem can enhance Ron's, Rosiland's, and Jack's development despite the disruptions in their lives. In addition, research indicates that self-esteem is a protective factor against the effects of child abuse (Fraser et al., 2004).

◆ *Intelligence.* Even in young children, a high IQ serves as a protective factor. For example, young children with high IQs were less likely to be affected by maternal psychopathology (Tiet et al., 2001). Others suggest that intelligence results in success, which leads to higher levels of self-esteem (Fraser, 2004). For young children, then, intelligence may contribute to mastery of skills and independence, which may enhance self-esteem. Intelligence may also protect children through increased problem-solving skills, which allow for more effective responses to adverse situations.

IMPLICATIONS FOR SOCIAL WORK PRACTICE

In summary, knowledge about early childhood has several implications for social work practice with young children:

- ◆ Become well acquainted with theories and empirical research about growth and development among young children.
- ◆ Continue to promote the elimination of poverty and the advancement of social justice.
- ◆ Collaborate with other professionals in the creation of laws, interventions, and programs that assist in the elimination of violence.
- ◆ Create and support easy access to services for young children and their parents.
- ◆ Assess younger children in the context of their environment.
- ◆ Become familiar with the physical and emotional signs of child abuse.
- ◆ Directly engage younger children in an age-appropriate intervention process.
- ◆ Provide support to parents and help facilitate positive parent/child relationships.
- ◆ Encourage and engage both mothers and fathers in the intervention process.
- ◆ Provide opportunities for children to increase self-efficacy and self-esteem.
- ◆ Help parents understand the potential effects of negative environmental factors on their children.

KEY TERMS

authoritarian parenting
authoritative parenting
child maltreatment
developmental delay
disengaged parenting
discipline
egocentrism
empathy

hostile aggression
instrumental aggression
lateralization
learning play
permissive parenting
perspective taking
physical aggression
preconventional level of
  moral reasoning

relational aggression
self-esteem
self-theory
sociodramatic play
symbolic play
transductive reasoning

Active Learning

1. Watch any child-oriented cartoon on television. Describe the apparent and implied messages (both positive and negative) available in the cartoon about race and ethnicity, and gender differences. Consider how these messages might affect gender and ethnic development in young children.

2. Observe preschool-age children at play. Record the types of play that you observe. How well do your observations fit with what is described about play in this chapter?

3. The case studies at the beginning of this chapter (Terri, Jack, and Ron and Rosiland) do not specify race or ethnicity of the families. How important an omission did that appear to you? What assumptions did you make about the racial and/or ethnic background of the families? On what basis did you make those assumptions?

WEB RESOURCES

National Family Resiliency Center, Inc. (NFSC)
www.divorceabc.com

Site presented by the NFSC contains information about support groups, resources for professionals, library of articles, news and events, KIDS Newsletter, and Frequently Asked Questions.

American Academy of Child & Adolescent Psychiatry
www.aacap.org

Site presented by American Academy of Child & Adolescent Psychiatry contains concise and up-to-date information on a variety of issues facing children and their families, including day care, discipline, children and divorce, child abuse, children and TV violence, and children and grief.

The Office for Studies in Moral Development and Education
tigger.uic.edu/~1nucci/MoralEd/office.html

Site presented by the Office for Studies in Moral Development and Education at the College of Education at the University of Illinois at Chicago contains an overview of Piaget's, Kohlberg's, and Gilligan's theories of moral development and the domain theory of moral development.

International Society for Child and Play Therapy
www.playtherapy.org

Site presented by the International Society for Child and Play Therapy contains reading lists, articles and research, recommended resources, and other related organizations.

Children's Defense Fund
www.childrensdefense.org

Site presented by the Children's Defense Fund, a private nonprofit child advocacy organization, contains information on issues, the Black Community Crusade for Children, the Child Watch Visitation Program, and a parent resource network.

U.S. Department of Health & Human Services
www.dhhs.gov

Site maintained by the U.S. Department of Health & Human Services contains information on child care, child support enforcement, and children's health insurance.

MIDDLE CHILDHOOD

Leanne Charlesworth, Jim Wood, and Pamela Viggiani

Key Ideas	177
Case Study 5.1: ■ Anthony Bryant's Impending Assessment	177
Case Study 5.2: ■ Brianna Shaw's New Self-Image	178
Case Study 5.3: ■ Manuel Vega's Difficult Transition	179
Historical Perspective on Middle Childhood	181
Middle Childhood in the Multigenerational Family	182
Development in Middle Childhood	183
Physical Development	183
Cognitive Development	186
Cultural Identity Development	191
Emotional Development	193
Social Development	194
The Peer Group	197
Friendship and Intimacy	198
Team Play	199
Gender Identity and Gender Roles	199
Middle Childhood & Formal Schooling	201
Formal Schooling and Cognitive Development	202
Formal Schooling and Diversity	204
Formal Schooling: Home and School	205
Formal Schooling: Schools Mirror Community	206
Special Challenges in Middle Childhood	209

Poverty	210
Family and Community Violence	212
Mental and Physical Challenges	215
Attention Deficit Hyperactivity Disorder (ADHD)	215
Autistic Spectrum Disorders	215
Emotional/Behavioral Disorder	217
Family Disruption	220
Risk Factors and Protective Factors in Middle Childhood	221
Implications for Practice	224
Key Terms	224
Active Learning	225
Web Resources	225

❖ How have our conceptions of middle childhood changed through time?

❖ What types of individual, family, school, community, and other systemic qualities are most conducive to positive development during middle childhood?

❖ During middle childhood, what factors heighten developmental risk for children, and what supports resilience?

KEY IDEAS

As you read this chapter, take note of these central ideas:

1. Values and beliefs regarding childhood in general, and middle childhood specifically, are shaped by historical and sociocultural context.

2. During middle childhood, a wide variety of bio/psycho/social/spiritual changes take place across the developmental domains.

3. As children progress through middle childhood, the family environment remains extremely important, while the community environment—including the school—also becomes a significant factor shaping development.

4. During middle childhood, peers have an increasingly strong impact on development; peer acceptance becomes very important to well-being.

5. Poverty, family or community violence, special needs, and family disruption create developmental risk for many children.

Case Study 5.1

Anthony Bryant's Impending Assessment

Anthony is a 6-year-old boy living in an impoverished section of a large city. Anthony's mother, Melissa, was 14 when Anthony was born. Anthony's father—James, 15 when Anthony was born—has always spent a great deal of time with Anthony. Although James now also has a 2-year-old daughter from another relationship, he has told Melissa that Anthony and Melissa are the most important people in his life. Once Anthony was out of diapers, James began spending even more time with him, taking Anthony along to visit friends and occasionally, on overnight outings.

James's father was murdered when he was a toddler and he rarely sees his mother, who struggles with a serious substance addiction and is known in the neighborhood as a prostitute. James lived with his

(Continued)

(Continued)

paternal grandparents until he was in his early teens, when he began to stay with a favorite uncle. Many members of James's large extended family have been incarcerated on charges related to their involvement in the local drug trade. James's favorite uncle is a well-known and widely respected dealer. James himself has been arrested a few times and is currently on probation.

Melissa and Anthony live with her mother. Melissa obtained her GED after Anthony's birth, and she has held a variety of jobs for local fast food chains. Melissa's mother, Cynthia, receives SSI because she has been unable to work for several years due to her advanced rheumatoid arthritis, which was diagnosed when she was a teenager. Melissa remembers her father only as a loud man who often yelled at her when she made noise. He left Cynthia and Melissa when Melissa was 4 years old, and neither has seen him since. Cynthia seemed pleased when Anthony was born and she has been a second mother to him, caring for him while Melissa attends school, works, and socializes with James and her other friends.

Anthony has always been very active and energetic, frequently breaking things and creating "messes" throughout the apartment. To punish Anthony, Cynthia spanks him with a belt or other object—and she sometimes resorts to locking him in his room until he falls asleep. Melissa and James are proud of Anthony's wiry physique and rough and tough play; they have encouraged him to be fearless and not to cry when he is hurt. Both Melissa and James use physical punishment as their main discipline strategy with Anthony, but he usually obeys them before it is needed.

Anthony entered kindergarten at the local public school last fall. When he started school, his teacher told Melissa that he seemed to be a very smart boy, one of the only boys in the class who already knew how to write his name and how to count to 20. It is now spring, however, and Melissa is tired of dealing with Anthony's teacher and other school staff. She has been called at work a number of times, and recently the school social worker requested a meeting with her. Anthony's teacher reports that Anthony will not listen to her and frequently starts fights with the other children in the classroom. Anthony's teacher also states that Anthony constantly violates school rules, like waiting in line and being quiet in the hallways, and he doesn't seem bothered by threats of punishment. Most recently, Anthony's teacher has told Melissa that she would like Anthony assessed by the school psychologist.

Case Study 5.2

Brianna Shaw's New Self-Image

When Brianna was born, her mother Deborah was 31 years old with a 13-year-old daughter (Stacy) from a prior, short-lived marriage. Deborah and Michael's relationship was relatively new when Deborah became pregnant with Brianna. Shortly after Deborah announced the pregnancy, Michael moved into her mobile home. Michael and Deborah initially talked about setting a wedding date and pursuing Michael's legal adoption of Stacy, whose father had remarried and was no longer in close contact.

Michael made it clear throughout Deborah's pregnancy that he wanted a son. He seemed very content and supportive of Deborah until around the time the couple found out the baby was a girl. In Stacy's view, Michael became mean and bossy in the months that followed. He started telling Stacy what to do, criticizing

Deborah's appearance, and complaining constantly that Deborah wasn't any fun anymore since she stopped drinking and smoking while she was pregnant.

During Brianna's infancy, the couple's relationship began to change even more rapidly. Michael was rarely home and instead spent most of his free time hanging out with old friends. When he did come by, he'd encourage Deborah to leave Brianna with Stacy so the two of them could go out like "old times." Even though her parents were Deborah's full-time day care providers and both Brianna and Stacy were thriving, Deborah was chronically exhausted from balancing parenting and her full-time job as a nursing assistant. Soon, whenever Michael came by, the couple frequently argued and their shouting matches gradually escalated to Michael threatening to take Brianna away. Michael was soon dating another woman and his relationship with Deborah and Stacy became increasingly hostile during the following four years.

The summer that Brianna turned 5, the local hospital closed down and Deborah lost her job. After talking with her parents, Deborah made the decision to move her daughters to Fairfield, a city four hours away from home. An old high school friend had once told Deborah that if she ever needed a job, the large hospital her friend worked for had regular openings and even offered tuition assistance. Within two months, Deborah had sold her mobile home, obtained a full-time position with her friend's employer, and signed a lease for a small townhouse in a suburb known for its excellent school system.

When Brianna started kindergarten in their new town, her teacher described her to Deborah as shy and withdrawn. Deborah remembered reading something in the school newsletter about a social skills group run by a school social worker, and she asked if Brianna could be enrolled. Gradually, the group seemed to make a difference and Brianna began to act more like her old self, forming several friendships during the following two years.

Today, Brianna is 8 years old and has just entered third grade. Brianna usually leaves for school on the bus at 8:00 a.m. and Deborah picks her up from an afterschool program at 5:45 p.m. When possible, Stacy picks Brianna up earlier, after her own classes at a local community college are over. Brianna still spends summers with her grandparents in the rural area where she was born. Academically, she has thus far excelled in school but a new concern is Brianna's weight. Brianna is 49 inches tall and weighs 72 pounds. Until the last year or so, Brianna seemed unaware of the fact that many people viewed her as overweight. In the last several months, however, Brianna has told Stacy and Deborah various stories about other children calling her "fat" and making other comments about her size. Deborah feels that Brianna is increasingly moody and angry when she is home. Brianna recently asked Deborah why she is "fat" and told Stacy that she just wishes she were dead.

Case Study 5.3

Manuel Vega's Difficult Transition

A slightly built 11-year-old Manuel is in seventh grade in Greenville, Mississippi. He speaks English moderately well. He was born in Texas where his mother, Maria, and father, Estaban, met. For Estaban, it has been an interesting journey from his home town in Mexico to Mississippi. For generations, Esteban's family lived and worked near Izucar de Matamoros, a small city in Mexico on the inter-American highway. During their teen years in Izucar de Matamoros, Estaban and his four younger brothers worked on the local sugar cane farms and in the sugar refineries. By the time he was in his early twenties, Estaban began to

(Continued)

(Continued)

look for better paying work and was able to get his license to haul products from Izucar de Matamoros to larger cities, including Mexico City. Estaban and one brother eventually moved to a medium-sized city where his employer, the owner of a small trucking company, provided an apartment for several of his single truckers.

After three productive years in the trucking industry, the company went bankrupt. With his meager savings, Estaban made arrangements to travel to Arizona to pursue his dream of owning his own trucking company. Working as a day laborer, he eventually made his way to Laredo, Texas where he met and married Maria. Although both Maria and Estaban's formal schooling ended relatively early, both acquired a basic command of English while living in Laredo. During the late 1970s, Maria and Estaban requested documentation for Estaban and after a lengthy process, they were successful.

Estaban and Maria began their family while Estaban continued to work at day labor construction jobs in and around Laredo. At home and with their relatives and neighbors, Maria and Estaban spoke Spanish exclusively. In their neighborhood, Maria's many relatives not only provided social support, but also helped Maria sell tamales and other traditional Mexican foods to locals and occasional tourists. Eventually, the family saved enough money for the purchase of a small truck that Estaban used to make deliveries of Maria's specialties to more distant restaurants. However, the family faced many competitors in the local Mexican food industry. Maria's Uncle Arturo urged the family to move to the Mississippi Delta where he owns Mi Casa, a Mexican restaurant and wholesale business. Uncle Arturo was hopeful that Maria would enrich his menu with her mastery of Mexican cuisine. He promised employment for Estaban, hauling Mexican specialty food staples to the growing number of Mexican restaurants in the Delta, ranging from Memphis to Biloxi.

Almost three years ago, Estaban and Maria decided to take Arturo up on his offer and together with their two sons, they moved to Greenville. Their older son Carlos never adjusted to school life in Mississippi. Now 16, Carlos did not return to school this fall. Instead, he began working full-time for his father loading and unloading the truck and providing his more advanced English language capacity to open up new markets for the business. At first Maria and Estaban resisted the idea of Carlos dropping out of school, but he was insistent. Carlos always struggled in school; he repeated a grade early on in his education and found most of his other subjects challenging. The family's new business, after thriving during their first year in the Delta, began having difficulties in the aftermath of Hurricane Katrina. However, recently several stores and restaurants on the gulf coast have returned to business as usual and are placing orders for products. Carlos knows the family finances have been in peril and that he is needed.

Carlos and his younger brother Manuel have always been close. Manuel yearns to be like his older brother and Carlos has always considered it his job to protect and care for his younger brother. Carlos sees in Manuel the potential for school success that he never had. He tells Manuel that he must stay in school to acquire the "book learning" that he could never grasp. But leaving the warm embrace of their former neighborhood in Texas for the Mississippi Delta has been hard for Manuel. Their tight knit family bonds are still in tact, but they are still struggling to understand how Delta culture operates. In Manuel's old school, most students and teachers spoke or knew how to speak Spanish and Manuel always felt he fit in. Now, Manuel is one of a small percentage of Spanish speaking students in his new school, where the vast majority of students and staff are African American and speak only English.

In the school setting, Manuel's new ESL teacher, Ms. Jones, is concerned about him. His teacher reports that he struggles academically and shows little interest in classroom activities or peers, often seeming sullen. Ms. Jones has observed that Manuel frequently appears to be daydreaming and when teachers try to talk with him, he seems to withdraw further. Ms. Jones knows that Manuel's records from Texas indicate that he was an outgoing, socially adjusted primary school student. However, his records also show that his reading and writing performance was below grade level starting in first grade. Ms. Jones has found that if she speaks with Manuel in Spanish while taking a walk around the school, he will share stories about his family and his old neighborhood and friends. To date, no educational or psychological assessments have taken place. When Manuel meets his social worker, he avoids eye contact and appears extremely uncomfortable.

⬚ Historical Perspective on Middle Childhood

Until the beginning of the twentieth century, children were viewed primarily in economic terms within most European countries and the United States (Fass & Mason, 2000). Emphasis was often placed on the child's productivity and ability to contribute to the family's financial well-being. Middle childhood represented a period during which children became increasingly able to play a role in maintaining or improving the economic status of the family and community. Beginning in the early twentieth century, however, a radical shift occurred in the Western world's perceptions of children. Children passing through middle childhood became categorized as "school age" and their education became a societal priority. Child labor and compulsory education laws supported and reinforced this shift in societal values. This shift has not taken place in many parts of the nonindustrialized world where children continue to play important economic roles for families. In Latin America, Africa, and some parts of Asia, childhood is short, and many children in middle childhood live and work on the streets (called "street children"). There is no time for the luxury of an indulged childhood. In rapidly industrializing countries, children must balance their economic productivity with time spent in school (Leeder, 2004).

Mirroring political ideals, the shift toward the public education of children was intended to be an equalizer, enabling children from a variety of economic backgrounds to become successful citizens. Public schools were to be free and open to all. Instead, however, they reflected traditional public ambiguity toward poverty and diversity, and they embodied particular value systems and excluded certain groups (Allen-Meares, Washington, & Walsh, 1996). In the United States, the first public schools were, in effect, open to European Americans only, and children from marginalized or nondominant groups rarely received advanced education. Today, schools continue to play a pivotal role in reinforcing segregation and **deculturalizing** various groups of children (Kozol, 2005; Spring, 2004). In essence, as schools pressure children from nondominant groups to assimilate, they play a role in intentionally or unintentionally destroying or severely limiting a culture's ability to sustain itself. These marginalized groups consistently achieve more poorly than the rest of the student population, a situation often referred to as the "achievement gap."

Today, the evolution of our perceptions of middle childhood continues. Although there is incredible diversity among children, families, and communities, generally speaking, middle childhood has come to be viewed in the United States as a time when education, play, leisure, and social activities should dominate daily life (Fass & Mason, 2000). Sigmund Freud perceived middle childhood as a relatively uneventful phase of development. But in the twenty-first century, middle childhood is recognized as a potentially turbulent time in children's lives.

The age range classified as middle childhood is subject to debate. In the United States, it is most often defined as the period beginning at approximately ages 5 or 6 and ending at approximately ages 10 to 12 (Berk, 2002a, 2002b; Broderick & Blewitt, 2006; Craig & Baucum, 2002). However, some assert that middle childhood begins a bit later than 6 (Allen & Marotz, 2003) and ends at the onset of puberty (Davies, 2004), which ranges tremendously among children.

Images of middle childhood often include children who are physically active and intellectually curious, making new friends and learning new things. But as Anthony Bryant, Brianna Shaw, and Manuel Vega demonstrate, middle childhood is filled with both opportunities and challenges. For some children, it is a period of particular vulnerability. In fact, when we think of school-aged children, images of child poverty and related school inequities, family and community violence, sexual victimization or **precociousness** (early development), learning challenges and physical and emotional ailments like depression, asthma, and Attention Deficit/Hyperactivity Disorder may dominate our thoughts. In some parts of the world, children between the ages of 6 and 12 are vulnerable to war, land mines, and forced enlistment as soldiers. They are also vulnerable to slave-like labor and being sold as sex workers in an international *child trafficking* economy (Human Rights Watch, 2006).

⬛ Middle Childhood in the Multigenerational Family

During middle childhood, the child's social world expands dramatically. Although the family is not the only relevant force in a child's life, it remains an extremely significant influence on development. Families are often in a constant state of change and so the child's relationships with family members and the environment that the family inhabits are likely to be different from the child's first experiences of family. For example, consider the changes in Anthony Bryant's, Brianna Shaw's, and Manuel Vega's families over time and the ways in which family relationships have been continually evolving.

How are Anthony, Brianna, and Manuel affected by their multigenerational families?

Despite the geographical distances that often exist between family members today, nuclear families are still emotional subsystems of extended, multigenerational family systems. The child's nuclear family is significantly shaped by past, present, and anticipated future experiences, events, and relationships (Carter & McGoldrick, 2005a). Profoundly important factors such as historical events, culture, and social structure often influence children through their family systems. And family members' experiences and characteristics trickle through families via generational ties. These experiences or characteristics may be biological in nature and therefore fairly obvious, or they may include more nebulous qualities such as acquired emotional strengths or wounds. For example, consider Brianna's maternal grandfather, who is African American and grew up with the legacy of slavery under Jim Crow laws and legal segregation in the United States, or Anthony's maternal grandmother, who as a child was repeatedly victimized sexually. Children become connected to events or phenomena such as a familial history of child abuse or a group history of discrimination and **oppression** (restrictions and exploitation), even in the absence of direct experiences in the present generation (see Crawford, Nobles, & Leary, 2003; Hass, 1990; Karson, 2001; McGoldrick, 2004).

Thus, the developing school-age child is shaped not only by events and individuals explicitly evident in present time and physical space but also by those events and individuals that have more directly influenced the lives of their parents, grandparents, great-grandparents, and beyond. These influences—familial, cultural, and historical in nature—shape all aspects of each child's development in an abstract and complex fashion.

▧ Development in Middle Childhood

New developmental tasks are undertaken in middle childhood and development occurs within the physical, cognitive, cultural identity, emotional, and social dimensions. Although each developmental domain is considered separately for our analytical purposes, changes in the developing child reflect the dynamic interaction continuously occurring across these dimensions.

Physical Development

During middle childhood, physical development continues steadily but children of the same chronological age may vary greatly in stature, weight, and sexual development. For most children, height and weight begin to advance less rapidly than during prior developmental phases, but steady growth continues. The nature and pace of physical growth during this period is shaped by both genetic and environmental influences in interaction (Craig & Baucum, 2002).

As children progress from kindergarten to early adolescence, their fine and gross motor skills typically advance. In the United States today, children in this age range are often encouraged to gain a high level of mastery over physical skills associated with a particular interest such as dance, sports, or music. However, medical professionals caution that school-age children continue to possess unique physical vulnerabilities related to the growth process and they therefore remain quite susceptible to injuries associated with excessive physical activity or training (Craig & Baucum, 2002).

Middle childhood is a developmental phase of entrenchment or eradication of many potent risk or protective factors manifesting in this developmental domain. Focusing on risk, for children residing in chronically impoverished countries and communities, issues such as malnutrition and disease threaten physical health. Seemingly innocuous issues such as poor dental hygiene or mild visual impairment may become more serious as they begin to impact other areas of development such as cognitive, emotional, or social well-being. In the United States, health issues such as asthma and obesity are of contemporary concern and often either improve or become severe during middle childhood.

▲ **Photo 5.1** During middle childhood, physical development continues steadily and children are encouraged to gain mastery over physical skills.

What impact do these differences in biological age have on psychological and social development during middle childhood?

Unintentional physical injuries change in nature but continue as a major threat to well-being (Berk, 2002b). In the United States, motor vehicle injuries and drowning are currently the leading causes of injury-related death among children ages 5 to 14 (National Center for Injury Prevention and Control, 2001). Nearly one-third of bicyclists killed in traffic accidents are children in this age range. Playground-related injuries are also common in middle childhood and are often severe or even fatal, including falls from playground surfaces and strangulation on playground equipment.

Moreover, school-age children gain new risks: almost one-third of rapes occur before age 12 and, among children ages 10 to 14, suicide is the third leading cause of death. Some speculate that the physical injuries unique to middle childhood may be indirectly facilitated by declines in adult supervision and adult over-estimation of children's safety-related knowledge and ability to implement safety practices. In addition, children's continued physical and cognitive (specifically, judgment and decision making processes) vulnerabilities combine, potentially, with an increasing propensity to engage in risk-taking activities and behaviors (Berk, 2002b; National Center for Injury Prevention and Control, 2001).

Middle childhood is the developmental phase that leads from *prepubescence* (the period prior to commencement of the physiological processes and changes associated with puberty) to *pubescence* (the period during which the child begins to experience diverse and gradual physical processes associated with puberty). Pubescence includes the growth of pubic hair for boys and girls, breast development for girls, and genitalia development for boys. Many of us may not think of middle childhood as the developmental phase during which puberty becomes relevant. Precocious puberty has traditionally been defined as puberty beginning before age 8 in girls and 9 in boys (Nakamoto, 2000). However, although ongoing consultation with a child's pediatrician or other health care provider is always recommended, recent research suggests that the initial signs of pubic hair and breast development may be considered normative when it begins as early as 7 to 8 years of age among non-Hispanic white girls and 6 to 7 years of age among non-Hispanic black girls (Nakamoto, 2000). Kaplowitz (2006) explains that "it now appears that the great majority of early-maturing girls (using the 8-years-old definition) are normal girls who are at the early end of the normal age distribution for pubertal onset" (p. 490).

Exhibit 5.1 summarizes recent research focusing on puberty onset differences according to race and gender. Understanding of sexual development and puberty trends broadens knowledge of development generally, as well as increases our ability to detect maturation patterns indicating a need for more thorough assessment, for example, to rule out endocrine pathology including growth disorders or hormone imbalances. Professionals working with children should be knowledgeable about the full spectrum of pubescence as well as related personal biases or misconceptions.

Exhibit 5.1	Puberty Onset Comparison					
	Median Age at Onset					
	Girls			Boys		
	Non-Hispanic White	Non-Hispanic Black	Mexican American	Non-Hispanic White	Non-Hispanic Black	Mexican American
Pubic Hair	10.6	9.4	10.4	12.0	11.2	12.3
Breast Development	10.4	9.5	9.8	—	—	—
Genitalia Development	—	—	—	10.0	9.2	10.3

SOURCE: Sun et al., 2002.

Focusing on racial differences, many studies have found that in the United States, non-Hispanic African American girls begin puberty earlier than other children (Adair & Gordon-Larsen, 2001; Benefice, Caius, & Garnier, 2004; Chumlea et al., 2003; Peck, 1997). However, Sun et al. (2002) point out that across gender and racial groups, children continue to *complete* their **secondary sexual development**, or development of secondary sex characteristics, at approximately the same age. This issue will receive further attention in Chapter 6.

A trend toward earlier age of puberty onset, particularly among girls, has brought much attention to the potential causes. Some have argued that the trend may be due to certain food-based or environmental chemicals known to impact hormonal activity (Wang, Needham, & Barr, 2005), or changing social conditions including family characteristics (Ellis & Garber, 2000; Moffitt, Caspi, Belsky, & Silva, 1992); popular media speculates that the sexualization of young girls may play a role (Irvine, 2006; Levin, 2005). Recently, an oft cited cause is a gradual increase in children's average Body Mass Index (BMI) and the related issue of childhood obesity.

There is evidence suggesting that a fat-protein called leptin may be the underlying link between the weight and puberty trend association. Kaplowitz (2006) explains that leptin levels typically rise in girls, but not boys, at the time of puberty and states "we can speculate that overweight girls with higher leptin levels are more likely to enter puberty and reach menarche at an earlier age. Such a connection between leptin and normal reproductive functioning makes evolutionary sense, in that it ensures that pregnancy will not occur unless there are adequate fat stores to sustain the viability of the fetus" (p. 490). However, Wang, Needham, and Barr (2005) caution that "the signaling pathway for leptin in the development of puberty is not known, and further work is necessary to define this mechanism and the difference in leptin levels among racial/ethnicity groups" (p. 1101). Wang, Needham, and Barr (2005) identify nutritional status; genetic predisposition, including race/ethnicity; and environmental chemical exposure as associated with age of puberty onset.

It should be noted that careful examination of puberty onset trends suggests that the "trend toward earlier onset of puberty in U.S. girls over the past 50 years is not as strong as some reports suggested" (Kaplowitz, 2006, p. 487). Indeed, within the United States, research suggests that there is evidence supporting this trend, but only to a certain point. Specifically, the average age of menarche decreased from approximately 14.8 years in 1877 to about 12.8 years in the mid 1960s (Kaplowitz, 2006). Most researchers have concluded that the general trend observed during this broad historical time period is due to health and nutrition improvement within the population as a whole. A recent examination of available data concludes that there is little evidence to support a clear continued decline in more recent years. Nevertheless, some have suggested that our public education and health systems should reconsider the timing and nature of health education for children because the onset of puberty may impact social and emotional development and has traditionally been associated with a variety of "risky and unhealthy behaviors" (Wang et al., p. 1101) among children and adolescents. Indeed a relationship, albeit complex, appears to exist between puberty and social development for both boys and girls (Felson, 2002; Kaltiala-Heino, Kosunen & Rimpela, 2003; Martin, 1996; McCabe & Ricciardelli, 2003). As they progress through puberty, girls in particular may be faced with new sexual attention from both peers and adults (American Association of University Women, 1995). Intervention focused on self-protection and individual rights and responsibilities may be beneficial, and schools committed to the safety of their students must diligently educate staff and students about sexual development, sexual harassment, and sexual abuse.

Middle childhood is the developmental phase when increased public attention and self-awareness is directed toward various aspects of physical growth, skill, or activity patterns and levels deemed outside the normal range. Because physical development is outwardly visible, it affects perceptions of self and the way a child is viewed and treated by peers and adults in a cyclical fashion. Physical development can also affect children's peer relationships. School-age children constantly compare themselves to others, and physical differences are often the topic of discussion. Whereas "late" developers may feel inferior about their size or lack of sexual development, "early" developers may feel awkward and out of place among their peers. Many children worry about being "normal." Reassurance by adults that physical development varies among people and that all development is "normal" is crucial.

Cognitive Development

For most children, the acquisition of cognitive abilities that occurs early in middle childhood allows the communication of thoughts with increasing complexity. Public education plays a major role in the cognitive development of children in the United States, if only because children attend school throughout the formative years of such development. When Anthony Bryant, Brianna Shaw, and Manuel Vega first entered school, their readiness to confront the challenges and opportunities that school presents was shaped by prior experiences. Anthony, for example, entered school generally prepared for the academic emphases associated with kindergarten. He was perhaps less prepared for the social expectations present in the school environment.

In Jean Piaget's (1936/1952) terms, children start school during the second stage (preoperational thought) and finish school when they are completing the fourth and final stage of cognitive development (formal operations). In the third stage (concrete operations), children are able to solve concrete problems using logical problem-solving strategies. By the end of middle childhood, they enter the formal operations stage and become able to solve hypothetical problems using abstract concepts (refer back to Exhibit 3.4 for an overview of Piaget's stages of cognitive development). School children rapidly develop conceptual thought, the ability to categorize complicated systems of objects, and the ability to solve problems (Allen-Meares, 1995).

Bergen and Coscia (2001) point out that as you observe children moving into and through middle childhood, you will note these rapid gains in intellectual processes and memory. These brain-produced shifts in the child's understanding of him or herself and the surrounding world are consistent with the transition into Piaget's concrete operational stage of cognitive development. Potential gains in cognitive development enable new learning in a variety of environments. For example, children gain enhanced ability to understand people, situations, and events within their surrounding environments. The task for caregivers and others within the child's environment is to recognize and respond to this ability sensitively by nurturing and supporting the child's expanding cognitive abilities.

▲ **Photo 5.2**   Middle childhood is a critical time for children to acquire a sense of self-confidence and develop conceptual thought.

Beyond Piaget's ideas, brain development and cognitive functioning during middle childhood have received relatively little attention when compared to research devoted to brain development in prior developmental phases. However, our ever-expanding general understanding of the human brain illuminates opportunities and vulnerabilities present throughout childhood. For example, professionals working with children are increasingly aware of the meaning and implications of *brain plasticity*. As pointed out in Chapter 3, infancy, toddlerhood, and early childhood appear to represent "sensitive periods" in brain development. By middle childhood, a child's brain development and functioning has been profoundly shaped by the nature of earlier experiences and development. And yet, remarkable **brain plasticity** continues, with brain structure and functioning capable of growth and refinement throughout life (Shonkoff & Phillips, 2000). The conceptual framework perhaps most useful to understanding this potential and the processes at play is nonlinear dynamic systems theory, also known as complexity or chaos theory (Applegate & Shapiro, 2005). Applied to this context, this theoretical perspective proposes that changes in one area or aspect of the neurological system may stimulate or interact with other neurological or broader physiological system components in an unpredictable fashion, potentially leading to unanticipated outcomes. Brain development follows a coherent developmental process, but brain plasticity in particular demonstrates the role of complex nonlinear neurological system dynamics and processes.

There are at least two aspects of brain development of particular interest when we focus on middle childhood. The first is the idea that different brain regions appear to develop according to different time lines. In other words, middle childhood may be a "sensitive period" for certain aspects of brain development not yet clearly understood. The second important idea is the notion that brain synapses (connections between cells in the nervous system) that are initially present as children enter this developmental phase may be gradually eliminated if they are not used. As reported in Chapter 3, there seems to be a pattern of *synaptogenesis,* or creation and fine-tuning of brain synapses, in the **human cerebral cortex** during early childhood which appears to be followed by a gradual pruning process that eventually reduces the overall number of synapses to their adult levels (Shonkoff & Phillips, 2000). Ongoing positive and diverse learning opportunities during middle childhood may help facilitate continued brain growth and optimal refinement of existing structures. The National Research Council of Medicine (Shonkoff & Phillips, 2000) argues that it is essential to recognize that although genetic factors and the nature and timing of early experiences matter, "more often than not, the developing child remains vulnerable to risk and open to protective influences throughout the early years of life and into adulthood" (p. 31).

Variations in brain development and functioning appear to play a critical role in learning abilities and disabilities as well as patterns of behavior (Bergen & Coscia, 2001). During middle childhood, identification and potential diagnosis of special needs, including issues such as Attention Deficit Hyperactivity Disorder and autism spectrum disorders, typically peak. In recent years, an area of public interest is gender or sex-based differences in brain functioning and, possibly, learning styles. This interest has been stimulated in part by evidence suggesting that boys are currently at higher risk than girls for poor literacy performance, special education placement, and school drop out (Weaver-Hightower, 2003).

Gurian (2001) and Sax (2005) have argued that brain-based cognitive processing, behavior, and learning style differences may be responsible for the somewhat stable trends observed in gender differences in educational achievement. The importance of sex, or gender, in shaping the human experience cannot be overstated. Gender is a profoundly important organizing factor shaping human development and its biological correlates may impact behavior and learning processes in ways we do not clearly understand. In particular, the nature and causes of educational achievement differences among girls and boys are "complex and the interconnections of the causes are poorly understood" (Weaver-Hightower, 2003, p. 487). Also, it is critically important to remember that among children, gender is but one of several personal and group characteristics relevant to understanding educational privilege specifically, as well as risk and protection generally.

Concern about the well-being of boys in schools has been stimulated, in part, by the assertion that in the late twentieth and early twenty-first centuries, boys' performance has been declining on indicators of educational achievement and attainment. Some argue that boys have suffered, in educational contexts, from the amount of attention dedicated to supporting girls' educational success during the late twentieth century (Sommers, 2000). Indeed, a variety of publications and educational initiatives in the late twentieth century attempted to correct the role that schools and other social institutions had traditionally played in placing girls at risk emotionally, socially, and academically (see American Association of University Women, 1995; Orenstein, 1994; Pipher, 1994; Sadker & Sadker, 1994).

There is speculation, however, that today's schools, in particular the early years of public schooling, privilege a predominately "female" learning style (Sax, 2005). On the other hand, evidence suggests that boys continue to receive advantage in a subtle fashion throughout the schooling experience (Sadker & Sadker, 1994; Guzzetti, Young, Gritsavage, Fyfe, & Hardenbrook, 2002). And while girls may "out perform" boys in certain areas, such as literacy (reading and writing), there is evidence that boys generally continue to "out perform" girls in the math, science, and technology domains (Barrs, 1994; Dee, 2005; Rowan, Knobel, Bigum, & Lankshear, 2002). In sum, careful analysis of contemporary data and shortcomings indicates that the differences between boys and girls are complex and there simply is not clear evidence of exclusively one-sided advantage or disadvantage (Bailey, 2002).

Several developmental theorists, including those listed in Exhibit 5.2, have described the changes and developmental tasks associated with middle childhood. According to these traditional theorists, thinking becomes more complex, reasoning becomes more logical, the child's sense of morality expands and develops into a more internally based system, and the ability to understand the perspectives of others emerges. However, shortcomings in the focus, methods, and findings of many traditional developmental theorists are today widely recognized (see Gibbs & Huang, 1989; Gilligan, 1982; Langford, 1995; Mowrer & Klein, 2001). In particular, much developmental research historically lacked rigor and did not devote sufficient attention to females and children belonging to nondominant groups.

A number of contemporary developmental theorists have focused on assessing the relevance and applicability of these developmental tasks to all children. Most agree that the central ideas of the theorists summarized in Exhibit 5.2 continue to be meaningful. For example, Erikson's thoughts remain widely recognized as relevant to our understanding of school-age children. In some areas, however, these developmental theories have been critiqued and subsequently expanded. This is particularly true in the area of moral development.

The best-known theory of moral development is Lawrence Kohlberg's stage theory (for an overview of this theory, refer back to Exhibit 4.1). Kohlberg's research on moral reasoning found that children do not enter the second level of *conventional moral reasoning,* or morality based on approval of authorities or upon upholding societal standards, until about age 9 or 10, sometime after they have the cognitive skills for such reasoning. Robert Coles (1987, 1997) expanded upon Kohlberg's work and emphasized the distinction between moral imagination—the gradually developed capacity to reflect on what is right and wrong—and moral conduct, pointing out that a "well-developed conscience does not translate, necessarily, into a morally courageous life" (p. 3). To Coles, *moral behavior* is shaped by daily experiences, developing in response to the way the child is treated in his or her various environments such as home and school. The school-age child often pays close attention to the discrepancies between the "moral voices" and actions of the adults in his or her world, including parents, friends' parents, relatives, teachers, and coaches. Each new and significant

Exhibit 5.2	Phases and Tasks of Middle Childhood	
Theorist	*Phase or Task*	*Description*
Freud (1938/1973)	Latency	Sexual instincts become less dominant; superego develops further.
Erikson (1950)	Industry versus inferiority	Capacity to cooperate and create develops; result is sense of either mastery or incompetence.
Piaget (1936/1952)	Concrete operational	Reasoning becomes more logical but remains at concrete level; principle of conservation is learned.
Piaget (1932/1965)	Moral realism and autonomous morality	Conception of morality changes from absolute and external to relative and internal.
Kohlberg (1969)	Preconventional and conventional morality	Reasoning based on punishment and reward is replaced by reasoning based on formal law and external opinion.
Selman (1976)	Self-reflective perspective taking	Ability develops to view own actions, thoughts, and emotions from another's perspective.

adult sets an example for the child, sometimes complementing and sometimes contradicting the values emphasized in the child's home environment.

Also, Gilligan (1982) has extensively criticized Kohlberg's theory of moral development as paying inadequate attention to girls' "ethic of care" and the keen emphasis girls often place on relationships and the emotions of others. Gilligan has argued that gender differences can be observed not necessarily in basic values or moral choices but in ethical thinking and decision making processes (Davies, 2004). Consistent with Gilligan's ideas, a number of developmental theorists have argued that girls moving through middle childhood must reconcile increasing emphasis and abilities in the area of abstract linear thinking with their **interrelational intelligence,** which is based on emotional and social intelligence and is similar to Howard Gardner's concept of interpersonal intelligence (Borysenko, 1996, p. 41). Such developmentalists, drawing upon feminist scholarship, point out that both girls and boys advance rapidly in the cognitive and moral developmental domains during middle childhood, but the genders may be distinct in their approaches to social relationships and interactions, and such differences may shape the nature of development in all domains (Borysensko, 1996; Davies, 2004; Gilligan, 1982; Taylor, Gilligan & Sullivan, 1995).

Many developmentalists have also examined the implications of advancing cognitive abilities for children's understanding of their group identities. Children become much more aware of ethnic identities and other aspects of diversity (such as socioeconomic status and gender identities) during their middle childhood years. Cultural awareness and related beliefs are shaped by the nature of experiences such as exposure to diversity within the family and community, including school, contexts. Unlike the preschoolers' attraction to "black and white" classifications, children progressing through middle childhood are increasingly capable of understanding the complexities of group memberships; in other words, they are cognitively capable of rejecting over-simplistic stereotypes and recognizing the complexities present within all individuals and groups (Davies, 2004). McAdoo (2001) asserts that, compared to children who identify with the majority group, children from nondominant groups are much more likely to possess awareness of both their own group identity or identities, as well as majority group characteristics. Thus, a now widely recognized developmental task associated with middle childhood is the acquisition of positive group identity or identities (Davies, 2004; Verkuyten, 2005). The terms *bicultural* or *multicultural competence* are widely used to refer to the skills children from nondominant groups must acquire in order to survive and thrive developmentally (Chestang, 1972; Lum, 2003a, 2003b; Norton, 1993).

Manuel speaks English as a second language and in some ways is representative of many school-age children. An estimated 47.0 million people age 5 and older in the United States, or approximately 18% of the population, speak a language other than English at home, a figure that is expected to increase steadily over time (Shin & Bruno, 2003). Multi and bilingual children in the United States have traditionally been thought to be at risk of developmental deficits. However, significant research evidence demonstrates that bilingualism may have a positive impact on cognitive development. Bilingual children often perform better than monolingual children on tests of analytical reasoning, concept formation, and cognitive flexibility (Hakuta, Ferdman, & Diaz, 1987). Moreover, bilingual children may be more likely to acquire capacities and skills that enhance their reading achievement (Campbell & Sais, 1995). With growing evidence of brain plasticity and the way that environmental demands change brain structures, researchers have begun to explore the relationship between bilingualism and the brain. They have found that learning a second language increases the density of grey matter in the left inferior parietal cortex. The earlier a second language is learned and the more proficient the person becomes, the more benefit to brain development (Mechelli et al., 2004). Despite such findings, however, too often bilingual children receive little support for their native language and culture in the school context.

Cultural Identity Development

For many European American children, ethnicity does not lead to comparison with others or exploration of identity (Rotheram-Borus, 1993). But for most children who are members of nondominant groups, ethnicity or race may be a central part of the quest for identity that begins in middle childhood and continues well into adolescence and young adulthood. By around age 7, cognitive advances allow children to view themselves and others as capable of belonging to more than one "category" at once, as capable of possessing two or more heritages simultaneously (Morrison & Bordere, 2001). As children mature, they may become more aware of not only dual or multiple aspects of identity but also of the discrimination and inequality to which they may be subjected. Such issues may in fact present overwhelming challenges for the school-age child belonging to a nondominant group. At a time when development of a sense of belonging is critical, these issues set some children apart from members of dominant groups and may increase the challenges they experience.

> How can cultural identity serve as a protective factor for children from nondominant groups?

Segregation based on ethnicity/race and social class is common in friendships at all ages, including middle childhood. Like adults, children are more likely to hold negative attitudes toward groups to which they do not belong. However, children, like adults, vary in the extent to which they hold ethnic and social class biases. Specific learning experiences appear to be influential in the development of childhood prejudice (Powlishta, Serbin, Doyle, & White, 1994). Verbalized prejudice declines during middle childhood as children learn to obey social norms against overt prejudice. However, children belonging to nondominant groups continue to face institutional discrimination and other significant challenges throughout this period of the life course (Bigler & Liben, 1993; Gutierrez, 2004; Harps, 2005).

A particular challenge for children like Manuel Vega may be blending contradictory values, standards, or traditions. Some children respond to cultural contradictions by identifying with the mainstream American culture (*assimilation*) in which they are immersed or by developing negative attitudes about their subcultural group memberships either consciously or subconsciously (*stereotype vulnerability*). Research evidence indicates that rejection of ethnic/race identity is particularly likely among members of nondominant groups lacking a supportive social movement that stresses group pride (Phinney, 1989). On the other hand, children whose experience in the mainstream culture challenges self-esteem and raises barriers to academic success may reject the dominant culture and define themselves in reaction against majority values (Matute-Bianchi, 1986). Other children begin to develop their own unique blend of group memberships and cultures. Individual reactions, like that of Manuel, will be shaped by the child's unique experiences and social influences. Blending the values of both dominant and nondominant groups in a manner that promotes self-esteem is possible but may be difficult and confusing for the school-age child (Bautista de Domanico, Crawford, & DeWolfe, 1994; Markstrom-Adams & Adams, 1995; Roebers & Schneider, 1999). It is a major developmental task to integrate dual or multiple identities into a consistent personal identity as well as a positive ethnic or racial identity (Gibbs & Huang, 1989).

Many models of identity development have been developed for children of mixed ethnicity, with new ideas and theories constantly emerging. It is clear that identity development for such children is diverse, extremely complex, and not well understood. As always, however, parents and professionals must start where the child is, with a focus on facilitating understanding and appreciation of heritage in order to promote development of an integrated identity and positive self-regard (Kopola, Esquivel, & Baptiste, 1994). Children should be provided with opportunities to explore their dual or multiple heritages and to select their own terms for identifying and describing themselves (Morrison & Bordere, 2001). Although studies have produced diverse findings, positive outcomes seem to be associated with supportive family systems and involvement in social and recreational activities that expose children to their heritage and lead to self-affirmation (Fuligni, 1997; Gibbs & Huang, 1989; Guarnaccia & Lopez, 1998; Herring, 1995).

Key tasks for adults, then, include educating children about family histories and supporting the creation of an integrated sense of self. Individuals and organizations within the child's social system can provide support by being sensitive to issues related to ethnic/racial origin and ethnic/racial distinctions; they can also help by celebrating cultural diversity and trying to increase the cultural sensitivity of all children. Such interventions appear to encourage fewer negative stereotypes of peers belonging to nondominant groups (Rotheram-Borus, 1993).

In general, it is critical to the positive identity development of all children, but particularly those from nondominant groups, that schools value diversity and offer a variety of experiences that focus on positive identity development (Morrison & Bordere, 2001). Ensuring that schools respect nondominant cultures and diverse learning styles is an important step. In order for schools to do this, all school staff must develop self-awareness. A variety of materials have been designed to facilitate this process among educators (see Lee,

Menkart & Okazawa-Rae, 1998; Matsumoto-Grah, 1992; Seefeldt, 1993) and other professionals (Fong, 2003; Lum, 2003b; Sue & McGoldrick, 2005).

The family environment of course plays a critical role in shaping all aspects of development, and the family is typically the vehicle through which cultural identity is transmitted. Children typically learn, through their families, how to view their ethnicity/race as well as that of others, as well as coping strategies to respond to potential or direct exclusion, discrimination, or racism (Barbarin, McCandies, Coleman, & Atkinson, 2004).

Emotional Development

> What are our societal expectations for emotional intelligence during middle childhood?

As most children move from early childhood into and through middle childhood, they experience significant gains in their ability to identify and articulate their own emotions as well as the emotions of others. Exhibit 5.3 summarizes several gains school-age children often make in the area of emotional functioning. It is important to recognize, however, that culture and other aspects of group identity may shape emotional development. For example, cultures vary in their acceptance of expressive displays of emotion.

Many children in this age range develop more advanced coping skills that help them when encountering upsetting, stressful, or traumatic situations. As defined by Daniel Goleman (1995), **emotional intelligence** refers to the ability to "motivate oneself and persist in the face of frustrations, to control impulse and delay gratification, to regulate one's moods and keep distress from swamping the ability to think, to empathize and to hope" (p. 34). To Goleman (2006), emotional and social intelligence are inextricably linked, and many other developmentalists agree. As a result, interventions used with children experiencing social difficulties often focus upon enhancing some aspect of emotional intelligence.

Goleman also asserts that social and emotional intelligence are key aspects of both moral reasoning and moral conduct. In other words, although often it may seem that advancing capacities in the moral domain occurs naturally for children, positive conditions and interactions must exist in a child's life in order for optimal emotional and social competencies to develop. Thus, a child like Anthony Bryant, with seemingly great academic

---

Exhibit 5.3	Common Emotional Gains During Middle Childhood

- Ability to mentally organize and articulate emotional experiences
- Cognitive control of emotional arousal
- Use of emotions as internal monitoring and guidance systems
- Ability to remain focused on goal directed actions
- Ability to delay gratification based on cognitive evaluation
- Ability to understand and use the concept of planning
- Ability to view tasks incrementally
- Use of social comparison
- Influence of internalized feelings (e.g., self-pride, shame) on behavior
- Capacity to tolerate conflicting feelings
- Increasingly effective defense mechanisms

SOURCE: Davies, 2004, pp. 369–372.

promise, may not realize his potential without timely intervention targeting the development of critical emotional competencies. These competencies include, for example, self-awareness, impulse control, and the ability to identify, express, and manage feelings, including love, jealousy, anxiety, and anger. Healthy emotional development can be threatened by a number of issues, including challenges such as significant loss and trauma. We increasingly recognize the vulnerability of school-age children to serious emotional and mental health issues. Assessment approaches that incorporate awareness of and attention to the possible existence of such issues are critical.

Fortunately, a substantial knowledge base regarding the promotion of positive emotional development exists. Many intervention strategies appear effective, particularly when they are preventive in nature and provided during or before middle childhood (see Hyson, 2004).

For example, Brianna Shaw, like too many children—particularly girls her age—is at risk of developing depression and could benefit from intervention focusing on the development of appropriate coping strategies. A number of interacting, complex biopsychosocial-spiritual factors shape vulnerability to ailments such as depression. Goleman (1995) argues that many cases of depression arise from deficits in two key areas of emotional competence: relationship skills and cognitive, or interpretive, style. In short, many children suffering from—or at risk of developing—depression likely possess a depression-promoting way of interpreting setbacks. Children with a potentially harmful outlook attribute setbacks in their lives to internal, personal flaws. Appropriate preventive intervention, based on a cognitive behavioral approach, teaches children that their emotions are linked to the way they think and facilitates productive, healthy ways of interpreting events and viewing themselves. For Brianna, such cognitive-behavioral oriented intervention may be helpful. Brianna also may benefit from a gender-specific intervention, perhaps with a particular focus upon relational resilience. Potter (2004) argues that gender-specific interventions are often most appropriate when the social problem is experienced primarily by one gender. She identifies eating disorders and depression as two examples of issues disproportionately impacting girls. Identifying the relevance of gender issues to Brianna's current emotional state and considering a gender-specific intervention strategy therefore may be appropriate. The concept of "relational resilience" is built upon relational-cultural theory's belief that "all psychological growth occurs in relationships;" the building blocks of relational resilience are "mutual empathy, empowerment, and the development of courage" (Jordan, 2005, p. 79).

Many school-age girls and boys also experience depression and other types of emotional distress due to a variety of factors, including **trauma** (severe physical or psychological injury) or significant loss. Children with close ties to extended family are particularly likely to experience loss of a close relative at a young age and therefore are more prone to this sort of depression. Loss, trauma, and violence may present serious obstacles to healthy emotional development. Research demonstrates the remarkable potential resilience of children (see Garmezy, 1994; Goldstein & Brooks, 2005; Kirby & Fraser, 2004; Luthar, 2003; Werner & Smith, 2001), but both personal and environmental attributes play a critical role in processes of resilience. To support the healthy emotional development of children at risk, appropriate multilevel prevention and intervention efforts are crucial.

Social Development

Perhaps the most widely recognized developmental task of this period is the acquisition of feelings of *self-competence*. Traditional developmentalists have pointed out that the school-age

How does a growing sense of competence promote the capacity for human agency in making choices?

child searches for opportunities to demonstrate personal skills, abilities, and achievements. This is what Erik Erikson (1963) was referring to when he described the developmental task of middle childhood as industry versus inferiority (refer back to Exhibit 3.6 for a description of all eight of Erikson's psychosocial stages). *Industry* refers to a drive to acquire new skills and do meaningful "work." The experiences of middle childhood may foster or thwart the child's attempts to acquire an enhanced sense of *mastery* and self-efficacy. Family, peer, and community support may enhance the child's growing sense of competence; lack of such support undermines this sense. The child's definitions of self and accomplishment vary greatly according to interpretations in the surrounding environment. But superficial, external bolstering of self-esteem is not all that children of this age group require. External appraisal must be supportive and encouraging but also accurate in order for children to value such feedback.

Some theorists argue that children of this age must learn the value of perseverance and develop an internal drive to succeed (Kindlon, 2003; Seligman, Reivich, Jaycox, & Gillham, 1995). Thus, opportunities to both fail and succeed must be provided, along with sincere feedback and support. Ideally, the developing school-age child acquires the sense of personal competence and tenacity that will serve as a protective factor during adolescence and young adulthood.

Families play a critical role in supporting development of this sense. For example, as the child learns to ride a bike or play a sport or musical instrument, adults can provide specific feedback and praise. They can counter the child's frustration by identifying and complimenting specific improvements and emphasizing the role of practice and perseverance in producing such improvements. Failures and setbacks can be labeled as temporary and surmountable rather than attributed to personal flaws or deficits. The presence of such feedback loops is a key feature of high-quality adult-child relationships, in the family, school, and beyond. Middle childhood is a critical time for children to acquire this sense of competence. In the process they gain an increasing awareness of their fit in the network of relationships in their surrounding environments. Each child experiences events and daily interactions that enhance or diminish feelings of self-competence. A systems perspective is critical to understanding the multiple influences on children's development during this period.

Children are not equally positioned as they enter this developmental phase, as Anthony Bryant's, Brianna Shaw's, and Manuel Vega's stories suggest. Developmental pathways preceding entry into middle childhood are extremely diverse. Children experience this phase of life differently based not only on differences in the surrounding environment—such as family structure and socioeconomic status—but also on their personality differences. A particular personality and learning style may be valued or devalued, problematic or nonproblematic, in each of the child's expanding social settings (Berk, 2002a, 2002b; Green, 1994). Thus, although Anthony, Brianna, and Manuel are moving through the same developmental period and facing many common tasks, they experience these tasks differently and will emerge into adolescence as unique individuals. Each individual child's identity development is highly dependent upon social networks of privilege and exclusion. There is a direct relationship between the level of control and power a child experiences and the degree of balance that is achieved in the child's emerging identity between feelings of power (privilege) and powerlessness (exclusion) (Johnson, 2005; Tatum, 1992). As children move toward adolescence and early adulthood, the amount of emotional, social, spiritual, and economic **capital**, or resources, acquired determines the likelihood of socioeconomic and other types of success as well as feelings of competence to succeed. Experiencing economically and socially just support systems is key to optimum development.

Middle childhood is a critical time in moral development, a time when most children become intensely interested in moral issues. Advancing language capability serves not only as a communication tool but also as a vehicle for more sophisticated introspection. Language is also a tool for positive assertion of self and personal opinions as the child's social world expands (Coles, 1987, 1997). In recent years, many elementary schools have added **character education** to their curricula. Such education often consists of direct teaching and curriculum inclusion of mainstream moral and social values thought to be universal in a community (e.g., kindness, respect, tolerance, and honesty). Renewed focus on children's character education is in part related to waves of school violence and bullying. Survey research with children suggests that, compared to children in middle and high school settings, children in elementary school settings are at highest risk of experiencing bullying, either as a perpetrator or victim (Astor, Benbenishty, Pitner, & Meyer, 2004).

At a broader level, federal and state legislative initiatives have encouraged school personnel to confront bullying and harassment in the school setting (Limber & Small, 2003). Schools have been particularly responsive to these initiatives in the wake of well-publicized incidents of school violence. Today, most schools have policies in place designed to facilitate efficient and effective responses to aberrant behavior, including bullying and violence. The content and implementation details of such policies, of course, vary widely.

There is plentiful evidence to suggest that "the bully" or "bullying" has existed throughout modern human history (Astor et al., 2004). During the late twentieth century, changes occurred within our views of and knowledge regarding bullying. In general, the public has become less tolerant of bullying, perhaps because of a fairly widespread belief that school shootings (such as the Columbine High School massacre) can be linked to bullying. Bullying is today recognized as a complex phenomenon, with both **direct bullying** (physical) and indirect bullying viewed as cause for concern (Astor et al., 2004). **Indirect bullying** is conceptualized as including verbal, psychological, and social or "relational" bullying tactics.

In recent years, new interest has centered on gender differences in bullying. Initially, attention was drawn to the previously underrecognized phenomenon of girls experiencing direct bullying, or physical aggression and violence, at the hands of other girls (Garbarino, 2006). Although both direct and indirect bullying crosses genders, more recent attention has centered on the widespread existence of indirect, or relational, bullying particularly among girls, and its potentially devastating consequences (Simmons, 2003; Underwood, 2003).

A positive outcome of recent attention to bullying is interest in establishing "best practices" in bullying prevention and intervention. Astor and colleagues (2004) argue that the United States is lagging behind other countries such as Norway, the United Kingdom, and Australia in implementing and evaluating comprehensive bullying prevention and intervention strategies; a benefit of our delayed status is our ability to learn from this international knowledge base. This knowledge base suggests that the most effective approaches to reducing bullying within a school is implementation of a comprehensive, school-wide prevention and intervention plan that addresses the contributing factors within all levels of the school environment (Espelage & Swearer, 2003; Plaford, 2006). In recent years, many school districts in the United States have implemented such initiatives and have experienced positive results (Beaudoin & Taylor, 2004).

As children increasingly view their lives as part of the network of lives within their environment, communities gain greater potential to provide important support and structure. Today, however, many communities provide as many challenges as opportunities for development. Communities in which challenges outweigh opportunities have been labeled as "socially toxic," meaning that they threaten positive development (Garbarino, 1995). In contrast, within a socially supportive environment, children have access to peers and adults who can lead them toward more advanced moral and social thinking. This development occurs in part through the modeling of *pro-social behavior,* which injects moral reasoning and social sensitivity into the child's accustomed manner of reasoning and behaving. Thus, cognitive and moral development is a social issue. The failure of adults to take on moral and spiritual mentoring roles contributes significantly to the development of socially toxic environments.

This type of moral mentoring takes place in the **zone of proximal development**—the theoretical space between the child's current developmental level and the child's potential level if given access to appropriate models and developmental experiences in the social environment (Vygotsky, 1986). Thus, the child's competence alone interacts dynamically with the child's competence in the company of others. The result is developmental progress. This continuous process of social interaction and shaping is consistent with systems theory or with a biological model of equilibration, where organisms develop as they respond to environmental stimuli in a constant process of equilibrium, disruption, and re-equilibration.

The Peer Group

Nearly as influential as family members during middle childhood are *peer groups*—collections of children with unique values and goals (Hartup, 1983). As children progress through middle childhood, peers have an increasingly important impact on such everyday matters as social behavior, activities, and dress. By this phase of development, a desire for group belongingness is especially strong. Within peer groups, children potentially learn three important lessons. First, they learn to appreciate different points of view. Second, they learn to recognize the norms and demands of their peer group. And, third, they learn to have closeness to a same-sex peer (Newman & Newman, 2006). Whereas individual friendships facilitate the development of critical capacities such as trust and intimacy, peer groups foster learning about cooperation and leadership.

> What role do peer groups play in developing the capacity for meaningful relationships in middle childhood?

Throughout middle childhood, the importance of *group norms* is highly evident (von Salisch, 2001). Children are sensitive, sometimes exceedingly so, to their peers' standards for behavior, appearance, and attitudes. Brianna Shaw, for instance, is beginning to devalue herself because she recognizes the discrepancy between her appearance and group norms. Often it is not until adolescence that group norms may become more flexible, allowing for more individuality. This shift reflects the complex relationship among the developmental domains. In this case, the association between social and cognitive development is illustrated by simultaneous changes in social relationships and cognitive capacities.

In most middle childhood peer groups, *dominance hierarchies* establish a social order among group participants. Those hierarchies may predict outcomes when conflict arises (Pettit, Bakshi, Dodge, & Coie, 1990; Savin-Williams, 1979); typically, more dominant children prevail. Furthermore, through reinforcement, modeling, and direct pressure to conform to expectations, children's dominance hierarchies contribute to socialization.

Again, through middle childhood, gains in cognitive abilities promote more complex communication skills and greater social awareness. These developments, in turn, facilitate more complex peer interaction, which is a vital resource for the development of **social competence**—the ability to engage in sustained, positive, and mutually satisfactory peer interactions. Positive peer relationships reflect and support social competence, as they potentially discourage egocentrism, promote positive coping, and ultimately serve as a protective factor during the transition to adolescence (Spencer, Harpalani, Fegley, Dell'Angelo, & Seaton, 2003).

Gender and culture influence the quantity and nature of peer interactions observed among school-age children (Potter, 2004). Sociability, intimacy, social expectations and rules, and the value placed on various types of play and other social activities are all phenomena shaped by both gender and culture. The relationship between gender and peer relationships has been studied fairly extensively, however, the specific ways in which culture influences the nuances of children's peer relationships remain unclear because the state of research in this area is significantly underdeveloped (Robinson, 1998).

Spencer et al. (2003) point out that children from nondominant groups are more likely to experience dissonance across school, family, and peer settings; for example, such children may experience language differences, misunderstandings of cultural traditions or expressions, and distinct norms, or rules, regarding dating behavior, peer intimacy, or cross-gender friendships. These authors also assert that although many youth experiencing dissonance across school, family, and peer systems may suffer from negative outcomes such as peer rejection or school failure, some may learn important coping skills that will serve them well later in life. In fact, the authors argue that given the clear trend toward increasing cultural diversity around the globe, "experiences of cultural dissonance and the coping skills they allow youth to develop should not be viewed as aberrant; instead, privilege should be explored as having a 'downside' that potentially compromises the development of coping and character" (p. 137).

A persistent finding is that, across gender and culture, peer acceptance is a powerful predictor of psychological adjustment. One well-known study asked children to fit other children into particular categories. From the results, the researchers developed five general categories of social acceptance: popular, rejected, controversial, neglected, and average (Coie, Dodge, & Coppotelli, 1982). Common predictors of popular status include physical appearance (Adams & Crane, 1980) and pro-social behaviors in the social setting (Newcomb, Bukowski, & Pattee, 1993; Rotenberg et al., 2004). Rejected children are those who are actively disliked by their peers. They are particularly likely to be unhappy and to experience achievement and self-esteem issues. Rejected status is strongly associated with poor school performance, antisocial behavior, and delinquency in adolescence (DeRosier, Kupersmidt, & Patterson, 1994; Ollendick, Weist, Borden, & Greene, 1992). For this reason, we should be concerned about Brianna Shaw's growing sense of peer rejection.

Support for rejected children may include interventions to improve peer relations and psychological adjustment. Most of these interventions are based on social learning theory and involve modeling and reinforcing positive social behavior—for example, initiating interaction and responding to others positively. Several such programs have indeed helped children develop social competence and gain peer approval (Lochman, Coie, Underwood, & Terry, 1993; Mize & Ladd, 1990; Wyman, Cross, & Barry, 2004; Young, Marchant, & Wilder, 2004).

Friendship and Intimacy

Throughout middle childhood, children develop their ability to look at things from others' perspectives. In turn, their capacity to develop more complex friendships—based on awareness of others' thoughts, feelings, and needs—emerges (Selman, 1976; von Salisch, 2001). Thus, complex and fairly stable friendship networks begin to form for the first time in middle childhood (Hartup, 1983). Although skills such as cooperation and problem solving are learned in the peer group, close friendships facilitate understanding and promote trust and reciprocity. Most socially competent children maintain and nurture both close friendships and effective peer group interaction.

As children move through middle childhood, friendship begins to entail mutual trust and assistance and thus becomes more psychologically rather than behaviorally based (Asher & Paquette, 2003; Damon, 1977). In other words, school-age children may possess close friendships based on the emotional support provided for one another as much as, if not more than, common interests and activities. The concept of friend is transformed from the playmate of early childhood to the confidant of middle childhood. Violations of trust during this period are often perceived as serious violations of the friendship bond. As children move out of middle childhood and into adolescence, the role of intimacy and loyalty in friendship becomes even more pronounced. Moreover, children increasingly value mutual understanding and loyalty in the face of conflict among peers (Berndt, 1988).

Team Play

The overall incidence of aggression during peer activities decreases during middle childhood, and friendly rule-based play increases. This transition is due in part to the continuing development of a **perspective-taking** ability, the ability to see a situation from another person's point of view. In addition, most school-age children are exposed to peers who differ in a variety of ways, including personality, ethnicity, and interests.

School-age children are able to take their new understanding of others' needs and desires into account in various types of peer interaction. Thus, their communication and interaction reflects an enhanced ability to understand the role of multiple participants in activities. These developments facilitate the transition to many rule-based activities, such as team sports (Rubin, Fein, & Vandenburg, 1983). Despite occasional arguments or fights with peers, involvement with team sports may provide great enjoyment and satisfaction. Participation in team sports during middle childhood may also have long-term benefits. One research team found a link between voluntary participation in team sports during middle childhood and level of physical activity in adulthood (Taylor, Blair, Cummings, Wun, & Malina, 1999). While participating in team sports, children also develop the capacity for interdependence, cooperation, division of labor, and competition (Van der Vegt, Eman, & Van De Vliert, 2001).

Gender Identity and Gender Roles

Although most children in middle childhood have a great deal in common based upon their shared developmental phase, girls and boys differ significantly in areas ranging from their self-understanding and social relationships to school performance and life aspirations (Potter, 2004). Among most school-age children, gender identity, or an "internalized psychological experience of being male or female," is quite well-established (Diamond & Savin-Williams, 2003, p. 105). But during middle childhood, boys and girls seem to follow different paths in gender role development. Often, boys' identification with "masculine" role attributes increases while girls' identification with "feminine" role attributes decreases (Archer, 1992; Levy, Taylor, & Gelman, 1995; Potter, 2004). For instance, boys are more likely than girls to label a chore as a "girl's job" or a "boy's job." As adults, females are the more androgynous of the two genders, and this movement toward androgyny appears to begin in middle childhood (Diamond & Savin-Williams, 2003; Serbin, Powlishta, & Gulko, 1993).

These differences have multiple causes, from social to cognitive forces. In the United States, during middle childhood and beyond, cross-gender behavior in girls is more socially acceptable than such behavior among boys. Diamond and Savin-Williams use the term "gender typicality," or the "degree to which one's appearance, behavior, interests, and subjective self-concept conform to conventional gender norms" (p. 105). Research to date suggests that for both genders, a traditionally "masculine" identity is associated with a higher sense of overall competence and better academic performance (Boldizar, 1991; Newcomb & Dubas, 1992). Diamond and Savin-Williams also emphasize the role of culture in this relationship, pointing out that this is likely due to the fact that traits associated with male, or for girls, "tomboy" status are those traits most valued in many communities. These traits include qualities such as athleticism, confidence, and assertiveness. Indeed, local communities with "more entrenched sexist ideologies" regarding male versus female traits are those in which boys exhibiting feminine or "sissy" behaviors are likely to suffer (p. 107).

A related issue is a disturbing trend noted among girls transitioning from middle childhood to adolescence. Specifically, in recent years, women's studies' experts have pointed out that school-age girls often seem to possess a "vibrant, feisty, and confident understanding of self" which gradually disintegrates as they increasingly "discredit their feelings and understandings, experiencing increased self-doubt" during early adolescence and subsequently becoming susceptible to a host of internalizing and externalizing disorders linked to poor self-esteem (Potter, 2004, p. 60). A number of studies and theories attempt to explain this shift in girls' self-image and mental health (see Pipher, 1994; Simmons, 2003), but Potter (2004) cautions against overgeneralization of the phenomena and in particular suggests that the trend may not apply widely across girls from differing ethnic groups, socioeconomic statuses, and sexual orientations.

Our understanding of the structure of gender roles is derived from various theoretical perspectives. An anthropological or social constructionist orientation illuminates the ways in which, throughout history, gender has shaped familial and societal systems and inevitably impacts individual development in an intangible yet profound fashion (Wertsch, del Rio & Alvarez, 1995). Cognitive theory suggests that at the individual level, self-perceptions emerge. Gender, as one component of self-perception, joins related *cognitions* to guide children's gender-linked behaviors. A behavioral perspective suggests that gender-related *behaviors* precede self-perception in the development of gender role identity; in other words, at a very young age, girls start imitating feminine behavior and *later* begin thinking of themselves as distinctly female, and boys go through the same sequence in developing a masculine identity. Gender schema theory (see Bem, 1993, 1998), an information-processing approach to gender, combines behavioral and cognitive theories, suggesting that social pressures and children's cognition work together to perpetuate gender-linked perceptions and behaviors.

Feminist psychodynamic theorists such as Nancy Chodorow (1978, 1989) have proposed that while boys typically begin to separate psychologically from their female caregivers in early childhood, most girls deepen their connection to and identification with their female caregivers throughout childhood. Such theorists propose, then, that as girls and boys transition into adolescence and face a new level of individuation, they confront this challenge from very different psychological places and girls are more likely to find the task emotionally confusing if not deeply overwhelming. This feminist, psychoanalytic theoretical orientation has been used to explain not only gender identity and role development, but also differences between boys and girls in their approaches to relationships, or relational orientations, and emotional expressiveness throughout childhood.

In general, due to expanding cognitive capacities, as children leave early childhood and progress through middle childhood, their gender stereotypes gradually become more flexible and most school-age children begin to accept that males and females can engage in the same activities and occupations (Carter & Patterson, 1982; Sagara, 2000). In addition, school-age children increasingly rely on unique characteristics, rather than a gender label, in attempting to predict the nature and behavior of a specific individual (Biernat, 1991; Potter 2004).

African American children may hold less stereotyped views of females than do European American children (Bardwell, Cochran, & Walker, 1986). In addition, children from middle and upper-income backgrounds appear to hold more flexible views of gender than children from lower-income backgrounds (Serbin et al., 1993).

The implications of gender stereotyping for individual gender role adoption are not clear cut. Even children well aware of community gender norms and role expectations may not conform to gender role stereotypes in their actual behavior (Diamond & Savin-Williams, 2003; Downs & Langlois, 1988; Serbin et al., 1993). Perhaps children acquire personal gender role preferences before acquiring knowledge of gender role stereotypes or perhaps they learn and interpret gender role stereotypes in very diverse ways. Our understanding of the complexities of gender and sexual identity development—and the relationships between the two during the life course—is in its infancy.

◪ Middle Childhood and Formal Schooling

Before discussing the role of formal schooling in the life of the school-age child in the United States and other relatively affluent societies, it is important to note that, in an era of a knowledge-based global economy, there continue to be large global gaps in opportunities for education. Although educational participation is almost universal between the age of 5 and 14 in affluent countries, 115 million of the world's children, most residing in Africa or South Asia, do not receive even a primary education (United National Development Program, 2005). There is a widening gap in average years of education between rich and poor countries (McMichael, 2004). The average child born in Mozambique in 2005 will receive four years of formal education, compared to eight years in South Asia, and 15 years in France (United Nations Development Program, 2005). Females will receive one year less of education, on average, than males in African and Arab countries and two years less in South Asia (United Nations Development Program, 2005), but females receive higher levels of education than males, on average, in most affluent industrialized countries (Sen, Partelow, & Miller, 2005).

Although development is framed by multiple human interactions at home and in the community, the current importance of formal schooling during middle childhood in advanced industrial countries cannot be overstated. Children entering school must learn to navigate a new environment quite different from the family. In school, they are evaluated on the basis of how well they perform tasks; people outside the family—teachers and other

▲ **Photo 5.3**   As children get older, schools are the primary context for development in middle childhood.

school staff as well as peers—begin shaping the child's personality, dreams, and aspirations (Good & Nichols, 2001). At the same time, the school environment may serve as an important resource for the physical, cognitive, emotional, and social tasks of middle childhood.

Success in the school environment is very important to the development of self-esteem. Anthony Bryant, Brianna Shaw, and Manuel Vega illustrate the potentially positive as well as painful aspects of schooling. Manuel and Brianna seem increasingly distressed by their interactions within the school environment. Often, difficulties with peers create or compound academic challenges. Brianna's school experience is becoming threatening enough that she may begin to withdraw from the environment, which would represent a serious risk to her continued cognitive, emotional, and social development.

As children move through the middle years, they become increasingly aware that they are evaluated on the basis of what they are able to do. In turn, they begin to evaluate themselves based on treatment by teachers and peers and on self-assessments of what they can and cannot do well (Barr & Parrett, 1995; Harter, 1988; Skaalvik & Skaalvik, 2004). School-age children consistently rate parents, classmates, other friends, and teachers as the most important influences in their lives (Harter, 1988). Thus, children are likely to evaluate themselves in a positive manner if they receive encouraging feedback from these individuals in their academic and social environments.

Formal Schooling and Cognitive Development

In the past few decades, school-age children have benefited from new research and theory focusing on the concept of intelligence. Traditional views of intelligence and approaches to intelligence testing benefited European American children born in the United States. Howard Gardner's work, however, represented a paradigm shift in the field of education. He proposed that intelligence is neither unitary nor fixed, and argued that intelligence is not adequately or fully measured by IQ tests. More broadly, in his theory of **multiple intelligences**, intelligence is "the ability to solve problems or fashion products that are of consequence in a particular cultural setting or community" (Gardner, 1993, p. 15). Challenging the idea that individuals can be described, or categorized, by a single, quantifiable measure of intelligence, Gardner proposed that at least eight critical intelligences exist: verbal/linguistic, logical/mathematical, visual/spatial, musical/rhythmic, bodily/kinesthetic, naturalist, interpersonal, and intrapersonal. This paradigm shift in the education field encouraged a culturally sensitive approach to students (Campbell, Campbell, & Dickinson, 1999) and a diminished role for standardized testing.

In its practical application, multiple intelligence theory calls for use of a wide range of instructional strategies that engage the range of strengths and intelligences of each student (Kagan & Kagan, 1998). Gardner specifically calls for matching instructional strategies to the needs and strengths of students, stretching the intelligences—or maximizing development of each intelligence—by transforming education curricula, and celebrating or (at a minimum) understanding the unique pattern of intelligences of each student.

> How might this increased emphasis on cognitive diversity alter the life course of students like Anthony, Brianna, and Manuel?

This last point is critical. Such understanding can facilitate self-knowledge and self-acceptance. Understanding and celebration of cognitive diversity, Gardner believes, will come from a transformation not only of curricula, or instructional methods, but also of the fundamental way in which adults view students and students view themselves and one another. Schools help children develop a positive self-evaluation by providing a variety of activities that allow children with different strengths to succeed. For example, schools that assess children in many areas, including those described by Gardner, may help children who have a deficit in one area experience success in another realm. Children can also be encouraged to evaluate themselves positively through the creation of individual student portfolios and through school initiatives that promote new skill development. Classroom and extracurricular activities can build on children's abilities and help them develop or maintain self-confidence (Barr & Parrett, 1995).

For example, most children benefit from diverse educational materials and varied activities that appeal to visual, auditory, and experiential learning styles. Such activities can include group work, student presentations, field trips, audiovisual presentations, written and oral skill activities, discussion, and lectures (Roueche & Baker, 1986). In recent years, *flexible grouping* is frequently employed. It draws on both heterogeneous and homogenous grouping and recognizes that each method is useful to achieve distinct objectives. Grouping strategies include pairing students, forming cooperative and collaborative groups, modeling lessons for students, conducting guided practice, and setting up subject-based learning laboratories. A teacher may draw on any appropriate technique during a class period, day, or week. These approaches represent an attempt to adapt instruction to meet diverse student needs. Students like Anthony Bryant, with more academic skill, may model effective methods of mastering academic material for less advanced students. Meanwhile, Anthony simultaneously learns more appropriate school behavior from his socially adept peers. Furthermore, this teaching method may help Anthony strengthen peer friendships—an important potential source of support as he confronts family transitions or conflict in the future.

On the other hand, schools can contribute to the development of a negative self-evaluation by emphasizing *norm-referenced testing*, judging students against other people taking the test, and providing little opportunity for skill development. Thus, in addition to calling for changes in instructional strategies, multiple intelligence theory calls for movement away from norm-referenced testing and toward more comprehensive assessments of diverse areas of student performance. Such assessment includes naturalistic, across-time observation and development of self-appraisal materials such as student portfolios (Lazear, 1994). This shift, however, has occurred in tandem with the standards movement within the

United States. Most schools and states have moved away from norm-referenced testing and toward *criterion-referenced testing,* which requires all graduating students to meet certain absolute scores and requirements. At present, all states have established some form of learning standards that all students must achieve in order to graduate from high school.

Formal Schooling and Diversity

Students like Manuel Vega face considerable challenges in the school setting. Manuel's ability to engage in the school environment is compromised, and many schools are ill equipped to respond to the issues confronting children like him. If Manuel is not supported and assisted by his school system, his educational experience may assault his healthy development. But if Manuel's personal and familial support systems can be tapped and mobilized, they may help him overcome his feelings of isolation in his new school environment. Carefully constructed and implemented interventions must be used to help Manuel. These interventions could include a focus on bridging the gap between his command of the rules of the informal register of English and the acquisition of formal standard English, without destroying his Spanish language base and his Mexican cultural heritage.

Today in the United States, Manuel's situation is not rare. About one in five elementary and high school students have at least one foreign-born parent (U.S. Census Bureau, 2001a) and in general, students are more diverse than ever before. There are many challenges facing children who have recently arrived in the United States, particularly those fleeing war-torn countries. Research suggests that immigrant and refugee children are at heightened risk of experiencing mental health challenges and school failure (Escobar, Hoyos-Nervi, & Gara, 2000; Fuligni, 1997; Guarnaccia & Lopez, 1998; Miller & Rasco, 2004; Pernice & Brook, 1996). Language difficulties and their consequences among such children are increasingly recognized. It has been established that children are best served when they are able to speak both their native language and the language of their host country (Vuorenkoski, Kuure, Moilanen, Penninkilampi, & Myhrman, 2000). The mental health status among immigrant populations, however, appears to be dependent on a wide number of factors.

In general, **acculturation**, or a process by which two or more cultures remain distinct but exchange cultural features (such as foods, music, clothing), is easier on children than **assimilation**, or a process by which the minority culture must adapt and become incorporated into the majority culture, particularly in the school environment. Communication and interaction between families and schools is always important (Bhattacharya, 2000; U.S. Department of Health & Human Services, 2000).

It is essential for schools and professionals to recognize the importance of language. Ruby Payne (2005) describes the many complex ways in which poverty in particular affects relationships between schools and children. She notes, for example, that virtually all children from nondominant groups, including lower-income Caucasian children, possess an informal **language register** that contains the communication rules needed to survive in the familial and cultural group to which the child belongs. Schools often ignore the potency of these informal registers as they work toward their mission of teaching the "formal register" of the dominant middle class, deemed necessary to survive in the world of work and school. The need for specific strategies to acknowledge and honor the "informal register," while teaching the formal, has been identified by several literacy researchers (see Gee, 1996; Knapp, 1995). These researchers emphasize the importance of teaching children to recognize their internal, or natural, "speech" and the "register" they use in the school environment. Identifying and mediating these processes is best accomplished in the context of a caring relationship (Noddings, 1984). By sensitively promoting an awareness of such differences in the home and school, teachers, social workers, and other adults can help children experience less confusion and alienation.

Formal Schooling: Home and School

Indeed, for all children, parental involvement in school is associated with better school performance (Domina, 2005). Schools serving diverse populations are becoming increasingly creative in their approaches to encouraging parent involvement, including the development of sophisticated interpretation and translation infrastructures (Pardington, 2002). Unfortunately, many schools lag behind, suffering from either inadequate resources or the consequences of exclusive and racist attitudes within the school and larger community environments (see Jones, 2001).

The link between school and home is important in poor and affluent neighborhoods alike, because school and home are the two major spheres in which children exist. The more similar these two environments are, the more successful the child will be at school and at home. Students who experience vastly different cultures at home and at school are likely to have difficulty accommodating the two worlds (Ryan & Adams, 1995). A great deal of learning goes on before a child enters school. By the time Anthony Bryant, Brianna Shaw, and Manuel Vega began school, they had acquired routines, habits, and cognitive, social, emotional, and physical styles and skills (Kellaghan, Sloane, Alvarez, & Bloom, 1993). School is a "next step" in the educational process.

The transition is relatively easy for many students because schools typically present a mainstream model for behavior and learning. As most parents interact with their children, they model and promote the behavior that will be acceptable in school. Children are taught the necessities of widely accepted social interactions, such as saying "thank you," "excuse me," and "please" (Comer, 1994; Payne, 2005). Many parents also teach their children the basic rules of the classroom, such as "sit in your chair" and "wait to speak until you are acknowledged." Children from such backgrounds are often well prepared for the school environment because, quite simply, they understand the rules; as a result, the school is accepting of them. Furthermore, the school environment helps reinforce rules and skills taught in the home environment, just as the home environment helps reinforce rules and skills taught in the school environment. Research indicates that this type of home-school continuity often predicts school success (Ameta & Sherrard, 1995; Comer, 1994; Epstein & Lee, 1995; Kellaghan et al., 1993; Ryan & Adams, 1995).

In contrast, children with a distinct background may not be fluent in mainstream speech patterns and may not have been extensively exposed to school rules or materials such as scissors and books. These children, although possessing skills and curiosity, are often viewed as inferior in some way by school personnel (Comer, 1994). Children viewed in this manner may begin to feel inferior and either act out or disengage from the school process (Finn, 1989). Because the school environment does not support the home environment and the home environment does not support the school environment, these children face an increased risk of poor school outcomes.

Schools that recognize the contribution of home to school success typically seek family involvement. Parents and other family members can help establish the motivation for learning and provide learning opportunities within the home environment (Constable & Walberg, 1996; Jones, 2001). Children whose parents are involved in their education typically succeed academically (Fan, 2001; Fan & Chen, 2001; Kurtz, 1988; Kurtz & Barth, 1989; Zellman & Waterman, 1998). Unfortunately, poor communication between parents, children, and schools may short-circuit parental involvement. Traditionally, schools asked parents only to participate in Parent Teacher Association meetings, to attend parent-teacher meetings, to act as helpers in the classroom, and to review notes and written communications sent home with the schoolchild. This sort of parental participation does not always facilitate meaningful, open communication. Schools can establish more meaningful relationships with parents by reaching out to them, involving them as partners in decision making and school governance, treating parents and other caregivers (and their children) with authentic respect, providing support and coordination to implement and sustain parental involvement, and connecting parents with resources (see Comer, 1980; Dupper & Poertner, 1997; Kellaghan et al., 1993; Patrikakou, Weisberg, Redding, & Walberg, 2005; Swap, 1993).

Formal Schooling: Schools Mirror Community

How do racism, classism, and sexism affect middle childhood development?

As microcosms of the larger U.S. society, schools mirror its institutional structures. Thus, schools often uphold racism, classism, and sexism (Bowles & Gintis, 1976; Harry, 2006; Keating, 1994; Ogbu, 1994). As discussed, cognitive development can be impacted by cultural factors specific to second language usage and gender socialization as well as racial and class identities. Students belonging to nondominant groups have often been viewed as inherently less capable and thus failed to receive the cognitive stimulation needed for optimal growth and development. This problem has led to lowered expectations, segregation, and institutionalized mistreatment throughout the history of schooling. At the federal and state levels, from the mid-1960s through 1980, specific legislation was developed to attempt to rectify the effects of the unequal treatment of a variety of groups.

In most parts of the country, however, members of historically mistreated groups (e.g. children with mental and physical challenges, children belonging to ethnic and racial minority groups) did not receive equal treatment, and they were forced to attend segregated and inferior schools throughout most of the twentieth century. Over time, various court rulings, most prominently the 1954 *Brown v. Board of Education* decision (347 U.S. 483), made equal, integrated education the right of all U.S. citizens, ruling that "separate but equal" has no place in public education. However, in the past 15 years, courts at both the state and federal levels have been lifting desegregation orders, arguing that separate can be equal or at least "good enough." As a result, today the school systems in the United States are more segregated by race than they were thirty years ago (Kozol, 2005). These court rulings as well as housing patterns and social traditions work against integrated public schooling. Schools continue to mirror the social systems with which they interact and thus often fall short of their democratic ideals. Informal segregation often persists in schools, and poor children still suffer in schools that frequently do not provide enough books, supplies, teachers, or curricula challenging enough to facilitate success in U.S. society (Kozol, 1991, 2005). The juxtaposition of inner-city and suburban schools continues to point to substantial divisions between economically rich and impoverished communities.

During all phases of childhood, children benefit from equal treatment and attention and suffer when **institutional discrimination**—the systemic denial of access to assets, economic opportunities, associations, and organizations based on minority status—is in place. Indeed even when African American and poor children, and children from predominantly Spanish speaking populations, were integrated into public school systems in the twentieth century, the process of *tracking* students assured that the vast majority of students of color and low socioeconomic status were relegated to less rigorous course sequences (Oakes, 1985; Owens, 1985). In addition, such division of students has often been based on standardized tests, which research suggests may be culturally and class biased. Students have also been divided based on school personnel reports. Such reports are often subjective and may inadvertently be based on assessments of students' dress, language, and behavior (Oakes, 1985; Oakes & Lipton, 1992). Throughout the history of public schooling, most teachers and other school staff have belonged to dominant groups, and consciously or unconsciously, they may have awarded privilege and preference to learning styles, language, and dress that they found familiar.

In short, post desegregation, tracking has traditionally served as a two-tiered system of ongoing educational inequality. Although it is necessary to understand the complexities of tracking, including both advantages and disadvantages (see Loveless, 1999; Wang, Walberg, & Reynolds, 2004), it is equally important to recognize that special education, noncollege-bound, and nonaccelerated classes have been disproportionately populated by historically excluded students. These classes too often prepared students to work only in low-skilled, low-paying jobs. Conversely, regular education, college-bound, and accelerated classes have been disproportionately white and middle or upper class. These classes typically prepare their members for college and leadership roles. Thus, the traditional structure of public education often both reflected and supported ethnic and class divisions within U.S. society (Kozol, 2005; Oakes, 1985; Oakes & Lipton, 1992; Winters, 1993).

For an example of the dangers of tracking, consider Anthony Bryant. His behavior puts him at risk for eventual placement in specialized classes for emotionally disturbed children, even though his behavior may be a normal part of his developmental process (Hosp & Reschly, 2003). Currently, his fairly infrequent aggressive behavior seems to be dealt with by school personnel appropriately, which may prevent an escalation of the problem. Intervention with Anthony's family members may also facilitate a consistent, positive family response to Anthony's behavior. However, the professionals making decisions at Anthony's school and in his community could begin to interpret his behavior as serious and threatening.

> What impact have these historical trends in public education had on middle childhood development?

Thus, Anthony faces an increased risk of placement outside the "regular" track. What could follow, through a series of steps intended by the school system to provide special programming for Anthony, is his miseducation based on a set of faulty cultural lenses that diagnose his needs and prescribe deficient remedies. The potential miseducation of Anthony is compounded by social patterns that have persisted for years and work against the success of African American males and immigrant youth in particular.

Many school systems have now recognized their historically unequal treatment of students and taken steps to reduce discrimination. One approach is *mainstreaming,* or *inclusion,* the practice of placing all children who could be assigned to special education classrooms into regular education classrooms (Sleeter, 1995). An increasingly common and innovative approach in the disability arena is the *collaborative classroom.* Children with and without disabilities are team-taught by both a "regular" and a "special" education teacher. Heterogeneous grouping helps prevent students of different races, socioeconomic classes, and genders from being separated and treated unequally. Different approaches to teaching academic content are used in hopes of accommodating a variety of learning styles and social backgrounds. Teachers, students, and other school personnel receive training on diversity. And sexual harassment policies have slowly been implemented and enforced in public schools. The policies are enforced by the requirement that all schools receiving federal funds designate a Title IX hearing officer to inquire about and, if warranted, respond to all allegations of harassment in its many forms.

Schools have also begun to include, in their curricula, content that reflects the diversity of their students. As the topic of diversity has become prominent in academic and popular discourse, educational materials are increasingly likely to include the perspectives of traditionally nondominant groups. As a result, more literature and history lessons represent females and minorities who have contributed to U.S. life.

In the last decade, clear and consistent educational research in the fields of literacy education and educational theory has also begun to detail effective instructional strategies and methodological approaches. Implementation of such research findings has disrupted the "stand and deliver," or lecture format, as the dominant approach to teaching and knowledge acquisition.

Schools located in areas with high rates of poverty have also been targeted for extra attention. *Full-service schools* attempt to provide school-based or school-linked health and social services for school children and their families (Dryfoos, 1994). Similarly, school-based family resource centers attempt to provide children, families, and communities with needed supports (Adler, 1993). Such provision of holistic family services illustrates public education's continuing effort to meet the ideal of equal and comprehensive education, allowing all U.S. children equal opportunity to achieve economic and social success.

A recent development of importance is that the U.S. Department of Education has launched a major initiative to close the achievement gap of historically excluded populations with the passage by Congress of the No Child Left Behind Education Act of 2001 (NCLB) as an extension of the Elementary and Secondary Education Act. Increasingly, schools have been refocused on English Language Arts and math skill development training by the national standards movement and advanced by the requirements of NCLB and its accountability arm, but to the potential detriment of educating the whole child (Guisbond & Neill, 2004).

The NCLB has shifted federal focus to school and teacher accountability for higher achievement, which is monitored by annual "high stakes" tests (grades 3 to 8 in reading and math to start, with the addition of science and other subjects subsequently). All children must take such standardized assessments and schools are required to disaggregate their results for each of five subpopulations including gender and students with disabilities, limited English proficiency, low socioeconomic status, as well as students who are black, Hispanic, American Indian/Alaskan Native, Asian/Pacific Islander, or white. Under the provisions of the law, school districts must meet annual yearly progress (AYP) goals for both aggregated and disaggregated data sets. Districts failing to meet such goals face consequences ranging from providing extra funding for parents to acquire support services to having a school closed down for consistently missing AYP targets. An additional contemporary change is that the federal government is emphasizing the concept of "scientifically-based educational research" as a base for educational decisions. As a result, educational research has been given higher status to influence educational policy than it has received in the past.

This push for educational accountability and its impact on the lives of children is complex and highly controversial. The application of the NCLB Act standards has spurred a number of organizations and states (e.g., the National Educational Association, Michigan, Connecticut, and Utah) to either sue the federal government or sharply criticize the act for raising state achievement requirements without adequate supporting funds or as a violation of states' rights. For children, this controversy is a moot point since the U.S. Department of Education currently shows few signs of altering expectations. The resulting adjustments to teaching methodology in order to prepare students for the annual assessments continue unabated.

However, a number of schools have adopted innovative practices designed to raise achievement of basic skills while attempting to meet the educational needs of all students. And yet only ten reform programs received the highest grade (defined as moderate or limited success) by the Comprehensive School Reform Quality Center and American Institutes for Research (2006) in their federally funded three year study of school reform programs. Two initiatives examined within this study serve as prime examples of the variety of philosophies that drive such schools. The Knowledge Is Power Program (KIPP) follows a prescription that demands that its students strictly adhere to a regimen of social behavior development coupled with long hours dedicated to mastering content-based curricula (Carter, 2000). On the other hand, Expeditionary Learning Schools (a consortium of 140 schools) immerse their students in problem-based learning that is linked to authentic experiences often consummated outside the walls of the school (Cousins, 2000; Levy, 2000). As this report suggests, most schools are struggling to balance a number of competing demands while meeting the standards of the NCLB Act. Evidence regarding the effectiveness of the NCLB Act will be examined during congressional hearings in 2007, when the act is considered for reauthorization.

▧ Special Challenges in Middle Childhood

In the last several decades in the United States, family structures have become more diverse than ever (Amato, 2003; Fields, 2004; Parke, 2003). The percentage of children living with both parents has steadily declined during the last four to five decades. According to the U.S. Census Bureau data, in 2002, 69% of children resided with two parents, 23% lived with only their mother, and 5% lived with only their father. About 4% of children do not live with either parent, and about one-half of these children have at least one grandparent in their household (Fields, 2003).

Dual-income families are now commonplace. Economic trends have forced more and more parents of young children into the workforce in order to make ends meet. Legislation requires single parents who receive public assistance to remain engaged in or re-enter the workforce. The school day often does not coincide with parents' work schedules, and recent research suggests that due to parental employment, more than half of school-age children regularly need additional forms of supervision when school is not in session. Most of these children either participate in a before or afterschool program or receive care from another relative (Lerner, Castellino, Lolli, & Wan, 2003). Many low- and middle-income families struggle to find affordable child care and often are forced to sacrifice quality child care for economic reasons (McWhirter et al., 1993; National Association of Child Care Resource and Referral Agencies, 2006; Wertheimer, 2003).

Unfortunately, available data suggest that the quality of child care experienced by the average child in the United States is less than ideal (Helburn & Bergmann, 2002; Vandell & Wolfe,

2000). This fact is particularly troubling because child care quality has been linked to children's physical health as well as cognitive, emotional, and social development (Burchinal, 1999; Hayes, Palmer, & Zaslow, 1990; Tout & Zaslow, 2003; Vandell & Wolfe, 2000). These findings apply not only to early childhood programs but also to before and afterschool programs for older children. Moreover, as children move from the early (ages 5 to 9) to later (10 to 12) middle childhood years, they are increasingly likely to take care of themselves during the before and afterschool hours (Lerner et al., 2003). Regular participation in a high quality before and afterschool program is positively associated with academic performance and in general, a significant body of research suggests that how school-age children spend their afterschool hours is strongly associated with the likelihood of engaging in risky behaviors (Lerner et al., 2003).

Inadequate child care is just one of the challenges facing school-age children—along with their families and communities—in the twenty-first century. Others include poverty, family and community violence, mental and physical challenges, and family disruption.

Poverty

The United Nations Children's Fund (2000a) is optimistic about a growing international consensus that poverty is "among the most important human rights challenges facing the world community" (p. 3). Indeed, foremost among threats to children's healthy development is poverty, which potentially threatens positive development in all domains (see Brooks-Gunn & Duncan, 1997; McLoyd, 1998; National Research Council, 1993; United Nations Children's Fund, 2000a, 2000b; Vandivere, Moore, & Brown, 2000).

> How does poverty serve as a risk factor in middle childhood?

Unfortunately, it is estimated that half of the children of the world live in poverty, many in extreme poverty (Bellamy, 2004). That children should be protected from poverty is not disputed; in the United States, this societal value dates back to the colonial period (Trattner, 1994). The nature of policies and programs targeted at ensuring the minimal daily needs of children are met, however, has shifted over time, as has our success in meeting this goal (Chase-Lansdale & Vinovskis, 1995; United Nations Children's Fund, 2000a).

In the United States, the late twentieth century brought a dramatic rise in the child poverty rate, which peaked in the early 1990s, declined for approximately a decade, and has gradually increased again during the early years of the twenty-first century (Koball & Douglas-Hall, 2006). In 2004, the national child poverty rate for the population as a whole was approximately 18%; in other words, approximately one in five children live in a family with an income below the federal poverty level (Fass & Cauthen, 2005).

As illustrated in Exhibit 5.4, Caucasian children comprise the majority of poor children in the United States. Young children and children from minority groups are statistically overrepresented among the population of poor children (Linver, Fuligni, Hernandez & Brooks-Gunn, 2004). This is a persistent modern trend; in other words, although in absolute numbers Caucasian children consistently compose the majority of poor children, children from Latino and African American families are consistently significantly overrepresented among all children in poverty. Typically, the percentage of African American or Latino children living in poverty is at least twice as high as the percentage of Caucasian children (Children's Defense Fund, 1996; Linver et al., 2004).

In general, the risk factors associated with child poverty are numerous, especially when poverty is sustained. Children who grow up in poverty are more likely to be born with low birth weight, to experience serious and chronic health problems, and to receive poorer health care and nutrition than children who grow up in better financial circumstances (Linver et al., 2004; United Nations Children's Fund, 2000b).

A number of perspectives attempt to explain the ways in which poverty impacts child development (Linver et al., 2004). Limited income constrains a family's ability to obtain or invest in resources that promote positive development. Poverty detrimentally impacts caregivers' emotional health and parenting practices. Individual poverty is correlated with inadequate family, school, and neighborhood resources and, thus, children experiencing family poverty are likely experiencing additional, cumulative risk factors. Each of these perspectives is valid and sheds light on the complex and synergistic ways in which poverty threatens optimal child development.

Exhibit 5.4	**U.S. Child Poverty Data 2005**			
Race	Children in Low-Income Families (by Race)	Number	Children in Poor Families (by Race)	Number
Black	61%	6,531,529	35%	3,685,360
Latino	61%	8,843,389	28%	4,108,988
White	26%	11,094,359	10%	4,223,801
Asian	28%	823,221	11%	323,148

Children in Low-Income Families in US			Children in Poor Families in US		
Age	Percent	Number	Age	Percent	Number
Under 6 years	42%	10,211,991	Under 6 years	20%	4,872,428
Over 6 years	37%	18,153,810	Over 6 years	16%	7,942,378

SOURCES: National Center for Children in Poverty, 2006c, 2006d.

NOTE: Low-income families are those with an income below 200% of the federal poverty level (i.e., incomes approximately twice that of the federal poverty level). Poor families are defined as families with incomes below the federal poverty level (FPL). The annual FPL is approximately $16,090 for a family of three and $19,350 for a family of four (see www.census.gov for more information).

Children who have spent any part of their prenatal period, infancy, or early childhood in poverty have often already encountered several developmental challenges by the time middle childhood begins. Children who enter, progress through, and leave middle childhood in poverty are at much greater risk of negative developmental outcomes than those who briefly enter and then exit poverty while still in middle childhood. In other words, evidence suggests that persistent and "deep," or extreme, poverty poses the most significant threat to healthy child development (Linver et al., 2004; United Nations Children's Fund, 2000a).

But what does it actually mean, to a child, to be poor? Being poor is a relative concept, the meaning of which is defined by perceptions of and real exclusion (Garbarino, 1992, 1995; Kozol, 2005). In most communities, one must be *not* poor in order to be fully engaged and included. Lack of income and certain goods deprive poor people of what is expected among those who belong; thus, poverty results in perceived and real inabilities and inadequacies. This is the essence of **relative poverty**, or the tendency to define one's poverty status in relation to others within one's social environment. Fundamentally, then, poverty is as much a social as an economic phenomenon. The social aspect of poverty has been extended by Payne (2005) to include emotional, spiritual, and support system impoverishment in addition to economic poverty. Such deficits in the developing child's background accumulate and result in impediments to the development of critical capacities including coping strategies. Unfortunately, income disparity—or the gap between the rich and the poor—has only continued to widen in recent years, both within and across countries around the globe (United Nations Children's Fund, 2000b).

The meaning of relative poverty for the school-age child is particularly profound. As evidence, James Garbarino (1995) points to an innocent question once asked of him by a child: "When you were growing up, were you poor or regular?" (p. 137). As the child struggles with the normal developmental tasks of feeling included and socially competent, relative poverty sends a persistent message of social exclusion and incompetence.

Family and Community Violence

What protective factors can buffer the effects of neighborhood violence on school-age children?

Children are increasingly witness or subject to violence in their homes, schools, and neighborhoods (Guterman & Cameron, 1997; Hutchison, 2007). Although child maltreatment and domestic violence have always existed, they have been recognized as social problems only recently. Community violence is slowly becoming recognized as a social problem of equal magnitude, affecting a tremendous number of children and families. Exposure to violence is a particular problem in areas where a lack of economic and social resources already produces significant challenges for children (Groves, 1997; Maluccio, 2006). Among children from war-torn countries, the atrocities witnessed or experienced are often unimaginable to children and adults who have resided in the United States all of their lives (see Gowen, 2001; Zea, Diehl, & Porterfield, 1997).

Witnessing violence deeply affects children, particularly when the perpetrator or victim of violence is a family member. In the United States, experts estimate that anywhere between 3 and 10 million children may be impacted each year, but no consistent, valid data source exists regarding children witnessing or otherwise exposed to domestic violence (Children's Defense Fund, 2000; Fantuzzo, Mohr, & Noone, 2000). But being a victim of violence is even more devastating, or fatal.

In the United States, children appear most susceptible to nonfatal physical abuse between the ages of 6 and 12. Some speculate that in the United States, at least, this association may be due to increased likelihood of public detection through school contact during these years. The number of children reported to child protective services (CPS) agencies annually is staggering. In 2003, CPS agencies across the United States received 2.9 million referrals, or reports, of suspected child abuse or neglect. This figure represents a reporting rate of 39.1 per 1,000 children. CPS agencies accepted approximately two-thirds of these reports for investigation or assessment purposes, ultimately identifying approximately 906,000 children as "confirmed" victims of abuse or neglect in 2003 (USDHHS ACYF, 2005). Child neglect is consistently the most common form of documented maltreatment, but it is important to note that victims typically experience more than one type of abuse or neglect simultaneously and therefore are appropriately included in more than one category. Maltreatment subtype trends are relatively stable over time; victims of child neglect consistently account for more than half of all child maltreatment victims (see Exhibit 5.5).

African American and Native American children are consistently overrepresented among confirmed maltreatment victims. Careful examination of this issue, however, has concluded that although children of color are disproportionately represented within the child welfare population, studies that are cognizant of the relationship between culture and parenting practices, that control for the role of poverty, and that examine child maltreatment in the general population find no association between a child's race or ethnicity and likelihood of child maltreatment. Thus, it is likely that the disproportionate representation of children of color within the child welfare system is caused by the underlying relationship between poverty and race or ethnicity (Thomlison, 2004).

A variety of factors contribute to child maltreatment and family violence (Belsky, 1980, 1984; Charlesworth, 2007; Hillson & Kuiper, 1994). These factors include parental, child, family, community, and cultural characteristics. Typically, the dynamic interplay of such characteristics leads to maltreatment, with the most relevant factors varying significantly depending upon the type of maltreatment examined. Thus, multiple theoretical perspectives, particularly the life course, ecological, systems, and stress and coping perspectives, are helpful for understanding situations of child maltreatment.

Not surprisingly, children who experience abuse have been found to report more unhappiness and troubled behavior than children who only witness abuse (Sternberg et al., 1993). Witnesses, in turn, report more adjustment difficulties than children who have neither been abused nor witnessed domestic violence. Because of the strong association between domestic violence and child maltreatment, however, many children are likely to experience these challenges to healthy development simultaneously (McCloskey, Figueredo, & Koss, 1995).

Exhibit 5.5	Child Maltreatment Subtypes

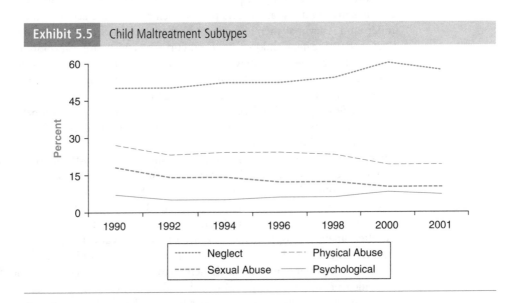

The impact of child maltreatment varies based on a number of factors, including but certainly not limited to, the type of maltreatment, the age of the child, and many other child, family, and community characteristics (Haugaard et al., 1997). The Centers for Disease Control and Prevention (CDC) (2005) has published a helpful overview of child maltreatment consequences, pointing out that experiencing maltreatment as a child is associated with an overwhelming number of negative health outcomes as an adult. These outcomes include an increased likelihood of using or abusing alcohol and other substances, disordered eating, depression, and susceptibility to certain chronic diseases.

Children who experience trauma, induced by either indirect or direct exposure to violence, may experience *post-traumatic stress disorder* (PTSD)—a set of symptoms that include feelings of fear and helplessness, reliving of the traumatic experience, and attempts to avoid reminders of the traumatic experience (Groves, 1997; Jenkins & Bell, 1997; Kaplan & Sadock, 1998). Researchers have also found changes in the brain chemistry of children exposed to chronic violence (Perry, 1997, 2006). Clearly, witnessing or experiencing violence adversely affects children in a number of areas, including the ability to function in school and the ability to establish stable social, including peer, relationships (Dyson, 1989; Guterman & Embry, 2004). Evidence suggests that perhaps as many as one-half of all children exposed to violence before the age of 10 develop psychiatric problems in adulthood (Davidson & Smith, 1990). Children who directly experience violence are at high risk of negative outcomes, but secondary exposure to violence and trauma—such as when a child's parents are suffering from PTSD—also may lead to negative outcomes for children (Hamblen, 2002; Monahon, 1997). In general, the intergenerational nature of family violence has been established (Herrenkohl et al., 2004). Childhood exposure to violence significantly increases the likelihood of mental health difficulties and violence perpetration or revictimization. Currently, the focus is on understanding the specific pathways of intergenerational processes (Coid et al., 2001; Heyman & Smith Slep, 2002; Lang, Stein, Kennedy, & Foy, 2004). It is clear that prolonged exposure to violence has multiple implications for child development. Children are forced to learn lessons about loss and death, perhaps before they have acquired the cognitive ability to understand. They may therefore come to believe that the world is unpredictable and violent, a belief that threatens children's natural curiosity and desire to explore the social environment. Multiple experiences in which adults are unable to protect them often lead children to conclude that they must take on such responsibility for themselves, a prospect that can easily overwhelm the resources of a school-age child.

Experiencing such helplessness may also lead to feelings of incompetence and hopelessness, to which children who experience chronic violence react in diverse ways. Responses may be passive, including withdrawal symptoms and signs of depression; or they may be active, including the use of aggression as a means of coping with and transforming the overwhelming feelings of vulnerability (Groves, 1997; Guterman & Cameron, 1997).

The emotional availability of a parent or other caretaker who can support the child's need to process traumatic events is critical. However, in situations of crisis stimulated by child maltreatment, domestic violence, and national or international violence, families are often unable to support their children psychologically. Even with the best of parental resources, moreover, children developing in violent and chronically dangerous communities continue to experience numerous challenges to development. The child's need for autonomy and independence is directly confronted by the parent's need to protect the child's physical safety. For example, hours spent indoors to avoid danger do not promote the much-needed peer relationships and sense of accomplishment, purpose, and self-efficacy so critical during this phase of development (Groves, 1997; Hutchison, 2007).

Mental and Physical Challenges

Although the term "disability" is still widely used in academic discourse and government policy, many are actively seeking to change popular discourse to reflect the need to see all children as possessing a range of physical and mental abilities. The use of the term disability establishes a norm within that range and labels those with abilities outside the norm as "disabled," which implies that group of individuals is "abnormal" and the group of individuals within the norm is "normal." Since the latest government data (U.S. Census Bureau, 2005) suggest that 6.7% of 5- to 20-year-olds, 12.7% of 21- to 64-year-olds, and 40.5% of those people 65 and older in the United States have some form of mental or physical "disability," such a label confines "normal" and "abnormal" to fixed categories that are not helpful to realizing a vision of a just and equal society. Just over one in ten children in the United States has difficulty performing one or more everyday activities, including for example, learning and self-care (Emmons, 2005; Hauser-Cram & Howell, 2003). Some of these difficulties are discussed below.

Attention Deficit Hyperactivity Disorder (ADHD)

ADHD is a commonly diagnosed childhood behavioral disorder impacting learning in the school environment. ADHD includes predominately inattentive, predominately impulsive-hyperactive, and combined inattentive-hyperactivity (American Psychiatric Association, 1994) (see Exhibit 5.6 for diagnostic criteria for ADHD). Estimates of the prevalence of ADHD among school-age children range from 3% to 12%, with highest incidence of ADHD diagnosis occurring between ages 5 and 10; compared to girls, boys are significantly more likely to receive a diagnosis of ADHD (Schneider & Eisenberg, 2006; Strock, 2006). ADHD is associated with school failure or academic underachievement, but the relationship is complex in part due to the strong relationship between ADHD and a number of other factors also associated with school difficulties (Barry, Lyman & Klinger, 2002; Hinshaw, 1992; LeFever, Villers, Morrow & Vaughn, 2002; Schneider & Eisenberg, 2006). Also, several studies suggest that the interpretation and evaluation of ADHD behaviors is significantly influenced by culturally-linked beliefs (Glass & Wegar, 2000; Kakouros, Maniadaki, & Papaeliou, 2004). In other words, the extent to which ADHD-linked behaviors are perceived as problematic varies according to individual and group values and norms.

Autistic Spectrum Disorders

In recent years, growing public attention and concern has focused upon autistic spectrum disorders. Among children ages 3 to 10, just over 3 per 1,000 children are diagnosed with autistic spectrum disorders; compared to girls, boys are three times as likely to receive such a diagnosis (Strock, 2004). Autism typically manifests and is diagnosed within the first two years of life; however, some children may not receive formal assessment or diagnosis until their early or middle childhood years. Like children with any special need or disability, children diagnosed with autistic spectrum disorders are extremely diverse; in particular, such children vary widely in terms of their intellectual and communicative abilities as well as the nature and severity of behavioral challenges (Volkmar, Paul, Klin, & Cohen, 2005).

Exhibit 5.6	Diagnostic Criteria for Attention Deficit/Hyperactivity Disorder

Either (1) or (2):

(1) **Inattention:** Six (or more) of the following symptoms of inattention have persisted for at least 6 months to a degree that is maladaptive and inconsistent with developmental level:
   - Often fails to give close attention to details or makes careless mistakes in schoolwork, work, or other activities
   - Often has difficulty sustaining attention in tasks or play activities
   - Often does not seem to listen when spoken to directly
   - Often does not follow through on instructions and fails to finish schoolwork, chores, or duties in the workplace (not due to oppositional behavior or failure to understand instruction)
   - Often has difficulty organizing tasks and activities
   - Often avoids, dislikes, or is reluctant to engage in tasks that require sustained mental effort (such as schoolwork or homework)
   - Often loses things necessary for tasks or activities (toys, school assignments, pencils, books, or tools)
   - Is often easily distracted by extraneous stimuli
   - Is often forgetful in daily activities

(2) **Hyperactivity-Impulsivity:** Six (or more) of the following symptoms of hyperactivity-impulsivity have persisted for at least 6 months to a degree that it is maladaptive and inconsistent with developmental level:

Hyperactivity
   - Often fidgets with hands or feet or squirms in seat
   - Often leaves seat in classroom or in other situations in which remaining seated is expected
   - Often runs about or climbs excessively in situations in which it is inappropriate (in adolescents or adults, may be limited to subjective feelings of restlessness)
   - Often has difficulty playing or engaging in leisure activities quietly
   - Is often "on the go" or often acts as if "driven by a motor"
   - Often talks excessively

Impulsivity
   - Often blurts out answers to questions before they have been completed
   - Often has difficulty awaiting turn
   - Often interrupts or intrudes on others (e.g., butts into conversations or games)
   - Some hyperactive-impulsive or inattentive symptoms that caused impairment were present before age 7
   - Some impairment from the symptoms is present in two or more settings (e.g., at school [or work] and at home)
   - There must be clear evidence of clinically significant impairment in social, academic, or occupational functioning
   - The symptoms do not occur exclusively during the course of a pervasive developmental disorder, schizophrenia, or other psychotic disorder and are not better accounted for by another mental disorder (e.g., mood disorder, anxiety disorder, dissociated disorder, or a personality disorder)

SOURCE: American Psychiatric Association, 1994.

Exhibit 5.7	Diagnostic Criteria for Autistic Disorder

A. A total of six (or more) items from (1), (2), and (3), with at least two from (1), and one each from (2) and (3):

(1) qualitative impairment in social interaction, as manifested by at least two of the following:
  (a) marked impairment in the use of multiple nonverbal behaviors such as eye-to-eye gaze, facial expression, body postures, and gestures to regulate social interaction
  (b) failure to develop peer relationships appropriate to developmental level
  (c) a lack of spontaneous seeking to share enjoyment, interests, or achievements with other people (e.g., by a lack of showing, bringing, or pointing out objects of interest)
  (d) lack of social or emotional reciprocity

(2) qualitative impairments in communication as manifested by at least one of the following:
  (a) delay in, or total lack of, the development of spoken language (not accompanied by an attempt to compensate through alternative modes of communication such as gesture or mime)
  (b) in individuals with adequate speech, marked impairment in the ability to initiate or sustain a conversation with others
  (c) stereotyped and repetitive use of language or idiosyncratic language
  (d) lack of varied, spontaneous make-believe play or social imitative play appropriate to developmental level

(3) restricted repetitive and stereotyped patterns of behavior, interests, and activities, as manifested by at least one of the following:
  (a) encompassing preoccupation with one or more stereotyped and restricted patterns of interest that is abnormal either in intensity or focus
  (b) apparently inflexible adherence to specific, nonfunctional routines or rituals
  (c) stereotyped and repetitive motor mannerisms (e.g., hand or finger flapping or twisting, or complex whole-body movements)
  (d) persistent preoccupation with parts of objects

B. Delays or abnormal functioning in at least one of the following areas, with onset prior to age 3 years: (1) social interaction, (2) language as used in social communication, or (3) symbolic or imaginative play.

C. The disturbance is not better accounted for by Rett's Disorder or Childhood Disintegrative Disorder.

SOURCE: American Psychiatric Association, p. 75.

In general, autism consists of impairment within three major domains: reciprocal social interaction, verbal and nonverbal communication, and range of activities and interests (Holter, 2004) (see diagnostic criteria in Exhibit 5.7).

Emotional/Behavioral Disorder

In many schools, the children perhaps presenting the greatest challenge to educators and administrators are those who consistently exhibit disruptive or alarming behavior yet do not clearly fit the criteria for a disability diagnosis. Although the U.S. Individuals with Disabilities Education Act (IDEA) includes a definition for "seriously emotionally disturbed" children, not all school professionals and government education agencies consistently agree with or use this definition (Young et al., 2004). In fact, the National Mental Health and Special Education Coalition has publicized a definition of "emotionally/behaviorally disordered" children, suggesting that this term and a set of diagnostic criteria could be used in place of the IDEA definition (see Exhibit 5.8).

Because of these definitional inconsistencies, it is extremely difficult to accurately estimate the number of school-age children falling within this population. Such estimates range from 0.05% to 6% of students.

Exhibit 5.8	Diagnostic Criteria for Emotional/Behavioral Disorder or Disturbance

Emotionally Disturbed

1. A condition exhibiting one or more of the following characteristics over a long period of time and to a marked degree, which adversely affects educational performance:
   a. An inability to learn which cannot be explained by intellectual, sensory, or health factors;
   b. An inability to build or maintain satisfactory interpersonal relationships with peers and teachers;
   c. Inappropriate types of behavior or feelings under normal circumstances;
   d. A general, pervasive mood of unhappiness or depression;
   e. A tendency to develop physical symptoms or fears associated with personal or school problems.

2. Includes children who are schizophrenic (or autistic). The term does not include children who are socially maladjusted, unless it is determined that they are seriously emotionally disturbed.

Emotional/Behavioral Disorder

1. A disability characterized by behavioral or emotional responses in school programs so different from appropriate age, culture, or ethnic norms that they adversely affect educational performance, including academic, social, vocational, or personal skills, and which:
   a. Is more than a temporary, expected response to stressful events in the environment;
   b. Is consistently exhibited in two different settings, at least one of which is school-related; and
   c. Persists despite individualized interventions within the education program, unless, in the judgment of the team, the child or youth's history indicates that such interventions would not be effective.

2. May include children or youth with schizophrenia disorders, affective disorders, anxiety disorders, or other sustained disturbances of conduct or adjustment when they adversely affect educational performance in accordance with Section I.

SOURCE: Young, Marchant, & Wilder, 2004, pp. 177–178.

Early identification and intervention, or provision of appropriate supportive services, are key protective factors for a child with special needs. In addition, the social environment more generally may serve as either a risk or protective factor, depending on its response to the child with a special need. Although difference of any sort is often noticed by children and adults, students with special needs or chronic illness are at particular risk for being singled out by their peers, and middle childhood is a critical time for such children. For children to acquire

What educational initiatives could minimize the risks associated with ADHD, autistic spectrum disorders, and other emotional/behavioral disorders?

a clear and positive sense of self, they need positive self-regard. The positive development of all children is facilitated by support at multiple levels to promote feelings of self-competence and independence (Goldstein, Kaczmarek, & English, 2002). Educating all children and adults about special needs and encouraging the support of all students may help to minimize negative attitudes and incidents (Gargiulo, 2005; Garrett, 2006).

Students who feel misunderstood by their peers are particularly likely to feel alone or isolated in the school setting. Students who are socially excluded by their peers often develop a dislike of school. Some students who are teased, isolated, or harassed on a regular basis may begin to withdraw or act out in order to cope with unpleasant experiences. Teachers, parents, and other school personnel who pay special attention to, and intervene with, students in this situation may prevent the escalation of such problems.

Children's adjustment to special needs is highly dependent on the adjustment of those around them. Families may respond in a number of ways to a diagnosis of a disability or serious illness. Often caregivers move through loss or grief stages; these stages may include: denial, withdrawal, rejection, fear, frustration, anger, sadness, adjustment, and acceptance (Ziolko, 1993). Awareness of and sensitivity to these stages is critical for those assessing the need for intervention. Typically, parents are helped by advocacy and support groups and access to information and resources.

Families of children with special needs also typically desire independence and self-determination for their children. Family empowerment was an explicit focus of the Education for All Handicapped Children Act (P.L. 94-142) of 1975 (Gallagher, 1993), which stresses parental participation in the development of an **individual education plan (IEP)** for each child. The IEP charts a course for ensuring that each child achieves as much as possible in the academic realm. The need to include the family in decision making and planning is also embodied in the IDEA of 1990 (reauthorized in 1997 and 2004), which replaced the Education for All Handicapped Children Act (Hauser-Cram & Howell, 2003). The IDEA requires that the IEP includes specific educational goals for each student classified as in need of special educational services. In addition, the IDEA assures all children the right to a free and appropriate public education and supports the placement of children with disabilities into integrated settings.

Prior to this act, the education of children with disabilities was left to individual states. As a result, the population labeled "disabled" and the services provided varied greatly. Today, however, through various pieces of legislation and several court decisions, society has stated its clear preference to educate children with special needs in integrated settings (*least restrictive environment*) to the maximum extent possible (Gent & Mulhauser, 1993).

A recent examination of the nature of inclusion nationwide concluded that during the last two decades, students with special needs (including learning disabilities) were much more likely to be formally identified, but only approximately 15 states clearly moved toward educating students with special needs in less restrictive settings (McLeskey, Hoppey, Williamson, & Rentz, 2004). Evaluations of the impact of inclusive settings on children's school success suggest positive academic gains for children with special needs and neutral impact on academic performance for children without identified special needs (McDonnel et al., 2003).

However, some caution against a "one size fits all" model of inclusion for all students with special needs, arguing that assessment of the optimal educational setting must be thorough and individualized. For example, some within the deaf community have argued that current full inclusion programs are unable "to meet the unique communication and social development needs of solitary deaf students" (Hehir, 2003, p. 36).

Hehir (2003) explains that while inclusion in statewide assessments has been shown to improve educational opportunities and achievement for some students with disabilities, "high-stakes" testing negatively impacts such progress if it alone is used as the basis for preventing students from being promoted a grade or graduating. In other words, standards-based reforms can positively impact students with disabilities if they improve the educational opportunities for all students. If such reforms, however, shift practice toward a system in which standardized testing is the only format through which student knowledge and capabilities are assessed, then many students, particularly those with special needs, are likely to suffer (Hehir, 2003, p. 40).

Family Disruption

Throughout history, most nuclear and extended families have succeeded in their endeavor to adequately protect and socialize their young. For too many children, however, the family serves as both a protective and risk factor due to unhealthy family attributes and dynamics. In the specific realm of family disruption, divorce was traditionally viewed as a developmental risk factor for children. Today, among U.S. children with married parents, approximately one-half experience the divorce of their parents (Amato, 2003). Between two-thirds and three-fourths of divorced parents marry a second time, and thus for many school-age children, divorce leads to new family relationships (Meyer & Garasky, 1993). The likelihood of divorce is even greater for second marriages, and approximately half of these children experience the end of a parent's second marriage. Many children experience the dissolution of their parents' nonmarital romantic relationships, and related attachments, without being counted in official "children of divorce" statistics or research. Although no reliable data on similar nonmarital relationship patterns exists, we can assume that similar trends exist among children's nonmarried parents and other caregivers.

Divorce and other types of family disruption often lead to a parade of new people and situations, including new housing and income arrangements and new family roles and responsibilities (Hetherington & Jodl, 1994). Family disruption may also immerse the child in poverty (Bianchi & McArthur, 1991). As the body of research on children and divorce grows in depth and breadth, it has become apparent that divorce and other types of family disruption may detrimentally or positively impact children depending on the circumstances preceding and following the divorce (Adam & Chase-Lansdale, 2002; Amato, 2003; Gilman, Kawachi, & Fitzmaurice, 2003). For example, if divorce brings an end to seriously dysfunctional spousal tension or violence and results in positive changes within the home environment, child outcomes may be positive. Alternatively, if the divorce disrupted a healthy, nurturing family system and led to declines in the emotional and financial health of the child's primary caregiver(s), child outcomes may be negative.

Historically, many children experienced family disruption due to the death of one or both parents (Amato, 2003). Although improvements in public health have significantly reduced the likelihood of parental death, a substantial number of children continue to experience the death of a primary caregiver. Compared to adults, children have less cognitive and other resources to cope with death and loss (Saldinger, Cain, Kalter, & Lohnes, 1999). For children coping with the death of a parent, the circumstances of the death and the adjustment of the remaining caregivers are critical variables impacting child outcomes (Hope & Hodge, 2006; Kwok et al., 2005). Also, in recent years, a number of studies have focused upon "children of suicide." This literature notes the potential long-term impacts of parental suicide on surviving children and identifies the ways in which outcomes may be carried through generations (Cain, 2006).

Many school-age children experience disruption of attachment relationships through other means. For example, approximately 800,000 children spend some amount of time in foster care each year (Child Welfare League of America, 2005). Some of these children spend lengthy periods of time in some type of foster care setting, while some children enter and leave foster care rapidly and only once during their childhoods, and still other children cycle in and out of their home and foster care settings repeatedly. Approximately one-third of the children in foster care at any time have been in substitute care for three years or more; approximately one-fifth of children in foster care are identified as unlikely to ever return home and are awaiting a permanent plan (Downs, Moore, McFadden, Michaud, & Costin, 2004).

Family disruption is stressful for all children. Great variation exists, however, in the circumstances preceding and following the family disruption, the nature of the changes involved, and how children respond to this type of stress. Critical factors in outcomes for children include social supports within the family and surrounding community, the child's characteristics, the emotional well-being of caregivers, and in general the quality of care received following the family disruption. In addition, because middle childhood spans a wide age range, school-age children exhibit a wide range of cognitive, emotional, and behavioral responses to divorce and other types of family disruption. They may blame themselves and experience anxiety or other difficult emotions, or they may demonstrate a relatively mature understanding of the reasons behind the events.

Children experiencing family disruption without supports or those who have experienced difficulties preceding the disruption are most likely to experience long-term emotional and behavioral problems. Children placed in foster care or otherwise exposed to traumatic or multiple losses are more likely to fall into this group (Webb & Dumpson, 2006). These children are likely to face additional stress associated with the loss of familiar space, belongings, and social networks (Groves, 1997). However, with appropriate support and intervention as well as the presence of other protective factors, many children experiencing family disruption adjust over time (Hetherington & Clingempeel, 1992).

▧ Risk Factors and Protective Factors in Middle Childhood

School-age children face a variety of risks that undermine their struggles to develop a sense of purpose and self-worth. These risks include poverty, prejudice, and violence (Garbarino, 1995). More generally, risk factors are anything that increases the probability of a problem condition, its progression into a more severe state, or its maintenance (Fraser, 2004). Risk factors are moderated, however, by protective factors, either internal or external, which help children resist risk (Fraser, 2004; Garmezy, 1993, 1994; Werner & Smith, 2001). Risk and protective factors can be biological, psychological, social, and spiritual in nature, and like all influences on development, they span the micro to macro continuum (Bronfenbrenner, 1979). Dynamic, always evolving, interaction occurs among risk and protective factors present in each dimension of the individual child and his or her environment.

Resilience—or "survival against the odds"—arises from an interplay of risk and protective factors and manifests as adaptive behavior producing positive outcomes (Fraser, 2004). A variety of factors influence resilience during middle childhood. Whether a factor presents risk or protection often depends on its interaction with other factors influencing the individual child. For example, a highly structured classroom environment run by a "strict" teacher may function as a protective factor for one child while simultaneously functioning as a risk factor for another child.

The life course and systems perspectives provide tools for understanding positive development during middle childhood. These perspectives also facilitate assessment and intervention efforts. As social workers, we must recognize that resilience is rarely an innate characteristic. Rather, it is a process (Egeland, Carlson, & Sroufe, 1993; Fraser, 2004) that may be facilitated by influences within the child's surrounding environment. Indeed, research suggests that high-risk behavior among children increases when they perceive declining family involvement and community support (Benson, 1990; Blyth & Roehlkepartian, 1993). A primary goal of the professions dedicated to child well-being must be facilitation of positive external supports for children and enhancement of the person/environment fit so as to maximize protective factors and minimize risk factors. Exhibit 5.9 summarizes major risk and protective factors identified as most relevant to childhood.

Exhibit 5.9	Potential Childhood Risk and Protective Factors

Risk	*Protective*
Child/Individual	**Child/Individual**
Prematurity, birth anomalies	Good health
Exposure to toxins in utero	
Chronic or serious illness	
Temperament: for example, difficult or slow to warm up	Personality factors: easy temperament; positive disposition; active coping style; positive self-esteem, good social skills; internal locus of control; balance between help seeking and autonomy
Mental retardation, cognitive delays, low intelligence	Above-average intelligence
Childhood trauma	History of adequate development
Antisocial peer group	Hobbies and interests
Gender	Good peer relationships

Risk	Protective
Parental/Family	**Parental/Family**
Insecure attachment	Secure attachment; positive and warm parent child relationship
Parent: insecure adult attachment pattern	Parent: secure adult attachment pattern
Single parenthood (with lack of support)	Parent(s) supports child in times of stress
Harsh parenting, maltreatment	Effective/positive (authoritative) parenting
Family disorganization; low parental monitoring	Household rules and structure, parental monitoring of child
Social isolation, lack of support	Support/involvement of extended family, including help with caregiving
Domestic violence	
High parental/interparental conflict	Stable relationship between parents
Separation/divorce, especially high-conflict divorce	
Parental psychopathology	Parent(s) model competence and good coping skills
Parental substance abuse	Family expectations of prosocial behavior
Parental illness	High parental expectations
Death of a parent or sibling	
Foster care placement	
Social/Environmental Risk Factors	**Social/Environmental Risk Factors**
Poverty/collective poverty	Middle-class or above socioeconomic status
Lack of access to adequate medical care, health insurance, and social services	Access to adequate health care and social services
Parental/community unemployment	Consistent parental/community employment
Inadequate child care	Adequate child care and housing
Inadequate housing	
Exposure to racism, discrimination, injustice	Family religious faith/participation
Low-quality schools	High-quality schools
Frequent change of residence and schools/ transient community	Supportive adults outside family who serve as role models/mentors to child
Exposure to environmental toxins	Presence of caring adult(s)
Exposure to dangerous neighborhood(s), community violence, media violence	Collective efficacy
	Competence in normative roles
Few opportunities for education or employment	Many opportunities for education and employment

SOURCE: Based on Davies, 2004, pp. 106–108; Fraser et al., 2004, pp. 36–49.

IMPLICATIONS FOR SOCIAL WORK PRACTICE

This discussion of middle childhood suggests several practice principles for social workers and other professionals working with children:

- Development is multidimensional and dynamic; recognize the complex ways in which developmental influences interact, and incorporate this understanding into your work with children.
- Support parents and other family members as critically important social, emotional, and spiritual resources for their children.
- Support family, school, and community attempts to stabilize environments for children.
- Incorporate identification of multilevel risk and protective factors into assessment and intervention efforts.
- Recognize and support resilience in children and families. Support the strengths of children and families and their efforts to cope with adversity.
- Recognize the critical influence of the school environment on growth and development, and encourage attempts by school personnel to be responsive to all children and families.
- Understand the important role of peer groups in psychosocial growth and development; facilitate the development and maintenance of positive peer and other social relationships.
- Understand the ways in which the organization of schools reflects and supports the inequalities present in society. Support schools in their efforts to end practices and policies, intended or unintended, that sustain and/or reinforce inequalities based on race, ethnicity, gender, disability, and socioeconomic status.
- Facilitate meaningful teacher-family-child communication and school responsiveness to children experiencing difficulties in the school environment.
- Understand the effects of family, community, and societal violence on children, and establish prosocial, nurturing, nonviolent environments whenever possible; provide opportunities for positive mentoring of children in the school and community environments.
- Become familiar with and implement best practices in areas such as trauma, loss and grief, social skill development, character education, and bullying prevention.
- Promote cultural competency, and help children and other adults recognize and respect all forms of diversity and difference.

KEY TERMS

acculturation
assimilation
brain plasticity
Brown v. Board of Education
capital
cerebral cortex
character education
deculturalizing
direct bullying

emotional intelligence
indirect bullying
individual education plan (IEP)
institutional discrimination
interrelational intelligence
language register
multiple intelligences
oppression
perspective taking

precociousness
relative poverty
secondary sexual development
social competence
trauma
zone of proximal development

Active Learning

1. In small groups, compare and contrast the risk and protective factors present for Anthony Bryant, Brianna Shaw, and Manuel Vega. Brainstorm multilevel interventions you would consider if you were working with each child.

2. Assign pairs of students to the story of either Anthony Bryant, Brianna Shaw, or Manuel Vega. Each pair should identify the relevance of the various developmental theorists, discussed in the chapter, to the assigned child, focusing on the theorist(s) whose idea(s) seem particularly relevant to the selected child. After approximately 20 minutes, form three small groups consisting of the pairs focusing on the same child. After comparing their similarities and differences, each group should report back to the full class.

3. Create a list of debate topics raised directly or indirectly in the chapter (e.g., school tracking, expansion of bilingual school curricula, educational assessment/standardized testing, federal spending or programs to address child poverty, gun control to reduce violence against children, family structure and family disruption, inclusion for children with special needs, etc.). Debates can take place between teams or individuals. Topics and "pro" or "con" designation can be assigned or chosen depending on the instructor's desired learning outcomes for the debate. Suggested times are two minutes to present a case for each side. Each team will also have one minute for rebuttal.

4. Use task rotation for important chapter issues like *community violence:* (1) How does child maltreatment or trauma impact childhood development? (2) How are child witnesses impacted by acts of violence? (3) What programs might schools employ to support students impacted by violence? (4) What interventions might a social worker pursue to help families impacted by violence? *Task rotation description:* Questions are posted on chart paper around the room. Each group starts at a question, discusses it, writes ideas in response on the chart paper and then after a short time (less than three minutes) is stopped and rotated to the next chart. At the next chart they are given a brief period of time to review the work of the previous group and add any ideas the first group missed. The groups are stopped and rotated until all groups read and add to all issues listed on the charts. Whole group review follows.

WEB RESOURCES

Forum on Child and Family Statistics
www.childstats.gov

Official Web site of the Federal Interagency Forum on Child and Family Statistics offers easy access to federal and state statistics and reports on children and families, including international comparisons.

Child Welfare Information Gateway
www.childwelfare.gov

Site presented by the Administration for Children and Families contains information and resources to protect children and strengthen families, including statistics, prevention information, state statutes, family-centered practice, and publications.

Search Institute
www.search-institute.org

Site presented by Search Institute, an independent, nonprofit, nonsectarian organization with the goal of advancing the well-being of adolescents and children, contains information on 40 developmental assets and methods for building assets for child and youth development.

Child Trauma Academy
www.childtraumaacademy.com

Site presented by the Child Trauma Academy contains information on the impact of child maltreatment on the brain and the physiological and psychological effects of trauma on children.

American Association of University Women
www.aauw.org

Site maintained by the American Association of University Women contains information on education and equity for women and girls, including a report card on Title IX, a law that banned sex discrimination in education.

CHAPTER 6

ADOLESCENCE

Susan Ainsley McCarter

Key Ideas	229
Case Study 6.1: ■ David's Coming-Out Process	230
Case Study 6.2: ■ Carl's Struggle for Identity	230
Case Study 6.3: ■ Monica's Quest for Mastery	231
The Social Construction of Adolescence Across Time and Space	232
The Transition From Childhood to Adulthood	232
Biological Aspects of Adolescence	233
Nutrition, Exercise, and Sleep	233
Puberty	236
The Adolescent Brain	237
Psychological Aspects of Adolescence	238
Psychological Reactions to Biological Changes	238
Changes in Cognition	240
Development of an Identity	241
Theories of Self and Identity	242
Identity Formation	245
Gender Differences	246
Social Aspects of Adolescence	247
Relationships With Family	247
Relationships With Peers	248

Relationships With Institutions   249
    School   249
    Work   251
    Leisure   251
    The Internet   253
Relationships With Culture   255
Spiritual Aspects of Adolescence   256
Issues, Challenges, and Problems During Adolescence   258
    Sexuality   259
        Masturbation   259
        Sexual Orientation   259
        Sexual Decision Making   261
        Oral Sex   263
        Pregnancy and Childbearing   264
        Sexually Transmitted Diseases   265
    Substance Use and Abuse   268
        Decision Making About Substance Use   270
        Consequences of Substance Use and Abuse   271
    Juvenile Delinquency   271
    Other Threats to Physical and Mental Health   273
        Violence   273
        Dating Violence and Statutory Rape   274
        Poverty and Low Educational Attainment   275
        Obesity and Eating Disorders   276
        Depression and Suicide   278
Risk Factors and Protective Factors in Adolescence   278
Implications for Social Work Practice   279
Key Terms   280
Active Learning   280
Web Resources   280

❖ How do biological, psychological, social, and spiritual dimensions affect the adolescent phase of the life course?

❖ Why do social workers need to understand theories of identity formation when working with adolescents?

❖ What unique challenges do adolescents face when confronted with issues of sexuality and substance use and abuse?

KEY IDEAS

As you read this chapter, take note of these central ideas:

1. Adolescence is characterized by significant physical change, increased hormone production, sexual maturation, improved cognitive functioning, formative identity development, increased independence, and possible experimentation with sex and substances.

2. During adolescence, increased hormone production results in a period called puberty, during which persons become capable of reproduction. Other physical changes during this period include skeletal, musculature, and fat distribution changes as well as development of primary and secondary sex characteristics.

3. Psychological changes during this period include reactions to physical, social, and cultural changes confronting the adolescent, as well as cognitive development, in which most individuals develop the abilities to contemplate the future, to comprehend the nature of human relationships, to consolidate specific knowledge into a coherent system, and to envision possible consequences from a hypothetical list of actions.

4. The greatest task of adolescence is identity formation—determining who one is and where one is going.

5. Adolescents in the United States spend nearly a third of their waking hours at school, where they should receive skills and knowledge for their next step in life, but a school that follows a Eurocentric educational model without regard for other cultures may damage the self-esteem of students from minority ethnic groups.

6. Among the physical and mental health risks to today's adolescents are violence, poor nutrition, obesity, eating disorders, depression, and suicide.

David's Coming-Out Process

The social worker at Jefferson High School sees many facets of adolescent life. Nothing much surprises her—especially not the way some of the kids hem and haw when they're trying to share what's really on their mind. Take David Cunha, for instance. When he shows up for his first appointment, he is simply asked to tell a bit about himself.

"Let's see, I'm 17," he begins. "I'm a forward on the varsity soccer team. What else do you want to know? My parents are from Bolivia and are as traditional as you can imagine. My dad, David Sr., teaches history and is the varsity baseball coach here at Jefferson. My mom is a geriatric nurse. I have a younger sister, Patti. Patti Perfect. She goes to the magnet school and is in the ninth grade."

"How are things at home?" his social worker asks.

"Whatever. Patti is perfect, and I'm a 'freak.' They think I'm 'different, arrogant, stubborn.' I don't know what they want me to be. But I don't think that's what I am. That may be because . . . because I'm gay. I haven't come out to my parents. That's all I need!"

This is obviously a difficult confession for David to make to an adult, but with a little encouragement he continues: "There are two other soccer players who are gay, and then we have some friends outside of soccer. Thank God! But basically when the whole team is together or when I'm with other friends, I just act straight. I talk about girls' bodies just like the other guys. I think that is the hardest. Not being able to be yourself. I'm at least glad that I've met other gay guys. It was really hard when I was about 13. I was so confused. I knew that men were supposed to be with women, not other men. What I was feeling was not 'normal,' and I thought I was the only one. I wanted to kill myself. That was a bad time."

David's tone changes. "Let's talk about something good. Let me tell you about Theo. I find Theo very attractive. I hope he likes my soccer build. I wonder if he would like to hang out together—get to know one another. He's a junior, and if we got together, the other guys would razz me about seeing a younger guy. But I keep thinking about him. And looking at him during practice. I just need to say something to him. Some guys off the team are going out Thursday night after practice. He hasn't been invited in the past. Maybe if I invite him, he'll come."

Carl's Struggle for Identity

Whereas David seeks out the social worker, Carl Fleischer, another 17-year-old, is sent to the social work office at the high school. He matter-of-factly shares that he is "an underachiever." He used to get an occasional B in his classes, but now it's mostly Cs with an occasional D.

When Carl is asked what he likes to do in his spare time, he replies, "I like to get high and surf the Net." Further probing elicits one-word answers until the social worker asks Carl about girlfriends. His face contorts as he slaps his ample belly: "I'm not exactly a sex symbol. According to my doctor, I'm a fatso. He says normal boys my age and height weigh at least 50 pounds less than I do. He also tells me to quit smoking and get some exercise. Whatever. My mom says I'm big-boned. She says my dad was the same way. I wouldn't know. I never met the scumbag. He left when my mom was pregnant. But you probably don't want to hear about that."

Carl won't say more on that topic, but with more prodding, he finally talks about his job, delivering pizzas two nights a week and on the weekends. "So if you need pizzas, call me at Antonio's. I always bring pies home for my mom on Tuesday and Friday nights. She works late those nights, and so we usually eat pizza and catch the Tuesday and Friday night lineups on TV. She lets me smoke in the house—cigarettes, not weed. Although I have gotten high in the house a couple times. Anyway, I am not what you would call popular. I am just a fat, slow geek and a pizza guy. But there are some heads who come into Antonio's. I exchange pies for dope. Works out pretty well: they get the munchies, and the pies keep me in with the heads."

Case Study 6.3

Monica's Quest for Mastery

Monica Golden, one of the peer counselors at Jefferson High, hangs around to chat after a meeting of the peer counselors. Monica is the youngest and tallest daughter in a family of five kids, with one younger brother. Monica's mother is the assistant principal at Grover Middle School, and her father works for the Internal Revenue Service. This year Monica is the vice president of the senior class, the treasurer for the Young Republicans, a starter on the track team, a teacher at Sunday school, and a Jefferson peer counselor.

When the social worker comments on the scope of these activities, Monica replies: "I really do stay busy. I worked at the mall last year, but it was hard to keep my grades up. I'm trying to get into college, so my family and I decided I shouldn't work this year. So I just babysit sometimes. A lot of my aunts and uncles have me watch their kids, but they don't pay me. They consider it a family favor. Anyway, I am waiting to hear back from colleges. They should be sending out the letters this week. You know, the fatter the envelope the better. It doesn't take many words to say, 'No. We reject you.' And I need to either get into a state school or get a scholarship so that I can use my savings for tuition."

Next they talk a little about Monica's options, and she shares that her first choice is Howard University. "I want to surround myself with black scholars and role models and my dream is to be a pediatrician, you know. I love kids," Monica says. "I tried tons of jobs—that's where I got the savings. And, well, those with kids I enjoyed the most. Like I said, I've worked retail at the mall. I've worked at the supermarket as a cashier. I've worked at the snack bar at the pool. And I've been babysitting since I was 12. That's what I like the most."

"I'd love to have kids someday. But I don't even have a boyfriend. I wear glasses. My parents say I don't need contacts; they think I'm being vain. Not that I don't have a boyfriend because I wear glasses. Guys think I'm an overachiever. They think I'm driven and demanding and incapable of having fun. That's what I've been told. I think I'm just ambitious and extroverted. But really, I just haven't had much time to date in high school. I've been so busy. Well, gotta run."

The Social Construction of Adolescence Across Time and Space

If we were asked to describe David Cunha, Carl Fleischer, and Monica Golden, attention would probably be drawn to their status as adolescents. The importance of that status has changed across time and cultures, however. Adolescence was invented as a psychosocial concept in the late nineteenth and early twentieth centuries as the United States made the transition from an agrarian to an urban-industrial society (Fass & Mason, 2000). Prior to this time, adolescents worked beside adults, doing what adults did for the most part (Leeder, 2004). This is still the case for adolescents in many nonindustrial societies today. As the United States and other societies became urbanized and industrialized, child labor legislation and compulsory education policies were passed, and adolescents were moved from the workplace to the school and became economically dependent on parents. The juvenile justice system was developed because juvenile offenders were seen as different from adult offenders, with less culpability for their crime because of their immaturity.

In 1904, G. Stanley Hall, an American psychologist, published *Adolescence: Its Psychology and Its Relations to Physiology, Anthropology, Sociology, Sex, Crime, Religion, and Education.*

How have our views on adolescence changed over time?	Hall proposed that adolescence is a period of "storm and stress," a period when hormones cause many difficulties. That seems to be the image of adolescence that permeates the popular culture in the United States. In the past 25 years, however, behavioral scientists have made intensive study of the adolescent period and have found that, although adolescence presents special challenges, most adolescents do not experience a long stormy period (Lerner & Galambos,

1998). At the same time, there is growing agreement that the societal context in which adolescence is lived out in the United States is becoming increasingly less supportive for adolescent development (Fass & Mason, 2000).

Sociologists caution against thinking of a monolithic adolescence. They suggest that, unfortunately, many adults dichotomize children and adolescents as "our own" children and "other people's" children (Graff, 1995). Our own children are expected to have "an innocent and secure childhood and dependent, prolonged adolescence" (Graff, 1995, p. 332). Other people's children are expected to be resilient in their childhood and accountable for their own behavior at increasingly younger ages, as we see in the declining ages for being treated as an adult in the criminal justice system. Sociologists conclude that there are multiple adolescences, with gender, race, and class as major influences on the ways they are constructed and their realities.

The Transition From Childhood to Adulthood

In industrialized countries, adolescence is described as the transitional period between childhood and adulthood. It is more than that, of course. It is a very rich period of the life course in its own right. For many, it is a thrilling time of life full of new experiences. The word *adolescence* originates from the Latin verb *adolescere,* which means "to grow into maturity." It is a period of life filled with transitional themes in every dimension of the configuration of person and environment: biological, psychological, social, and spiritual. These themes do not occur independently or without affecting one another. For example, David Cunha's experience may be complicated because he is gay and because his family relationships are strained, but it is also strengthened by his supportive friendships and his participation in athletics. Carl Fleischer's transition is marked by several challenges—his weight, his substance use, his lack of a relationship with his father, his academic performance—but also by the promise of his developing computer expertise and entrepreneurial skills. Monica Golden's movement through adolescence may be eased by her academic, athletic, and social success, but it also could be taxed by her busy schedule and high expectations for herself.

Many cultures have specific **rites of passage**—ceremonies that demarcate the transition from childhood to adulthood. Often these rites include sexual themes, marriage themes, themes of becoming a man or a woman, themes of added responsibility, or themes of increased insight or understanding. For example, among the Massai ethnic group in Kenya and Tanzania, males and females are both circumcised at about age 13, and males are considered junior warriors and sent to live with other junior warriors (Leeder, 2004). In the United States, Jews celebrate the bar mitzvah for boys and bas mitzvah for girls at the age of 13 to observe their transition to adulthood and to mark their assumption of religious responsibility. Many Latino families, especially of Mexican heritage, celebrate *quincianera*, during which families attend Mass with their 15-year-old daughter, who is dressed in white and then presented to the community as a young woman. Traditionally, she is accompanied by a set of Padrinos, or godparents, who agree to support her parents in guiding her during this time. The ceremony is followed by a reception at which her father dances with her and presents her to the family's community of friends (Garcia, 2001; Zuniga, 1992).

Mainstream culture in the United States, however, has few such rites. Many young adolescents go through confirmation ceremonies in Protestant and Catholic churches. Otherwise, the closest thing to a rite of passage may be getting a driver's license, graduating from high school, registering to vote, graduating from college, or getting married. But these events all occur at different times and thus do not provide a discrete point of transition. Moreover, not all youth participate in these rites of passage.

Even without a cultural rite of passage, all adolescents experience profound biological, psychological, psychosocial, social, and spiritual changes. In advanced industrial societies, these changes have been divided into three phases: early adolescence (ages 11 to 14), middle adolescence (ages 15 to 17), and late adolescence (ages 18 to 20). Exhibit 6.1 summarizes the typical biological, psychological, and social developments in these three phases. Of course, adolescent development varies from person to person and with time, culture, and other aspects of the environment. Yet, deviations from the normative patterns of adolescent change may have psychological ramifications, because adolescents are so quick to compare their own development to that of their peers.

⧆ Biological Aspects of Adolescence

Adolescence is a period of great physical change, marked by a rapid growth spurt in the early years, maturation of the reproductive system, redistribution of body weight, and continuing brain development. Adequate care of the body during this exciting time is of paramount importance.

> What is the impact of biological age on psychological age, social age, and spiritual age during adolescence?

Nutrition, Exercise, and Sleep

At any stage along the life course, the right balance of nutrition, exercise, and sleep is important. As the transition from childhood to adulthood begins,

Exhibit 6.1	Typical Adolescent Development		
Stage of Adolescence	*Biological Changes*	*Psychological Changes*	*Social Changes*
Early (11 to 14)	Hormonal changes Beginning of puberty Physical appearance changes Possible experimentation with sex and substances	Reactions to physical changes, including early maturation Concrete/present-oriented thought Body modesty Moodiness	Changes in relationships with parents and peers Less school structure Distancing from culture/tradition Seeking sameness
Middle (15 to 17)	Completion of puberty and physical appearance changes Possible experimentation with sex and substances	Reactions to physical changes, including late maturation Increased autonomy Increased abstract thought Beginning of identity development Preparation for college or career	Heightened social situation decision making Consideration of physical attractiveness
Late (18 to 20)	Slowing of physical changes Possible experimentation with sex and substances	Formal operational thought Continuation of identity development Moral reasoning	Very little school/life structure Beginning of intimate relationships Renewed interest in culture/tradition

▲ **Photo 6.1**   Peer relationships contribute to adolescents' identities, behaviors, and personal and social competence.

adolescent bodies undergo significant biological changes from their brains to the hair follicles on their legs and everywhere in between. Yet few adolescents maintain a healthy balance during their time in adolescent flux. In their book, *Healthy Teens, Body and Soul: A Parent's Complete Guide* (2003), Andrea Marks and Betty Rothbart suggest that to go FAR in life— teens need the three health basics of FUEL, ACTIVITY, and REST. They assert that many young people skimp on nutritious food and overload on junk food, lounge for hours in front of a television or computer, or stay up late and fail to get enough sleep, and then wonder why they are too heavy or too thin, lack energy, are irritable or depressed, and can't improve their grades (p. 33). And the authors note that these actions can lead to bigger problems: an adolescent who eats poorly and does not exercise may feel sluggish, even if he or she gets enough sleep, an overweight teen often feels too awkward to exercise, a sleep-deprived teen might reach for too many sweets (or caffeine) for quick energy boosts and then end up with energy crashes (or caffeine addiction), a teen who exercises but doesn't get enough iron could lack the energy to achieve fitness goals, a young female athlete intent on lifelong fitness runs the risk of bone injury now and in the future if she doesn't get enough calcium, a motivated adolescent who stays up late to study may never score as high on exams as an equally smart friend who is in bed by ten (p. 33).

Recognizing the need for intervention, the U.S. Department of Health and Human Services and the Department of Agriculture have begun some campaigns aimed at adolescent nutrition. They outline some of their recommendations in the Dietary Guidelines for Americans 2005 (U.S. Department of Health and Human Services/U.S. Department of Agriculture, 2005). For adolescents, they recommend consuming 2 cups of fruit and 2.5 cups of vegetables a day (for a 2,000 calorie intake); choosing a variety of fruits and vegetables each day selecting from all five vegetable subgroups—dark green, orange, legumes, starchy vegetables, and other vegetables— several times a week; consuming 3 or more ounce equivalents of whole-grain products per day; consuming 3 cups per day of fat-free or low-fat milk or equivalent milk products; limiting fat intake to between 25% to 35% of calories with most fats coming from sources of polyunsaturated and monounsaturated fatty acids, such as fish, nuts, and vegetable oils; and consuming less than 2,300 mg (approximately 1 tsp of salt) of sodium per day.

Yet, the National Youth Risk Behavior Survey for 2005 (CDC, 2006c) suggests that nationwide only 20.1% of young people in grades 9–12 had eaten fruits and vegetables at least five times a day and only 16.2% had drunk at least three glasses of milk a day during the preceding week. Many U.S. youth say they don't have time to eat breakfast or that they aren't hungry in the morning. Yet the research is rather convincing, indicating that students who eat breakfast obtain higher test scores and are less likely to be tardy or absent from school (Meyers, Sampson, Weitzman, Rogers, & Kayne, 1989; Lonzano & Ballesteros, 2006).

In terms of activity, the recommendation is for most people of every age to engage in regular physical activity and reduce sedentary activities to promote health, psychological well-being, and a healthy body weight. Physical fitness should be achieved by including cardiovascular conditioning, stretching exercises for flexibility, and resistance exercises or calisthenics for muscle strength and endurance. And the specific recommendation for adolescents is to engage in at least 60 minutes of physical activity on most, preferably all, days of the week (U.S. Department of Health and Human Services/U.S. Department of Agriculture, 2005).

So, are teens exercising? Nationwide, 35.8% of high school students reported being physically active for a total of at least 60 minutes a day on at least five of the seven days preceding the survey, 68.7% had participated in at least 20 minutes of vigorous physical activity on at least three of the seven days preceding the survey, and 9.6% had not partici-pated in any vigorous or moderate physical activity during the seven days preceding the survey (CDC, 2006c).

How about rest? Many adolescents feel that sleep is not as important as whatever else is going on in their lives. Researchers assert that adolescents in the United States are the most sleep-deprived segment of a very sleep-deprived society (National Institutes of Health, 2001). According to the National Sleep Foundation (2006), puberty changes sleep patterns and needs such that adolescents require 8.5 to 9.25 hours of sleep each night, and shifts in circadian rhythms cause teens to be more alert late at night and to wake later in the morn-ing, resulting in an increase in daytime sleepiness.

Yet, survey data show that only 20% of U.S. adolescents get at least 9 hours of sleep on school nights. U.S. sixth graders get an average of 8.4 hours of sleep on school nights, and U.S. high school seniors get an average of only 6.9 hours on school nights, which gives them 12 hours of sleep deficit over the course of a week (National Sleep Foundation, 2006). More than half of teens are aware that they are sleep deprived, but 90% of parents report that their teens are getting enough sleep much of the time. School performance is affected by insuffi-cient sleep. More than a quarter of high school students fall asleep at school at least once a week, and students who get sufficient sleep have higher grades on average than students with sleep deficit. Mood is also affected by insufficient sleep; teens who get nine or more hours of sleep per night report more positive moods than students who get insufficient sleep (National Sleep Foundation, 2006).

As suggested above, the risks of sleep deprivation are varied, and they can be serious (National Institutes of Health, 1997). Drowsiness or fatigue is a principle cause of at least 100,000 police-reported traffic collisions annually, killing more than 1,500 Americans and injuring 71,000 more. Drivers 25 and younger cause more than half of the crashes attributed to drowsiness (National Sleep Foundation, 2005). Teens who feel sleepy are at increased risk for substance use, including caffeine, nicotine, and alcohol (Carskadon, 1990). Adolescents with-out sufficient sleep who consume alcohol are at greater risk of injury than those who have had sufficient sleep because sleep deprivation has been shown to heighten the effects of alcohol (Roehrs, Beare, Zorick, & Roth, 1994). Sleep-deprived youth may also present with symptoms which are similar to ADHD and thus run the risk of misdiagnosis (Marks & Rothbart, 2003).

Puberty

Those "raging hormones of adolescence" that we hear about are truly influential at this time of life. The hypothalamus, pituitary gland, adrenal glands, and **gonads** (ovaries and testes) begin to interact and stimulate increased hormone production. Although androgens are typ-ically referred to as male hormones and estrogens as female hormones, males and females in fact produce all three major **sex hormones**: androgens, progestins, and estrogens. Sex hor-mones affect the development of the gonads, functioning of the gonads (including sperm production and ova maturation), and mating and child-caring behavior.

However, during **puberty** (the years during which adolescents become capable of repro-duction), increased levels of androgens in males stimulate the development and functioning of the male reproductive system; increased levels of progestins and estrogens in females stim-ulate the development and functioning of the female reproductive system. Specifically, testosterone, which is produced in males by the testes, affects the maturation and function-ing of the penis, prostate gland, and other male genitals; the secondary sex characteristics;

and the sex drive. Estrogen, which is produced in females by the ovaries, affects the maturation and functioning of the ovaries, uterus, and other female genitals; the secondary sex characteristics; and child-caring behaviors.

Primary sex characteristics are those directly related to the reproductive organs and external genitalia. For boys, these include growth of the penis and scrotum. During adolescence, the penis typically doubles or triples in length. Girls' primary sex characteristics are not so visible but include growth of the ovaries, uterus, vagina, clitoris, and labia.

Secondary sex characteristics are those not directly related to the reproductive organs and external genitalia. Secondary sex characteristics are enlarged breasts and hips for girls, facial hair and deeper voices for boys, and hair and sweat gland changes for both sexes. Female breast development is distinguished by growth of the mammary glands, nipples, and areola. The tone of the male voice lowers as the larynx enlarges and the vocal cords lengthen. Both boys and girls begin to grow hair around their genitals and then under their arms. This hair begins with a finer texture and lighter color and then becomes curlier, coarser, and darker. During this period, the sweat glands also begin to produce noticeable odors.

Puberty is thought to begin with the onset of menstruation in girls and production of sperm in boys. Menstruation is the periodic sloughing off of the lining of the uterus. This lining provides nutrients for the fertilized egg. If the egg is not fertilized, the lining sloughs off and is discharged through the vagina. However, for a female to become capable of reproduction, she must not only menstruate but also ovulate. Ovulation, the release of an egg from an ovary, usually does not begin until several months after **menarche**, the onset of menstruation. For males to reproduce, **spermarche**—the onset of the ability to ejaculate mobile sperm—must occur. Spermarche does not occur until after several ejaculations.

Females typically first notice breast growth, then growth of pubic hair, then body growth, especially hips; they then experience menarche, then growth of underarm hair, and finally an increase in production of glandular oil and sweat, possibly with body odor and acne. Males typically follow a similar pattern, first noticing growth of the testes, then growth of pubic hair, body growth, growth of penis, change in voice, growth of facial and underarm hair, and finally an increase in the production of glandular oil and sweat, possibly with body odor and acne.

Generally, females begin puberty about two years earlier than males. Normal pubertal rates (meaning they are experienced by 95% of the population) are for girls to begin menstruating between the ages of 9 and 17 and for boys to produce sperm between the ages of 11 and 16 (Rew, 2005). The age at which puberty begins has been declining in this century, but there is some controversy about the extent of this shift (Newman & Newman, 2006).

In addition to changes instigated by raging sex hormones, adolescents experience growth spurts. Bones are augmented by cartilage during adolescence, and the cartilage calcifies later, during the transition to adulthood. Typically, boys develop broader shoulders, straighter hips, and longer forearms and legs; girls typically develop narrower shoulders and broader hips. These skeletal differences are then enhanced by the development of additional upper body musculature for boys and the development of additional fat deposits on thighs, hips, and buttocks for girls. These changes account for differences in male and female weight and strength.

The Adolescent Brain

Recent magnetic resonance imaging (MRI) studies are revealing new findings regarding adolescent brain development (Gogtay et al., 2004; Rapoport et al., 1999). As discussed in earlier chapters, researchers have known for some time that the early brain overproduces gray matter from development in the womb to about 3-years-old, is highly plastic and thus shaped by experience, and goes through a pruning process. The neural connections or synapses that get exercised are retained, whereas the ones which are not exercised are eliminated. New brain research suggests that the adolescent brain undergoes another period of overproduction of gray matter just prior to puberty and then a second version of pruning. This process, like the infant's, is also affected by the individual's interactions with the outside world (Lidow, Goldman-Rakic, & Rakic, 1991; Rapoport et al., 1999; Seeman, 1999).

Research also shows that teens' gray matter changes in different functional brain areas at different times in development. The gray matter growth spurt just prior to puberty predominates in the frontal lobe which controls planning, decision making, impulse control, language, memory, and reasoning. While the gray matter volume and metabolism diminish, neural activity during certain tasks becomes more focused and efficient (Casey, 1999; Luna et al., 2001; Rubia et al., 2000). A recent small scale longitudinal research project at the National Institutes of Health indicates that "higher order" brain centers, like the prefrontal cortex, that inhibit risky behavior don't fully develop until young adulthood (Gogtay et al., 2004).

> How do changes in the brain during adolescence affect the capacity to exercise human agency in making choices?

Gray matter growth has been found in the temporal lobe, which is specialized for language, and in the parietal lobe, which is specialized for spatial relations, between the ages of 6 and 13 (Thompson et al., 2000). This growth diminished significantly after age 12. Brain researcher Dr. Jay Giedd surmised that "If a teen is doing music or sports or academics, those are the cells and connections that will be hardwired. If they're lying on the couch or playing video games or MTV, those are the cells and connections that are going to survive" (cited in Koelling, 2004, p. 22). In addition, MRI scans show that teens with a rare childhood onset from of schizophrenia have four times the gray matter loss in the frontal lobe as normally occurs (Rapoport et al., 1999).

Psychological Aspects of Adolescence

Psychological development in adolescence is multifaceted. Adolescents have psychological reactions, sometimes dramatic, to the biological, social, and cultural dimensions of their lives. They become capable of and interested in discovering and forming their psychological selves. They may show heightened creativity, as well as interest in humanitarian issues, ethics, religion, and reflection and record keeping, as in a diary (Rew, 2005). Three areas of psychological development are particularly noteworthy: reactions to biological changes, changes in cognition, and the development of a self and an identity.

Psychological Reactions to Biological Changes

Imagine—or remember—being a sweaty, acne-ridden, gangly teenager whose body is changing every day and who is concerned with fitting in and being normal. The penis comparisons in the boys' locker room and the discussions of breasts, bras, and periods in the girls' locker room are examples of how adolescents try to cope with biological change.

Because the onset and experience of puberty vary greatly, adolescents need reassurance regarding their own growth patterns. Some adolescents will be considered early maturers, and some will be considered late maturers. There are psychological and social consequences of early and late maturing for both males and females, but the research findings are not always consistent. Earlier research found several positive consequences for boys who matured early, including greater opportunities for leadership and higher self-esteem (Brooks-Gunn, 1988; Richards & Larson, 1993). More recent research presents a different picture, indicating that early maturing boys have more hostility, more depression and anxiety, more substance abuse and other deviant behaviors (Cota-Robles, Neiss, & Rowe, 2002; Ge, Conger, & Elder, 2001; Wichstrom, 2001). The differences in findings could indicate a cohort effect, but it is also possible that both sets of findings are accurate—that early maturing boys have more opportunities for leadership and also that they are more likely to get drawn into high-risk behavior.

For girls, early maturation often brings awkwardness (Alsaker, 1992; Brooks-Gunn, Petersen, & Eichorn, 1985) and even psychological distress (Ge, Conger, & Elder, 1996; Hayward et al., 1997). Early maturing girls may be taller and heavier than other girls and may find themselves having to wear a bra before their friends who want to wear a bra even pick one out. In addition to the psychological impact, early maturing girls may also feel early sexual pressure. Late maturing girls seem to be the least affected of all boys and girls. They seem to be given more psychological space to develop at their own pace. One research team found that the timing of puberty does not play as big a role in the emotional well-being of girls as aspects of the social context (Booth, Johnson, Granger, Crouter, & McHale, 2003).

Adolescents trying to make psychological accommodations to the dramatic biological changes they are experiencing benefit greatly from the compassion and support of caring adults. Judy Blume's *Are You There, God? It's Me, Margaret* (1970) captures the mixed feelings that some girls experience with their first menstrual period and models useful adult support. The book ends with the following scene:

> Then I looked down at my underpants and I couldn't believe it. There was blood on them. Not a lot—but enough. I really hollered, "Mom—hey Mom—come quick!"
>
> When my mother got to the bathroom she said, "What is it? What's the matter?"
>
> "I got it," I told her.
>
> "Got what?"
>
> I started to laugh and cry at the same time. "My period. I've got my period!" My nose started running and I reached for a tissue.
>
> "Are you sure, Margaret?" my mother asked.
>
> "Look—look at this," I said, showing her my underpants.
>
> "My God! You've really got it. My little girl!" Then her eyes filled up and she started sniffling too. "Wait a minute—I've got the equipment in the other room. I was going to put it in your camp trunk, just in case."
>
> "You were?"
>
> Then I got dressed and looked at myself in the mirror. Would anyone know my secret? Would it show? Would Moose, for instance, know if I went back outside to talk to him? Would my father know right away when he came home for dinner? I had to call Nancy and Gretchen and Janie right away. Poor Janie! She'd be the last of the [group] to get it. And I'd been so sure it would be me! How about that! Now I am growing for sure. Now I am almost a woman! (pp. 147–148)

This fictional representation mirrors what Karin Martin (1996) calls a "normative cultural scenario." A girl is "supposed to begin her period at home, with a supportive, informative mother, with knowledge of what is happening to her, with pads (or occasionally tampons) available" (p. 24). Margaret was indeed prepared, but not everyone has this experience. In any case, the reactions of significant others influence how the adolescent female begins to think and feel about her changing body.

From the male perspective, masturbation is a similarly sensitive topic. A young man interviewed by Martin (1996) had this to say:

> I pretty much knew everything. I was only worried about getting AIDS through like masturbating or something [laughs], but umm, I actually talked to my dad about that, so I wasn't really worried about anything after sixth grade. [Researcher asks what his dad said when he talked to him.] He said, he sort of laughed. He told me stories about how he used to do it too, and he said, "No, you can't get AIDS from doing that." And so I was happy, and he was happy, and that sort of opened the door for whatever conversations. (p. 50)

How the topic of masturbation is handled by adolescents and their families and peers may have lasting effects. Like Margaret's experience with menarche, this young man's situation was managed by a compassionate parent. A range of responses are possible, however, and some of them create enduring problems with attitudes toward the body and sex.

Changes in Cognition

During adolescence, most individuals develop cognitive abilities beyond those of childhood (Keating, 2004), including these:

- Contemplation of the future
- Comprehension of the nature of human relationships
- Consolidation of specific knowledge into a coherent system
- Ability to envision possible consequences from a hypothetical list of actions (foresight)
- Abstract thought
- Empathy
- Internal control

Many of these abilities are components of Jean Piaget's fourth stage of cognitive development called formal operational thought (see Exhibit 3.4 for an overview of Piaget's stages of moral development). *Formal operational thought* suggests the capacity to apply hypothetical reasoning to various situations and the ability to use symbols to solve problems. David Cunha, for example, demonstrated formal operational thought when he considered the possibility of getting to know Theo. He considered the reactions from his other friends if he were to get together with Theo; he examined his thoughts, and he formulated a strategy based on the possibilities and on his thoughts.

Whereas younger children focus on the here-and-now world in front of them, the adolescent brain is capable of retaining larger amounts of information. Thus, adolescents are capable of hypothesizing beyond the present objects. This ability also allows adolescents to

▲ **Photo 6.2** Physical change, formative identity development, increased independence, are but a few factors that characterize adolescence.

engage in decision making based on a cost/benefit analysis. In one study, seventh through twelfth graders were asked to use a cost/benefit analysis to make decisions regarding sexual activity (Small, Silverberg, & Kerns, 1993). The data suggest that perceived costs are more important to sexual decision making than perceived benefits.

Adolescent cognition, however, mirrors adolescence in the sense that it is multifaceted. In addition to the increased capacity for thought, adolescents also bring with them experience, culture, personality, intelligence, family values, identity, and so on. If we conceptualize adolescent cognitive development along a linear continuum from simple intuitive reasoning to advanced, computational, rational, and objective reasoning (Case, 1998; Moshman, 1998), we miss many other facets of individuals and the influences on their cognition. For example, research suggests that older adolescents may not be more objective than younger adolescents, perhaps because irrational cognitive tendencies and biases increase with age (Baron, Granato, Spranca, & Teubal, 1993; Klaczynski, 2000; Klaczynski & Fauth, 1997). Older adolescents have more stereotypes, intuitions, memories, and self-evident truths that they may employ in processing information.

Development of an Identity

Adolescents are fundamentally concerned with the question, "Who am I?" **Identity** is a combination of what you're born with and into; who you associate with; how others see you; what you've done; your attitudes, traits, abilities, habits, tendencies, and preferences; and

How do factors such as gender, race, ethnicity, and social class affect identity development?

what you look like. You might consider the issue of defining a self or an identity to be a psychosocial concept because it is a psychological task of adolescence developed in social transactions. What does the identity we so laboriously construct during adolescence do for us? Identity has five common functions (Adams & Marshall, 1996, p. 433):

1. To provide a structure for understanding who one is

2. To provide meaning and direction through commitments, values, and goals

3. To provide a sense of personal control and free will

4. To enable one to strive for consistency, coherence, and harmony between values, beliefs, and commitments

5. To enable one to recognize one's potential through a sense of future possibilities and alternative choices

Mature adults often incorporate all five functions of identity.

Theories of Self and Identity

A number of prominent psychologists have put forward theories that address self or identity development in adolescence. Exhibit 6.2 provides an overview of five theorists: Freud, Erikson, Marcia, Piaget, and Kohlberg. All five help to explain how a concept of self or an identity develops, and all five suggest that it cannot develop fully before adolescence. Piaget and Kohlberg suggest that some individuals may not reach these higher levels of identity development at all.

Sigmund Freud (1905/1953) thought of human development as a series of five psychosexual stages in the expression of libido (sensual pleasure). The fifth stage, the genital stage, occurs in adolescence, when reproduction and sexual intimacy become possible.

Building on Freud's work, Erik Erikson (1950, 1959, 1963, 1968) proposed eight stages of psychosocial development (refer back to Exhibit 3.6). He viewed psychosocial crisis as an opportunity and challenge. Each Eriksonian stage requires the mastery of a particular developmental task related to identity. His fifth stage, identity versus role diffusion, is relevant to adolescence. The developmental task is to establish a coherent sense of identity; failure to complete this task successfully leaves the adolescent without a solid sense of identity.

James Marcia (1966, 1980) expounded upon Erikson's notion that adolescents struggle with the issue of identity versus role diffusion. Marcia proposed that adolescents vary in how easily they go about developing personal identity, and described four stages of identity development in adolescents:

1. *Identity diffusion.* No exploration of or commitment to roles and values

2. *Foreclosure.* Commitment made to roles and values without exploration

3. *Moratorium.* Exploration of roles and values without commitment

4. *Identity achievement.* Exploration of roles and values followed by commitment

Exhibit 6.2	Theories of Self or Identity in Adolescence	
Theorist	*Developmental Stage*	*Major Task or Processes*
Freud	Genital stage	To develop libido capable of reproduction and sexual intimacy
Erikson	Identity versus role diffusion	To find one's place in the world through self-certainty versus apathy, role experimentation versus negative identity, and anticipation of achievement versus work paralysis
Marcia	Ego identity statuses	To develop one of these identity statuses: identity diffusion, foreclosure, moratorium, or identity achievement
Piaget	Formal operational thought	To develop the capacity for abstract problem formulation, hypothesis development, and solution testing
Kohlberg	Postconventional morality	To develop moral principles that transcend one's own society: individual ethics, societal rights, and universal principles of right and wrong

Jean Piaget proposed four major stages leading to adult thought (refer back to Exhibit 3.4 for an overview of Piaget's stages). He expected the last stage, the stage of formal operations, to occur in adolescence, enabling the adolescent to engage in more abstract thinking about "who I am." Piaget (1972) also thought that adolescents begin to use formal operational skills to think in terms of what is best for society.

Lawrence Kohlberg (1976, 1984) expanded on Piaget's ideas about moral thinking to describe three major levels of moral development (refer back to Exhibit 4.1 for an overview of Kohlberg's stage theory). Kohlberg thought that adolescents become capable of **postconventional moral reasoning**, or morality based on moral principles that transcend social rules, but that many never go beyond conventional morality, or morality based on social rules.

These theories have been influential in conceptualizations of identity development. On perhaps a more practical level, however, Morris Rosenberg, in his book *Conceiving the Self* (1986), provides a very useful model of identity to keep in mind while working with adolescents—or perhaps to share with adolescents who are in the process of identity formation. Rosenberg suggests that identity comprises three major parts, outlined in Exhibit 6.3:

- **Social identity** is made up of several elements derived from interaction with other people and social systems.
- **Dispositions** are self-ascribed aspects of identity.
- **Physical characteristics** are simply one's physical traits, which all contribute a great deal to sense of self.

Exhibit 6.3	Rosenberg's Model of Identity	
Social Identity	*Dispositions*	*Physical Characteristics*
Social statuses: Basic classifications or demographic characteristics, such as sex, age, and socioeconomic status	Attitudes (e.g., conservatism, liberalism)	Height
		Weight
	Traits (e.g., generosity, bravery)	Body build
Membership groups: Groups with which the individual shares an interest, belief, origin, or physical or regional continuity (e.g., groups based on religion, political party, or race)	Abilities (e.g., musical talent, athletic skill)	Facial features
	Values (e.g., efficiency, equality)	
Labels: Identifiers that result from social labeling (as when the boy who skips school becomes a delinquent)	Personality traits (e.g., introversion, extroversion)	
	Habits (e.g., making lists, getting up early)	
Derived statuses: Identities based on the individual's role history (e.g., veteran, high school athlete, or Harvard alumnus)	Tendencies (e.g., to arrive late, to exaggerate)	
Social types: Interests, attitudes, habits, or general characteristics (e.g., jock, geek, head, playboy, or go-getter)	Likes or preferences (e.g., romance novels, pizzas)	
Personal identities: Unique labels attached to individuals (e.g., first name, first and last names, social security number, fingerprints, or DNA)		

Source: Rosenberg, 1986.

Exhibit 6.4	Examples of Adolescent Identity		
Element of Identity	*David*	*Carl*	*Monica*
Social Identity			
Social statuses	Male, 17, middle class	Male, 17, working class	Female, 17, upper middle class
Membership groups	Bolivian American, gay	European American, heads	African American, Christian, Young Republicans
Labels	Freak	Fatso, underachiever, smoker	Overachiever
Derived statuses	Soccer player	Pizza deliverer	Senior class vice president, baby-sitter, supermarket cashier, track athlete
Social types	Jock	Geek, head (affiliate)	Brain, go-getter
Personal identity	David Cunha	Carl Fleischer	Monica Golden
Disposition	Athletic	Underachiever, not popular, fat, slow, likes to get high, likes to surf the Internet	Athletic, ambitious, extroverted, likes children
Physical characteristics	Soccer build	Overweight	Tall

Exhibit 6.4 uses Rosenberg's model to analyze the identities of David Cunha, Carl Fleischer, and Monica Golden. Notice that disposition is an element of identity based on self-definition. In contrast, a label is determined by others, and physical characteristics are genetically influenced. David has an athletic body and thinks of himself as athletic, but his parents—and perhaps others—label him as a freak. He is working to incorporate the fact that he is different into his identity. Carl has been labeled as a fatso, an underachiever, and a smoker. He seems to have incorporated these negative labels into his identity. Monica has been labeled as an overachiever, but she does not absorb the negative label, reframing it instead as ambitious.

Identity Formation

How do adolescents construct an identity? We can think of adolescent identity formation as a trip to the salad bar of life. As adolescents move through the salad bar, they first have to decide on a base of iceberg lettuce or maybe romaine or perhaps spinach. Then they exercise more free will: broccoli, carrots, or tomatoes? cheese? croutons? sunflower seeds?

Scholars suggest that identity formation is structured by the sociocultural context (Adams & Marshall, 1996; Baumeister & Muraven, 1996). Thus, the options offered by any given salad bar will vary depending on the restaurant. Think about David, Carl, and Monica. What is the sociocultural context of their trip to the salad bar? What salad ingredients can they choose, given the restaurant they find themselves in?

For those salad options that individuals are able to choose—for those aspects of identity that we shape ourselves—individuals have four ways of trying on and developing a preference for certain identities:

1. *Future orientation.* By adolescence, youth have developed two important cognitive skills: they are able to consider the future and they are able to construct abstract thoughts. These skills allow them to choose from a list of hypothetical behaviors based on the potential outcomes resulting from those behaviors. David Cunha demonstrates future orientation in his contemplation regarding Theo. Adolescents also contemplate potential future selves.

2. *Role experimentation.* According to Erikson (1963), adolescence provides a psychosocial moratorium—a period during which youth have the latitude to experiment with social roles. Thus, adolescents typically sample membership in different cliques, build relationships with various mentors, take various academic electives, and join assorted groups and organizations—all in an attempt to further define themselves. Monica Golden, for example, sampled various potential career paths before deciding on becoming a pediatrician.

3. *Exploration.* Whereas role experimentation is specific to trying new roles, exploration refers to the comfort an adolescent has with trying new things. The more comfortable the individual is with exploration, the easier identity formation will be.

4. *Self-evaluation.* During the quest for identity, adolescents are constantly sizing themselves up against their peers. Erikson (1968) suggested that the development of identity is a process of personal reflection and observation of oneself in relation to others. George Herbert Mead (1934) suggested that individuals create a **generalized other** to represent how others are likely to view and respond to them. The role of the generalized other in adolescents' identity formation is evident when adolescents act on the assumed reactions of their

families or peers. For example, what Monica Golden wears to school may be based not on what she thinks would be most comfortable or look the best but rather on what she thinks her peers expect her to wear. Thus, she does not wear miniskirts to school because "everyone" (generalized other) will think she is "loose."

There are certainly added complexities during the identity formation of minority youth. Arthur Jones (1992) suggests that "the usual rifts between young adolescents (ages 13 to 15) and their parents are sometimes more intense in middle-class African American families, especially those in which middle-class economic status is new for the parents. This is because the generation gap is more exaggerated" (p. 29). Consider Monica Golden, who is an upper-middle-class, African American teenager in a predominantly white high school. What are some of the potential added challenges of Monica's adolescent identity formation? Is it any wonder that she is hoping to attend Howard University, a traditionally black college, where she could surround herself with African American role models and professional support networks?

Gender Differences

Adolescence, like early childhood in Chapter 4, is a time of significant gender identification and much has been written lately in the United States about the specific experiences of either adolescent boys or adolescent girls (Garbarino, 1999, 2006; Kindlon & Thompson, 1999; Pipher, 1994; Pollack, 1999; Rimm, 1999; Wiseman, 2002). Exercise caution, however, with these types of works as some may present an exaggerated perspective for either gender experience.

Mary Pipher (1994), in her book *Reviving Ophelia: Saving the Selves of Adolescent Girls*, suggests that "girls today are much more oppressed. They are coming of age in a more dangerous, sexualized and media-saturated culture. They face incredible pressures to be beautiful and sophisticated, which in junior high means using chemicals and being sexual. As they navigate a more dangerous world, girls are less protected" (p. 12).

Similar sentiments are presented regarding the forces that threaten adolescent boys in *Raising Cain: Protecting the Emotional Life of Boys* (Kindlon & Thompson, 1999) and *Real Boys: Rescuing Our Sons From the Myths of Boyhood* (Pollack, 1999). The authors see boys in the United States who are hurting, sad, afraid, angry, and silent in a society that expects them to be tough and confident. Amid statistics that suggest increasing numbers of adolescent boys at risk for suicide, alcohol and drug abuse, violence, and loneliness, Kindlon and Thompson feel that "boys, beginning at a young age, are systematically steered away from their emotional lives toward silence, solitude, and distrust" (p. xv). They advocate giving boys the space and permission to be active and the emotional vocabulary and tools to develop in their social world. Pollack (1999) adds that boys should be allowed, encouraged, and supported in demonstrating all of their emotions.

As we work with adolescents and strive to be responsive to their particulars, we need to begin to consider what role being female or being male may play in who they are and what may be happening in their lives. How would David Cunha's situation be different if he were a lesbian versus a gay male? What if Carl Fleischer was Carol? How are weight issues different for women and men? Are they different? And do successful black men have different experiences or expectations from successful black women? What if Monica Golden were male?

▧ Social Aspects of Adolescence

The social environment—family, peers, certain institutions, culture, and so on—is a significant element of adolescent life. For one thing, as already noted, identity develops through social transactions. For another, as adolescents become more independent and move into the world, they develop their own relationships with more elements of the social environment.

Relationships With Family

Answering the question, "Who am I?" includes a consideration of the question, "How am I different from my brothers and sisters, my parents, and other family members?" For many adolescents, this question begins the process of **individuation**—the development of a self or identity that is unique and separate. David Cunha seems to have started the process of individuation; he recognizes that he may not want to be what his parents want him to be. He does not yet seem comfortable with this idea, however. Carl Fleischer is not sure how he is like and different from his absent father. Monica Golden has begun to recognize some ways that she is different from her siblings, and she is involved in her own personal exploration of career options that fit her dispositions. It would appear that she is the furthest along in the individuation process.

Separation from parents has four components (Moore, 1987):

1. *Functional independence.* Literally being able to function with little assistance or independently from one's parents. An example would be getting ready for school: selecting an appropriate outfit, getting dressed, compiling school supplies, and feeding oneself.

2. *Attitudinal independence.* Not merely having a different attitude from parents, but developing one's own set of values and beliefs. An example might be choosing a presidential candidate based not on your parents' choice but on your values and beliefs.

3. *Emotional independence.* Not being dependent on parents for approval, intimacy, and emotional support. Emotional independence might mean discovering your own way to overcome emotional turmoil—for example, listening to your favorite CD after a fight with your girlfriend or boyfriend rather than relying on support from your parents.

4. *Conflictual independence.* Being able to recognize one's separateness from parents without guilt, resentment, anger, or other negative emotions. Conflictual independence is being comfortable with being different. Thus, instead of ridiculing your dad for wearing those shorts to the picnic, you are able to go to the picnic realizing that you would not wear those shorts but that your father's taste in shorts is not a reflection on you.

The concept of independence is largely influenced by culture. And mainstream culture in the United States places a high value on independence. However, as social workers, we need to recognize that the notion of pushing the adolescent to develop an identity separate from family is not acceptable to all cultural groups in the United States, including Italians, Jews, and Latinos (McGill & Pearce, 1996). Many Asian Indian families may view adolescent struggles for independence as a disloyal cutting off of family and culture (Hines et al., 2005). Our assessments of adolescent individuation should be culturally sensitive. Likewise, we must be realistic in our assessments of the functional independence of adolescents with mental and physical disabilities.

Even when it is consistent with their cultural values, not all adolescents are able to achieve functional independence, attitudinal independence, emotional independence, and conflictual independence. Instead, many maintain a high level of conflict. Conflict is particularly evident in families experiencing additional stressors, such as divorce and economic difficulties (Flanagan, 1990; Smetana, Killen, & Turiel, 1991). Conflict also plays out differently in different arenas. Research suggests that, compared with childhood, adolescent conflict regarding chores, appearance, and politeness decreases overall; conflict regarding substance use stays the same; and conflict regarding finances increases (Galambos & Almeida, 1992).

Adolescent struggles for independence can be especially potent in multigenerational contexts (Preto, 2005). These struggles typically come at a time when parents are in midlife and grandparents are entering late adulthood and both are facing stressors of their own. Adolescent demands for independence may reignite unresolved conflicts between the parents and the grandparents and stir the pot of family discord. The challenge for the family is to stay connected while also allowing the adolescent to widen contact with the world. Most families make this adjustment well, but often after an initial period of confusion and disruption.

> How can families stay connected to their adolescents while also honoring their struggle for independence and increased agency in making choices?

The Society for Research on Adolescence prepared an international perspective on adolescence in the twenty-first century and reached three conclusions regarding adolescents and their relationships with their families:

♦ Families are and will remain a central source of support to adolescents in most parts of the world. Cultural traditions that support family cohesion, such as those in the Middle East, South Asia, and China, remain particularly strong, despite rapid change. A great majority of teenagers around the world experience close and functional relationships with their parents.

♦ Adolescents are living in a wider array of diverse and fluid family situations than was true a generation ago. These include divorced, single-parent, remarried, gay and lesbian, and multi-local families. More adolescents live in households without men. As a result of AIDS, regional conflicts, and migratory labor, many adolescents do not live with their parents.

♦ Many families are becoming better positioned to support their adolescents' preparation for adulthood. Smaller family sizes result in adults devoting more resources and attention to each child. Parents in many parts of the world are adopting a more responsive and communicative parenting style, which facilitates development of interpersonal skills and enhances mental health (Larson, Wilson, & Mortimer, 2002).

Relationships With Peers

Most adolescents would rather be anywhere with their peers than anywhere with their parents. In the quest for autonomy and identity, adolescents begin to differentiate themselves from their parents and associate with their peers. And whereas children seek same-sex peer groups, adolescents begin socializing more with opposite-sex peers. Peer relationships contribute to adolescents' identities, behaviors, and personal and social competence.

Peer relationships are a fertile testing ground for youth and their emerging identities (Brown, 2004). Many adolescents seek out a peer group with compatible members, and

▲ **Photo 6.3** Peer relationships are a fertile testing ground for youth and their emerging identities.

inclusion or exclusion from certain groups can affect their identity and overall development. David Cunha's peer groups include the soccer team and a group of gay males from school. Carl Fleischer seems to be gravitating toward the "heads" for his peer group—although this choice appears to be related to a perception of rejection by other groups. Monica Golden enjoys easy acceptance by several peer groups: the peer counselors at high school, the senior class officers, the Young Republicans, and the track team.

For some adolescents, participation in certain peer groups influences their behavior negatively. Peer influence may not be strong enough to undo protective factors, but if the youth is already at risk, the influence of peers becomes that much stronger (Rew, 2005). Sexual behaviors and pregnancy status are often the same for same-sexed best friends. Substance use is also a behavior that most often occurs in groups of adolescents. The same is true for violent and delinquent behaviors (Garbarino, 1999; Klein, 1995).

Relationships With Institutions

As adolescents loosen their ties to parents, they develop more direct relationships in other arenas such as school, employment, leisure, and the Internet.

School

In the United States, as well as other wealthy nations, youth are required to stay in school through a large portion of adolescence. The situation is quite different in many poor nations, however, where children may not even receive a primary school education (United Nations Development Program, 2005).

In their time that is spent at school, adolescents are gaining skills and knowledge for their next step in life, either moving into the workforce or continuing their education. In school, they also have the opportunity to evolve socially and emotionally; school is a fertile ground for practicing future orientation, role experimentation, exploration, and self-evaluation.

Middle schools have a very structured format and a very structured environment; high schools are less structured in both format and environment, allowing a gradual transition to greater autonomy. The school experience changes radically, however, at the college level. Many college students are away from home for the first time and are in very unstructured environments. David Cunha, Carl Fleischer, and Monica Golden have had different experiences with structure in their environments to date. David's environment has required him to move flexibly between two cultures. That experience may help to prepare him for the unstructured college environment. Carl has had the least structured home life. It remains to be seen whether that has helped him to develop skills in structuring his own environment, or left him with insufficient models for doing so. Monica is accustomed to juggling multiple commitments and should have little trouble with the competing attractions and demands of college.

School is also an institutional context where cultures intersect, which may create difficulties for students who are not familiar or comfortable with mainstream culture. That is most likely an important contributing factor to the low high school graduation rates of youth of color. Recent research by the Civil Rights Project at Harvard University indicates that 75% of white students graduate from high school compared to approximately half of black, Hispanic, and Native American youth (Orfield, Losen, Wald, & Swanson, 2004). You may not realize how Eurocentric the educational model in the United States is until you view it through a different cultural lens. We can use a Native American lens as an example. Michael Walkingstick Garrett (1995) uses the experiences of the boy Wind-Wolf as an example of the incongruence between Native American culture and the typical education model:

> Wind-Wolf is required by law to attend public school. . . . He speaks softly, does not maintain eye contact with the teacher as a sign of respect, and rarely responds immediately to questions, knowing that it is good to reflect on what has been said. He may be looking out the window during class, as if daydreaming, because he has been taught to always be aware of changes in the natural world. These are interpreted by his teacher as either lack of interest or dumbness. (p. 204)

What are some ways that different cultural expectations regarding education affect adolescent development?

Children in the United States spend less time in school-related activities than do Chinese or Japanese children and have been noted to put less emphasis on scholastic achievement. Some researchers attribute oft-noted cross-cultural differences in mathematics achievement to these national differences in emphasis on scholastics (Fuligni & Stevenson, 1995). For adolescents, scholastic interest, expectations, and achievements may also vary, based not only on nationality but also on gender, race, ethnicity, economic status, and expectations for the future. Girls have been found to be more invested in school activities than boys (Shanahan & Flaherty, 2001). In a study of students in 33 middle and high schools, African American and Hispanic students were found to be more disengaged from school than Asian and white students, and economically disadvantaged teenagers were found to be more disengaged than more economically advantaged students (Csikszentmihalyi & Schneider, 2000). Recent longitudinal research found that adolescents with a future orientation and expectations of further schooling, marriage, and good citizenship devote a greater percentage of their time to school-related activities (Shanahan & Flaherty, 2001).

A 1988 report, *The Forgotten Half,* by the William T. Grant Foundation, cited 1980 census data that half of U.S. adults 25 and over had no formal education beyond high school and were vulnerable to a lifetime of poverty. Through the early 1990s, vocational education in the United States was stigmatized as the high school track for students with poor academic capabilities, special needs, or behavioral problems (Gamoran & Himmelfarb, 1994). Congress and most educators, however, believe that broadening the segment of the student population that participates in vocational education and adding academic achievement and postsecondary enrollment to the traditional objectives of technical competency, labor market outcomes, and general employability skills will improve the quality of these programs

(Lynch, 2000). Recently, the National Women's Law Center has reported that there is pervasive sex segregation in high school vocational programs in the United States, with girls clustered in programs that train them for lower-paying jobs ("Sex Bias," 2002).

Work

Like many adolescents, Carl and Monica also play the role of worker in the labor market. Work can provide an opportunity for social interaction and greater financial independence. It may also lead to personal growth by promoting notions of contribution, responsibility, egalitarianism, and self-efficacy and by helping the adolescent to develop values and preferences for future jobs—answers to questions like "What kind of job would I like to have in the future?" and "What am I good at?" (Mortimer & Finch, 1996, p. 4). For example, Monica tried many jobs before deciding that she loves working with children and wants to become a pediatrician. In addition, employment may also offer the opportunity to develop job skills, time management skills, customer relation skills, money management skills, market knowledge, and other skills of value to future employers.

In July 2006, 21.9 million U.S. youth ages 16 to 24 were employed for an employment rate of 59.2% of the civilian noninstitutional population (Bureau of Labor Statistics, 2006). The rate fell almost 11 points between July 1989 and July 2003 but has remained fairly constant from 2003 to 2006. Being in the labor force means the individual is working either full-time or part-time as a paid employee in an ongoing relationship with a particular employer, such as working in a supermarket. Individuals are not considered to be in the labor force if they work in "freelance jobs" that involve doing tasks without a specific employer, such as babysitting or mowing lawns. Broken down by gender and race the employment rate for July 2006 was 61.9% for young men, 56.5% for young women, 63.3% for whites, 43.5% for blacks, 42.8% for Asians, and 55.2% for Latinos (Bureau of Labor Statistics, 2006).

The U.S. Department of Labor has launched a new initiative called YouthRules! that seeks to promote positive and safe work experiences for young workers. Their guidelines may be the social policy result of research that suggests that for youth, work, in spite of some positive benefits, may also detract from development by cutting into time needed for sleep, exercise, maintenance of overall health, school, family relations, and peer relations. Adolescents who work more than 10 hours per week have been found to be at increased risk for poor academic performance, psychological problems such as depression, anxiety, fatigue, and sleep difficulties, as well as physical problems such as headaches, stomachaches, and colds. They are also more likely to use cigarettes, alcohol, or other drugs, regardless of ethnicity, socioeconomic status (SES), or age (Mortimer & Finch, 1996). Although we cannot draw causal conclusions, Carl Fleischer is a good example of this linkage: he works more than 10 hours a week and also has declining grades and uses tobacco and marijuana.

Leisure

A sizable portion of an adolescent's life is spent in leisure pursuits. These activities often have great influence on various aspects of the individual's development, such as identity formation, and psychological and behavioral functioning (Bartko & Eccles, 2003). Cross-national research indicates that there are national differences in the way adolescents use nonschool time (Verma & Larson, 2003). For example, Korean and Japanese youth spend more time on homework and preparation for college entrance exams than U.S. or European youth (Lee, 2003). Compared to European teens from 12 countries, U.S. teens spend less time on schoolwork, less time in reading for leisure, more time in paid employment, and more time hanging out with friends (Flammer & Schaffner, 2003; Larson & Seepersad, 2003). Japanese and U.S. youth spend a great deal of time on extracurricular activity, particularly organized sports, based on a cultural belief that these activities build character (Larson & Seepersad, 2003; Nishino & Larson, 2003). Across national lines, girls tend to have more chores and spend more time in the arts than boys, and boys spend more time in sports and with electronic media than girls (Silbereisen, 2003).

One research team (Bartko & Eccles, 2003) examined the nonschool activity profiles of 918 adolescents from Washington, D.C., across 11 different activity domains. Using cluster analysis, they identified a typology of six unique activity profiles:

Sports Cluster: highly involved in sports, and also in spending time with friends

School Cluster: highly involved in school-based clubs, homework, and reading for pleasure

Uninvolved Cluster: activity levels below the mean in all 11 activity domains

Volunteer Cluster: highly involved in volunteer activities

High-involved Cluster: highly involved in a range of activities, including community-based clubs, sports, homework, reading, chores, volunteering, and religious activities; low involvement in unstructured activities

Working Cluster: highly involved in paid work, and low levels of involvement in other activity domains

There were no race differences in activity choices, but there were gender differences. Males were overrepresented in the Sports Cluster and Uninvolved Cluster. Females were overrepresented in the School Cluster, Volunteer Cluster, and High-involved Cluster. The parents of the High-involved Cluster had higher educational attainment than students in the other clusters. Psychological and behavioral functioning was associated with the activity profiles of the respondents. Respondents in the School and High-involved clusters had the highest grade point averages, and Uninvolved respondents had the lowest grade point averages. Behavior problems were more often reported by respondents in the Sports, Uninvolved, and Work clusters. The highest rates of depression were found in the Uninvolved Cluster.

Another study examining the relationship between leisure and identity formation for adolescents found that the patterns of influence are different for girls and boys (Shaw, Kleiber, & Caldwell, 1995). Participation in sports and physical activities has a positive effect on identity development for female adolescents but shows no effect for males. Watching television has a negative effect on identity development for male adolescents but shows no effect for females. And involvement in social activities and other leisure activities was not significantly correlated with identity development for either gender.

Access to leisure activities varies. Leisure activities for rural adolescents are different from leisure activities for urban youth, for example. Adolescents living in urban areas have greater access to transportation and to public recreational activities and programs. Rural youth lack this access and thus rely more heavily on school-related leisure activities (Garton & Pratt, 1991). Access to leisure activities also increases with SES.

Whatever an adolescent's gender, region, or SES, however, research suggests that those who consider their leisure time to be boring are more likely to use substances (Iso-Ahola & Crowley, 1991). They are also more likely to drop out of school (Widmer, Ellis, & Trunnell, 1996).

The Internet

In the 1990s and first years of the twenty-first century, there was enormous growth in the use of the Internet. Increasingly, teens are using the Internet to complete schoolwork, obtain general information, play games, and socialize. In 2004, it was estimated that two-thirds of households in the United States had access to the Internet (Croteau & Hoynes, 2006). And with children and teenagers comprising one of the fastest growing groups of Internet users, researchers estimate that almost 25 million youth in the United States between the ages of 10 and 17 are regular Internet users today (Wolak, Mitchell, & Finkelhor, 2006). Nationwide, 21.1% of high school students said they played video or computer games or used a computer for something other than school work for more than three hours on an average school day (CDC, 2006c).

▲ **Photo 6.4** Leisure activities often have great influence on identity formation as well as psychological and behavioral functioning.

There is empirical evidence that the Internet fosters social connections and identity development, is an important source for adolescent health information, and provides opportunities for practicing leadership skills (Borzekowski, Fobil, & Asante, 2006; Greenfield & Zheng, 2006; Gross, 2004). On the other hand, parents, school officials, and legislators have become increasingly concerned that adolescents will see sexually explicit material on the Internet, and be sexually exploited or otherwise harassed via the Internet. In 1999 and 2000 researchers Wolak, Mitchell, and Finkelhor conducted the first Youth Internet Safety Survey (YISS-1) with a national sample of over 1,500 youth ages 10 to 17 who used the Internet at least once a month for the past six months. A second Youth Internet Safety Survey (YISS-2) was conducted in 2005 by the same researchers, again using a sample of over 1,500 youth ages 10 to 17 (Wolak et al., 2006). Some of the main findings of YISS-2 are presented below:

91% of the youth had home Internet access, compared to 74% in YISS-1

74% had access in three or more places, compared to 51% in YISS-1

86% of the youth had used the Internet in the past week, compared to 76% in YISS-1

23% reported using the Internet more than two hours at a time, compared to 13% in YISS-1

49% used the Internet five to seven days a week, compared to 31% in YISS-1

30% visited online chat rooms, compared to 56% in YISS-1

34% saw sexual material online that they did want to see in the past year, up from 25% in YISS-1, despite the increased use of filtering, blocking, and monitoring software

34% communicated online with people they did not know in person, compared to 40% in YISS-1

One in seven youth received unwanted sexual solicitation, compared to one in five in YISS-1

4% received aggressive sexual solicitations, which attempted offline contact, compared to 3% in YISS-1

4% reported that online solicitors asked them for nude or sexually explicit photographs of themselves; this information was not collected in YISS-1

9% were the victims of online harassment and/or bullying, compared to 6% in YISS-1

28% had made rude or nasty comments to someone on the Internet, compared to 14% in YISS-1

YISS-2 also found a large increase in the posting or sending of personal information or pictures between 2000 and 2005. In 2005, 34% had posted their real names, home addresses, telephone number, or their school names; 45% had posted their date of birth or age; and 18% had posted pictures of themselves. In 2000, only 11% had posted personal information and only 5% had posted pictures of themselves. This increase reflects the rise of personal profile sites such as MySpace, Friendster, and Xanga. Wolak, Mitchell, and Finkelhor (2003) surmise that "adolescents may be especially drawn to online relationships because of their intense interest in forming relationships, and because the expansiveness of cyberspace frees them from some of the constraints of adolescence by giving them easy access to a world beyond that of their families, schools and communities" (p. 106). Unfortunately, adolescents are also vulnerable to unethical marketers who engage in such tactics as bundling digital pornography material with game demos and other products that youth are likely to download (Wolak et al., 2006). Researchers have also found that sex offenders target young teenagers by playing on their desire for romance and interest in sex (Wolak et al., 2006). The adolescents who are most vulnerable to these advances are girls who have high levels of conflict with their parents or who are highly troubled and boys with low levels of communication with their parents or who are highly troubled (Wolak et al., 2003).

Relationships With Culture

Adolescents in the United States who are not of European American background face additional challenges as they encounter the many changes of adolescence. The greatest challenges may be faced by immigrants. Following a five-year longitudinal study of immigrants, Patricia Arrendondo (1984) proposed the following three factors as necessary for satisfactory adjustment to a new culture:

1. Willingness and ability to confront the issue of belonging versus estrangement

2. Ability to rely on the values of the native culture

3. Supportive family relationships

Among the challenges facing immigrant youth is deciding what their relationship will be with their native culture and the mainstream culture. They generally have these options (Garrett, 1995):

- *Traditional.* Speaking in their native language and practicing traditional beliefs and practices
- *Transitional.* Speaking both their native language and English and not participating fully in either traditional practices or mainstream culture
- *Bicultural.* Participating in both native culture and mainstream culture
- *Assimilated.* Practicing only mainstream culture and values

For some youth, this decision is not theirs to make; it is imposed on them by family and community.

Many youth seek to distance themselves from their minority culture in early adolescence in order to emphasize their similarities with peers. These youth may then readopt their native culture in late adolescence if their self-concept and identity are adequately formed and allow the reconnection. For some youth, their heritage is a source of great pride; for others, it carries shame. These responses certainly affect the sense of self or identity of minority adolescents.

Some youth may be more likely to withdraw from the challenges of accessing mainstream culture rather than confronting those challenges and seeking workable options. Multiethnic (Markstrom-Adams & Adams, 1995), Mexican American (Abraham, 1986), and Native American (Markstrom & Mullis, 1986) youth are especially likely to have this

How can social workers use research like this to understand risk and protection in minority youth?

response. Their perception that their options in mainstream culture are limited may pose psychological risk, depending on factors such as perceptions of their ethnic group's social status, available support systems, structures and patterns of family interactions, psychological characteristics of the individual, and explicit and implicit societal policies (Miller, 1992).

Researchers have recently taken an interest in how adolescents of different racial and ethnic backgrounds cope with stress. Paula Chapman and Ronald Mullis (2000) investigated racial differences in coping styles among a sample of lower-middle-class white and African American adolescents who resided in rural communities in a southern state. Their findings indicate important racial differences in coping with stress, but caution must be used in interpreting their findings. African Americans were the majority racial group in the communities from which the sample was drawn, and the researchers were probably tapping minority-majority differences in coping styles, as well as racial differences. Keeping that in mind, Chapman and Mullis found that African American adolescents reported using several coping strategies more frequently than white adolescents: diversions, self-reliance, spiritual support, close friends, demanding activities, solution of family problems, and relaxation. White adolescents used two coping strategies more frequently than African American adolescents: ventilating feelings and avoidance. White females, as well as African American adolescents of both genders, reported more use of social support than white males. No racial differences were found in self-esteem. This research, and earlier work on which it was based, should alert white social workers to recognize the strengths in the coping styles of racial minority youth. Moreover, while recognizing the difficulties that may exist for minority youth, social workers must also be alert to the ethnocentrism that may be inherent in typical intervention strategies.

✎ Spiritual Aspects of Adolescence

Another potential facet of adolescent development is spirituality or religiosity. As adolescents become capable of advanced thinking and begin to contemplate their existence, identity, and future, many also undertake spiritual exploration. Sociology of religion researchers suggest that adolescents are a population that many religious organizations particularly target in order to exert influence in their lives, and adolescence and young adulthood are the life stages when religious conversion is most likely to take place (Smith, Denton, Faris, & Regnerus, 2002, p. 597).

How important is it for social workers to assess the spirituality of adolescents with whom they work?

The National Study of Youth and Religion (NSYR) is the most comprehensive study of spirituality and religion among U.S. adolescents to date. Supported by the Lilly Endowment, this study began in August 2001 and is funded through December 2007. The first wave of data collection was conducted from July 2002 to April 2003. It is a nationally representative, random-digit-dial method, telephone survey of 3,290 English- and Spanish-speaking teenagers ages 13 to 17 and of their parents living in all 50 states. It also includes more than 250 in-depth, face-to-face interviews of a subsample of survey respondents. The second wave included 78% of the original respondents and was conducted from June 2005 to November 2005. Much of the second wave analysis is still being completed.

The NSYR found that the vast majority of U.S. teenagers identify themselves as Christian (52% Protestant, various denominations, and 23% Catholic). Sixteen percent are not religious. In addition, 2.8% identify themselves with two different faiths, 2.5% are Mormon, 1.5% are Jewish, and other minority faiths (Jehovah's Witness, Muslim, Eastern Orthodox, Buddhist, Pagan or Wiccan, Hindu, Christian Science, Native American, Unitarian Universalist) each comprised less than 1% of the representative sample. Four out of ten U.S. adolescents say they attend religious services once a week or more, pray daily or more, and are currently involved in a religious youth group. Eighty-four percent of the surveyed youth believe in God whereas 12% are unsure about belief about God, and 3% do not believe in God.

The bulk of the NSYR data are analyzed in the book, *Soul Searching: The Religious and Spiritual Lives of American Teenagers* by Smith and Denton (2005) who reached these empirical conclusions:

Religion is a significant presence in the lives of many U.S. teens today.

Teenage religiosity in the United States is extraordinarily conventional and very few youth appear to be pursuing 'spiritual but no religious' personal quests.

The religious diversity represented by U.S. adolescents is no more varied today than it has been for a very long time.

The single most important social influence on the religious and spiritual lives of adolescents is their parents.

The greater the supply of religiously grounded relationships, activities, programs, opportunities, and challenges available to teenagers the more likely teenagers will be religiously engaged and invested.

At the level of subjective consciousness, adolescent religious and spiritual understanding and concern seem to be generally very weak.

It is impossible to adequately understand the religious and spiritual lives of U.S. teenagers without framing that understanding to include the larger social and institutional contexts that form their lives.

Significant differences [exist] in a variety of important life outcomes between more and less religious teenagers in the United States. (pp. 260–263)

Michael Donahue and Peter Benson (1995) found similar effects of religion on the well-being of adolescents (controlling for sociodemographic variables). They found a link between religiousness and "prosocial values and behavior." Religious adolescents are less likely to think of or attempt suicide, to abuse substances, to become prematurely involved in sexual activity, and to become "delinquent" (p. 145). In a similar vein, psychologist James Garbarino (1999) found a spiritual emptiness in violent adolescent males, whom he calls "lost boys." Garbarino advocates using spiritual values to build a positive attachment between boys and their communities, and working to make the boys' social environment (family, school, community) more competent to meet their needs. Garbarino believes this practice will anchor boys in empathy and socially engaged, moral thinking (p. 238).

For many youth, spirituality may be closely connected to culture. Jose Cervantes and Oscar Ramirez (1992) suggest that interventions with adolescents and their families should be consistent with their spirituality. For example, family therapy based on an understanding of mestizo spirituality and of the philosophy of *curanderismo* might profitably be used to guide clinical practice with Mexican American families.

The **mestizo perspective** "allows for an introspective attitude fostering culturally sanctioned inclination toward wholeness, harmony, and balance in one's relationship with self, family, community, and the physical and social environment. This attitude is embedded within a consciousness that understands learning from one's life history, diversity, and multicultural struggle" (Cervantes & Ramirez, 1992, p. 106). It is based on the following five tenets:

1. Every person has a valuable life story to tell and lesson to learn. There is a Mexican proverb, "Cada cabeza un mundo," which suggests that each person's life and experience is unique and important.

2. Harmony with the physical and social environment is crucial to psychological adjustment and reflects a recognition of balance and respect for all living things.

3. Openness to diversity fosters a multicultural attitude of mutual respect and acceptance of all peoples.

4. A willingness to learn from diversity advances the humanistic agenda of the people.

5. A theistic cosmology protects, influences, and engages all of life.

Curanderismo is a holistic folk medicine philosophy (Carrasco, 1990; Cervantes & Ramirez, 1992; De La Cancela & Martinez, 1983; Perrone, Stockel, & Krueger, 1989). It is based on the following beliefs (Cervantes & Ramirez, 1992, pp. 114–115):

- Divine will is central and the individual's responsibility is to have good intentions and do good deeds. If the individual deviates from this responsibility, misfortune and illness may result.
- Social, emotional, and physiological successes or difficulties are also the result of the individual's interpersonal relationships within the family and community.
- Supernatural forces can positively or negatively influence the individual, and the individual can take steps to restore balance with these forces.
- There is no separation between mind and body, and this union is inextricably linked to the divine.

Although adolescents may not seem to be guided by their spirituality or religiosity, they may have underlying spiritual factors at work. As with any biological, psychological, or social aspect of the individual, the spiritual aspect of youth must be considered to gain the best understanding of the whole person.

⬚ Issues, Challenges, and Problems During Adolescence

The adolescent period is quite complex all on its own, and substance use, juvenile delinquency, and other threats to physical and mental health further complicate the picture. Again, not all adolescents face all of these issues, and those who do face some of them follow no strict time line. We do know, however, that adolescents who are considered at risk may be more susceptible than others to these challenges or problems of adolescence. In the introduction to her book *Adolescents at Risk,* Joy Dryfoos (1990) states:

> Many children are growing up in the United States today without a hope of enjoying the benefits that come with adulthood. They are not learning the skills necessary to participate in the educational system or to make the transition into the labor force. They cannot become responsible parents because they have limited experience in family life and lack the resources to raise their own children. The gap between achievers and nonachievers is expanding. A new class of "untouchables" is emerging in our inner cities, on the social fringes of suburbia, and in some rural areas: young people who are functionally illiterate, disconnected from school, depressed, prone to drug abuse and early criminal activity, and eventually, parents of unplanned and unwanted babies. (p. 3)

Although sexual development is a natural part of adolescence, managing sexuality presents a challenge to many adolescents.

Sexuality

Sexual identity is a significant component in the transition to adulthood. For the adolescent, sexual identity encompasses becoming familiar with the physical changes of puberty, recognizing one's sexual orientation, and making decisions about sexual activity; it may also include dealing with pregnancy and childbearing, sexually transmitted disease, and acquaintance rape.

Masturbation

As the pubertal hormones cause changes throughout the body, adolescents spend time becoming familiar with those changes. For many, exploration includes **masturbation**, the self-stimulation of the genitals for sexual pleasure. Almost 50% of boys and 30% of girls report masturbating by age 13; boys masturbate earlier and more often than girls (Leitenberg, Detzer, & Srebnik, 1993). The gender difference has been found to be even greater in Bangkok, Thailand, where 79% of male secondary students report masturbating, compared to 9% of females (O-Prasetsawat & Petchum, 2004).

However, masturbation has negative associations for some boys and girls. Many girls do not like to touch or look at their genitals, so it makes sense that fewer masturbate. For boys, any negative or anxious associations with sex at adolescence are usually in regard to masturbation (Martin, 1996). Thus, masturbation may have psychological implications for adolescents, depending on the way they feel about masturbation and on how they think significant others feel about it. Female college students who are high in religiosity report more guilt about masturbation than female college students who are low in religiosity (Davidson, Moore, & Ullstrup, 2004).

Sexual Orientation

During adolescence, many individuals, both homosexual and heterosexual, have homosexual experiences, but not all form a sexual orientation based on those experiences. About 6.8% of youth responding to the U.S. National Health Survey reported having experienced same-sex attractions or same-sex relationships, but only a small group reported same-sex sexual behaviors, and even fewer identified themselves as gay, lesbian, or bisexual (cited in Savin-Williams & Diamond, 2004).

Still, adolescence is the time when most people develop some awareness of their sexual orientation. In their comprehensive investigation of gay and lesbian sexuality, Marcel Saghir and Eli Robins (1973) found that most adult gay men and lesbians reported the onset of homosexual arousal, homosexual erotic imagery, and homosexual romantic attachment during early adolescence before age 15. More recent research has produced similar findings (Diamond, 2000; Herdt & Boxer, 1996). Recent studies indicate, however, that gay and lesbian youth may be "coming out" and accepting the homosexual identity at earlier ages than in prior eras (Taylor, 2000). One study found that the average age for both gay males and lesbians to accept the homosexual identity is 16 (Herdt & Boxer, 1996).

Gay and lesbian youth typically suffer from the awareness that they are different from most of their peers in an aspect of identity that receives a great deal of attention in our culture (Ryan & Futterman, 1998). Consider David Cunha's conflict over his homosexuality. Dennis Anderson (1994) suggests that a "crisis of self-concept occurs because the gay adolescent senses a sudden involuntary joining to a stigmatized group" (p. 15). He goes on to elaborate:

To some gay and lesbian adolescents the experience of watching boys and girls in school walk hand-in-hand down the hallway, while their own desires must be kept secret, produces feelings of rage and sadness that are difficult to resolve. In addition to having no opportunity to experience social interactions with gay or lesbian peers, there is little likelihood that they will see gay or lesbian adult role models in their day-to-day lives. Low self-esteem, academic inhibition, truancy, substance abuse, social withdrawal, depressed mood, and suicidal ideation are not unusual and may be difficult to differentiate from depressive disorders. (p. 18)

Recall David Cunha's feelings of abnormality, isolation, depression, and suicidal thoughts in regard to his sexual orientation. As an adolescent, he is struggling to develop a sense of identity, including sexual identity, but society discourages him from expressing what he finds.

Parents are often not very helpful to their gay and lesbian children:

Unlike teenagers from other oppressed minority groups, gay teenagers find little or no support or understanding at home for their societal difference. Most often, family members are the most difficult people to reveal sexual orientation to, and are often the last to know. Considering the consequences, this is often a wise choice. Many teenagers who reveal their sexual orientation (or "come out") to their parents face extreme hostility, violence or sudden homelessness. (O'Conor, 1994, p. 10)

To forestall such damaging responses, the Parents, Families and Friends of Lesbians and Gays (PFLAG) (2001), a social movement with the goal of promoting a more supportive environment for gay males and lesbians, produced a brochure titled *Read This Before Coming Out to Your Parents*. This brochure lists 12 questions to ponder prior to coming out, reproduced in Exhibit 6.5. These are heavy questions for any adolescent, and few nonfamilial supports are available to assist adolescents in resolving their questions related to sexual orientation or easing the process of coming out. Researchers have found, as we might expect, that adolescents who feel close to their parents and supported and accepted by them are more likely to come out to their parents (Waldner & Magruder, 1999). And, parental acceptance is very important to continued identity development (Floyd, Stein, Harter, Allison, & Nye, 1999).

Exhibit 6.5	Questions to Ponder Prior to Coming Out

1. Are you sure about your sexual orientation?

2. Are you comfortable with your gay sexuality?

3. Do you have support?

4. Are you knowledgeable about homosexuality?

5. What's the emotional climate at home?

6. Can you be patient?

7. What's your motive for coming out now?

8. Do you have available resources?

9. Are you financially dependent on your parents?

10. What is your general relationship with your parents?

11. What is their moral societal view?

12. Is this your decision?

SOURCE: Parents, Families and Friends of Lesbians and Gays, 2001.

Sexual minority youth report more depression, hopelessness, and suicidal thinking and behavior than heterosexual adolescents (Safren & Heimberg, 1999). One recent study of 21,927 sexually active adolescents in Minnesota found that gay, lesbian, and bisexual (GLB) young people were more than twice as likely as non-GLB to attempt suicide. Among males, 29% of the GLB youth and 12.6% of non-GLB youth reported suicide attempts. Among females, 52.4% of the GLB youth and 24.8% of non-GLB youth reported suicide attempts (Eisenberg & Resnick, 2006). The researchers also found that the GLB youth reported significantly lower levels of such protective factors as family connectedness, adult caring, and school safety as the non-GLB youth. They concluded that sexual orientation would not be a serious risk factor for suicide if GLB youth had access to these important protective factors.

Sexual Decision Making

The decision to engage or not to engage in sexual activity is yet another decision that most adolescents make. Biological, psychological, social, cultural, spiritual, and moral factors all play a part in the decision. Biologically, changes in hormone production and the reaction to the changes in appearance based on hormones have been cited as possible catalysts for sexual activity (Ponton & Judice, 2004). Psychologically, adolescents are involved in making a wide range of decisions and developing their own identities, and sexuality is just one more decision. Socially, youth are influenced by the attitudes toward sexual activity that they encounter in the environment, at school; among peers, siblings, and family; in their clubs/organizations; in the media; and so on. When and how they begin to engage in sexual activity is closely linked to what they perceive to be the activities of their peers (Ponton & Judice, 2004; Rew, 2005). Research also suggests that youth who are not performing well in school are more likely to engage in sexual activity than are those who are doing well

▲ **Photo 6.5**   Social aspects of adolescence—The social environment and relationships with peers contributes significantly to personal competence.

(Rew, 2005). Finally, beliefs and behaviors regarding sexuality are also shaped by one's culture, religion/spirituality, and value system. Ponton and Judice (2004) suggest that "a nation's attitude about adolescent sexuality plays an important role in the adolescent's sexual development and affects the laws, sexual media, sexual services, and the interaction of religion and state as well as the type of education that they receive in their schools" (p. 7).

The U.S. Youth Risk Behavior Survey suggests that nationwide, 46.8% of high school students have had sexual intercourse during their life, 6.2% had sexual intercourse for the first time before age 13, 14.3% have had sexual intercourse with more than four persons during their life, and 33.9% are sexually active during the last three months (CDC, 2006c). Of the 33.9% of high school students who indicated that they are currently sexually active, 62.8% report that either they or their partner used a condom during last sexual intercourse, 17.6% reported that either they or their partner had used birth control pills to prevent pregnancy before last intercourse, and 23.3% had drunk alcohol or used drugs before their last sexual intercourse (CDC, 2006c).

Data suggest that, on average, adolescents in the United States experience first sexual intercourse slightly earlier than adolescents in other industrialized countries; the average age of first intercourse in the United States was found to be 15.8 years, compared to 16.2 in Germany, 16.8 in France, and 17.7 in the Netherlands (Berne & Huberman, 1999). In the United States, 70% of females who had sex before age 13 did so nonvoluntarily (Alan Guttmacher Institute, 1999). One study found that the majority of teens in the United States who are sexually active wish they had waited until they were older to begin to have sexual intercourse (National Campaign to Prevent Teen Pregnancy, 2002).

As compared to the already high rates of adolescent sexual involvement in North America and Europe, there is recent research to suggest that rates of adolescent sexual involvement have been increasing in Latin America, sub-Saharan Africa, and East and Southeast Asia (Larson et al., 2002). And although sexual relationships remain heavily sanctioned for adolescents, primarily girls, in the Middle East and South Asia, research also points to increased cross-gender interaction among urban youth in these regions (Larson et al., 2002).

Regardless of nation or milieu, there is most certainly a need for adolescents to develop skills for healthy management of sexual relationships. Early engagement in sexual intercourse has some negative consequences. The earlier a youth begins engaging in sexual intercourse, the more likely he or she is to become involved in delinquent behavior, problem drinking, and marijuana use (Costa, Jessor, Donovan, & Fortenberry, 1995). Young age, as well as use of substances, is associated with an increased number of sexual partners and nonuse of condoms (Shrier, Emans, Woods, & DuRant, 1996). Findings like these suggest that adolescents who report first sexual intercourse before age 13 are more likely to have nine or more sexual partners by the age of 20 (Shrier et al., 1996).

Rates of sexual activity among teens in the United States are fairly comparable to those in Western Europe, yet the incidence of adolescent pregnancy, childbearing, and STDs in the United States far exceeds the level of most other industrialized nations (Feijoo, 2001). For instance, the Netherlands, France, and Germany have far better sexual outcomes for teens than the United States. Teens in those countries begin sexual activity at slightly later ages and have fewer sexual partners than teens in the United States. The teen pregnancy rate in the United States is eight times greater than the pregnancy rate in the Netherlands and Japan, nearly five times greater than the rate in Germany, nearly four times greater than the rate in France, and twice as high as England, Wales, or Canada. The teenage abortion rate in the United States is nearly seven times the rate in the Netherlands, nearly three times the rate in France, and nearly eight times the rate in Germany. There are similar differences in rates of sexually transmitted diseases among teens when comparing the United States to European countries (Advocates for Youth, 2002a; Alan Guttmacher Institute, 2006a). This discrepancy is probably related to three factors: teenagers in the United States make less use of contraception than teens in European countries, reproductive health services are more available in European countries, and sexuality education is more comprehensively integrated into all levels of education in most of Europe than in the United States (Feijoo, 2001; Huberman, 2001). It should be noted, however, that between 1995 and 2002, there was a decline in the percentage of U.S. teens having sexual intercourse before age 15, down from 19% to 13% for females and from 21% to 15% for males (Alan Guttmacher Institute, 2006a).

Oral Sex

The popular press, including *The New York Times* and *The Washington Post*, has reported that oral sex has gained popularity among adolescents (Jarrell, 2000; Stepp, 1999). This information has, for the most part, been anecdotal, because as adolescent sexuality researcher Lisa Remez, contends, obtaining parent consent to surveys about the sexual activity of their minor children can be difficult. There is a generalized fear that asking young people about sex will somehow lead them to choose to have sex, and the federal government has been reluctant to sponsor controversial research about the noncoital sexual behaviors of adolescents (Remez, 2000).

However, the 2002 National Survey of Family Growth (NSFG) was able to collect data on oral sex among people ages 15 to 44, and the data have been analyzed and reanalyzed by several organizations. The consensus is that the data show that 22% of females and 24% of males ages 15 to 19 who haven't had sexual intercourse have engaged in heterosexual oral sex. In addition, 83% of females and 88% of males who have had sexual intercourse have also engaged in heterosexual oral sex. It was also found that fewer than one in ten adolescents who engaged in oral sex used condoms to protect against STDS (Mosher, Chandra, & Jones, 2005).

These findings raise some important questions for social workers who work with adolescents. Do adolescents think oral sex is less intimate—reserving sexual intercourse for that special person but engaging in fellatio and cunnilingus more casually? Adolescents know that oral sex prevents pregnancy, but are they aware that most sexually transmitted diseases can also be contracted orally? What are the psychosocial effects of rape via coerced oral sex—do adolescents consider this rape if they don't consider oral sex, as sex?

Pregnancy and Childbearing

> What factors might be producing this recent decline in the teen birthrate?

Approximately 750,000 adolescent girls ages 15 to 19 become pregnant each year in the United States (Alan Guttmacher Institute, 2006a). This is a pregnancy rate of 75 per 1,000 15- to 19-year-old women, a 36% decline since the peak in 1990. And this pregnancy rate varies by race and ethnicity with the pregnancy rate of black (134 per 1,000) and Hispanic (131 per 1,000) females being almost three times that of white non-Hispanic females (48 per 1,000). Of teen pregnancies, 57% end in birth, 29% end in abortion, and 14% end in miscarriage (Alan Guttmacher Institute, 2006a). Exhibit 6.6 demonstrates U.S. birth rates (rather than pregnancy rates) in 2002 by age and race/ethnicity. This demonstrates that the large majority of babies born to teen mothers have mothers who are 18 to 19 years old.

As discussed in Chapter 2, adolescent pregnancies carry increased physical risks to mother and infant, including less prenatal care and higher rates of miscarriage, anemia, toxemia, prolonged labor, premature delivery, and low birth weight. In many Asian, eastern Mediterranean, African, and Latin American countries, the physical risks of adolescent pregnancy are mitigated by social and economic support (Hao & Cherlin, 2004). In the United States, however, adolescent mothers are more likely than their counterparts elsewhere to drop out of school, to be unemployed or underemployed, to receive public assistance, and to have subsequent pregnancies and lower educational and financial attainment. Teenage fathers may also experience lower educational and financial attainment (Bunting & McAuley, 2004).

The developmental tasks of adolescence are typically accomplished in this culture by going to school, socializing with peers, and exploring various roles. For the teenage mother, these avenues to development may be radically curtailed. The result may be long-lasting disadvantage. Consider Monica Golden's path. She obviously loves children and would like to have her own someday, but she would also like to become a pediatrician. If Monica were to become pregnant unexpectedly, an abortion would challenge her religious values and a baby would challenge her future goals.

Exhibit 6.6	U.S. Births per 1,000 Women, 2002	
Race/Ethnicity	Ages 15–17	Ages 18–19
All races	23.2	72.8
White non-Hispanic	13.1	51.9
Black non-Hispanic	41.0	110.3
Hispanic	50.7	133.0

SOURCE: Martin et al., 2003.

Sexually Transmitted Diseases

Youth have always faced pregnancy as a consequence of their sexual activity, but other consequences now include infertility and death as a result of **sexually transmitted diseases (STDs)**. The majority of sexually active adolescents used contraception the first time they had sexual intercourse, 74% of females and 82% of males, and even more at the most recent sexual intercourse, 83% of females of 91% of males (Alan Guttmacher, 2006a). The condom is the most common form of contraception used. However, as discussed earlier, the NSFG study found that only one in ten adolescents use protection when engaging in oral sex (Mosher et al., 2005). Health and sex education at home and in the schools often does not prepare adolescents for the difficult sexual decisions they must make, and they may be particularly ill-informed about STDs (Berne & Huberman, 2000).

Data collection on STDs is complicated for several reasons. Only five STDs—chlamydia, gonorrhea, syphilis, hepatitis A, and hepatitis B—are required to be reported to state health departments and the U.S. Centers for Disease Control and Prevention (CDC), and these conditions are not always detected and reported. Some STDs, such as chlamydia and HPV, are often asymptomatic and go undetected. In addition, many surveys are not based on representative samples (Alan Guttmacher Institute, 2006b; Weinstock, Berman, & Cates, 2004). Therefore, the data presented in this discussion are the best estimates available. And, the best estimates available indicate that adolescents and young adults ages 15 to 24 constitute 25% of the sexually active population but account for almost half of the STD diagnoses each year (Weinstock et al., 2004). Although rates of gonorrhea, chlamydia, and syphilis are above average in this age group, three STDs together account for nearly 90% of the new STDs among 15- to 24-year-olds each year; they are HPV, trichomoniasis, and chlamydia (Weinstock et al., 2004). We discuss these three here as well as HIV which is on the rise among adolescents.

◆ *Chlamydia.* Chlamydia trachomatis, or T-strain Mycoplasma, is the most commonly reported infectious disease in the United States. Approximately 3 million new infections occur each year (Weinstock et al., 2004). The national rate of reported chlamydia in 2004 was 319.6 cases per 100,000 people, an increase of 5.9% from 2003's 301.7 cases. And the age group with the highest chlamydia infection rate was females ages 15 to 19 with a rate of 2,761.5 per 100,000 people (CDC, 2005a). The disease is typically transmitted through sexual contact, but can also be spread nonsexually, through contact with the mucus or feces of an infected person. The symptoms of chlamydia include vaginal itching and discharge in women (although most women remain asymptomatic) or a thin, whitish discharge in men (approximately 40% remain asymptomatic). These symptoms appear one to three weeks after contact. Chlamydia is most often treated with antibiotics like azithromycin or doxycycline, but if left untreated can result in pelvic inflammatory disease (PID). Almost 40% of women with untreated chlamydia infections develop PID and 20% of those may become infertile (Hillis & Wasserheit, 1996).

♦ *HPV.* Human Papillomavirus actually refers to a group of viruses, which has more than 100 different strains, more than 30 of which are sexually transmitted. Approximately 6.2 million Americans get a new genital HPV infection each year. The CDC reports that at least 50% of sexually active men and women acquire genital HPV infection at some point in their lives and by age 50, at least 80% of women will have had a genital HPV infection (CDC, n.d.a). Estimating adolescent rates of HPV infection is difficult, but it has been estimated that approximately 30% of sexually active female adolescents are infected with HPV (Weinstock et al., 2004). Genital HPV infection may be contracted during vaginal or anal intercourse or during childbirth. Most people who have a genital HPV infection do not show any signs or symptoms and therefore can unknowingly transmit the disease to sexual partners. Some people get visible genital warts. The warts usually begin as flesh-colored, painless bumps in the genital area that may then resemble tiny cauliflower florets. After sexual contact with an infected person, warts may appear within weeks or months or most often—not at all (CDC, n.d.a). Pap tests may reveal precancerous circumstances caused by HPV in women but currently there are no tests to detect HPV in men. HPV has no cure. The warts, however, can be treated with imiquimod cream, podophyllin, podofilox, fluorouracil cream, trichloroacetic acid or with surgical, laser, or freezing treatments. Because the virus is always present in the body of someone who is infected, however, the warts often come back after treatment. Early treatment may prevent cancer of the cervix, vulva, or penis. In June of 2006, the FDA approved the use of a vaccine for females ages 9 to 26 which may prevent four strains of the human papillomavirus, which together cause 70% of cervical cancers and 90% of genital warts (FDA, 2006).

♦ *Trichomoniasis.* It is estimated that there were 7.4 million new cases of trichomoniasis in the United States in 2000, and that 25% of those cases occurred in 15- to 24-year-olds (Weinstock, 2004). Trichomoniasis is caused by Trichomonas vaginalis, a single-celled protozoan parasite. The parasite is transmitted by penis-to-vagina intercourse or vulva-to-vulva contact with an infected partner. Women can be infected by either men or women, but men are only infected by women. The vagina is the most common site of the infection in women, and the urethra is the most common site of infection in men (CDC, n.d.b). Most men with trichomoniasis do not have symptoms, but some men may have a temporary irritation inside the penis, mild discharge, or burning after urination or ejaculation. Symptoms are more common in women who may have a yellow-green vaginal discharge with a strong odor, discomfort during intercourse and urination, or irritation and itching in the vaginal area. In order to detect a trichomoniasis infection in men and women, a health care provider must conduct a physical examination and a laboratory test to diagnose the disease. Trichomoniasis can usually be cured with metronidazole and both partners should be treated at the same time to eliminate the parasite (CDC, n.d.b).

◆ *HIV/AIDS.* The human immunodeficiency virus (HIV) attacks the immune system and is the virus that causes acquired immunodeficiency syndrome (AIDS). HIV also reduces the body's ability to combat other diseases. Transmission of the virus can occur through unprotected sexual contact, shared drug paraphernalia, perinatal transmission from an HIV-infected mother to fetus or to newborn during childbirth, and through breastfeeding. Early in the HIV/AIDS epidemic, blood transfusions were another significant method of transmission, but safety measures have almost eliminated this as a method of transmission in the United States (Hutchison & Kovacs, 2007). In 2004, 50% of all newly diagnosed HIV/AIDS cases globally occurred in persons between the ages of 15 and 24 (UNAID, 2005). In the United States in that same year, 14% of all persons with newly diagnosed infections were under 25, but the number of people living with HIV/AIDS increased for the age group 15 to 19 between 2001 and 2004 (CDC, 2006d). Refer to Exhibit 6.7 to see the racial disparity in the U.S. AIDS infection rates for youth ages 13 to 19. Although white non-Hispanic youth comprise 63% of the U.S. adolescent population, they only make up 13% of the adolescent AIDS cases, whereas black non-Hispanic youth only comprise 15% of the adolescent population but 73% of the adolescent AIDS cases. In 2006, a little less than 1 million persons are living with HIV/AIDS in the United States, an estimated 252,000–312,000 HIV-infected persons in the United Sates are unaware of their HIV infection, and an estimated 40,000 new HIV infections are expected to occur this year (CDC, 2006d). Most people infected with HIV carry the virus for years before it destroys enough CD4+ T cells for AIDS to develop. Symptoms of HIV infection may include swollen lymph nodes, unexplained weight loss, loss of appetite, persistent fevers, night sweats, chronic fatigue, unexplained diarrhea, bloody stools, skin rashes, easy bruising, persistent and severe headaches, and unexplained chronic dry cough, all of which can result from opportunistic infections. As of 2006, there is no cure for AIDS. There are several anti-HIV drugs that can slow the immune system destruction, but these have not been tested extensively with children or adolescents.

Some social workers who work with adolescents may encounter issues of STD infection, but all social workers who work with adolescents should discuss STD prevention. Teaching communication skills to youth will probably benefit them the most, but in addition, they should be educated to:

◆ Recognize the signs and symptoms of STDs
◆ Refrain from sexual contact if they suspect themselves or a partner of having any of these signs or symptoms and instead get medical attention as soon as possible
◆ Use a latex condom correctly during sexual activity
◆ Have regular checkups that include STD testing

For AIDS information, the U.S. Public Health Service has a confidential toll-free hotline in English (1-800-342-2437) and in Spanish (1-800-344-7432). The American Social Health Association provides an STD hotline at 1-800-227-8922, where callers can obtain STD information in English or Spanish without leaving their names.

Exhibit 6.7	Facts about AIDS and Adolescents

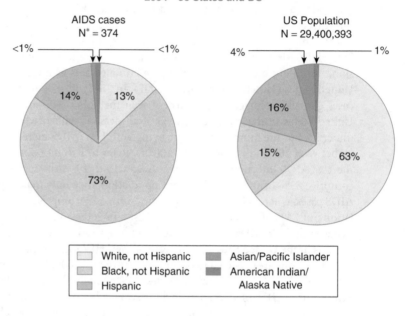

Proportion of AIDS Cases and Population Among Adolescents
13 to 19 Years of Age, by Race/Ethnicity Reported in
2004—50 States and DC

SOURCE: Centers for Disease Control and Prevention, http://www.cdc.gov/hiv/topics/surveillance/resources/slides/adolescents/index.htm

Substance Use and Abuse

Throughout this book, you have encountered a multiplicity of factors that contribute to the way individuals behave. Substance use is yet another variable in that mix. For example, Carl Fleischer's use of tobacco and marijuana has several likely effects on his general behavior. Tobacco may make him feel tense, excitable, or anxious, and these feelings may amplify his concern about his weight, his grades, and his family relationships. On the other hand, the marijuana may make Carl feel relaxed, and he may use it to counteract or escape from his concerns.

High school students in the United States have a higher rate of illicit drug use than youth in other industrialized countries (Johnston, O'Malley, Bachman, & Schulenberg, 2004, 2005). However, in the past five years (2001–2006), there has been a 23% decline in past month use of any illicit drug by students in the 8th, 10th, and 12th grades in the United States (see Exhibit 6.8). Cigarette smoking continues to fall and is now at the lowest level since the data have been collected. Between 2001 and 2006, past month use of marijuana declined by nearly 25% among students in 8th, 10th, and 12th grades. During this same period, lifetime, past year, and past month use of steroids declined in all three groups, and ecstasy use decreased by more than 50% in all three groups. Methamphetamine use continues to decline among adolescents. There is some news that is not so good, however. Oxycontin (a narcotic) use increased from 1.3% to 2.6% of 8th graders, 9.7% of 12th graders abuse vicodin (another narcotic), and 7% of 12th graders abuse cold medicines (National Institute on Drug Abuse, 2006). Alcohol continues to be the most widely used of all the drugs included in the Monitoring the Future studies. In 2005, one-sixth (17%) of the 8th graders indicated drinking once or more in the prior 30 days, as did a third (33%) of the 10th graders, and nearly half (47%) of the 12th graders (Johnston, O'Malley, Bachman, & Schulenberg, 2006).

Adolescents typically follow a pattern of substance use (Kandel & Logan, 1984, 1991; O'Malley, Johnston, & Bachman, 1991), beginning with tobacco, coffee, and alcohol. Thus, tobacco is considered a gateway drug to further substance use and abuse. Although cigarette use has been declining, according to a Youth Tobacco Survey conducted by the Office on Smoking and Health (2000), 80% of tobacco users began use before the age of 18.

Adolescence is the primary risk period for initiating the use of other substances as well (Shedler & Block, 1990), and some researchers contend that experimental use of some licit and illicit drugs may even be considered a normative behavior among U.S. teenagers. Each year approximately 3.3 million youth between the ages of 12 and 17 begin drinking alcohol, and alcohol use increases with age (CASA, 2002). Among high school seniors who had ever

| Exhibit 6.8 | Trends in Illegal Drug Use in 8th, 10th, and 12th Graders in the United States |

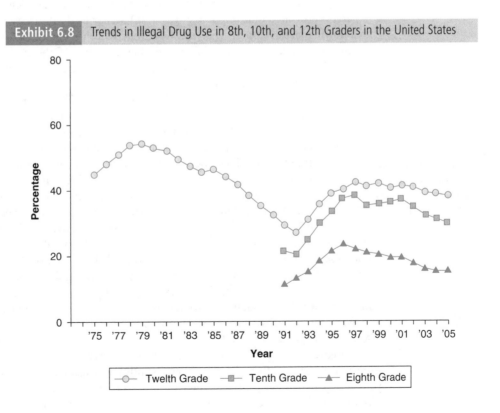

SOURCE: The Monitoring the Future Study, the University of Michigan.

tried alcohol, 91.3% are still drinking in the 12th grade; of those students who had ever been drunk, 83.3% are still getting drunk in the 12th grade. Current alcohol use is nearly identical for male (40.2%) and female (41%) 9th graders, as is binge drinking for male (21.7%) and female (20.2%) 9th graders. Caucasian (52.5%) and Latino (52.8%) youth have comparable alcohol use rates, with lower rates for African American youth (39.9%). Eighth graders in rural areas are 29% more likely than their urban counterparts to have used alcohol and are 70% more likely to have been drunk (CASA, 2002).

Despite industry claims that alcohol is not marketed to children, animation, adolescent humor, and rock music are prevalent in alcoholic beverage advertising. Moreover, in the first six months of 2001, 217 varieties of "malternatives" (such as Rick's Spiked Lemonade, Tequiza, Hooper's Hooch, Smirnoff Ice, Skyy Blue) were approved by the Bureau of Alcohol, Tobacco, and Firearms (CASA, 2002). Forty-one percent of youth ages 14 to 18 have tried these sweet-tasting and colorfully packaged alcoholic beverages (CASA, 2002).

Decision Making About Substance Use

When asked why youth choose to use alcohol, adolescents cite the following reasons: to have a good time with friends, to relieve tension and anxiety, to deal with the opposite sex, to get high, to cheer up, and to alleviate boredom. When asked why youth use cocaine, the additional responses were to get more energy and to get away from problems. Overall drug use at a party is also cited quite often as a reason (O'Malley et al., 1991; Segal & Stewart, 1996). The following factors appear to be involved in adolescents' choice of drugs: the individual characteristics of the drug, the individual characteristics of the user, the availability of the drug, the current popularity of the drug, and the sociocultural traditions and sanctions regarding the drug (Segal & Stewart, 1996).

Adolescents who choose to abuse substances seem to differ from those who do not. In a 12-year longitudinal study, Richard Jessor (1987) found that adolescent problem drinkers differ from other adolescents in their personal qualities, their social environment,

> What are the risk factors for substance abuse in adolescence?

and their other patterns of behavior. Problem drinkers are less likely to hold traditional values about education, religion, or conformity. They perceive large differences between their family's values and their peers' values, are more influenced by their peers, and have peers who are also engaged in problem drinking. Finally, problem drinkers are also more likely to participate in other risk-taking behaviors, such as sexual activity and delinquency (Jessor, 1987). More recently, Jessor and colleagues have tested the stability of these findings using six adolescent samples that range the years from 1974 to 1992, two national samples and four local community samples. Even though there were significant changes in the sociohistorical context over the years of the six samples, the researchers found that the personal and environmental correlates of problem drinking remained the same across all samples, and were the same correlates as summarized above from Jessor's longitudinal study (Donovan, Jessor, & Costa, 1999).

Moreover, some adolescents are clearly more at risk for substance abuse than others. American Indian youth and Alaska Native youth begin using alcohol and other drugs at a younger age than other youth, use them more frequently, use a greater amount, and use more different substances in combination with each other (Cameron, 1999; Novins, Beals, Shore, & Manson, 1996). The death rate due to substance abuse among American Indian youth is twice that of other youth (Pothoff et al., 1998). In response to this social need, drug treatment to Native American teens is undergoing a rapid change, with direct service provided by the tribes, employing mainly American Indian staff, and using traditional Indian healing approaches in combination with standard addiction treatment approaches (Novins et al., 1996; Novins, Fleming, Beals, & Manson, 2000). It is too early to know how successful these new approaches will be.

Consequences of Substance Use and Abuse

Chemical substances pose a profound threat to the health of adolescents, because substance abuse affects metabolism, internal organs, the central nervous system, emotional functioning, and cognitive functioning (Segal & Stewart, 1996). Alcohol and opiates can cause severe intoxication, coma, and withdrawal symptoms. Sedative drugs can depress the nervous and respiratory systems; withdrawal may lead to disturbances in breathing, heart function, and other basic body functions. Intravenous use of cocaine has been linked to adolescent cases of hepatitis, HIV, heart inflammation, loss of brain tissue, and abnormally high fever. Extended use of inhalants can cause irreparable neuropsychological damage. And finally, substances can weaken the immune system and increase a youth's likelihood of disease or general poor health.

Substance abuse has significant psychosocial implications for adolescents as well:

> [It] compromises their adjustment and school performance, contributes to low achievements, poor academic performance and high school dropout. It disrupts normal psychosocial functioning, decreases social support, limits participation in age-appropriate activities, reduces psychological resources and produces anxiety, tension, and low self-esteem. Substance induced psychological reactions interfere with eating and sleeping, modify health related behavior and may be a cause of serious psychiatric disorders. (Segal & Stewart, 1996, p. 202)

As mentioned earlier, substance use can also affect the decision to engage in sexual activity. After substance use, youth are more likely to engage in sexual activity and are less likely to use protection; thus, they are more likely to become pregnant or impregnate and to contract a sexually transmitted disease (Brooks-Gunn & Furstenberg, 1989; Segal & Stewart, 1996; Shrier et al., 1996). In general, adolescents who use tobacco products, alcohol, marijuana, and other substances are more likely to be sexually active and to have more sexual partners (CASA, 2002; Lowry et al., 1994).

Juvenile Delinquency

Almost every adolescent breaks the rules at some time—disobeying parents or teachers, lying, cheating, and perhaps even stealing or vandalizing. As we've seen, many adolescents smoke cigarettes and drink alcohol and some skip school or stay out past curfew. For some adolescents, this behavior is a phase, passing as quickly as it appeared. Yet for others, it becomes a pattern and a probability game. Although most juvenile delinquency never meets up with law enforcement, the more times young people offend, they more likely they are to come into contact with the juvenile justice system.

In the United States, persons older than 7 but younger than 18 can be arrested for anything for which an adult can be arrested. (Children under 7 are said not to possess *mens rea*, which means "guilty mind," and thus are not considered capable of criminal intent.) In addition, they can be arrested for what are called **status offenses**, such as running away from home, skipping school, violating curfew, and possessing tobacco or alcohol—behaviors not considered crimes when engaged in by adults. When adolescents are found guilty of committing either a crime (by adult standards) or a status offense, we refer to their behavior as **juvenile delinquency**.

The Office of Juvenile Justice and Delinquency Prevention reports that in 2003, U.S. law enforcement agencies made an estimated 2.2 million arrests of persons under the age of 18 (Snyder & Sickmund, 2006) which is 11% fewer than the number of arrests in 1999. According to FBI arrest statistics, juveniles accounted for 16.4% of all arrests in 2002. For violent crimes, persons under age 18 were arrested for 9.6% of murder/non-negligent manslaughter arrests, 16.7% of forcible rape arrests, 23.1% of robbery arrests, and 13% of aggravated assault arrests. Additional juvenile arrest rates for 2002 include: 30% of burglary arrests, 49.4% of arson arrests, 38.3% of vandalism arrests, and 21.4% of weapons arrests (Snyder & Sickmund, 2006).

According to the 2006 National Report for Juvenile Offenders and Victims by the U.S. Department of Justice and the Office of Juvenile Justice and Delinquency Prevention (OJJDP):

- By age 17, 33% of all youth said they had been suspended from school at least once, 18% had run away from home (i.e., had at least once left home and stayed away overnight without a parent's prior knowledge or permission), and 8% had belonged to a gang.
- By age 17, a greater proportion of juveniles reported that they had committed an assault with the intent of seriously hurting the person than reported ever having run away from home, sold drugs, carried a handgun, stolen something worth more than $50, or belonged to a gang.
- Males were significantly more likely than females to report ever being suspended from school (42% vs. 24%) or ever belonging to a gang (11% vs. 6%) and were four times more likely to report ever carrying a handgun (25% vs. 6%).
- White youth were significantly less likely than black or Hispanic youth to report ever belonging to a gang.
- With the exception of selling drugs, the proportions of youth who reported committing the above behaviors at age 17 are either the same or less than the proportions reporting the same behaviors at earlier ages (Snyder & Sickmund, 2006).

The juvenile arrest rate for all offenses reached its highest level of the last two decades in 1996 and has been steadily declining since (Snyder & Sickmund, 2006). In 2003, there were 6,573 total arrests for every 100,000 youths ages 10 to 17 in the United States. The highest violent crimes arrest rate for juveniles was reached in 1994 and the juvenile arrest rate for violent crimes in 2003 was 273 per 100,000, a decrease of 48% since 1994. And this trend is echoed in the 2003 arrest rates for property crime index offenses, vandalism, and the status offense—running away. This is despite a steady increase in the U.S. juvenile population.

Between 1995 and 2015, the population of persons under age 18 is expected to increase by 8% (Snyder & Sickmund, 2006).

Historically, gang membership has been one way to become established and defend the ethnic neighborhood. In 2000, the National Youth Gang Survey estimated that more than 24,500 gangs were active in the United States (Egley, 2002). In 1999, 47% of gang members in the United States were Hispanic, 31% were African American, 13% were Caucasian, 7% were Asian, and 2% were "other." It is important to note, however, that in 1999 only 37% of gang members were juveniles (under 18), and 63% were adults (18 and over) (Egley, 2002). Indeed, each wave of immigration in the United States has had its own incarnation of gangs, and most early gang members have been young adults (Huff, 1996). Gangs have been a mixed blessing for ethnic communities, however. They provide some necessary services for their neighborhoods, but they also bring the threat of violence, and for juveniles, delinquency.

Although most crime committed by gangs is nonviolent, it is the violent gang behavior that is best known to the public (U.S. Department of Health and Human Services, 2001c). Among cities with populations over 250,000 with persistent gang problems, 47% reported an increase in gang-related homicides from 1999 to 2000 (Egley, 2002).

And in 2006, OJJDP researchers Snyder and Sickmund (2006) again found that some problem behaviors cluster—or are likely to contribute to other problem behaviors. They found that juveniles who reported belonging to a gang were twice as likely as other juveniles to have committed a major theft, three times more likely to have sold drugs, four times more likely to have committed a serious assault, and five times more likely to have carried a handgun (p. 72).

Other Threats to Physical and Mental Health

Threats to adolescent health and well-being include not only pregnancy, STDs, and substance abuse, which have already been discussed, but also violence, poverty and low educational achievement, problems with nutrition, and suicide.

Violence

In 2002, on average, four juveniles were murdered daily in the United States. That was the third leading cause of death for juvenile ages 12 to 17 with only unintentional injury and suicide killing more young people (Snyder & Sickmund, 2006). An estimated 1,600 persons under age 18 were murdered in the United States in 2002—10% of all persons murdered that year. About one-third (36%) of these juvenile murder victims were female. About 1 in 10 (8%) were ages 12 to 14, and 4 in 10 (43%) were ages 15 to 17. More than half (51%) of juvenile murder victims in 2002 were white, 45% were black, and 4% were either American Indian or Asian. With white youth comprising 78% of the U.S. resident juvenile population in 2002 and black youth comprising 16%, the murder rate for black youth in 2002 was more than four times the white murder rate (see Exhibit 6.9). This disparity was seen across victim age groups and increased with victim age. Over three quarters of juvenile homicides are committed with firearms (Snyder & Sickmund, 2006).

These murders are not happening at schools, however, so although school shootings have received media attention and have thus increased public concern for student safety, school-related violent deaths account for less than 1% of homicides among school-aged children and youth (Anderson et al., 2001). In fact, in 2001, students were safer in school and

Exhibit 6.9	Homicide Rates for Black and White Youth, 2002		
	2002 Homicide Rate*		
Victim Age	*White*	*Black*	*Black to White Ratios*
0–17	1.4	6.0	4.2
0–5	1.9	6.5	3.4
6–11	0.4	1.6	3.6
12–14	0.7	2.8	4.4
15–17	3.3	18.1	5.5

SOURCE: Snyder & Sickmund, 2006, p. 22

* Homicide rates are the number of homicides per 100,000 juveniles in the age group.

on their way to and from school than they were in 1992 because crimes against juveniles fell substantially between 1992 and 2001 both in and out of school (Snyder & Sickmund, 2006).

Juveniles are, however, more likely than adults to be both victims and perpetrators of violence. A 2005 Bureau of Justice Statistics (BJS) report (Baum, 2005) summarized National Crime Victimization Survey data for the years 1993–2003 to document the trends in nonfatal violent victimizations of youth ages 12 to 17. On average from 1993 through 2003, juveniles ages 12 to 17 were about 2.5 times more likely than adults (i.e., ages 18 and older) to be the victim of a nonfatal violent crime. That means that in a typical group of 1,000 youth ages 12 to 17, 84 experienced nonfatal violent victimizations, compared with 32 per 1,000 persons ages 18 and older (Baum, 2005).

Data collected in 2005 as part of the Youth Risk Behavior Survey (YRBS) reveal that on at least one of the 30 days preceding the survey, 18.5% of high school students had carried a weapon and 5.4% had carried a gun. And during the 12 months that preceded the survey, 3.6% had been in a physical fight for which they had to be treated by a doctor or nurse (CDC, 2006c). The CDC adds that in 2004, more than 750,000 young people ages 10 to 24 were treated in emergency departments for injuries sustained due to violence (CDC, 2006c).

Even if they are not perpetrators or direct victims of violence, many U.S. adolescents witness violence. One study of 935 urban and suburban youth found that over 45% had witnessed a shooting or stabbing or other serious act of violence during the previous year (O'Keefe, 1997). Moreover, participating in violence and or witnessing violence can be a significant predictor of aggressive acting-out behavior for both male and female adolescents (O'Keefe, 1997) as well as a significant source of depression, anger, anxiety, dissociation, posttraumatic stress, and total trauma symptoms (Fitzpatrick & Boldizar, 1993; Singer, Anglin, Song, & Lunghofer, 1995).

Dating Violence and Statutory Rape

Acquaintance rape can be defined as forced, manipulated, or coerced sexual contact by someone known to the victim. Women between 16 and 24 are the primary victims of acquaintance rape, but junior high school girls are also at great risk (U.S. Department of Justice Bureau of Justice Statistics, 2000).

Nationwide in 2005, 9.2% of high school students responded to the YRBS that they had been hit, slapped, or physically hurt on purpose by their boyfriend or girlfriend at least once over the course of the 12 months that preceded the survey (CDC, 2006c). Young women, ages 16 to 24, experience the highest rates of relationship violence (Rennison & Welchans, 2000). One study found that approximately one in five female high school students reported being physically and/or sexually abused by a dating partner (Silverman, Raj, Mucci, & Hathaway, 2001).

Date rape accounts for almost 70% of the sexual assaults reported by adolescent women; 38% of those women are between 14 and 17 years old (Levy, 1991). The YRBS data reveals that 7.5% of the students stated that they had been physically forced to have sexual intercourse when they did not want to. Overall, the prevalence of having been forced to have sexual intercourse was higher among black (9.3%) than white (6.9%) students. The prevalence of having been forced to have sexual intercourse was higher among 11th grade (7.9%) and 12th grade (9.0%) than 9th grade (6.1%) students; higher among 12th grade (9.0%) than 10th grade (7.2%) students (CDC, 2006c).

One research team found that predictors of unwanted sexual activity may include reaching menarche at an early age, being sexually active, having sexually active same-sex friends, having poor peer relationships, and being emotionally fragile or distressed. The researchers conclude that parents, teachers, counselors, the legal system, and communities should be informed of the seriousness of this problem and should adequately address it (Vicary, Klingaman, & Harkness, 1995).

Although much research supports the notion that the majority of female victims know their assailants (Mynatt & Algeier, 1990), stranger rape is overrepresented in FBI statistics because acquaintance rape is much less likely to be reported. Stranger rape is also more likely to involve the use of a weapon and to result in physical injury to the victim (Mynatt & Algeier, 1990). Because of their underreporting, date rape and dating violence may be even more prevalent among adolescents than we have data to suggest. Yet researchers have found that adolescent girls who report a history of experiencing dating violence are more likely to exhibit other serious health risk behaviors (Silverman et al., 2001).

Statutory rape occurs when individuals have voluntary and consensual sexual relations and one individual is either too young or otherwise unable (e.g., mentally retarded) to legally consent to the behavior. The majority of victims of statutory rape are females ages 14 to 15 whereas 82% of the rape perpetrators of female victims were adults ages 18 and older (Snyder & Sickmund, 2006). Not only were most offenders adults, but most were also substantially older than their victims. About half of the male offenders of female victims in statutory rapes reported to law enforcement were at least six years older than their victims. For male victims, the difference was even greater; in these incidents, half of the female offenders were at least nine years older than their victims (Snyder & Sickmund, 2006).

Poverty and Low Educational Attainment

Additional threats to physical and mental health may also stem from poverty and low educational attainment, both of which are rampant in the nonindustrialized world. In the United States, 12% of all persons lived at or below their poverty thresholds in 2002. This proportion was far greater for persons under age 18 (18%) than for those ages 18 to 64 (11%) and those above age 64 (10%) (Snyder & Sickmund, 2006).

The education institution is becoming a prime force in perpetuating, if not exacerbating, economic inequalities. A 2006 report by the Education Trust indicates that current trends in the education institution are the principle reason that there is less upward mobility in the social class structure in the United States today than there was 20 years ago, and less mobility in the United States than in any European nation except England (Haycock, 2006). High school graduation rates are a key measure of whether schools are making adequate yearly progress (AYB) under the provisions of the No Child Left Behind (NCLB) legislation (see Chapter 5 for a fuller discussion of NCLB). As it turns out, most school districts do not have a system for calculating graduation rates, and there are major holes in their reported data. Furthermore, several researchers have analyzed the reported state data and found that all states inflated their graduation rates, ranging from a 1% to a 33% inflation rate (Hall, 2005). These researchers estimate that graduation rates for students who entered high school in 2000 ranged from 51% in South Carolina to 86% in New Jersey. More than half of nongraduates were African American, Latino, or Native American, indicating an over-representation because these groups together comprise about one-third of students in public school nationally. Even when students in impoverished rural and urban neighborhoods graduate, their high schools may not have offered the types of courses that college admissions departments require. There is also a critical shortage of teachers who are trained to teach English language learners who often must navigate very large high school settings (Hood, 2003).

Obesity and Eating Disorders

As suggested earlier, the dietary practices of some adolescents put them at risk for overall health problems. These practices include skipping meals, usually breakfast or lunch; snacking, especially on high-calorie, high-fat, low-nutrition snacks; eating fast foods; and dieting. Poor nutrition can affect a youth's growth and development, sleep, weight, cognition, mental health, and overall physical health.

An increasing minority of adolescents in the United States is obese and the risks and consequences can be profound (Hedley et al., 2005; James, 2006; Must & Strauss, 1999; Ogden, Flegal, Carroll, & Johnson, 2002). The 1999–2002 National Health and Nutrition Examination Survey (NHANES), as reported in the National Center for Health Statistics (2004), found that an estimated 16% of children and adolescents ages 6 to 19, over 9 million, are overweight (defined as BMI-for-age at or above the 95th percentile of the CDC Growth Charts). This represents a 45% increase from the NHANES III 1988–1994 statistics and is triple what the proportion was in 1980 (National Center for Health Statistics, 2004).

It is important to note that this is a worldwide trend. According to a recent report (James, 2006), almost half of the children in North and South America, about 38% of children in the European Union, and about 20% of children in China, will be overweight by 2010. Significant increases are also expected in the Middle East and Southeast Asia. Mexico, Brazil, Chile, and Egypt have rates comparable to fully industrialized countries:

> We seem at present to be very poor at developing coherent and effective methods for helping families with overweight and obese children to grow normally. Is this because, like adults, children's brain mechanisms controlling their body fat are steadily becoming reset so that children also entrain themselves at a new higher weight or is it that in so many countries it is difficult to induce a progressive

improvement in the microenvironment within which children live because the pervasive pressures to overeat inappropriate foods and constrain children's activity are so overwhelming? (James, 2006, p. 9)

This chapter has emphasized how tenuous self-esteem can be during adolescence, but the challenges are even greater for profoundly overweight or underweight youth. Overweight adolescents may suffer exclusion from peer groups and discrimination in education, employment, marriage, housing, and health care (DeJong, 1993). Carl Fleischer has already begun to face some of these challenges. He thinks of himself as a "fat, slow geek" and assumes females would not be interested in him because of his weight.

Research is exposing the breadth of the problem. Thirteen percent of the high school students in the nationwide sample of the YRBS are overweight (CDC, 2006c). Yet, 31.5% of that same sample described themselves as slightly or very overweight and 45.6% were trying to lose weight. Moreover, within the 30 days preceding the survey, 12.3% of the high schools students had gone without eating for 24 hours or more, 6.3% had taken diet pills, powders, or liquids and 4.5% had vomited or taken laxatives to lose weight or to keep from gaining weight (CDC, 2006c).

Girls' body dissatisfaction reflects the incongruence between the societal ideal of thinness and the beginning of normal fat deposits in pubescent girls. Joan Brumberg (1997) used unpublished diaries to do a historical analysis of femaleness in adolescence. Her analysis suggests a strong trend for girls in the United States to define themselves more and more through their appearance. She suggests that we now have a situation in which girls are reaching sexual maturity at a younger age in a highly sexualized culture that exploits girls' normal sensitivity to their changing bodies, often using the prepubescent female body as a sexual symbol. And using that prepubescent female as the ideal may be why the American Psychiatric Association (APA) suggests that most eating disorders like **anorexia nervosa** and **bulimia nervosa** begin in adolescence (APA, 2000).

◆ Anorexia nervosa means literally "loss of appetite due to nerves," but the disorder is actually characterized by a dysfunctional body image and voluntary starvation in the pursuit of weight loss. According to the *Diagnostic and Statistical Manual of Mental Disorders* (*DSM-IV*) (APA, 1994), the essential features of anorexia nervosa are that "the individual refuses to maintain a minimally normal body weight, is intensely afraid of gaining weight, and exhibits a significant disturbance in the perception of the shape or size of his or her body" (p. 539).

◆ Bulimia nervosa is characterized by a cycle of binge eating; feelings of guilt, depression, or self-disgust; and purging (producing vomiting or evacuation of the bowels). The *DSM-IV* (APA, 1994) suggests that individuals with bulimia nervosa are also excessively influenced by body shape and weight, and exhibit binge eating followed by purging at least twice a week for at least three months.

The American Psychiatric Association (2000) estimates that 0.5% to 3.7% of women suffer from anorexia nervosa in their lifetime and about 1% of female adolescents have anorexia nervosa. An estimated 1.1% to 4.2% of women have bulimia nervosa in their lifetime. And 50% of people who have had anorexia nervosa develop bulimia or bulimic patterns (APA, 2000).

Depression and Suicide

Epidemiological studies suggest that as many as 8.3% of adolescents in the United States may have a major depressive disorder. Parents are less likely to recognize depression in their adolescents than the adolescents themselves. During adolescence, girls are about twice as likely as boys to have a major depressive disorder (National Institute of Mental Health [NIMH], 2000). The diagnoses may not accurately reflect the prevalence of male depression, however, because many "tough" male adolescents may find it hard to verbalize, admit, or identify feelings related to depression (Morales, 1992, p. 147). Research suggests that African American and Mexican American youth may be at increased risk for depression (Roberts, Roberts, & Chen, 1997).

Adolescent depression may also be underdiagnosed, among males and females alike, because it is difficult to detect. Many parents and professionals expect adolescence to be a time of ups and downs, moodiness, melodrama, anger, rebellion, and increased sensitivity. There are, however, some reliable outward signs of depression in adolescents: poor academic performance, truancy, social withdrawal, antisocial behavior, changes in eating or sleeping patterns, changes in physical appearance, excessive boredom or activity, low self-esteem, sexual promiscuity, substance use, propensity to run away from home, and excessive family conflict. Additional symptoms of depression not unique to adolescence include pervasive inability to experience pleasure, severe psychomotor retardation, delusions, and a sense of hopelessness (Kaplan & Sadock, 1998).

The many challenges of adolescence sometimes prove overwhelming. We have already discussed the risk of suicide among gay male and lesbian adolescents. Nationwide, during the 12 months preceding the YRBS survey, 28.5% of high school students reported having felt so sad or hopeless almost every day for two weeks or more that they stopped doing some usual activities (CDC, 2006c). And again in the 12 months preceding the survey, 16.9% had seriously considered attempting suicide, 13% had made a suicide plan, 8.4% had actually attempted suicide, and 2.3% had made a suicide attempt which resulted in an injury, poisoning, or overdose that had to be treated by a doctor or nurse (CDC, 2006c). Overall, suicide is the third leading cause of death for adolescents in the United States (NIMH, 2000). In 2001, 3,971 youth ages 15 to 24 took their own lives (Anderson & Smith, 2003). Of those 3,971 deaths, 86% were male and 14% were female, and 54% used firearms. During that same year, American Indian and Alaskan Natives had the highest rate of suicides (Anderson & Smith, 2003).

◪ Risk Factors and Protective Factors in Adolescence

There are many pathways through adolescence; both individual and group-based differences result in much variability. Some of the variability is related to the types of risk factors and protective factors that have accumulated prior to adolescence. Emmy Werner and associates (see Werner & Smith, 2001) have found, in their longitudinal research on risk and protection, that females have a better balance of risk and protection in childhood, but the advantage goes to males during adolescence. Their research indicates that the earlier risk factors that most predict poor adolescent adjustment are a childhood spent in chronic poverty, alcoholic and psychotic parents, moderate to severe physical disability, developmentally disabled siblings, school problems in middle childhood, conflicted relationships with peers, and family

What are the implications of research on risk and protection for social work program development?

disruptions. The most important earlier protective factors are easy temperament, positive social orientation in early childhood, positive peer relationships in middle childhood, nonsex-typed extracurricular interests and hobbies in middle childhood, and nurturing from nonparental figures.

Much attention has also been paid to the increase in risk behaviors during adolescence (Lerner & Galambos, 1998). In the United States, attention has been called to a set of factors that are risky to adolescent well-being and serve as risk factors for adjustment in adulthood as well. These factors include use and abuse of alcohol and other drugs; unsafe sex, teen pregnancy, and teen parenting; school underachievement, failure, and dropout; delinquency, crime, and violence; and youth poverty. The risk and resilience research indicates, however, that many youth with several of these risk factors overcome the odds. Protective factors that have been found to contribute to resilience in adolescence include family creativity in coping with adversity, good family relationships, faith and attachment to religious institutions, social support in the school setting, and school-based health services. As social workers, we will want to promote these protective factors while, at the same time, work to prevent or diminish risk factors.

IMPLICATIONS FOR SOCIAL WORK PRACTICE

Adolescence is a vulnerable period. Adolescents' bodies and psyches are changing rapidly in transition from childhood to adulthood. Youth are making some very profound decisions during this life course period. Thus, the implications for social work practice are wide ranging.

- When working with adolescents, meet clients where they are "at," because that place may change frequently.
- Be familiar with typical adolescent development and with the possible consequences of deviations from developmental time lines.
- Be aware of, and respond to, the adolescent's level of cognition and comprehension. Assess the individual adolescent's ability to contemplate the future, to comprehend the nature of human relationships, to consolidate specific knowledge into a coherent system, and to envision possible consequences from a hypothetical list of actions.
- Recognize that the adolescent may see you as an authority figure who is not an ally. Develop skills in building rapport with adolescents.
- Assess the positive and negative effects of the school environment on the adolescent in relation to such issues as early or late maturation, popularity/sociability, culture, and sexual orientation.
- Where appropriate, advocate for change in maladaptive school settings, such as those with Eurocentric models or homophobic environments.
- Provide information, support, or other interventions to assist adolescents in resolving questions of sexual identity and sexual decision making.
- Where appropriate, link youth to existing resources, such as extracurricular activities, education on STDs, prenatal care, and gay and lesbian support groups.
- Provide information, support, or other interventions to assist adolescents in making decisions regarding use of tobacco, alcohol, or other drugs.
- Develop skills to assist adolescents with physical and mental health issues, such as nutritional problems, obesity, eating disorders, depression, and suicide.

◆   Participate in research, policy, and advocacy on behalf of adolescents.
◆   Work at the community level to develop and sustain recreational and social pro-
      grams and places for young people.

KEY TERMS

acquaintance rape	juvenile delinquency	rites of passage
anorexia nervosa	masturbation	secondary sex
bulimia nervosa	menarche	characteristic
curanderismo	mestizo perspective	sex hormones
dispositions	physical characteristics	sexually transmitted
generalized other	postconventional	diseases (STDs)
gonads	moral reasoning	social identity
identity	primary sex characteristic	spermarche
individuation	puberty	status offenses

Active Learning

1. Recalling your own high school experiences, which case study individual would you most identify with—David, Carl, or Monica? For what reasons? How could a social worker have affected your experiences?

2. Visit a public library and check out some preteen and teen popular fiction or magazines. Which topics from this chapter are discussed and how are they dealt with?

3. Have lunch at a local high school cafeteria. Be sure to go through the line, eat the food, and enjoy conversation with some students. What are their concerns? What are their notions about social work?

WEB RESOURCES

Adolescence Directory On-Line
education.indiana.edu/cas/adol/adol/html
Site presented by the Center for Adolescent Studies at Indiana University contains an electronic guide to information on adolescent issues, including breaking news, conflict and violence, mental health issues, health issues, and resources for counselors and teens.

Puberty Information for Boys and Girls
www.aap.org/family/puberty.htm
Site presented by the American Academy of Pediatrics contains general information on the process of puberty for both boys and girls as well as advocacy issues and current research.

CDC Health Topic: Adolescents and Teens
www.cdc.gov/node.do/id/0900f3ec80le457a
Site maintained by the Centers for Disease Control and Prevention contains links to a variety of health topics related to adolescents, including reproductive health, teen pregnancy, working teens, physical activity in adolescence, and youth smoking.

Adolescent Health and Mental Health
www.fenichel.com/adolhealth.shtml

Site presented by Dr. Michael Fenichel of the University of Nebraska-Lincoln contains links to information on adolescence and peer pressure, eating disorders, anxiety and panic, trauma, and depression.

Youth Risk Behavior Surveillance System (YRBSS)
www.cdc.gov/HealthyYouth/yrbs/index.htm

Site presented by the National Center for Chronic Disease Prevention and Health Promotion contains latest research on adolescent risk behavior.

ABA Juvenile Justice Center
www.abanet.org/crimjust/juvjus/home.html

Site presented by the American Bar Association Juvenile Justice Center contains current events related to juvenile justice, and information on topics such as girls in the juvenile justice system, juvenile death penalty, and zero tolerance.

CHAPTER 7

YOUNG ADULTHOOD

Holly C. Matto

Key Ideas		285
Case Study 7.1: ■ Jerome's Break from School		286
Case Study 7.2: ■ Ben's New Environment		286
Case Study 7.3: ■ Carla's Transition to Parenthood		287
A Definition of Young Adulthood		288
Theoretical Approaches to Young Adulthood		290
Erikson's Psychosocial Theory		290
Levinson's Theory of Life Structure		291
Arnett's "Emerging" Adulthood		292
Cultural Variations		294
Multigenerational Concerns		295
Physical Functioning in Young Adulthood		296
The Psychological Self		298
Cognitive Development		298
Spiritual Development		299
Identity Development		301
Social Development and Social Functioning		302
Relationship Development in Young Adulthood		305
Romantic Relationships		306
Parenthood		309
Mentoring		311
Work and the Labor Market		312
Immigration and Work		313

Role Changes and Work 314
Race, Ethnicity, and Work 314
Risk Factors and Protective Factors in Young Adulthood 316
Implications for Social Work Practice 317
Key Terms 318
Active Learning 318
Web Resources 318

❖ Why is it important for social workers to understand transitional markers associated with young adulthood from a *multidimensional* perspective, recognizing systemic-structural impacts on development as well as the psychosocial factors that are traditionally studied?

❖ How do social class, culture, and gender affect the transition to adulthood?

❖ Given that our educational institution serves as gatekeeper to economic opportunities, what are the ways in which our educational system identifies and responds to the changing labor market trends in order to create viable long-term opportunities for all of society's young adults?

KEY IDEAS

As you read this chapter, take note of these central ideas:

1. A new phase called "emerging adulthood" (ages 18 to 25) has been proposed as a time when individuals explore and experiment with different life roles, occupational interests, educational pursuits, religious beliefs, and relationships—with more focus than in adolescence but without the full commitment of young adulthood.

2. Traditional transitional markers associated with young adulthood have included obtaining independent housing, establishing a career, developing significant partnerships that lead to marriage, and becoming a parent; current research suggests that financial independence and authority in decision making are the markers considered important by emerging adults.

3. In young adulthood, cognitive capacities become more flexible; "moral conscience" expands in social awareness, responsibility, and obligation; and religious beliefs are often reexamined.

4. Identity development continues into adulthood and is not static, but is dynamic and ever evolving through significant interpersonal relationships.

5. Young adults struggle with the Eriksonian psychosocial crisis of intimacy versus isolation—the challenge of finding meaningful connections to others without losing oneself in the process.

6. Labor force experience and connection in young adulthood is associated with psychological and social well-being; advanced education is becoming increasingly important in attaining quality jobs.

7. Discrimination and multilevel racism-related stressors can directly and indirectly affect entry into young adulthood.

Jerome's Break From School

Jerome Walters is a 20-year-old white male living in a moderate-sized Midwest town. He went to college for a couple of years, but found it just wasn't for him and left to take a management position in his uncle's construction business. Jerome knows he will probably have to go back to school someday, but was excited at the prospect of doing something "more meaningful" in the real work world. He doesn't believe this job will be his lifelong career, but he says he feels good about having a steady paycheck, being able to have his own place, and being financially independent from his parents. Jerome has a strong work ethic (he usually gets to the construction site at 7:00 A.M. and works well into the evening), but lives by the mantra "work hard and play hard."

Jerome spends a lot of his free time with his friends, and says that having a family of his own right now is the furthest thing from his mind. Some of Jerome's friends from high school have children, and the emotional and financial stresses that he sees them endure lead him to say that he enjoys his freedom too much to be tied down right now. Jerome was dating a woman his age for about a year, but their relationship ended because he was not willing to get married. He is now in and out of dating relationships, each usually lasting a few months.

Jerome's parents have been divorced since he was 7 years old. He says he is not close to his father, who was physically abusive to him during his childhood, and says he "has never gotten along" with his stepmother. However, Jerome has a very close relationship with his mother, who is living with and caring for his ill grandmother. Jerome makes a point to see his mother and grandmother every Sunday.

Jerome is not very involved in his community and does not belong to a church, but he and a few work friends play basketball several nights a week at the local YMCA. Jerome says that, for the most part, he is comfortable with his life right now, but he has come to the family and youth services bureau to participate in an outpatient substance awareness group because the courts have determined that his use of alcohol and marijuana has "gotten out of control." Jerome is currently fulfilling his 10-week court-mandated participation in this group as a result of a recent drug possession charge, and he is one of the few group members who presents as engaged in the treatment, despite openly stating that he does not have a substance abuse problem.

Ben's New Environment

Ben Hahn is a 23-year-old second-generation Korean American. He comes from a very large family, all of whom live in a small rural community. They own the local grocery market, and Ben's two older brothers help in managing the store.

When Ben graduated from high school, he vowed to move out of the town and away from the "small-minded people who inhabit it." Ben says that he never really felt like he fit in during his high school years, partly because of his "immigrant" status and partly because he is gay. Ben had only a few close friends in

high school, did not date, and dreamed of moving to New York City upon graduation. He did fairly well in his schoolwork and was admitted to a large state school close to New York City. Ben's family was proud that he graduated from high school and that he planned to go to college, but they were upset that he chose to move so far away from his family.

During college, Ben became much more comfortable socially, became active in student politics, and found a niche in the college running club. On the running team Ben met Michael, who became a close friend, and over time, they became romantically involved. Ben and Michael did everything together—they shared a lot of the same academic and political interests and enjoyed intense political debates. Throughout his college years, Ben saw his family only infrequently, mostly at holiday breaks, and never brought Michael with him.

Ben continued to do well academically and, after finishing college, decided to go to graduate school in New York City for a master's degree in urban planning. His partner moved into the city with him, and they currently share an apartment near Ben's university. Ben and Michael are actively involved in gay social clubs, a city running club, and a community civic association. Ben wants to establish stronger ties with his parents and siblings back home but also feels as though he has "grown out of" that environment. He is afraid they will not understand all the changes he has been through in college and graduate school and that they will not accept his sexual identity or partnership. In addition, Ben knows that his parents still hold onto the expectation that he will come home when he finishes his graduate program.

Case Study 7.3

Carla's Transition to Parenthood

Carla Aquino is a 30-year-old Latina living in a large West Coast city. She graduated from the local college with a degree in business and is currently employed as an accountant. She has been married for four years to a man she met through her church and is four months pregnant with her first child.

In the midst of her excitement about the new baby, Carla is anxious about how she will juggle the new caretaking responsibilities with her career aspirations. She knows she wants both to have a meaningful career and to be a good mother but is very concerned about managing multiple demanding roles. Her husband, a consultant, works long hours and travels frequently for his job. Carla has discussed with the social worker at the company Employee Assistance Program the disruption, strain, and lack of continuity she feels in their marriage as a result of her husband's intense work schedule, but she also knows that he makes good money and she respects the fact that he enjoys his work.

Carla and her husband are actively involved in their church group, where they meet monthly with other young adults for spirituality discussions. They also participate in the church's various outreach projects, and Carla volunteers two hours each week with Streetwise Partners. However, they live in a very transient part of the city, and she is struggling to develop more meaningful connections with neighbors.

One of Carla's close friends, Marissa, was just diagnosed with breast cancer, which came as a shock to family and friends, because Marissa is only in her late 20s and does not have a family history of cancer.

(Continued)

(Continued)

Carla has had a lot of difficulty dealing with her friend's diagnosis, and worries about her own risks for breast cancer, as she remembers her aunt had a malignant tumor removed two years ago.

Carla's mother died of liver failure the year before Carla graduated from high school, but Carla's father is still alive and is a significant support in her life. Most of Carla's extended family live nearby or in towns outside the central city, although some relatives still live in the Dominican Republic. Carla's mother-in-law, Jan, lives close by and just recently got divorced after 27 years of marriage. Jan relies heavily on her son and daughter-in-law for emotional (and some financial) support during this life transition.

Carla and her husband both say that they are having trouble dealing with the myriad roles they are faced with (such as young professionals, marriage partners, supportive family members), and are considering how the new role of first-time parents will affect their current lives and future life choices.

⬚ A Definition of Young Adulthood

Defining young adulthood and the transitional markers that distinguish this period from adolescence and middle adulthood has been the challenge and life's work of a number of developmental scholars. A broad challenge has been to determine a framework for identifying the developmental characteristics of young adulthood. For example, is a young adult one who has reached a certain biological or legal age? One who has achieved specific physiological and psychological milestones? Or perhaps one who performs certain social roles? Research, theory, and scholarly thinking about young adulthood presents a variety of perspectives related to each of these dimensions. Current research suggests that the transitional markers that have traditionally defined adulthood in decades past, such as marriage and childbearing, are no longer the most salient markers characterizing the young adult in today's society (e.g., see Settersten, Furstenberg, & Rumbaut, 2005). For example, in 1960, three-fourths (77%) of women and 65% of men left home, completed school, became financially independent, got married, and had at least one child by age 30. In 2000, not even half (46%) of women and 31% of men had done so by age 30 (Furstenberg, Kennedy, McCloyd, Rumbaut, & Settersten, 2003, cited in Draut, 2005, p. 6).

> Is it biological age, psychological age, social age, or spiritual age that best defines young adulthood?

Typical chronological ages associated with young adulthood are 22 to 34 (Ashford, LeCroy, & Lortie, 2006) or 18 to 34 (Settersten et al., 2005), and the international chronological standard for defining adulthood is age 18 (Lloyd, Behrman, Stromquist, & Cohen, 2006). And researchers estimate that the 18- to 24-year-old cohort will increase by 21% by 2010 (Sum, Fogg, & Mangum, 2000). Some scholars define young adulthood even more broadly, from the age of 17 to about 40 (Levinson, 1978). Other scholars assert that such broad ranges encompass too much variety of experience:

> If ages 18 [to] 25 are young adulthood, what would that make the thirties? Young adulthood is a term better applied to the thirties, which are still young but are definitely adult in a way that the years 18 [to] 25 are not. It makes little sense to lump late teens, twenties, and thirties together and call the entire period young adulthood. The period from ages 18 to 25 could hardly be more distinct from the thirties. (Arnett, 2000, p. 479)

In this book, however, we are using a broad range of approximately 18–40. Although a wide chronological age range can be useful in providing some chronological boundaries around this developmental period, from a life course perspective it is more useful to examine the social role transitions, important life events, and significant turning points associated with young adulthood. The major challenges facing young adults are attaining independent financial stability and establishing autonomy in decision making, although attaining financial independence is becoming more delayed as advanced educational credentials are increasingly necessary to secure quality employment (Arnett, 2004). Young adults ages 18 to 25 agree when asked about what they see as markers of entry into young adulthood (Arnett, 1998). Young persons who do not attend college are as likely as college students to say that making independent decisions based on their own values and belief systems is important for defining adult status (Arnett, 2000). Other social role changes young people face during the transition from adolescence to adulthood include:

◆ Leaving home and becoming responsible for housing
◆ Taking on work and/or education tasks
◆ Marrying or committing to a significant partnership
◆ Raising children and caring for others
◆ Starting a career
◆ Making time commitments to their families of origin and to their newly created families

Some scholars also define young adulthood as the point at which young persons become functioning members of the community, demonstrated by obtaining gainful employment, developing their own social networks, and establishing independent housing (Halpern, 1996). From a psychosocial perspective, this period is seen as a time of progressive movement out of an individualized and egocentric sense of self and into greater connection with significant others. Social role transitions in young adulthood are summarized in Exhibit 7.1.

Timing of these transitions and psychological readiness for adopting adult roles are important factors in the individual's life course trajectory. However, research indicates that individual variation in the timing and sequence of transitions—when and in what order the individual leaves home, starts a career, and forms a family, for example—does not have large-scale effects on the individual's eventual socioeconomic status (Marini, 1989). These findings contradict the popular notion that people who don't "grow up" on schedule will never

---

Exhibit 7.1	Social Role Transitions in Young Adulthood

- Leaving home
- Gaining financial independence
- Gaining independence in decision making
- Pursuing an education or vocational skills
- Making a partnership commitment
- Becoming a parent
- Renegotiating relationships with parents
- Engaging with the community and the wider social world

"amount to much." However, the timing and sequencing of child-bearing, entry into post-secondary educational institutions, and labor market attachment may have wide-ranging effects on economic viability and security over the long-term. For example, very young single-parents employed in full-time, low-wage work without adequate access to affordable quality childcare or health care will be faced with difficulty in affording and finding time for the additional higher education necessary to obtain employment with better wages, better benefits, and better work schedules (e.g., see Edin & Lein, 1997).

Nevertheless, young adulthood is a challenging and exciting time in life. Young people are confronted with new opportunities and the accompanying stressors associated with finances, occupational planning, educational pursuits, development of significant relationships, and new family roles (Havighurst, 1972). Kenneth Keniston, an eminent developmental scholar writing in the late 1960s, during an era of student activism and bold social expression, described young adulthood as a time of struggle and alienation between an individual and society (Keniston, 1966). Young adulthood remains a period of intrapersonal and interpersonal questing as well as a period of critiquing and questioning of social norms. Young persons grapple with decisions across several polarities: independence versus relatedness, family versus work, care for self versus care for others, and individual pursuits versus social obligations.

▧ Theoretical Approaches to Young Adulthood

Two prominent developmental theories, promulgated by Erik Erikson and Daniel Levinson, specifically address this life course phase.

Erikson's Psychosocial Theory

Erik Erikson's psychosocial theoretical framework is probably one of the most universally known approaches to understanding life course development. Young adulthood is one of Erikson's original eight stages of psychosocial development (refer back to Exhibit 3.6). Erikson described it as the time when individuals move from the identity fragmentation, confusion, and exploration of adolescence into more intimate engagement with significant others (Erikson, 1968, 1978).

Individuals who successfully resolve the crisis of **intimacy versus isolation** are able to achieve the virtue of love. An unsuccessful effort at this stage may lead the young adult to feel alienated, disconnected, and alone. A fear that exists at the core of this crisis is that giving of oneself through a significant, committed relationship will result in a loss of self and diminution of one's constructed identity. To successfully pass through this stage, young adults must try out new relationships and attempt to find a way to connect with others in new ways while preserving their individuality (Erikson, 1978; Fowler, 1981).

> How is the capacity for intimacy affected by earlier social relationships?

In Jerome Walters's case, he seems to be struggling with this problem-solving process. He is tentatively trying out new relationships yet unwilling to fully commit to any one relationship. It appears that Jerome is still exploring and expanding his own individual pursuits, and enjoys both his alone time and social time with friends. Jerome is also very connected to his work, and the psychological attachment and time commitment to his job may prevent him from developing more intimate personal relationships.

Levinson's Theory of Life Structure

Daniel Levinson (1978) describes adulthood as a period of undulating stability and stress, signified by transitions that occur at specific chronological times during the life course. He initially developed his theory based on interviews with men about their adult experiences; later he included women in the research (1996). From his research he developed the concept of **life structure,** which he described as the outcome resulting from specific decisions and choices made along the life course in such areas as relationships, occupation, and childbearing. He considered the ages of 17 to 33 to be the **novice phase** of adulthood. The transition into young adulthood, which occurs during the ages of 17 to 22, includes the tasks of leaving adolescence and making preliminary decisions about relationships, career, and belief systems; the transition out of this phase, which occurs about the age of 30, marks significant changes in life structure and life course trajectory.

During the novice phase, young persons' personalities continue to develop, and they prepare to differentiate (emotionally, geographically, financially) from their families of origin (Levinson, 1978). The transition to adulthood takes hold primarily in two domains: work and relationships. Levinson suggested that it may take up to 15 years for some individuals to resolve the transition to adulthood and to construct a stable adult life structure.

Building on Levinson's concepts, others have noted that cultural and societal factors affect life structure choices during young adulthood by constraining or facilitating opportunities (Newman & Newman, 2006). For example, socioeconomic status, parental expectations, availability of and interactions with adult role models, neighborhood conditions, and community and peer group pressures may all contribute to a young person's decisions about whether to marry early, get a job or join the military before pursuing a college education or advanced training, or delay childbearing. Social and economic factors may directly or indirectly limit a young person's access to alternative choices, thereby rigidifying a young person's life structure. Along these lines, many researchers discuss the strong link between social capital and human capital, suggesting that a family's "wealth transfer" or extent of familial assets, such as the ability to pay for children's college education, is influential in opening up or limiting young adults' opportunities for advanced education and viable employment (Lui, Robles, Leondar-Wright, Brewer, & Adamson, 2006; Rank, 2005).

All three of the case studies at the beginning of the chapter reveal decision making that will affect life structure. Ben Hahn is currently struggling with what he perceives his parents' expectations to be (for him to move home to be with his family after completing his education) and his own desires to maintain the independent lifestyle he has constructed for himself. Jerome Walters sees his friends who have children as struggling with pressures to make ends meet, and decides to put his own family plans on hold. And Carla Aquino may find herself curtailing some of her career aspirations in order to fulfill her familial obligations and responsibilities as a new parent. Especially in young adulthood, life structures are in constant motion, changing with time and evolving as new life circumstances unfold.

Decisions made during the young adulthood transition, such as joining the military, forgoing postsecondary education or delaying childbearing, may not accurately or completely represent a young person's desired life structure or goals. Social workers need to explore goal priorities and the resources and obstacles that will help or hinder the individual in achieving these goals. Social workers are also often called on to help young adults negotiate conflicting, incompatible, or competing life roles throughout this novice phase, such as renegotiating family and work responsibilities as parenthood approaches.

▲ **Photo 7.1**   Recent graduates—Young adulthood remains a period of intrapersonal and interpersonal questing as well as a period for critiquing and questioning social norms.

Arnett's "Emerging" Adulthood

A number of prominent developmental scholars who have written about the stages of adolescence and young adulthood in advanced industrial countries have described phenomena called "prolonged adolescence," "youthhood," or "psychosocial moratorium," which represent an experimentation phase of young adulthood (Arnett, 2000; Erikson, 1968; Settersten et al., 2005; Sheehy, 1995). Jeffrey Jensen Arnett has gone one step further, defining a phase he terms **emerging adulthood** in some detail (Arnett, 2000; Arnett, 2004; Arnett & Tanner, 2005). He describes emerging adulthood as a developmental phase distinct from both adolescence and young adulthood, occurring between the ages of 18 and 25 in industrialized societies (Arnett, 2000, p. 470). There is considerable variation in personal journeys from emerging adulthood into young adulthood, but most individuals make the transition by age 30 (Arnett, 2000). Arnett conceptualized this new phase of life based on research showing that a majority of young persons ages 18 to 25 believe they have not yet reached adulthood and that a majority of people in their 30s do agree they have reached adulthood.

> What historical trends are producing "emerging adulthood"?

According to Arnett, emerging adulthood is a period of prolonged exploration of social and economic roles. Emerging adults try out new experiences related to love, work, financial responsibilities, and educational interests without committing to any specific lasting plan. The social role experimentation of adolescence becomes further refined, more focused, and more intense, although commitment to adult roles is not yet solidified. Arnett explains this adulthood transition using an organizing framework that includes cognitive, emotional, behavioral, and role transition elements (Arnett & Taber, 1994).

Most young persons in emerging adulthood are in education, training, or apprentice-ship programs working toward an occupation; most individuals in their 30s have established a more solid career path and are moving through occupational transitions (e.g., promotion to leadership positions and recognition for significant accomplishments). Studies do show more occupational instability during the ages 18 to 25 as compared to age 30 (Rindfuss, Cooksey, & Sutterlin, 1999).

Although marriage has traditionally been cited as a salient marker in the adulthood transition, current research shows that marriage has not retained its high status as the critical benchmark of adulthood. Today, independent responsibility for decision making and finances seems to be more significant in marking this transition than marriage is (Arnett, 1998). Overall, the emphasis in emerging adulthood is on trying out new roles without the pressure of making any particular commitment (Schwartz, Cote, & Arnett, 2005). The transition, then, from *emerging* adulthood into *young* adulthood is marked by solidifying role commitments. Newer research shows that, across race and ethnicity, the difference between those who follow a **default individualization** pathway (adulthood transitions defined by circumstance and situation, rather than individual agency) versus a **developmental individualization** pathway (adulthood transitions defined by personal agency and deliberately charted growth opportunities in intellectual, occupational, and psychosocial domains), is a firmer commitment to goals, values, and beliefs for those in the developmental individuation pathway (Schwartz et al., 2005, p. 204). In addition, these researchers found that personal agency, across race and ethnicity, is associated with a more flexible and exploratory orientation to adulthood commitments, and is less associated with premature closure and circumscribed commitment.

Residential stability and mobility is another theme of this transition. Emerging adults in their early 20s may find themselves at various times living with family, living on their own in independent housing arrangements yet relying on parents for instrumental support, and living with a significant partner or friends. Indeed, residential instability and mobility is typically at its height in the mid-20s (Rindfuss et al., 1999). Thus, a traditional definition of the separation-individuation process may not be appropriately applied to emerging adulthood. True "separation" from the family of origin may appear only toward the end of young adulthood or, perhaps for some, during the transition to middle adulthood.

Ben Hahn's college experience exemplifies these transitions. It allowed him to test his interests through campus activities and engagements, which helped direct him into more focused relationships and educational pursuits. He has tried out a new geographical environment. However, Ben has still not emerged in the occupational world as a solid employee, as he is still in the process of obtaining his graduate degree. He demonstrates more refined focus and commitment, yet not strong or stable roots.

Demographic changes over the past several decades, such as delayed marriage and childbearing, have made young adulthood a significant developmental period filled with complex changes and possibilities (Arnett, 2000; Sheehy, 1995). Current global demographic trends suggest a similar picture. Overall, globally, family size has decreased, the timing of first marriage is being delayed, including a decrease in teenage marriages, and there are overall decreases in adolescent labor accompanied by increases in educational attainment; although, in some countries like Pakistan, the delay in first marriage has been attributed to a rise in the rate of adolescent girls in the labor market (see Lloyd et al., 2006; White, 2003). In addition, there is similarity in adulthood transitioning trends between developing countries and more economically developed countries, with East Asian countries showing the highest trend similarities and sub-Saharan African showing the least similarities (Behrman & Sengupta, 2006). Specifically, there has been an increased reliance on finding employment outside the family, an emphasis on more formal schooling, rather than family-based learning, a decreased gender gap, and greater transiency in young adulthood (Behrman & Sengupta, 2006).

Arnett's theoretical perspective accounts for this prolongation of role experimentation and exploration during young adulthood within work, educational, relationship, family, and community domains. It also provides a framework for understanding the ebb and flow of a young person's journey toward increased stability. Endorsing the inevitability and normalcy of an experimental phase is important. Traditional models of human development that rely heavily on such criteria as enduring independent residence, stable employment, and new family formation may need to be revisited and updated in coming decades to expand on Arnett and colleagues' insights.

Cultural Variations

Another advantage of the theory of emerging adulthood is that it recognizes diversity. Individual routes of development (the timing and sequence of transitions) are contingent on socialization processes experienced within family, peer groups, school, and community.

| How do culture and socioeconomic status affect the transition to adulthood? |

Specifically, environmental opportunities, expressed community attitudes, and family expectations may all influence the timing and sequencing of transitions during emerging adulthood. Socially constructed gauges of adulthood—such as stable and independent residence, completion of education, entry into a career path, and marriage or significant partnership—hold varying importance across families and cultures.

For some young persons, decisions may be heavily weighted toward maintaining family equilibrium. For example, some may choose not to move out of the family home and establish their own residence in order to honor the family's expectation that children will continue to live with their parents, perhaps even into their 30s. This is a reality that Ben Hahn faces. For others, successful adult development may be defined through the lens of pragmatism; a young person may be expected to make decisions based on immediate, short-term, utilitarian outcomes. For example, they may be expected to enter the labor force and establish a career in order to care for a new family and release the family of origin from burden.

Culture and gender are significant influences on roles and expectations (Arnett & Taber, 1994). Social norms may sanction the postponement of traditional adult roles (such as marriage) or may promote marriage and childbearing in adolescence. There may be different family expectations about what it means to be a "good daughter" or "good son," and these expectations may be consistent or inconsistent with socially prescribed gender roles, potentially creating competing role demands. For example, a young woman may internalize her family's expectations of going to college and having a career while at the same time being aware of her family's expectations that her brothers will go directly into a job to help support the family and her college expenses. In addition, this woman may internalize society's message that women can "do it all"—have a family and career and yet see her friends putting priority on having a family and raising children. As a result, she may feel compelled to succeed in college and a career to make good on the privilege that her brothers did not have while at the same time feeling anxious about putting a career over creating a new family of her own.

Carla Aquino seems to be struggling to uphold several Latina social norms, as seen through her emotional and financial commitments to her immediate and extended family, efforts to maintain a meaningful connection to her church, and creation of a family of her own. However, the multiple role demands experienced are considerable, as her own personal goals of maintaining a professional identity, being a good wife, and giving back to the community compete for Carla's time and emotional energy.

Some environments may offer limited education and occupational opportunities. Economic structures, environmental opportunities, family characteristics, and individual abilities also contribute to variations in transitioning during emerging adulthood. Young adults with developmental disabilities tend to remain in high school during the adulthood transitioning years of 18 to 21, as compared to their peers without such disabilities who are more likely to continue on to college or enter the workforce. Research suggests that more inclusive post-secondary environments, that offer higher education opportunities for young adults with developmental disabilities and the necessary accommodations for such adults to succeed, can increase their social and academic skills, as well as facilitate productive interactions between young adults with and without disabilities (Casale-Giannola & Kamens, 2006). Some studies have shown that Latina mothers of young adults with developmental disabilities encourage family-centered adulthood transitioning, with less emphasis on traditional markers of independence and more emphasis on the family's role in the young adults' ongoing decision making, with such mothers reporting that their young adults' social interactions were more important to them than traditional measures of productivity (Rueda, Monzo, & Shapiro, 2005).

Individuals who grow up in families with limited financial resources, or who are making important transitions during an economic downturn, have less time for lengthy exploration than others do and may be encouraged to make occupational commitments as soon as possible. Indeed, research shows that childhood socioeconomic status is an important mediating factor in young adult transitions (Smyer, Gatz, Simi, & Pedersen, 1998). For example, Astone, Schoen, Ensminger, and Rothert (2000) examined the differences between "condensed" (or time-restricted) and "diffuse" (or time-open) human capital development, with findings suggesting that a diffuse educational system offers opportunities for school reentry across the life course, which may be beneficial to young people who do not immediately enter higher education due to family or economic reasons, such as going into the military or entering the labor force. And, more specifically, they found that military service after high school increased the probability of returning to higher education for men, but not for women.

A family's economic background and resources is strongly associated with the adult status of the family's children; high correlations exist between parents' income and occupational status and that of their children (Rank, 2005). For example, about one-third (34%) of youth from low-income families go on to college compared to 83% of youth from high-income families (Hair, Ling, & Cochran, 2003). Individuals with greater financial stability often have more paths to choose from and may have more resources to negotiate the stressors associated with this developmental period. In counseling Jerome, this may be a factor to investigate.

Multigenerational Concerns

In today's society, young persons are increasingly becoming primary caretakers for elderly family members. Such responsibilities can dramatically affect a young adult's developing life structure. Family life, relationships, and career may all be affected (Dellmann-Jenkins, Blankemeyer, & Pinkard, 2001, p. 1). The demographic trend of delaying childbearing, with an increase of first births for women in their 30s and 40s and a decrease of first births to women in their 20s (Ashford et al., 2006), suggests that young adults are also likely to face new and significant role challenges as primary caretakers for their own aging parents.

The concern is that young adults will face a substantial caregiving burden, trying to help their aging parents with later-in-life struggles while nurturing their own first children. We might see a shorter period of "emerging adulthood" for many people, which would mean that they have less opportunity to explore, to gain a sense of independence, and to form new families themselves. There may be less support for the notion of giving young people time to get on their feet and establish a satisfactory independent adulthood. In addition, young adults may increasingly experience the emotional responsibilities of supporting late-in-life divorcing parents or parents deciding to go back to school at the same time these young adults may be considering advanced educational opportunities themselves. Carla Aquino and her husband are clearly facing these multigenerational role demands as they become the main social support for Jan at the same time that they are trying to get ahead in their careers and prepare for their new baby. Luckily, Carla and her husband have the financial resources and an adequate support network themselves (Carla's father, some extended family, and their church) to help with logistical problem solving, such as finding day care, and to help them deal effectively with the emotional stressors of these role demands.

Physical Functioning in Young Adulthood

Physical functioning is typically at its height during early adulthood. But as young adults enter their 30s, an increased awareness of physical changes—changes in vision, endurance, metabolism, and muscle strength—is common (e.g., Ashford et al., 2006). With new role responsibilities in family, parenting, and career, young adults may also spend less time in exercise and sports activities than during adolescence and pay less attention to their physical health. And at the same time, young adults ages 18 to 34 are the least insured when it comes to health care coverage as compared to any other age cohort (Draut, 2005). However, many young adults make an effort to maintain or improve their physical health, committing to exercise regimens and participating in wellness classes (such as yoga or meditation). They may choose to get more actively involved in community recreational leagues in such sports as hockey, soccer, racquetball, and ultimate Frisbee. Sometimes physical activities are combined with participation in social causes, such as Race for the Cure runs, AIDS walks, or organized bike rides.

Behavioral risks to health in emerging and young adulthood may include unprotected sex. The potential for STDs, including HIV, is related to frequent sexual experimentation, substance use (particularly binge drinking), and smoking or use of other tobacco products. There are 121 million people in the United States, age 12 or older, who are current drinkers (50.3%) and 19.1 million people who are illicit drug users (7.9%); and recent data show that young adults ages 18 to 25 account for the highest rates of binge drinking, heavy drinking, and cigarette use, with the peak prevalence age of 21. In addition, data show that young adults ages 18 to 22 who are in college are more likely to binge drink or drink heavily than those young adults not enrolled in college (Substance Abuse and Mental Health Services Administration [SAMHSA], 2005).

▲ **Photo 7.2**   Young adults may choose to get more actively involved in community recreational leagues.

Recent data from the Drug Abuse Warning Network (DAWN) showed that 2 million drug-related emergency department (ED) visits occurred in 2004. Cocaine, then marijuana, heroin, stimulants, and other drugs represent an ordered account of the drug-prevalence linked to these ED visits (DHHS, 2006a). The National Hospital Ambulatory Medical Care Survey showed an increase from 1993 to 2003 of 19% in ED visits by adults ages 22 to 49, with 11.4% of alcohol-related ED visits accounted for by adolescents and young adults under age 21 and half (53.2%) occurring by adults ages 21 to 44. Young adults ages 15 to 24 had the highest injury-related emergency ED visits, with two–thirds (66.7%) of alcohol-related visits characterized by injury. In addition, African Americans, across age cohorts, had an 86% higher rate of ED utilization compared to that of whites (McCaig & Burt, 2005). Combined, the data seem to indicate that young adults are at high risk for accidents and related health injuries associated with drug use.

Other health concerns include Type I diabetes ("juvenile diabetes"), typically diagnosed in children and young adults. Although this type of diabetes is less prevalent than Type II (diagnosed in older adults), young adults do have a risk of getting Type I diabetes in their 20s. Adults who are diagnosed with diabetes will have to adjust to lifestyle changes, such as more consistent exercise, modified diets, and monitoring of blood sugar levels.

Data from the American Cancer Society show that breast cancer rates for women ages 20 to 39 have not changed significantly over the past decade. Although women under age 40 are not usually at high risk for breast cancer, young women should have an understanding of the signs, symptoms, and risk factors associated with breast cancer and be vigilant of their own health as they age into middle adulthood.

In working with young adults who do have a health-related illness, social workers will want to assess the client's relationship to the illness and evaluate how the treatments are affecting the psychosocial developmental tasks of young adulthood (Dunbar, Mueller, Medina, & Wolf, 1998). For example, an illness may increase a young person's dependence on others at a time when independence from parents is valued, individuals may have concerns about finding a mate, societal stigma associated with the illness may be intense at a time when the individual is seeking more meaningful community engagements, and adjustment to the possibilities of career or parenthood delays may be difficult.

In addition, young adult partners who struggle with infertility problems may have to confront disappointment from family members and adjust to feelings of unfulfilled social and family expectations. Costs of treatment may be prohibitive, and couples may experience a sense of alienation from peers who are moving rapidly into parenthood and child rearing.

> How does infertility alter the young adults phase of the life course?

▨ The Psychological Self

Young adulthood is a time when an individual continues to explore personal identity and his or her relationship to the world. Cognition, spirituality, and identity are intertwined aspects of this process.

Cognitive Development

Psychosocial development will depend on cognitive and moral development, which are parallel processes (Fowler, 1981). Young adulthood is a time when individuals expand, refine, and challenge existing belief systems, and the college environment is especially fertile ground for such broadening experiences (Perry, 1994). Late adolescents and young adults are also entering Piaget's formal operations stage, during which they begin to develop the cognitive ability to apply abstract principles to enhance problem solving and to reflect on thought processes (refer back to Exhibit 3.4 for an overview of Piaget's stages of cognitive development). These more complex cognitive capabilities, combined with a greater awareness of personal feelings, characterize cognitive development in young adulthood (Labouvie-Vief, 1986).

The abstract reasoning capabilities of adulthood and the awareness of subjective feelings can be applied to life experiences in ways that help individuals negotiate life transitions, new roles, stressors, and challenges (Labouvie-Vief, 1986; Schaie, 1982). You might think of the development in cognitive processing from adolescence to young adulthood as a gradual switch from obtaining information to using that information in more applied ways (Arnett & Taber, 1994). Young adults are better able to see things from multiple viewpoints and from various perspectives than adolescents are.

With increasing cognitive flexibility, young adults begin to solidify their own values and beliefs. They may opt to retain certain traditions and values from their family of origin while letting go of others in order to make room for new ones. Ben Hahn is going through some of this tension as he prepares to confront his parents' traditional expectations. In the past, Ben dealt with his feeling that he did not fit in by removing himself geographically from the source of the problem. Through his college years, he has had more freedom psychologically, emotionally, and socially to find his niche, and is now at a point where he is trying to make sense of it all. His challenge is to reconcile the knowledge he has gained about himself (his sexual identity, political beliefs, career aspirations, geographic preferences) with the realities of his family ties. He is ready to revisit what he had let go of in its entirety at an earlier time, armed with new ideologies and values of his own.

During this sorting out process, young adults are also defining what community means to them and what their place in the larger societal context might be like. Individuals begin establishing memberships in, and attachments to, select social, service, recreational, and faith communities. Research indicates that religious beliefs, in particular, are reevaluated and critically examined in young adulthood, with individuals sorting out beliefs and values they desire to hold onto and those they choose to discard (Hodge, Johnson, & Luidens, 1993). However, there is a danger that discarded family beliefs may not be replaced with new meaningful beliefs (Arnett, 2000). Many emerging adults view the world as cold and disheartening and are somewhat cynical about the future. With this common pitfall in mind, we can take comfort from Arnett's finding that nearly all the 18- to 24-year-olds who participated in his study believed that they would ultimately achieve their goals at some point in the future (Arnett, 2000).

In terms of moral development, Lawrence Kohlberg (1976) categorized individuals ages 16 and older as fitting into the postconventional stage, which has these characteristics (refer back to Exhibit 4.1 for an overview of Kohlberg's stages of moral reasoning):

- Greater independence in moral decision making
- More complex contemplation of ethical principles
- Development of a "moral conscience"
- Move from seeking social approval through conformity to redefining and revising values and selecting behaviors that match those values
- Recognition of larger systems and appreciation for community
- Understanding that social rules are relativistic, rather than rigid and prescribed

Young adults begin to combine the principle of utility and production with the principle of equality, coming to the realization that individual or group gain should not be at the detriment of other individuals or social groups.

How does continued moral development affect the capacity for human agency in making choices?

Kohlberg's research indicates that people do not progress in a straight line through the stages of moral development. Late adolescents and young adults may regress to conventional moral reasoning as they begin the process of critical reflection. In any case, successful resolution of the adolescent identity crisis, separation from home, and the willingness and ability to take responsibility for others are necessary, but not sufficient, conditions for postconventional moral development (Kohlberg, 1976).

Spiritual Development

As mentioned earlier, young adulthood is a time when individuals explore and refine their belief systems. Part of that process is development of **spirituality,** a focus on that which gives meaning, purpose, and direction to one's life. Spirituality manifests itself through one's ethical obligations and behavioral commitment to values and ideologies. It is a way of integrating values relating to self, other people, the community, and a "higher being" or "ultimate reality" (Hodge, 2001). Spirituality has been found to be associated with successful marriage (Kaslow & Robison, 1996), considerate and responsible interpersonal relations (Ellison, 1992), positive self-esteem (Ellison, 1993), and general well-being (George, Larson, Koenig, & McCullough, 2000).

Spirituality develops in three dimensions related to one's connection with a higher power (George et al., 2000; Hodge, 2001):

1. *Cognition.* Beliefs, values, perceptions, and meaning related to work, love, and life

2. *Affect.* Sense of connection and support; attachment and bonding experiences; psychological attachment to work, love, and life

3. *Behavior.* Practices, rituals, and behavioral experiences

Generally, consistency across all three dimensions is necessary for a vigorous spiritual life. For Carla Aquino, for example, it is not enough just to attend church (behavior) or just to subscribe to a defined belief set (cognition); she also needs to feel that she is "making a difference" through her church service projects (affect).

Research has shown that religious behavioral practices are correlated with life course stages. One study found that religiosity scores (reflecting beliefs, practices, and personal meaning) were higher for a group of young adults (ages 18 to 25) than for a group of adolescents (ages 14 to 17) (Glover, 1996), suggesting a growing spiritual belief system with age. Individuals making the transition from adolescence into young adulthood seem to place a particularly high value on spirituality. In addition, religious participation has been found to increase with age, even within the young adulthood stage (Gallup & Lindsay, 1999; Stolzenberg, Blair-Loy, & Waite, 1995).

In an attempt to understand the development of spirituality, James W. Fowler (1981) articulated a theory of six stages of faith development. Fowler's research suggested that two of these stages occur primarily in childhood and two others occur primarily during late adolescence and young adulthood. Fowler's stages are very closely linked with the cognitive and moral development paradigms of Piaget and Kohlberg. Adolescents are typically in a stage characterized by **synthetic-conventional faith,** during which faith is rooted in external authority. Individuals ages 17 to 22 usually begin the transition to **individuative-reflective faith**, a stage when the person begins to let go of the idea of external authority and looks for authority within the self (Fowler, 1981). During this time, young adults establish their own belief system and evaluate personal values, exploring how those values fit with the various social institutions, groups, and individuals with whom they interact.

The transition from synthetic-conventional faith to individuative-reflective faith usually occurs in the early to mid-20s, although it may occur in the 30s and 40s, or may never occur at all (Fowler, 1981). An individual's faith development depends on his or her early attachments to other people, which serve as templates for understanding one's connection to more abstract relationships and which help shape these relationships. Faith growth, therefore, is heavily related to cognitive, interpersonal, and identity development.

The process also depends on crises confronted in the 20s and 30s; challenges and conflict are critical for change and growth in faith. In one study, young adult women who were HIV-positive were interviewed in order to explore coping strategies, women's experiences of living with the diagnosis, and life transformations or changes (Dunbar et al., 1998). The majority of women discussed the spiritual dimensions activated by their illness, such as renewing relationships, developing a new understanding of the self, experiencing heightened connections with nature and higher powers, and finding new meaning in the mundane. The interviews revealed several themes related to spiritual growth, including "reckoning with death," which led to the will to continue living and renewed "life affirmation"; finding new meaning in life; developing a positive sense of self; and achieving a "redefinition of relationships." These young women found new meaning and purpose in their lives, which gave them renewed opportunities for social connection (Dunbar et al., 1998).

Identity Development

Identity development is generally associated with adolescence and is often seen as a discrete developmental marker, rather than as a process spanning all stages of the life course. However, identity development—how one thinks about and relates to oneself in the realms of love, work, and ideologies—continues well into adulthood. Ongoing identity development is necessary to make adult commitments possible, to allow individuals to abandon the insular self, and to embrace connection with important others. In addition, continuing identity development is an important part of young adults' efforts to define their life's direction (Glover, 1996).

The classic work of James Marcia (1966) defined stages of identity formation in terms of level of exploration and commitment to life values, beliefs, and goals (as discussed in Chapter 6) as follows:

- Diffused (no exploration; no commitment)
- Foreclosed (no exploration; commitment)
- Moratorium (exploration; no commitment)
- Achievement (exploration; commitment)

Marcia (1993) has stated that people revisit and redefine their commitments as they age. As a result, identity is not static, but dynamic, open, and flexible.

Research exploring this notion that identity formation is a process that continues deep into adulthood shows several interesting outcomes. In one study the researchers interviewed women and men between the ages of 27 and 36 to explore the process of commitment in five domains of identity: religious beliefs, political ideology, occupational career, intimate relationships, and lifestyle (Pulkkinen & Kokko, 2000). Results showed that men and women differed in their overall commitment to an identity at age 27. Women were more likely to be classified in Marcia's "foreclosed" identity status, and men were more likely to be classified in the "diffused" identity status. However, these gender differences diminished with age, and by age 36, foreclosed and achieved identity statuses were more prevalent than diffused or moratorium statuses for both men and women. This trend of increasing commitment with age held constant across all domains except political ideology, which showed increased diffusion with age. Also, across ages, women were more likely than men to be classified in the achieved identity status for intimate relationships; for men, the diffused identity status for intimate relationships was more prevalent at age 27 as compared to age 36.

The young adult who is exploring and expanding identity experiences tension between independence and self-sufficiency on one hand and a need for connection with others and reliance on a greater whole on the other. Young adults are often challenged to find comfort in connections that require a loosening of self-reliant tendencies. Some suggest that the transition into adulthood is signified by increased self-control while simultaneously submitting to the social conventions, structure, and order of the larger community.

Another study of the development of identity well into adulthood used a sample of women in their 20s (Elliott, 1996). The researchers found that the transition into young adulthood excites new definitions of identity and one's place in society, leading to potential changes in self-esteem and psychological self-evaluations. Although self-esteem tends to remain stable in young adulthood, several factors appeared to influence self-esteem in a positive or negative direction:

- Marriage may have a positive effect on self-esteem if it strengthens a young adult's economic stability and social connectedness.
- Parenthood is likely to have a negative effect if the role change associated with this life event significantly increases stresses and compromises financial stability.
- Receiving welfare is likely to decrease a young woman's self-esteem over time.
- Employment may mitigate the negative effects brought about by the transition into parenthood.

Employment tends to expand one's self-construct and identity and can offer a new parent additional social support as well as a supplemental source of validation. However, the extent to which employment will operate as a stress buffer is contingent on the occupational context and conditions. Certainly, good-quality jobs with benefits may enhance, and are unlikely to harm, a woman's psychological well-being (Elliott, 1996). However, dead-end, low-paying jobs do not help with the stresses of parenthood and have the potential to undermine a young woman's self-esteem.

Social workers need to be aware of how peoples' work life impinges on their development of identity. In our case example, Carla Aquino is beginning the process of exploring family benefits provided by her place of employment as she prepares for the new baby. She knows that some of her friends work in environments that have on-site day care, but she does not think her company has that service. She is aware that her work is central to her identity, but she also recognizes that she and her husband must find a way to balance their commitments to work and family.

⊠ Social Development and Social Functioning

There are, of course, many paths to early adulthood, and not all arrive at this phase of the life course with equal resources for further social role development. This section looks at some of the special challenges faced by young adults as they negotiate new social roles, and the impact on social functioning in young adulthood—particularly in regard to interpersonal relationships and work attachment.

What factors put individuals at risk when making the transition to adulthood?

Research has shown that problem behavior in young adults is linked to challenges experienced in negotiating new social roles (Hammer & Vaglum, 1990; Kandel, Davies, Karus, & Yamaguchi, 1986; Sampson & Laub, 1990). For example, although Jerome Walters seems to be maintaining a sense of well-being currently through his connection to the work world, family members, and friends, the shift he is experiencing in becoming a responsible caregiver for his family and taking on financial independence, while still wanting to preserve the freedom of adolescent exploration without commitment, puts Jerome in a vulnerable period of transition. One behavioral expression of this transitional stress is his increased frequency of drinking and smoking marijuana with his friends. However, it is often times difficult to definitively capture the direction of influence. For example, does prior "deviant" behavior create difficulties in committing to work, or does a failure in finding a good job lead to problematic behaviors?

The Child Trends study (Hair et al., 2003) on educationally disadvantaged youth identifies six categories of vulnerable youth making the transition to adulthood: out-of-school youth, youth with incarcerated parents, young welfare recipients, youth transitioning out of incarceration, runaway/homeless youth, and youth leaving foster care (p. 15). The largest group was out-of-school youth, although there is considerable overlap among these vulnerable categories. Many of these educationally disadvantaged youth lack parental monitoring, supervision, and support that would help facilitate the transition into adulthood. Along these lines, poor social functioning in young adulthood appears to be linked to a variety of difficulties in making the transition to new roles (Ronka & Pulkkinen, 1995):

- Problems in school and family in adolescence lead to social functioning problems in young adulthood.
- Unstable employment for males is associated with strained relationships, criminality, and substance abuse.
- Men who have many behavioral problems in young adulthood can be differentiated from young adult males who do not exhibit behavioral problems by several childhood factors, such as aggressive history, problems in school and family, and lack of formal educational attainment.

It is estimated that approximately half of 18-to 24-year-olds have not completed a high school education, have not moved on to college, or moved on to more advanced vocational training (Hair et al., 2003). The transition to young adulthood from the secondary school environment can be challenging, particularly for students with learning disabilities. They drop out of high school at a higher rate than students without these challenges. Results from a qualitative study suggest some reasons why (Lichtenstein, 1993), one being that many students with learning disabilities worked while in high school, often because employment provided an environment where they could gain control over decision making, exercise authority, garner support, and increase self-esteem—outcomes that such students were not able to experience in the traditional educational system. In this study, working during the high school years was related to later employment but was also related to the risk of dropping out of high school altogether before graduation. These findings suggest a need for a well-tailored individual education plan (IEP) for each learning-disabled youth that outlines how that person can best make the transition out of high school and which postschool opportunities might be appropriate, as well as better transitioning services and active follow-up. In addition, the parents of students with learning disabilities need to be educated on their rights, and parent advocacy efforts within the school need to be strengthened (Lichtenstein, 1993).

The Child Trends study (Hair et al., 2003) cites 12 empirically evaluated programs that operate to facilitate adulthood transitioning for youth, to include: Alcohol Skills Training Program; Job Corps; JOBSTART; Job Training Partnership Act; New Chance; Nurse Home Visitation Program; Ohio Learning, Earning and Parenting Program; School Attendance Demonstration Project; Youth Corps; AmeriCorps; Skill-Based Intervention on Condom Use; and Teenage Parent Demonstration. These programs primarily focus on educational and employment gains, and most showed solid gains in employment and improvement in school attendance and completion of GED or gaining of a high school diploma, but not definitive gains in increasing earnings or job retention. Specifically, the Youth Corps program showed the most significant outcomes for African American males who earned higher incomes from their employment, had better employment relationships, and were more likely to have attained advanced education than those who did not participate in the program. Latino males who participated in the program also showed increased employment and work promotions as compared to those who did not participate, while white males actually showed negative effects from participation as they were less likely to be employed and received lower earnings from their work. African American, Latina, and white females all benefited from participation, showing increased work hours and higher educational aspirations (Hair et al., 2003).

Another special population that is likely to face challenges in making the transition into young adulthood is young persons with more severe emotional difficulties. They often have trouble forming meaningful interpersonal relationships, maintaining employment, managing physical health needs, and gaining financial independence. Research shows that disability diagnosis and severity may influence social outcomes. For example, young adults with severe mental retardation and coexisting impairments tend to show the most limited leisure involvement and date less frequently than those young adults with cerebral palsy, hearing loss, or epilepsy (Van Naarden Braun, Yeargin-Allsopp & Lollar, 2006).

Many young adults with developmental and/or emotional disabilities may have tenuous experience with the labor market and weakened connections to work. Often their families do not have sufficient resources to help them make the transition from high school, potentially delaying the youth's opportunity to live independently. Many of these young persons do not have a stable support network, and as a result, they are at higher than usual risk for homelessness (Davis & Vander Stoep, 1997). In a 20-year longitudinal study following a cohort of individuals with developmental delays who were first diagnosed at age 3, both parents and their young adult children expressed concern about the young adults' social isolation and inability to find gainful employment. Many of the young adults were concerned about not having enough peer involvement and too much parental involvement in their lives. Three types of parent-young adult relationships tended to emerge: (1) *dependent* relationships, which were comfortable to the young adults in that parents responded to needs in appropriate quality and quantity; (2) *independent* relationships, which were comfortable to the young adults in that parents responded to young adult needs only in times of crisis; and (3) *interdependent* relationships, which was the most conflictual of the three types and was characterized by young adult resentment of parental involvement (Keogh, Bernheimer & Guthrie, 2004).

Another group of youth at risk in the transition from late adolescence to early adulthood are those with poor relationships with their parents. Emotional intimacy in the parent-child relationship has been found to be important in the development of self-esteem, with the benefits lasting into adulthood. However, engaging and satisfying employment seems to mediate a poor parent-child relationship, increasing the youth's well-being (Roberts & Bengston, 1993).

Youth with unstable attachments to adult caregivers, like many foster care youth who are transitioning out of the foster care system, have a great need for developmentally appropriate and culturally sensitive supportive services as they make the transition into young adulthood. Social workers should examine the ways in which formal services facilitate the transition to adulthood for youths who have no informal supports. Certainly, terminating services to these youths at the age of majority, without making arrangements for them to receive adult services, will undermine the efforts made during the youth's adolescence and put these individuals at a disadvantage as young adults (Davis & Vander Stoep, 1997). Particularly for individuals with developmental disabilities, there may be a strong need for services to continue on into young adulthood (Keogh et al., 2004).

Finally, the immigration experience for youth may pose a risk during the adulthood transition. Research shows that more than one-third (38.2%) of young adult Latinos do not have a high school degree, and immigration transition and associated stressors, as well as socioeconomic barriers may be contributing factors. As social workers, we must ask about the context of the immigration experience and examine how it influences young adult development. For example: Was immigration a choice? Were there family separations along the way and what was the nature of such separations? What motivated the immigration experience? Was there a change in the family's socioeconomic and/or role statuses? What are the hardships encountered in the new country? Are these hardships experienced differently by different members of the same family? What is the level of the family's and individual members' acculturation (Chapman & Perreira, 2005)? It is important to assess for the extent of intergenerational stress that may have developed from the immigration experience as studies show that both high and low levels of acculturation are associated with risk behaviors such as substance abuse and mental health problems (Chapman & Perreira, 2005).

Relationship Development in Young Adulthood

Erikson's concept of intimacy, which relies on connection with a significant partner, is at the core of relationship development during early adulthood. Typically, young adults develop sustained commitments to others and come to recognize a responsibility for others' well-being. This developmental process may manifest as thoughtful awareness in the early years, changing to more active behavioral commitment in later years—for example, caring for children or aging parents, getting involved in the community, and taking on social obligations.

Intimacy, which can be defined as a sense of warmth or closeness, has three components: interdependence with another person, self-disclosure, and affection (Perlman & Fehr, 1987). Intimacy may take the form of cognitive/intellectual intimacy, emotional intimacy, sexual intimacy, physical intimacy apart from a sexual relationship, and spiritual intimacy. When reflecting on intimate relations, some people talk about finding a "soul mate"; feeling intensely connected; sharing values, beliefs, and philosophical inquiries; and feeling as though the relationship has strong direction and purpose.

Establishing intimacy is a multifaceted process. Exhibit 7.2 lists some of the tasks involved in fostering an intimate relationship with someone. The ability to perform these tasks depends not only on personal abilities but also on external factors, such as the individual's family background. Research has found several family factors in adolescence to be important in the ability to develop intimate relationships during young adulthood: (1) a positive relationship with the mother (e.g., effective, clear communication with her, as well as mutual respect and empathy), and (2) adaptability of the family unit (e.g., good habits of conflict resolution and appropriate discipline) (Robinson, 2000). The young adult's ability to develop intimate relationships also depends on favorable environmental conditions, such as having adequate resources to accommodate stressors, handle life responsibilities, and deal effectively with the multiple life transitions of this developmental stage.

Exhibit 7.2	Tasks in Fostering Intimacy

- Effectively negotiating expectations for the relationship
- Negotiating roles and responsibilities
- Making compromises
- Prioritizing and upholding values
- Deciding how much to share of oneself
- Identifying and meeting individual needs
- Identifying and meeting partnership needs
- Renegotiating identity
- Developing trust and security
- Allowing for reciprocal communication
- Making time commitments to partner
- Effectively resolving conflict and solving problems
- Demonstrating respect, support, and care

An individual's family relationships and attachment to the family unit as a whole are transformed during young adulthood. The family's life cycle stage and the psychosocial development of individual members will influence the nature of family relationships in young adulthood. Generally, though, young adults may see parents, siblings, and relatives less frequently as work, romantic attachments, and new family responsibilities take precedence. With greater independence, geographic distance may also preclude more visits. Thus, time spent together may center around holiday celebrations. As traditional family roles evolve, young adults may take more active responsibility for holiday preparations. They may find themselves wanting to spend less time with old friends and more time with family. As young adults have children, holiday activities and family interactions may increasingly focus on the new generation.

Romantic Relationships

Romantic relationships are a key element in the development of intimacy during early adulthood. **Romantic love** has been described as a relationship that is sexually oriented, is "spontaneous and voluntary," and occurs between equal partners (Solomon, 1988). Satisfaction in romantic partnerships depends on finding a delicate balance between positive and negative interactions across time (Gottman, 1994).

In the United States, heterosexual romantic love has traditionally been considered a precursor to marriage. However, a recent trend in romantic relationships is to have sex earlier but marry later. By the mid-1990s, more than half of all marriages occurred after a period of

▲ **Photo 7.3**   A family wedding photo—The transition from emerging adulthood to young adulthood is marked by solidifying role commitments, such as marriage.

cohabitation (Steinhauer, 1995). It is important to remember, however, that in many parts of the world and among many recent immigrant groups to the United States, marriage is arranged and not based on romantic courtship. There are many other variations in relationship development as well, represented by single-parent families, childless couples, gay/lesbian partnerships, couples who marry and choose to live apart to establish individual career tracks, and couples where partners are in different life stages (e.g., early adulthood and middle adulthood).

In the past, increasing education decreased women's likelihood of marrying, but recent data suggest a reversal of that trend. The cohort of women who recently graduated from college, both black and white, are likely to marry later than women of their cohort without a college education, but their rate of eventual marriage will be higher (Goldstein & Kenney, 2001). The researchers interpret this trend to indicate that marriage is increasingly becoming a choice only for the most educated members of society. Given the advantages of a two-earner family, this trend may contribute toward the widening economic gap in our society.

An increasing awareness of variation in relationships has prompted research into all sorts of romantic attachments. One focus is homosexual relationships. One study that identified three "scripts" in lesbian relationships helps to differentiate romantic attachment from other kinds of intimacy (Rose & Zand, 2000): (1) the "romance" script combines emotional intimacy and sexual attraction. It is characterized by an attenuated dating period and quick commitment to a relationship; (2) "friendship" is a script in which individuals fall in love and are

How does sexual orientation affect young adult development?

emotionally committed, though sexual behaviors are not necessarily a part of the relationship. Research shows that this is the most common script among lesbians, emphasizing emotional intimacy over sexuality. Women have suggested that the ambiguity implicit in this script often makes defining the relationship difficult; (3) "sexually explicit" focuses on sexual attraction and leaves emotional intimacy at the periphery. This script is void of any direct expression of future commitment. These scripts are summarized in Exhibit 7.3.

Exhibit 7.3	Lesbian Relationship Development
Script	*Descriptor*
Romance	Emotional and sexual attraction; quick commitment
Friendship	Emotional commitment; sexual behavior may or may not be part of relationship
Sexually Explicit	Sexual attraction is focal point; emotional intimacy secondary

SOURCE: Adapted from Rose & Zand, 2000.

Lesbian and gay partnering becomes more complex if the coming out process begins in early adulthood. The individuals involved have to negotiate through their parents' emotional reactions and responses at the same time as the new relationship is developing. One study found that lesbian and gay partners are less likely to identify family as a significant social support as compared to heterosexual couples (Kurdek, 2004). One possible reason is that siblings and other relatives may be forced to confront their own comfort, biases, and values associated with the young adult's relationship. If gay and lesbian couples decide to have children, their own parents will inevitably be forced to confront the homosexual identity in order to develop their grandparent role with the new child.

Even in families where "acceptance" has taken root, people in the family's social network may have limited understanding that is difficult to work through. Family members who thought they had come to terms with the young adult's homosexual identity may find themselves harboring anger, hurt, disappointment, or confusion about how the young person's life trajectory is affecting their own life trajectories.

Other complicating factors related to gay and lesbian relationship development can be connections with the larger community and with the gay and lesbian community itself. Current legal inequities—such as the lack of legal sanction for marriage-like partnerships, the associated lack of benefits (e.g., survivorship and inheritance rights and housing loans), and the lack of authority in decision making for gay and lesbian partners (in such matters as child custody and health care/medical procedures)—can cause additional external strain on new couples. In the 2006 election, voters in seven states (Colorado, Idaho, South Carolina, South Dakota, Tennessee, Wisconsin, and Virginia) approved a ban on same-sex marriage legislation that amends the states' constitutions to define marriage as a "union between one man and one woman" and, in some cases, specifies prohibition of recognizing legal status for unmarried persons. One state opted for language to specify prohibition of the legislature from recognizing "civil unions, domestic partnerships, or other quasi-marital relationships." Arizona was the only state in the 2006 election where citizens voted down the proposed ban (proposition 107), with only a slight majority (51.8%) of the votes.

Currently, only Massachusetts has recognized same-sex marriages, but prohibits non-residents from marrying if such a marriage would not be recognized in the couples' own state. Vermont, Connecticut, and California have legal unions which offer marriage rights, and Maine, Hawaii, and Washington, D.C. also have legal unions with some marriage rights recognized. As recently as December of 2006, New Jersey passed a law allowing civil unions, which confer all the constitutional rights and responsibilities of marriage to same-sex couples. To be sure, these amendment developments have been politically powerful and publicly polarizing, with some state citizenry equally divided in their opinions on whether same-sex couples should be granted legal rights of marriage, and other state citizenry more clearly divided, with over 80% of some state voters endorsing such bans (e.g., Tennessee).

The legal impact of these political wranglings on gay and lesbian adults' rights has been described, but how a young adult's family status is defined in legal terms by society may also influence other decision making processes, such as choice of community or residential neighborhood, childbearing decisions, employment choices, and options during times of unemployment (e.g., if one partner's benefits, such as health insurance, are not legally available to the other partner when one young adult loses a job). In addition, impact may be experienced at the mezzo level via various systems' (e.g., school, health care, child care centers) interactions with same-sex parents if there is a lack of recognition of the rights of both parents in decision making for their child.

Regardless of the sexuality of young adult clients, social workers need to consider the client's partner when exploring intimacy issues (LaSala, 2001). These partners may be a valuable resource in matters relating to the partnership itself as well as relations with the family of origin. Social workers also need to assess the adequacy of a young adult's support system across multiple dimensions and to identify and respond to any perceived gaps. Although marriages and partnerships typically expand a young adult's social support network, this might not be the case for all individuals, and social workers should be cautious about making such assumptions.

Parenthood

Parenting is an interactive process, with reciprocal parent-child and child-parent influences (Maccoby, 2002). The multiple role transitions that mark entry into parenthood during young adulthood can be both exciting and challenging, as new familial interdependencies evolve. New social obligations and responsibilities associated with caretaking affect the relationship between the young adult partners and between the young adults and their parents.

Often, the nature of the partners' relationship before parenthood will determine how partners will manage the demands of these changing roles (Durkin, 1995). Adjustment to parenthood, and successful role reorganization, depends on five dimensions (Cowan, 1991):

1. Individual factors, such as how role changes affect one's sense of self

2. Quality of the partners' relationship (e.g., how the couple negotiates responsibilities and their decision making capabilities)

3. Quality of the relationship between the young adults and their children

4. Quality of each partner's relationships with his/her family of origin

5. Quality of external relationships (e.g., school, work, community)

How partners negotiate the division of labor along gender lines also influences parenting and marital satisfaction. Much of the parenting literature has focused on the role strain mothers face in maintaining work commitments alongside new parenting responsibilities. Some new literature has focused on the more positive aspects of mothers' participation in the workforce (Zaslow & Emig, 1997). However, fatherhood and the positive impact of paternal parenting on both child well-being and on the father's own successful male adult development need further exploration.

According to the most recent statistics from the National Survey of Family Growth, about two-thirds (64%) of men ages 15 to 44 had a first child in their 20s. One-quarter of black fathers had a first child before age 20 compared to one-fifth of Latino fathers and 11% of white males. One-fifth of children in two-parent families have their father as their primary caregiver (Halle, 2002). Just over one-third (37%) of black fathers were married when they had their first child, as compared to three-quarters (77%) of white fathers and half (52%) of Latino fathers (Department of Health and Human Services [DHHS], 2006b). The Rochester Youth Development Study (Thornberry, Smith, & Howard, 1997) estimated that over one-quarter (28%) of public school males become fathers by the age of 19, and other studies show that adolescent fatherhood is a risk factor for delinquency (Stouthamer-Loeber & Wei, 1998), and is associated with weakened school attachment and lower wages (Pirog-Good, 1996). In addition, lower socioeconomic status, aggressive behavior, and low academic achievement are antecedents to teen fatherhood (Xie, Cairns, & Cairns, 2001). Weinman, Buzi, and Smith (2005) found that young fathers have significant mental health needs and address the importance of fatherhood education, advocating for a "social marketing" approach that delivers educational messages to male youth indigenously within targeted communities.

Research on tasks associated with responsible fathering identify the provision of economic and emotional support to children, basic caregiving, offering guidance and control, and "being there" (or being present) as most important to the fathering role as defined by young fathers and linked to successful fathering (Peart, Pungello, Campbell, & Richey, 2006). Fathers who are highly involved with their children often describe their peers' parents as being influential in their own development as a father (Masciadrelli, Pleck, & Stueve, 2006). Further research needs to account for the presence of male **fictive kin** (nonrelatives that are considered family) and their role in helping young adults develop as fathers, and to document the strengths of special populations of fathers, such as young African American fathers (see Connor & White, 2006).

Some evidence of paternal parenting styles was provided in a longitudinal study of father-child relationships based on interviews with 240 working-class families (Snarey, 1993). Results showed that 35% of fathers in the study were "not very active," 41% reported being "substantially involved," and 24% were "highly involved" in fatherhood activities. Data showed that fathers were more involved during childhood as compared to adolescence or infancy. Socioemotional support was the most common support that fathers provided during activities shared with their children, followed by physical/athletic support and intellectual/academic support.

As for mothers, the evidence suggests that maternal employment may have a positive influence on her sense of self, leading to better outcomes for her children. With these findings in mind, it becomes necessary to identify groups for whom employment opportunities may be limited. Parents of children with disabilities fall into this category. Research shows that 12% of children in the United States have at least one developmentally related functional limitation that requires special attention and care (Hogan & Msall, 2002). Parenting a child with a functional disability demands extra care, which may decrease a parent's opportunity to enter or continue participation in the labor market. One study suggested that two-thirds of families with a child who has a functional limitation will experience significant changes in labor force participation (Hogan & Msall, 2002).

Low-income mothers are another group for whom maternal employment is significantly related to child well-being (Zaslow & Emig, 1997). Employment often creates child care difficulties. However, characteristics associated with positive parenting (e.g., the mother's ability to express warmth to the child, her lack of depressive symptoms, and the quality of her verbal interaction with the child) have been found to mediate the ill effects on child well-being that may arise in welfare-to-work programs, which sometimes leave low-income mothers with poor child care options (McGroder, Zaslow, Moore, Hair, & Ahluwalia, 2002). Other studies have found that parents who have more social support are better at parenting (Marshall, Noonan, McCartney, Marx, & Keefe, 2001).

Helping young adults to develop parenting efficacy may help them overcome environmental conditions and improve their children's well-being. Unfortunately, research shows that one of the biggest gaps in independent living services for young adults transitioning out of foster care is in parenting skills development (the other was housing preparation) (Georgiades, 2005). Another study compared the effects of increasing the mother's parenting efficacy in white and black families characterized by a weak marriage and living in economically disadvantaged neighborhoods (Ardelt & Eccles, 2001). The black families showed greater benefits in the form of increased academic success for their children. Parenting efficacy also contributed more to positive child outcomes in black families with a compromised marriage than in black families where the marriage was strong and secure. Parenting-related protective factors in Latino families include respect, familism, and biculturalism (Chapman & Perreira, 2005).

Mentoring

Although young adults seek out older adult mentors in work as they begin establishing themselves in new careers, young persons also often serve as mentors themselves. Serving as a mentor can help young adults move through the adulthood transition by facilitating new experiences and helping them to develop new roles that require "taking care of others" as opposed to "being taken care of" themselves. As young adults refine their ideologies, beliefs, and values, they form group affiliations consistent with their emerging identity, career, relationships, community, and religious and political views.

Some examples of current groups and mentoring programs young adults might get involved in include 20 Something, a gay/lesbian young adult social group; Young Democrats/Young Republicans political groups; YMCA/YWCA; and Big Brothers/Big Sisters youth mentoring programs. Service-related groups young adults may choose to become involved with include Junior Achievement, a nonprofit organization that brings young adults together with elementary school students to teach children economic principles, and Streetwise Partners, where young adults help low-income and unemployed persons with job skills training. College students may also get actively involved in Habitat for Humanity projects or student associations such as the College Hispanic American Society, Campus Crusaders for Christ, and Association of Black Students, which spearhead philanthropic and community-integration activities.

Work and the Labor Market

The transition into the world of work is an important element of social development during early adulthood. A young adult's opportunity for successful adulthood transitioning into the labor market depends on a variety of dimensions, to include **human capital** (talents, skills, intellectual capacity, social development, emotional regulatory capacity), as well as **community assets** such as public infrastructure (e.g., adequate transportation to get to work), community networks, and educational opportunities. In addition, family capital is important. "Transformative assets," or those family contributions that aid in deferring the immediate economic costs of long-term investments such as a college education or the down payment for a house, are differentially spread across race, with half of white families giving young adults this investment edge, while data show that only 20% of black families are able to do so (Lui et al., 2006). This coupled with the fact that, in some states, children of undocumented immigrants do not receive in-state tuition for higher education, makes the prospects of getting into and affording a college education out of reach for many young adults, and erodes their longer-term access to asset growth and economic stability.

Given that our educational institution operates as society's gatekeeper to economic opportunities, we need to examine how our educational system is preparing our youth for future employment, as well as how and to whom such opportunities are afforded. For example, what kind of jobs are our youth getting and what educational and vocational paths lead to these jobs? Are we effectively and appropriately matching educational and vocational opportunities to the current economic landscape, so that all youth transitioning into the adult world of work can benefit? Does our educational system effectively track and keep pulse on changing labor market trends, identify careers with long-term gains (e.g., with benefits and growth potential), and then create the appropriate education and training experiences necessary to be attractive in competing for these jobs? In other words, if factors associated with gaining assets include access to education, jobs, promotions, credit, and safety net/benefits such as health care (Lui et al., 2006, p. 229), and asset accumulation leads to prosperity and economic stability (Rank, 2005), we need to examine how differential education and training tracks might be influencing lifelong economic and labor market trajectories, keeping certain groups entrenched in poverty.

Indeed, as important as individual factors are in the transition to work, the changing labor market and structural shifts in the economy may have an even greater influence by shaping a young person's opportunities for finding and maintaining productive work. Work in industry and manufacturing has been diminishing for four decades now, and the number of jobs in the service sector has increased (Portes & Rumbaut, 2001). Manufacturing jobs once offered unskilled youth with relatively little education an opportunity for good wages, employment benefits, and job security. However, the service sector is divided between low-wage, temporary or part-time service jobs, and work opportunities that call for advanced, technical skills. Today there is a high labor market demand for low-wage, low-skill jobs as well as a high demand among employers for workers with more specialized and technical skills (Portes & Rumbaut, 2001).

The dilemma facing disadvantaged youth entering adulthood is vexing. Labor market attachment is not only the surest route to material well-being (for example, according to Shapiro [2004] once basic living expenses are accounted for, each additional dollar of annual income generates $3.26 in net worth over a person's lifetime), but labor market attachment also has been

> How do factors such as gender, race, ethnicity, and disability affect transitions into the labor market?

▲ **Photo 7.4** A major challenge facing young adults is attaining independent financial stability and establishing autonomy and decision making.

found to be significantly related to mental health and psychosocial well-being. One study looked at factors associated with well-being and adjustment between ages 16 and 21. The study found that experiences of unemployment were significantly associated with thoughts of suicide, substance abuse, and crime (Fergusson, Horwood, & Woodward, 2001). Benefits of work include increased self-esteem, increased social interaction, and external validation through social recognition.

Increasingly, therefore, youths' life trajectories will be determined by access to advanced education and then good jobs. Jerome Walters, at age 20, realizes that society demands education. But right now he is not worried about having dropped out of college, and he enjoys his work. He feels as though he has plenty of time to go back. In addition, his uncle needs Jerome's help and is not encouraging Jerome to go back to school. Although Jerome's mother would like to see him complete his education someday, she believes that what he really needs right now is a steady job.

Immigration and Work

Alejandro Portes and Ruben G. Rumbaut (2001), in their timely book *Legacies: The Story of the Immigrant Second Generation,* based on results from the Children of Immigrants Longitudinal Study (CILS), note that the structural labor market change of the past few decades disproportionately affects immigrants, particularly youth in late adolescence who will be emerging into this new occupational landscape. "Increasing labor market inequality implies that to succeed socially and economically, children of immigrants today must cross, in the span of a few years, the educational gap that took descendents of Europeans several generations to bridge" (p. 58). An important finding from the CILS is the contrast in job selection between older and younger generations of immigrants. Today's young people are more likely to turn down "traditional immigrant jobs" that are seen as unfulfilling, in contrast to older immigrants who often felt compelled to take any job available in their youth without such questioning (Portes & Rumbaut, 2001).

Another study investigated how migration affects the earnings prospects of Latino men making the transition into young adulthood (Padilla & Jordan, 1997). Specifically, seeking work opportunities in more favorable socioeconomic environments during early adulthood was found to be associated with decreased likelihood of poverty in adulthood. Increased education and cognitive ability were also associated with a decreased likelihood of being in poverty during the transition into adulthood.

It is important for social workers to understand the social and economic conditions that immigrant youth face. This large and growing group, born from the surge in immigration of recent decades, faces special challenges as young adults under recent economic conditions.

Role Changes and Work

A number of other factors are related to the type of work young adults secure, and thus their occupational prestige and income earned later in life. Across race and gender, educational attainment has a strong effect. Marriage itself is not a significant predictor of occupational prestige or earnings for males or females. Women who marry between ages 24 and 26 usually have higher earnings than women who marry earlier; but for males, entry into marriage before age 24 was associated with higher earnings than marriage at later ages (Marini, 1989). Parenthood showed no association with occupational prestige for either sex but negatively affected the income of women. Family role changes (marriage, parenthood) occurring before work transitions appear to have no relationship with individual socioeconomic status (SES). However, experience in the work force positively affects occupation and earnings (Marini, 1989).

For the social worker, it would be important to examine to what extent culture affects educational and work-related opportunities and timing sequences. Social workers also need to explore with individuals the extent of role overload that may exist. For example, an additional effect of employment on low-income earners may be the added expense that occurs when work and family pressures collide. Exploring the unique costs and benefits of employment decisions for each individual, recognizing the larger family context, can be helpful. Social workers should also assess clients' coping strategies and ask clients for their perceptions about how identified stressors are affecting the individual and family.

Race, Ethnicity, and Work

The associations among race, ethnicity, and work attachment have received some attention. While first generation Mexican immigrants earn incomes that are half that of white males, second generation immigrants typically earn three-quarters that of white men and more than black men. About 40% of first generation Mexican immigrants ages 16 to 20 are in school or college as compared to two-thirds of second generation immigrants in this age cohort (Of Meat, Mexicans and Social Mobility, 2006).

Labor force connection tends to be weakest for black males who have little formal education and who lack work experience (Laseter, 1997). Of course, the economic restructuring of past decades has made good-quality jobs for young adults without specialized skills hard to come by. Other barriers for young black men include discrimination in hiring, absence of adult mentors in the community who might help socialize youth toward work roles, a disconnect from a good-paying job with benefits, diminished self-efficacy related to perceptions of constricted economic opportunities, hopelessness about finding quality jobs, and the presence of alternative informal and more prosperous economic options (e.g., drug dealing, gambling). All may decrease the youth's ability or motivation to pursue formal work opportunities. But that is not to say that young black men do not want to succeed in the world of work:

> Young black men want jobs and wages comparable to white young men, and their reluctance to take inferior jobs, despite less experience, lengthens their period of unemployment. They share middle-class values and aspirations. The problem is how to achieve those aspirations. (Laseter, 1997, p. 74)

Racism may be a factor in job prospects for young black males as well. Sociological studies have shown that white men with a prison record are more likely to be hired for a job than black men without a prison record (Lui et al., 2006). Racism can directly tax individuals and families and can indirectly deplete their buffering resources and weaken solutions to managing direct stressors (Harrell, 2000). Stressors and resources change over the life course, however, and social workers need to be able to assess the ways in which individuals and families are able to adapt to such changes.

Although social workers need to understand the effects of oppressive living conditions and environmental stressors on all groups, they should be aware of the disproportionate number of African Americans living in such conditions. Regardless of SES, African American males have the lowest well-being scores of any group studied (white women and men, African American women and men) (Woody & Green, 2001). Their low scores are potentially explained by social conditions such as stigma, constrained economic opportunities, health-related discrepancies, and a perception of lack of control over their lives. It is dually important, however, for social workers to understand the range of diversity within the African American community along many social dimensions, including SES, in order to avoid perpetuating the stereotypes that further stigmatize this diverse group.

In addition, social workers should be aware of how social assistance is unequally distributed, and should work toward eliminating such disparities. For example, of those exiting welfare, whites are twice as likely as blacks or Latinas to receive child care or transportation transitional assistance. In addition, the median wage for a white welfare exiter between 1997–1999 was $7.31/hour compared to $6.88 and $6.71 for African American and Latina exiters respectively (Lui et al., 2006). Other research shows that when women who leave Temporary Assistance to Needy Families (TANF) are employed in steady jobs and remain employed over time, their wages increase with this longevity in the work world (Corcoran, Danziger, Kalil, & Seefeldt, 2000). However, the reality is that many young women leaving TANF do not enter long-term continuous employment due to a variety of barriers, such as maternal and child physical and/or mental health problems, unaffordable/ inaccessible/or poor quality child care, or unreliable transportation (Corcoran et al., 2000). Without addressing these problems, the *long-term* wage stability and economic viability of these families remain in question. The living wage social movement that continues to gain momentum will help bring more public awareness and hopefully policy change to these issues.

Risk Factors and Protective Factors in Young Adulthood

A longitudinal study that followed a cohort of individuals born in 1955 from infancy to age 40 identified clusters of protective factors at significant points across the life course (see Exhibit 7.4) that are associated with successfully making the transition to adulthood (Werner & Smith, 2001). The researchers identified high-risk individuals and then determined the specific factors that influenced their positive adaptation to adulthood at age 32. The protective factors included successful early social, language, and physical development; good problem-solving skills in middle childhood; educational and work expectations and plans by age 18; and social maturity and a sense of mastery and control in late adolescence. Family factors included stable maternal employment when the child was 2 to 10 years old, access to a variety of social support sources, and the child's sense of belonging within the family unit at age 18. Community factors included having access to nurturing, caring adults in one's community, including the presence of adult mentors, and having access to "enabling," as opposed to "entrapping," community niches (see Saleeby, 1996).

> How can social workers help to provide protective factors for the adult transition?

Other researchers have identified similar protective factors associated with successful developmental transitions into emerging adulthood and young adulthood, to include childhood IQ, parenting quality, and socioeconomic status. Adaptation in emerging adulthood, specifically, is associated with an individual's planning capacity, future motivation, autonomy, social support, and coping skills (Masten et al., 2004).

Risk factors that researchers found to be associated with the transition to adulthood included low family income during infancy, poor reading achievement by age 10, problematic school behavior during adolescence, and adolescent health problems (Werner & Smith, 2001). For men, an excessive number of stressful events, living with an alcoholic or mentally ill father, and substance abuse contributed to problematic coping in early adulthood. Other

Exhibit 7.4	Common Core Protective Factors Predicting Adult Adaptation	
	Individual Characteristics	*Caregiving Context*
Infancy	Autonomy; social competence Health status	Maternal competence Emotional support # of stressful events
Middle childhood	Academic proficiency Health status	Emotional support to child (extended family; mentor) # of stressful events
Adolescence	Self-efficacy Health status	Emotional support to child (peer relations; feelings about family) # of stressful events
Young adulthood	Temperament Health status	Emotional support (quality of partner, work, & community relationships) # of stressful events

Source: Adapted from Werner & Smith, 2001, pp. 161–163.

studies have found that adolescent fatherhood can be a risk factor for delinquency, which, in turn, can lead to problematic entry into adulthood (Stouthamer-Loeber & Wei, 1998). For women, a sibling death in early childhood, living with an alcoholic or mentally ill father, and a conflicted relationship with the mother were significant risk factors for successful coping at age 32 (Werner & Smith, 2001).

A recent study of the effects of war on adult mental health reveals other risk factors that social workers should be aware of. Although some researchers have found that military service often provides youth a positive opportunity in transitioning into adulthood (Werner & Smith, 2001) and frequently leads to facilitating a young adult's return to higher education (Astone et al., 2000), the ravages of war experienced during military service can pose significant mental health risk. For example, Hoge, Auchterlonie, and Milliken (2006) examined the prevalence of mental health problems and service utilization among military personnel who recently returned from service in Iraq, and found that one-fifth (19.1%) of those returning from Iraq had at least one mental health problem, with about one-third (35%) of those adults accessing mental health services during their first year back home. In addition, those personnel who were assessed as having a mental health condition were more likely to subsequently leave the military as compared to those personnel who returned home without a mental health condition. Therefore, it appears that although military service can be a positive path for many transitioning youth, the nature and quality of a youth's military experience may influence later physical and mental health outcomes, as well as work trajectory decisions (e.g., to leave the military early). It appears that military service in a time of war may be a risk factor rather than protective factor. In addition, the availability of, access to, and quality of mental health care for military personnel upon their return home may also contribute to the severity of wartime service as a risk factor.

Knowledge of risk and protective factors related to the adulthood transition can help social workers assess young adult clients' current challenges, vulnerabilities, strengths, and potentials. Gaining an accurate understanding of the client's developmental history provides guidance to the social worker in formulating appropriate goals and intervention strategies. It is important to remember to check out your own assumptions of "risk" with clients in order to clarify the unique impact such experiences have on individual clients.

IMPLICATIONS FOR SOCIAL WORK PRACTICE

This discussion of young adulthood suggests several practice principles for social workers:

- Recognize that social roles during emerging adulthood may be different from those later in young adulthood.
- Explore cultural values, family expectations, attitudes toward gender roles, and environmental constraints/resources that may influence life structure decisions and opportunities when working with young adult clients.
- Assess specific work, family, and community conditions as they pertain to young adult clients' psychological and social well-being; be aware of any caregiving roles young adults may be playing.
- Where appropriate, help young adults to master the tasks involved in developing intimate relationships.

- ◆ Where appropriate, assist young adults with concerns about differentiating from family of origin and do so in a culturally sensitive manner.
- ◆ Work with other professionals to advocate for policies that promote transitional planning and connect youth to the labor market, particularly for youth aging out of foster care placements, correction facilities, group home environments, or other formal residential mental health settings.
- ◆ Take the initiative to develop mentoring programs that build relations between young adults and younger or older generations.
- ◆ Take the initiative to develop parenting classes for first-time parents, and recognize and develop the unique strengths of fathers, especially in mentoring teen fathers' to increase parenting skills.

KEY TERMS

community assets	fictive kin	life structure
default individualization	human capital	novice phase
developmental	individuative-reflective faith	romantic love
individualization	intimacy	spirituality
emerging adulthood	intimacy vs. isolation	synthetic-conventional faith

Active Learning

1. Identify one current social issue as portrayed in the media (e.g., housing, immigration policies, health care access or coverage or affordability, living wage) and explore how this social issue uniquely affects young adults.

2. Create your own theory of young adulthood. What are some of the important characteristics? What makes someone a young adult? What differentiates this stage from adolescence and middle adulthood? Start the process by answering the following question: "Do you consider yourself to be an adult?"

3. Choose one of the case studies at the beginning of the chapter (Jerome Walters, Ben Hahn, or Carla Aquino). Change the gender for that case without changing any other major demographic variable. Explore how your assumptions change about the individual's problems, challenges, and potential. Now choose a different case. Change the race or ethnicity for that case and again explore your assumptions. Finally, using the remaining case, change the SES and again explore how your assumptions change.

WEB RESOURCES

Network on Transitions to Adulthood
http://www.transad.pop.upenn.edu/about/index.htm

Site presented by the Network on Transitions to Adulthood, examines the policies, programs, and institutions influencing the adulthood transition; contains fast facts and information on research initiatives. The Network is funded by the John D. and Catherine T. MacArthur Foundation and is chaired by University of Pennsylvania sociologist, Frank Furstenberg.

National Guard Youth ChalleNGe Program
http://www.ngycp.org

Site that reports on success stories of a multistate program that targets youth who have dropped out of high school to provide them with a five-month residential program and ongoing mentoring services to facilitate their entry into employment, higher education/training, or the military.

AmeriCorps NCCC (National Civilian Community Corps)
http://www.americorps.org/about/programs/nccc.asp

Site details one of AmeriCorps' programs for young adults ages 18 to 24, offering full-time residential community service opportunities. Target goals include developing youths' leadership capacity through intensive and directed community service.

High School and Beyond Survey
http://nces.ed.gov/surveys/hsb

Site of the National Education Longitudinal Studies program of the National Center for Education Statistics, provides data and reports from their longitudinal projects that have tracked the educational and personal development of youth transitioning into adulthood.

National Gay and Lesbian Task Force
http://www.thetaskforce.org

Site presented by the National Gay and Lesbian Task Force contains information about the task force, news and views, special issues, state and local organizations, and special events.

National Survey of Family Growth
http://www.cdc.gov/nchs/nsfg.htm

Site of The National Center for Health Statistics offers reports, other publications, and data from their CDC-sponsored Survey documenting family formation issues in adulthood, such as fertility and family planning, sexual behavior and health.

Sloan Work and Family Research Network
http://wfnetwork.bc.edu

Site presented by the Sloan Work and Family Research Network of Boston College contains a literature database, research newsletter, resources for teaching, research profiles, and work and family links. Part of the Network's mission is to inform policy makers on key family-work issues.

National Fatherhood Initiative
http://www.fatherhood.org/default.asp

Site of the National Fatherhood Initiative, provides numerous resources and links to other fatherhood sites; discusses educational and outreach campaigns underway to promote involved fathering and family well-being.

Child Trends
http://www.childtrends.org

Site of Child Trends, a nonprofit research organization located in Washington, D.C., provides data and reports focused on child well-being and marriage/family, to include fatherhood and parenting.

MIDDLE
ADULTHOOD

Elizabeth D. Hutchison

Key Ideas	323
Case Study 8.1: ■ Viktor Spiro, Assuming New Responsibilities as He Turns 40	324
Case Study 8.2: ■ Helen Tyson, Struggling to Be a "Good Mother" at 42	326
Case Study 8.3: ■ Robert Johnson, Enjoying Fatherhood at 48	327
The Changing Social Construction of Middle Adulthood	328
Changing Age Demographics	329
A Definition of Middle Adulthood	330
Culture and the Construction of Middle Adulthood	331
Theories of Middle Adulthood	332
Erikson's Theory of Generativity	333
Jung's and Levinson's Theories of Finding Balance	334
Life-Span Theory and the Gain-Loss Balance	334
Biological Changes and Physical and Mental Health in Middle Adulthood	336
Changes in Physical Appearance	336
Changes in Mobility	337
Changes in the Reproductive System and Sexuality	337
Changes in Health Status	340
Intellectual Changes in Middle Adulthood	345
Personality Changes in Middle Adulthood	346
The Argument for Personality Stability	347
The Argument for Personality Change	347

Evidence for Stability and Change in Midlife Personality   348
Whitbourne's Identity Process Model   349
Spiritual Development in Middle Adulthood   350
Relationships in Middle Adulthood   353
Middle Adulthood in the Context of the Multigenerational Family   355
Relationships With Spouse or Partner   357
Relationships With Children   358
Relationships With Parents   359
Other Family Relationships   360
Relationships With Friends   361
Community/Organizational Relationships   362
Work in Middle Adulthood   362
Risk Factors and Protective Factors in Middle Adulthood   365
Implications for Social Work Practice   367
Key Terms   367
Active Learning   367
Web Resources   368

❖ How are increased longevity, coupled with a declining birthrate, altering the life course phase of middle adulthood in affluent societies?

❖ What do social workers need to know about biological, psychological, social, and spiritual changes in middle adulthood?

❖ What are the antecedent risk factors and protective factors that affect resilience in middle adulthood as well as the effects of midlife behavior on subsequent health and well-being?

KEY IDEAS

As you read this chapter, take note of these central ideas:

1. Increased life expectancy and a declining birthrate in the United States and other industrial countries are leading to a trend of "mass longevity" and a large cohort of adults in midlife; very recently, this trend has led to an intense research interest in middle adulthood.

2. Theories about middle adulthood propose that midlife adults are deeply involved in care and concern for the generations to come and that midlife is a time when individuals attempt to find balance in opposing aspects of their lives.

3. Most biological systems reach their peak in the mid-20s, and gradual declines begin after that; by age 50, biological change becomes physically noticeable in most people, particularly changes in physical appearance, mobility, the reproductive system, and in vulnerability to chronic disease.

4. Middle adulthood is the period of peak performance of four mental abilities: inductive reasoning, spatial orientation, vocabulary, and verbal memory. Perceptual speed and numerical ability decline in middle adulthood.

5. There is good evidence of both stability and change in personality in middle adulthood; one often noted personality change during middle adulthood is a gender crossover in personality.

6. Theory and research suggest that humans have the potential for continuous spiritual growth across the life course, with midlife adults having the capacity to recognize many truths and become more oriented to service to others.

7. The most central roles in middle adulthood are related to family and paid work.

Viktor Spiro, Assuming New Responsibilities as He Turns 40

Viktor Spiro was born in a village outside of Tirana, Albania, and lived most of his life, as did many Albanians in the Stalinist state, amidst very impoverished conditions. He was the youngest of four children, with two sisters and a brother 12 years his senior. Viktor describes his childhood as "normal," until he sustained a serious head injury after falling from a tractor when he was 13. He experienced an increasing depression following his hospitalization; his school performance declined and he withdrew from his friends. When Viktor was 20, his older brother died from a rare gastrointestinal illness, another traumatic event that exacerbated Viktor's depression and substance abuse. He subsequently went AWOL from his military post and fled to Greece, where he continued to drink heavily and was reportedly hospitalized at a psychiatric facility.

Because his father was a U.S. citizen, Viktor was able to immigrate to the United States in his late 20s, after the dissolution of Albania's repressive communist regime. He secured a job as a painter, but the language barrier and fast paced life left him feeling vulnerable. Struggling to cope, Viktor made a series of suicide attempts and was arrested after lunging for the gun of a police officer who was trying to help him. Viktor claims that he did not intend to harm the officer, but that he saw the gun as a quick means to end his own life. Viktor's suicide attempts and arrest led to the beginning of a long relationship with mental health services (MHS). He was diagnosed with Bipolar Disorder with Psychotic Features, made more suicide attempts, was hospitalized, and lived in a group home.

After a few years, Viktor's father and mother, Petro and Adriana, moved to the United States to reunite with Viktor and his sister Maria. Viktor moved into an apartment with his parents and showed some signs of improved adjustment, including advances in his use of English and steady employment secured through the MHS job service program. However, his first-hand exposure to the worsening state of Petro's vascular dementia proved very traumatic. Then, Petro broke his hip and was in a nursing home briefly. He may have benefited from more advanced care and rehabilitation in a nursing facility, but his family could not wait to get him home. Supporting an elderly family member at an institution was culturally unacceptable.

Viktor and his father were both referred to a residential program to obtain counseling and case management services. The family was transferred here approximately eight months after Viktor's most recent suicide attempt. His social worker learned that Viktor had accrued over $140,000 in hospital bills and was still on "medical leave" from his job. The family had no significant income other than Petro's monthly $400 social security check and Adriana's stipend from Social Services to "take care" of her husband. Viktor shared that he had deep regrets about his latest suicide attempt and could not put himself or his family through this again. He felt that he was at a turning point and needed to take on more responsibility as he approaches 40, especially with caring for his ailing parents. Viktor and Adriana were thankful for the agency's help, and insisted on "payment" in the form of having his social worker break bread with the family, and lighting incense in prayer for the agency workers.

It soon became clear that Adriana is the backbone of this family. The social worker tried to find ways to help Adriana lighten her load, but Adriana let him know that caring for the family is her role. Although the family is quite dependent on the agency to navigate their social environment, the home is Adriana's environment, and she finds purpose and a clearly defined role as keeper of the house as she acclimates to life in the United States.

As Viktor and his social worker met regularly, Viktor became more aware of his mother's struggles to fulfill family needs and began to do more in the house. Adriana began to trust the social worker's commitment to her family, and with Viktor translating, the social worker learned that Adriana wears her black dress and gold crucifix on a daily basis in mourning for her deceased son. Adriana called her life "unlucky," as she recounted the death of her first born, the chronic depression and strokes that have afflicted her husband over the past 40 years, and Viktor's ongoing struggles with his mental illness. Although the Spiro family clearly has experienced much suffering and trauma, their incredible strength and resolve are impressive. They are very affectionate and exhibit an enduring love for one another, demonstrating much resiliency in the laughter that often fills the apartment during mealtimes and in the family's optimism that their "luck" will change.

Viktor began to reveal a more reflective, insightful side during his recovery. He confided to his treatment team that he was hearing voices for nearly six months prior to his last suicide attempt, but didn't tell anyone. He hoped the voices would just "go away." Viktor was able to communicate more freely about his emotions and no longer seemed preoccupied with past anxiety about being discovered by the military or with guilt regarding his brother's premature passing. His social worker and job coach assisted him with transition back into the work force, and he eventually obtained the medical clearance to return to his dishwashing job, resuming the role as the primary breadwinner for the family. This was a real lift to Viktor's self-esteem. The Spiro family experienced another financial lift with the news of a total forgiveness of Viktor's outstanding hospital bills.

While the Spiro family was enjoying their improving situation, the treatment team worked with Viktor to expand his social network outside the family. Viktor had been spending all of his time with his parents in their apartment when he was not working. As his confidence grew with his psychiatric improvement, however, he became more receptive to suggestions about weekend social activities coordinated by the agency. Viktor tried out a couple of the groups and enjoyed the activities and chance to form new relationships. He quickly immersed himself in a variety of weekend activities that involved shopping, movies, athletics, and cultural events.

The social worker assisted Viktor with the long process of reapplying for naturalization, after learning that he did not provide INS with the required documents on his previous application. With his improved mental state, Viktor was able to concentrate on studying for the citizenship test, which he passed. His citizenship ceremony was a wonderful day for Viktor and his family, and he made a poignant speech about dreaming of this day as a teenager watching CHIPS reruns in Albania.

The Spiro family clearly enjoyed the series of positive events for Viktor, but soon they faced another change of events. Petro developed pneumonia and respiratory failure, and was placed on a respirator. He was eventually taken off the respirator successfully, but his physician indicated that he may not have long to live. The Spiros are once again grief stricken and want to take Petro home immediately. They struggle to understand the medical issues, and need assistance to interpret such figurative language as "the end is near," and to grasp the concept of a Do Not Resuscitate Order. Viktor grieves for his father, but his handling of this crisis is a remarkable change from the impulsive and often dangerous behavior he had previously exhibited when responding to stressful situations. However, Viktor and his family will need help to deal with end of life issues, in the context of his mental illness and the ongoing cultural barriers. Adriana and Viktor draw on Greek Orthodox faith and rituals during this difficult time.

—Derek Morch
Social Work Student

Helen Tyson, Struggling to Be a "Good Mother" at 42

Helen Tyson was the youngest of four girls. She lived with her parents and sisters in a low socioeconomic area in a northeast suburb of Melbourne, Australia. Helen's family was of Anglo-Australian origin and she describes them as "battlers" and says "Mum and Dad did it tough, but always loved us and did the best they could."

Helen describes herself as "wild" as an adolescent, "out partying instead of studying." About 9 p.m. one Thursday evening when she was 16, she was traveling to a friend's place on the train when she was forced into a car by a number of men, driven to an empty factory, and repeatedly raped and bashed over a period of six hours. The men then dumped her at the railway station. A taxi driver found her and drove her to a hospital and the police were called. Helen says that her parents were "fantastic," but she believed the attack was "karma for being wild." She knew the identity of "a couple of the men"—she had seen them at parties and was aware that they had been involved in similar incidents with other young women. Although she was fearful about possible repercussions, she cooperated with the police. The police investigations found evidence that these young men were involved in a consistent pattern of rape and intimidation of young women in the area. The men were charged with sexual offences against Helen and three other young women. During the period leading up to the trial, Helen's friends and family received a number of warnings advising her not to continue to cooperate with the police. The men were subsequently convicted and jailed.

Helen received counseling at a sexual assault service for six months after the rape. She said "it helped" and she felt "okay" with the support of her family and friends. Initially she was terrified and frightened to be on her own, and needed someone to remain with her at all times. The counseling focused on this, and she felt that she had achieved something when she was able to go to a job interview on her own. She ceased counseling at this stage. Her schoolwork was affected, however, and she left school after completing Year 11. She had a couple of short-term jobs but was always anxious about people's intentions. She stopped work when she married Jim at age 20. She met Jim at a cousin's wedding and says that because he was older, she "felt safe with him." She told him about the rape and then they agreed not to refer to it again. Helen says that she always wanted to be a "good mother" and felt that this would prove that she was "okay" and not "damaged goods." She felt that to be a "good mother" would ameliorate some of the "badness" of being raped. She describes her pregnancies as fine, noting that she was relieved to be advised to have caesarean births; she felt uncomfortable about a vaginal birth because her vagina seemed "damaged."

Helen and Jim have been married for 22 years, and they own their own home. Jim is the owner and operator of a small courier business that he operates with one van. Helen has not worked outside the home but volunteered at her children's schools and worked at the various clubs in which her children were involved. This gave her satisfaction and made her feel that she was a "good mother." Helen says her marriage with Jim is "good" and thinks that he has been a good provider and father to the children. She has never enjoyed their sexual relationship but likes the fact that they are "good friends."

Helen and Jim have three children, Samantha, age 20, Will, age 18, and Sarah, age 16. Samantha recently moved out of home to live with her boyfriend, Joe. Will left school after completing Year 12. He did not apply for any tertiary (college-bound) courses and has had intermittent employment since. He had learning difficulties at school and currently has symptoms of depression. He has lost confidence and spends lots of time in his room. Jim and Helen have tried to help him find work through their friends and contacts but nothing has been successful. Sarah works part-time in a sandwich bar and is still at secondary school. She has recently started going out at night with friends. Helen describes Sarah as "bright," and, "she's the one most like me."

Helen's parents provided a great deal of emotional, financial, and practical support to her and Jim, and Helen was devastated when her mother died of breast cancer 12 months ago. Her father has since become physically frail and has shown some loss of cognitive function. He still lives close to Helen and she and her three sisters provide support for him—taking turns to clean, provide food, and so forth. Helen has no close friends and says she finds it difficult to trust people. She relies on her sisters for support.

Helen has had great difficulty accepting Samantha's boyfriend. He is from the same ethnic background as the men who raped her and while she can say "I know he's not like that," she is still concerned about cultural attitudes to women and about her emotional response to him. Helen feels that she cannot talk to Samantha about this because she does not want Samantha to know that she had been raped, saying, "Children should be protected from things like that." Helen is also frightened that knowledge of the rape would change how Samantha sees her. Helen missed Samantha when she moved out, she is worried about Will, concerned that he has lost direction, and she is terrified that the same thing will happen to Sarah that happened to her when she was 16. The issues in her children's' lives are causing her to question whether or not she is a "good mother." Jim says he "loves" her but he has recently started to question the point of their relationship.

Helen had never been back to the railway station where she was abducted until very recently. She had avoided traveling in that area, but one night Sarah phoned for a lift from the train station and Jim was busy. Helen tried to find someone else to pick Sarah up, but eventually went herself. This precipitated a crisis. Helen started having flashbacks to the rapes, insomnia, and panic attacks. Her general physician has diagnosed depression and suggested that she contact the sexual assault service from which she received counseling at age 16.

—Lesley Hewitt, Lecturer
Department of Social Work
Monash University, Melbourne, Australia

Case Study 8.3

Robert Johnson, Enjoying Fatherhood at 48

Robert Johnson was born into a stable black working-class family. His father was a longtime laborer in the steel industry, with an income that allowed the family to maintain a middle-class lifestyle. Robert's mother was a full-time housewife. Robert currently lives about two miles from his parents and keeps in close touch with them and with his two younger sisters and their families. He is proud of and grateful for the type of upbringing he was provided with by his hardworking parents.

(Continued)

(Continued)

Robert's father had the good fortune, as many other black male workers did, of getting into the relatively high-paying, unionized steel industry before it began to crumble. Drawing on the equity accumulated in the family's modest home, he was able to provide financial assistance for Robert to attend college. Robert was the first member of his family to attend college, and now he has undergraduate and law degrees from a prestigious university.

With a good education, strong earning potential, and a positive self-image, Robert worked steadily toward building the kind of independence that is characteristic of the U.S. middle class. He set his career goals high: to become a partner in his respected law firm. Soon after beginning work at the law firm, Robert set about repaying his school loans. At the same time, he began building his own investment program for the future.

After living together for three years, Robert and Cindy Marsh, an interior decorator, felt financially secure enough to get married. Soon after they were married, they bought a house. Once the house was furnished and Robert became a partner in the law firm, Robert and Cindy began to plan to have children. They were excited about this prospect and confident that they would make excellent parents. As the months went by and Cindy did not get pregnant, they became increasingly distressed. They attended a fertility clinic for about a year but found that their relationship was suffering from the constant pressure to become pregnant.

Finally, Robert and Cindy decided to go away for an extended vacation and take time to think about their plan to have children. They talked about their sadness over their inability to get pregnant, their love for each other, and their desire to share their many resources with children. They decided to work with children at their church, and they also began working toward adoption at Family Services, Inc. Their adoption of 3- and 5-year-old brothers, Craig and James, was finalized four years ago, and Robert and Cindy are kept busy juggling work and parenting. They are happy to be living so close to Robert's extended family and appreciate the opportunity to raise their sons in the warm embrace of nearby grandparents, uncles, aunts, and cousins. There is some worry, however, as both Robert's and Cindy's parents begin to have some rather serious health problems. Cindy has needed to make several trips to Texas in recent months to assist her mother who is receiving treatment for breast cancer. Also, Craig and James had some emotional and behavioral problems in the first year after the adoption, but with the help of a social worker, the family has adapted well. Robert has begun to volunteer at Family Services, Inc. as a co-facilitator of a new parent group, and he and Cindy continue to work with children at their church.

⊠ The Changing Social Construction of Middle Adulthood

Although their life paths have been very different, Viktor Spiro, Helen Tyson, and Robert Johnson are all in the life course phase of middle adulthood. Not so long ago, middle adulthood was nearly an unstudied terrain. Recently, however, due to a confluence of demographic trends and research accomplishments, there has been intense interest in the middle adult years in affluent societies. Although we still have only a hazy picture of middle adulthood, that picture is coming into better focus.

Changing Age Demographics

In 1900, the median age of the U.S. population was 23 and the average life expectancy was 47.3 years (U.S. Census Bureau, 1999). By 1950, the median age was 30.2 years and average life expectancy was 68.2 years (National Center for Health Statistics, 2001a). By 2000, the median age was 35.3 and the average life expectancy was 76.9. And by 2006, the median age was 36.4 years and the average life expectancy at birth was 77.9 years (CIA, 2006). These changing demographics are presented visually in Exhibit 8.1. These data do not mean that no one lived past what we now consider middle age in 1900. The average life expectancy in 1900 was deflated by high rates of infant mortality. Indeed, in 1900, 18% of the population of the United States was 45 years old or older. This compares to 28% in 1950 and 34% in 2000. Living past age 45 is not new, but more people are doing it. David Plath (1980) describes the current demographic trend in the United States, which exists as well in northern and western Europe and in Japan, as a trend toward "mass longevity." This trend has an enormous impact on our understanding of the adult life course (Wahl & Kruse, 2005). Although he did not become a parent until his mid-40s, Robert Johnson assumes that he will live to see his children well into adulthood.

> How might these changing demographics affect the midlife phase of the life course?

Exhibit 8.1   Changing Life Expectancy and Median Age

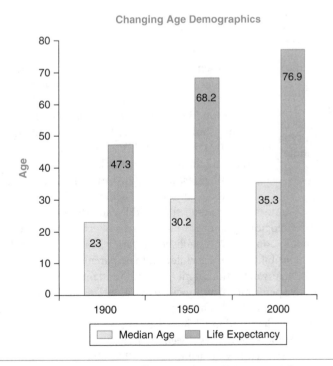

Changing Age Demographics

SOURCE: Based on U.S. Census Bureau, 1999, and National Center for Health Statistics, 2001b.

This trend of increased life expectancy is juxtaposed with another important demographic trend, declining birthrate (Moen & Wethington, 1999). These two trends together have produced the large baby-boom generation currently moving through midlife in record numbers. The 50- to 54-year age group was the fastest growing age group from 1990 to 2000, with an increase of 55%, and the 45- to 49-year age group was the second fastest growing group, with a 45% increase. In 2000, there were over 96 million adults between the ages of 35 and 59, representing 34% of the U.S. population (U.S. Census Bureau, 2001b).

Longevity and birthrates vary across global populations. Mass longevity and declining birthrates hold true in advanced industrial societies, but in poor and less-developed societies, the trends are radically different. International data show a high life expectancy of 83.5 years in Andorra and a low of 33.9 years in Botswana in 2005 (CIA, 2006). In that same year, the average life expectancy was less than 50 years in no fewer than 31 countries. Social workers who work in the international arena or with immigrant families will need to develop appropriate understanding of how the life course varies across world populations.

Given the trend in mass longevity and the current large cohort of adults in midlife, it is not surprising that researchers have begun to take a serious interest in the "lengthy central period" (Lachman, 2001a, p. xiii) of the human life course. Beginning in the 1990s, an interdisciplinary group of researchers in North America and Europe launched several large research projects to move our understanding of middle adulthood from mythology to science (see Brim, Ryff, & Kessler, 2004; Lachman, 2001b; Willis & Martin, 2005). These researchers span the fields of anthropology, economics, genetics, neurology, psychology, and sociology.

A Definition of Middle Adulthood

Before we go further, we need to pause and consider *who* is included in middle adulthood. In the most general sense, we are talking about people who are in midlife, or the central part of the life course. Beyond that, we do not have generally agreed upon ages to include in middle adulthood. The most frequently used definition of middle adulthood includes those persons who are between the ages of 40 and 60, but some scholars use a lower limit as young as age 30 and an upper limit as late as age 70 (Dittmann-Kohli, 2005). The National Council on Aging (2000) found that one third of their sample in their 70s think of themselves as middle-aged, and other researchers have found that the older one is, the later the reported age of middle adulthood (Lachman & Bertrand, 2001).

> Is biological age, psychological age, social age, or spiritual age the best marker for middle adulthood?

Some authors argue that middle adulthood should not be thought of in terms of chronological age, but instead in terms of achieving certain developmental tasks. Generally, midlife adults have established a family, settled into and peaked in a career, and taken responsibility for their children, their parents, and their community (Staudinger & Bluck, 2001). Any definition of middle adulthood must also include biological aging processes, subjective perceptions, and social roles, as well as historical and generational contexts (Moen & Wethington, 1999). This suggestion is consistent with the major themes of a life course perspective discussed in Chapter 1 of this book.

Some authors have been critical of any approach to defining middle adulthood that includes such a wide age range as 40 to 60 or older (e.g., Staudinger & Bluck, 2001). They suggest that the beginning of midlife is very different from the latter part of midlife, and that lumping these parts of the life course together may lead to contradictory findings. They call for a division of middle adulthood into early midlife and late midlife (Kohli & Künemund, 2005; Lachman, 2004). You may recall a similar concern about the boundaries of young adulthood noted in Chapter 7. Late adulthood, which is divided into late adulthood and very late adulthood in this book, encompasses an even larger age span, potentially from 65 to 100+. As longevity increases, the adult portion of life is likely to be divided into finer and finer phases.

Culture and the Construction of Middle Adulthood

With the identification of a middlehood, societies must construct roles for, and make meaning of, middle adulthood. There is evidence that middle adulthood has been incorporated into views of the life course since at least the early Middle Ages (Dittmann-Kohli, 2005). In his book *Welcome to Middle Age! (And Other Cultural Fictions)*, Richard Shweder (1998) suggests that middle age is a "cultural fiction" and the fiction does not play out the same way in all cultures. He does not use "fiction" to mean false, but to mean, instead, that ideas about middle age are "fabricated, manufactured, invented, or designed" (p. x). Shweder suggests that the European American cultural construction of middle adulthood casts it primarily in terms of chronology (middle age), biology, and medicine. He argues that this cultural construction is a story of mental and physical decline. Other cultures, he suggests, organize the life course, including middle adulthood, in terms of "a social history of role transitions" (p. xi), focusing particularly on family roles.

▲ **Photo 8.1** Middle-aged workers are deeply affected by changes in the job market and must be proactive in maintaining and updating their job skills.

Consider how middle adulthood is defined and understood in three cultures: upper-caste Hindu in rural India, middle-class Japanese, and middle-class Anglo American (Menon, 2001):

◆ Asian Indian Hindu beliefs and practices differ greatly according to region and caste, but middle adulthood is not defined as a separate, clearly distinguished life phase as it is in the United States. To the extent that it is recognized, it is thought of as "maturity" and seen in relation to transitions in family roles. Women become senior wives, and men replace their fathers as head of the family, responsible for family decision making and for the family's interaction with the community. Maturity is considered to be the best time in the life course.

◆ In Japan, aging is associated with power and creativity. This view of aging is tied to two central beliefs. First, life is about becoming, not being, and all phases of the life course offer "endless opportunities for continual personal improvement," to reach for human perfection (Menon, 2001, p. 52). A second central belief is that aging is a natural process. Although the Japanese recognize some loss and decline with the passing of years, the general view of middle adulthood is that it is the "prime of life," a time of fullness, activity, and spiritual growth.

◆ Empirical research about the meaning of midlife in the United States suggests two divergent cultural beliefs: one view sees middle adulthood as a positive time of having accumulated resources for coping; the other view sees middle adulthood as a negative time of decline and loss. This latter view of decline and loss (of being "over the hill") often seems to permeate popular culture (Gullette, 1998). However, much of the recent research on middle adulthood reveals an attempt to recast middlehood as the "prime of life." What images come to mind when you think of middle adulthood? Do you think first of sagging chins, wrinkles, reading glasses, thinning or graying hair, hot flashes, loss of sex drive, and so on, or do you think first of emotional and spiritual maturity that gives power and creativity? What images do you think Viktor Spiro, Helen Tyson, and Robert Johnson hold of middle adulthood?

Comparing views of middlehood in these three cultures helps us recognize that our taken-for-granted views of this life course phase are, indeed, highly influenced by culture. It also alerts us to the possibility that our clients from different cultural groups may have different expectations for midlife roles. However, it is important to note that the above descriptions cover relatively privileged groups within wider cultures. There is evidence that conceptions of the adult life course vary across social class lines within a given society. Clearly, location in the global economy, war, and the AIDS pandemic are factors that have different impacts on different groups of people around the globe and can lead to very different constructions of middle adulthood.

▧ Theories of Middle Adulthood

Few theories focus directly on middle adulthood, but a number of theories address middle adulthood as a part of a larger developmental framework. Themes from three of those theories are presented here.

Erikson's Theory of Generativity

According to Erik Erikson's (1950) life span theory, the psychosocial struggle of middle adulthood is **generativity** versus stagnation (refer back to Exhibit 3.6 for an overview of Erikson's psychosocial stage theory). Generativity is the ability to transcend personal interests to provide care and concern for younger and older generations; it encompasses procreation, productivity, and creativity (Erikson, 1982, p. 67). Generative adults provide "care, guidance, inspiration, instruction, and leadership" (McAdams, 2001, p. 395) for future generations. Failure to find a way to contribute to future generations, or to make a contribution to the general well-being, results in self-absorption and a sense of stagnation. Erikson saw generativity as an instinct that works to perpetuate society. With some help, Viktor Spiro is beginning to practice generativity in his relationship with his parents. For Helen Tyson, generativity is expressed in care of her father and her children. Generativity seems to be a very conscious experience for Robert Johnson and he is finding a variety of ways to enact it. As a social worker, however, you will most likely encounter people who struggle with a sense of stagnation in middle adulthood.

> How does generativity affect the capacity for interdependence?

Dan McAdams and Ed de St. Aubin (1992, 1998) have presented a model of generativity that includes the seven components found in Exhibit 8.2. McAdams and de St. Aubin (1992, 1998) see generativity coming from both the person (personal desire) and the social and cultural environment (cultural demand).

Even though Erikson outlined middlehood generativity in 1950, generativity was not a subject of empirical investigation until the 1980s. There is limited longitudinal research to answer the question, are midlife adults more generative than people in other life course phases? Most of the cross-sectional research on generativity reports greater generativity during middle adulthood than in young adulthood or late adulthood (see review in McAdams, 2001), but other researchers have found that generativity continues to grow past middle adulthood (Sheldon & Kasser, 2001). One notable exception is a cross-sectional study in which the researchers found that although midlife adults scored significantly higher than young adults and older adults on an overall measure of generativity, young adults scored just as high as midlife adults on some measures of generativity related to having concerns about making a

---

Exhibit 8.2   McAdams and de St. Aubins's Seven Components of Generativity

1. Inner desire for immortality and to be needed

2. Cultural demand for productivity

3. Concern for the next generation

4. Belief in the species

5. Commitment

6. Action: creating, maintaining, or offering

7. Development of a generative life story

SOURCE: Adapted from McAdams, Hart, & Maruna, 1998.

contribution to the world (McAdams, de St. Aubin, & Logan, 1993). One longitudinal study (Stewart & Vandewater, 1998) found that *generativity motivation* decreased over time in two cohorts of college-educated women, but generative actions increase. The researchers suggest that young adults may have a generative spirit but lack the material, social, or emotional resources to accomplish generative goals until they reach middle adulthood. Although it is possible that the generative spirit wanes over time, resources for generative action increase. At any rate, research consistently finds that the cultural expectation in the United States is that adults become more generative in midlife (McAdams & de St. Aubin, 1998).

Research also finds that generativity is associated with gender, class, and race. Several researchers (Marks, Bumpass, & Jun, 2004; McAdams & de St. Aubin, 1992; McKeering & Pakenham, 2000) have found that men who had never been fathers scored particularly low on measures of generativity, but not being a mother did not have the same effect for women. Generativity has been found to increase with educational level (Keyes & Ryff, 1998). Black adults have been found to score higher on some measures of generativity than white adults (Cole & Stewart, 1996; Hart, McAdams, Hirsch, & Bauer, 2001).

Jung's and Levinson's Theories of Finding Balance

Both Carl Jung and Daniel Levinson suggest that middle adulthood is a time when individuals attempt to find balance in their lives in several ways. Jung (1971) sees middle adulthood as a time when we discover and reclaim parts of the self that were repressed in the search for conformity in the first half of life. He emphasizes the importance of gender identity in middle adulthood. Adults begin to move from the stereotyped gender-role behavior of young adulthood to a more androgynous behavioral repertoire at this age. Jung also suggested that **extroversion,** or orientation to the external world, and **introversion,** or orientation to the internal world, come into greater balance in middle adulthood. He suggested that the challenges of establishing family and work roles demands extroversion in young adulthood, but in middle adulthood individuals tend to turn inward and explore their own subjective experience.

Daniel Levinson (Levinson, 1986, 1990; Levinson & Levinson, 1996; Levinson, Darrow, Klein, Levinson & McKee, 1978) conceptualizes the life course as a sequence of eras, each with its own biopsychosocial character (Levinson & Levinson, 1996) with major changes from one era to the next. Changes do occur within eras, but these changes are small and do not involve major revision of the life structure. Adult life is composed of alternating periods of relative stability and periods of transition. As mentioned in Chapter 7, a key concept of Levinson's theory is life structure, by which he means "the underlying pattern or design of a person's life at a given time" (Levinson & Levinson, 1996, p. 22). In most cases, family and occupation are the central components in the life structure, but people vary widely in how much weight they assign to each. During the transition to middle adulthood, individuals often try to give greater attention to previously neglected components. That seems to be what Robert Johnson and Cindy Marsh were doing when they decided to become parents. Levinson sees this transition in terms of balancing four opposing aspects of identity: young versus old, creation versus destruction, feminine versus masculine, and attachment versus separating (Levinson, 1977).

Life-Span Theory and the Gain-Loss Balance

Life-span theory has much in common with the life course perspective introduced in Chapter 1 of this book. It is more firmly rooted in psychology, however, whereas the life course perspective has more multidisciplinary roots. Life-span theory is based in ongoing transactions between persons and environments and begins with the premise that development is lifelong. Six central propositions of the life-span theory as they relate to middle adulthood are summarized in Exhibit 8.3.

Exhibit 8.3	Central Propositions of Life-Span Theory as They Relate to Middle Adulthood

- Human development is lifelong and no age period is supreme in the developmental trajectory. Midlife cannot be studied in isolation; it must be studied in terms of both its antecedents and its consequences.
- Development involves both gains and losses. In midlife, there is a tie in the relationship between gains and losses.
- Biological influences on development become more negative, and cultural support becomes more important, with increasing age in adulthood. A distinction can be made between early and late midlife.
- With increasing age in adulthood, there is an overall reduction in resources. At midlife, adults must put a major effort into managing resources.
- Even though challenges increase and biological resources decrease in midlife, there is still possibility for change.
- The experience of midlife adults may depend on cultural and historical contexts.

Source: Adapted from Staudinger & Bluck, 2001, pp. 17–18.

We focus here particularly on the proposition that in midlife there is a tie in the balance of gains and losses (Staudinger & Bluck, 2001). Life-span researchers have raised the question, what is the balance of gains and losses in midlife (Baltes, Lindenberger, & Staudinger, 1998)? For example, there is good evidence of gains in self-esteem and emotional maturity and of losses in biological functioning. There is beginning agreement that across adulthood, the balance shifts from a dominance of developmental gains in early midlife to a dominance of developmental losses in late midlife (e.g., Heckhausen, 2001; Staudinger & Bluck, 2001). It is important to note, however, that gains or losses are defined and given meaning in cultural contexts and are influenced by both group-based and individual-based attributes. One might wonder how Viktor Spiro, Helen Tyson, and Robert Johnson see the gain-loss balance in early midlife.

With professional help, Viktor Spiro seems to be making some gains in emotion regulation, economic security, relationships, and comfort in his adopted country but is facing loss in the form of the rapidly declining health of his father. Helen Tyson sees gain in the stability of her marriage, but she seems more focused on losses, the loss of her mother and declining control over her children. It is quite possible that the reactivation of an earlier traumatic experience and the accompanying depression is contributing to her focus on losses. Robert Johnson, who is approaching late midlife, has many biological, social, emotional, and spiritual resources for coping with challenges and seems to be focused on gains rather than losses in several spheres. This is beginning to change, however, as his parents and Cindy begin to face serious health problems.

As we review the research on changes in middle adulthood in the remaining sections of this chapter, it is important to note that it is hard to know whether what we are learning about midlife is tied to a specific cohort, the baby boomers. Research on middle adulthood is quite new, and there are no long-term longitudinal studies available of earlier cohorts of midlife adults. Among the factors to keep in mind as you read research results is that the baby boomers (born 1946–1964) represent a very large cohort, and have, throughout their adulthood, faced more competition for jobs and other resources than earlier cohorts.

⬚ Biological Changes and Physical and Mental Health in Middle Adulthood

There have been dramatic changes in the last few decades in the numbers of adults who enjoy healthy and active lives in the years between 45 and 65 and beyond. However, some physical and mental decline does begin to occur. Most biological systems reach their peak performance in the mid-20s. Age-related changes over the next 20 to 30 years are usually gradual, accumulating at different rates in different body systems. The changes are the result of interactions of biology with psychological, sociocultural, and spiritual factors, and individuals play a very active role in the aging process throughout adulthood, as we can see in the life trajectories of Viktor Spiro, Helen Tyson, and Robert Johnson. However, by the age of 50, the accumulation of biological change becomes physically noticeable in most people.

> What factors have led to changes in biological age in middle adulthood?

The biggest stories in biological functioning and physical and mental health in middle adulthood are changes in physical appearance; changes in mobility; changes in the reproductive system; and changes in health, more specifically the beginnings of chronic disease. There are enormous individual differences in the timing and intensity of these changes, but some changes affect almost everyone, such as presbyopia for both men and women and menopause for women.

Changes in Physical Appearance

Probably the most visible signs of physiological changes in middle adulthood are changes in physical appearance (see, e.g., Merrill & Verbrugge, 1999; Whitbourne, 2001). The skin begins to sag and wrinkle as it loses its firmness and elasticity. Small, localized areas of brown pigmentation, often called aging spots, may appear in parts of the body exposed to sunlight. As the sebaceous glands that secrete oils become less active, the skin becomes drier. Hair on the head often becomes thinner and grayer, and hair may appear in places where it is not wanted, such as ears, thicker clumps around the eyebrows, and the chin on women. Many midlife adults wear glasses for the first time because of the decreased ability to focus on near objects (presbyopia) that occurs in most adults between the ages of 45 and 55.

There are significant changes in body build as midlife adults begin to lose height and gain weight. Beginning in their 40s, people lose about one half inch in height per decade, due to loss of bone material in the vertebrae. Starting about age 20, there is a tendency to gain weight until about the mid-50s. Body fat begins to accumulate in the torso and accounts for a greater percentage of weight in middle adulthood than in adolescence and early adulthood. In the late 50s, people tend to begin to lose weight, but this weight loss comes from loss of lean body mass (bone and muscle) rather than from loss of fat.

Changes in skin can be minimized by using sunscreen, skin emollients, applications of vitamin E, facial massages, and by smoking cessation. Increasingly, affluent baby boomers are using procedures such as plastic surgery and Botox to maintain a youthful appearance. Changes in body build can be minimized by involvement in aerobic exercise and resistance training to improve muscle tone, reduce fat, and offset bone loss. The current recommendation is 30 to 60 minutes of exercise three to four days per week.

Changes in Mobility

Beginning in the 40s, losses in muscles, bones, and joints start to have an impact on mobility. A progressive loss of muscle mass leads to loss of strength beginning at about age 45, and muscle strength continues to decline at the rate of 12% to 15% per decade thereafter (Whitbourne, 2001). The most apparent loss of muscle strength occurs in the legs and back (Merrill & Vertrugge, 1999). By engaging in strength training, midlife adults can minimize the loss of muscle mass. An effective strength training program involves two to three workouts per week.

Maximum bone density is reached in early adulthood, and there is a progressive loss of bone mineral after that. The rate of bone loss accelerates in the 50s. Microcracks begin to develop in the bones in response to stress, and bones also begin to lose their elasticity. By the end of middle adulthood, bones are less strong and more brittle. The rate of bone loss is about two times greater in women than in men, linked to the loss of estrogens after menopause. Bone loss tends to be greater in people with fair skin, and black women have higher bone mineral than white women or Hispanic women. Bone loss is accelerated by smoking, alcohol use, and poor diet. It is slowed by aerobic activity, resistance training, increased calcium intake in young adulthood, and use of vitamin D (Whitbourne, 2001).

Changes in the joints begin to occur before skeletal maturity, but without injury, no obvious symptoms appear until the 40s. The cartilage that protects joints begins to degenerate, and an outgrowth of cartilage starts to develop and interfere with ease of movement. Unlike muscles, joints do not benefit from constant use. To prevent unnecessary wear and tear on joints, it is important to wear the proper footwear when engaging in exercise activities and to avoid repetitive movements of the wrists. Flexibility exercises help to expand the range of motion for stiff joints. Exercises to strengthen the muscles that support joints also help to minimize the mobility problems associated with changes in joints.

Changes in the Reproductive System and Sexuality

Perhaps the most often noted biological change in middle adulthood is the lost or diminished reproductive capacity (see, e.g., Finch, 2001; Rossi, 2004a). Although both men and women experience reproductive changes during adulthood, the changes are more gradual for men than for women.

What effect do these sex differences in changes in the reproductive system have on middle adulthood?

The pattern reported for men is a gradual decline in testosterone beginning in early adulthood and continuing throughout life (Finch, 2001; Merrill & Verbrugge, 1999). The quantity of viable sperm begins to decrease in the late 40s or 50s, and most births are fathered by men younger than 60 years (Finch, 2001; Merrill & Verbrugge, 1999).

The picture is somewhat different for women. In middle adulthood, women's capacity to conceive and bear children gradually declines until menopause, when the capacity for conceiving children ends (although reproductive technology to extend a woman's reproductive life may eventually become more generally available). **Menopause** is the permanent cessation of menstruation, and for research purposes is usually defined as 12 consecutive months with absence of menstruation (Rossi, 2004a). The median age of menopause is 50 or 51 years; it occurs between the ages of 45 and 55 in 90% of women in the United States.

Although less gradual than the decline in reproductive capacity in men, menopause is a more gradual process than often recognized (Avis, 1999; Rossi, 2004a). The menopause process begins when the woman is in her 30s. At this time, called **premenopause,** the woman begins to have occasional menstrual cycles without ovulation, or the production of eggs. This change usually goes without notice.

By the mid- to late 40s, the supply of egg cells is depleted, ovarian production of hormone slows, and more and more menstrual cycles occur without ovulation. The menstrual cycle becomes irregular, some menstrual periods are skipped, and the production of estrogen drops. In this period, known as *perimenopause*, changes in the reproductive system begin to be noticed (Gyllstrom, Schreiner, & Harlow, 2006). The World Health Organization (1996) defines **perimenopause** as the period of time that begins immediately prior to menopause, when there are biological and clinical indicators that reproductive capacity is reaching exhaustion, and continues through the first year after the last menstrual period. One study using longitudinal data reported the median age for the beginning of perimenopause as 47.5 years (McKinlay, Brambilla, & Posner, 1992).

In popular culture, menopause is seen as a major milestone, a prominent biological marker, for women; it is popularly called the "change of life." Cross-cultural studies suggest widely differing experiences with menopause, with many non-Western cultures viewing it as a positive change, ushering in a time of greater freedom for women, a time when they are allowed greater participation in the world beyond the family (Rossi, 2004a). In contrast, the Euro American perspective over time has focused on menopause as loss, decay, and more recently deficiency (estrogen deficiency) (Avis, 1999). In this tradition, menopause is assumed to be universally associated with hot flashes, night sweats, vaginal dryness, insomnia, fatigue, anxiety, depression, irritability, memory loss, difficulty concentrating, and weight gain.

Although perimenopause, and purported associated symptoms and discomforts, has received much attention in the popular media in recent years, it has not been the subject of intensive scientific study. Menopause did not receive much attention either until the 1980s. This increased interest seems to come from a confluence of factors. Chief among those factors is that the current baby boom generation of women, who are now in middlehood, have, as a cohort, asserted their control over their reproductive lives and challenged taboos about sexuality. Two other influential factors include epidemiological studies that identified estrogen decline in menopause as a risk factor for osteoporosis and cardiovascular disease, and the development of medications for the "treatment" of menopause. To date, however, research on the connection between menopause and most of the symptoms believed to be a consequence is far from conclusive.

Existing research suggests considerable variation in signs and symptoms of menopause across cultures. One recent large national research project compared menopausal symptoms across racial and ethnic groups in the United States, including Caucasian, African American, Chinese, Japanese, and Hispanic women (Avis et al., 2001; Bromberger et al., 2001). The researchers found that the Caucasian women reported significantly more psychosomatic symptoms than women from the other racial and ethnic groups. African American women were significantly more likely to report hot flashes or night sweats. These findings are consistent with earlier cross-cultural and cross-national research (Flint, 1975; Payer, 1991; Vatuk,

1992). It is hard to tease out the relative contribution of cultural beliefs about menopause from different patterns of diet and exercise. For example, Japanese diets are lower in fat and higher in phytoestrogens than diets in Canada and the United States (Adlercreutz, Hamalaiven, Gorback, & Grodin, 1992).

Existing research also reports considerable individual variations in the signs and symptoms of menopause in the United States. Data from one longitudinal study in the United States report that only 19% of postmenopausal women report never experiencing a hot flash, but only 19% of those who experienced hot flashes report that the hot flashes were a problem (McKinlay et al., 1992). Data from this study indicate that the rate of hot flash reporting increases as the menstrual cycle becomes more irregular during perimenopause, peaking at about 50% just before menopause. Similar findings occurred in more recent research that found that half of peri- and postmenopausal women reported no hot flashes (Rossi, 2004a). This research project found that women who have high levels of menstrual pain in earlier stages of their lives, women who are especially sensitive to internal and environmental factors, and women who have stressful roles at home are more likely to experience five symptoms (hot flashes, sweating a lot, insomnia, irritability, and discomfort during intercourse) during the peri- and postmenopausal period.

Longitudinal research on depression and menopause indicates that there is a moderate increase in depression during perimenopause, but most women who become depressed during perimenopause had prior episodes of depression (Avis, Brambilla, McKinlay, & Vass, 1994). The researchers did find, however, that women who experienced a long perimenopausal period, lasting at least 27 months, were at greater risk of depression than women who experienced a shorter perimenopausal period. Existing research indicates that sleep disturbance is associated with menopause, but the exact mechanism for that association is not clear. Some research suggests that the sleep disturbance is directly related to hot flashes, finding that menopausal women who do not report hot flashes also do not report sleep disturbance (Shaver, Giblin, Lentz, & Lee, 1988).

Research does indicate that vaginal lubrication decreases as women age (Laumann, Paik, & Rosen, 1999). With lower estrogen levels, the blood supply to the vagina and surrounding nerves and glands is reduced. The tissues become thinner and drier and cannot produce sufficient lubrication for comfortable intercourse. There is also increased risk of infection unless estrogen replacement or an artificial lubricant is used. Longer periods of foreplay can also help with this situation.

Some social critics suggest that our latest construction of menopause as deficiency is a medical construction: menopause as disease (see, e.g., Bell, 1990). The treatment for the "disease of menopause" is hormone replacement therapy. There are two primary types of hormone therapy for menopause: estrogen alone (ERT) or estrogen combined with progestin (hormone replacement therapy, or HRT). ERT was introduced first in the 1940s, and was promoted widely by pharmaceutical companies and by popular books such as *Feminine Forever* (Wilson, 1966) in the 1960s. In the 1970s, several research studies reported that ERT increased women's risk for endometrial cancer (Mack et al., 1976; Smith, Prentice, Thompson, & Hermann, 1975; Ziel & Finkle, 1975). In response to these studies, pharmaceutical companies discovered that combining estrogen with progestin could prevent the excessive buildup of estrogen that increased the risk for endometrial cancer. HRT then became the recommended treatment for menopausal women who still have an intact uterus, and use of HRT more than doubled between 1982 and 1992 and continued to increase at the beginning of the twenty-first century (Rossi, 2004a).

Although manufacturers of hormone products had advertised the benefits to physical and mental health from HRT, recent research has found quite a different story. Existing research on HRT suggests that women should be cautious about using it (Rexrode & Manson, 2002; Rossi, 2004a). In the United States, the Women's Health Initiative (WHI) was involved in a large, ongoing study, scheduled to last for 8.5 years, comparing hormone therapy with a placebo. But in a surprising move, they called a halt to their study after 5.2 years in the summer of 2002 because the health risks exceeded the health benefits. HRT was found to increase the risks of coronary heart disease, breast cancer, stroke, and pulmonary embolism. These risks are weighed against the slight positive effects on colorectoral cancer, endometrial cancer, and hip fracture (Hlatky, Boothrody, Vittinghoff, Sharp, & Whooley, 2002; National Institutes of Health, 2002; Okie, 2002; Rossi, 2004a).

Recently, some researchers have begun to explore another alternative to HRT, selective estrogen replacement modulators (SERMs), such as raloxifene and tamoxifen. These newer alternatives are thought to have a more targeted effect on bone loss (Johnson, 2006). It is important to note that lifestyle changes have also been shown to reduce the risks related to hormonal changes during menopause: quitting smoking, exercising, reducing cholesterol intake, taking calcium supplements, and losing weight.

The physical changes in middle adulthood require some adjustments in the sexual lives of midlife men and women. Beginning in their late 50s, men begin to experience a gradual slowdown in sexual responses. This includes decreased frequency and intensity of orgasms, increased difficulty in achieving erection, and longer time needed before achieving subsequent erection. For women, the vaginal dryness that often occurs during menopause may cause painful intercourse. Many couples adjust well to these changes, however, and with children out of the home, may find that their sexual lives become less inhibited and more passionate. The sex lives of midlife adults may benefit from improved self-esteem that typifies middle adulthood and, in relationships of some longevity, from better understanding of the desires and responses of the sexual partner. Currently, there are a number of treatments available to assist with deficient sexual responses in men, including Viagra and testosterone supplements, as well as a number of products being developed (Lux, Reyes, Morgentaler, & Levine, 2007; Stroberg, Hedelin, & Ljunggren, 2006).

Changes in Health Status

As we can see in the stories of Viktor Spiro, Helen Tyson, and Robert Johnson, who are all in early midlife, health during middle adulthood is highly variable. There are some positive changes: the frequency of accidents declines, as does susceptibility to colds and allergies. On the other hand, although many people live through middle adulthood with little disease or disability, the frequency of chronic illness, persistent symptoms, and functional disability begins to rise in middlehood. And the death rate increases continuously over the adult years, as demonstrated by death rates in the United States reported in Exhibit 8.4. You will also note that there are significant gender and race differences in the death rates in middle adulthood, with men having higher death rates than women in both white and black populations, and blacks of both genders having alarmingly higher death rates than their white counterparts. Data for other racial and ethnic groups are not reported because of inconsistencies in reporting race on death certificates.

> What might be some reasons for these race and gender differences in health in middle adulthood?

Exhibit 8.4	Death Rate (per 100,000 Persons) in Selected Age Groups in 2004					
		Male			*Female*		
Age Group	*Overall*	*Overall*	*Black*	*White*	*Overall*	*Black*	*White*
25 to 34 Years	100.5	137.2	249.1	124.9	62.7	110.2	56.1
35 to 44 Years	191.1	239.9	391.6	225.6	142.4	253.8	128.6
45 to 54 Years	423.1	539.1	945.8	500.6	311.1	554.3	283.4
55 to 64 Years	905.9	1121.2	1932.0	1061.0	705.9	1126.3	670.6
65 to 74 Years	2165.6	2647.0	3791.5	2589.4	1761.3	2365.4	1725.4

SOURCE: Minino, Heron, & Smith, 2006.

In the past century, there has been a change in the types of diseases that are likely to affect health across the life course in affluent countries. In the early 1900s, when life expectancy was in the mid-40s, most deaths were caused by infectious diseases, such as pneumonia, tuberculosis, and influenza (CDC, 1999b). With the increase in life expectancy, chronic disease plays a more important role in the great stretch of middle adulthood and beyond. People are now living long enough to experience a chronic illness: "We are now living well enough and long enough to slowly fall apart. . . . [T]he diseases that plague us now are ones of slow accumulation of damage—heart disease, cancer, cerebrovascular disorders" (Sapolsky, 1998, p. 2).

The prevalence of chronic conditions increases with each decade from middle adulthood on. (Note: *Prevalence* measures the proportion of a population that has a disease at a point in time. *Incidence* measures the number of new cases of a disease or condition over a period of time, such as one year.) There is an increase in potentially fatal chronic conditions, as well as nonfatal chronic conditions. The important role of chronic illness as cause of death is demonstrated in Exhibit 8.5, which reports the five leading causes of death for age groups in the United States. Except for accident, suicide, and homicide, all the leading causes of death are chronic diseases: heart disease, cancer, HIV/AIDS, cerebrovascular disease (stroke), diabetes, chronic lower respiratory disease (COPD), and Alzheimer's disease. With advancing age, chronic conditions replace accidents, suicide, and homicide as primary causes of death.

There are also important gender and race differences in causes of death throughout adulthood. Cancer is a more common cause of death for women than for men, beginning in early adulthood and continuing into middle adulthood. Death due to accidents is more common among men than women beginning in early adulthood and continuing into middle adulthood. Homicide and HIV/AIDS play a more prominent role in the deaths of blacks than of whites in young and middle adulthood. Suicide plays a more prominent role in the deaths of whites than of blacks. It is important to note that these racial differences may be partly due to differences in socioeconomic status between whites and blacks (Anderson, 2001).

It is important to note that there are some global differences in causes of death. The World Health Organization (WHO, 2003a) reports on the leading causes of death in developed and developing countries. Heart disease is the number one cause of death and cerebrovascular disease is the number two cause of death in both developed and developing

Exhibit 8.5	Five Leading Causes of Death and Percentage of Total Deaths in Age Groups in United States, 2004
15 to 24 Years	Accidents (46.1%)
	Homicide (14.8%)
	Suicide (12.8%)
	Cancer (5.1%)
	Heart Disease (3.0%)
25 to 44 Years	Accidents (22.7%)
	Cancer (14.7%)
	Heart Disease (12.7%)
	Suicide (9.2%)
	HIV/AIDS (5.8%)
45 to 64 Years	Cancer (33.1%)
	Heart Disease (22.8%)
	Accidents (5.8%)
	Diabetes (3.7%)
	Stroke (3.7%)
65 and Over	Heart Disease (30.4%)
	Cancer (21.8%)
	Stroke (7.4%)
	COPD (6.1%)
	Alzheimer's (3.7%)

SOURCE: Minino et al., 2004, pp. 29–30.

countries. In developed countries, cancer, lower respiratory infections, and COPD are the next most common causes of death in that order. In developing countries, lower respiratory infections, perinatal conditions, and HIV/AIDS are the next most common causes of disease in that order. It is also important to note that in developing countries, diarrhoeal disease, tuberculosis, and malaria are among the top 10 causes of death, a situation not currently found in developed countries. These data indicate that chronic illness is the major cause of death around the globe, but infectious diseases continue to be a major challenge in less affluent nations that lack access to safe water and adequate sanitation.

Exhibit 8.6 indicates that, in the United States, most of the common chronic conditions in middle adulthood are not fatal, however. Men have been reported to have a higher prevalence of fatal chronic conditions in middle adulthood than women, and women have been reported to have a higher prevalence of nonfatal chronic conditions (Merrill & Verbrugge, 1999). Overall, women in middle adulthood have higher rates of arthritis, sinusitis, and allergies than men but lower rates of heart disease and hearing impairments (Summer, O'Neill, & Shirey, 1999). There are also racial differences in the most common chronic conditions in middle adulthood, with diabetes more common among blacks and heart disease more common among white males. Although most midlife adults do not experience limitations from chronic conditions, limits on activity generally increase from early midlife to later midlife. Data from household interviews of a sample of civilian noninstitutionalized children and adults in the United States indicate that 13.1% of adults 45 to 54 years old and 21.1% of adults 55 to 64 years old reported some limitation of activity caused by chronic conditions (National Center for Health Statistics, 2001b). As socioeconomic status decreases, limitations of activity due to chronic conditions become more common.

Exhibit 8.6	Five Most Common Chronic Conditions in Black and White Men and Women Ages 45 to 74 in the United States		
Black Men	*White Men*	*Black Women*	*White Women*
Hypertension	Hypertension	Hypertension	Arthritis
Arthritis	Hearing impairments	Arthritis	Hypertension
Orthopedic impairments	Arthritis	Sinusitis	Sinusitis
Diabetes	Orthopedic impairments	Orthopedic impairments	Orthopedic impairments
Sinusitis	Heart disease	Diabetes	Hay Fever

SOURCE: Summer et al., 1999.

The WHO uses the concept of Disability Adjusted Life Year (DALY) to measure the sum of the years lost due to premature death *plus* the number of years spent in states of poor health or disability. There is much international evidence that socioeconomic position is a powerful predictor of both mortality and poor health (morbidity) (Marmot & Fuhrer, 2004). The WHO has calculated the worldwide leading causes of DALYs for males and females 15-years-old and older; these are reported in Exhibit 8.7. It is important to note that the WHO data include mental health as well as physical health conditions whereas health statistics in the United States do not. Therefore, the WHO data are useful because they give a better picture of the impact of unipolar depressive disorders and alcohol use disorders on global health. The stories of Viktor Spiro and Helen Tyson demonstrate the important impact that mental health conditions can have on life trajectories. It is important to note, however, that the data in Exhibit 8.7 are for ages 15 years and older, and not just for middle adulthood. For example, road traffic accidents and violence are much more common causes of death in adolescent and young adult males than in middle adult males. A longitudinal study in the Netherlands found that mental health tends to improve across the life course, but a minority of midlife adults shows persistently high levels of depressive symptoms and loneliness across the middle adult years (Deeg, 2005). These researchers, like many other researchers of middle adulthood, emphasize that reporting average results can mask the great variability in middle adult trajectories.

Viktor Spiro struggled with depression and substance abuse before he immigrated to the United States, and, as happens with many immigrants, the multiple losses and demands associated with the immigration experience exacerbated his mental health problems. As Karen

Exhibit 8.7	Leading Causes of Disease Burden (DALYS) for Males and Females Ages 15 Years and Older, Worldwide, 2002

Males	Females
1. HIV/AIDS	1. Unipolar depressive disorders
2. Ischaemic heart disease	2. HIV/AIDS
3. Cerebrovascular disease	3. Ischaemic heart disease
4. Unipolar depressive disorders	4. Cerebrovascular disease
5. Road traffic injuries	5. Cataracts
6. Tuberculosis	6. Hearing loss, adult onset
7. Alcohol use disorders	7. COPD
8. Violence	8. Tuberculosis
9. COPD	9. Osteoarthritis
10. Hearing loss, adult onset	10. Diabetes mellitus

Source: World Health Organization, 2003b.

Aroian and Anne E. Norris (2003) note, "Depression significantly impairs immigrants' ability to adapt to the new country and has serious emotional and economic consequences for immigrants and their families" (p. 420). Aroian and Norris found high levels of depression in a sample of immigrants from the former Soviet Union; they also found that the severity and longevity of depressive symptoms were correlated with the level of immigration-related stressors. They concluded that mental health interventions with depressed immigrants should focus on relieving these stressors by focusing on such practical issues as learning English and obtaining employment, as well as on emotional issues like loss, trauma, and feeling at home in the new country. Viktor was lucky to find mental health professionals who did just this, assisting him to get debt forgiveness and attain citizenship, while also working on issues of emotion regulation and expanding his social network.

Helen Tyson survived a traumatic experience at age 16, and seems to have gotten through young adulthood without the flashbacks and panic attacks she has recently experienced. It does appear, however, that since her attack she has reduced her involvement with the external world, which is another symptom of posttraumatic stress disorder (PTSD). Researchers have found that "midlife is a particularly high-risk period for either delayed onset or reactivated PTSD" (Solomon & Mikulincer, 2006, p. 664). Helen is facing an impending change in her life structure, which has been focused on active mothering. Such transitions often invite a period of reminiscence and review of one's life. This review may bring suppressed traumatic memories to the surface. In addition, Helen's recent loss of her mother, the declining health of her father, and the sense of loss of control over her children may be breaking through the defenses that have helped her avoid painful memories. In addition, she may have been triggered by having Sarah arrive at the age of her attack, especially given that she sees much of herself in Sarah. A recent longitudinal investigation of PTSD symptoms among combat veterans found that the symptoms decreased by the third year following combat trauma but had been reactivated in many veterans in the 20-year follow-up. It is important for social workers to recognize the possibility of delayed and reactivated PTSD in their midlife clients. This will be particularly important in the years ahead as veterans of the Iraq war become clients in every social service sector.

▧ Intellectual Changes in Middle Adulthood

Perhaps no domain of human behavior in middle adulthood arouses more concern about the balance of gains and losses than intellectual functioning. A trip to your local pharmacy will confront you with the variety of supplements and herbal remedies that are marketed to midlife adults with promises of maintaining mental alertness and mental acuity. And yet, middle-aged adults are often at the peak of their careers and filling leadership roles. The most recent presidents of the United States were men older than 50.

Research on cognitive changes in middle adulthood are recent, but there is growing and clear evidence that cognitive performance remains stable for the majority of midlife adults (Martin & Zimprich, 2005; Willis & Schaie, 2005). However, a significant subset of midlife adults shows important gain in cognitive functioning, and another significant subset shows important decline (Willis & Schaie, 2005). The amount of gain and decline varies across different types of cognitive functioning. For example, one study found that depending on the specific cognitive skill, the proportion of midlife adults who were stable in performance ranged from 53% to 69%, the proportion who gained ranged from 6% to 16%, and the proportion who declined ranged from 15% to 31% (Willis & Schaie, 2005).

Researchers are finding that individual differences in intellectual performance increase throughout middle adulthood (Martin & Zimprich, 2005). These increasing variations are related to both biological factors and environmental factors. Several biological risk factors have been identified for cognitive decline in midlife—including hypertension, diabetes, high cholesterol, and the APOE gene (a gene that has been associated with one type of Alzheimer's disease). Several protective factors have also been identified, most of them social in nature, including education, work or other environments that demand complex cognitive work, and physical exercise (Willis & Schaie, 2005). These findings are consistent with increasing evidence of brain plasticity throughout the life course, and suggest that cognitive decline can be slowed by engaging in activities that train the brain.

The Seattle Longitudinal Study (SLS) is studying intellectual changes from the early 20s to very old age by following the same individuals over time as well as drawing new samples at each test cycle. Willis and Schaie (1999) summarize the findings about changes for selected mental abilities across the life course, paying attention to gender differences. By incorporating data on new participants as the survey progresses, they are also able to study generational (cohort) differences, addressing the question, is the current baby boom midlife cohort functioning at a higher intellectual level than their parent's generation?

Willis and Schaie summarize the findings for six mental abilities:

1. *Vocabulary:* ability to understand ideas expressed in words

2. *Verbal Memory:* ability to encode and recall language units, such as word lists

3. *Number*: ability to perform simple mathematical computations quickly and accurately

4. *Spatial Orientation*: ability to visualize stimuli in two- and three-dimensional space

5. *Inductive Reasoning*: ability to recognize and understand patterns in and relationships among variables to analyze and solve logical problems

6. *Perceptual Speed*: ability to quickly make discriminations in visual stimuli

The research shows that middle adulthood is the period of peak performance of four of the six mental abilities: inductive reasoning, spatial orientation, vocabulary, and verbal memory. Two of the six mental abilities, perceptual speed and numerical ability, show decline in middle adulthood, but the decline in perceptual speed is much more dramatic than the decline in numerical ability. The authors note that the mental abilities that improve in middle adulthood—inductive reasoning, spatial orientation, vocabulary, and verbal memory—are among the more complex, higher-order mental abilities.

There are gender differences in the changes in mental abilities during middle adulthood. On average, men reach peak performance somewhat earlier than women. Men reach peak performance on spatial orientation, vocabulary, and verbal memory in their 50s, and women reach peak performance on these same mental abilities in their early 60s. On the other hand, on average, women begin to decline in perceptual speed somewhat earlier than men, in their 20s compared to the 30s for men. The improvement in mental abilities in middle adulthood is more dramatic for women than for men. Across the adult life course, women score higher than men on vocabulary, verbal memory, perceptual speed, and inductive reasoning. Men, on the other hand, score higher than women across the adult life course on spatial orientation. There is some evidence that cognitive decline in middle adulthood is predictive of cognitive impairment in late adulthood (Willis & Schaie, 2005).

Willis and Schaie (1999) also report on cohort differences in the selected mental abilities. They found that the baby boom cohort scored higher on two of the abilities, verbal memory and inductive reasoning, than their parents' generation did at the same chronological age. The baby boomers also scored higher than their parents on spatial orientation, but these differences were smaller than those for verbal memory and inductive reasoning. There were virtually no cohort differences on vocabulary and perceptual speed. The boomers did not score as well as their parents' generation on numerical ability, and the authors note that this is a continuation of a negative trend in numerical ability since the early 1900s found in other studies.

> What factors might be producing this historical trend toward declines in numerical ability?

▧ Personality Changes in Middle Adulthood

Does it appear to you that Viktor Spiro, Helen Tyson, and Robert Johnson, have grown "more like themselves" over their life course trajectories, or do you see changes in their personalities as they travel the life course? Little attention has been paid to the issue of personality in middle adulthood until quite recently. The literature that does exist on the topic consists largely of an argument about whether personality is stable or dynamic during middle adulthood. One theoretician (Whitbourne, 1986) has focused in recent years on identity processes in middle adulthood.

The Argument for Personality Stability

The idea that personality is stable in middle adulthood is an old one, rooted in Freud's psychoanalytic theory that saw personality as determined sometime in middle childhood. In this view, personality change past the age of 50 was practically impossible. The idea that personality is stable throughout adulthood comes from another very different approach to personality, commonly known as **trait theory**. According to this view, personality traits are enduring characteristics that are rooted in early temperament and are influenced by genetic and organic factors, but that remain relatively consistent across the life course. Recent empirical studies have focused on the degree to which individuals exhibit five broad personality traits, often referred to as the Big Five personality traits (Dorner, Mickler, & Studinger, 2005; Judge, Higgins, Thoresen, & Barrick, 1999; Roberts, Robins, Trzesniewski, & Caspi, 2003):

1. *Neuroticism:* moody, anxious, hostile, self-conscious, and vulnerable

2. *Extroversion:* outgoing, friendly, lively, talkative, and active

3. *Conscientiousness:* organized, responsible, hardworking, persistent, and careful

4. *Agreeableness:* cooperative, cheerful, warm, caring, trusting, and gentle

5. *Openness to experience:* creative, imaginative, intelligent, adventurous, and nonconforming

Avshalom Caspi's **contextual model** also proposes personality stability across the life course, but it presents a different explanation for that stability (Caspi, 1987; Caspi & Roberts, 1999). Caspi and colleagues assert that personality influences both the environments we select for ourselves and how we respond to those environments. Personality leads us to choose similar environments over time, and these similar environments reinforce our personal styles.

The Argument for Personality Change

Some psychoanalysts have broken with Freud and proposed that personality continues to change across adulthood. More specifically, they propose that middle adulthood is a time when the personality ripens and matures. Most notable of these are Carl Jung, Erik Erikson, and George Vaillant. All three are consistent with humanistic models of personality that see middle adulthood as an opportunity for continued growth. Jung conceptualizes middle adulthood as a time of balance in the personality. Although Erikson sees early life as important, he suggests that societal and cultural influences call for different personal adaptations over the life course. Vaillant (1977, 2002) suggests that with age and experience, **coping mechanisms**, or the strategies we use to master the demands of life, mature. He divides coping mechanisms into *immature mechanisms* (denial, projection, passive aggression, dissociation, acting out, and fantasy) and *mature mechanisms* (sublimation, humor, altruism, and suppression). He proposes that as we age across adulthood, we make more use of mature coping mechanisms such as altruism, sublimation, and humor and less use of immature coping mechanisms such as denial and projection. Definitions for both the immature and mature coping mechanisms are found in Exhibit 8.8.

Exhibit 8.8	Coping Mechanisms

Immature Coping Mechanisms

Acting out. Ideas and feelings are acted on impulsively rather than reflectively.

Denial. Awareness of painful aspects of reality are avoided by negating sensory information about them.

Dissociation. Painful emotions are handled by compartmentalizing perceptions and memories, and detaching from the full impact.

Fantasy. Real human relationships are replaced with imaginary friends.

Passive-aggression. Anger toward others is turned inward against the self through passivity, failure, procrastination, or masochism.

Projection. Unacknowledged feelings are attributed to others.

Mature Coping Mechanisms

Altruism. Pleasure is attained by giving pleasure to others.

Mature humor. An emotion or thought is expressed through comedy, allowing a painful situation to be faced without individual pain or social discomfort.

Sublimation. An unacceptable impulse or unattainable aim is transformed into a more acceptable or attainable aim.

Suppression. Attention to a desire or impulse is postponed.

SOURCE: Vaillant, 1977, 2002.

As you might imagine, life course theorists see possibilities for personality change in middle adulthood, as individuals experience life events and culturally influenced role changes. In fact, Daniel Levinson (Levinson, 1977, 1986; Levinson & Levinson, 1996), influenced by both Erikson and Jung, proposed that many adults experience a life event he called a "midlife crisis" in the transition to middle adulthood.

Evidence for Stability and Change in Midlife Personality

What can we conclude about personality in middle adulthood? Is it marked by stability or change? The available research suggests that we should think of the midlife personality in terms of both stability and change.

Research on the Big Five personality traits suggests that there is long-term stability in terms of the ranking of traits. For example, a person who is high in agreeableness at one point in adulthood will continue to be high in agreeableness across the life course (Costa & McCrae, 1994; Dorner et al., 2005; Roberts et al., 2003). However, there is some evidence that there is a slight drop in consistency during early midlife, suggesting that this might be a period of the life course that is more conducive to personality change than other adult phases (Dorner et al., 2005). Researchers have studied the genetic basis of the Big Five traits and found a small genetic contribution, particularly for neuroticism and agreeableness (Jang et al., 2001). In addition, a 40-year longitudinal study drawn from the Berkeley Guidance Study—which collected data during late childhood and again during young adulthood and middle adulthood—found a great deal of personality consistency over time (Caspi, 1987).

Nevertheless, a number of both cross-sectional and longitudinal studies report age-related changes in personality traits in middle and late adulthood (Costa & McCrae, 1994; Dorner et al., 2005; McCrae et al., 1999; Roberts et al., 2003). Extroversion (activity and thrill seeking), neuroticism (anxiety and self-consciousness), and openness to experience have been found to decline with age starting in middle adulthood. On the other hand, agreeableness has been found to increase with age, and conscientiousness and emotional stability have been found to peak in middle adulthood (Dorner et al., 2005; Lachman & Bertrand, 2001). What's more, these patterns of age-related changes in personality have been found in cross-cultural research that included samples from Germany, Italy, Portugal, Croatia, and South Korea (McCrae et al., 1999).

Some researchers have found gender differences in personality traits to be greater than age-related differences (Lachman & Bertrand, 2001). Women score higher than men in agreeableness, conscientiousness, extroversion, and neuroticism. Men, on the other hand, score higher than women on openness to experience. These gender differences in personality have been found in 26 cultures, but the magnitude of differences varied across cultures. The researchers were surprised to find that the biggest gender differences occurred in European and North American cultures, where traditional gender roles are less pronounced (Costa, Terracciano, & McCrae, 2001).

In spite of these gender differences, a number of researchers have found evidence for a gender-role shift during middle adulthood, as hypothesized by Jung, who suggested that in midlife both men and women become more androgynous. In fact, one research team found that scales measuring femininity and masculinity were among the scales that revealed the most change between the ages of 43 and 52 (Helson & Wink, 1992). Women were found by these and other researchers to increase in decisiveness, action orientation, and assertiveness during midlife. Men have been found to increase in nurturance and affiliation by some researchers (Havighurst, Neugarten, & Tobin, 1968; Neugarten & Gutmann, 1968). Writing from a different perspective, Joan Borysenko (1996), a cellular biologist, provides evidence for a gender crossover in personality in midlife that she attributes to changes in levels of sex hormones. On the other hand, some researchers have found no gender role crossover for men (Lowenthal, Thurnher, & Chiriboga, 1975), and recent research suggests that it is motherhood and not age that promotes femininity in women (Roberts, Helson, & Klohnen, 2002).

Although there is evidence that midlife adults often engage in review and reappraisal, there is much disagreement about whether that review and reappraisal is serious enough to constitute the midlife crisis proposed by Levinson and others. Most researchers who have studied this issue take a middle ground, suggesting that some midlife adults do reach crisis level in midlife, but in general, the idea of midlife crisis has been greatly overstated (see, e.g., Sterns & Huyck, 2001). Research on turning points in adulthood suggest that they are most likely to occur in young adulthood (Wethington, Kessler, & Pixley, 2004).

Whitbourne's Identity Process Model

Susan Whitbourne and colleagues (Whitbourne, 1986; Whitbourne & Connolly, 1999) propose that identity plays a central role in adult personality stability and change. Drawing on Piaget's theory of cognitive development, they suggest that identity continues to develop throughout adulthood through the processes of assimilation and accommodation. **Assimilation** is the process through which individuals incorporate new experiences into their existing identity. **Accommodation**, on the other hand, is the process through which an individual changes some aspect of identity in response to new experiences. Three identity styles are identified, based on the way that midlife individuals respond to new experiences (Whitbourne & Connolly, 1999):

1. *Assimilative identity style.* Midlife individuals see themselves as unchanging and may either deny the physical and other changes they are experiencing or rationalize them as something else.

2. *Accommodative identity style.* Midlife individuals overreact to physical and other changes, and this undermines their identity and leaves it weak and incoherent.

3. *Balanced identity style.* Midlife individuals, combining goals and inner purpose with the flexibility to adapt to new experiences, recognize the physical and other changes of aging, engage in good health maintenance to minimize risk and enhance protection, and accept what cannot be changed.

It appears that earlier losses and trauma may have predisposed Viktor Spiro and Helen Tyson to an accommodative identity style. As he enters middle adulthood, with professional help, Viktor appears to be making some movement toward a more balanced identity style. It seems quite likely that Helen Tyson's counselor will be attempting to help her do the same. On the other hand, Robert Johnson appears to have a balanced identity style. He moved with both purpose and flexibility to meet his goal of becoming a parent and has been open to new ways of expressing generativity.

How does a balanced identity style relate to human agency in making choices?

✑ Spiritual Development in Middle Adulthood

Religion and a search for connectedness play a major role in Robert Johnson's life. Religion is also very important in the life of Viktor Spiro's mother, and both he and his mother are drawing strength from their Greek Orthodox faith as they deal with Petro's declining health. The same is true of many midlife adults. The major world religions associate spiritual growth with advancing age (see, e.g., Biggs, 1999; Isenberg, 1992; Post, 1992; Thursby, 1992). And yet, until very recently, the burgeoning U.S. literature on middle adulthood had almost entirely overlooked the issue of spiritual development; this continues to be the case in the European literature. The primary effort has been models of spiritual development that propose that humans have the potential for continuous spiritual growth across the life course.

For example, James Fowler's Theory of Faith Development (1981) proposes six stages of faith. The first two stages occur primarily in childhood. These are the four stages that can occur in adulthood:

1. *Synthetic-conventional faith.* The basic worldview of this faith stage is that spiritual authority is found outside the individual. In this faith stage, the individual relies on a pastor or rabbi or other spiritual leader to define morality. Many people remain in this faith stage throughout their lives and never progress to the other stages.

▲ **Photo 8.2**   Family prayer—Religion and spiritual connectedness often play a major role in the lives of midlife adults.

2. *Individuative-reflective faith.* The adult no longer relies on outside authority and begins to look for authority within the self, based on moral reasoning. The individual also takes responsibility for examining the assumptions of his or her faith.

3. *Conjunctive faith.* In this stage, the individual looks for balance in such polarities as independence and connection, recognizes that there are many truths, and opens out beyond the self in service to others. Fowler proposes that many people never reach the stage of **conjunctive faith**, and if they do, they almost never reach it before middle adulthood.

4. *Universalizing faith.* In Fowler's final stage, **universalizing faith**, individuals lead selfless lives based on principles of absolute love and justice. Fowler notes that only rare individuals reach this stage.

Fowler's theory has received support in cross-sectional research but has not yet been put to test in longitudinal research. Therefore, it should be applied with caution, recognizing that it may reflect the influences of historical time on faith development.

Interestingly, Fowler's description of conjunctive faith overlaps with theories of middle adulthood previously discussed in this chapter. For example, the reference to balance calls to mind the theories of Jung and Levinson, who saw middle adulthood as a time of bringing balance to personality and life structure. In addition, the idea of opening oneself in service to others is consistent with Erikson's idea of generativity as the psychosocial struggle of middle adulthood (Biggs, 1999; Dollahite, Slife, & Hawkins, 1998). Drawing on Jung, one theorist proposes that late midlife is "a time when our energy naturally moves beyond the concerns of our nuclear family into a concern with the world family" (Borysenko, 1996, p. 185). The emphasis is on spirituality as a state of "being connected." Using data from a national survey of midlife adults in the United States, one researcher has found a strong correlation between regular participation in religious activities and community volunteer service, particularly in terms of making financial contributions to community organizations and charities (Rossi, 2004b).

One of the few studies of spiritual development in middle adulthood was described in Wade Clark Roof's *A Generation of Seekers* (1993), which reported on the "spiritual journeys of the baby boom generation" in the United States. Roof emphasizes the likelihood of cohort effects in this study. Drawing on survey data and interview responses, Roof suggested that the baby boom generation was "changing America's spiritual landscape" (Roof, 1993, p. 50). He reported that most baby boomers grew up in religious households, but 58% of his sample dropped their relationships with religious institutions for at least two years during their adolescence or young adulthood. Roof acknowledges that earlier generations have also dropped out of religion during early adulthood, but not in the numbers found in his sample of baby boomers. He suggests that the turmoil of the 1960s and 1970s, with a youth culture that questioned authority, is probably largely responsible for the high rate of dropout among baby boomers. Roof found that about one-fourth of his sample that had dropped out had returned to religious activities by the end of the 1980s. For many of them, their return seemed to be related to having children at home.

Roof found that religious affiliation and activity did not tell the whole story about the spiritual lives of baby boomers, however. Regardless of religious affiliation, baby boomers were involved in an intense search for personal meaning (Roof, 1993). But for many of Roof's sample, the current spiritual quest was a very personal, introspective quest—one that embraced a wide range of nontraditional as well as traditional beliefs.

In a follow-up study with the same sample from 1995 to 1997, Roof (1999) found that many boomers had shifted in their religious affiliation again. More than half of the earlier dropouts who had returned to religious activities by the late 1980s had dropped out again. But, on the other hand, one half of those who had dropped out in the 1980s had returned to religious activities by the mid-1990s. Presence of children in the home again seemed to be the factor that motivated a return to religion.

Roof suggests that the baby boomers are leading a shift in U.S. religious life away from an unquestioning belief to a questioning approach, and toward a belief that no single religious institution has a monopoly on truth. That shift is certainly not total at this point, however. Roof identifies five types of contemporary believers from his sample: 33% are born-again or Evangelical Christians, 25% are old-line mainstream believers, 15% are dogmatists who see one truth in the doctrine and form of their religious tradition, 15% are metaphysical seekers, and 12% are nonreligious secularists. Thus, almost three quarters of his sample could be classified as more or less unquestioning adherents of a particular system of beliefs but with an increasing trend toward recognition of the legitimacy of multiple spiritual paths. It is important to note that religion plays a much more central role in the lives of adults in the United States than it does in European countries (Reid, 2004).

Unfortunately, Roof does not analyze racial and ethnic differences in religious and spiritual expression for his baby boom sample. Others have found evidence, however, of strong

What does Roof's research suggest about spiritual age in middle adulthood?

racial and ethnic differences (Gallup & Lindsay, 1999). Black baby boomers have been much more constant in their religious beliefs and participation than white baby boomers and are far more likely to consider religion very important in their lives. Although not as steadfast as their black cohorts, Hispanic baby boomers have also been less fluid in their religious activity than their non-Hispanic white cohorts. Robert Johnson, who has been steadfast in his religious belief and activity throughout his life, is typical of black baby boomers.

▧ Relationships in Middle Adulthood

In contemporary life, both women and men fulfill multiple social roles in midlife (Antonucci, Akiyama, & Merline, 2001). The most central roles are related to family and paid work. Relationships with family, friends, and coworkers are an important part of life in middle adulthood.

In an analysis of longitudinal data, Elizabeth Paul (1997) found seven categories of relationships to be important to the well-being of midlife adults: relationships with mother, father, siblings, extended family, spouse or partner, children, and friends. Most midlife adults were involved in five or more of these types of relationships at one time or another, but the nature of the mix of relationships and their importance for personal well-being changed over time in complex ways. Paul concludes that people may need a variety of relationships for their psychological well-being.

Toni Antonucci and colleagues (Antonucci & Akiyama, 1987, 1997; Kahn & Antonucci, 1980) suggest that we each travel through life with a **convoy**, or a network of social relationships that protect, defend, aid, and socialize us. In one study, these researchers asked respondents in a representative sample of people ages 8 to 93 to map their convoys of support, using three concentric circles surrounding the individual respondent (Antonucci & Akiyama, 1997). In the inner circle, the respondents were asked to identify people who were so close and important to them that they could not imagine living without them. In the middle circle, respondents were asked to name people who were not quite that close but still very close and important to them. In the outer circle, respondents were asked to name people who were not as close as those in the two inner circles but who were still important enough that they came to mind as members of the support network.

Exhibit 8.9 demonstrates how Robert Johnson might respond to the request to map his current convoy. You can probably appreciate that he would map his convoy differently at different points in his life. A diagram of Viktor Spiro's convoy would include more formal helping professionals than we see in Robert's convoy. A diagram of Helen Tyson's convoy would call attention to the lack of friends in her convoy.

The size and structure of a person's convoy appear to vary with age and other demographic characteristics. For example, compared with other age groups, midlife adults (in a group ages 35 to 49 and a group ages 50 to 64) reported, on average, the largest convoys (Antonucci & Akiyama, 1997). The older midlife age group reported slightly fewer people in their convoys (average of almost 10) than the younger midlife age group (average of over 11). In both age groups, women reported more people in their convoys than men. The difference between men and women was larger in the 35 to 49 age group than in any other adult age group. What may be more important is that the gender differences show up in the closest inner circle, with midlife women reporting, on average, one more person in the inner circle than midlife men. There are also racial and ethnic differences. Whites have been found to

| Exhibit 8.9 | Hypothetical Convoy for Robert Johnson, Age 48 |

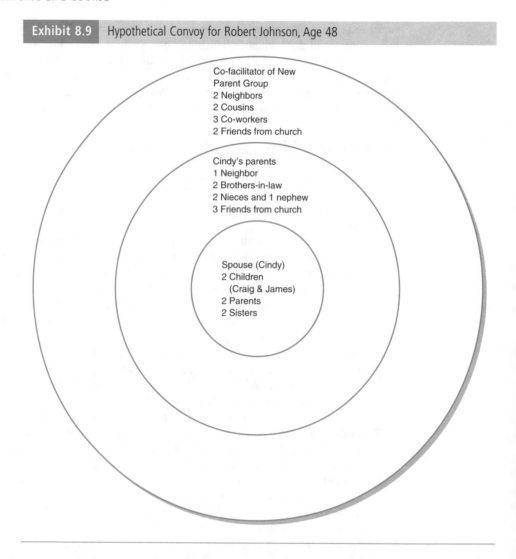

have larger convoys than African Americans, and the convoys of African American adults have a higher proportion of kin in them than the convoys of white adults (Antonucci et al., 2001). According to these findings, Robert Johnson has a very rich convoy, and seems to defy both the gender and racial trends in convoy size. One cross-national research project on convoys also indicates the important role of culture. In Japan, young adults in their 20s were the age group reporting the largest convoy of support (Antonucci & Akiyama, 1995). Another study conducted in Taiwan suggests that in our very mobile times, when younger generations leave home to follow jobs in global cities, some people may have only one or two circles in their convoys (Chen, 2006). Certainly, it is important to understand the very dynamic nature of convoys in the lives of many people in a globalized world.

Most of the other research that has been done on midlife adult relationships is based on the premise that the marital relationship is the focal relationship in middle adulthood.

Consequently, too little is known about other familial and nonfamilial relationships. Recently, however, gerontologists have suggested that a variety of relationships are important to adults in late adulthood, and this hypothesis has led to preliminary investigations of a variety of relationships in middle adulthood (Paul, 1997). In the following sections, we look first at multigenerational family relationships and then review the limited research on friendship and community and organizational relationships.

Middle Adulthood in the Context of the Multigenerational Family

Because of increasing longevity, multigenerational families are becoming more common. By the early 1990s, three-quarters of adults ages 50 to 54 in the United States had a family with at least three generations; about 40% had families with four generations (Sweet & Bumpass, 1996). Similarly, in Germany, 80% of adults ages 40 to 54, and 76% of adults 55 to 69, have three-generation families (Kohli & Künemund, 2005). With a declining birthrate, the multigenerational family becomes increasingly vertical, with more generations but fewer people in each generation. This is the picture in all industrialized countries; the historical pyramid shape of the family has been replaced by a beanpole shape (tall and thin) (Putney & Bengtson, 2003). There is also increasing complexity in the multigenerational family, with divorces and remarriages adding a variety of step-relationships to the mix.

There is much popular speculation that family ties are weakening as geographic mobility increases. Research in the United States and Germany suggests, however, that there is more intergenerational solidarity than we may think (Bengtson, 2001; Putney & Bengtson, 2001; Kohli & Künemund, 2005). Certainly, we see much intergenerational solidarity in the

▲ **Photo 8.3** Quality time—Theories about middle adulthood propose that it is a time when individuals attempt to find balance in their lives.

families of Viktor Spiro, Helen Tyson, and Robert Johnson. Using a national representative sample in the United States, Bengtson and colleagues have identified five types of extended family relationships. About one-quarter (25.5%) of the families are classified as *tightly knit*, and another quarter (25.5%) are classified as *sociable*, meaning that family members are engaged with each other but do not provide for, and receive concrete assistance from, each other. The remaining families are about evenly split among the *intimate-but-distant* (16%); *obligatory*, or those who have contact but no emotional closeness or shared belief system (16%); and *detached* (17%) classifications. It is important to note that no one type of extended family relationships was found to be dominant, suggesting much diversity in intergenerational relationships in the United States. Ethnicity is one source of that variation. For example, black and Hispanic families report stronger maternal attachments than are reported in white families, and they are also more likely to reside in multigenerational households (Putney & Bengtson, 2003). One researcher has also found much diversity in intergenerational relationships in Taiwan (Chen, 2006).

Another way of categorizing extended families is as collectivist oriented or individualistic (Pyke & Bengtson, 1996). In families with a strong collectivist orientation, kinship ties and family responsibilities take precedence over nonfamily roles. In families with a strong individualistic orientation, personal achievement and independence take precedence over family ties. The researchers found that most families were some mix of collectivist and individualistic.

Despite the evidence that intergenerational family relationships are alive and well, there is also evidence that many family relationships include some degree of conflict. One longitudinal study concluded that about one in eight adult intergenerational relationships can be described as "long-term lousy relationships" (Bengtson, 1996).

After studying multigenerational family relationships for several decades, Bengtson (2001) suggests that, with increased marital instability and a declining birthrate, multigenerational family relationships are once again becoming more important in the United States and may replace some nuclear family functions. We should perhaps think of the multigenerational family as a "latent kin network" (Bengtson, 2001, p. 12) that may be activated only at times of crisis. Of course, strong multigenerational families are still the norm in many parts of the world, and many immigrant groups bring that approach to family life with them to the United States.

The trend toward multiple generations in extended families has particular relevance for midlife adults, who make up the generation in the middle. Several researchers (see, e.g., Fry, 1995; Rosenthal, 1985) have found that midlife adults are the kinkeepers in multigenerational families and that this holds true across cultures. **Kinkeepers** are family members who work at keeping family members across the generations in touch with one another and who make sure that both emotional and practical needs of family members are met. Historically, when nuclear families were larger, kinkeepers played an important role in working to maintain ties among large sibling groups. With increased longevity and multiple generations of families, kinkeepers play an important role in the multigenerational family, working to maintain ties across the generations, ties among grandparents, parents, children, grandchildren, siblings, aunts, uncles, nieces, nephews, and cousins.

Researchers have found that most kinkeepers are middle-aged women (Aronson, 1992; Gerstel & Gallagher, 1993; Ross & Rossi, 1990). Women help larger numbers of kin than men and spend three times as many hours helping kin (Gerstel & Gallagher, 1993). Because of this kinkeeping role, midlife women have been described as the "sandwich generation" (Brody,

1985). This term was originally used to suggest that midlife women are simultaneously caring for their own children as well as their parents. Recent research suggests that with demographic changes, few women still have children at home when they begin to care for parents, but midlife women continue to be "sandwiched" with competing demands of paid work roles and intergenerational kinkeeping (Kohli & Künemund, 2005; Putney & Bengston, 2001).

Helen Tyson and her sisters are all middle-aged women who play important kinkeeping roles in their extended family. They provide increasing assistance to their frail father and guidance and assistance of various kinds to their children. In addition, they take the initiative to plan extended family holiday get-togethers. The sisters are lucky to be able to share these kinkeeping roles because they now must balance assistance to their father with the needs of their own children.

Relationships With Spouse or Partner

In recent decades, there has been an increased diversity of marital statuses at midlife. Some men and women have been married for some time, some are getting married for the first time, some are not yet married, some will never marry, some were once married but now are divorced, some are in a second or third marriage, and some are not married but are living in a long-term committed relationship with someone of the same or opposite sex (Antonucci et al., 2001). Only one in 20 adults ages 40 to 59 have never been married (Marks et al., 2004). Adults like Viktor Spiro who have struggled with mental health issues are more likely than other adults to be single.

For heterosexual marriages, midlife appears to be a time of both good news and bad news. On the one hand, midlife has been found to be the time of peak marital happiness (White & Edwards, 1993). Marital happiness has a first peak in the first few years, drops off during the child-rearing years, and peaks again after the last child is launched. Midlife marriages seem to combine friendship, companionship, shared interests, tolerance, and equality (Dowling, 1996). Likewise, midlife gay and lesbian partnerships have been described as "more companionable and less passionate" (Blacker, 2005, p. 304) than young adult gay and lesbian partnerships.

On the other hand, the divorce rate is high during midlife for the baby boom generation. There is a dramatic increase in divorce 15 to 18 years after marriage and again 25 to 28 years after marriage (Shapiro, 1996). The first increase occurs at a time when there are usually adolescent children in the family. The second increase occurs at a time when the couple has typically launched young adult children. Although many marriages flourish once the children have been launched, some marriages cannot survive without the presence of children to buffer conflicts in the marriage. Men at midlife report more marital satisfaction than women at midlife (Antonucci & Akiyama, 1997), and most divorces are initiated by women (Carter & McGoldrick, 2005a). Longitudinal research has found that baby boom women are less satisfied with their marriages than their mother's were at midlife, reminding us of the importance of considering cohort effects when reporting life course trends (Putney & Bengtson, 2003).

Although there is a period of adjustment to divorce, midlife adults cope better with divorce than young adults (Marks & Lambert, 1998). Some individuals actually report improved well-being after divorce (Antonucci et al., 2001). It is true, however, that the financial consequences of divorce for women are negative (Scott, 1997). After divorce, men are more likely to remarry than women, and whites are more likely to remarry than African Americans.

Relationships With Children

Although a growing number of midlife adults, like Robert Johnson, are parenting young or school age children, most midlife adults are parents of adolescents or young adults. Parenting adolescents can be a challenge, and launching young adult offspring from the nest is a happy experience for most families. It is a family transition that has been undergoing changes in the past 20 years, however, coming at a later age for the parents and becoming more fluid in its timing and progress (Antonucci & Akiyama, 1997).

In the United States and the industrialized European countries, it became common for young adults to live outside the family prior to marriage in the 1960s, as was the case with

What factors are producing these trends in family life?

Robert Johnson. Then, in the 1980s, two trends became evident: increased age at first leaving home and increased incidence of returning home. Popular culture has used phrases such as "prolonged parenting," "cluttered nest," "boomerang generation," and "adultolescents" to describe these trends (Putney & Bengtson, 2001, 2003). Recent data indicate that 30% to 40% of parents between the ages of 40 and 60 in the United States live with their adult children. Approximately half of these young adult children have never left home, and the other half have left home but returned one or more times. About 40% of recent cohorts of young adults have returned home at least once after leaving home (Putney & Bengtson, 2001). A very similar trend exists in Northern Europe; of parents ages 50 to 59, 28% in Denmark, 36% in Sweden, and 48% in Germany and Austria live with adult children. In contrast, 79% of parents in the same age group live with adult children in Spain and 82% in Italy (Kohli & Künemund, 2005).

These shifts in the timing of young adult launching from the family home have created uncertainty in the expectations of both parents and young adults about realistic age norms for this family transition. In general, parents are more positive than their young adult children about living together. Fathers, in particular, seem to derive satisfaction from living with their young adult children (Spitze, Logan, Joseph, & Lee, 1994). Young adults who live with their parents report slightly less affection toward their parents than do nonresident young adults (White & Rogers, 1997).

Attitudes toward coresidence of young adults with their parents are influenced by ethnicity and religion. Every group in the United States is more supportive of the arrangement than white, nonfundamentalist Protestants (Goldscheider & Lawton, 1998). Hispanics and non-Hispanic Catholics are the groups with the most positive attitudes toward young adults living with parents. Blacks have ambiguous attitudes: although black families tend to be more collectivist oriented than white families, among low-income blacks preference for coresidence is confounded with inadequate resources in the family. Although attitudes in Germany, France, the Netherlands, and Great Britain are similar to the attitudes of white, nonfundamentalist Protestants in the United States, young adults in Italy and Spain are expected to remain in the parental home until they form their own family, as are young adults from Asian cultures (Goldscheider, 1997). Conflicts with adolescent and young adult children often develop when midlife immigrant parents wish to maintain these cultural traditions (Antonucci et al., 2001).

Although marital happiness has been found to increase after adult children leave the house, staying closely connected to their children is important for the well-being of midlife adults (White & Edwards, 1993). In general, mothers have closer relationships with their young adult children than fathers, and divorced fathers have been found to have weaker emotional attachments with their adult children than either married fathers or divorced mothers (Putney & Bengtson, 2003; Silverstein & Bengtson, 1997). Young adults are more likely to continue living with parents if the family is "intact" than if the parents are divorced; the presence of a stepparent further decreases the likelihood of coresidence (Aquilino, 1990). Although the dominant culture in the United States emphasizes the importance of the marital relationship, some suggest that the parent-child relationship is the "single most important kinship tie in Western industrial societies," particularly because marital relationships are becoming less stable (Bahr, Dechaux, & Stiehr, 1994, p. 116).

It is also important to note the common exchange of material resources between generations. Viktor Spiro and his parents are pooling resources to stay afloat economically. Helen Tyson and her husband received financial assistance from her midlife parents during the early years of their marriage. Robert Johnson received financial assistance from his midlife parents to attend college. Recent research in Germany suggests that intergenerational financial transfers are common and often sizable, with midlife and late life adults particularly providing financial assistance to adult children with poor economic position (Kohli & Künemund, 2005).

Relationships With Parents

Most research shows that middle-aged adults are deeply involved with their aging parents (Antonucci & Akiyama, 1997; Kohli & Künemund, 2005; Marks et al., 2004). As suggested in the stories of Viktor Spiro, Helen Tyson, and Robert Johnson, the nature of the relationship with aging parents changes over time. Aging parents provide comfort, aid, and support for their midlife children, particularly while the parents are in their 60s and 70s (see, e.g., Akiyama, Antonucci, & Campbell, 1990; Bengtson & Harootyan, 1994). Viktor Spiro lives with his parents and receives much emotional support from his mother. Helen Tyson feels lost without the emotional support of her mother who died a year ago. Robert Johnson received much emotional support from his parents when he was making the transition to parenting. But as the parents' health begins to deteriorate, they turn more to their midlife children for help, as is currently the case for Viktor, Helen, and Robert. In one study in the United States (Marks, 1998), about one in eight employed midlife adults reported giving personal care for one month or more to a disabled or frail relative. By age 54, one in three reported providing this type of care at some point in the past. A German study found that caring for elderly family members peaks between the ages of 50 to 54 (Kohli & Künemund, 2005).

Traditionally, and typically still, caregivers to aging parents are daughters or daughters-in-law (Blacker, 2005). This is the case, even though by 1997, over 75% of women between the ages of 45 and 54 were employed (U.S. Bureau of Labor Statistics, 1997). At least one researcher found that unmarried women are more likely to be called upon to be the primary caregiver than other daughters (Allen, 1989). In spite of competing demands from spouses and children, providing limited care to aging parents seems to cause little psychological distress (Marks, 1998). Extended caregiving, on the other hand, has been found to have a negative effect on the emotional well-being of married women (Putney & Bengtson, 2001).

Culture plays a role in whether providing care to aging parents is experienced as a burden. Both collectivist-oriented and individualistic families meet the caregiving needs of their elders, but their motivations and processes differ (Pyke & Bengtson, 1996). Collectivist families engage in caregiving out of affection, often share the caregiving among family members, and experience little caregiver burden. This seems to be the situation for Helen Tyson and her sisters, and for Robert and Cindy Johnson. Individualistic families, on the other hand, engage in caregiving out of a sense of obligation, often use formal care, and are more likely to report caregiver burden. Collectivist-oriented families, such as Latino, Asian American, African American, and Native American families, normalize family caregiving. Individualistic families, such as those of Irish and Czech background, value individual independence and find elder care particularly troublesome to both caregiver and care recipient (McGoldrick, Giordano, & Pearce, 1996). Even in collectivist-oriented families, however, midlife caregivers are at high risk for stress-related illnesses. Greene (1991) has identified the issues presented in Exhibit 8.10 as points of stress for midlife caregivers.

Other Family Relationships

Midlife is typically a time of launching children and a time when parents die. It is also a time when new family members get added by marriage and the birth of grandchildren. Until recently, however, family relationships other than marital relationships and parent-child relationships have received little research attention. One notable exception is the line of research that studies extended kinship systems (Hatchett & Jackson, 1993; Paz, 1993). The grandparent-grandchild relationship has received the next greatest amount of research attention, followed by a growing body of research on sibling relationships.

For those adults who become grandparents, the onset of the grandparent role typically occurs in their 40s or 50s, or increasingly in their 60s. This role is often gratifying to midlife adults, especially women. One study found that relationships with grandchildren are particularly important for the well-being of midlife women (Paul, 1997). Another study found that grandmothers have more affection for their grandchildren than do grandfathers (Silverstein & Long, 1998). Other researchers have noted two potential problems for grandparents. First, if adult children divorce, custody agreements may fail to attend to the rights of grandparents

---

Exhibit 8.10	Points of Stress for Midlife Caregivers

- *Shift in generational intimacy.* Caregivers learn personal details and provide intimate care.
- *Shift in power and responsibility.* Power passes from elder parents to their midlife children as midlife adults assume some caregiving responsibilities.
- *Financial burden.* If midlife caregivers provide financial assistance to their parents, they may do so at the time that they are paying college tuitions and saving for retirement.
- *Competing roles.* Caregivers may also be employees, students, volunteers, mothers, partners, and homemakers.
- *Emotional ambivalence.* Providing intimate physical care can stimulate a variety of emotions, including embarrassment, anger, and guilt.
- *Confrontation of one's own aging.* Watching their parents age make midlife adults more mindful of their aging processes.

SOURCE: Based on Greene, 1991.

for visitation (Bergquist, Greenberg, & Klaum, 1993). Second, if adult children become incapacitated by substance abuse, illness, disability, or incarceration, grandparents may be recruited to step in to raise the grandchildren. The number of children cared for by grandparents in the United States has risen dramatically in the past 30 years. In one national representative sample, 30% of black grandmothers, 19% of Hispanic grandmothers, and 12% of white grandmothers reported that they had been surrogate parents for a grandchild at some point in their lives (Szinovacz, 1998). Vern Bengtson (2001) asserts that grandparents play an important socializing role in families, and that this role will most likely continue to grow in importance in the near future.

Most midlife adults have at least one sibling. Sibling relationships have been found to be important for the well-being of both men and women in midlife (Paul, 1997). Siblings often drift apart in young adulthood, but contact between siblings increases in late midlife (Carstensen, 1998; Cicerelli, 1995). They are often brought together around the care and death of aging parents. Their collaboration at such times may bring them closer together or may stir new as well as unresolved resentments. Although step- and half-siblings tend to stay connected to each other, their contact is less frequent than the contact between full siblings.

Viktor Spiro's sister was an important lifeline for him when he immigrated to the United States, but tensions developed during the time when Viktor was suicidal. Their mutual concern about their father's health is drawing them closer again. Helen Tyson and her sisters have remained close over the years, and, indeed, Helen's sisters have been her major source of support. Currently, their collaboration around the care of their father is an important point of mutual interest. Robert Johnson has close relationships with his sisters and their families, and these relationships continue to be important as the siblings face concerns about their parents' health.

Relationships With Friends

Midlife adults have more family members in their social convoys than do younger and older adults, but they also continue to report at least a few important friendships (Adams & Allan, 1998). In an attempt to account for this phenomenon, one theorist suggests that midlife adults become more selective about their relationships (Carstensen, 1992). The emphasis shifts from having a large number of friends to having a smaller number of more intimate friends. This idea has some support from research (Carney & Cohler, 1993), but midlife friendships are studied less than friendships in other life phases (Sherman, de Vries, & Lansford, 2000). It is important to remember that midlife adults report larger social convoys than any other adult age group, but the bulk of those convoys are intergenerational family members. This gives credence to the suggestion that midlife adults have less time than other adult age groups for friendships (Antonucci et al., 2001).

Friendships appear to have an impact on midlife well-being for both men and women, although they do not seem to be as important as close familial relationships (Julian, 1992). For instance, the adequacy of social support, particularly from friends, at age 50 predicts physical health for men at age 70 (Vaillant, 1998). Likewise, midlife women who have a confidant or a close group of female friends report greater well-being than midlife women without such interpersonal resources (McQuaide, 1998). Women who report positive feelings toward their women friends also have fewer depressive symptoms and higher morale than women who report less positive feelings toward female friends (Paul, 1997). Whether good feelings toward friends protect against depression or depression impairs the quality of friendships remains to be determined, however.

Given this research, it appears that as Robert Johnson approaches 50, his wide circle of friends, as well as family, bode well for his continuing good health. On the other hand, the research indicates that Helen Tyson's lack of friends, and inability to trust others enough to develop friendships, may be a risk factor for continued depression. This is an issue that she and her counselor may want to address. Viktor Spiro's recent participation in social events is providing him an opportunity to expand his social convoy and appears to be adding an important dimension to his life circumstances.

It appears that the importance of friends in the social convoy varies by sexual orientation, race, and marital status. Friends are important sources of support in the social convoys of gay and lesbian midlife adults, often serving as an accepting "chosen family" for those who have traveled the life course in a homophobic society (Johnson & Colucci, 1999; Kimmel & Sang, 1995; Weston, 1991). These chosen families provide much care and support to each other, as evidenced by the primary caregiving they have provided in times of serious illness such as AIDS and breast cancer (McGoldrick, 2005). Friends also become family in many African American families. In one study, two-thirds of the black participants reported having *fictive kin*, or friends who are neither biologically nor romantically related to the family but who are adopted as family and given the same rights and responsibilities as family members (Chatters & Jayakody, 1995). Friendships also serve an important role in the social convoys of single midlife adults, serving as a chosen family rather than a "poor substitute" for family (Berliner, Jacob, & Schwartzberg, 2005; Marks & Lambert, 1998).

> Why is it important for social workers to recognize the role of fictive kin in the lives of their clients?

Community/Organizational Relationships

Little information is available about midlife relationships in the community and within organizations, but it is increasingly recognized that these relationships are important in the lives of midlife adults (Antonucci et al., 2001). The two most frequently cited places for forming friendships are workplace and neighborhood (Fischer & Phillips, 1982). Mentoring younger employees at work has been found to provide a good forum for the expression of generativity (McDermid, Heilbrun, & DeHaan, 1997). Contacts with neighbors and with volunteer associations are positively correlated with health and well-being in middle adulthood, as in other periods of the adult life course. Black midlife women have been found to score higher on political participation than white middle-aged women in one cross-sectional study. The relationship between this participation and well-being deserves further study (Cole & Stewart, 1996). Participation in a religious community is consistently found to be associated with health and well-being (Antonucci et al., 2001). Participation in voluntary associations becomes a more important part of the social convoy after retirement (Moen, 1997). Alice Rossi (2004b) found that social class makes a difference in the nature of relationships in middle adulthood. Lower income persons are more likely than more affluent persons to be involved in hands-on caregiving to family and friends, and affluent persons are more likely than their lower income peers to be involved in contributing time and money to the larger community.

▧ Work in Middle Adulthood

Like Viktor Spiro and Robert Johnson, the majority of midlife adults engage in paid labor. In the United States, only 20% of people between the ages of 40 and 59 and 24% of people between the ages of 51 and 59 are unemployed. Of those who are unemployed, 54% are retired but have been employed sometime in the past five years and 46% are dependents who have not been employed in the past 20 years. Nonemployed midlife men are more likely to be retired (85%) than nonemployed midlife women (44%). That ratio may change in future midlife cohorts, however, given the trend toward convergence of the work patterns for women and men (Elman & O'Rand, 1998).

Work and retirement have different meanings for different people. Among the meanings work can have are the following (Friedmann & Havighurst, 1954):

- A source of income
- A life routine and way of structuring time
- A source of status and identity
- A context for social interaction
- A meaningful experience that provides a sense of accomplishment

Given these meanings, employment is an important role for midlife adults in many parts of the world, for men and women alike (Dittmann-Kohli, 2005; Kim & Moen, 2001). Helen Tyson and her counselor might want to consider whether returning to paid work would benefit Helen at this time, perhaps providing a source of status and identity, a context for social interaction, and a sense of accomplishment. These possible benefits would have to be weighed against the stress of balancing work and family.

In affluent societies, the last few decades have seen a continuing decline in the average age of retirement, particularly for men (Kim & Moen, 2001; Moen, 2004). This trend exists alongside trends of lengthening of years of both midlife and late adulthood and the fact that adults are entering midlife healthier and better educated than in previous eras. Improved pension plans are at least partially responsible for this trend, but in the United States, there is a growing gap in pension coverage. Between 1979 and 1993, the gap in pension coverage between workers with less than 12 years of education and workers with 16 years or more of education more than quadrupled (O'Rand, 2003). Governmental policies minimize the pension gap in European countries (Heinz, 2003).

Overall, the work patterns of middle-aged workers in the United States have changed considerably in the past three decades. Four trends stand out (Elman & O'Rand, 1998):

1. *Greater job mobility among middle-aged workers.* Changes in the global economy have produced job instability for middle-aged workers. In the late twentieth century, corporate restructuring, mergers, and downsizing revolutionized the previous lockstep career trajectories, and produced much instability in midcareer employment (Moen, 2003). Midlife white-collar workers who had attained midlevel management positions in organizations have been vulnerable to downsizing and reorganization efforts aimed at flattening organizational hierarchies. Midlife blue-collar workers have been vulnerable to changes in job skill requirements as the global economy shifts from an industrial base to a service base. Within these broad trends, gender, class, and race have all made a difference in the work patterns of midlife adults (Elman & O'Rand, 1998). Women are more likely than men to have job disruption throughout the adult life course, although those with higher education and higher income are less vulnerable to job disruption. Race is a factor in the midlife employment disruption for men but not for women. Although black men have more job disruptions than white men, there are no race differences for women when other variables

are controlled. Research indicates that loss of work in middle adulthood is a very critical life event that has negative consequences for emotional well-being (Dittmann-Kohli, 2005).

2. *Greater variability in the timing of retirement.* Like many others in his age group, Robert Johnson has given some thought to the idea that he could retire in his late 50s. Today, many other midlife adults anticipate working into their late 60s or early 70s. The decision to retire is driven by both health and financial status (more particularly, the availability of pension benefits) (Han & Moen, 1999; Moen, 2003). The National Academy on an Aging Society (Sterns & Huyck, 2001) found that 55% of persons in the United States who retired between the ages of 51 and 59 reported a health condition as a major reason for retirement. Although availability of a pension serves as inducement for retirement, men and women who work in physically demanding jobs often seek early retirement whether or not they have access to a pension. Some leave the workforce as a result of disability and become eligible for Social Security disability benefits.

3. *Blurring of the lines between working and retirement.* Many people now phase into retirement. Some middle-aged retirees return to work in different occupational fields than those from which they retired. Others leave a career at some point in middle adulthood for a part-time or temporary job. Increasing numbers of middle-aged workers leave a career position because of downsizing and reorganization and find reemployment in a job with less financial reward, a "bridge job" that carries them into retirement (Moen, 2003; Sterns & Huyck, 2001). As many as half of all the people who permanently retire have left these lower-quality jobs (Elman & O'Rand, 1998).

4. *Increasing educational reentry of midlife workers.* This trend has received little research attention. However, workers with high levels of educational attainment prior to middle adulthood are more likely than their less-educated peers to retrain in middle adulthood (Elman & O'Rand, 1998). This difference is consistent with the theory of cumulative advantage; those who have accumulated resources over the life course are more likely to have the resources for retraining in middle adulthood. But in this era of high job obsolescence, relatively few middle-aged adults will have the luxury of choosing to do one thing at a time; to remain marketable, many middle-aged adults will have to combine work and school.

These trends aside, there is both good news and bad news for the middle-aged worker in the beginning of the twenty-first century. Research indicates that middle-aged workers have greater work satisfaction, organizational commitment, and self-esteem than younger workers (Dittmann-Kohli, 2005). Robert Johnson appears to be a good example of this finding. However, with the current changes in the labor market, employers are ambivalent about middle-aged employees. Employers may see middle-aged workers as "hard-working, reliable, and motivated" (Sterns & Huyck, 2001, p. 476). But they also often cut higher-wage older workers from the payroll as a short-range solution for reducing operating costs and staying competitive.

For some midlife adults, like Viktor Spiro, the issue is not how they will cope with loss of a good job but rather how they can become established in the labor market. In the previous industrial phase, poverty was due to unemployment. In the current era, the major issue is the growing proportion of low-wage, no-benefit jobs. Black men with a high school education or less have been particularly disadvantaged in the current phase of industrialization, largely because of the declining numbers of routine production jobs. Adults like Viktor, with disabilities, have an even harder time finding work that can support them (West, 1991). Even with legislation of the past two decades, much remains to be done to open educational and work opportunities to persons with disabilities. In addition, Viktor has had to contend with language and cultural barriers.

▲ **Photo 8.4**   Research indicates that middle-aged workers often have greater work satisfaction, organizational commitment, and self-esteem than younger workers.

Thus, middle-aged workers, like younger workers, are deeply affected by a changing labor market. Like younger workers, they must understand the patterns in those changes and be proactive in maintaining and updating their skills. As researchers are finding, however, that task is easier for middle-aged workers who arrive in middle adulthood with accumulated resources (e.g., Elman & O'Rand, 1998; Moen, 2003). Marginalization in the labor market in adulthood is the result of "cumulative disadvantage" over the life course. Unfortunately, adults like Viktor Spiro who have employment disruptions early in the adult life course tend to have more job disruption in middle adulthood as well.

⬚ Risk Factors and Protective Factors in Middle Adulthood

From a life course perspective, midlife behavior has both antecedents and consequences. Earlier life experiences can serve either as risk factors or as protective factors for health and well-being during middle adulthood. And midlife behaviors can serve either as risk

Why is it important for social workers to understand both antecedents and consequences of midlife behavior?

factors or as protective factors for future health and well-being. The rapidly growing body of literature on risk, protection, and resilience based on longitudinal research has recently begun to add to our understanding of the antecedents of midlife behavior.

One of the best known programs of research is a study begun by Emmy Werner and associates with a cohort born in 1955 on the island of Kauai, Hawaii. The research participants turned 40 in 1995, and Werner and Ruth Smith (2001) capture their risk factors, protective factors, and resilience in *Journeys from Childhood to Midlife*. They summarize their findings by suggesting that they "taught us a great deal of respect for the self-righting tendencies in human nature and for the capacity of *most* individuals who grew up in adverse circumstances to make a successful adaptation in adulthood" (p. 166). At age 40, compared to previous decades, the overwhelming majority of the participants reported "significant improvements" in work accomplishments, interpersonal relationships, contributions to community, and life satisfaction. Most adults who had a troubled adolescence had recovered by midlife. Many of these adults who had been troubled as youth reported that the "opening of opportunities" (p. 168) in their 20s and 30s had led to major *turning points*. Such turning points included continuing education at community college, military service, marriage to a stable partner, religious conversion, and survival despite a life-threatening illness or accident. At midlife, participants were still benefiting from the presence of a competent, nurturing caregiver in infancy, as well as from the emotional support along the way of extended family, peers, and caring adults outside the family.

Although this research is hopeful, Werner and Smith (2001) also found that one of six of the study cohort was doing poorly at work and in relationships. The earlier risk factors associated with poor midlife adjustment include severe perinatal trauma, small for gestational age birth weight, early childhood poverty, serious health problems in early childhood, problems in early schooling, parental alcoholism and/or serious mental illness, health problems in adolescence, and health problems in the 30s. Viktor Spiro's early life produced several of these risk factors: early childhood poverty, health problems in adolescence, and his father's chronic depression. For men, the most powerful risk factor was parental alcoholism from birth to age 18. Women were especially negatively affected by paternal alcoholism during their adolescence. It is interesting to note that the long-term negative effects of serious health problems in early childhood and adolescence were just beginning to show up at age 40. We are also learning, as we see with Helen Tyson, that some negative effects of childhood and adolescent trauma may not present until early midlife.

Several studies have also examined the effects of midlife behavior, specifically the effects on subsequent health (Stamler et al., 1999; Vita, Terry, Hubert, & Fries, 1998). They have found a number of health behaviors that are risk factors for more severe and prolonged health and disability problems in late adulthood. These include smoking, heavy alcohol use, diet high in fats, overeating, and sedentary lifestyle. Economic deprivation and high levels of stress have also been found to be risk factors throughout the life course (Auerback & Krimgold, 2001; Spiro, 2001). A health behavior that is receiving much research attention as a protective factor for health and well-being in late adulthood is a physical fitness program that includes stretching exercises, weight training, and aerobic exercise (Whitbourne, 2001).

IMPLICATIONS FOR SOCIAL WORK PRACTICE

This discussion has several implications for social work practice with midlife adults:

- Be familiar with the unique pathways your clients have traveled to reach middle adulthood.
- Recognize the role that culture plays in constructing beliefs about appropriate midlife roles and assist clients to explore their beliefs.
- Help clients to think about their own involvement in generative activity and the meaning that this involvement has for their lives.
- Become familiar with biological changes and special health issues in middle adulthood. Engage midlife clients in assessing their own health behaviors.
- Be aware of your own beliefs about intellectual changes in middle adulthood and evaluate those against the available research evidence.
- Be aware of both stability and the capacity for change in personality in middle adulthood.
- Help clients assess the role that spirituality plays in their adjustments in middle adulthood and, where appropriate, to make use of their spiritual resources to solve current problems.
- Engage midlife clients in a mutual assessment of their involvement in a variety of relationships, including romantic relationships, relationships with parents, relationships with children, other family relationships, relationships with friends, and community/organizational relationships.
- Collaborate with social workers and other disciplines to advocate for governmental and corporate solutions to work and family life conflicts.

KEY TERMS

accommodation	extroversion	perimenopause
assimilation (identity)	generativity	premenopause
conjunctive faith	introversion	trait theory
contextual model	kinkeepers	universalizing faith
convoy	life-span theory	
coping mechanism	menopause	

Active Learning

1. Think about how you understand the balance of gains and losses in middle adulthood. Interview three midlife adults ranging in ages from 40 to 60 and ask them whether they see the current phase of their lives as having more gains or more losses over the previous phase.

2. Draw your social convoy as it currently exists with three concentric circles:
   - Inner circle of people who are so close and important to you that you could not do without them
   - Middle circle of people who are not quite that close but are still very close and important to you

- Outer circle of people who are not as close and important as those in the two inner circles but still close enough to be considered part of your support system
- What did you learn from engaging in this exercise? Do you see any changes you would like to make in your social convoy?

3. What evidence do you see of antecedent risk factors and protective factors that are affecting the midlife experiences of Viktor Spiro, Helen Tyson, and Robert Johnson? What evidence do you see of current behaviors that might have consequences, either positive or negative, for their experiences with late adulthood.

WEB RESOURCES

Max Planck Institute for Human Development
www.mpib-berlin.mpg.de/index_js.en.htm

Site presented by the Max Planck Institute for Human Development, Berlin, Germany, contains news and research about life course development.

Network on Successful Midlife Development
www.midmac.medharvard.edu

Site presented by the John D. and Catherine T. MacArthur Foundation Research Network on Successful Midlife Development (MIDMAC) contains an overview of recent research on midlife development and links to other human development research projects.

Boomers International
boomersint.org

Site presented by Boomers International: World Wide Community for the Baby Boomer Generation contains information from the trivial to the serious on the popular culture of the baby boomer generation.

MEDLINEplus: Hormone Replacement Therapy
www.nlm.nih.gov/medlineplus/hormonereplacementtherapy.html

Site presented by the National Institute on Aging contains the latest news on research on hormone replacement therapy to treat menopause in midlife women.

Families and Work Institute
www.familiesandwork.org

Site presented by the Families and Work Institute contains information on work-life research, community mobilization forums, information on the Fatherhood Project, and frequently asked questions.

Seattle Longitudinal Study
geron.psu.edu/sls/index.html

Site at Pennsylvania State University presents information on the Seattle Longitudinal Study and publications from the study.

CHAPTER

9

LATE ADULTHOOD

Michael Melendez

Peter Maramaldi

Matthias J. Naleppa

Key Ideas	371
Case Study 9.1: ■ The Smiths in Early Retirement	372
Case Study 9.2: ■ Ms. Ruby Johnson, Caretaker for Three Generations	373
Case Study 9.3: ■ The Moros' Increasing Needs for Care	374
Demographics of the Older Population	374
Cultural Construction of Late Adulthood	379
Psychosocial Theoretical Perspectives on Social Gerontology	382
Biological Changes in Late Adulthood	386
Health and Longevity	387
Age-Related Changes in Physiology	389
Psychological Changes in Late Adulthood	391
Personality Changes	391
Intellectual Changes, Learning, and Memory	392
Mental Health and Mental Disorders	394
Social Role Transitions and Life Events of Late Adulthood	396
Families in Later Life	396
Grandparenthood	399
Work and Retirement	401
Caregiving and Care Receiving	404
Widowhood	405
Institutionalization	405

The Search for Personal Meaning 407
Resources for Meeting the Needs of Elderly Persons 408
    Informal Resources 408
    Formal Resources 409
Risk Factors and Protective Factors in Late Adulthood 411
Implications for Social Work Practice 413
Key Terms 413
Active Learning 414
Web Resources 414

❖ How will the trend toward increased longevity affect family life and social work practice?

❖ What do social workers need to understand about the biological, psychological, social, and spiritual changes in late adulthood and the coping mechanisms used to adapt to these changes?

❖ What formal and informal resources are available for meeting the needs of elderly persons?

KEY IDEAS

As you read this chapter, take note of these central ideas:

1. Unlike in earlier historical eras, many people in the United States and other industrialized countries today reach the life phase of late adulthood, and the older population is a very heterogeneous group, including the young-old (65 to 74 years), the middle-old (75 to 84 years), and the oldest-old (85 and above). In this chapter, we consider the young-old and the middle-old.

2. The cumulative effect of health disparities based on race, ethnicity, gender, and socioeconomic status impacts the quality of aging for significant subpopulations of older people in the United States and around the world.

3. The most commonly discussed psychosocial theories of social gerontology are disengagement, activity, continuity, social construction, feminist, social exchange, life course, and age stratification theories; the most common theories of biological aging are the genetic theories, molecular/cellular theories, and system theories.

4. All systems of the body appear to be affected during the aging process.

5. It has been difficult to understand psychological changes in late adulthood without long-term longitudinal research, but recent longitudinal research suggests that with age and experience, individuals tend to use more adaptive coping mechanisms.

6. Families play an important role in late adulthood, and as a result of increased longevity, multigenerational families are more common than ever.

7. Although most persons enter retirement in late adulthood, some individuals continue to work even after they are eligible to retire, either out of financial necessity or by choice.

8. Older adults rely on a number of both informal and formal resources to meet their changing needs.

The Smiths in Early Retirement

The Smiths are a European American couple in their early retirement years who have sought out couples counseling. Lois Smith is 66 and Gene Smith is 68 years of age. They have lived in the same quiet suburban neighborhood since they married 20 years ago. When they met, Gene was a widower and Lois had been divorced for three years. They have no children from this marriage but three children from Lois's first marriage. The Smiths are grandparents to the three children of their married daughter, who lives four hours away. Their two sons are both single and also live in a different city. The Smiths visit their children frequently, but family and holiday gatherings usually take place at the Smiths' house.

The Smiths live in a comfortable home, but their neighborhood has changed over the years. When they bought the house, many other families were in the same life stage, raising adolescent children and seeing them move out as young adults. Many of the neighbors from that time have since moved, and the neighborhood has undergone a change to young families with children. Although the Smiths feel connected to the community, they do not have much interaction with the people in their immediate neighborhood. Only one other neighbor, a woman in her mid-80s, is an older adult. This neighbor has difficulty walking and no longer drives a car. The Smiths help her with chores around the house and often take her shopping.

Until her divorce, Lois had focused primarily on raising her children. After the divorce at age 43, she needed to enter the job market. Without formal education beyond high school, she had difficulty finding employment. She worked in a number of low-paying short-term jobs before finding a permanent position as a secretary at a small local company. She has only a small retirement benefit from her 12 years on that job. Gene had worked as bookkeeper and later assistant manager with a local hardware store for more than 30 years. Although their combined retirement benefits enable them to lead a comfortable retirement, Gene continues to work at the hardware store on a part-time basis.

The transition into retirement has not been easy for the Smiths. Both Gene and Lois retired last year, which required them to adjust all at once to a decrease in income. Much more difficult, however, has been the loss of status and feeling of void that they are experiencing. Both were accustomed to the structure that was provided by work. Gene gladly assists in his former company on a part-time basis, but he worries that his employer will think he's getting too old. Lois has no plans to reenter the workforce. She would like her daughter to live closer so she could spend more time with the grandchildren. Although the infrequency of the visits with the grandchildren has placed some strain on Lois's relationship with her daughter, especially in the period following her retirement, Lois has now begun to enjoy the trips to visit with her daughter as a welcome change in her daily routine. But those visits are relatively infrequent, and Lois often wishes she had more to do.

Ms. Ruby Johnson, Caretaker for Three Generations

Ms. Ruby Johnson is a handsome woman who describes herself as a "hard-boiled, 71-year-old African American" who spent the first 30 years of her life in Harlem, until she settled in the Bronx, New York. She married at 19 and lived with her husband until her 30th birthday. During her initial assessment for case management services, she explained her divorce with what appeared to be great pride. On her 29th birthday, Ruby told her husband that he had one more year to choose between "me and the bottle." She tolerated his daily drinking for another year, but when he came home drunk on her 30th birthday, she took their 6-year-old daughter and left him and, she explained, "never looked back."

Ruby immediately got a relatively high-paying—albeit tedious—job working for the postal service. At the same time, she found the Bronx apartment, in which she has resided for the past 41 years. Ruby lived there with her daughter, Darlene, for 18 years until she "put that girl out" on what she describes as the saddest day of her life.

Darlene was 21 when she made Ruby the grandmother of Tiffany, a vivacious little girl in good health. A year later, Darlene began using drugs when Tiffany's father abandoned them. By the time Darlene was 24, she had a series of warnings and arrests for drug possession and prostitution. Ruby explained that it "broke my heart that my little girl was out there sellin' herself for drug money." Continuing the story in an unusually angry tone, she explained that "I wasn't gonna have no 'hoe' live in my house."

During her initial interview, Ruby's anger was betrayed by a flicker of pride when she explained that Darlene, now 46, has been drug free for more than 20 years. Tiffany is 25 and lives with her husband and two children. They have taken Darlene into their home to help Ruby. Ruby flashed a big smile when she shared that "Tiffany and Carl [her husband] made me a great-grandma twice, and they are taking care of Darlene for me now." Darlene also has a younger daughter—Rebecca—from what Ruby describes as another "bad" relationship with a "no good man." Rebecca, age 16, has been living with Ruby for the past two years since she started having difficulty in school and needed more supervision than Darlene was able to provide.

In addition, about a year ago, Ruby became the care provider for her father, George. He is 89 and moved into Ruby's apartment because he was no longer able to live independently after his brother's death. On most weeknights, Ruby cooks for her father, her granddaughter, and everyone at Tiffany's house as well. Ruby says she loves having her family around, but she just doesn't have half the energy she used to have.

Ruby retired five years ago from the postal service, where she worked for 36 years. In addition to her pension and Social Security, she now earns a small amount for working part-time providing child care for a former coworker's daughter. Ruby explains that she has to take the extra work in order to cover her father's prescription expenses not covered by his Medicare benefits, and help pay medical/prescription bills for Tiffany's household. Tiffany and Carl receive no medical benefits from their employers and are considering lowering their income in order to qualify for Medicaid benefits. Ruby wants them to keep working, so she has been trying to use her connections to get them jobs with the postal service. Ruby reports this to be her greatest frustration, because her best postal service contacts are "either retired or dead."

Although Ruby's health is currently stable, she is particularly concerned that it may worsen. She is diabetic and insulin dependent and worries about all the family members for whom she feels responsible. During the initial interview, Ruby confided that she thinks that her physical demise has begun. Her greatest fear is death; not for herself, she says, but for the effect it would have on her family. She then asked her social worker to help her find a way to ensure their well-being after her death.

The Moros' Increasing Needs for Care

Frank Moro is an 82-year-old married man who lives with his 80-year-old wife, Camille, in their own home. Both Frank and Camille are second-generation Italian Americans. Frank had a stroke one year ago that resulted in a right-side paralysis. He has several other limiting medical conditions, including arthritis, hypertension, and a partial loss of vision. He perceives his health to be fair, even though his level of functioning in activities of daily living is very low. He needs assistance in using the toilet, rising from a chair, getting in and out of bed, moving around, and personal care. Frank has a wheelchair that he rarely uses. He shows a slight cognitive decline on a standardized measurement tool. Camille is the primary caregiver, assisting her husband in his personal care, helping him in and out of bed, and assisting him with toileting. The two sons who live in the area also provide assistance, especially with home repairs and financial arrangements.

Frank was referred by his physical therapist to a case management program. Since his stroke, he is not able to ambulate independently. His wife and sons have reported being overwhelmed by round-the-clock caregiving.

During the first home visit, his social worker identified several needs: Frank needed assistance with his personal care and mobility, and he did not use his wheelchair. Furthermore, Camille needed some respite. After exploring Frank's personal care needs, the social worker told the Moros about the services available to them. Then the three of them agreed to undertake a couple of tasks: the social worker would contact a home health aide to set up a meeting, and the Moros would discuss their needs and make arrangements with the home health aide. These tasks were completed quickly, and the aide began providing services within a week.

Two other target problems would be met by the same solution. After some discussion, it was decided that Frank would benefit from medical adult day care, which could assist in maintaining his mobility. Day care would also provide respite for Camille. Implementing this plan took a little longer, however, because the Moros had to visit an adult day care center, apply, and arrange for transportation before Frank could begin to attend.

Another area of need, identified by Camille, related to Frank's unwillingness to use the wheelchair. In his culture, he said, men do not advertise physical limitations and dependence on others. His self-esteem as well as cultural factors seemed to be hindering efforts to increase his mobility. With a great deal of persuasion, the social worker helped Frank see the benefits of using a wheelchair, and he finally agreed to try it out for a few days. Although he began very reluctantly, after several weeks Frank got used to the wheelchair. He uses it on a daily basis now and concedes that it has significantly enhanced his independence.

Demographics of the Older Population

Every client in these stories could be considered old, and yet, they are functioning in different ways and at different levels. In the context of U.S. society, the term *old* can have many meanings. These meanings reflect attitudes, assumptions, biases, and cultural interpretations of what it means to grow older. In discussing life course trajectories, we commonly use the terms *older population* or *elderly persons* to refer to those over 65 years of age. But an

Olympic gymnast is "old" at age 25, a president of the United States is "young" at age 50, and a 70-year-old may not consider herself "old" at all.

Late adulthood is perhaps a more precise term than *old*, but it can still be confusing because of the 50-year range of ages it may include. *Late adulthood* is considered to start at 65 and continue through the 85-and-older range. Many people today reach the life stage of late adulthood. In 2000, there were approximately 420 million people 65 years or older in the world (Aldwin & Gilmer, 2004). Globally, the United States is fairly young as wealthy nations go, with just over 12% of its population 65 and older. Most European countries average 15% of their population as 65 or older. Japan and Italy's older population stands at 19% of the total population (Federal Interagency Forum on Aging Related Statistics, 2004). The enormous increase in life expectancy is not unique to the United States. Nor is it occurring only in the developed world. Most nations of the world have a growing older population; half of the population over 65 lives in nonindustrialized or newly industrializing countries. However, this is changing, and by 2030, it is anticipated that the industrialized world will have twice the number of older adults of the nonindustrialized world (Aldwin & Gilmer, 2004). Disability rates are declining among the older population in the United States, Japan, and a number of European nations, contributing to an extended life expectancy rate internationally (American Association of Retired Persons, 2003).

According to the U.S. Census, the 85 and older population is the fastest growing segment of the aging population, projected to increase from 4.2 million in 2000 to 8.9 million in 2030 (Administration on Aging, 2006a). There are increasing numbers of people 100 years and older, a 73% increase from 1990 figures. As of 2003, persons reaching age 65 have an average life expectancy of an additional 18.5 years (19.8 years for females and 16.8 for males). A child born in 2003 could expect to live 77.6 years, about 30 years longer than a child born in 1900 (Administration on Aging, 2005).

Increased life expectancy is a product of a number of factors: decrease in mortality of children and young adults, decreased mortality among the aging, improved health technology, and other factors. Life expectancy also varies by race, gender, and socioeconomic status. On average whites can expect to live five and a half years longer than minority groups in the United States. The gap is anticipated to narrow to a point where life expectancy for whites is two years longer than for blacks (Administration on Aging, 2006b; George, 2005; Rieker & Bird, 2005, Williams, 2005).

Just a century ago, it was uncommon to reach 65. The first population census of the United States, conducted in 1870, estimated about 3% of the population to be over 65 years of age. Today, more than three-fourths of all persons in the United States live to be 65 (Walker, Manoogian-O'Dell, McGraw, & White, 2001). The U.S. Census Bureau estimates that in the next 25 years, the elderly population will double to 72 million. By 2030 one in five people in the United States will be 65 or older. People in the United States are living longer, have lower rates of disability, are less likely to live in poverty, and on average have higher levels of education than in the past (Administration on Aging, 2005; U.S. Census Bureau, 2004). These salutary developments are not without social and economic implications for both the aging and general population.

> What factors are leading to this trend toward increased longevity?

Age structure, the segmentation of society by age, will affect the economic and social condition of the nation, especially as it regards dependence. An interesting side effect of the growing elderly population is a shifting **dependency ratio**—a demographic indicator that expresses the degree of demand placed on society by the young and the aged combined (Morgan & Kunkel, 1996). There are three dependency ratios: the elderly dependency ratio, the number of elders 65 and older per 100 people ages 18 to 64; the child dependency ratio, the number of children under 18 per 100 persons ages 18 to 64; and the total dependency ratio, the combination of both of these categories.

The nature of the U.S. dependency ratio has changed gradually over the past century, as the percentage of children in the population has decreased and the percentage of dependent older adults has increased. As Exhibit 9.1 demonstrates, the elderly dependency ratio is predicted to continue to increase at a fairly rapid pace in the near future. U.S. Census projections indicate small increases of elderly dependency from 20.9 per 100 persons age 18 to 64 in 1995 to 21.2 per 100 in 2010. Steep increases are projected for 2010 to 2030 with stability occurring at the level of 36 per 100 by 2050. The child dependency ratio has shown a modest "U" trend. There were about 43 persons under 18 per 100 persons ages 18 to 64 in 1995 with an anticipated drop to 39 per 100 by 2010 and expected increase to 43 by 2030. The overall dependency ratio is expected to stabilize to about 79 per 100 persons ages 18 to 64 between 2030 and 2050 (Administration on Aging, 2006b). The social and economic implications of this increase in the dependency ratio are the focus and concern of many scholars and policy makers.

The older population encompasses a broad age range, and is often categorized into subgroups: the young-old (age 65 to 74), the middle-old (age 75 to 84), and the oldest-old (over 85).

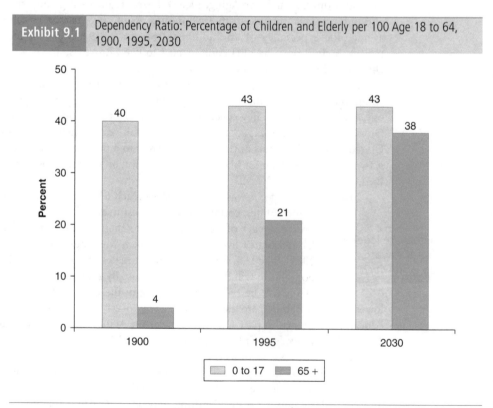

| Exhibit 9.1 | Dependency Ratio: Percentage of Children and Elderly per 100 Age 18 to 64, 1900, 1995, 2030 |

SOURCE: Administration on Aging, 2006b.

The Smiths and Ruby Johnson exemplify the young-old, the Moros the middle-old. In this chapter, we discuss those persons in the young-old and middle-old categories, ages approximately 65 to 84. Very late adulthood is discussed in Chapter 10, covering ages 85 and over.

The U.S. society is one of the most racially and ethnically diverse societies in the world. By 2050 it has been predicted that 48% of the general population will be minorities with approximately one-third of the older adults reflecting minority communities. The aging population reflects these shifting trends in the general population. The data available from 2004 indicate that 18% of adults over age 65 are nonwhite, with 8% non-Hispanic black, 6% Hispanic, almost 3% Asian and Pacific Islander, and 1% indigenous Americans (Administration on Aging, 2006a). As demonstrated in Exhibit 9.2, racial and ethnic composition of older adults is projected to change profoundly by 2050. This change reflects the decline in the white elderly (from 83% of older Americans to 72% in the year 2030 and 66% by 2050), as well as dramatic increases in all other categories. The U.S. Census Bureau estimates that between 2000 and 2050, the Hispanic population will be the fastest growing subpopulation, accounting for 18% of older adults by 2050. Hispanics will be a larger and older group than the black non-Hispanic population of elders that is projected to be 12%. Nine percent of elders will be non-Hispanic Asian and Pacific Island persons, and 1% indigenous/Native Americans (Administration on Aging, 2005, 2006c, 2006d). Proportionally, 6.8% of the populations of minorities are older as compared to 15% of the white population. In 2004, 18.7% of the elderly people of color were living in poverty, twice that of the total older population whose poverty rate is at 9.8% (Administration on Aging, 2006c, 2006d).

| Exhibit 9.2 | Racial Makeup of U.S. Elderly Population, 2004, 2050 |

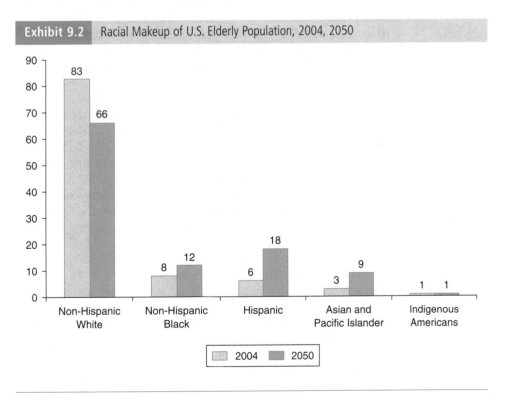

Source: Administration on Aging, 2006b, 2006c, 2006d.

There are a number of factors that account for this ethnic and racial shift in the U.S. population. They include high fertility rates among black, Hispanic, and Asian populations; low mortality rates among Asians and Hispanics; and the influence of immigration rates on Asian and Hispanic populations (Administration on Aging, 2006b). The number of immigrants age 60 and older has risen over the past thirty years, for approximately 70,000 immigrants in 2001 were elderly compared to 20,000 in 1969. In 2001, upon arrival in the United States, nearly 7% of immigrants were age 60 or older. Additionally, the number of immigrants admitted as parents of U.S. citizens increased from 45,000 in 1986 to over 80,000 in 2001 (Wilmoth & Longino, 2006).

Among the older population in the United States, women—especially those in very late adulthood (85 and older)—continue to outnumber men across all racial and ethnic groups. Census data analyzed in 2004 indicate that older women (21.1 million) outnumber older men (15.2 million). In 2000, the sex ratio stood at 82 males per 100 females in the age group 65 to 74. The proportion of men drops with age, with 65 men for every 100 women in the 75 to 84 age group, and 41 men for every 100 women in the 85 years and older age group. As long as men exceed women in mortality rates, women will outnumber men among the elderly, especially in the oldest-old group of 85 years or more (Administration on Aging, 2005; U.S. Census Bureau, 2004).

One of the biggest gender differences in life circumstances of older adults is the difference in marital status. Older men are more likely to be married than older women. According to census data from 2003, 76% of men 65 or older were married as compared to 42% of women. As people age the overall proportion of those married decreases (Federal Interagency Forum on Aging-Related Statistics, 2004). This is an important consideration, because marital status influences a person's emotional and economic status, living arrangement, and caregiving needs. As of 2004, the rate of divorce and separation for older Americans was 10.6%. This figure has doubled since 1980, when it stood at 5.3%. Approximately 11% of women and 10% of men age 65 or older were divorced in 2004 (Administration on Aging, 2005).

Gender, race, and ethnicity have a significant effect on the economic status of elderly individuals. In general, poverty rates increase with age across the late adult years. As of 2004, 9.8% of elderly persons were below the poverty level, a statistically significant drop from 10.5% in 2003. An additional 6.7% of elderly persons are classified as "near poor" (income levels between poverty level and 125% of that level). The poverty rate for

> **How are gender, race, ethnicity, and social class related in late adulthood?**

persons 65 to 74 was 9%, 12% for the population between the ages of 65 to 74, and 14% for those ages 85 and older. However, elderly men have a significantly lower poverty rate than elderly women (7% vs. 17%).

The poverty rates also differ for racial groups. One in 12 (7.5%) elderly whites was poor in 2004, as compared to 23.9% of elderly African Americans, 13.6% of Asians, and 18.7% of Hispanics. Almost 40% of those older adults with the highest poverty levels were older   African American and Hispanic women living alone (Administration on Aging, 2005). Although it was initially thought that trends indicated that the poverty rate was declining for all racial and ethnic groups of older adults, there is mounting evidence of increasing economic disparities across groups (Schoeni, Martin, Andreski, & Freedman, 2005; Wilmoth & Longino, 2006).

The geographic distribution of the elderly population varies considerably by states across the United States. In 2004, about half (52%) of older U.S. adults were concentrated in nine states: California, Florida, New York, Texas, Pennsylvania, Ohio, Illinois, Michigan, and New Jersey (Administration on Aging, 2005). Between 1990 and 2000, every state experienced population increases in the proportion of age 65 and older, ranging from a 1% increase in Rhode Island to a 79% increase in Nevada. Only the District of Columbia showed a decrease in the proportion of people age 65 and older. The greatest regional increases in percentages of older people occurred in the West (20%) and the South (16%). Increases occurred at significantly lower rates in the Midwest (7%) and the Northeast (5%). Between 1994 and 2004, eight states had a 20% increase in their 65 and older population: Nevada, Alaska, Arizona, New Mexico, Colorado, Delaware, Utah, and Idaho (U.S. Census Bureau, 2004).

Residential mobility has a significant impact on the distribution of the elderly population. However, older adults are less likely to change residence than any other age group. In 2004, only 4.4% of older persons moved as opposed to 14.3% of the population under 65. More than half (53.7%) of older adults who moved stayed within the same county and 76% remained in the same state (Administration on Aging, 2005). Nevertheless, migration of older persons to states such as Florida after retirement contributes to its high percentage of elderly residents. On the other hand, high percentages of elderly residents in some other regions are the result of outward migration by younger people (Hobbs & Damon, 1997).

Residential mobility can also lead to changing age structures within neighborhoods and thus affect the elderly person's life. A recent study noted that the role of neighborhood structural context, as measured by poverty, residential stability, and aged-based demographic concentration, was predictive of the health and well being of elders (Subramanian, Kubzansky, Berman, Fay, & Kawachi, 2006). For example, the Smiths used to be a "typical" family in their neighborhood. Now, as one of only two households with elderly occupants, they are the exception.

▧ Cultural Construction of Late Adulthood

The ethnic/racial diversity of the older population in the United States underscores the complexity and importance of taking cultural differences in perceptions of aging into account. A

> How important is social age in defining late adulthood?

salient example of cultural differences in approaches to aging is the contrasts between traditional Chinese and mainstream U.S. beliefs and values. China has been described in anthropological literature as a "gerontocracy," wherein older people are venerated, given deference, and valued in nearly every task. Benefiting from the Confucian values of filial piety, older people hold a revered position in the family and society.

By contrast, consider the traditional cultural influences in the United States, where individualism, independence, and self-reliance are core values that inherently conflict with the aging process. In the United States, older people have traditionally been collectively regarded as dependent, and cultural values dictate that older people living independently are given higher regard than those requiring assistance. As people age, they strive to maintain the independence and avoid—at all costs—becoming a burden to their family. Older people in the United States typically resort to intervention from private or social programs to maintain their independence rather than turning to family. By contrast, Chinese elders traditionally looked forward to the day when they would become part of their children's household, to live out their days being venerated by their families (Kao & Lam, 1997).

No discussion of comparisons between cultures would be complete without mention of differences that occur within groups. An individual Chinese person might value independence.

▲ **Photos 9.1a & b**   Family relationships have been found to be closer and more central for older women than for older men.

And an individual in the United States might be closer to the Confucian value of filial piety than traditional U.S. values. Additionally, processes such as acculturation, assimilation, and bicultural socialization further influence the norms, values, expectations, and beliefs of all cultural groups, including that which is considered the dominate cultural norm. Globalization of economics and information exchange also impact and change the cultural norms of other countries so that culture must be construed as something that is dynamic, fluid, emergent, improvisational, and enacted (Laird, 1998). In fact, U.S. values of aging appear to be shifting, influenced in part by political and market forces. In the United States, we are now bombarded with contradictory information about aging—media presentations of long-lived, vibrant older adults are juxtaposed with media presentations of nursing home horror stories (Vaillant, 2002).

In his recent book, *Aging Well*, George Vaillant (2002) raises the question, "Will the longevity granted to us by modern medicine be a curse or a blessing?" (p. 3). The answer, he suggests, is influenced by individual, societal, and cultural values, but his research makes him optimistic. Vaillant reports on the most long-term longitudinal research available, the Study of Adult Development. The study includes three separate cohorts of 824 persons, all of whom have been studied since adolescence:

1. *268 socially advantaged graduates of Harvard University born about 1920.* These research participants were selected for their physical and psychological health as they began college.

2. *456 socially disadvantaged inner-city men born in 1930.* These research participants were selected because they were nondelinquent at age 14. Half of their families were known to five or more social agencies, and more than two-thirds of their families had been recent public welfare recipients.

3. *90 middle-class intellectually gifted women born about 1910.* These participants were selected for their high IQs when they were in California elementary schools.

A significant limitation of the study is the lack of racial and ethnic diversity among the participants, who are almost exclusively white. The great strength of the study is its ability to control cohort effects by following the same participants over such a long period of time.

Much of the news from the Study of Adult Development is good news. Vaillant reminds us that Immanuel Kant wrote his first book of philosophy at 57, Titian created many art works after 76, Ben Franklin invented bifocals at 78, and Will Durant won a Pulitzer Prize for history at 83. Unless they develop a brain disease, the majority of older adults maintain a "modest sense of well-being" (p. 5) until a few months before they die. Older adults are also less depressed than the general population. Many older adults acknowledge hardships of aging but also see a reason to continue to live. Vaillant concludes that "positive aging means to love, to work, to learn something we did not know yesterday, and to enjoy the remaining precious moments with loved ones" (p. 16). Although he found many paths to successful aging, Vaillant identifies six traits for "growing old with grace," found in Exhibit 9.3.

> How much choice do we have over the six traits for "growing old with grace"?

Vaillant reports that he had originally planned to study only the rate of physical deterioration as individuals age. He had absorbed the cultural bias that aging was only about decay. He recounts a letter he received from one study participant, who wrote, "You ask us what we can no longer do . . . but I detect little curiosity about our adaptability, our zest for life, how our old age is, or isn't, predictable from what went before" (p. 36). This feedback influenced Vaillant to pursue the possibilities in late adulthood, without denying the special hardships of this life phase. Note that this study participant and other members of the current generation of older adults are exercising human agency and, in the process, producing changes in some of the culture of aging in the United States.

A more recent study using longitudinal data from the Americans' Changing Lives study (ACL) continues to examine the question of the impact of life expectancy and quality of life as a person ages. This is a nationally representative sample of adults age 25 years and older, first interviewed in 1986 and re-interviewed in 1989, 1994, and 2001/2002 (House, Lantz, & Herd, 2005). The ACL was designed to address one central dilemma of research on aging and health: whether increased life expectancy in the United States and other developed nations

Exhibit 9.3	Six Traits for Growing Old With Grace

1. Caring about others and remaining open to new ideas

2. Showing cheerful tolerance of the indignities of old age

3. Maintaining hope

4. Maintaining a sense of humor and capacity for play

5. Taking sustenance from past accomplishments while remaining curious and continuing to learn from the next generation

6. Maintaining contact and intimacy with old friends

Source: Vaillant, 2002, pp. 310–311.

foreshadowed a scenario of longer life but worsening health with the result of increasing chronically ill and functionally limited and disabled people requiring expensive medical and long term care—or whether, through increased understanding of psychosocial as well as biomedical risk factors, the onset of serious morbidity and attendant functional limitation and disability could be potentially postponed or "compressed."

These authors focused on socioeconomic disparities in health changes through the middle and later years. They represent a set of scholars who are examining a theoretical concept of cumulative advantage and disadvantage and its role in understanding differential aging among various populations (Hatch, 2005; Wickrama, Conger, & Abraham, 2005). They argue that multiple interacting factors throughout the life course impact the quality of the health of older individuals. For example, early poverty, lifetime of poverty, poor environmental conditions, poor education, race, and gender have a direct impact on how a person will age. It is not a simple linear causal track, but instead reflects the complexity of interacting risk and protective factors.

Reviewing research findings from the ACL study, House et al., (2005) examined the impact of two factors related to socioeconomic status (SES), education and income, on poor health. They found that overall socioeconomic disparities do impact health outcomes rather than the reverse. Additionally, they found that education has a greater impact than income on the onset of functional limitations/disabilities. Income, however, has a greater impact on the progression of functional limitations. Finally, the impact of educational disparities on the onset of functional limitations increased strikingly in later middle and early old age, with more highly educated individuals postponing limitations and thus compressing the number of years spent with limitations (pp. 55–84).

Other authors (George, 2005; Rieker & Bird, 2005; Williams, 2005) argue that SES is not the sole explanatory factor for the quality of aging. George argues that SES is only one form of social stratification, arguing that gender and race/ethnicity are other important forms of stratification. Although they are significantly related to SES, their associations with health extend beyond SES in complex ways. Race and gender are partial determinants of SES. However they are "ascribed statuses" that involve basic obstacles and barriers to opportunities and resources associated with better aging. Additionally, these ascribed statuses contend with overt forms of and micro-aggressions associated with racism and sexism. For these authors, this raises the question as to whether race and gender are more fundamentally associated with illness and poor quality of aging than the more general category of SES.

Psychosocial Theoretical Perspectives on Social Gerontology

How social workers see and interpret aging will inspire our interventions with older adults. **Social gerontology**—the social science that studies human aging—offers several theoretical perspectives that can explain the process of growing old. Eight predominant theories of social gerontology are introduced here. An overview of the primary concepts of each theory is presented in Exhibit 9.4.

1. *Disengagement theory.* **Disengagement theory** suggests that as elderly individuals grow older, they gradually decrease their social interactions and ties and become increasingly

Exhibit 9.4	Psychosocial Theoretical Perspectives on Social Gerontology
Theory	*Primary Concept*
Disengagement theory	Elderly persons gradually disengage from society.
Activity theory	Level of life satisfaction is related to level of activity.
Continuity theory	Elderly persons continue to adapt and continue their interaction patterns.
Social construction theory	Self-concepts arise through interaction with the environment.
Feminist theory	Gender is an important organizing factor in the aging experience.
Social exchange theory	Resource exchanges in interpersonal interactions change with age.
Life course perspective	Aging is a dynamic, lifelong process characterized by many transitions.
Age stratification perspective	Society is stratified by age, which determines people's roles and rights.

self-preoccupied (Cumming & Henry, 1961). This is sometimes seen as a coping mechanism in the face of ongoing deterioration and loss (Tobin, 1988). Considering Frank Moro, for example, you might interpret his initial lack of initiative to increase his mobility by using the wheelchair as a sign of his disengagement from others. It also could simply be a normative depressive reaction to a new loss from which he will recover. In addition, society disengages itself from older adults. Although disengagement is seen as a normative and functional process of transferring power within society, the theory does not explain, for example, the fact that a growing number of older persons, like Gene and Lois Smith, continue to assume active roles in society (Hendricks & Hatch, 2006). Disengagement theory has received much criticism and little research support.

2. *Activity theory.* **Activity theory** states that higher levels of activity and involvement are directly related to higher levels of life satisfaction in elderly people (Havighurst, 1968). If they can, individuals stay active and involved, and carry on as many activities of middle adulthood as possible. There is growing evidence that examining and promoting physical activity is associated with postponing functional limitation and disability (Benjamin, Edwards, & Bharti, 2005). Activity theory has received some criticism for not addressing relatively high levels of satisfaction for individuals like Ms. Johnson, whose level of activity is declining. It also does not address the choice made by many older individuals to adopt a more relaxed lifestyle.

An alternative construct for measuring quality of aging is the concept of self-efficacy. Self-efficacy is the perception, or belief, that one has the ability to produce, and to regulate events in one's life and achieve desired goals. Having a sense of mastery and competence can be associated with a whole range of activities, not just physical activity. Brandtstadter (2006) argues that self-efficacy is more predictive of positive aging than life satisfaction.

3. *Continuity theory.* **Continuity theory** was developed in response to critiques of the disengagement and activity theories. According to continuity theory, individuals adapt to changes by using the same coping styles they have used throughout the life course, and they adopt new roles that substitute for roles lost because of age (Neugarten, Havighurst, & Tobin,

▲ **Photo 9.2**   Variables that often predict healthy aging include practicing healthy habits such as exercising, eating well, maintaining a healthy weight, and not smoking or abusing alcohol.

1968). Individual personality differences are seen as a major influence in adaptation to old age. Those individuals who were active earlier in life stay active in later life, whereas those who adopted a more passive lifestyle continue to do so in old age. Older adults also typically retain the same stance concerning religion and sex as they always did. Current scholarship considers the interaction between personal and contextual factors that promote or impede the accomplishment of desired goals and new roles, recognizing that individuals have control over some contextual factors but not others (Brandtstadter, 2006). Continuity theory might help counsel someone like Lois Smith. Just as she adapted actively to her divorce by reentering the job market later in life, she might actively seek new roles in retirement. She might find great satisfaction in volunteering in her church and in being a grandmother.

4. *Social construction theory.* **Social construction theory** aims to understand and explain the influence of social definitions, social interactions, and social structures on the individual elderly person. This theoretical framework suggests that ways of understanding are shaped by the cultural, social, historical, political, and economic conditions in which knowledge is developed, thus values are associated with various ways of understanding (Dean, 1993). Conceptions about aging arise through interactions of an individual with the social environment (Dannefer & Perlmutter, 1990). For instance, George Vaillant's conceptions of aging changed as he followed research participants into late adulthood. His emphasis on the negative aspects of aging was counterbalanced by a respondents' own sense of a fulfilling life. The recent conceptualization of "gerotranscendence" is an example of the application of social constructionist theory to aging. The idea of gerotranscendence holds that human development extends into old age and does not simply end or diminish with aging. In one

focus group process, Wadensten (2005) found that participants identified the concept of gerotranscendence as salient and beneficial to them because it gave them a more positive view of aging, allowing them to affirm themselves as they are.

5. *Feminist theory.* Proponents of **feminist theories** of aging suggest that gender is a key factor in understanding a person's aging experience. They contend that because gender is a critical social stratification factor with attendant power, privilege, and status that produces inequalities and disparities throughout the life course, we can only understand aging by taking gender into account (Arber & Ginn, 1995). Gender is viewed as influencing the life course trajectory by impacting access and opportunity, health disparities, disparities in socioeconomic opportunities, and by creating a lifelong condition of "constrained choice" (Rieker & Bird, 2005). Gabriela Spector-Mersel (2006) argues that in Western societies, older persons have been portrayed as "ungendered." Older men are in a paradoxical position because the metaphors for old age are the opposite of the metaphors for masculinity in these societies. Think, for example, about Camille Moro's experience as a caregiver to her husband and about Ms. Johnson's experience as a single older woman. How might their personal situations differ if they were men?

6. *Social exchange theory.* **Social exchange theory** is built on the notion that an exchange of resources takes place in all interpersonal interactions (Blau, 1964; Homans, 1961). This theory is rooted in an analysis of values developed from a market-driven capitalist society. Individuals will only engage in an exchange if they perceive a favorable cost/benefit ratio or if they see no better alternatives (Hendricks, 1987). As individuals become older, however, the resources they are able to bring to the exchange begin to shift. Exchange theory bases its explanation of the realignment of roles, values, and contributions of older adults on this assumption. For example, many older persons get involved in volunteer activities; this seemingly altruistic activity may also be seen as fulfilling an emotional need that provides a personal gain. Older individuals who withdraw from social activities may perceive their personal resources as diminished to the point where they have little left to bring to an exchange, thus leading to their increasing seclusion from social interactions. As social workers, then, it is important to explore how Frank and Camille Moro are dealing with the shift in resources within their relationship.

7. *Life course perspective.* From the **life course perspective**, the conceptual framework for this book, aging is a dynamic, lifelong process. Human development is characterized by multidirectionality, multifunctionality, plasticity, and continuity in the person's experiences of gains and losses over the life course (Greve & Staudinger, 2006). Individuals go through many transitions in the course of their life span. Human development continues through aging and involves the interaction of person-specific factors, social structures, and personal agency (Hendricks & Hatch, 2006). The era they live in, the cohort they belong to, and personal and environmental factors influence individuals during these transitions.

8. *Age stratification perspective.* The framework of **age stratification** falls into the tradition of the life course perspective (Foner, 1995; Riley, 1971). Stratification is a sociological concept that describes a given hierarchy that exists in a given society. Social stratification is both multidimensional and interactive as individuals occupy multiple social locations with varying amounts of power, privilege, and status. The age stratification perspective suggests that, similar to the way society is structured by socioeconomic class, it is also stratified by age. Roles and

rights of individuals are assigned based on their membership in an age group or cohort. Individuals proceed through their life course as part of that cohort. The experience of aging differs across cohorts because cohorts differ in size, composition, and experience with an ever-changing society. Current scholarship argues that social stratifications of gender, race/ethnicity, and socioeconomic status are pertinent stratifications to consider in aging, given the cumulative effect of disparities that are the result of such stratification (George, 2005).

▧ Biological Changes in Late Adulthood

Every day, our bodies are changing. In a sense, then, our bodies are constantly aging. As social workers, however, we need not be concerned with the body's aging until it begins to affect the person's ability to function in her or his world, which typically begins to occur in late adulthood. There are more than a dozen biological theories of why our bodies age. In this discussion, we follow Carolyn Aldwin and Diane Gilmer's (2004) lead and consider three categories of theories: genetic theories, molecular/cellular theories, and system-level theories.

> How important is the impact of biological age on the experience of the late adult phase of the life course?

Genetic theories of biological aging propose that there are genetically determined differences between species in the maximum life span, for example a maximum life span of about 120 years for humans and about 30 days for a fruit fly (Aldwin & Gilmer, 2004, p. 46). It is not yet clear what mechanisms are involved in regulating aging and death, but several possibilities are being forwarded. **Programmed aging theories** propose that cells cannot replicate themselves indefinitely. A slowing down in the replication of cells occurs as we become older. Hayflick (1994) has proven that some human cells can only divide a limited number of times, approximately 50 times. **Random error theories** propose that physiological aging occurs because of damaging processes that become more frequent in late adulthood but are not a part of a genetic unfolding process.

Molecular/cellular theories of biological aging, as the name suggests, propose that biological aging is caused by molecular or cellular processes. One of the most popular theories in this category is the *free radical theory.* Free radicals are reactive oxygen species (ROS) that are created during the oxidation process in cells. ROS are unstable and highly chemically reactive and they cause damage when they attach to other molecules. The free radical theory proposes that there is an increased concentration of free radicals with age, because aging cells create more free radicals, aging cells have less ability to generate antioxidants, and cellular repair is less efficient in aging cells. There is some experimental support for the free radical theory (Cristafalo, Tresini, Francis, & Volker, 1999). Another theory in this category is *waste product accumulation theory,* which proposes that as we age, waste products build up in the body's cells and interfere with bodily functioning and sometimes lead to cell death (Whitbourne, 2001). A third theory in this category is *autoimmune theory,* which proposes that the aging body loses some of its ability to recognize foreign bacteria, viruses, and other invaders. The body also starts to attack some of its own healthy cells by producing antibodies against itself, thus possibly producing autoimmune diseases.

System level theories of biological aging propose that aging is caused by processes operating across biological systems. The *homeostasis approach* operates on the premise that to be stable, organisms must maintain good communication among the various organ systems. This communication is largely organized by the autonomic nervous system through the neuroendocrine system. With age, a number of systems may show slower responses and, over time, may begin to show exaggerated responses and take longer to return to baseline. Target organs may become less responsive to neuroendocrine signals (Taffett, 1996). One of the earliest theories of biological aging was the *wear and tear theory*, which proposes that with continual use our organs and joints simply wear out. This theory was once in great favor but has not held up well in empirical research. If this were the whole story, athletes would have shorter lives than sedentary individuals. What research does show is that abuse of a system will shorten its life span. Consequently, *stress theory*, which has good empirical support, has replaced wear and tear theory. Stress theory proposes that prolonged exposure to both physiological and psychosocial stress hastens aging in many organ systems, as a result of the toxic effects of stress-related hormones (Sapolsky, 1998).

However the complex process of physiological aging is described, it has an impact on the functional capacity of both the body and the mind.

Health and Longevity

Mortality rates—the frequency at which death occurs within a population—have declined significantly for all segments of the population in the United States during the last century. Between 1981 and 2001, the overall age-adjusted death rates for all causes of death for individuals 65 years and older declined by 12%. In this age bracket, death rates from heart disease and stroke declined by approximately one-third. However, the death rates for some diseases increased, such as diabetes mellitus by 43% and chronic lower respiratory diseases by 62%. In 2001, the leading causes of death for people 65 and older were, in descending order, heart disease, cancer, stroke, chronic lower respiratory diseases, influenza/pneumonia, and diabetes. Overall death rates in 2001 were higher for older men than for older women (Federal Interagency Forum on Aging-Related Statistics, 2004; National Health Statistics, 2005).

As mortality has decreased, **morbidity**—the incidence of disease—has increased. In other words, the proportion of the population suffering from age-related chronic conditions has increased in tandem with the population of elderly persons. In 1995, for people 70 years or older, the most prevalent and debilitating chronic conditions in descending order were arthritis (58%), hypertension (51%), heart disease (31%), cancer (21%), and diabetes (16%). Chronic illnesses are long-term, rarely cured, and costly health conditions (National Health Statistics, 2005).

The prevalence of chronic conditions varies significantly by gender, race, and ethnicity. For example, older women report higher levels of hypertension, asthma, chronic bronchitis, and arthritic symptoms than older men. Older men are more likely to identify heart disease, cancer, diabetes, and emphysema. There are also racial and ethnic differences. Non-Hispanic blacks report higher levels of hypertension (66% compared to 49%) and diabetes (23% compared with 14%) than non-Hispanic whites. Hispanics (24%) report higher levels of diabetes than whites (14%). Between 1992 and 2002, the prevalence of certain conditions among ethnic/racial minorities has increased, including a 50% increase in hypertension and a 16% increase in diabetes (Federal Interagency Forum on Aging-Related Statistics, 2004). As of 2002, arthritis was reported by 68% of non-Hispanic African Americans, 58% of non-Hispanic whites, and 50% of Hispanics. Interestingly, cancer is more prevalent among whites, reported by 21% of non-Hispanic whites, 11% of Hispanics, and 9% of non-Hispanic African Americans (Federal Interagency Forum on Aging-Related Statistics, 2004). Physical decline is also associated with SES, but it is difficult to separate SES from race and ethnicity because minority groups tend to be overrepresented in lower SES groups (Wilmoth

& Longino, 2006; George, 2005). Vaillant (2002) found the physical conditions of his inner-city men ages 68 to 70 to be similar to the physical conditions of the women and the Harvard men ages 78 to 80.

▲ **Photo 9.3**   Social workers need to be concerned with aging if and when it affects a person's ability to function in his or her world.

A chronic condition can have considerable impact on a family system. In Ms. Johnson's case, the seven people for whom she cares—including two toddlers, an adolescent, an adult daughter who is functionally impaired, a granddaughter and her husband who both are at risk of leaving the workforce, and an aging father—are all affected by her chronic diabetes. This case illustrates the untold impact of chronic conditions in aging populations that are rarely described by national trend reports.

For many people, illness and death can be postponed through lifestyle changes. In recent years, the importance of preventing illness by promoting good health has received considerable attention (Agency for Healthcare Research and Quality [AHRQ], 2006). The goals of health promotion for older adults include preventing or delaying the onset of chronic disease and disability; reducing the severity of chronic diseases; and maintaining mental health, physical health, and physical functioning as long as possible (Greve & Staudinger, 2006; Hendricks & Hatch, 2006; McAuley et al., 2006). Ways to promote health in old age include improving dietary habits, increasing activity levels and physical exercise, stopping smoking, and obtaining regular health screenings (blood sampling, blood pressure measurement, cancer screening, glaucoma screening). An important finding has been the roles of self-efficacy, sense of mastery, positive attitude, and social supports in improving the quality of life and delaying functional limitation and disability (Brandtstadter, 2006; Collins & Smyer, 2005; Fiksenbaum, Greenglass & Eaton, 2006; McAuley et al., 2006).

Age-Related Changes in Physiology

All systems of the body appear to be affected during the aging process. Consider the *nervous system*. In the brain, neurons and synapses are the transmitters of information throughout the nervous system. Because neurons are not replaced by the body after birth, the number of neurons decreases throughout the life span (Santrock, 1995). The result is a slow decrease of brain mass after age 30. Because we are born with many more neurons and synapses than we need to function, problems usually do not arise. Also, if the older adult develops brain deficits in one area of the brain, he or she may make up for these deficits by increasing activity in other brain regions (Whitbourne, 2001). However, a neurological injury or disease may result in more permanent and serious consequences for an older person. This is just one of the changes that may affect the brain, spinal cord, nerves, and mechanisms controlling other organs in the body. There is also evidence of stress-related increases in norepinephrine in the aging brain, resulting in difficulty returning to baseline after stressful events (Aldwin & Gilmer, 2004).

Our *cardiovascular system* also changes in several ways as we become older. The cardiac output—the amount of blood pumped per minute—decreases throughout adult life, and the pulse slows with age (Whitbourne, 2001). The arteries become less elastic and harden, which can result in arteriosclerosis. Fatty lipids accumulate in the walls of the blood vessels and make them narrower, which can cause atherosclerosis. As a result of these changes, less oxygen is available for muscular activities (Whitbourne, 2001). With advancing age, it takes longer for the blood pressure and heart rate to return to normal resting levels after stressful events (Aldwin & Gilmer, 2004).

The *respiratory system* too changes with age. Beginning at about 20 years of age, a person's lung capacity decreases throughout the lifespan (Whitbourne, 2001). The typical decrease from age 20 to age 80 is about 40% for a healthy person.

The most important age-related change in our *skeletal system* occurs after age 30, when the destruction of bones begins to outpace the reformation of bones. The gradual decrease in bone mass and bone density can cause osteoporosis (Whitbourne, 2001). It is estimated that bone mineral content decreases by 5% to 12% per decade from the 20s through the 90s. One result is that we get shorter as we age. As the cartilage between the joints wears thin, arthritis, a chronic inflammation of the joints, begins to develop. Although many individuals suffer from some form of arthritis in their 40s, the symptoms are often not painful until late adulthood. Some of these changes can be ameliorated by diet and exercise and by avoiding smoking and alcohol (Aldwin & Gilmer, 2004; Whitbourne, 2001).

With increasing age, the *muscular system* declines in strength and endurance. As a consequence, an elderly person may become fatigued more easily. In addition, muscle contractions begin to slow down, which contributes to deteriorating reflexes and incontinence. However, the muscular system of older individuals can be successfully strengthened through weight training and changes in diet and lifestyle (Whitbourne, 2001).

Changes in the neurological, muscular, and skeletal systems have an impact on the *sensory system* and the sense of balance, which contributes to the increase in accidental falls and bone fractures in late adulthood. Vision decreases with age, and older persons need more light to reach the retina in order to see. The eye's adaptation to the dark slows with age, as does visual acuity, the ability to detect details (Aldwin & Gilmer, 2004). Age-related decreases in hearing are caused by degenerative changes in the spiral organ of the ear and the associated nerve cells. Many older adults have a reduced ability to hear high-pitched sounds

(Aldwin & Gilmer, 2004). Age-related changes in taste appear to be minimal (Aldwin & Gilmer, 2004). Differences may reflect individual factors, such as exposure to environmental conditions like smoking, periodontal disease, or use of medications, rather than general processes of aging. The smell receptors in the nose can decrease with age, however, and become less sensitive.

The *integumentary system* includes the skin, hair, and nails. The skin comprises an outer layer (epidermis) and an inner layer (dermis). With age, the epidermis becomes thinner and pigment cells grow and cluster, creating age spots on the skin (Aldwin & Gilmer, 2004). The sweat and oil-secreting glands decrease, leaving the skin drier and more vulnerable to injury (Whitbourne, 2001). Much of the fat stored in the hypodermis, the tissue beneath the skin, is lost in age, causing wrinkles. The skin of an older person often feels cool because the blood flow to the skin is reduced (Aldwin & Gilmer, 2004).

Sexual potency begins to decline at age 20, but without disease, sexual desire and capacity continue in late adulthood. According to a 1998 survey, half of all persons in the United States age 60 or older are sexually active. Among those who are sexually active, 74% of the men and 70% of the women report that they are as satisfied or more satisfied with their sex lives now than they were in their 40s (National Council on the Aging, n.d.). Vaillant (2002) reports that *frequency* of sexual activity decreases, however. He found that partners in good health at 75 to 80 often continue to have sexual relations, but that the average frequency is approximately once in every 10 weeks. Interestingly, Vaillant also found that among the women in his study, mastering the life task of generativity, rather than mastering the task of intimacy, was the predictor of regular attainment of orgasm.

Contemporary views on the physiology of aging focus on longevity. Anti-aging medicine focuses on developing interventions that will delay age-related pathology or other changes that are not officially listed as disease or decreases in bone and muscle mass. Science and technology are achieving gains that show great promise for the future. However, to date, there is no evidence that these gains have increased the maximum life span of humans (International Longevity Center-USA, 2002). Some of the more promising gains in this area include the following (Dychtwald, 1999):

- Supernutrition is the only technique that has extended life in humans with consistency. Supernutrition involves properly dosed dietary supplements of multivitamins and multiminerals, along with restricted fats and fresh, whole, unprocessed foods. The convergence of nutritional sciences and the emphasis on preventive medicine is likely to yield a new generation of supernutritional foods in the not-so-distant future.
- Hormone therapy is already used in some medical conditions today. Further breakthroughs with the use of estrogen, testosterone, melatonin, dehydroepiandrosterone (DHEA), and human growth hormone (HGH) are currently investigated but are wrought with potentially dangerous side effects to date.
- Gene manipulation will potentially have the greatest impact of all interventions on human aging. But despite recent advances in gene mapping, the technology is not yet developed enough for large-scale human applications.
- Bionics would have seemed like science fiction a generation ago, but the convergence of biological science and engineering may produce limbs and organs to replace those worn out or deteriorated with age.

♦ Organ or tissue cloning is an approach similar to bionics. Tissue cloning has particular appeal for brain diseases such as Parkinson's or Alzheimer's because it could provide patients with healthy neural tissue identical to their own.

In each of these areas, significant research efforts are being conducted the world over (Dychtwald, 1999). Whether any of these technologies will come into widespread use is uncertain. It is certain that economic and ethical considerations and debates will be as unprecedented as the technologies themselves.

⊠ Psychological Changes in Late Adulthood

Without good longitudinal research, it has been difficult to understand psychological changes in late adulthood. Because cross-sectional research cannot control for cohort effects, we need to exercise great caution in interpreting findings of age differences in human psychology. Three areas that have received a lot of attention are changes in personality, changes in intellectual functioning, and mental health and mental disorders in late adulthood.

Personality Changes

A couple of theorists have addressed the issue of how personality changes as individuals age. As noted in Chapter 8, Erik Erikson's (1950) life-span theory proposes that the struggle of middle adulthood is generativity versus stagnation (refer back to Exhibit 3.6 for an overview of Erikson's stages of psychosocial development). You may recall that generativity is the ability to transcend personal interests to guide the next generation. The struggle of late adulthood, according to Erikson, is **ego integrity versus ego despair**. *Integrity* involves the ability to make peace with one's "one and only life cycle" and to find unity with the world. Erikson (1950) also noted that from middle adulthood on, adults participate in a "wider social radius," with an increasing sense of social responsibility and interconnectedness. Some support was found for this notion in a 50-year follow-up of adult personality development (Haan, Millsap, & Hartka, 1986). The researchers found that in late adulthood, three aspects of personality increased significantly: outgoingness, self-confidence, and warmth. A recent study examining the association of chronological aging with positive psychological change supported the idea that some forms of positive psychological change are normative across the life span and that older people know clearly what values are most important and that they pursue these objectives with a more mature sense of purpose and ownership (Sheldon, 2006).

Vaillant (2002) has also considered the personality changes of late adulthood. He found that for all three of the cohorts in the Study of Adult Development, mastery of generativity tripled the likelihood that men and women would find their 70s to be a time of joy instead of despair. He also proposes that another life task, Keeper of the Meaning, comes between generativity and integrity. The **Keeper of the Meaning** takes on the task of passing on the traditions of the past to the next generation. In addition, Vaillant suggests that humans have "elegant unconscious coping mechanisms that make lemonade out of lemons" (2002, p. 91). As discussed in Chapter 8, Vaillant reports that with age and experience, individuals tend to use more adaptive coping mechanisms. This idea is supported by Fiksenbaum et al. (2006), who see successful coping as an essential aspect of aging.

Do you have any "keepers of the meaning" in your multigenerational family?

The proposition that coping mechanisms mature with age requires further longitudinal research. And indeed, Vaillant finds support for this idea in his Study of Adult Development. He found that over a 25-year period, the Harvard men made significant increases in their use of altruism and humor and significant decreases in their use of projection and passive aggression. Overall, he found that 19 of 67 Harvard men made significant gains in use of mature coping mechanisms between the ages of 50 and 75, 28 men were already making strong use of mature mechanisms at age 50, use of mature mechanisms stayed the same for 17 men, and only 4 out of the 67 men used less mature coping mechanisms with advancing age. Vaillant (1993) in part attributed this maturation in coping to the presence of positive social support and the quality of their marriages. These findings are consistent with findings from another longitudinal study of aging that found that in late adulthood, participants became more forgiving, more able to meet adversity cheerfully, less prone to take offense, and less prone to venting frustrations on others (McCrae & Costa, 1990). Langle and Probst (2004) suggest that this might be the result of older adults being required to face fundamental questions of existence because coping with the vicissitudes of life loom ever larger during aging.

In Chapter 8, we read that there are controversies about whether personality changes or remains stable in middle adulthood. There are similar controversies in the literature on late adulthood. Using longitudinal research, Vaillant (2002) found evidence for both change and continuity of personality. He suggests that personality has two components: temperament and character (p. 284). Temperament, he concludes, doesn't change, and adaptation in adolescence is one of the best predictors of adaptation in late adulthood. Studies on depression, anxiety, and suicidal ideation in late adulthood support this idea that coping and adaptation in adolescence is a good predictor of later life temperament (Lynch, Cheavens, Morse, & Rosenthal, 2004; Cheung & Todd-Oldehaver, 2006; Wickrama et al., 2005). On the other hand, character, or adaptive style, does change, influenced both by experiences with the environment and the maturation process. Vaillant (2002) attributes this change in adaptive style over time to the fact that many genes are "programmed to promote plasticity," or the capacity to be shaped by experience (p. 285). One personality change that was noted in Chapter 8 to occur in middle age is gender role reversal, with women becoming more dominant and men becoming more passive. This pattern has also been noted in late adulthood.

Intellectual Changes, Learning, and Memory

Answering the question about how our intellectual capabilities change in late adulthood is a complex and difficult task. One often-cited study on age-related intellectual changes found that fluid intelligence declines with age, but crystallized intelligence increases (Horn, 1982). **Fluid intelligence** is the capacity for abstract reasoning and involves such things as the ability to "respond quickly, to memorize quickly, to compute quickly with no error, and to draw rapid inferences from visual relationships" (Vaillant, 2002, p. 238). **Crystallized intelligence** is based on accumulated learning and includes the ability to reflect and recognize (e.g., similarities and differences, vocabulary) rather than to recall and remember. This theory has received much criticism, however, because it was based on a cross-sectional comparison of two different age groups. Researchers who followed a single cohort over time found no general decline of intellectual abilities in late adulthood (Schaie, 1984). Rather, they found considerable individual variation. Other longitudinal research has found that fluid intelligence declines earlier than crystallized intelligence, which has been found to remain the same at 80 as at 30 in most healthy older adults (Vaillant, 2002).

Learning and memory are closely related; we must first learn before we can retain and recall. Memory performance, like the impact of aging on intelligence, demonstrates a wide degree of variability. One study suggests that the effects of aging on the underlying brain processes related to retention and recall are dependent on individual memory performance, and the researchers call for further investigation of performance variability in normal aging (Duarte, Ranganath, Trujillo, & Knight, 2006). When we process information, it moves through several stages of memory (Kaplan & Sadock, 1998; Palsson, Johansson, Berg, & Skoog, 2000; Winkler & Cowan, 2005):

- *Sensory memory.* New information is initially recorded in sensory memory. Unless the person deliberately pays attention to the information, it is lost within less than a second. There seems to be little age-related change in this type of memory.
- *Primary memory.* If the information is retained in sensory memory, it is passed on to the primary memory, also called recent or short-term memory. Primary memory has only limited capacity; it is used to organize and temporarily hold information. Working memory refers to the process of actively reorganizing and manipulating information that is still in primary memory. Although there are some age-related declines in working memory, there seems to be little age-related decline in primary memory.
- *Secondary memory.* Information is permanently stored in secondary memory. This is the memory we use daily when we remember an event or memorize facts for an exam. The ability to recall seems to decline with age, but recognition capabilities stay consistent.
- *Tertiary memory.* Information is stored for extended periods, several weeks or months, in tertiary memory, also called remote memory. This type of memory experiences little age-related changes.

Another way to distinguish memory is between intentional and incidental memory. **Intentional memory** relates to events that you plan to remember. **Incidental memory** relates to facts you have learned without the intention to retain and recall. Research suggests that incidental memory declines with old age, but intentional memory does not (Direnfeld & Roberts, 2006).

Another element of intellectual functioning studied in relation to aging is *brain plasticity,* the ability of the brain to change in response to stimuli. Research indicates that even older people's brains can rewire themselves to compensate for lost functioning in particular regions, and in some instances, may even be able to generate new cells. As a result, people are capable of lifelong learning, despite myths to the contrary. Typically researchers have used years of education as the proxy and predictor of decline in cognitive ability, memory, and executive function. Manly, Schupf, Tang, and Stern (2006) found that literacy was a better predictor of learning, memory, retention, and cognitive decline than educational years. This is especially salient for minority ethnic groups whose access to formal education may be limited. However, adult education and intellectual stimulation in later life may actually help maintain cognitive health. Not only are humans capable of lifelong learning, but the stimulation associated with learning new things may reduce the risk of impairments (Institute for the Study of Aging, 2001).

For reasons that are unknown, the rate at which the human brain can receive and process information slows with age. However, contemporary thinking about cognitive

vitality is based on the assumption that having a clear mind is more important than processing speed to quality of life—especially for older women and men, hence the concern about
dementia, a brain disease in which memory and cognitive abilities deteriorate over time.
Dementia is greatly feared because it is disruptive and has the effect of robbing people of
their personality. It is estimated that 24.3 million people worldwide have dementia, and that
there are 4.6 million new cases every year (Joshi & Morley, 2006). One research team found
that in Canada as many as 64% of community-dwelling older adults with dementia are not
diagnosed as such (Sternberg, Wolfson, & Baumgarten, 2000). However, the best estimates
available suggest that the incidence of dementia is between 0.7 and 3.5 per 1,000
per year for persons ages 65 to 69, and doubles about every five years (Joshi & Morley, 2006).
Epidemiological studies indicate that Alzheimer's disease (AD) is the most common form
of dementia, responsible for 75% of cases (Nourhashemi, Sinclair, & Vellas, 2006). AD is
thought to be the third most expensive illness in the United States, costing between $60 bil-
lion and $100 billion annually (Joshi & Morley, 2006).

The initial stage of cognitive dysfunction is called *age-associated memory impairment*
(AAMI). It is followed by even greater memory loss and diagnosed as *mild cognitive impairment* (MCI), which may progress to dementia. The rate of decline in cognitive and functional skills is predictive of mortality among nondemented older adults. The risk increases
with dementia (Schupf et al., 2006). AAMI and MCI involve memory loss alone, whereas
dementia results in disruption of daily living and an inability to function normally. MCIs
have been thought not to constitute dementia but to be a transitional stage between normal
cognitive functioning and Alzheimer's disease. Studies have identified a subset of amnesic
MCI as evidence of early stage AD (Morris, 2006). Further development in early prediction
of AD has characterized declining functions by examining both duration and quantitative
changes in different domains of functioning (McArdle, Small, Backman & Fratiglioni, 2005).
Neuro-pathological lesions have been found to contribute independently both to Alzheimer's
and non-Alzheimer's disease (White et al., 2005). Further research is being conducted to
understand and refine the onset of disease process in cognition.

Risk factors for cognitive decline and dementia include genetic factors; female gender;
medical conditions, including, but not limited to, hypertension, heart disease, and diabetes;
lifestyle choices such as smoking or substance abuse; psychological and psychosocial factors
such as low educational achievement, lack of physical activity, lack of social interaction and
leisure activities, and excessive response to stress (Institute for the Study of Aging, 2001).

Mental Health and Mental Disorders

A number of longitudinal studies indicate that, without brain disease, mental health
improves with age (Vaillant, 2002). Although older adults are more predisposed to certain
brain diseases such as dementia, these disorders are not a part of the normal aging process.
However, the prevalence of mental disorders in residents of long-term care facilities is over
80% (Conn, 2001). Although few institutionalized individuals with mental disorders receive
care from mental health professionals, many of the more common mental disorders associated with older age can be diagnosed and treated in elderly persons much as they would be
in earlier adulthood (Aldwin & Gilmer, 2004). Given the aging of the population, the need
for gero-psychiatric research and clinical practice is sure to increase.

Some of the more commonly diagnosed mental disorders in late adulthood include the
following:

◆ *Anxiety.* Anxiety in older adults is similar to that in the younger population. Diagnosis and treatment, however, are often more complex and difficult, because anxiety in older adults often does not follow any direct stimulus. Rather, anxiety is frequently an indication of an underlying mental or physical disorder (Tueth, 1993). Situational stressors that may trigger anxiety in older adults include financial concerns, physical stressors, and loss and loneliness. Symptoms of anxiety include tension, worry, apprehension, and physiological symptoms such as dizziness, gastrointestinal distress, palpitations, urinary disturbance, sweating, and tremors. One recent study found that non-Hispanic whites had twice the rate of anxiety symptoms as either non-Hispanic blacks or Hispanics (Ostir & Goodwin, 2006).

◆ *Depression.* The most common mental health problem in older adults is depression, and major depression is the leading cause of suicide in late adulthood (Blazer, 1995). Symptoms of depression include sadness and depressed mood, loss of interest, weight loss, insomnia, and fatigue. To be diagnosed, the depressive episode has to persist for at least two weeks. Many depressive episodes in older adults are associated with problems in coping with difficult life events, such as death of a loved person or physical illness. Comparison of white and black older persons found that lower education and functional disability were common risk factors for severe depressive symptoms for both groups, and sense of mastery and satisfaction with support were common protective factors. Advanced age was a risk factor for whites but not for blacks, and being female and being less religious were risk factors for blacks but not for whites (Jang, Borenstein, Chiriboga & Mortimer, 2005). This is yet another reminder of the important role of religious coping among many blacks. Comparison of older adults in the United States and Japan found that multiple roles were more detrimental to the mental health of the Japanese elders than to U.S. elders (Kikuzawa, 2006).

◆ *Delirium.* One of the two most prevalent cognitive disorders in the elderly population (Kaplan & Sadock, 1998), **delirium**, is characterized by an impairment of consciousness. The syndrome has a sudden onset (a few hours or days), then follows a brief and fluctuating course that includes impairment of consciousness, and has the potential for improvement when the causes are treated. Prevalent causative factors include not only central nervous system disturbances but also outside factors such as toxicity from medications, low oxygen states, infection, retention of urine and feces, undernutrition and dehydration, and metabolic conditions (Joshi & Morley, 2006). The prevalence of delirium is high among hospitalized elderly persons, with approximately 30% to 40% of hospital patients over age 65 experiencing an episode (Kaplan & Sadock, 1998).

◆ *Dementia.* The other most prevalent cognitive disorder among older adults is dementia, which was discussed earlier in the context of memory loss. Dementia has a slower onset than delirium and is not characterized by an impairment of consciousness. Rather, dementia is characterized by multiple impairments of the person's cognitive functioning. Reversible dementia is caused by factors such as drug and alcohol use, a brain tumor, hypothyroid, syphilis or AIDS, or severe depression, and the cognitive decline is reversible if identified and treated early enough (Joshi & Morley, 2006). Irreversible dementia is not curable. In the advanced stages, the person may repeat the same words over and over again, may have problems using appropriate words, and may not recognize a spouse or other family members. At the same time, the person may still be able to recall and vividly describe events that happened many years ago.

◆ *Substance abuse.* Alcohol is the drug of choice among today's older adults. The prevalence of at-risk drinking is approximately 15% among the older adults; 5% can be defined as abusing or dependent on alcohol with the remaining 10% considered to be at risk of abuse or dependence. Elders with severe dependency are less likely than younger people to seek treatment from a specialty clinic (National Institute of Alcohol Abuse and Alcoholism [NIAAA], 2005). Substance abuse is the second most frequent reason (after depression) for admitting older adults to an inpatient psychiatric facility (Moss, Mortens, & Brennan, 1993). The general consumption of alcohol is lower for older adults than for younger adults, but many heavy drinkers do not reach old age, and alcohol abuse is often more hidden among older adults. The consequence of alcoholism for older adults is higher risk of stroke, injury, falls, suicide, and potential interactions with the development of dementia (NIAAA, 2005). There is a tendency for families and society to minimize the seriousness of the problem and to convey such notions as "He's too old to change," "If I were old I would drink too," or "Don't take away her last pleasure." These attitudes often prevent efforts to intervene. Contrary to these common attitudes, however, many older persons respond as well to treatment as younger adults do.

⊠ Social Role Transitions and Life Events of Late Adulthood

Transitions are at the center of the life course perspective, and people experience many transitions, some of them very abrupt, in late adulthood. Retirement, death of a spouse or partner, institutionalization, and one's own death are among the most stressful events in human existence, and they are clustered in late adulthood. Several other events are more benign but may still enter into the social worker's analysis of the changing configuration of person and environment represented by each case. Despite the concern of the impact of the loss of social roles, studies have demonstrated that older adults generally adapt to late life role transitions and maintain emotional well-being (Hinrichsen & Clougherty, 2006).

Families in Later Life

As you saw with the Smiths, the Moros, and Ms. Johnson, families continue to play an important role in the life of an older person. With increased longevity, however, the post-empty nest and post-retirement period lengthens (Walsh, 2005). Thus, the significance of the marital or partner relationship increases in late adulthood. As older individuals are released from their responsibilities as parents and members of the workforce, they are able to spend more time together. Some studies have suggested a U-shaped curve of marital satisfaction, with the highest levels during the first period of the marital relationship and in late adulthood, and lower levels during the childbearing years (Bengtson, Rosenthal, & Burton, 1990). Moreover, overall satisfaction with the quality of life seems to be higher for married elderly individuals than for the widowed or never married. For married couples, the spouse is the most important source of emotional, social, and personal support in times of illness and need of care.

Thirty percent (9.7 million) of noninstitionalized older Americans live alone. The most common living arrangement for men over 65 is with their wife; in 2003, 73% of men over 65 lived with their spouse (Administration on Aging, 2005). The picture is different for older women, who are twice as likely as older men to be living alone. By age 75, over one-half of women are living alone.

▲ **Photo 9.4**   As older adults are released from responsibilities as parents and members of the workforce, they are able to spend more time together.

Living arrangements for older adults vary by race and ethnicity. In 2004, the proportion of white and black women living alone was similar, about 41%. Fewer older Hispanic women lived alone (25%) and even fewer Asian and Pacific Island women lived alone (21%) (Administration on Aging, 2005). Older black and Hispanic women are less likely than white women to live with a spouse (Himes, 2001). Older Asian women are more likely to live with relatives than women of other races. Black men are three times more likely to live alone than Asian men who are three times more likely to live with relatives than men from other races (Federal Agency Forum on Aging-Related Statistics, 2004). A complex relationship between culture, socioeconomic status, and individual personality has to be considered in accounting for the ethnic and racial differences in living arrangements. Drawing inferences based solely on cultural differences is overly simplistic given the use of racial categories devised by the General Accounting Office as proxies for cultural identity.

Family relationships have been found to be closer and more central for older women than for older men. Mother-daughter relationships have been found to be particularly strong (Silverstein & Bengtson, 2001). Additionally, friendship appears to be a more important protective factor for older women than older men. Friendships have been associated with lower levels of cognitive impairment and increased quality of life satisfaction (Beland, Zunzunegui, Alvardo, Otero, & del Ser, 2005).

The never married constitute a very small group of the current elderly population. It will further decrease for some time as the cohort of baby boomers, with its unusually high rate of marriage, enters late adulthood (Bengtson, Rosenthal, & Burton, 1990). However, the proportion of elderly singles and never married will probably increase toward the middle of the next century, because the cohort that follows the baby boomers has had an increase in the number of individuals remaining single.

Singlehood due to divorce in late adulthood is increasing, however, as divorce is becoming more socially accepted in all population groups. As in all stages of life, divorce in later life may entail financial problems, especially for older women, and it may be especially difficult to recuperate financially in postretirement. Divorce also results in a change of kinship ties and social networks, which are important sources of support in later life. The incidence of remarriage after divorce or widowhood is significantly higher for older men than for older women. The fact that there are more elderly women than men contributes to this trend. Even if older adults are not themselves divorced, they may need to adjust to the enlarged and complicated family networks that come from the divorces and remarriages of their children and grandchildren (Walsh, 2005).

One group of older adults that has often been neglected in the discussion of late adulthood is elderly gay men and lesbians. Estimates of the proportion of gay men and lesbians among elderly persons are similar to those for younger age groups (Teitelman, 1995). Being faced not only with ageist but also with homophobic attitudes, elderly gay men and lesbians may be confronted by a double jeopardy. Eligibility requirements for many services to elderly adults continue to be based on a norm of heterosexuality. Although growing in number, services catering directly to older gay or lesbian persons are still few and far between in many parts of the country. But the most problematic aspect of being an elderly homosexual may be the lack of societal sanction to grieve openly when the partner dies (Barranti & Cohen, 2001; Humphreys & Quam, 1998; Teitelman, 1995).

Sibling relationships play a special role in the life of older adults. Siblings share childhood experiences and are often the personal tie with the longest duration. Siblings are typically not the primary source of personal care, but they often play a role in providing emotional support. Sibling relationships often change over the life course, with closer ties in preadulthood and later life and less involvement in early and middle adulthood. Women's ties with siblings have been found to be more involved than those of men (Cicerelli, 1995).

Relationships with children and grandchildren are also significant in late adulthood. The "myth of the golden age" in the United States suggests that in the past, older people were more likely to live in a multigenerational family, be well taken care of, and have valued emotional and economic roles. This heartwarming picture is a myth, however, because people died earlier and multigenerational families were less prevalent than they are in our era of increased longevity (Hareven, 2000). Furthermore, even in the past, elderly individuals valued independent living, and they typically resided in separate households from their adult children, although they usually lived in close proximity.

In fact, multigenerational families have become more common in recent years, resulting in more interactions and exchanges across generations. Contrary to common belief, intergenerational exchanges between adult children and elderly parents are not one-directional. Children often take care of their elderly parents, but healthy elderly persons also provide significant assistance to their adult children, as is the case with Ms. Johnson. Research on elderly parents living with their adult children suggests that for the young-old, more assistance flows from the elderly parents to the adult children than the other way around (Speare & Avery, 1993). In another study (Ward, Logan, & Spitze, 1992), older parents living with their adult children reported doing more than three-quarters of the housework. Patterns of coresidence between parents and adult children vary by race. Non-Hispanic white elderly are the least likely to coreside with their children; Asian elderly are the most likely to live with their children (Speare & Avery, 1993).

Grandparenthood

In some cases, older people such as Ms. Johnson are assuming full responsibility for parenting their grandchildren, because their children have problems with drugs, HIV infection, or crime. Beginning in the early 1990s, the U.S. Census Bureau began to note an increasing number of children under 18 living with grandparents, rising from 3% of children under age 18 in 1970 to 5.5% in 1997 (Bryson & Casper, 1999). About 1.53 million older people in the United States live in a household in which a grandchild is present. Approximately 50% of this number resides in parent-maintained households (Administration on Aging, 2005). A little over one-quarter are primary caregivers for their grandchildren (U.S. Census 2004). This has been viewed by some as a negative trend, but there is no inherent reason why grandchildren receiving care from grandparents is problematic, and, indeed, across time and place, grandparents have sometimes been seen as appropriate caregivers. Many cultural groups often have multigenerational households that are not predicated on dysfunction within the family. Recall that large percentages of Asian, Hispanic, and black elders live with family members, not their spouse. It does appear, however, that the current trend is influenced by the growth of drug use among parents, teen pregnancy, and the rapid rise of single-parent families (Bryson & Casper, 1999). As a result, new physical, emotional, and financial demands are placed on grandparents with already limited resources. Some speculate that custodial grandparents may also be caring for their own impaired adult child, because two-thirds of grandparent-headed households have a member of the "skipped generation" in residence (Burnette, 1999).

Grandparenthood is a normative part of the family life cycle, but the majority of grandparents do not coreside with their grandchildren. The timing of grandparenthood influences the way it is experienced and the roles and responsibilities that a grandparent will take on. Predominately, many first-time grandparents are middle-aged adults in their early 50s. However, the census data from 2004 indicate that grandparenthood has been documented as beginning as young as age 30 (U. S. Census, 2004). Yet, others do not become grandparents until they are 70 or 80 years old. Because individuals are enjoying longer lives, more and more assume the role of grandparent, and they assume it for more years. Many spend the same number of years being a grandparent as being a parent of a child under the age of 18.

> **How do culture, social class, and gender affect grandparenting styles?**

In general, being a grandparent is a welcome and gratifying role for most individuals, but it may increase in significance and meaning for an older person. The Smiths, for example, both enjoy being grandparents, and Lois Smith especially gains pleasure and satisfaction from her role as grandmother to her daughter's children.

Family researchers have begun to take a strong interest in the grandparenting role, but little is actually known about grandparent-grandchild relationships. A classic study of middle-class grandparents in the early 1960s identified several styles of grandparents: formal grandparents, fun seekers, distant figures, surrogate parents, and mentors (Neugarten & Weinstein, 1964).

A more recent study by Margaret Mueller and her associates has focused particularly on the relationships between grandparents and adolescent grandchildren; the average age of grandparents in this study was 69 years old (Mueller, Wilhelm, & Elder, 2002). This study identified five dimensions of the grandparenting role in 451 families: face-to-face contact, activities done together, intimacy, assistance, and authority/discipline. Each of these grandparenting dimensions is defined in Exhibit 9.5. Using a statistical clustering method, the researchers identified five styles of grandparenting:

1. *Influential grandparents* are highly involved in all aspects of grandparenting, scoring high on all five dimensions. These grandparents constituted 17% of the sample. Ms. Johnson is grandparenting Rebecca in this manner.

2. *Supportive grandparents* are highly involved in the lives of their grandchildren but do not see themselves in a role of disciplinarian or authority figure. About a quarter of the sample fit this pattern.

3. *Passive grandparents* are moderately involved in their grandchildren's lives, but they do not provide instrumental assistance and do not see themselves as discipline/authority figures. About 19% of the sample fit this pattern. Lois and Gene Smith seem to be following this pattern of grandparenting.

4. *Authority-oriented grandparents* see their role as authority figures as the central component in their grandparenting, and they are relatively inactive in their grandchildren's lives compared with both influential and supportive grandparents. These grandparents constitute about 13% of the sample.

5. *Detached grandparents* are the least involved of the grandparents, scoring lowest on all the dimensions of grandparenting. This was the largest group, comprising about 28% of the sample.

Exhibit 9.5	Dimensions of Grandparenting Role
Dimension	*Definition*
Face-to-face contact	How often grandparents see their grandchildren
Activities done together	Participation in shared activities, such as shopping, working on projects together, attending grandchildren's events, teaching the grandchild a skill
Intimacy	Serving as confidant, companion, or friend; discussing grandparent's childhood
Assistance	Providing instrumental assistance, such as financial aid and/or interpersonal support
Discipline and authority	Disciplining the grandchild or otherwise serving as an authority figure

SOURCE: Based on Mueller et al., 2002.

This research is helpful because it demonstrates that the grandparent role may be played in many different ways. A number of factors may influence the style of grandparenting, including geographic proximity, ages of grandparents and grandchildren, number of grandchildren, and family rituals. There is a major drawback to the sample, however; it is entirely white and midwestern. It does not, therefore, address the possibility of cultural variations in grandparenting roles. For example, Caribbean immigrants' grandparents are often the primary attachment figures in many families.

A smaller-scale study of grandparenting in 17 Native American families, including Sioux, Creek, Seminole, Choctaw, and Chickasaw, partially addresses the issue of cultural variation (Weibel-Orlando, 2001). Like the research of Mueller and her associates, this study identified five styles of grandparenting:

1. *The distanced grandparent* lives at considerable geographic distance from grandchildren but also has psychological and cultural distance. This type of grandparenting is not common among Native Americans. It is most likely to occur if the family has migrated to an urban area and the grandparents return to their ancestral homeland after retirement.

2. *The ceremonial grandparent* also lives at considerable geographic distance from grandchildren but visits regularly. Intergenerational visits are times for ethnic ceremonial gatherings, and grandparents model appropriate ceremonial behavior.

3. *The fictive grandparent* assumes the elder role with children who are not biologically related. These grandparents may have no grandchildren of their own or may live at a great distance from their biological grandchildren.

4. *The custodial grandparent* lives with the grandchildren and is responsible for their care. This style of grandparenting is usually the result of parental death, incapacitation, or abandonment, and is based on necessity rather than choice.

5. *The cultural conservator grandparent* actively pursues the opportunity to have grandchildren live with her (all such grandparents were women in this study) so that she might teach them the Native American way of life.

Think about your relationships with your grandparents. How would you characterize their grandparenting styles? Did you have different types of relationships with different grandparents? Did your grandparents have different types of relationships with different grandchildren? What might explain any differences?

Work and Retirement

Until the twentieth century, the average worker retired about three years before death. In 1890, 90% of men in the United States over age 70 were still in the workforce. Increased worker productivity, mass longevity, and Social Security legislation changed that situation,

How do these social trends affect the late adult phase of the life course?

however, and by 1986, only 31% of 65-year-old men were in the workforce. As of 2004, only 14.4 % of U.S. adults 65 and older were still in the work force—18% of men and 10% of women. However, in the age group 65 to 74, 25% of men and 15% of women were still in the labor force (U.S. Census, 2004). In the past century, with the combined impact of increased longevity and earlier retirement, the average number of years spent in retirement before death is almost 15 years (Vaillant, 2002).

Retirement patterns vary with social class, however. Vaillant found that only 20% of his sample of surviving inner-city men were still in the workforce at age 65, but half of the sample of Harvard men were still working full time at 65. The inner-city men retired, on average, five years earlier than the Harvard men. Poor health often leads to earlier retirement among less advantaged adults (Sterns & Huyck, 2001). In addition, higher levels of education make workers eligible for more sedentary jobs, which are a better fit with the declining energy levels in late adulthood (Vaillant, 2002).

Data about retirement have been based on the work patterns of men, probably because women's labor force involvement has been less uniform. Current trends reflect the history of women's involvement in the workforce with many "baby boomers" having never worked or worked intermittently. A trend was noted in the early 1990s, however, in which labor force participation rates for men over 50 were falling while labor force participation rates of women over 50 were increasing. The greatest increase of women workers in the 55 to 61 age range occurred between 1963 and 2003, up from 44% to 63%. During the same period, the labor force participation of women increased from 29% to 39% among women ages 62 to 64 and from 17% to 23% for women ages 65–69. The gap between male and female labor participation has narrowed from 46% in 1963 to 12% in 2003 (Federal Interagency Forum on Aging-Related Statistics, 2004). The decline in labor force participation of men can be accounted for by a number of factors, including eligibility for retirement at age 62 and greater wealth generated by workers, consequently permitting retirement (Federal Interagency Forum on Aging-Related Statistics, 2004).

The "appropriate" age for retirement in the United States is currently understood to be age 65. This cultural understanding has been shaped by Social Security legislation enacted in 1935. However, the 1983 Social Security Amendments included a provision for a gradual increase in the age at which a retired person could begin receiving social security retirement benefits. Exhibit 9.6 shows the schedule for increasing the age for receiving full benefits. In arguing for this legislative change, members of Congress noted increased longevity and improved health among older adults (Federal Interagency Forum on Aging-Related Statistics, 2004).

Certainly, some older individuals continue to work for many years after they reach age 65 (Morgan & Kunkel, 1996). Individuals who continue to work fall into two groups: those who could afford to retire but choose to continue working and those who continue to work because of a financial need. Older adults of the first group usually receive great satisfaction in sharing their knowledge and expertise, and gain a feeling of purpose from being productive. Members of the second group continue to work out of necessity. Because economic status in old age is influenced by past employment patterns and the resultant retirement benefits, this second group consists of individuals who had lower-paying employment throughout their lives. This group also includes elderly divorced or widowed women who depended on their husband's retirement income and are now faced with poverty or near poverty. Lifelong gender inequality in wages contributes to inequality in pension and retirement funds (Wilmoth & Longino, 2006). Gene Smith falls into the first category, because he continued working even though he and his wife had sufficient combined benefits to retire. However, Lois Smith's own benefits would not have enabled her to lead a financially comfortable retirement if she were not married, and she would probably face some financial hardship if she were to become a widow. Ruby Johnson continues to be employed on a part-time basis out of financial necessity.

When we think about retirement, we often picture individuals cleaning up their desks to stop working completely and sit in a rocking chair on the front porch. Yet, there are many ways of retiring from the workforce. Some individuals do cease work completely, but others continue with part-time or part-year employment. Others may retire for a period and then reenter the labor market, as Gene Smith did when his former employer offered him a

Exhibit 9.6	Amended Age to Receive Full Social Security Benefits (1983)
Year of Birth	*Full Retirement Age*
1937 and earlier	65
1938	65 and 2 months
1939	65 and 4 months
1940	65 and 6 months
1941	65 and 8 months
1942	65 and 10 month
1943–1954	66
1955	66 and 2 months
1956	66 and 4 months
1957	66 and 6 months
1958	66 and 8 months
1959	66 and 10 month
1960 and later	67

SOURCE: Social Security Administration, n.d.

part-time position. Retirement is a socially accepted way to end an active role in the workforce. Most persons retire because of advancing age, mandatory retirement policies, health problems, a desire to pursue other interests, or simply a wish to relax and lead the life of a retiree.

Individuals vary in whether they view retirement as something to dread or something to look forward to. Most often, however, retirement is a positive experience. Vaillant (2002) argues that "retirement is highly overrated as a life problem" (p. 220). He found no evidence in his longitudinal research that retirement is bad for physical health; in fact, for every person who indicated that retirement was bad for her or his health, four retirees indicated that retirement had improved their health. Vaillant did note, however, four conditions under which retirement is stressful (p. 221):

1. Retirement was involuntary or unplanned.

2. There are no other means of financial support besides salary.

3. Work provided an escape from an unhappy home life.

4. Retirement was precipitated by preexisting bad health.

As Vaillant notes, these conditions are present among only a fraction of retirees, but those are the retirees with whom social workers are likely to come into contact.

Vaillant found that retirement has generally been very rewarding for many of the participants of his study. Four basic activities appear to make retirement rewarding:

1. Replacing work mates with another social network

2. Rediscovering how to play

3. Engaging in creative endeavors

4. Continuing lifelong learning

Vaillant also suggests that retirement would be less stressful if the culture provided rituals for the transition, as it does for other life transitions. While some people with a long tenure in a job are given retirement parties by their employers, Vaillant found little evidence of significant rituals in his research.

Caregiving and Care Receiving

As retirement unfolds, declining health may usher in a period of intensive need for care. The majority of older adults with disabilities live in the community and receive predominately informal care from spouses, children, and extended family. The percentage of older adults receiving informal or formal caregiving actually declined from 15% in 1984 to 11% in 1999. Over 90% of those older adults with disabilities who received care between 1984 and 1999 received primarily informal caregiving in combination with some formal caregiving. Two-thirds of this group received only informal caregiving (Federal Interagency Forum on Aging-Related Statistics, 2004). Eighty percent of older adults who need long-term care receive that care in the community rather than in an institution. Women are the primary source of caregiving in old age (Walsh, 2005). Daughters are more likely than sons to take care of elderly parents. Moreover, elderly men tend to be married and thus are more likely to have a wife available as caregiver.

Caregiving can be an around-the-clock task and often leaves caregivers overwhelmed and exhausted. Camille Moro is a good example of the burden that can be experienced by an elderly spouse. Programs that can assist caregivers like Camille in reducing their exceptional levels of stress have received much attention. Many programs combine educational components—for example, information about and training in adaptive coping skills—with ongoing support through the opportunity to share personal feelings and experiences. Respite programs for caregivers are also available. In-home respite programs provide assistance through a home health aide or a visiting nurse. Community-based respite is often provided through adult day care and similar programs.

How can such programs buffer the stress of caregiving and care receiving?

When caregiving becomes too overwhelming, a nursing home placement may be pursued. Yet, caregiving often continues after a family member enters a nursing home. Although caregivers are relieved from direct care, they continue to be involved in the emotional and social aspects of care in the nursing home.

Stress and burden are not experienced only by the caregiver. The care recipient also often experiences significant strain. Requiring care is a double loss: the person has lost the capability to perform the tasks for which he or she needs assistance and the person has also lost independence. Having to rely on others for activities that one has carried out independently throughout adult life can be the source of tremendous emotional and psychological stress. Some individuals respond by emotional withdrawal; others become agitated and start blaming others for their situation. The levels of stress that an elderly care recipient may experience depend on "(1) personal and situational characteristics of the elderly recipient; (2) characteristics of the caregiver; (3) social support provided to caregiver and recipient; (4) aspects of the relationship between family caregiver and recipient; and (5) characteristics of caregiving" (Brubaker, Gorman, & Hiestand, 1990, p. 268).

Think of Frank Moro. His stress was amplified by culturally defined norms promoting independence, individuality, and pride. Helping Frank overcome his uneasiness about receiving assistance and support was a matter of asking him to verbalize his worries, listening to him express his feelings, and looking together at ways that he could overcome his uneasiness in small steps. Getting him to accept a wheelchair also reduced his stress by increasing his independence. Such assistive technology can often greatly reduce the care recipient's reliance on help and thus decrease her or his stress.

Widowhood

Widowhood is more common among women than men. Almost half (43%) of all older women in 2004 were widows. This was four times the rate of widowers (2 million widowers compared to 8.4 million widows) (Administration on Aging, 2005). The death of a spouse has been found to be the most stressful event in a person's life. In most cases, it is the loss of someone with whom the individual has shared a major part of life. Moreover, the marital relationship is one of the most important relationships for a person in later life. Because they have a longer life expectancy, more women than men face this life event.

Losing a spouse signifies the end of one phase in a person's life course and the beginning of a new phase called widowhood. It requires the individual to readjust to a new social role and a new way of relating to others. Those who saw the world through the eyes of a spouse have to learn to see everything from a new perspective. Widowhood also confronts the person with his or her own mortality. There is evidence that the loss of a spouse is associated with subsequent illness and earlier mortality (Martikainen & Valkonen, 1996), but a recent Finnish study found this to be true for women but not for men (Vahtera et al., 2006). Loss, grief, and bereavement are discussed in greater detail in Chapter 10.

Adjustment to widowhood is facilitated by a person's own inner strength, family support, a strong network of friends and neighbors, and membership in a church or an active community. The family is the most important source of emotional, social, and financial support during this time.

Widowhood may be especially difficult if the surviving spouse provided intensive caregiving for a prolonged period. In this case, the partner's death may be a relief from the burdensome caregiving task, but it may also mean the loss of a role and sense of purpose. In addition, during the period of intensive caregiving, the survivor may have had to give up many social interactions and thus have a shrunken social support network.

Institutionalization

Another myth of aging is that older individuals are being abandoned and neglected by their families and being pushed into nursing homes to get them out of the way. Fewer elderly persons are institutionalized than we generally assume, but the risk for entering a nursing home increases significantly with age. During the past decade, the percentages of older people living in nursing homes actually declined from 5.1% in 1990 to 4.5% in 2000, but the total number has increased due to the rapid growth in the aged population (Federal Interagency Forum on Aging-Related Statistics, 2004). However, the risk of entering a nursing home does continue to increase with age. Only 1.1% of older adults between the age of 65 and 74, compared with 18.2% of those 85 and older, live in nursing homes. Additionally 5% of older adults live in self-described senior housing, many of which have supportive services (Administration on Aging, 2005). There have been many efforts to reduce disability that can result in nursing home placement (Agency for Healthcare Research and Quality, 2006). It remains to be seen whether Gene Smith, Lois Smith, Ms. Johnson, Frank Moro, or Camille Moro will spend some time before death in a nursing home.

Most children and spouses do not use nursing homes as a dumping ground for their elderly relatives. They turn to nursing homes only after they have exhausted all other alternatives. Nor is institutionalization a single, sudden event. It is a process that starts with the need to make a decision, continues through the placement itself, and ends in the adjustment to the placement (Naleppa, 1996).

Researchers have taken a close look at the factors that predict a person's entry into a nursing home. Among the most important are the condition and needs of the elderly individual. Functional and behavioral deficits, declining health, previous institutionalization, and advanced age all contribute to the decision to enter a nursing home. Family characteristics that are good predictors of institutionalization include the need for 24-hour caregiving, caregiver feelings of distress, caregiver health and mental status, and caregiving environment (Naleppa, 1996). Marital status is a strong predictor of institutionalization for elderly men. Unmarried and never married men have the highest risk of entering a nursing home (Dolinsky & Rosenwaike, 1988; Hanley, Alecxih, Wiener, & Kennell, 1990). Individuals without a spouse who live alone in the community are at a higher risk of entering a nursing home than those living with spouses, family members, or friends (Montgomery & Kosloski, 1994).

The placement decision itself is emotionally stressful for all involved and can be viewed as a family crisis. Yet, it can be considered a normative part of the family life cycle. The process of making a placement decision itself unfolds in four stages: "the recognition of the potential for institutionalization; discussion of the institutionalization option; implementation of action steps toward institutionalization; and placement of the relative in the institutional setting" (Gonyea, 1987, p. 63). Because many nursing home placements are arranged from the hospital for an elderly individual who entered the hospital expecting to return home, many people may not have time to progress well through these stages. For those who unexpectedly enter a nursing home from the hospital, it may be advisable to arrange a brief visit home to say farewell to their familiar environment. While society has developed rituals for many occasions, unfortunately no rituals exist for this difficult life transition.

Entering a nursing home means losing control and adjusting to a new environment. How well a person adjusts depends on many factors. If the elderly individual sees entering the nursing home in a favorable light and feels in control, adjustment may proceed well. Frequent visits by relatives and friends also help in the adaptation to the new living arrangement. Despite the commonly held belief that families do not visit their relatives, continued family involvement seems to be the norm. About two-thirds of nursing home residents receive one or more visitors a week, and only a very small group is never visited (Bitzan & Kruzich, 1990).

▧ The Search for Personal Meaning

As adults become older, they spend more time reviewing their life achievements and searching for personal meaning. In gerontology, the concept of **life review** as a developmental task of late adulthood was introduced by Robert Butler (1963). He theorized that this self-reflective review of one's life is not a sign of losing short-term memory, as had been assumed. Rather, life review is a process of evaluating and making sense of one's life. It includes a reinterpretation of past experiences and unresolved conflicts. Newer forms of clinical interventions rooted in narrative theory underscore the importance of providing structure, coherence, and opportunity for meaning making of one's experience that "storying" provides (Morgan, 2000). Social workers can influence a more positive outcome of a life review through relationship, empathic listening and reflection, witness to the story, and providing alternative reframes and interpretations of past events. For example, promoting a story of resiliency as a lifelong process helps to reframe stories that support successful mastery of challenges and compensatory recovery in the face of adversity (O'Leary, & Bhaju, 2006; Wadensten, 2005).

The life review can lead to diverse outcomes, including depression, acceptance, or satisfaction (Butler, 1987). If the life review is successful, it leads the individual to personal wisdom and inner peace. But the reassessment of one's life may also lead to despair and depression. This idea that the process of life review may lead to either acceptance or depression is similar to the eighth stage of Erikson's theory of adult development; through the life review, the individual tries to work through the conflict between ego integrity (accepting oneself and seeing one's life as meaningful) and despair (rejecting oneself and one's life).

The ways in which individuals review their lives differ considerably. Some undertake a very conscious effort of assessing and reevaluating their achievements; for others, the effort may be subtle and not very conscious. Regardless of how they pursue it, life review is believed to be a common activity for older adults that occurs across cultures and time.

The concept of **reminiscence** is closely related to life review. Most older persons have a remarkable ability to recall past events. They reminisce about the past and tell their stories to anyone who is willing to listen, but they also reminisce when they are on their own. This reminiscing can serve several functions (Sherman, 1991):

- ◆ Reminiscing may be an enjoyable activity that can lift the spirits of the listener and of the person telling the story.
- ◆ Some forms of reminiscing are directed at enhancing a person's image of self, as when individuals focus on their accomplishments.
- ◆ Reminiscing may help the person cope with current or future problems, letting her or him retreat to the safe place of a comfortable memory or recall ways of coping with past stressors.
- ◆ Reminiscing can assist in the life review, as a way to achieve ego integrity.

Reminiscing combines past, present, and future orientations (Sherman, 1991). It includes the past, which is when the reviewed events occurred. However, the construction of personal meaning is an activity that is also oriented to the present and the future, providing purpose and meaning to life. A recent study examined the association between reminiscence frequency, reminiscence enjoyment or regret, and psychological health outcomes. The study found that reminiscence enjoyment was positively associated with psychological health outcomes. High frequency of reminiscence and having regret were associated with poor psychological health (Mckee et al., 2005)

Another factor in the search for personal meaning is religious or spiritual activity. Cross-sectional research has consistently found that humans become more religious or spiritual in late adulthood (Gallup & Lindsay, 1999). Vaillant's (2002) longitudinal research did not find support for this idea, however. He found that the importance of religion and spirituality, on average, did not change in the lives of his study participants over time. He suggests that the cross-sectional finding may be picking up a cohort effect, and that subsequent cohorts of older adults may be less religious or spiritual in adolescence and young adulthood than the current cohort of older adults was. What Vaillant fails to address is whether his cohort reaches a higher faith stage in late adulthood, as developmental theorists would suggest.

☒ Resources for Meeting the Needs of Elderly Persons

The persons in the case studies at the beginning of this chapter needed several kinds of assistance. Lois and Gene Smith, for example, needed some counseling to help them settle comfortably into retirement together. Gene went back to work to fill some of his leisure hours, but Lois needed some suggestions about the volunteer opportunities that could give meaning to her life. The Moros' needs were quite different. Frank is confronted with several chronic conditions for which he needs assistance. Much of this assistance has been provided by his wife. Camille, in turn, needs some respite services to prevent her from being overwhelmed by the demands of giving care. Ms. Johnson requires a level of assistance most practically provided by effective and comprehensive case management.

The types of support and assistance that elderly persons receive can be categorized as either formal or informal resources. Formal resources are those provided by formal service providers. They typically have eligibility requirements that a person has to meet in order to qualify. Some formal resources are free, but others are provided on a fee-for-service basis, meaning that anyone who is able to pay can request the service. Informal resources are those provided through families, friends, neighbors, churches, and so forth. Elderly persons receive a considerable amount of support through these informal support networks.

Informal Resources

The family is the most important provider of informal resources for many older individuals. It is estimated that 80% to 90% of the care provided to elderly persons living in the community is provided by family members (Allen, Blieszner, & Roberto, 2001). Usually family members can provide better emotional and social support than other providers of services. Family members know the person better and are more available for around-the-clock support. Different family members tend to provide different types of assistance. Daughters tend to provide most of the caregiving and are more involved in housekeeping and household chores. Sons are more likely to provide assistance with household repairs and financial matters.

What types of social service programs can enhance informal supports for older adults?

However, the family should not be considered a uniformly available resource or support. Not all family networks are functional and able to provide needed support. As Ms. Johnson's story illustrates, even when family members are involved in the elderly person's life, they may place additional demands on the older person instead of relieving the burden. The increased presence of women in the labor market places them in a particularly difficult position—trying to balance the demands of raising children, taking care of their parents, and being part of the workforce. Furthermore, the size of the family network available to support elderly persons is decreasing as a consequence of the decreasing average number of children in a family (Walsh, 2005).

A second source of informal resources is friends and neighbors, who often provide a significant amount of care and assistance. Although they may be less inclined than family members would be to provide personal care, friends and neighbors like Gene and Lois Smith often offer other forms of assistance, such as running errands or performing household chores. Sometimes a system of informal exchanges evolves—for example, an elderly woman invites her elderly neighbor over for meals while he mows her lawn and drives her to medical appointments.

Finally, informal resources are also provided by religious and community groups. Religious-related resources include social and emotional support through group activities and community events. It is this form of support that an active retired person like Lois Smith finds most helpful. In addition, some religious groups are involved in providing more formal resources, such as transportation or meal services.

Formal Resources

The second type of support for older adults is the formal service delivery system, which offers a wide range of services. Four different Social Security trust funds are the backbone of formal resources to older people in the United States:

1. *Old-Age and Survivors Insurance (OASI).* The retirement and survivors' component of the U.S. Social Security system is a federally administered program that covers almost all workers. To qualify, a person must have worked at least 10 years in employment covered by the program. The benefit is based on the individual's earnings and is subject to a maximum benefit amount. Through cost-of-living adjustments, the amount is adjusted annually for inflation. Many older individuals are able to supplement this benefit with private pension benefits.

2. *Hospital Insurance Trust Fund (Medicare Part A).* This fund covers a major part of the cost of hospitalization, as well as a significant part of the costs of skilled nursing facility care, approved home health care, and under certain conditions, hospice care. Depending on the type of service needed, beneficiaries pay a one-time copayment or a percentage of the actual costs. Most beneficiaries do not need to pay a monthly premium (Kingson & Berkowitz, 1993).

3. *Supplementary Medical Insurance. Medicare Part B* covers medical costs such as physicians' services, inpatient and outpatient surgery, and ambulance services, as well as laboratory services, medically necessary home health care, and outpatient hospital treatment. Beneficiaries pay a small monthly premium (Kingson & Berkowitz, 1993). Some services require a copayment or a deductible. *Medicare Part D,* a result of the Medication Prescription Drug Improvement and Modernization Act of 2003, became effective on January 1, 2006. It was designed to provide older adults and people with disabilities access to prescription drug coverage. Rather than being administered by the federal government, as in the case of Part A and Part B, Part D is being administered by private insurance plans that are then reimbursed

by the Centers for Medicare and Medicaid Services (CMS) (U.S. Department of Health and Human Services, 2006). Participants have choices of a number of private insurance plans, but the choices, to date, are not straightforward. Plans with the lowest premiums may not cover the drugs needed by a particular participant. In addition, plans may change their drug prices frequently. In 2007, the initial coverage is limited to drug costs of $2,400, and catastrophic coverage does not pick up until drug costs reach $3,850, placing considerable financial burden on many older beneficiaries (Medicare Advocacy, 2007). This situation has been called the "donut" problem.

4. *Disability insurance.* This component provides benefits for workers younger than 62 with a severe long-term disability. There is a five-month waiting period, but the benefits continue as long as the disability exists.

> How do these federal programs serve as protective factors in late adulthood?

In addition, Supplementary Social Security Income (SSI) is a financial need-based program that provides cash benefits to low-income, aged, blind, and disabled persons. It is not part of the Social Security trust funds but is a federal welfare program.

Other formal services are available regionally. Here is an overview of some of the most important ones:

♦ *Adult day care.* Some elderly individuals have conditions that prevent them from staying at home while their caregiver is at work, or the caregiver may benefit from respite. Two forms of adult day care exist for such situations. *The social adult day care model* provides meals, medication, and socialization, but no personal care. *The medical adult day care model* is for individuals who need medical care, nursing services, physical or occupational therapy, and more intensive personal care.

♦ *Senior centers.* Community forums for social activities, educational programs, and resource information are available even in small communities.

♦ *Home health care services.* Several types of home health care are available, varying greatly in level of assistance and cost. They range from homemakers who assist with household chores, cleaning, and errands to registered nurses who provide skilled nursing service, use medical equipment, and provide IV therapy.

♦ *Hospice programs.* The purpose of a hospice program is to provide care to the terminally ill. Through inpatient or outpatient hospice, patients typically receive treatment by a team of doctors, nurses, social workers, and care staff.

♦ *Senior housing.* An elderly person may require a change in his or her living arrangement for a number of reasons, and several alternative living arrangements are available. Senior apartments and retirement communities are for persons who can live independently. They typically offer meals and housekeeping services, but no direct care. Many offer transportation, community rooms, and senior programs.

♦ *Adult homes.* For seniors in need of more assistance, adult homes usually have rooms, rather than apartments, and provide meals, medication management, and supervision.

♦ *Health-related senior facilities.* For those in need of nursing care and intensive assistance with activities of daily living, residents live in private or semiprivate rooms, and share living and dining rooms. Medications, meals, personal care, and some therapeutic services are provided. Included in this category is the growing number of *assisted living facilities,* which may provide small apartments as well as single rooms. The skilled nursing facility provides the highest level of care, including nursing and personal care and an array of therapeutic services. Several noninstitutional alternatives to the nursing home exist, including *adult foster care* programs that operate in a similar way to foster care programs for children and adolescents.

◆ *Nutrition programs.* Deficits in nutrition can affect a person's health and the aging process. Nutritional services are provided through a number of programs, the best known being Meals on Wheels (Wacker, Roberto, & Piper, 1997).

◆ *Transportation services.* Public and private providers offer transportation for elderly persons with mobility problems.

◆ *Power of attorney.* Some elderly persons have difficulty managing their legal and financial affairs. A **power of attorney (POA)** is a legal arrangement by which a person appoints another individual to manage his or her financial and legal affairs. The person given the POA should be a person the client knows and trusts. Standard POA forms are available at stationery stores, but the POA can be tailored to the individual's situation. It then needs to be notarized, a service provided by attorneys and some banks. A POA can be limited (for a limited time period), general (no restrictions), or durable (begins after the client reaches a specified level of disability) (Wacker et al., 1997).

With so many types of services available, the social worker's most daunting task is often assessing the elderly person's needs. It may also be a challenge, however, to find quality services that are affordable. Thus, advocacy on behalf of older adults remains a concern of the social work profession.

⊠ Risk Factors and Protective Factors in Late Adulthood

Chapter 8 suggests that midlife behavior has both antecedents and consequences. The same can be said for late adulthood. Early life experiences can serve either as risk factors or as protective factors for health and well-being during late adulthood. And late adult behaviors can serve either as risk factors or as protective factors for future health and well-being.

As the longest-term longitudinal research available on late adult behavior, Vaillant's Study of Adult Development (2002) provides the clearest understanding of the antecedents of late adult well-being. Like Emmy Werner, who has studied a cohort until midlife (see Chapter 8), Vaillant is impressed with the self-righting tendencies in human nature. He summarizes the antecedent risk factors and protective factors for late adulthood in this way: "What goes right in childhood predicts the future far better than what goes wrong" (p. 95). He also suggests that unhappy childhoods become less important over the stages of adulthood. Consequently, Vaillant suggests that it is more important to count up the protective factors than to count up the risk factors. Although he found childhood experiences to diminish in importance over time, Vaillant also found that much of the resilience, or lack thereof, in late adulthood is predicted by factors that were established by age 50. He suggests that risk factors and protective factors change over the life course.

Exhibit 9.7 lists six variables that Vaillant was surprised to find did not predict healthy aging and seven factors that he did find to predict healthy aging. Some of the factors that did not predict healthy aging did predict good adjustment at earlier adult stages. In terms of stress, Vaillant found that if we wait a few decades, many people recover from psychosomatic illness. In terms of parental characteristics, he found that they are still important for predicting adaptation at age 40 but not by age 70. In terms of both childhood temperament and general ease in social relationships, he found that they are strong predictors of adjustment in young adulthood but no longer important at age 70.

On the other hand, Vaillant found that the seven factors on the right side of Exhibit 9.7, collectively, are strong predictors of health 30 years in the future. He also found that each variable, individually, predicted healthy aging, even when the other six variables were statistically controlled. Vaillant has chosen to frame each of these predictive factors in terms of protection; he sees risk as the flip side of protection. He notes the danger of such a list of protective factors: that it be used to "blame the victim" rather than provide guidance for aging well. He sees the list of predictors as "good news," however, because they all represent something that can be controlled to some extent.

By following cohorts across the period of young-old and middle-old, Vaillant (2002) also has some suggestions about the consequences of late adult behavior. We have already taken a look at his prescription for growing old gracefully. In addition, he notes the following personal qualities in late adulthood to bode well for continued well-being:

- Good self-care
- Future orientation, ability to anticipate, plan, and hope
- Capacity for gratitude and forgiveness
- Capacity for empathy, to imagine the world as the other sees it
- Desire to do things with people rather than to them

Exhibit 9.7	Variables That Affect Healthy Aging
Variables That Do Not Predict Healthy Aging	*Variables That Do Predict Healthy Aging*
Ancestral longevity	Not smoking, or stopping young
Cholesterol	Using mature coping mechanisms
Stress	Not abusing alcohol
Parental characteristics	Healthy weight
Childhood temperament	Stable marriage
General ease in social relationships	Some exercise
	Years of education

SOURCE: Vaillant, 2002.

IMPLICATIONS FOR SOCIAL WORK PRACTICE

Several practice principles for social work with older adults can be recommended:

- When working with an older adult, take into account the person's life history.
- Develop self-awareness of your views on aging and how different theoretical perspectives may influence your practice.
- Be conscious that age-related social roles change over time and that they vary for different cohorts.
- Identify areas in which you can assist an elderly client in preventing future problems, such as health-related difficulties.
- Develop an understanding of and skills to assess the difference between the physical, biological, psychological, and socioemotional changes that are part of normal aging and those that are indicative of a problematic process. Develop an understanding of how such factors may affect the intervention process.
- Develop an understanding of the different types of families in later life. Because older adults continue to be part of their families, it may be beneficial to work with the entire family system.
- Develop an understanding of the retirement process and how individuals adjust differently to this new life stage.
- Carefully assess an elderly person's caregiving network. Be conscious of the difficulties that the caregiving situation poses for both the caregiver and the care recipient. Be conscious of the potential for caregiver burnout, and familiarize yourself with local caregiver support options.
- Develop an understanding of the process of institutionalizing an older adult. Be careful not to label it as an act of abandonment. Rather, be aware that institutionalization is stressful for all involved and is typically done only as a last resort. Develop an understanding of the process of adaptation to nursing home placement and skills to assist an older adult and his or her family with that adaptation.
- When assessing the need for service, be conscious of the availability of formal and informal support systems. Develop an understanding and knowledge of the formal service delivery system.
- Avoid treating older persons as if they were incapable of making decisions simply because they may not be able to carry out the decision. Rather, involve them to the maximum extent possible in any decisions relating to their personal life and care, even if they are not able to carry out the related actions.

KEY TERMS

activity theory	dependency ratio	fluid intelligence
age stratification perspective	disengagement theory	genetic theories of
continuity theory	(of aging)	biological aging
crystallized intelligence	ego integrity versus ego	incidental memory
delirium	despair	intentional memory
dementia	feminist theory (of aging)	keeper of the meaning

(Continued)

(Continued)

life review
molecular/cellular theories
   of biological aging
morbidity
mortality rate
power of attorney (POA)

programmed aging
   theories
random error theories
reminiscence
social construction theory
   (of aging)

social exchange theory
   (of aging)
social gerontology
system level theories of
   biological aging

Active Learning

1. Think about the three case studies presented at the outset of this chapter (Smith, Johnson, and Moro). Which theory/theories of social gerontology seems to be the best fit with each of these individuals?

2. Think of examples of how older adults are presented in the media (TV, movies, advertisements). How are they typically characterized? What does this say about our society's views on aging? Think of examples of how older adults could be presented in an age-appropriate way in the media. Develop a short script for an advertisement that features older adults.

3. Think about your own extended family. What roles do the members of the oldest generation play in the family? How do the different generations interact, exchange resources, and influence each other? How do the different generations deal with their role changes and life transitions as they age? In what ways do the different generations support and hinder each other in life transitions?

WEB RESOURCES

National Institute on Aging
www.nia.nih.gov

Site presented by the National Institute on Aging (NIA) contains information about the NIA, news and events, health information, research programs, funding and training, and National Advisory Council on Aging.

National Council on the Aging
www.ncoa.org

Site presented by the National Council on the Aging (NCOA) contains information on advocacy, programs, publications, and a number of good links to other aging resources.

Social Security Online
www.ssa.gov

Site maintained by the U.S. Social Security Administration contains benefits information and online direct services.

AgingStats.Gov
www.agingstats.gov

Site presented by the Federal Interagency Forum on Aging-Related Statistics covers 31 key indicators of the lives of older people in the United States and their families.

Agency for Health Care Research and Quality
www.ahrq.gov

Site provides consumer, patient, and clinical practice information focused on specific populations: aging, women, and rural health.

American Association of Retired Persons
www.aarp.org

Organizational site provides a wide range of resources from health technology, travel, legal, and policy and advocacy.

U.S. Administration on Aging
www.aoa.gov

Site accesses information about older Americans Act, federal legislation and range of programs and statistics.

National Academy of Aging Society
www.agingsociety.org

Organization provides clear unbiased research and analysis focused on public policy issues arising from the aging of America's and world population.

Center on Aging Society - Older Hispanic Americans
http://ihcrp.georgetown.edu/agingsociety/pubhtml/hispanics

Site that presents research results on chronic conditions of older Latino Americans.

National Center and Caucus on Black Aged
www.ncba-aged.org

Site contains aging news for policy makers, legislators, advocacy groups, minority professionals and consumers addressing finances, caregiving, intergenerational issues, and governmental programs.

VERY LATE
ADULTHOOD

Pamela J. Kovacs

Key Ideas	419
Case Study 10.1: ■ Carmen Ruiz Is Institutionalized	420
Case Study 10.2: ■ Bina Patel Outlives Her Son	421
Case Study 10.3: ■ Pete Mullin Loses His Sister's Support	421
Very Late Adulthood: Charting New Territory	422
Very Late Adulthood in Historical and Cultural Perspective	423
What We Can Learn From Centenarians	427
Functional Capacity in Very Late Adulthood	429
Relationships in Very Late Adulthood	431
Relationships With Family and Friends	431
Intimacy and Sexuality in Very Late Adulthood	433
Relationships With Organizations and Community	434
The Housing Continuum	434
Spirituality in Very Late Adulthood	435
The Dying Process	437
Advance Directives	439
Care of People Who Are Dying	440
End-of-Life Signs and Symptoms	441
Loss, Grief, and Bereavement	443
Theories and Models of Loss	445
Culture and Bereavement	448

The Life Course Completed   449
Implications for Social Work Practice   450
Key Terms   450
Active Learning   450
Web Resources   451

❖ What are some of the reasons for the fast growth and increased diversity among very late-life adults, and what are some of the main challenges associated with increased longevity?

❖ What are some of the implications for intimacy among very late-life adults as their families and peers die and they become less mobile and independent?

❖ When working with clients in very late adulthood, what do social workers need to know about how people respond to crises such as severe illness, acquired disability, and loss?

KEY IDEAS

As you read this chapter, take note of these central ideas:

1. People 85 and older are the fastest growing segment of the older adult population. Never have so many people lived so long.

2. Among very late-life adults, women outnumber men five to two, and four out of five centenarians are women.

3. Because the more frail individuals die sooner, those surviving to very late adulthood tend to be a relatively robust group, but they face an increased incidence of chronic disease and disability.

4. In very late adulthood, individuals continue to desire and need connections to other people.

5. In very late adulthood, spirituality is often associated with making meaning of loss and finding a way to stay connected to others.

6. Very late adulthood is the one life course phase when dying is considered "on time," and very late-life adults seem to have less denial about the reality of death than those in other age groups.

7. Theoreticians and researchers continue to try to understand the multidimensional process of grief.

Carmen Ruiz Is Institutionalized

Carmen Ruiz has lived in the same ground floor apartment, next to the city bus station, since she immigrated to the United States in the mid-1950s. When she reflects on her 89 years, she reminisces about growing up on a farm in Puerto Rico, raising her family, and then moving to the United States with her husband when she was 41 years old. Carmen has lived on her own since her husband died 20 years ago, and her two sons returned to Puerto Rico upon their retirement a few years ago. She is the last family member of her generation who is still alive. Carmen's granddaughter, Gloria, who is 45 years old, lives in a nearby suburb and visits regularly. Although Carmen does not understand or speak English, she manages by only interacting with Spanish-speaking individuals and uses services provided in her language. When she requires assistance with English, she calls Gloria.

Carmen was recently hospitalized for six days because of complications related to a recurring heart condition. The original plan was to discharge Carmen to a nursing home for a short-term stay for rehabilitation. But at Gloria's request, that plan was changed, and Carmen was discharged to her apartment with home health aides, visiting nurse services, and in-home physical therapy and occupational rehabilitation services. Now, four weeks later, Carmen is feeling better, and she is back in her routine, shopping in the community, sitting on the steps talking with neighbors, and tending to her own health needs.

The social worker assigned to Carmen's case was involved in the discharge planning and is still following her through long-term care services. After Carmen's discharge, Gloria asked to speak with the social worker, due to growing concern about her grandmother's safety in the apartment. She explained that Carmen has her own unique form of logic, which is "inviolate and untouchable." Gloria thinks that Carmen "invents her own world and you either buy into it or get frozen out." Absolutely everything has to be at Carmen's convenience. The minute she steps into her primary care doctor's office, having made an appointment or not, the doctor must see her right away or she leaves. While Carmen was in the hospital, she became more and more confused, at times not remembering where she was. Since being discharged, Carmen's memory has continued to fail. Several times she has left the stove burning unattended. In-home health care services are an option right now, but soon Carmen will need constant supervision and assistance. Thus, Gloria has made the very difficult decision to pursue a nursing home placement.

When the social worker spoke to Carmen about these issues, she expressed anger and resentment. No one in her family had lived in a nursing home before, and it was not the way she had planned to spend her last years. She insisted that she will stay in her apartment until "God" takes her. Finally, after three incidents where the police had to help Carmen find her way back to the apartment, and a smoky oven fire, Carmen said that God appeared to her and told her that she could leave the apartment.

Fortunately, the social worker found a nursing home with a Spanish-speaking staff and an immediate opening. Carmen moved from her apartment of almost 50 years to the nursing home. Carmen's first days there were painfully difficult. She had to share a room with a woman experiencing dementia, who repeated the same phrases over and over again. During the day, Carmen did not want to spend any time in her new room. So, in addition to being upset about losing her independence and the hope of returning home, she felt trapped in an unfamiliar environment without a place to retreat. During these first days, Carmen felt very lonely and had a hard time finding companionship among the nursing home residents. Her social worker encouraged her to establish some new routines to take the place of her old ones. Gloria continues to visit Carmen daily, and they spend time together on the weekends. They continue to be close and are planning to spend a weekend together when Gloria's father visits from Puerto Rico.

Case Study 10.2

Bina Patel Outlives Her Son

Bina Patel is a 90-year-old immigrant who moved to the United States 25 years ago from India with her son and his family. Like many other South Asian older adults, Bina prefers to reside with her adult children and values the mutual interdependency among generations common in their culture. Upon arriving in this country at age 65, Bina, a widow, played a critical role in the family, providing child care, assisting with meals and various household tasks, and offering companionship and support for her adult children. True to her cultural tradition, Bina expects adult children—especially sons—to provide for parents in their old age, and believes that the role of the elder is to provide crucial functions such as passing on wisdom and guidance to children and grandchildren, and being constantly available to them.

Bina had been in remarkably good health until she had a mild stroke last year. She was managing well at home with weekly physical therapy and her family's assistance with bathing. She and her family have been unprepared for her longevity; and in fact it appears that she will outlive her son, who at age 69 was recently diagnosed with pancreatic cancer with a prognosis of 6 to 12 months to live. Her daughter-in-law is home full-time with Bina, but does not drive, and currently is emotionally distraught over her husband's rapid decline. Bina's two grandchildren, who are in their 30s, have relocated with their own families due to employment. They are in frequent telephone contact, but they live a two-hour plane ride away and are busy with work and children's school and activities. Although this family has traditionally handled their family needs on their own or with the help of a small South Asian network, the son's decline in health has caused tremendous concern regarding Bina's future well-being.

The hospital social worker has been asked to meet with the son and daughter-in-law during his hospitalization to explore possible sources of assistance during the son's pending decline as well as to help strategize for Bina's anticipated increased need of physical care, given her recent decline in cognitive and physical capacity.

Case Study 10.3

Pete Mullin Loses His Sister's Support

Pete Mullin and Lucy Rauso, brother and sister, ages 96 and 92, have lived together since the death of Lucy's husband, Tony, 25 years ago. Pete and Lucy are second-generation Irish Catholic Americans and Tony Rauso was Italian American. Pete was married in his 30s, but had lived alone since his divorce at age 55. Pete and Lucy were both in their early 70s when they decided to pool their limited savings and retirement income to buy a condominium in south Florida. The promise of lower cost of living and milder winters, and the fact that many of their friends had moved or died, made it easier for Lucy and Pete to leave the community in Massachusetts where they had spent their entire lives.

Pete has been estranged from his one daughter since his divorce but is in touch with a granddaughter who "found" him when she moved to Florida a few years ago. Lucy has one surviving son in New Jersey and several grandchildren who provide limited financial support and some social support via phone calls and an occasional visit. Pete has enjoyed his life and, despite some difficulty with his vision and hearing, manages to get around well in his familiar surroundings. He is especially fond of tending his orchids in the back porch.

(Continued)

(Continued)

Lucy has just been hospitalized with chronic heart failure and is not expected to make it through the night. A neighbor has brought Pete to the ICU to be with Lucy. Pete states that together he and Lucy managed to provide for each other and served as each other's durable power of attorney, health care surrogate, and in general made it possible for each of them to remain in their home. He wonders what will happen to him after Lucy's death. He knows that many people his age live in nursing homes, but he prefers to stay in his own home. He wonders if the Meals on Wheels will still come to the home, because their eligibility was based on Lucy's diagnosis of chronic heart failure. He hopes he will die soon and quickly like Lucy.

The social worker employed for the Meals on Wheels program has been asked to make a home visit within the week following Lucy's death to reassess Pete's eligibility for services. The social worker had not realized how much social work would involve working with people who have experienced a major loss, whether death of a loved one as in Pete's case, or the accompanying losses that come with illness, disability, and aging.

⧆ Very Late Adulthood: Charting New Territory

At 89, 90, 92, and 96, Carmen Ruiz, Bina Patel, Lucy Rauso, and Pete Mullin are charting new territory. They are a part of the rapidly growing population over age 85. Bina Patel—and perhaps Carmen Ruiz, Pete Mullin, and Lucy Rauso as well—has surprised herself, as well as her family, by living so long. Never have so many people lived to be so old.

How does the fact that the current cohort of very late-life adults are charting new territory affect their experience with this life course phase?

In the first edition of this book (1999), the chapter on late adulthood covered all persons 65 and older. The fact that subsequent editions present this content in two chapters ("Late Adulthood" and "Very Late Adulthood") indicates the scope and rapidity of the demographic changes taking place in the United States and other late industrial societies. Only within the past 10 to 15 years have some researchers begun to methodically consider age distinctions after age 65 or 75.

This chapter summarizes some of the emerging literature on very late adulthood. (Much of what appears in the previous chapter on late adulthood applies as well.) However, current knowledge about very late adulthood is limited. After all, until recently there were not enough adults over 85 to warrant special study. And at the current time, we do not have any longitudinal studies that have followed a cohort from early adulthood deep into very late adulthood. Consequently, it is impossible to tease out the cohort effects in the available cross-sectional research.

One issue that comes up at all adult stages is, what ages are you including? As you have seen throughout this book, chronological markers of age are arbitrary at best, and influenced by biological age, psychological age, social age, and spiritual age. But it is fairly standard to think of 85 and older as old old, oldest old, or very late adulthood. In this chapter, we use "very late adulthood" to describe the life course phase. For the most part, we use "very late-life adults" to describe people in this life course phase, but we also use "old old" and "oldest old" when citing work where those terms are used. Keep in mind that chronological age may not be the best marker for categorizing very late-life adults, however (Pipher, 1999). Loss of health might be a better criterion for categorization as very late adulthood or old old. Nevertheless, in keeping with the other chapters in the book, this chapter uses a chronological distinction.

The drawback to using a chronological marker for entry into very late adulthood is that the path through very late adulthood is quite diverse, and for many people over 85, ill health is not a central theme of their lives. In his book *Aging Well,* George Vaillant (2002) reminds us that:

- ◆ Frank Lloyd Wright designed the Guggenheim Museum at age 90.
- ◆ Dr. Michael DeBakey obtained a patent for a surgical innovation when he was 90.
- ◆ Pablo Casals was still practicing cello daily at 91.
- ◆ Leopold Stokowski signed a six-year recording contract at 94.
- ◆ Grandma Moses was still painting at 100.

In addition, we would add that:

- ◆ Sarah and Elizabeth Delany (1993) published their book *Having Our Say: Our First 100 Years* when Sarah (Sadie) was 103 and Elizabeth (Bessie) was 101.
- ◆ Sadie Delany (1997) published *On My Own at 107: Reflections on Life Without Bessie* at the age of 107.

So, there is much variation in the age at which health issues take on great importance. Carmen Ruiz and Bina Patel reached this stage in their late 80s, Lucy Rauso reached it in her early 90s, and it does not yet seem to have overtaken Pete Mullin in his mid-90s. But sooner or later in very late adulthood, health issues and impending death become paramount.

With our current ways of living, such as busy and pressured work schedules and families geographically scattered, late industrial societies are not organized to make aging easy. That portion of the physical environment attributable solely to human efforts was designed, in the main, by and for those in young and middle adulthood, not for children, persons with various types of disabilities, or older adults. Not only is the current cohort of very late-life adults charting new territory, but as a society we are also charting new territory that will become more and more familiar when the large baby boom generation reaches very late adulthood. What can we learn from people who reach 85 and beyond, and what do social work practitioners need to know to provide meaningful interventions?

As Erik Erikson suggested, we have one and only one life cycle (at least in this incarnation). Sooner or later, each of us will complete that life cycle and die. For some of us, that death will come quickly, but for others, death will come after a protracted period of disease and disability. One of the life tasks of late adulthood is to come to terms with that one and only life cycle, and the evidence suggests that most very late-life adults do that remarkably well. We began this book with a discussion of conception and birth, the starting line of the life course, and in this chapter we end the book with a discussion of death and dying, the finish line of the life course.

⊠ Very Late Adulthood in Historical and Cultural Perspective

There have always been those who outlive their cohort group, but greater numbers of people are surpassing the average life expectancy and more are becoming centenarians. Although very few persons age 100 years were known to exist in the United States in 1900, by 2000 there were an estimated 61,000 (Dunkle, Roberts, & Haug, 2001). Between 1990 and 2000, the largest percentage of growth in the U.S. population occurred in the baby boom 50- to 54-year-old age group, which grew 55%. The 90- to 94-year-old age group grew 45%, as did another baby boom group, the 45- to 49-year-old age group (U.S. Census Bureau, 2001b). According to the U.S. Census, the 85-and-older population is currently the fastest growing segment of the aging population (Administration on Aging, 2006a).

Growth in the midlife age groups is the result of the high birthrates in the baby boom generation. But what accounts for the fact that persons 85 and older are the fastest growing segment of the older adult population? Several factors contribute to the growth among old-old adults, including better health care in early and middle years, earlier diagnosis and improved technology for treatment and overall health care, and improved health habits, including less smoking, less consumption of alcohol and saturated fats, and increased exercise in some groups. In addition, fewer people die of infectious diseases. Although more older adults are living with chronic illnesses, fewer have debilitating illnesses (Hooyman & Kiyak, 2005).

The U.S. Census data refers to persons 65 and older as "elderly" and those 85 and older as the "oldest old" (Federal Interagency Forum on Aging-Related Statistics, 2004). Between 1900 and 1994, the elderly population in the United States increased elevenfold compared to threefold for those under age 65. Of interest to this chapter, however, is that from 1960 to 1994, persons aged 85 and older (the oldest old) increased by 274% compared to 100% for those 65 and older and 45% for the total population. The oldest old population is projected to grow from 4.2 million in 2000 to nearly 21 million by 2050, due in part to the baby boomers moving into this category after 2030.

Because both group-based and individual differences within this age group are great, one is cautioned against stereotyping very late-life adults in an attempt to describe them (Field & Gueldner, 2001). For instance, gender and racial/ethnic differences are embedded within these overall statistics. Life expectancy at birth in the United States in 1991 was about 80 years for white females, 74 years for black females, 73 years for white males, and 65 years for black males. Among very late-life adults, women outnumber men five to two, and four out of five centenarians are women. At this point, very late adulthood is largely a woman's territory. Pete Mullin is an exception to this trend. Culturally, the most significant fact is that very late-life adults, like other age groups, are becoming more diverse. The percent by racial category for 2003 and the projected percentage for 2050 are as follows for the population age 65 and over: non-Hispanic white 83%/61%; black 8%/12%; Hispanic 6%/18%; Asian 3%/8%; and all other races 1%/3% (Federal Interagency Forum on Aging-Related Statistics, 2004). These trends should eventually lead to more diversity among the old old.

Census data such as these are of interest to researchers studying *ethnogerontology*, the study of the causes, processes, and consequences of race, national origin, and culture on individual and population aging (Hooyman & Kiyak, 2005). Poverty is another indicator of interest with the older population, given decreased earning power and increased health related expenses. In terms of gender, older women (12%) were more likely than older men (8%) to live in poverty in 2002. Overall, the poverty rate increased with age with 9% of people 65 to 74 and 12% of those over 75 years of age living in poverty (Federal Interagency Forum on Aging-Related Statistics, 2004).

Chapter 1 suggests that one of the themes of the life course perspective is that individual and family development must be understood in historical context. It is particularly important when we interact with very late-life adults to be aware of the historical worlds in which their life journeys have taken place. To help us to keep this in mind, Exhibit 10.1 captures some historical events faced by the current cohort of 89-year-olds (as of June 2006). Of course, many of these events have also been shared by young adults, midlife adults, and late-life adults, but at different life phases.

Exhibit 10.1	Historical Events Witnessed by an 89-Year-Old Born in 1917 (as of 2006)

When He or She Was . . .	*Historical Event*
An infant	The United States enters World War I.
3	Women win the right to vote in the United States.
6	The National Woman's Party launches a campaign for an equal rights amendment.
	First shopping center opens in Kansas City.
11	First color motion picture is demonstrated.
A teenager	Mount Rushmore is completed.
	"Star Spangled Banner" is adopted as national anthem.
	The Great Depression becomes a worldwide phenomenon.
	Social Security legislation is passed.
20-something	American Medical Association approves birth control.
	New York's La Guardia Airport opens.
	U.S. Supreme Court rules blacks are entitled to first class services on railroad trains.
	United States enters World War II after the attack at Pearl Harbor.
	GI Bill is signed, giving broad benefits to returned servicemen.
30-something	Minimum wage is raised from 40 to 75 cents.
	U.S. Supreme Court outlaws racial segregation in public schools.
	Rosa Parks refuses to relinquish her seat to a white man on a bus in Montgomery, Alabama.
	Jonas Salk develops polio vaccine.
40-something	Russia sends first satellite into space, and the United States follows soon behind.
	The computer microchip is invented.
	BankAmericard and American Express issue credit cards.
	Alaska and Hawaii become the 49th and 50th states.
	President Kennedy becomes the first Catholic president of the United States.
	John Glenn becomes the first American to orbit Earth.
	Black Civil Rights Movement reaches its peak.
	National Organization for Women (NOW) is formed.
	United States involvement in Vietnam deepens.
	Lyndon Johnson begins a War on Poverty.
50-something	First human heart transplant takes place.
	Antiwar sentiment against U.S. involvement in Vietnam intensifies.
	Student protest movement against war and racism spreads.
	Neil Armstrong walks on the moon.

(Continued)

Exhibit 10.1	(Continued)

When He or She Was . . .	Historical Event
50-something	Thousands flock to music festival at Woodstock, New York.
	Computerized axial tomography (CAT) scan is developed.
	Watergate break-in ultimately causes Richard Nixon to resign.
	OPEC imposes a six-month oil embargo on the United States.
	Roe v. Wade imposes constitutional protections on abortion.
	Saturday Night Live television show debuts.
60-something	First "test-tube baby" is born.
	The World Health Organization announces that smallpox has been eradicated worldwide.
	CNN, the first 24-hour TV news channel, is launched.
	IBM introduces the first generation of personal computers.
	MTV is created.
	Sandra Day O'Connor becomes the first woman on the U.S. Supreme Court.
	Astronaut Sally Ride is the first U.S. woman to travel in space.
	Crack cocaine addiction becomes a serious problem.
	Terrorism becomes a fact of life.
	The space shuttle *Challenger* explodes immediately after takeoff.
70-something	Communism loses its hold in Eastern Europe, and the Soviet Union disintegrates.
	The Americans with Disabilities Act recognizes the civil rights of persons with disabilities.
	The U.S. wages Operation Desert Storm to liberate Kuwait from Iraq.
	Basketball star "Magic" Johnson announces on TV that he had contracted AIDS.
	Islamic terrorists bomb New York's World Trade Center, killing five people.
	The computer-based worldwide network (Internet) revolutionizes communications.
	Former President Ronald Reagan reveals he is suffering from Alzheimer's disease.
	War veteran Timothy McVeigh bombs the Alfred P. Murrah Building in Oklahoma City.
	President Bill Clinton signs legislation that ends "welfare as we knew it."
	The Taliban gains control in Afghanistan.
80-something	Researchers in Great Britain clone a sheep.
	President Clinton is impeached after a sex scandal with a White House intern.
	The stock market hits unprecedented highs, before deflating.
	On September 11, 2001, terrorists fly hijacked airplanes into the World Trade Center in New York City and the Pentagon.
	Scandals at major big businesses in the United States reveal accounting fraud and greed.
	President George W. Bush wages war on Iraq despite U.S. and worldwide protests

SOURCE: Based on National Geographic Society, 1998.

Chapter 1 also discusses the concept of *cohort effects,* which suggests that a historical event affects one cohort differently than it affects subsequent cohorts because of the life phase in which it occurred. Let's look, for example, at the wide use of the computerized worldwide network (the Internet). It was experienced:

- By the current cohort of 85-year-olds when they were in their 70s
- By the current cohort of 65-year-olds when they were in their 50s
- By the current cohort of 45-year-olds when they were in their 30s
- By the current cohort of 25-year-olds when they were in their teens
- By the current cohort of 10-year-olds as a staple of life from infancy

What differences do you think this cohort effect makes for cognitive and social development?

Individuals' cultural backgrounds also play a role in their perceptions of very late adulthood. Remember that Carmen Ruiz's first 41 years were spent in Puerto Rico, and Bina Patel lived the first 65 years of her life in India—both places in which the very old are expected to live out their lives under the care of their extended families. In contrast, Pete Mullin and Lucy Rauso relocated from Massachusetts to Florida in their 70s, moving away from family and friends. Social workers need to try to understand clients' years in these prior settings and any important historical markers in those settings. They also need to know something about migration experiences as well.

▧ What We Can Learn From Centenarians

"Forget about Generation X and Generation Y. Today, the nation's most intriguing demographic is Generation Roman numeral C—folks age 100 and over" ("Aging," 2002, p. 1). Phrases such as "master survivors" and "successful agers" have been used to describe those who reach their 80s.

Those who reach their 100s are "expert agers" (Poon et al., 1992, p. 7).

> How will this longevity trend alter our views on appropriate roles for other adult phases?

In the United States, the number of centenarians doubled in the 1980s and again in the 1990s, with a total of 70,000 reported in 2002 ("Aging," 2002). In the next 50 years, midrange projections anticipate that over 800,000 people in the United States could reach the century mark. The number is expected to grow to 834,000 by 2050 and double every 10 years thereafter (Coles, 2004). Other industrialized countries report similar trends. Future editions of human behavior textbooks might in fact report on another group that demographers are now counting—supercentenarians, people age 110 and over (Coles, 2004).

More than counting numbers, researchers want to know the answers to fundamental questions about human health and longevity such as:

- What does it take to live a long life?
- How much do diet, exercise, and other lifestyle factors matter compared with "good" genes and other genetic factors?
- What is the quality of life among very late-life adults?
- What role do individual characteristics such as gender, personality, and socioeconomic status play in longevity?

▲ **Photo 10.1** Fred Hale, Sr. smiles as his great-great-grandaughters arrive to celebrate his 113th birthday. In the United States, the number of centenarians doubled in the 1980s and again in the 1990s, with a total of 70,000 reported in 2002.

How does the gender gap affect the experience of very late adulthood?

◆ What is the role of social support, religion and spirituality, and social environment in longevity?
◆ Basically, what is the secret?

Much of what is known about centenarians comes from the work of Leonard Poon and his colleagues in the Georgia Centenarian Study (1992) and from the New England Centenarian Study (Perls & Wood, 1996). These and other centenarian studies are trying to understand the interrelationship between multiple variables such as family longevity, gender, environmental support, adaptational skills, individual traits, life satisfaction, and health.

These studies reveal that because the more frail individuals die sooner, those remaining are a relatively robust group. While these "extra" years are for the most part healthy years, several studies report high levels of dementia (66% in one study and 51% in another) and cardiovascular disease (72%), urinary incontinence (60%), and osteoarthritis (54%). What is more notable, however, is that the period of serious illness and disability for those who make it to 100 tends to be brief ("Aging," 2002). Some factors thought to contribute to centenarians' robustness are physical activity such as walking, biking, golfing, and swimming, as well as mental exercise such as reading, painting, and playing a musical instrument.

However, 100 is still old and life expectancy is short at 100, with most only living one to two more years. In the New England Study, 75% of the people were still living at home and taking care of themselves at 95. By age 102, this number had dropped to 30%—which is still quite remarkable.

The gender gap in very late adulthood widens further past the age of 100, with female centenarians outnumbering males nine to one. However, men who reach their 100th birthday are, on the whole, more healthy than their female counterparts, reporting lower incidence of dementia and other serious medical problems. Estrogen may give women an edge in longevity. Another possibility is that there may be some protective genes in the X chromosome, of which women have two but men only one. Others theorize that menstruation and systems related to childbirth better equip women to eliminate toxins from the body. Another hypothesis is that genetics are relatively neutral, but women tend to be more social, and these connections are thought to be critical in weathering old age ("Aging," 2002). Cross-cultural studies in which differences in diet, physical activity, and other lifestyle factors can be compared will be important in helping researchers better understand the influence of these multiple contributing variables.

▨ Functional Capacity in Very Late Adulthood

Although persons who reach 85 years of age and older demonstrate resilience in the simple fact of their longevity, they continue to face an increased incidence of chronic illness and debilitation with age. Chapter 9 provides a good overview of changes in physiology and mental functioning that begin to occur in late adulthood and only become more prevalent with advancing age. Unfortunately, much of the available information does not distinguish the 85 and older cohort group from the larger 65 and older group. We do know that the likelihood of living in a nursing home increases with age. Among nursing home residents, about 13% are between 65- and 74-years-old, 35% are between 75 and 84, and 51% are 85 and older (U.S. Census Bureau, 2004). Many late life adults enter a nursing home for a period of convalescence after hospitalization and then return to home or another setting.

In a national survey of older adults, respondents were asked to rate their health from *excellent* to *poor*. In the 75 to 84 age group, 71% of non-Hispanic whites, 54% of non-Hispanic blacks, and 50% of Hispanics rated their health as either good, very good, or excellent. The ratings were very similar for each group among the group 85 or older; 67% of non-Hispanic whites, 52% of non-Hispanic blacks, and 53% of Hispanics rated their health as either good, very good, or excellent (Federal Interagency Forum on Aging-Related Statistics, 2004).

In another research project, trend data from a four wave National Long Term Care Survey indicate a high level of disability among older adults 85 and over, but the rate of disability declined over a 15-year period from 62.0% in 1984 to 55.5% in 1999 (Spillman, 2004). There was no decline in limitations in **activities of daily living (ADL)**, or basic self-care activities, but declines did occur in limitations in **instrumental activities of daily living (IADL)**, which are more complex everyday tasks. (Exhibit 10.2 lists common ADLs and IADLs.) About the same percentage of 85 and older adults received human assistance with at least one ADL in 1984 (19.9%) and 1999 (18.5%). However, the percentage using ADL equipment increased from 1.9% in 1984 to 5.7% in 1999. The percentage receiving human assistance with IADLs declined from 16.6% in 1984 to 9.8% in 1999. There was no change in the use of community IADL equipment, which occurred in about 1% of the 85 and over population. The percentage of this population in institutions remained at about 20% during this 15-year period.

In general, all persons experience **primary aging**, or changes that are a normal part of the aging process. There is a recognized slowing with age—slowing of motor responses, sensory responses, and intellectual functioning. "Older individuals can do what younger ones can, but it takes more time. The causes of the slowing are not fully understood, although animals of all species become slower as they age" (Seifert, Hoffnung, & Hoffnung, 1997, p. 589). For example, the percentage of older adults in the United States with significant visual loss increases during late and very late adulthood: 9% among the 65- to 75-year-olds, 16% among the 75- to 84-year-olds, and 28% among those over 85. Similarly, in terms of hearing, 23% of 65- to 74-year-olds, 34% of 75- to 84-year-olds, and 51% of persons 85 and older experience significant hearing loss.

In addition, many experience **secondary aging** caused by health-compromising behaviors such as smoking or environmental factors such as pollution (Seifert et al., 1997).

Exhibit 10.2	Common Activities of Daily Living (ADLs) and Instrumental Activities of Daily Living (IADLs)

Activities of Daily Living

Bathing

Dressing

Walking a short distance

Shifting from a bed to a chair

Using the toilet

Eating

Instrumental Activities of Daily Living

Doing light housework

Doing the laundry

Using transportation

Handling finances

Using the telephone

Taking medications

How much control do we have over secondary aging?

Access to health care, ample and nutritious food, safe and affordable housing, safe working conditions, and other factors that influence the quality of life also affect longevity.

Although late adulthood is a time of loss of efficiency in body systems and functioning, the body is an organism that repairs and restores itself as damage occurs. Those persons who live to be 85 and older may be blessed with a favorable genetic makeup. But they may also have found ways to compensate, to prevent, to restore, and to maintain other health-promoting behaviors. One cross-sectional study of individuals age 85 and over found that most report well-being despite their physical and social losses (Johnson & Barer, 1997). Most very late-life adults come to think of themselves in ways that fit their circumstances. They narrow the scope of their activities to those that are most cherished, and they carefully schedule their activities to make the best use of their energy and talents.

Sooner or later, however, most very late-life adults come to need some assistance with ADLs and IADLs. As a society, we have to grapple with the question of who will provide that assistance. Currently, most of the assistance is provided by family members. But as families grow smaller, fewer adult children exist to provide such care. A number of family theorists have begun to wonder how multigenerational families might adjust their relationships and better meet long distance caregiving needs (Harrigan & Koerin, in press; MetLife/National Alliance for Caregiving, 2004; Pipher, 1999).

▧ Relationships in Very Late Adulthood

Much of what is presented in Chapter 9 under the section called Families in Later Life applies also to very late adulthood. Research that looks specifically at relationship patterns among very late-life adults is limited, but two themes are clear (Carstensen, 2001):

How do current social arrangements threaten and/or support the desire for social connections among very late-life adults?

1. Individuals continue to desire and need connections to other people throughout life.

2. In very late adulthood, people interact with others less frequently, but old-old adults make thoughtful selections about the persons with whom they will interact.

After intensive interviews with groups that she labeled as young-old and old-old, Mary Pipher (1999) concludes that "the situations that work for people in the young-old stage are not feasible for the old-old. Young-old people may love their mountain cabin or Manhattan townhouse, but old-old people need relatives nearby" (p. 32). That is one of the issues that will need to be explored as our society charts the new demographic territory.

Relationships With Family and Friends

Social isolation is considered to be a powerful risk factor not only for the development of cognitive and intellectual decline in very late adulthood but also for physical illness (McInnis-Dittrich, 2005). A sense of connectedness with family and friends can be achieved in person, on the phone, and more recently via chat rooms, blogs, and e-mail. The focus in this section is on relationships with people; however, remember that pets, plants, and other connections with nature bring comfort to any age group, including older adults.

Pertinent to very late-life adults is the increased likelihood that one will have lost spouses/partners, friends, and other family members to death, illness, debilitation, or relocation. Loss is more prevalent during this stage than at other times of life, but there is also greater opportunity for intergenerational family contact as four-, five-, and six-generation families become more common.

Siblings often provide companionship and caregiving for each other, as Pete Mullin and Lucy Rauso did in the case study. Siblings are comforting because they are part of one's cohort and also have experienced many of the same family events. In addition, siblings tend to be the most long-standing relationships in a person's life (Cicerelli, 1995; Hooyman & Kiyak, 2005). Obviously, sibling relationships may range from loving and close to ambivalent, distant, or even hostile. Sharing responsibility for aging parents may create greater closeness between siblings or increase tension. There is some evidence that sibling relationships are especially important sources of support among members of lower socioeconomic groups. Close relationships with sisters in very late adulthood have been found to be positively related to positive mental health, but close relationships with brothers have not been found to have the same benefit (Cicerelli, 1995).

Relationships with adult children are another important part of the social networks of very late-life adults. However, one study of a predominantly white sample in San Francisco found that older people prefer to be independent from their children when possible, with adult children serving more as managers of social supports than providing direct care

▲ **Photo 10.2**   Relationships with adult children are a very important part of social networks for very late-life adults.

(Johnson & Barer, 1997). Very late-life adults in the United States are in fact institutionalized more often for social reasons than for medical reasons (Hooyman & Kiyak, 2005). One reason for this is that approximately one in five women 80 and older has been childless throughout her life or has outlived her children. In addition, baby boomers and their children tended to have more divorces and fewer children, decreasing the caregiving options for their parents and grandparents (Hooyman & Kiyak, 2005). Racial and ethnic variations exist, however. As in Bina Patel's case, families with a collectivist heritage prefer to have elderly parents reside with their grown children. It is important to understand and honor historical and cultural expectations of each family when addressing the caregiving and health care needs of aging members.

Relationships with friends remain important in very late adulthood. In general, women have fewer economic resources, but more social resources, and richer, more intimate relationships than do older men (Hooyman & Kiyak, 2005). But over time, women tend to outlive partners, friends, and other key members of their social support system, often being left to deal with end-of-life decisions at an advanced age, without the social and perhaps financial support of earlier life.

Relationships with a domestic partner become much less likely in very late adulthood than in earlier phases of life. Very late-life adults have the potential to have shared 60 to 70 years with a spouse or partner, but one study found that was the case for no more than 20% of a white sample in San Francisco (Johnson & Barer, 1997). Such long-term relationships, where they do exist, present the risk of tremendous loss when one member of the relationship dies. (Widowhood is presented in more detail in Chapter 9.) Because women outnumber men five to two over the age of 85, heterosexual men stand a greater chance of starting a new relationship than heterosexual women. With the current gender demographics, lesbian domestic partnerships have the greatest opportunity for continued long-term relationships in very late adulthood.

Intimacy and Sexuality in Very Late Adulthood

Given the scarcity of men and the fact that many partners and friends have died, many persons 85 and older, especially women, are more alone in this life stage than at other times in their lives. The implications for intimacy and sexuality for heterosexual women are significant. Although minimal research has been conducted specifically about intimacy and sexuality with this age group, some tentative conclusions can be drawn from literature on aging. In particular, a summer 2002 issue of *Generations* focused on "Intimacy and Aging," including the expressions of intimacy in a variety of relationships, challenges related to physical and mental illness, gay and lesbian relationships, and separation of couples due to institutionalization.

Intimacy can be seen as much broader than sexuality, which has been identified as only one of five major components of intimacy (Moss & Schwebel, cited in Blieszner & deVries, 2001). These are the five major components of intimacy in this view:

1. *Commitment.* Feeling of cohesion and connection

2. *Affective intimacy.* A deep sense of caring, compassion, and positive regard and the opportunities to express the same

3. *Cognitive intimacy.* Thinking about and awareness of another, sharing values and goals

4. *Physical intimacy.* Sharing physical encounters ranging from proximity to sexuality

5. *Mutuality.* A process of exchange or interdependence

Closeness is inherent in cognitive, affective, and physical intimacy. Communication, or self-disclosure, facilitates intimacy.

Although sexuality is only one aspect of intimacy, it deserves additional attention; it should not be neglected, as it often is in our interaction with older adults: "Sexuality is a major quality-of-life issue, even into advanced age" (Bortz & Wallace, 1999, p. 167). It is important for social workers to assess the impact of physical and psychosocial conditions on the sexual interest level, satisfaction, and performance of older adults. Medical conditions such as heart disease, diabetes, arthritis, chronic pain, depression, and medications prescribed to address these and other conditions may reduce or restrict movement or sexual function as well as impact pleasure. (Ducharme, 2001; Hooyman & Kiyak, 2005). Because of these conditions, some very late-life adults are relieved to move into a less sexualized type of intimacy (Pipher, 1999).

Some of the more common psychosocial factors associated with reduced sexual desire or sexual dysfunction include restrictive beliefs about sexuality and aging, role changes due to illness or disability in one or both of the partners, anxiety about sexual function, and psychological disorders. Depression and substance abuse are especially prevalent in older adults with sexual dysfunction. Also, cultural ideals about body image and perceived sexual attractiveness make it more difficult for some older adults to embrace age-related changes (Zeiss & Kasl-Godley, 2001). Many older adults grew up in a time when older people were generally expected to be asexual or not interested in forming new romantic attachments. This cultural conditioning may make it difficult to accept today's greater openness about sexual and romantic relationships, sexual orientation, and varying partnership choices at all ages (Huyck, 2001).

Relationships With Organizations and Community

Relationships with the wider world peak in young and middle adulthood. They grow more constricted as access to social, occupational, recreational, and religious activities becomes more difficult due to decreased mobility and independence, and as the physical and cognitive impairments associated with age increase. As mobility declines, community-based programs like Meals on Wheels can become important resources to people like Pete Mullin and Lucy Rauso, providing them not only with essential resources such as food but serving also as a connection to the community.

One organizational relationship becomes more likely with advancing age, however. As people live longer and need greater assistance, many move into some form of institutional care. When reading the following discussion about the housing continuum, consider the benefits and the challenges each option presents.

◪ The Housing Continuum

As people live longer, the likelihood of illness and disability increases; spouses, partners, and friends die, and the chance of needing more support than is available to the very late-life adults in their own home increases. Review the section on informal and formal resources in Chapter 9 for a description of the variety of options along the continuum as needs for assistance increase.

Other than skilled nursing care reimbursed by Medicare and other health insurance, the majority of assistance that people need must be paid for privately. Financing is a major problem for low-income and even many middle-income people. Women, especially women of color, are overrepresented in lower socioeconomic categories, and in very late adulthood, safe, affordable housing options are a serious concern for them, as was the case for Carmen Ruiz. But even Pete Mullin and Lucy Rauso found housing a problem until they moved in together and pooled their resources.

> How do gender, race, ethnicity, and social class affect access to physical assistance in very later adulthood?

Current trends indicate that in the future, the following housing options will be in greater demand and hopefully more readily available (Hogstel, 2001):

- ◆ Shared housing, shared expenses, and support by family members and friends
- ◆ Options for care and assistance in the home with education and support available to family and other informal caregivers
- ◆ Housing options such as assisted living facilities, which provide 24-hour assistance, and continuing care retirement communities, which offer a range of services and options for aging in place, without a large initial investment

Here:

her short-term memory loss. But I also know that she has been questioning the meaning of her life and wondering about her own death, especially since the recent death of her 58-year-old son to cancer.

The following discussion about spirituality refers to aging in general, not specifically to the very late-life adults, but is included in this chapter because of the connection between aging, loss, spirituality, and meaning making. It is when faced by crises—particularly those of severe illness, disability, and/or loss—that one tends to reexamine the meaning of life (Ai, 2000). And while illness, disability, and loss occur throughout life, these challenges tend to accumulate and come at a faster pace during very late adulthood.

Many definitions of spirituality exist. Some social work educators suggest that spirituality refers to the way in which persons seek, find, create, use, and expand personal meaning in the context of their universe, with each person having a unique spiritual style (Ellor, Netting, & Thibault, 1999). More simply, spirituality represents the way in which people seek meaning and purpose in their lives (Bullis, 1996; Canda & Furman, 1999; Sheridan, 2008). Simmons (2005) reminds us to find a definition or association with the word "spirituality" that fits for each person, given that for some older adults the term may have negative connotations. Based on qualitative interviews with older women, Moremen (2004–2005) concluded that "spiritual questioning—independent of organized religion, significant loss, or impending death—is a natural part of the aging process as one approaches the end of the life span" (p. 309). Dalby (2006) notes that some aspects of spirituality pertain across the life course; however, the following tasks, needs, or changes become more relevant with aging: integrity, humanistic concern, changing relationships with others and greater concern for younger generations, relationship with a transcendent being or power, self transcendence, and coming to terms with death.

Spirituality late in life is often associated with loss (Armatowski, 2001, p. 75). Over time, losses accumulate in the following areas:

- Relationships: to children, spouses and partners, friends, and others
- Status and role: in family, work, and society
- Health: stamina, mobility, hearing, vision, and other physical and cognitive functions
- Control and independence: finances, housing, health care, and other decision-making arenas

Whether incremental or sudden, these losses can be difficult for members of a society where personal autonomy, independence, and sense of control are highly valued. Ironically, this increased focus on spirituality often coincides with decreased mobility and independence and diminishing social contact, limiting access to church services and other opportunities for spiritual fulfillment and social support (Harrigan & Farmer, 2000; Watkins, 2001). Spirituality that develops over a lifetime is most responsive to the challenges and the immediacies of old age (Koenig & Brooks, 2002). Consider, for example, the way that Carmen Ruiz depended on her relationship with God to make the difficult decisions she faced when she could no longer care for herself in her own home.

This search for meaning is a central element of Erik Erikson's (1963) eighth and final developmental task, referred to as maturity. It involves the challenge of *ego integrity versus ego despair* and centers on one's ability to process what has happened in life and accept these experiences as integral to the meaning of life. Other important spiritual challenges facing elders include transcendence beyond oneself and a sense of connectedness to others (McInnis-Dittrich, 2005). An elderly person's struggle to maintain independence and the ability to make choices in the face of multiple challenges, versus becoming dependent on others, is both psychosocial and spiritual, calling for a social work response addressing both. It is important to remember that culture, race, religious upbringing, and other life experiences may influence each person's spiritual journey.

Fischer (1993) suggests that for older adults, the meaning of spirituality often takes the form of these five themes of advice:

1. Embrace the moment.

2. Find meaning in past memories as part of constructing meaning in your life.

3. Confront your own limitations.

4. Seek reconciliation and forgiveness.

5. Reach out to others through prayer or service.

These themes suggest a process of slowing down, looking back, and reaching out—steps that make sense developmentally as one nears the end of life. Over time, people tend to review their lives, some informally, and others more formally. The more formal life review involves helping people shape their memories and experiences for others, usually family and loved ones. Whether shared orally or in writing, social workers, family members, or others who share a closeness with a person often help facilitate this process of reflection and meaning making (Hooyman & Kiyak, 2005).

The subject of spirituality is separated in this chapter from the subject of dying to emphasize the point that spirituality is not just about preparing for death. Rather, it is about finding meaning in life, transcending oneself, and remaining connected to others (McInnis-Dittrich, 2005).

▧ The Dying Process

The topic of death and dying is almost always in the last chapter of a human behavior textbook, reflecting the hope that death will come as late as possible in life. Obviously, people die in all stages of life, but very late adulthood is the time when dying is considered "on time."

Despite our strong cultural predisposition toward denial of the topic, and perhaps in response to this, there have been a plethora of efforts to talk about death, most notably Elisabeth Kübler-Ross's book *On Death and Dying* in 1969. In recent years, efforts like the Project on Death in America (PDIA) funded by the Soros Foundation and end of life initiatives funded by the Robert Wood Johnson Foundation have set out to change mainstream attitudes. The mission of PDIA is to understand and transform the culture and experience of dying and bereavement. It promotes initiatives in research, scholarship, the humanities, and the arts, and fosters innovations in the provision of care, education, and policy. Television programs such as the Public Broadcasting Service's *On Our Own Terms: Moyers on Dying* have facilitated public education and community dialogue.

On a more individual level, many factors influence the ways in which a person adjusts to death and dying, including one's religion and philosophy of life, personality, culture, and other personal traits. Adjustment may also be affected by the conditions of dying. A person with a long terminal illness has more time and opportunity to accept and prepare for his or her own death, or that of a loved one, than someone with an acute or sudden death.

The following adjectives used to describe death are found in both the professional and popular literature: good, meaningful, appropriate, timely, peaceful, sudden, and natural. One can be said to die well, on time, before one's time, and in a variety of ways and places. This terminology reflects an attempt to embrace, acknowledge, tame, and integrate death into one's life. Other language is more indirect, using euphemisms, metaphors, medical terms, and slang, and reflects a need to avoid directly talking about death?—suggesting the person is "lost," has "passed away," or has "expired" (DeSpelder & Strickland, 2005). It is important for a social worker to be attentive to words that individuals and families choose because they often reflect one's culture and/or religious background, and comfort level.

As with life, the richness and complexity of death is best understood from a multidimensional framework involving the biological, psychological, social, and spiritual dimensions (Bern-Klug, 2004; Bern-Klug, Gessert, & Forbes, 2001). The following conceptualizations of the dying process help capture the notion that dying and other losses, and the accompanying bereavement, are processes that differ for each unique situation, yet share some common aspects.

In *On Death and Dying*, Kübler-Ross (1969) described stages that people tend to go through in accepting their own inevitable death or that of others, summarized in Exhibit 10.3. While these stages were written with death in mind, they have application to other loss-related experiences, including the aging process. Given time, most individuals experience these five reactions, although not necessarily in this order. People often shift back and forth between the reactions rather than experience them in a linear way, get stuck in a stage, and/or skip over others. Kübler-Ross suggests that, on some level, hope of survival persists through all stages.

Exhibit 10.3	Stages of Accepting Impending Death

Denial: The person denies that death will occur: "This is not true. It can't be me." This denial is succeeded by temporary isolation from social interactions.

Anger: The individual asks, "Why me?" The person projects his or her resentment and envy onto others and often directs the anger toward a supreme being, medical caregivers, family members, and friends.

Bargaining: The individual starts bargaining in an attempt to postpone death, proposing a series of deals with God, self, or others: "Yes, me, but I will do . . . in exchange for a few more months."

Depression: A sense of loss follows. Individuals grieve about their own end of life and about the ones that will be left behind. A frequent reaction is withdrawal from close and loved persons: "I just want to be left alone."

Acceptance: The person accepts that the end is near and the struggle is over: "It's okay. My life has been . . . ."

SOURCE: Based on Kübler-Ross, 1969.

Although these reactions may fit people in general, very late-life adults appear to experience far less denial about the reality of death than other age groups (McInnis-Dittrich, 2005). As they confront their limitations of physical health and become socialized to death with each passing friend and family member, most very late-life adults become less fearful of death. Unfortunately, some professionals and family members may not be as comfortable expressing their feelings related to death and dying, which may leave the elder feeling more isolated.

In addition to expressing feelings about death, some very late-life adults have other needs related to dying. A fear of prolonged physical pain or discomfort, as well as fear of losing a sense of control and mastery, trouble very late-life adults most. Some have suggested that older adults who are dying need a safe and accepting relationship in which to express the fear, sadness, anger, resentment, or other feelings related to the pending loss of life and opportunity, especially separation from loved ones (Bowlby, 1980).

Ira Byock (1997, 2004) writes about the importance of certain tasks when facing death, as well as in everyday life given that we never know how much time we have. These tasks address affirmation (I love you; do you love me?); reconciliation (I forgive you; do you forgive me?); and saying goodbye. Farber, Egnew, and Farber (2004) prefer the notion of a "respectful death" over a "good death," proposing a process of respectful exploration of the goals and values of individuals and families rather than a prescription for successfully achieving a "good death." This approach reminds us of the importance of a social worker's nonjudgmental relationship that recognizes the uniqueness of each person's situation.

Advance Directives

On a more concrete level, social workers can help patients and families discuss, prepare, and enact health care **advance directives**, or documents that give instructions about desired health care if, in the future, individuals cannot speak for themselves. Such discussions can provide an opportunity to clarify values and wishes regarding end-of-life treatment. Ideally, this conversation has started prior to very late adulthood (see Chapter 9 regarding a power of attorney and other health care decision-making processes). If not, helping people communicate their wishes regarding life-sustaining measures, who they want to act on their behalf when they are no longer competent to make these decisions, and other end-of-life concerns helps some people feel empowered.

> How do advance directives promote a continued sense of human agency in making choices?

Since the passage of the Patient Self-Determination Act in 1990, hospitals and other health care institutions receiving Medicare or Medical Assistance funds are required to inform patients that should their condition become life-threatening, they have a right to make decisions about what medical care they would wish to receive (McInnis-Dittrich, 2005). The two primary forms of advance directive are the living will and the durable power of attorney for health care.

A **living will** describes the medical procedures, drugs, and types of treatment that one would choose for oneself if able to do so in certain situations. It also describes the situations for which the patient would want treatment withheld. For example, one may instruct medical personnel not to use any artificial means or heroic measures to keep one alive if the condition is such that there is no hope for recovery. Although a living will allows an individual to speak for oneself in advance, a durable power of attorney designates someone else to speak for the individual.

The promotion of patient rights as described above has helped many patients feel empowered and comforted some family members, but this topic is not without controversy. Because the laws vary from state to state, laypersons and professionals must inquire about the process if one relocates. Also, rather than feeling comforted by knowing a dying person's wishes, some family members experience the burden of difficult decision making that once was handled by the physician. Advance directives are not accepted or considered moral by some ethnic, racial, and religious groups. Because of historical distrust of the white medical establishment, some African American and Hispanic families have preferred life-sustaining treatment to the refusal of treatment inherent in advance directives. Among some religious groups, the personal control represented in advance directives is seen to interfere with a divine plan and is considered a form of passive suicide. As discussed below, social workers must approach each patient and family with an openness to learn about their values and wishes. Volker (2005) cautions health care providers to consider the relevancy of Western values, such as personal control over one's future, in the lives of non-Western patient groups.

Care of People Who Are Dying

Although some associate hospice and palliative care with "giving up" and there being "nothing left to do," in fact **palliative care** is active care of patients who have received a diagnosis of a serious, life-threatening illness. It is a form of care focusing on pain and symptom management as opposed to curing disease. Palliative care attends to the psychological, social, and spiritual issues in addition to the physical needs. The goal of palliative care is achievement of the best possible quality of life for patients and their families.

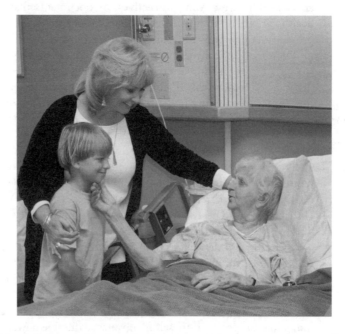

▲ **Photo 10.4**   Palliative care is a form of pain and symptom management as opposed to curing disease. The patient and the family is the unit of care.

Hospice is one model of palliative care, borrowed from the British, that began to address the needs of dying persons and their loved ones in the United States in the mid-1970s. It is more a philosophy of care than a place, with the majority of persons receiving hospice services where they live, usually in their home or a nursing home. It is typically available to persons who have received a prognosis of six months or less and who are no longer receiving care directed toward a cure. For instance, the hospital social worker may want to give Bina Patel and her daughter-in-law information about hospice care, as an additional support during her son's illness. Exhibit 10.4 summarizes the key ideas that distinguish hospice care from more traditional care of the dying.

Exhibit 10.4	Key Ideas of Hospice Care

- The patient and the family (as defined by the patient) are the unit of care.
- Care is provided by an interdisciplinary team composed of physician, nurse, nurse's aide, social worker, clergy, volunteer, and other support staff who attend to the spectrum of biopsychosocial and spiritual needs of the patient and family.
- The patient and family have chosen hospice services and are no longer pursuing aggressive, curative care, but selecting palliative care for symptom management.
- Bereavement follow-up is part of the continuum of care available to family members after the patient's death.

SOURCE: Based on Lattanzi-Licht, Mahoney, & Miller, 1998; McInnis-Dittrich, 2005.

The National Hospice and Palliative Care Organization (NHPCO) estimates that the United States had 3,650 operational hospice programs in 2004 serving most rural, suburban, and urban communities. In 2000, approximately one in four people who died in the United States received hospice services. Hospice continues to predominantly serve people with cancer (46%), but increasingly, noncancerous causes of death are included for conditions such as end-stage heart disease (12.2%), dementia (8.9%), lung disease (7.1%), end-stage kidney disease (3.1%), and debility (8.2%) (NHPCO, 2006).

Health disparities have been noted in hospice care, as in other health care settings, with persons of color historically being underserved. Initiatives through NHPCO, the Soros Foundation's Faculty Scholar program, as well as the Robert Wood Johnson Foundation's Promoting Excellence in End-of-Life Care, have focused on program development specific to the needs of patients and families in African American, Hispanic, Native American, and other communities that have been underserved by more traditional hospice programs (Crawley et al., 2000; NHPCO, 2006).

Palliative care programs are emerging in hospital settings to address pain and symptom management in patients who might not fit the hospice criteria. Some hospitals have palliative care units specializing in management of short-term, acute symptoms; others have palliative care consultative services that bring their expertise to medical, oncology, pediatric, and other units throughout the hospital.

End-of-Life Signs and Symptoms

Family members and others caring for a person who is dying often experience a great deal of anxiety when they do not have adequate information about the dying process. Most families appreciate knowing what to expect, and honest, factual information can help allay their fears of the unknown (Kovacs & Cagle, 2005; Proot et al., 2004). Pete Mullin, for instance, might benefit by knowing what to expect during his vigil with his sister. Many hospice services provide written information about symptoms of death for those families anticipating the death of a loved one at home. Exploring how much information people have and want is an important part of the social worker's assessment.

Obviously, each individual situation will differ, but the following general information about symptoms of impending death, summarized in Exhibit 10.5, helps people prepare (Bon Secours Hospice, 2002; Foley, 2005):

- *Temperature and circulation changes.* The patient's arms and legs may become cool to the touch, and the underside of the body may darken in color as peripheral circulation slows down. Despite feeling cool to touch, the patient is usually not aware of feeling cold and light bed coverings usually provide sufficient warmth.
- *Sleeping.* The dying patient will gradually spend more time sleeping and at times may be difficult to arouse as metabolism decreases. The patient will gradually retreat from the surroundings. It is best to spend more time with the patient during the most alert times.
- *Vision and hearing.* Clarity of vision and hearing may decrease. The patient may want the lights on as vision decreases. Hearing is the last of the five senses to be lost, so it should not be assumed that an unresponsive patient cannot hear. Speech should be soft and clear, but not louder than necessary. Many patients talk until minutes before death and are reassured by the exchange of words between loved ones.
- *Secretions in the mouth and congestion.* Oral secretions may become more profuse and collect in the back of the throat. Most people are familiar with the term *death rattle,* a result of a decrease in the body's intake of fluids and inability to cough up normal saliva. Tilting the head to the side and elevating the head of the bed will ease breathing. Swabbing the mouth and lips also provides comfort.
- *Incontinence.* Loss of bowel and bladder function may occur around the time of death or as death is imminent, as the muscles begin to relax. The urine will become very dark in color. If needed, pads should be used to keep skin clean and dry.
- *Restlessness and confusion.* The patient may become restless or have visions of people or things that do not exist. These symptoms may be a result of a decrease in the oxygen circulation to the brain and a change in the body's metabolism. Someone should stay with the patient, reassuring the person in a calm voice, telling the person it is okay to let go, and using oxygen as instructed. Soft music, back rubs, and gentle touch may help soothe the patient. The patient should not be interfered with or restrained, yet prevented from falling.
- *Eating, drinking, and swallowing.* Patients will have decreased need for food and drink. It may be helpful to explain that feeding will not improve the condition, and in fact may exacerbate symptoms. Slight dehydration may be beneficial in reducing pulmonary secretions and easing breathing. Dehydration also generally results in mild renal insufficiency that is mildly sedating. To withhold food and water feels counterintuitive, however, because food and water are usually equated with comfort and sustaining life. Ice chips, small sips of water, and small amounts of food that have meaning to the patient and family are more helpful than forcing food or liquids.

◆ *Breathing changes.* Breathing may become irregular, with periods of 10 to 30 seconds of no breathing. This symptom is very common and indicates a decrease in circulation and buildup of body waste products. Elevating the head of the bed and turning the patient on his or her side often helps relieve irregular breathing patterns.

◆ *Pain.* Frequent observation will help determine if the patient is experiencing pain. Signs of discomfort include moaning, restlessness, and a furrowed brow. Medication should be given as instructed or the nurse or physician should be contacted if pain persists.

Exhibit 10.5	Signs and Symptoms of Impending Death

- Lowered temperature and slowed circulation
- Deeper and longer periods of sleep
- Decreased acuity of vision and hearing
- Increased secretions in the mouth and congestion
- Incontinence
- Restlessness and confusion
- Reduced need for eating and drinking and difficulty swallowing
- Irregular and interrupted breathing
- Increased signs of pain

SOURCES: Bon Secours Hospice, 2002; Foley, 2005.

Dying may take hours or days; no one can predict the time of death even when the person is exhibiting signs and symptoms of dying. The following are signs that death has occurred:

◆ Breathing stops
◆ Heart stops beating
◆ Bowel or bladder control is lost
◆ No response to verbal commands or shaking
◆ Eyelids may be slightly open with eyes fixed on a certain spot
◆ Mouth may fall open slightly as the jaw relaxes

Such explicit discussion of death with those attending a dying family member or close friend may seem upsetting, but this knowledge is also comforting and can help ease the anxiety related to the fear of the unknown. Dying persons are also comforted knowing that their family members have the informational, medical, and social support they need to help them in their caregiving role. It is also helpful to have funeral plans in place so that at the time of death one phone call to the mortuary facilitates the process.

▨ Loss, Grief, and Bereavement

Loss is a common human experience. There is a great deal of ethnographic evidence that people of all cultures have strong, painful reactions to the death of the people to whom they are emotionally attached (Counts & Counts, 1991). Sadness, loneliness, disbelief, and anxiety are only a few of the feelings a person may experience in times of bereavement. The challenge is not to make grief the problem, thereby pathologizing someone's experience, but to understand the complexities related to death in a society that has grown increasingly old age and death avoidant (McKnight, 1995). So, we offer the following with the caution to avoid turning someone's grief into a problem, but to help the individual understand it as a normal part of life.

Grief, bereavement, and mourning are words that are often used interchangeably, perhaps because no one word "reflects the fullness of what a death introduces into the life of an individual, family or community" (Silverman, 2004, p. 226). We offer the following definitions to help distinguish the various aspects of this process:

* **Loss.** The severing of an attachment an individual has with a loved one, a loved object (such as a pet, home, or country), or an aspect of one's self or identity (such as a body part or function, physical or mental capacity, or role or position in family, society, or other context) (Stroebe, Stroebe, & Hansson, 1993). Silverman (2004) suggests that loss doesn't happen to us; rather it is "something we must make sense out of, give meaning to, and respond to" (p. 226).
* **Bereavement.** The state of having suffered a loss.
* **Grief.** The normal internal reaction of an individual experiencing a loss. Grief is a complex coping process, is highly individualized (Stroebe et al., 1993), and is an expected period of transition (Silverman, 2004).
    * **Mourning.** The external expression of grief (Stroebe et al., 1993); the "mental work following the loss of a loved one . . . social process including the cultural traditions and rituals that guide behavior after a death" (Silverman, 2004, p. 226).

▲ **Photo 10.5** Many factors influence the way in which a person adjusts to death and dying, including one's religion and philosophy of life, personality, and other traits.

The rituals associated with death vary in historical and cross-cultural context (Counts & Counts, 1991). In some cultures, the dead are buried; in other cultures, the dead are burned and the ashes are spread. In some places and times, a surviving wife might have been burned together with her husband. In the United States, death rituals can be as different as a traditional New Orleans funeral, with street music and mourners dressed in white, or a somber and serene funeral with hushed mourners dressed in black. Some cultures prescribe more emotional expression than others. Some cultures build ritual for expression of anger, and some do not. However, the death rituals in most cultures include the following (Counts & Counts, 1991):

* Social support provided to grievers
* Ritual and ceremony used to give meaning to death
* Visual confrontation of the dead body
* A procession

Did these earlier experiences with loss serve as either risk factors or protective factors for coping with current losses?

Throughout life, we are faced with many losses, some that occur by death but many that occur in other ways as well. For example, Bina Patel lost a homeland when she immigrated to be near her children, and she lost some physical functioning after her stroke. Carmen Ruiz lost her home, her privacy, and her routines when she moved into the nursing home. Pete Mullin lived through the losses related to divorce and retirement. Recently, the burgeoning literature on loss, grief, and bereavement has recognized that there may be similar processes for grieving all losses, including those that occur for reasons other than death. Loss is one of the most important themes in our work as social workers. For example, we encounter loss due to foster care placement, divorce, disease and disability, migration and immigration, forced retirement, and so on.

Theories and Models of Loss

A variety of theorists have sought to make sense of the complex experience of loss. Much of the literature on grief and bereavement for the past century has been influenced by Sigmund Freud's (1917/1957) classic article "Mourning and Melancholia." Freud described the "work of mourning" as a process of severing a relationship with a lost person, object, or ideal. He suggested that this happens over time as the bereaved person is repeatedly faced with situations that remind him or her that the loved person (object or ideal) has, indeed, been lost. From this classic work came the idea of a necessary period of **grief work** to sever the attachment bond, an idea that has been the cornerstone of a number of stage models of the grief process.

In the United States, Erich Lindemann (1944) was a pioneer in grief research. Through his classic study of survivors of a fire at the Cocoanut Grove Lounge in Boston, he conceptualized grief work as both a biological and psychological necessity. The common reactions to loss that he identified included the following:

- Somatic distress, occurring in waves lasting from 20 minutes to an hour, including tightness in throat, choking and shortness of breath, need for sighing, empty feeling in abdomen, lack of muscular power, and intense subjective distress
- Preoccupation with image of deceased, yearning for the lost one to return, wanting to see pictures of the deceased or touch items that are associated with the deceased
- Guilt
- Hostile reactions, toward the deceased as well as toward others
- Loss of patterns of conduct, where the ability to carry out routine behaviors is lost

Lindemann proposed that grief work occurs in stages, an idea that has been popular with other theorists and researchers since the 1960s. A number of stage models of grief have been proposed, and four are presented in Exhibit 10.6. As you can see, although the number and names of stages vary somewhat among theorists and researchers, in general the stage models all agree that grief work progresses from disbelief and feelings of unreality, to painful and disorganizing reactions, to a kind of "coming to terms" with the loss. Parkes (2002) notes that stages or phases run the risk of being misused when taken too literally; however, they have served to remind us that grief is a process that people "need to pass through on the way to a new view of the world" (p. 380).

Exhibit 10.6	Four Stage Models of Grief			
Typical Stages of Stage Models of Grief	Erich Lindemann (1944)	Elisabeth Kübler-Ross (1969)	John Bowlby (1980)	Therese Rando (1993)
Disbelief and feelings of unreality	Shock and disbelief	Denial and isolation	Numbness	Avoidance
Painful and disorganizing reactions	Acute mourning	Anger Bargaining Depression	Yearning Disorganization Despair	Confrontation
A kind of "getting over" the loss	Resolution	Acceptance	Reorganization	Accommodation

J. William Worden (2001) took a somewhat different approach, writing about the "tasks of mourning" rather than stages of mourning. He considered *task* to be more consistent with Freud's concept of grief work given that the mourner needs to take action and do something rather than passively move through grief. Worden suggests that the following four tasks of mourning are important when a person is adapting to a loss:

Task I: To accept the reality of the loss. Working through denial takes time, because this involves an intellectual and an emotional acceptance. Some people have traditional rituals that help with this process.

Task II: To work through to the pain of grief. Because people are often uncomfortable with the outward displays of grief, our society often interferes with this task. People often seek a geographic cure or quickly replace the lost person in a new relationship but often still have this task to complete.

Task III: To adjust to an environment in which the deceased is missing. This includes filling roles previously filled by the deceased and making appropriate adjustments in daily activities. In terms of roles, many widows report being thrown the first time they have to cope with a major home repair. Regarding adjustments in daily activities, many bereaved persons report that they find themselves automatically putting the favorite foods of the deceased in their grocery carts.

Task IV: To emotionally relocate the deceased and move on with life. This task was best described by Sadie Delany after the loss of her beloved sister, Bessie, "I don't want to get over you. I just want to find a way to live without you" (Delany with Hearth, 1997).

In the past couple of decades, there has been a critique of the idea of grief work. A highly influential article, "The Myths of Coping With Loss" (Wortman & Silver, 1989), disputed two major themes of the traditional view of grief work: distress is an inevitable response to loss, and the failure to experience distress is a sign of improper grieving.

In fact, a number of researchers have found that those who show the highest levels of distress immediately following a loss are more likely than those who show little distress to be depressed several years later. In another vein, Silverman (2004) challenges the notion of "tasks" which suggests something can be completed, recommending that we focus instead on "issues and processes" (p. 237).

Within this grieving process, Camille Wortman and Roxanne Silver (1990) proposed that at least four different patterns of grieving are possible:

1. *Normal grief.* Relatively high level of distress soon after the loss, followed by a relatively rapid recovery

2. *Chronic grief.* High level of distress continuing over a number of years

3. *Delayed grief.* Little distress in the first few months after the loss, but high levels of distress at some later point

4. *Absent grief.* No notable level of distress either soon after the loss or at some later time

In their research, Wortman and Silver (1990) found absent grief in 26% of their bereaved participants, and other researchers have had similar findings (Levy, Martinkowski, & Derby, 1994). These same researchers have found a high rate (over 30%) of chronic grief.

Given these critiques of traditional models of grief, theorists and researchers have looked for other ways to understand the complex reactions to loss. Recently, the study of bereavement has been influenced by developments in the study of stress and trauma reactions. Research on loss and grief has produced the following findings (Bonanno & Kaltman, 1999):

- It is the evaluation of the nature of the loss by the bereaved survivor that determines how stressful the loss is.
- How well a coping strategy works for dealing with loss depends on the context and the nature of the person-environment encounter.
- Maintaining some type of continued bond with the deceased, a strong sense of the continued presence of the deceased, may be adaptive.
- The capacity to minimize negative emotions after a loss allows the bereaved to continue to function in areas of personal importance.
- Humor can aid in the grief process by allowing the bereaved to approach the enormity of the loss without maximizing psychic pain or alienating social support.
- In situations of traumatic loss, there is a need to talk about the loss, but not all interpersonal relationships can tolerate such talk.

In summary, grief is a multidimensional process—a normal life experience—that theorists and practitioners continue to try to understand. There seems to be general agreement that culture, past experience, gender, age, and other personal characteristics influence how one copes with loss.

Culture and Bereavement

It is important to be informed about the impact of each individual's culture and how religious and spiritual practices affect the individual bereavement process. Historically, because of sensitivity about racial issues, there has been some hesitancy to address issues of race and ethnicity in the health care arena. Unfortunately, when ethnic differences are not taken into consideration, too often it is assumed that the norm is white and middle class.

Why is it important for social workers to learn about cultural variations in grief and bereavement?

As the United States becomes increasingly multiracial and ethnically diverse, you will need to continually inform yourself about cultural, ethnic, and religious traditions of individuals and families with whom you work so as to avoid becoming unintentionally ethnocentric. Del Rio (2004) reminds us that our own view of reality is "always socially constructed, does not account for all the phenomena of life, and should not take precedence over a client's view of reality" (p. 441). Given the tremendous diversity within groups as well as among them, the individual and the family are your best teachers. Ask them, "What do I need to know about you (your family, cultural, or religious and spiritual traditions) so that I can be of help to you?"

Some suggest that all people feel the same pain with grief, but that cultural differences shape our mourning rituals, traditions, and behavioral expresses of grief (Cowles, 1996). In the United States, we tend to psychologize grief, understanding it in terms of sadness, depression, anger, and other emotions (McKnight, 1995). There may be a cohort divide in the United States on this issue, however, and the current generation of very late-life adults are often much more matter-of-fact about death than younger adults are (Pipher, 1999). In China and other Eastern societies, grief is more often somatized, or expressed in terms of physical pain, weakness, and other physical discomfort (Irish, Lundquist, & Nelsen, 1993). We need to be aware of the possibility of somatization when working with many clients from different cultures, as well as with some older adults of Anglo heritage.

Cultural variation also exists regarding the acceptable degree of emotional expression of grief, from "muted" to "excessive" grief, with many variations between these two ends of the continuum. Gender differences exist in many cultures, including the dominant U.S. culture, where men have learned to be less demonstrative with emotions of grief and sadness than women (Murray, 2001).

Mourning and funeral customs also differ a great deal. For example, among African Americans, customs vary depending on whether the family is Southern Baptist, black Catholic, northern Unitarian, black Muslim, or Pentecostal (Perry, 1993). Perhaps because of some vestiges of traditional African culture and slavery, and a strong desire to celebrate the person's life and build up a sense of community, funerals are important external expressions of mourning in many black communities.

The complex, and at times impersonal, health care system in the United States often is insensitive to cultural traditions. In some cultures, proper handling of the body, time to sit with the deceased, and other traditions are important. For example, the Hmong believe that proper burial and worship of ancestors directly influence the safety and health of the surviving family members. They believe that the spiritual world coexists with the physical world. Because they believe that each person has several souls, it is important that the souls be "sent back appropriately" (Bliatout, 1993, p. 83).

Tremendous diversity exists within the Hispanic cultures in the United States, depending upon country of origin, degree of acculturation, and religious background. Historically, conquest and death have been an important part of the history of Mexican, Cuban, Guatemalan, and other cultures (Younoszai, 1993). Mexican culture, for example, celebrates the Day of the Dead with colorful traditions honoring those who have died. Additional saints' days provide ongoing bereavement opportunities.

Given approximately 350 distinct Native American tribes in the United States and more than 596 different bands among the First Nations in Canada, and because of the differing degrees of acculturation and religious practices from one group to another, it is difficult to provide useful generalizations about this cultural group (Brokenleg & Middleton, 1993). Although most Native Americans believe in an afterlife, the Navajo do not. Some tribes believe that talking directly about death helps the death occur. This belief makes discussing hospice and end-of-life plans challenging.

These are only a few examples of the rich diversity among some of the peoples in our increasingly multiethnic society. You cannot possibly know all the specific traditions, but it is important to assume that you do not know, and therefore to inquire of the family how you can assist them.

⬚ The Life Course Completed

In this book, we have explored the seasons of the life course. These seasons have been and will be altered by changing demographics. Current demographic trends have led to the following predictions about the future of the life course (Hogstel, 2001):

- ◆ The size and inevitable aging of the baby boom generation will continue to drive public policy debate and improve services for very late-life adults.
- ◆ Women will continue to live longer than men.
- ◆ Educational attainment levels of the very late-life adult will increase, with more women having been in the labor force long enough to have their own retirement income.
- ◆ Six-generation families will be common, although the generations will live in geographically dispersed settings, making care for very late-life adults difficult.
- ◆ Fewer family caregivers will be available for very late-life adults because the baby boomers and their children tended to marry later and have fewer children. At the same time, the need for informal or family caregiving to supplement formal care will be increasing.
- ◆ Assessment and management of health care, as well as health care education, will increasingly be available via telephone, computer/Internet, and television, providing greater access in remote areas but running the risk of rendering the service more impersonal.

As a society, we have a challenge ahead of us, to see that newborns begin the life course on a positive foot and that everyone reaches the end of life with the opportunity to see his or her life course as a meaningful whole. As social workers, we have a responsibility to take a look at our social institutions and evaluate how well they guarantee the opportunity for each individual to meet basic needs during each season of life, as well as whether they guarantee the opportunity for interdependence and connectedness appropriate to the season of life.

IMPLICATIONS FOR SOCIAL WORK PRACTICE

All the implications for practice listed in Chapter 9 on late adulthood apply in very late adulthood as well. In addition, the following practice principles focus on the topics of spirituality, relationships, the dying process, and loss, grief, and bereavement:

- Given the link between aging, disability, loss, and spirituality, consider doing a spiritual assessment to find ways to help very late-life adults address increasing spiritual concerns.
- Assess the impact of loss in the lives of your very late-life clients—loss of partners, friends, children, and other relationships, but also loss of role, status, and physical and mental capacities.
- Recognize and be delighted when very late-life adults are grateful for their "extra time."
- Assess the loneliness and isolation that may result from cumulative loss.
- Be informed about available formal and informal resources to help minimize isolation for older adults.
- Be aware of your own feelings about death and dying so that you may become more comfortable being physically and emotionally present with clients and their loved ones.
- Identify literature, cultural experiences, key informants, and other vehicles for ongoing education about your clients' cultural, ethnic, and religious practices that are different from your own. Remember, the client may be your best teacher.
- Assume that the very late-life adult continues to have needs for intimacy. Stretch your conceptualization of intimacy to include any relationship the person might have, wish for, or grieve, including a spouse or partner, friends, children, self, and community.

KEY TERMS

activities of daily living (ADL)	grief work	loss
advance directive	hospice	mourning
bereavement	instrumental activities of daily living (IADL)	palliative care
grief	living will	primary aging
		secondary aging

Active Learning

1. Take an inventory of your assumptions about what it is like to be 85 and older. What are your biggest fears? What do you think would be the best part of reaching that age? Think about how these assumptions might influence your feelings about working with clients in very late adulthood.

2. You have recently been hired as the social worker at an assisted living facility, and Carmen Ruiz, Bina Patel, and Pete Mullin have all recently moved in. All three are unhappy to be there, preferring their prior living arrangements. Bina's son and Pete's sister recently died. You want to help them share some of their recent experiences related to loss but want to be sensitive to the diversity in life experience that they bring with them. What barriers might you face in accomplishing your goal? What are some ways that you might begin to help them?

3. Think about possible relationships between poverty, gender, sexual orientation, and race as one ages in the United States today. Identify ways that social workers can influence policies that affect housing, health care, and other essential services directly related to quality of life in very late-life adulthood.

WEB RESOURCES

AARP
www.aarp.org

Site maintained by American Association of Retired Persons contains health and wellness information, information on legislative issues, and links to online resources regarding aging.

APA ONLINE Aging Issues Office
www.apa.org/pi/aging

Site presented by the Office of Aging of the American Psychological Association contains news briefs, publications, and links to aging organizations.

Hospice Foundation of America
www.hospicefoundation.org

Site maintained by the Hospice Foundation of America contains information on locating hospice programs, a newsletter, and links to a variety of hospice-related resources.

The National Hospice and Palliative Care Organization
www.nhpco.org

Site maintained by the National Hospice and Palliative Care Organization contains information on the history and current development of hospice and palliative care programs, advance directives, grief and bereavement, caregiving, and other related topics.

Center to Advance Palliative Care
www.capc.org

Site presented by the Center to Advance Palliative Care contains information on the Project on Death in America, as well as descriptions of physician, nursing, social work, and pastoral care roles on interdisciplinary teams; information for the development of palliative care services.

Solutions for Better Aging
www.caregivers.com

Site maintained by AgeNet Inc., a good place for both family and professional caregivers to start when seeking information about financing caregiving services, purchasing products helpful in providing care, contains linkage to online caregiver support groups and other topics.

Hospice Net
www.hospicenet.org

Site maintained by Hospice Net provides information for dying persons, their families, and professionals about the hospice movement, advance directives, pain and symptom management, and the grieving process.

National Association of Social Workers
www.naswdc.org/aging.asp

Site provides access to resources related to aging and social work practice, including some online courses.

National Center for Gerontological Social Work Education
www.Gero-EdCenter.org

Site maintained by the Council on Social Work Education Gero-Ed Center (National Center for Gerontological Social Work Education) provides resources for aging and end-of-life care.

REFERENCES

Abdel-Latif, M. E., Bajuk, B., Oel, J., Vincent, T., Sutton, L., & Liu, K. (2006). Does rural or urban residence make a difference to neonatal outcome in premature birth? A regional study in Australia. *Archives of Disease in Childhood: Fetal and Neonatal Edition, 91*(4), F251–F256.

Abel, E. L., & Sokol, R. J. (1987). Incidence of fetal alcohol syndrome and economic impact of FAS-related anomalies. *Drug and Alcohol Dependence, 19*, 51–70.

Abraham, K. (1986). Ego differences among Anglo-American and Mexican-American adolescents. *Journal of Adolescence, 9*(2), 151–166.

Achievements in Public Health: 1900–1999. (1999). Healthier mothers and babies. *Morbidity and Mortality Weekly, 49*(38), 849–858.

Adair, L. S., & Gordon-Larsen, P. (2001). Maturational timing and overweight prevalence in US adolescent girls. *American Journal of Public Health, 9*(4), 642–644.

Adam, E. K., & Chase-Lansdale, L. P. (2002). Home sweet home(s): Parental separations, residential moves, and adjustment problems in low-income adolescent girls. *Developmental Psychology, 38*(5), 792–805.

Adams, G. R., & Crane, P. (1980). An assessment of parents' and teachers' expectations of preschool children's social preference for attractive or unattractive children and adults. *Child Development, 51*, 224–231.

Adams, G. R., & Marshall, S. K. (1996). A developmental social psychology of identity: Understanding the person-in-context. *Journal of Adolescence, 19*, 429–442.

Adams, R., & Allan, G. (1998). *Placing friendship in context.* New York: Cambridge University Press.

Adler, L. (1993). Introduction and overview. *Journal of Education Policy, 8*(5–6), 1–16.

Adlercreutz, H., Hamalaiven, O., Gorback, S., & Grodin, B. (1992). Dietary phytoestrogens and the menopause in Japan. *Lancet, 339*, 1233.

Administration on Aging. (2005). *A profile of older Americans: 2005.* Washington, DC: U.S. Department of Health and Human Services.

Administration on Aging. (2006a). *A statistical profile of older Americans aged 65+* Washington, DC: U.S. Department of Health and Human Services. Retrieved July 7, 2006, from http://www/aoa/gov/prof/Statistics

Administration on Aging. (2006b). *Aging in the 21st century—Demography.* Washington, DC: U.S. Department of Health and Human Services. Retrieved July 7, 2006, from http://www/aoa/gov/prof/Statistics/future_growth/aging21/demography.asp

Administration on Aging. (2006c). *A statistical profile of Hispanic older Americans aged 65+.* Washington, DC: U.S. Department of Health and Human Services. Retrieved July 7, 2006, from http://www/aoa/gov/prof/Statistics

Administration on Aging. (2006d). *A statistical profile of black older Americans aged 65+.* Washington, DC: U.S. Department of Health and Human Services. Retrieved July 7, 2006, from http://www/aoa/gov/prof/Statistics

Advocates for Youth. (2002a). *Adolescent sexual health in Europe and the U.S.: Why the difference?* Retrieved June 6, 2002, from http://www.advocatesforyouth.org

Advocates for Youth. (2002b). *Adolescent contraceptive use.* Retrieved June 6, 2002, from http://www.advocatesforyouth.org

Agency for Healthcare Research and Quality. (2006). Preventing disability in the elderly with chronic disease. *Research in Action,* Issue 3. Retrieved July 7, 2006, from http://www .ahrq.gov/research/elderis.htmAging

Ahrons, C. (2005). Divorce: An unscheduled family transition. In B. Carter & M. McGoldrick (Eds.), *The expanded life cycle: Individual, family, and social perspectives* (3rd ed., pp. 381–398). Boston: Allyn & Bacon.

Ai, A. L. (2000). Spiritual well-being, spiritual growth, and spiritual care for the aged: A cross-faith and interdisciplinary effort. *Journal of Religious Gerontology, 11*(2), 3–28.

Ainsworth, M., Blehar, M., Waters, E., & Wall, S. (1978). *Patterns of attachment: A psychological study of the strange situation.* Hillsdale, NJ: Lawrence Erlbaum.

Akiyama, H., Antonucci, T., & Campbell, R. (1990). Exchange and reciprocity among two generations of Japanese and American women. In J. Sokolovski (Ed.), *Cultural context of aging: Worldwide perspectives* (pp. 127–138). Westport, CT: Greenwood Press.

Alan Guttmacher Institute. (1999). *Teen sex and pregnancy.* Retrieved June 6, 2006, from http://www.agi-usa.org/pubs/fb_teen_sex.html.

Alan Guttmacher Institute. (2005). *Facts in brief: Contraceptive use.* Retrieved December 13, 2006, from http://www.guttmacher.org/pubs/fb_const_use.html

Alan Guttmacher Institute. (2006a). *Facts on American teens' sexual and reproductive health.* Retrieved November 29, 2006, from http://www.guttmacher.org/pub/fb_ATSRH.html

Alan Guttmacher Institute. (2006b). *Facts on sexually transmitted infections in the United States.* Retrieved November 20, 2006, from http://www.guttmacher.org/pbus/fb_sti.html

Aldwin, C., & Gilmer, D. (2004). *Health, illness, and optimal aging: Biological and psychosocial perspectives.* Thousand Oaks, CA: Sage.

Alexander, G. R., Kogan, M., Bader, D., Carol, W., Allen, M., & Mor, J. (2003). US birth weight/gestational age-specific neonatal mortality: 1995–1997 rates for whites, Hispanics, and blacks. *Pediatrics, 111*(1), 191–192.

Alink, L., Mesmon, J., & van Zeijl, J. (2006). The early childhood aggression curve: Development of physical aggression in 10- to 50-month-old children. *Child Development, 77*(4), 954–966.

Allen, E. K., & Marotz, L. R. (2003). *Developmental profiles: Pre-birth through twelve* (4th ed.). Canada: Delmar Learning/Thomson.

Allen, K., Blieszner, R., & Roberto, K. (2001). Families in the middle and later years: A review and critique of the research in the 1990s. *Journal of Marriage and the Family, 62,* 911–926.

Allen, K. (1989). *Single women; family ties.* Newbury Park, CA: Sage.

Allen-Meares, P. (1995). School failure and special populations. In P. Allen-Meares (Ed.), *Social work with children and adolescents* (pp. 143–164). White Plains, NY: Longman.

Allen-Meares, P., Washington, R. O., & Walsh, B. (1996). *Social work services in schools* (2nd ed.). Englewood Cliffs, NJ: Prentice Hall.

Alsaker, F. D. (1992). Pubertal timing, overweight, and psychological adjustment. *Journal of Early Adolescence, 12,* 396–419.

Altken, R. J., Wingate, J. K., De Iullis, G. N., Koppers, A. J., & McLaughlin, E. A. (2006). Cis-unsaturated fatty acids stimulate reactive oxygen species generation and lipid peroxidation in human spermatozoa. *The Journal of Clinical Endocrinology and Metabolism, 91*(10), 4154–4163.

Alwin, D., & McCammon, R. (2003). Generations, cohorts, and social change. In J. Mortimer & M. Shanahan (Eds.), *Handbook of the life course* (pp. 23–49). New York: Kluwer Academic/ Plenum Publishers.

Aly, H., Massaro, A. N., & El-Mohandes, A. A. (2006). Can delivery room management impact the length of hospital stay in premature infants? *Journal of Perinatology, 26*(10), 593–596.

Amato, P. R. (2003). Family functioning and child development: The case of divorce. In R. M. Lerner, F. Jacobs, & D. Wertlieb (Eds.), *Handbook of applied developmental science, Vol. 1* (pp. 319–338). Thousand Oaks, CA: Sage.

American Academy of Child & Adolescent Psychiatry. (1995). *Facts for families: Fact no. 10. Teen suicide.* Washington, DC: Author.

American Academy of Family Physicians. (2005). *Natural family planning.* Retrieved on August 5, 2006, from http://familydoctor.org/126.xml?printxml

American Academy of Pediatrics. (1999). *Caring for your baby and young child.* New York: Bantam.

American Academy of Pediatrics. (2001a). Condom use by adolescents. *Pediatrics, 107*(6), 1463.

American Academy of Pediatrics. (2004). Policy statement: Hospital stay for healthy term newborns. *Pediatrics, 113*(3), 1434–1435.

American Academy of Pediatrics-Committee on Adolescence. (2005). Emergency contraception: Policy statement. *Pediatrics, 116*(4), 1026–1035.

American Association of Retired Persons. (2003). *Global aging: Achieving its potential.* Washington, DC: Author.

American Association of University Women. (1995). *How schools shortchange girls.* New York: Marlowe.

American College of Nurse-Midwives. (2006). *A brief history of nurse-midwifery in the United States.* Retrieved July 29, 2006, from http://www.mymidwife.org/index.cfm?id=10

American Medical Association. (2002). *Emergency contraception.* Retrieved September 9, 2002, from http://www.ama-assn.org/special/contrmergenca/support/ppfa/emergenc.htm

American Psychiatric Association. (1994). *Diagnostic and statistical manual of mental disorders (DSM-IV)* (4th ed.). Washington, DC: Author.

American Psychiatric Association Work Group on Eating Disorders. (2000). Practice guidelines for the treatment of patients with eating disorders (revision). *American Journal of Psychiatry, 157*(1 Suppl), 1–39.

American Society for Reproductive Medicine. (2002, October 12–17). *Highlights from the ASRM 58th Annual Meeting.* Seattle, Washington. Retrieved November 6, 2002, from http://www.asrm.org/Media?Press/1700000babies.html

American Society for Reproductive Medicine. (2002). Human immunodeficiency virus and infertility treatment. *Fertility and Sterility, 77*(2), 218–222.

Ameta, E. S., & Sherrard, P. A. (1995). Inquiring into children's social worlds: A choice of lenses. In B. A. Ryan, G. R. Adams, T. P. Gullotta, R. P. Weissberg, & R. L. Hampton (Eds.), *The family-school connection: Theory, research, and practice* (pp. 29–74). Thousand Oaks, CA: Sage.

Anderson, C. (2005). Single-parent families: Strengths, vulnerabilities, and interventions. In B. Carter & M. McGoldrick, *The expanded family life cycle: Individual, family, and social perspectives* (3rd ed., pp. 399–416). Boston: Allyn & Bacon.

Anderson, D. A. (1994). Lesbian and gay adolescents: Social and developmental considerations. *High School Journal, 77*(1–2), 13–19.

Anderson, J., Santelli, J., & Morrow, B. (2006). Trends in adolescent contraceptive use: Unprotected sex and poorly protected sex, 1991–2003. *Journal of Adolescent Health, 38*(6), 734–739.

Anderson, M., Kaufman, J., Simon, T. R., Barrios, L., Paulozzi, L., Ryan, G., et al. and the School-Associated Violent Deaths Study Group. (2001). School-associated violent deaths in the United States, 1994–1999. *Journal of American Medical Association, 286,* 2695–2702.

Anderson, R. (2001, October 12). Deaths: Leading causes for 1999. *National Center for Disease Control National Vital Statistics Report, 49*(11).

Anderson, R. E., & Anderson, D. A. (1999). The cost-effectiveness of home birth. *Journal of Nurse Midwifery, 44*(1), 30–35.

Anderson, R. N., & Smith, B. L. (2003). Deaths: Leading causes for 2001. *National Vital Statistics Report, 52*(9), 1–86.

Andrews, L. B. (1994). *Assessing genetic risks: Implications for health and social policy.* Washington, DC: National Academy Press.

Ankum, W. M. (2000). Diagnosing suspected ectopic pregnancy. *British Medical Journal, 321*(7271), 1235–1237.

Antonucci, T., & Akiyama, H. (1987). Social networks in adult life and a preliminary examination of the convoy model. *Journal of Gerontology: Social Sciences, 42,* S519–S527.

Antonucci, T., & Akiyama, H. (1995). Convoys of social relations: Family and friendships within a life span context. In R. Blieszner & V. Bedford (Eds.), *Handbook of aging and the family* (pp. 355–371). Westport, CT: Greenwood Press.

Antonucci, T., & Akiyama, H. (1997). Concern with others at midlife: Care, comfort, or compromise? In M. Lachman & J. James (Eds.), *Multiple paths of midlife development* (pp. 145–169). Chicago: University of Chicago Press.

Antonucci, T., Akiyama, H., & Merline, A. (2001). Dynamics of social relationships in midlife. In M. Lachman (Ed.), *Handbook of midlife development* (pp. 571–598). New York: Wiley.

Api, O., Unal, O., Api, M., Ergin, B., Alkan, N., Kars, B., et al. (2006). Ultrasonograpic appearance of cervical pregnancy following successful treatment with methotrexate. *Ultrasound in Obstetrics and Gynecology, 28*(6), 845–848.

Applegate, J. S., & Shapiro, J. R. (2005). *Neurobiology for clinical social work: Theory and practice.* New York: W.W. Norton & Co.

Aquilino, W. (1990). The likelihood of parent-adult child coresidence: Effects of family structure and parental characteristics. *Journal of Marriage and the Family, 52,* 405–419.

Arber, S., & Ginn, J. (1995). *Connecting gender and aging: A sociological approach.* Philadelphia: Open University Press.

Archer, J. (1992). Childhood gender roles: Social content and organization. In H. McGurk (Ed.), *Childhood social development* (pp. 31–62). Hillsdale, NJ: Erlbuam.

Ardelt, M., & Eccles, J. S. (2001). Effects of mothers' parental efficacy beliefs and promotive parenting strategies on inner-city youth. *Journal of Family Issues, 22*(8), 944.

Argetsinger, A. (2001, August 27). An oversupply of undergrads. *Washington Post,* pp. A1, A5.

Armatowski, J. (2001). Attitudes toward death and dying among persons in the fourth quarter of life. In D. O. Moberg (Ed.), *Aging and spirituality: Spiritual dimensions of aging theory, research, practice, and policy* (pp. 71–83). New York: Haworth Pastoral Press.

Armstrong, E. M. (2000). Lessons in control: Prenatal education in the hospital. *Social Problems, 47*(4), 583–611.

Arnett, J. J. (1998). Learning to stand alone: The contemporary American transition to adulthood in cultural and historical context. *Human Development, 41*(5), 295–297.

Arnett, J. J. (2000). Emerging adulthood: A theory of development from the late teens through the twenties. *American Psychologist, 55*(5), 469–480.

Arnett, J. J. (2004). *Emerging adulthood: The winding road from the late teens through the twenties.* New York: Oxford University Press.

Arnett, J. J., & Taber, S. (1994). Adolescence terminable and interminable: When does adolescence end? *Journal of Youth & Adolescence, 23*(5), 517–538.

Arnett, J. J., & Tanner, J. L. (2005). *Emerging adults in America: Coming of age in the 21st century.* Washington, DC: American Psychological Association.

Aroian, K., & Norris, A. (2003). Depression trajectories in relatively recent immigrants. *Comprehensive Psychiatry, 44*(5), 420–427.

Aronson, J. (1992). Women's sense of responsibility for the care of old people: But who else is going to do it? *Gender and Society, 6,* 8–29.

Arrendondo, P. M. (1984). Identity themes for immigrant young adults. *Adolescence, 19,* 977–993.

Asher, S., & Paquette, J. (2003). Loneliness and peer relations in childhood. *Current Directions in Psychological Science, 12,* 75–78.

Ashford, J. B., LeCroy, C. W., & Lortie, K. L. (2001). *Human behavior in the social environment* (2nd ed.). Belmont, CA: Wadsworth.

Ashford, J. B., LeCroy, C. W., & Lortie, K. L. (2006). *Human behavior in the social environment: A multidimensional perspective* (3rd ed.). Pacific Grove, CA: Brooks/Cole.

Ashton, D. (2006). Prematurity-infant mortality: The scourge remains. *Ethnicity and Disease, 16*(2 Suppl 3), S3–58-62.

Astone, N. M., Schoen, R., Ensminger, M., & Rothert, K. (2000). School reentry in early adulthood: The case of inner-city African Americans. *Sociology of Education, 73,* 133–154.

Astor, R. A., Benbenishty, R., Pitner, R. O., & Meyer, H. A. (2004). Bullying and peer victimization in the schools. In P. Allen-Meares & M.W. Fraser (Eds.), *Intervention with children and adolescents: An interdisciplinary perspective* (pp. 417–448). Boston: Allyn & Bacon.

Atchley, R. C. (1976). *The sociology of retirement.* Cambridge, MA: Schenkman.

Auerbach, J., & Krimgold, B. (Eds.). (2001). *Income, socioeconomic status, and health.* Washington, DC: National Policy Association.

Australian Government: Department of Family and Community Services: Office for Women. (2006). *What the Australian government is doing for women.* Retrieved November 2, 2006, from http://www.ofw.facs.gov.au/publications/budget2005/booklet.pdf

Avis, N. (1999). Women's health at midlife. In S. Willis & J. Reid (Eds.), *Life in the middle: Psychological and social development in middle age* (pp. 105–146). San Diego, CA: Academic Press.

Avis, N., Brambilla, D., McKinlay, S., & Vass, K. (1994). A longitudinal analysis of the association between menopause and depression: Results from the Massachusetts Women's Health Study. *Annals of Epidemiology, 4,* 214–220.

Avis, N., Stellato, R., Crawford, S., Bromberger, Ganz, P., Cain, V., & Kagawa-Singer, M. (2001). Is there a menopausal syndrome? Menopausal status and symptoms across racial/ethnic groups. *Social Science & Medicine, 52*(3), 345.

Awsare, N. S., Krishnan, J., Boustead, G. B., Hanbury, D. C., & McNicholas, T. A. (2005). Complications of vasectomy. *Annals of the Royal College of Surgeons of England, 87*(6), 406–410.

Bada, H. S., Das, A., Bauer, C. R., Shankaran, S., Lester, B. M., Gard, C. C., et al. (2005). Low birth weight and preterm births: Etiological fraction attributable to prenatal drug exposure. *Journal of Perinatology, 25*(10), 631–637.

Bahr, H., Dechaux, J., & Stiehr, K. (1994). The changing bonds of kinship: Parents and adult children. In S. Langlois (Ed.), *Convergence or divergence? Comparing recent social trends in industrial societies* (pp. 115–171). Buffalo, NY: McGill-Queen's University Press.

Bailey, J., & Zucker, K. (1995). Childhood sex-typed behavior and sexual orientation: A conceptual analysis and quantitative review. *Developmental Psychology, 31*, 43–55.

Bailey, S. M. (2002). Foreword. In *The Jossey-Bass reader on gender and education* (pp. xxi–xxiv). San Francisco: Jossey-Bass.

Baillargeon, R. (1987). Object permanence in 3½ and 4½ month old infants. *Developmental Psychology, 23*, 655–664.

Baillargeon, R. (2004). Infants' physical world. *Current Directions in Psychological Science, 13*, 89–94.

Bain, M. D., Gau, D., & Reed, G. B. (1995). An introduction to antenatal and neonatal medicine, the fetal period and perinatal ethics. In G. B. Reed, A. E. Claireaux, & F. Cockburn (Eds.), *Diseases of the fetus and newborn* (2nd ed., pp. 3–23). London: Chapman & Hall.

Baker, A. (1990). The psychological impact of the Intifada on Palestinian children in the occupied West Bank and Gaza: An exploratory study. *American Journal of Orthopsychiatry, 60*, 496–505.

Bakhru, A., & Stanwood, N. (2006). Performance of contraceptive patch compared with oral contraceptive pill in a high-risk population. *Obstetrics and Gynecology, 108*(2), 378–386.

Baltes, P., Lindenberger, U., & Staudinger, U. (1998). Life-span theory in developmental psychology. In R. Lerner (Ed.), *Handbook of child psychology* (5th ed., pp. 1029–1143). New York: Wiley.

Bandura, A. (1977). Self-efficacy: Toward a unifying theory of behavioral change. *Psychological Review, 84*, 191–215.

Bandura, A. (1977). *Social learning theory.* Englewood Cliffs, NJ: Prentice-Hall.

Bandura, A. (1986). *Social foundations of thought and action: A social cognitive theory.* Englewood Cliffs, NJ: Prentice-Hall.

Bandura, A. (2002). Social cognitive theory in cultural context. *Applied Psychology: An International Review, 51*(2), 269–290.

Barak, B., & Stern, B. (1986). Subjective age correlates: A research note. *The Gerontologist, 26*(5), 571–578.

Baranowski, T. (1983). Social support, social influence, ethnicity, and the breastfeeding decision. *Social Science & Medicine, 17*, 1599–1611.

Barbarin, O., McCandies, T., Coleman, C., & Atkinson, T. (2004). Ethnicity and culture. In P. Allen-Meares and M. W. Fraser (Eds.), *Intervention with children and adolescents: An interdisciplinary perspective* (pp. 27–53). Boston: Allyn & Bacon.

Bardwell, J. R., Cochran, S. W., & Walker, S. (1986). Relationship of parental education, race, and gender to sex role stereotyping in five year old kindergartners. *Sex Roles, 15*, 275–281.

Barker, K. K. (1998). "A ship upon a stormy sea": The medicalization of pregnancy. *Social Science & Medicine, 47*(8), 1067–1076.

Baron, J., Granato, L., Spranca, M., & Teubal, E. (1993). Decision-making biases in children and early adolescents: Exploratory studies. *Merrill-Palmer Quarterly, 39*, 22–46.

Barr, R. D., & Parrett, W. H. (1995). *Hope at last for at-risk youth.* Boston: Allyn & Bacon.

Barranti, C., & Cohen, H. (2001). Lesbian and gay elders: An invisible minority. In R. Schneider, N. Kropf, & A. Kisor (Eds.), *Gerontological social work: Knowledge, service setting, and special populations* (pp. 343–368). Belmont, CA: Brooks/Cole.

Barrs, M. (1994). Introduction: Reading the difference. In M. Barrs & S. Pidgeon (Eds.), *Reading the difference: Gender and reading in elementary classrooms* (pp. 1–11). York, ME: Stenhouse Publishers.

Barry, T. D., Lyman, R. D., & Klinger, L. G. (2002). Academic underachievement and Attention-Deficit/Hyperactivity Disorder: The negative impact of symptom severity on school performance. *Journal of School Psychology, 40*(3), 259–283.

Barth, R. (1994). Long-term in home services. In D. J. Besharov (Ed.), *When drug addicts have children* (pp. 175–194). Washington, DC: Child Welfare League of America.

Bartko, W. T., & Eccles, J. (2003). Adolescent participation in structured and unstructured activities: A person-oriented analysis. *Journal of Youth and Adolescence, 32*(4), 233–241.

Bartley, M., Blane, D., & Montgomery, S. (1997). Health and the life course: Why safety nets matter. *British Medical Journal, 314*(7088), 1194–1196.

Barton, L., & Hodgman, J. E. (2005). The contribution of withholding or withdrawing care to newborn mortality. *Pediatrics, 116*(6), 1487–1492.

Bassali, R., & Benjamin, J. (2002, July 12). Failure to thrive. *EMedicine Journal, 3*(7). Retrieved August 21, 2002, from www.emedicine.com/PED/topic738.htm

Batson, C. D., Schoenrade, P., & Ventis, W. L. (1993). *Religion and the individual: A social-psychological perspective.* New York: Oxford University Press.

Baum, K. (2005, August). *Juvenile victimization and offending. 1993–2003* (Special Report. National Crime Victimization Survey. NCJ 209468). Washington, DC: U.S. Department of Justice, Office of Justice Programs, Bureau of Justice Statistics.

Baumeister, R. F., & Muraven, M. (1996). Identity as adaptation to social, cultural, and historical context. *Journal of Adolescence, 19,* 405–416.

Baumrind, D. (1971). Current patterns of parental authority. *Developmental Psychology Monographs, 41*(1, Pt. 2).

Bausch, R. S. (2006). Predicting willingness to adopt a child: A consideration of demographic and attitudinal factors. *Sociological Perspectives, 49*(1), 47–56.

Bautista de Domanico, Y., Crawford, I., & DeWolfe, A. (1994). Ethnic identity and self-concept in Mexican-American adolescents: Is bicultural identity related to stress or better adjustment? *Child & Youth Care Forum, 23*(3), 197–206.

Beatson, J., & Taryan, S. (2003). Predisposition to depression: The role of attachment. *Australian and New Zealand Journal of Psychiatry, 37,* 219–225.

Beaudoin, M., & Taylor, M. (2004). *Breaking the culture of bullying and disrespect, grades K–8: Best practices and successful strategies.* Thousand Oaks, CA: Corwin Press.

Beckman, D., & Brent, R. (1994). Effects of prescribed and self-administered drugs during the second and third trimesters. In G. Avery, M. Fletcher, & M. MacDonald (Eds.), *Neonatology: Athophysiology and management of the newborn* (4th ed., pp. 197–206). Philadelphia: Lippincott.

Behrman, J., & Sengupta, P. (2006). Documenting the changing contexts within which young people are transitioning to adulthood in developing countries: Convergence toward developed economies? In C. B. Lloyd, J. R. Behrman, N. Stromquist, & B. Cohen (Eds.), *The changing transitions to adulthood in developing countries: Selected studies* (pp. 13–55). Washington, DC: National Research Council.

Beland, F., Zunzunegui, M., Alvardo, B. Otero, A., & del Ser, T. (2005). Trajectories of cognitive decline and social relations. *Journals of Gerontology: Series B: Psychological Sciences and Social Sciences, 60*(6), 320–330.

Bell, S. (1990). Sociological perspectives on the medicalization of menopause. *Annals of New York Academy of Sciences, 592,* 173–178.

Bellamy, C. (2004). *The state of the world's children 2005.* New York: The United Nations Children's Fund.

Belsky, J. (1980). Child maltreatment: An ecological integration. *American Psychologist, 35,* 320–335.

Belsky, J. (1984). The determinants of parenting: A process model. *Child Development, 55*(1), 83–96.

Belsky, J. (1987). Infant day care and socioemotional development: The United States. *Journal of Child Psychology and Psychiatry, 29,* 397–406.

Belsky, J., & Braungart, J. M. (1991). Are insecure-avoidant infants with extensive day care experience less stressed by and more independent in the strange situation? *Child Development, 62,* 567–571.

Belsky, J., Campbell, S., Cohn, J., & Moore, G. (1996). Instability of infant-parent attachment security. *Developmental Psychology, 32,* 921–924.

Bem, S. L. (1993). *The lenses of gender: Transforming the debate on sexual inequality.* New Haven, CT: Yale University Press.

Bem, S. L. (1998). Gender schema theory and its implications for child development: Raising gender-aschematic children in a gender-schematic society. In D. L. Anselmi & A. L. Law (Eds.), *Questions of gender: Perspectives and paradoxes.* Boston: McGraw Hill.

Benefice, E., Caius, N., & Garnier, D. (2004). Cross-cultural comparison of growth, maturation, and adiposity. *Public Health Nutrition, 74*(4), 479–485.

Benenson, J. (1993). Greater preference among females than males for dyadic interaction in early childhood. *Child Development, 64,* 544–555.

Bengtson, V. (1996). Continuities and discontinuities in intergenerational relationships over time. In V. Bengtson & K. Schaie (Eds.), *Adulthood and aging* (pp. 246–268). New York: Springer.

Bengtson, V. (2001). Beyond the nuclear family: The increasing importance of multigenerational bonds. *Journal of Marriage and Family, 63,* 1–16.

Bengtson, V., & Harootyan, R. (1994). *Intergenerational linkages: Hidden connections in American society.* New York: Springer.

Bengtson, V., Rosenthal, C., & Burton, L. (1990). Families and aging: Diversity and heterogeneity. In R. H. Binstock & L. K. George (Eds.), *Handbook of aging and the social sciences* (3rd ed., pp. 263–287). San Diego, CA: Academic Press.

Benjamin, K., Edwards, N. C., & Bharti, V. K. (2005). Attitudinal, perceptual, and normative beliefs influencing the exercise decisions of community-dwelling physically frail seniors. *Journal of Aging and Physical Activity, 13*(3), 276–293.

Benson, P. L. (1990). *The troubled journey: A portrait of 6th-12th grade youth.* Minneapolis, MN: Search Institute.

Benson, P. L., Yeager, R. J., Wood, P. K., Guerra, M. J., & Manno, B. V. (1986). *Catholic high schools: Their impact on low-income students.* Washington, DC: National Catholic Educational Association.

Bergen, D., & Coscia, J. (2001). *Brain research and childhood education: Implications for educators.* Olney, MD: Association for Childhood Education International.

Bergquist, W., Greenberg, E., & Klaum, G. (1993). *In our fifties: Voices of men and women reinventing their lives.* San Francisco: Jossey-Bass.

Berk, L. E. (2002a). *Infants and children: Prenatal through middle childhood* (4th ed.). Boston: Allyn & Bacon.

Berk, L. E. (2002b). *Infants, children, & adolescents* (4th ed.). Boston: Allyn & Bacon.

Berk, L. E. (2005). *Infants, children & adolescents* (5th ed.). Boston: Pearson.

Berkeley Planning Associates. (1996). *Priorities for future research: Results of BAs' Delphi survey of disabled women.* Retrieved November 6, 2002, from http://www.ncddr.org/rr/women/priorities.html

Berliner, K., Jacob, D., & Schwartzberg, N. (2005). The single adult and the family life cycle. In B. Carter & M. McGoldrick (Eds.), *The expanded family life cycle: Individual, family, and social perspectives* (3rd ed., pp. 362–372). Boston: Allyn & Bacon.

Berndt, T. J. (1988). Friendships in childhood and adolescence. In W. Damon (Ed.), *Childhood development today and tomorrow* (pp. 332–348.). San Francisco: Jossey Bass.

Berne, L., & Huberman, B. (1999). *European approaches to adolescent sexual behavior & responsibility.* Washington, DC: Advocates for Youth.

Berne, L., & Huberman, B. (2000). Lessons learned: European approaches to adolescent sexual behavior and responsibility. *Journal of Sex Education & Therapy, 25*(2–3), 189–199.

Bern-Klug, M. (2004). The ambiguous dying syndrome. *Health and Social Work, 29*(1), 55–65.

Bern-Klug, M., Gessert, C., & Forbes, S. (2001). The need to revise assumptions about the end of life: Implications for social work practice. *Health and Social Work, 26*(1), 38–48.

Berryman, J. C., & Wendridge, K. (1991). Having a baby after 40: A preliminary investigation of women's experience of pregnancy. *Journal of Reproduction and Infant Psychology, 9,* 3–18.

Berryman, J. C., & Wendridge, K. (1996). Pregnancy after 35 and attachment to the fetus. *Journal of Reproduction and Infant Psychology, 14,* 133–143.

Bertrand, J., Floyd, R. L., & Weber, M. K. (2005, October 28). Guidelines for identifying and referring persons with Fetal Alcohol Syndrome. *Centers for Disease Control, 54*(RR11), 1–10.

Best, K. (2002). Medical barriers often unnecessary: Barriers with no scientific basis can limit choice and endanger health (facilitating contraception choice). *Network, 21*(3), 4–14.

Betts, S. (2002). *Childhood immunizations.* Unpublished manuscript.

Bhathena, R. K., & Guillebaud, J. (2006). Contraception for the older woman: An update. *Climacteric: The Journal of the International Menopause Society, 9*(4), 264–276.

Bhattacharya, G. (2000). The school adjustment of South Asian immigrant children in the United States. *Adolescence, 35,* 77–85.

Bianchi, S., & McArthur, E. (1991). Family disruption and economic hardship: The short-run picture for children. *Current Population Reports, P-70*(23).

Biernat, M. (1991). Gender stereotypes and the relationship between masculinity and femininity: A developmental analysis. *Journal of Personality and Social Psychology, 61,* 351–365.

Biggs, S. (1999). *The mature imagination: Dynamics of identity in midlife and beyond.* Philadelphia: Open University Press.

Bigler, R. S., & Liben, L. S. (1993). A cognitive-developmental approach to racial stereotyping and reconstructive memory in Euro-American children. *Child Development, 64,* 1507–1518.

Billingsley, A. (1999). *Mighty like a river: The black church and social reform.* New York: Oxford University Press.

Bishop, K. (1993). Psychosocial aspects of genetic disorders: Implications for practice. *Families in Society, 74,* 207–212.

Bitzan, J. E., & Kruzich, J. M. (1990). Interpersonal relationships of nursing home residents. *The Gerontologist, 30,* 385–390.

Blacker, L. (2005). The launching phase of the life cycle. In B. Carter & M. McGoldrick (Eds.), *The expanded family life cycle: Individual, family, and social perspectives* (3rd ed., pp. 287–306). Boston: Allyn & Bacon.

Blandford, J. M., & Gift, T. L. (2006). Productivity losses attributable to untreated chlamydial infection and associated pelvic inflammatory disease in reproductive-aged women. *Sexually Transmitted Diseases, 33*(10), S117–S121.

Blass, E., & Ciaramitaro, V. (1994). A new look at some old mechanisms in human newborns: Taste and tactile determinants of state, affect, and action. *Monographs of the Society for Research in Child Development, 59*(1), v–81.

Blau, P. M. (1964). *Exchange and power in social life.* New York: Wiley.

Blazer, D. G. (1995). Depression. In G. L. Maddox (Ed.), *The encyclopedia of aging: A comprehensive resource in gerontology and geriatrics* (2nd ed., pp. 265–266). New York: Springer.

Bliatot, B. (1993). Hmong death customs: Traditional and acculturated. In D. Irish, K. Lundquist, & V. Nelsen (Eds.), *Ethnic variations in dying, death, and grief: Diversity in universality* (pp. 77–99). Washington, DC: Taylor & Francis.

Blieszner, R., & deVries, B. (2001). Perspectives on intimacy. *Generations, 25*(2), 7–8.

Blinn, C. (1997). *Maternal ties: A selection of programs for female offenders.* Lanham, MD: American Correctional Association.

Bloom, B., & Steinhart, D. (1993). *Why punish the children? A reappraisal of the children of incarcerated mothers in America.* San Francisco: National Council on Crime and Delinquency.

Bloom, L. (1998). Language acquisition in its developmental context. In W. Damon, D. Kuhn, & R. Siegler (Eds.), *Handbook of child psychology (5th ed.): Vol. 2. Cognition, perception, and language* (pp. 309–370). New York: Wiley.

Booth, A., Johnson, D., Granger, A., Crouter, A., & McHale, S. (2003). Testosterone and child and adolescent adjustment: The moderating role of parent-child relationships. *Developmental Psychology, 39*(1), 85–98.

Blume, J. (1970). *Are you there, God? It's me, Margaret.* New York: Dell.

Blyth, D. A., & Roehlkepartian, E. C. (1993). *Healthy communities, healthy youth.* Minneapolis, MN: Search Institute.

Boldizar, J. P. (1991). Assessing sex typing and androgyny in children: The children's sex role inventory. *Developmental Psychology, 27,* 505–515.

Bon Secours Hospice. (2002). *Signs and symptoms of approaching death.* Richmond, VA: Author.

Bonanno, G., & Kaltman, S. (1999). Toward an integrative perspective on bereavement. *Psychological Bulletin, 125*(6), 760–776.

Bonne, O. B., Rubinoff, B., & Berry, E. M. (1996). Delayed detection of pregnancy in patients with anorexia nervosa: Two case reports. *International Journal of Eating Disorders, 20,* 423–425.

Borke, H. (1973). The development of empathy in Chinese and American children between 3 and 6 years of age: A cross-cultural study. *Developmental Psychology, 9,* 102–108.

Bortz, W. M., & Wallace, D. H. (1999). Physical fitness, aging, and sexuality. *Western Journal of Medicine, 170*(3), 167–169.

Borysenko, J. (1996). *A woman's book of life: The biology, psychology, and spirituality of the feminine life cycle.* New York: Riverhead Books.

Borzekowski, D., Fobil, J., & Asante, O. (2006). Online access by adolescents in Accra: Ghanian teens' use of the Internet for health information. *Developmental Psychology, 42*(3), 450–458.

Bos, H., van Balan, F., & Visser, A. (2005). Social and cultural factors in infertility and childlessness. *Patient Education and Counseling, 59*(3), 223–225.

Bowlby, J. (1969). *Attachment and loss.* New York: Basic Books.

Bowlby, J. (1980). *Attachment and loss: Loss, sadness, and depression* (Vol. 3). New York: Basic Books.

Bowlby, J. (1982). *Attachment and loss* (Vol. 1). New York: Basic Books.

Bowles, S., & Gintis, H. (1976). *Schooling in capitalist America: Educational reform and the contradictions of economic life.* New York: Basic Books.

Bradley, L. A. (1995). Changing American birth through childbirth education. *Patient Education and Counseling, 25*(1), 75–82.

Bradley, R., Whiteside, L., Mundfrom, D., Casey, P., Kelleher, K., & Pope, S. (1994). Early indications of resilience and their relation to experiences in the home environments of low birthweight, premature children living in poverty. *Child Development, 65*, 346–360.

Bradley, S. (2000). *Affect regulation and the development of psychopathology.* New York: Guilford Press.

Brandtstadter, J. (2006). Adaptive resources in later life: Tenacious goal pursuits and flexible role adjustment. In M. Csikszentmihalyi & I. Csikszeentmihalyi (Eds.), *A life worth living: Contributions to positive psychology* (pp. 143–164). New York: Oxford Press.

Brantlinger, E. (1992). Professionals' attitudes toward the sterilization of people with disabilities. *Journal of the Association for Severe Handicaps, 17*(1), 4–18.

Braungart, J., Plomin, R., DeFries, J. C., & Fulker, D. (1992). Genetic influences on testerrated infant temperament as assessed by Bayley's Infant Behavior Record: Nonadoptive and adoptive siblings and twins. *Developmental Psychology, 28*, 40–47.

Brazelton, T. B. (1983). *Infants and mothers: Differences in development.* New York: Delta/Seymour Lawrence.

Bredekamp, S. (Ed.). (1992). *Developmentally appropriate practice in early childhood programs serving children from birth through age 8.* Washington, DC: National Association for the Education of Young Children.

Bright Futures. (n.d.). *Early childhood: Growth and physical development.* Retrieved December 4, 2006, from http://www.brightfutrues.org/physicalactivity/ec/1.html

Brim, O., Ryff, C., & Kessler, R. (Eds.). (2004). *How healthy are we? A national study of well-being at midlife.* Chicago: University of Chicago Press.

Brinch, M., Isager, T., & Tolstrup, K. (1988). Anorexia nervosa and motherhood: Reproduction pattern and mothering behavior of 50 women. *Acta Psychiatrica Scandinavica, 77*, 611–617.

Broderick, P. C., & Blewitt, P. (2006). *The life span: Human development for helping professionals* (2nd ed.). Upper Saddle River, NJ: Pearson.

Brody, E. (1985). Parent care as normative family stress. *The Gerontologist, 25*(1), 19–29.

Brokenleg, M., & Middleton, D. (1993). Native Americans: Adapting, yet retaining. In D. Irsih, K. Lundquist, & V. Nelsen (Eds.), *Ethnic variations in dying, death, and grief: Diversity in universality* (pp. 101–112). Washington, DC: Taylor & Francis.

Bromberger, J., Meyer, P., Kravitz, H., Sommer, B., Cordal, A., Powell, L., et al. (2001). Psychological distress and natural menopause: A multiethnic community study. *American Journal of Public Health, 91*(9), 1435.

Bronfenbrenner, U. (1979). *The ecology of human development: Experiments by nature and design.* Cambridge: Harvard University Press.

Brooks, J. L., Hair, E. C., & Zaslow, M. J. (2001, July). *Welfare reform's impact on adolescents: Early warning signs.* (Child Trends Research Brief). Washington, DC: Child Trends.

Brooks-Gunn, J. (1988). Antecedents and consequences of variations in girls' maturational timing. *Journal of Adolescent Health, 9,* 365–373.

Brooks-Gunn, J., & Duncan, G. (1997). The effects of poverty on children. *Future of Children, 7*(2), 55–71.

Brooks-Gunn, J., & Furstenberg, F. (1989). Adolescent sexual behavior. *American Psychologist, 44,* 249–257.

Brooks-Gunn, J., Petersen, A. C., & Eichorn, D. (1985). The study of maturational timing effects in adolescence. *Journal of Youth and Adolescence, 14,* 149–161.

Brown, B. B. (2004). Adolescent's relationships with peers. In R. M. Lerner & L. Steinberg (Eds.), *Handbook of adolescent psychology* (2nd ed., pp. 363–394). New York: Wiley.

Brown, J. (2003). The self-enhancement motive in collectivistic cultures: The rumors of my death have been greatly exaggerated. *Journal of Cross-Cultural Psychology, 34,* 603–605.

Brown, J., Dutton, K., & Cook, K. (2001). From the top down: Self-esteem and self-evaluation. *Cognition and Emotion, 15,* 615–631.

Brown-Guttovz, H. (2006). Myths and facts about ectopic pregnancy. *Nursing, 36*(8), 70.

Brubaker, E., Gorman, M. A., & Hiestand, M. (1990). Stress perceived by elderly recipients of family care. In T. H. Brubaker (Ed.), *Family relationships in later life* (2nd ed., pp. 267–281). Newbury Park, CA: Sage.

Brumberg, J. (1997). *The body project: An intimate history of American girls.* New York: Random House.

Brunner, E. (1997). Stress and the biology of inequality. *British Medical Journal, 314*(7092), 1472–1476.

Bryson, K., & Casper, L. (1999). *Coresident grandparents and grandchildren.* Washington, DC: U.S. Census Bureau.

Buchmann, M. (1989). *The script of life in modern society: Entry into adulthood in a changing world.* Chicago: University of Chicago Press.

Buekens, P., Xiong, X., & Harville, E. W. (2006). Hurricanes and pregnancy. *Birth, 22,* 91–93.

Buitendijk, S. E., Offerhaus, P. M., van Dommelen, P., & van der Pal-de-Bruin, K. M. (2005). Maternal factors and the probability of a planned home birth. *British Journal of Gynaecology: An International Journal of Obstetrics and Gynaecology, 112*(6), 748–753.

Bullis, R. K. (1996). *Spirituality in social work practice.* Washington, DC: Taylor and Francis.

Bullis, R. K., & Harrigan, M. (1992). Religious denominational policies on sexuality. *Families in Society, 73,* 304–312.

Bunting, L., & McAuley, C. (2004). Teenage pregnancy and motherhood: The contribution of child support. *Child and Family Social Work, 9,* 201–215.

Burchinal, M. R., Peisner-Feinberg, E. S., Bryant, D. M., & Clifford, R. M. (2000). Children's social and cognitive development and child care quality: Testing for differential associations related to poverty, gender, or ethnicity. *Applied Developmental Science, 4,* 149–165.

Burchinal, M. R. (1999). Childcare experiences and developmental outcomes. *Annals of the American Academy of Political Science, 563,* 73–98.

Bureau of Labor Statistics, U.S. Department of Labor. (2006, August 25). *Bureau of Labor Statistics News: Employment and unemployment among youth summary.* Washington, DC: Author.

Burnette, D. (1999). Custodial grandparents in Latino families: Patterns of service use and predictors of unmet needs. *Social Work, 44*(1), 22–34.

Buss, L., Tolstrup, J., Munk, C., Bergholt, T., Ottesen, B., Gronbaek, M., et al. (2006). Spontaneous abortion: A prospective cohort study of younger women from the general population in Denmark: Validation, occurrence and risk determinants. *Acta Obstetricia Et Gynaecologica Scandinavica, 85*(4), 467–475.

Bustan, N. M. (1994). Maternal attitudes toward pregnancy and the risk of neonatal death. *American Journal of Public Health, 84*, 411–414.

Butler, R. N. (1963). The life review: An interpretation of reminiscence in the aged. *Psychiatry, 26*, 65–70.

Butler, R. N. (1987). Life review. In G. L. Maddox (Ed.), *The encyclopedia of aging: A comprehensive resource in gerontology and geriatrics* (2nd ed., pp. 397–398). New York: Springer.

Byock, I. (1997). *Dying well: Peace and possibilities at the end of life.* New York: Riverhead Books.

Byock, R. (2004). *The four things that matter most: A book about living.* New York: Free Press.

Cahill, D., & Wardle, P. (2002). Management of infertility. *British Medical Journal, 325*(7354), 28–32.

Cain, A. C. (2006). Parent suicide: Pathways of effects into the third generation. *Psychiatry, 69*(3), 204–227.

Call, J. (1995). On becoming a good enough infant. *Infant Mental Health Journal, 16*(1), 52–57.

Calman, L., & Tarr-Whelan, L. (2005). *Early childhood education for all: A wise investment.* Retrieved May 3, 2007, from http://web.mit.edu/workplacecenter/docs/Full%Report.pdf

Cameron, L. (1999). Understanding alcohol abuse in American Indian/Alaskan native youth. *Pediatric Nursing, 25*(3), 297.

Campbell, L., Campbell, B., & Dickinson, D. (1999). *Teaching and learning through multiple intelligences* (2nd ed.). Needham Heights, MA: Allyn & Bacon.

Campbell, R., & MacFarlane, A. (1986). Place of delivery: A review. *British Journal of Obstetrics and Gynaecology, 93*(7), 675–683.

Campbell, R., & Sais, E. (1995). Accelaterated metalinguistic (phonological) awareness in bilingual children. *British Journal of Developmental Psychology, 13*, 61–68.

Campbell, S. (2002). *Behavioral problems in preschool children* (2nd ed.). New York: Guilford Press.

Canda, E. (1997). Spirituality. In *Encyclopedia of social work: 1997 supplement* (19th ed.). Washington, DC: National Association of Social Workers Press.

Canda, E. R., & Furman, L. D. (1999). *Spiritual diversity in social work practice.* New York: Free Press.

Canino, I., & Spurlock, J. (1994). *Culturally diverse children and adolescents.* New York: Guilford Press.

Carey, T. A. (1994). "Spare the rod and spoil the child." Is this a sensible justification for the use of punishment in child rearing? *Child Abuse and Neglect, 18*, 1005–1010.

Carney, J., & Cohler, B. (1993). Developmental continuities and adjustment in adulthood: Social relations, morale, and the transformation from middle to late life. *The course of life: Late adulthood* (Vol. 6, pp. 199–226). Madison, CT: International Universities Press.

Carrasco, D. (1990). *Religions of Mesoamerica.* New York: Harper Collins.

Carskadon, M. A. (1990). Adolescent sleepiness: Increased risk in a high-risk population. *Alcohol, Drugs and Driving, 5*(4), 317–328.

Carstensen, L. (1992). Social and emotional patterns in adulthood: Support for socioemotional selectivity theory. *Psychology and Aging, 7*, 331–338.

Carstensen, L. (1998). A life-span approach to social motivation. In J. Heckhausen & C. Dweck (Eds.), *Motivation and self-regulation across the life span* (pp. 341–364). New York: Cambridge University Press.

Carstensen, L. (2001). Selectivity theory: Social activity in life-span context. In A. Walker, M. Manoogian-O'Dell, L. McGraw, & D. White (Eds.), *Families in later life: Connections and transitions* (pp. 265–275). Thousand Oaks, CA: Pine Forge.

Carter, B., & McGoldrick, M. (2005a). *The expanded family life cycle: Individual, family and social perspectives* (3rd ed.). Boston: Allyn & Bacon.

Carter, B., & McGoldrick, M. (2005b). The divorce cycle: A major variation in the American family life cycle. In B. Carter & M. McGoldrick (Eds.), *The expanded family life cycle: Individual, family, and social perspectives* (3rd ed., pp. 373–380). Boston: Allyn & Bacon.

Carter, D. B., & Patterson, C. J. (1982). Sex roles as social conventions: The development of children's conceptions of sex-role stereotypes. *Developmental Psychology, 18,* 812–824.

Carter, S. (2000). *No excuses: Lessons from 21 high-performing, high poverty schools.* Washington, DC: The Heritage Foundation.

Cartlidge, P. H., & Stewart, J. H. (1995). Effect of changing the stillbirth definition on evaluation of perinatal mortality rates. *The Lancet, 346,* 486–488.

CASA. (2002). *CASA 2002 teen survey.* New York: National Center on Addiction and Substance Abuse at Columbia University (CASA).

Casale-Giannola, D., & Kamens, M. W. (2006). Inclusion at a university: Experiences of a young woman with Down Syndrome. *Mental Retardation, 44*(5), 344–352.

Case, R. (1998). The development of conceptual structures. In D. Kuhn & R. Siegler (Eds.), *Handbook of child psychology: Vol. 2. Cognition, perception, and language* (5th ed., pp. 745–800). New York: Wiley.

Casey, B. (1999). Images in neuroscience. Brain development, XII: Maturation in brain activation. *American Journal of Psychiatry, 156,* 504.

Caspi, A. (1987). Personality in the life course. *Journal of Personality and Social Psychology, 53*(6), 1203–1213.

Caspi, A., & Roberts, B. (1999). Personality continuity and change across the life course. In L. A. Pervin & O. P. John (Eds.), *Handbook of personality: Theory and research* (2nd ed., pp. 300–326). New York: Guilford Press.

Cavanaugh, J. (1996). *Adult development and aging* (3rd ed.). Pacific Grove, CA: Brooks/Cole.

Centers for Disease Control and Prevention. (1997, March 7). Analysis of the third National Health and Nutrition Examination Survey, 1988–1994 (NHAMES III). *Morbidity and Mortality Weekly Report, 46*(9), 11–32.

Centers for Disease Control and Prevention. (1999a). *1999 assisted reproductive technology success rates.* Retrieved September 9, 2002, from http://www.cdc.gov/nccdphp/drh/art.htm

Centers for Disease Control and Prevention. (1999b). *Chronic diseases and their risk factors: The nation's leading causes of death.* Atlanta, GA: Author.

Centers for Disease Control and Prevention. (2000). *Abortion surveillance: Preliminary analysis: United States, 1997.* Retrieved November 6, 2002, from http://www.infoplease.com/ipa/A0764203.html

Centers for Disease Control and Prevention, National Center for Injury and Prevention and Control. (2005a). *Child maltreatment: Fact sheet.* Retrieved May 2, 2005, from http://www.cdc.gov/ncipc/factsheets/cmfacts.htm

Centers for Disease Control and Prevention. (2005b). Trends in reportable sexually transmitted diseases in the United States, 2004. National Surveillance Data for Chlamydia,

Gonorrhea, and Syphillis. *Sexually Transmitted Disease Surveillance, 2004.* Atlanta: U.S. Department of Health and Human Services, Centers for Disease Control and Prevention.

Centers for Disease Control and Prevention. (2006a, October 3). *Preterm transcript.* Retrieved December 12, 2006, from http://www2a.cdc.gov/podcasts/pdf/preterm_con sumer_10–3-06_transcript.pdf

Centers for Disease Control and Prevention. (2006b). *Breastfeeding: Data and statistics: Breastfeeding practices—Results from the 2005 National Immunization Survey.* Retrieved December 11, 2006, from http://www.cdc.gov/breastfeedomgdat/NIS_data/data_2005.htm

Centers for Disease Control and Prevention. (2006c, June 9). Youth risk behavior surveillance—United States, 2005. *Morbidity and Mortality Weekly Report, 55*(SS-5), 1–112.

Centers for Disease Control and Prevention. (2006d). Cases of HIV infection and AIDS in the United States, 2004). *HIV/AIDS Surveillance Report* (Vol. 16). Atlanta: U.S. Department of Health and Human Services, Centers for Disease Control and Prevention.

Centers for Disease Control and Prevention. (n.d.a). *Sexually transmitted diseases. Genital HPV Infection—CDC Fact Sheet.* Retrieved January 5, 2007, from http://www.cdc.gov/ std/HPV/STDFact-HPV.htm

Centers for Disease Control and Prevention. (n.d.b). *Sexually transmitted diseases. Trichomoniasis—CDC Fact Sheet.* Retrieved January 5, 2007 from http://www.cdc.gov/ std/trichomonas/STDFact-Trichomoniasis.htm

Central Intelligence Agency. (2006). *The world fact book.* Retrieved December 19, 2006, from https://cia.gov/cia//publications/factbook/geos/us.html

Cervantes, J., & Ramirez, O. (1992). Spirituality and family dynamics in psychotherapy with Latino children. In L. Vargas & J. Koss-Chioino (Eds.), *Working with culture: Psychotherapeutic interventions with ethnic minority children and adolescents.* San Francisco: Jossey-Bass.

Chadiha, L., & Danziger, S. (1995). The significance of fathers for inner-city African-American mothers. *Child and Adolescent Social Work Journal, 12*(2), 83–100.

Chadwick, R., Levitt, M., & Shickle, D. (1997). *The right to know and the right not to know.* Brookfield, VT: Avebury.

Champion, J. D., Piper, J., Holden, A., Korte, J., & Shain, R. N. (2004). Abused women and risk for pelvic inflammatory disease. *Western Journal of Nursing Research, 26*(2), 176–195.

Champion, J. D., Piper, J., Holden, A., Shain, R. N., Perdue, S., & Dorte, J. E. (2005). Relationship of abuse and pelvic inflammatory disease risk behavior in minority adolescents. *Journal of the American Academy of Nurse Practitioners, 17*(6), 234–241.

Chang, G., McNamara, T., Orav, E., & Wilkins-Haug, L. (2006). Alcohol use by pregnant women: Partners, knowledge and other predictors. *Journal of Studies of Alcoholism, 67*(20), 245–251.

Chang, L. (2001). The development of racial attitudes and self concepts of Taiwanese preschoolers (China). *Dissertation Abstracts International: Section A: Humanities & Social Sciences, 61*(8-A), 3045.

Chang, S. H., Cheng, B. H., Lee, S. L., Chuang, H. Y., Yang, C. Y., Sung, F. C., et al. (2005). Low blood lead concentration in association with infertility in women. *Environmental Research 101*(3), 380–386.

Chapman, P., & Mullis, R. (2000). Racial differences in adolescent coping and self-esteem. *Journal of Genetic Psychology, 161*(2), 152–160.

Chapman, M. V., & Perreira, K. M. (2005). The well-being of immigrant Latino youth: A framework to inform practice. *Families in Society, 86,* 104–111.

Charlesworth, L. (2007). Child maltreatment. In E. Hutchison, H. Matto, M. Harrigan, L. Charlesworth, & P. Viggiani (Eds.), *Challenges of living: A multidimensional working model for social workers* (pp. 105–139). Thousand Oaks, CA: Sage.

Chase-Lansdale, P. L., & Vinovskis, M. A. (1995). Whose responsibility? An historical analysis of the changing roles of mothers, fathers, and society. In P. L. Chase-Lansdale & J. Brooks-Gunn (Eds.), *Escape from poverty: What makes a difference for children?* (pp. 11–37). New York: Cambridge University Press.

Chasnoff, I. (1998). Silent violence: Is prevention a moral obligation? *Pediatrics, 102,* 145–148.

Chatfield, J. E. (2002). FDA approves weekly birth control patch. *American Family Physician, 65*(12), 329.

Chatters, L., & Jayakody, R. (1995). Commentary: Intergenerataional support within African-American families: Concepts and methods. In V. Bengtson, K. Schaie, & L. Burton (Eds.), *Adult intergenerational relations: Effects of social change* (pp. 97–118). New York: Springer.

Cheap IVF needed: Editorial. (2006, August). *Nature, 442*(31), 958. Retrieved October 28, 2006, from http://www.nature.com.proxy.lib.odu.edu/nature/journal/v442/n7106/pdf/442958a.pdf

Chen, C. (2006). A household-based convoy and the reciprocity of support exchange between adult children and noncoresiding parents. *Journal of Family Issues, 27*(8), 1100–1136.

Chestang, L. (1972). *Character development in a hostile environment.* Chicago: University of Chicago Press.

Chethik, M. (2000). *Techniques of child therapy: Psychodynamic approaches* (2nd ed.). New York: Guilford Press.

Cheung, G., & Todd-Oldehaver, C. (2006). Personality trait of harm avoidance in late-life depression. *International Journal of Geriatric Psychiatry, 21*(2), 192–193.

Child Trends. (n.d.). *Trends in sexual activity and contraceptive use among teens.* Washington, DC: Author. Retrieved August 19, 2002, from http://www.childtrends.org

Child Welfare League of America. (2005). *Statement of the Child Welfare League of American for House Subcommittee on Human Resources of the Committee on Ways and Means for the hearing on federal foster care financing.* Retrieved December 27, 2006, from http://www.cwla.org/advocacy/fostercare050609.htm

ChildbirthSolutions, Inc. (n.d.). *Fertility awareness methods: Natural family planning.* Retrieved December 13, 2006, from http://www.childbirthsolutions.com/articles/preconception/fertilityawareness/index.php

Children's Defense Fund. (1996). *The state of America's children, 1996.* Washington, DC: Author.

Children's Defense Fund. (1997). *The state of America's children, 1997.* Washington, DC: Author.

Children's Defense Fund. (2000). *Yearbook 2000: The state of America's children.* Washington, DC: Author.

Children's Defense Fund. (2001). *The state of America's children, 2001.* Washington, DC: Author.

Chodorow, N. (1978). *The reproduction of mothering: Psychoanalysis and the sociology of gender.* Berkeley: University of California Press.

Chodorow, N. (1989). *Feminism and psychoanalytic theory.* New Haven, CT: Yale University Press.

Chomsky, N. (1968). *Language and mind.* New York: Harcourt Brace Jovanovich.

Chowdhury, F. (2004). The socio-cultural context of child marriage in a Bangladeshi village. *International Journal of Social Welfare, 13,* 244–253.

Christiansen, O. B., Nielsen, H. S., & Kolte, A. M. (2006). Future directions of failed implantation and recurrent miscarriage research. *Reproductive Biomedicine Online, 13.*

Chudacoff, H. (1989). *How old are you?* Princeton, NJ: Princeton University Press.

Chugani, H., Behen, M., Muzik, O., Juhasz, C., Nagy, F., & Chugani, D. (2001). Local brain functional activity following early deprivation: A study of post-institutional Romanian orphans. *Neuroimage, 14*, 1290–1301.

Chumlea, W. C., Schubert, C. M., Roche, A. F., Kulin, H. E., Lee, P. A., Himes, J. H., et al., (2003). Age at menarche and racial comparisons in US girls. *Pediatrics, 111*(1), 110–113.

Cicerelli, V. (1995). *Sibling relationships across the life span.* New York: Plenum Press.

Clare, R., Mazzucchelli, T., Studman, L., & Sanders, M. (2006). Behavioral family intervention for children with developmental disabilities and behavioral problems. *Journal of Clinical Child and Adolescent Psychology, 35*(2), 180–193.

Clark, H. (2001). Residential substance abuse treatment for pregnant and postpartum women and their children: Treatment and policy implications. *Child Welfare, 80*(2), 179–198.

Clark, K., & Clark, M. (1939). The development of consciousness of self and the emergence of racial identification in Negro preschool children. *Journal of Social Psychology, 10*, 591–599.

Clark, M. K., Dillon, J. Sowers, M., & Nichols, S. (2005). Weight, fat mass, and central distribution of fat increase when women use depotmedroxprogesterone acetate for contraception. *International Journal of Obesity, 29*(10), 1252–1258.

Clarke, J., & Craven, A. (2005). The gender balance. *Geography Review, 19*(1), 2–5.

Clarke-Stewart, K. A. (1988). "The 'effects' of infant day care reconsidered" reconsidered: Risks for parents, children, and researchers. *Early Childhood Research Quarterly, 3*(3), 293–318.

Clarke-Stewart, K. A. (1989). Infant day care: Maligned or malignant? *American Psychologist, 17*, 454–462.

Clearinghouse on International Developments in Child, Youth and Family Policies at Columbia University. (2002). *Child Policy International.* Retrieved June 7, 2002, from http://www.childpolicyintl.org

Cockey, C. D. (2005). On the edge: Premature births hit record high: One in eight newborn premature. *AWHONN Lifelines, 9*(5), 365–367.

Coid, J., Petruckevitch, A., Feder, G., Chung, W. S., Richardson, J., & Moorey, S. (2001). Relation between childhood sexual and physical abuse and risk of revictimisation in women: A cross-sectional survey. *The Lancet, 358*, 450–454.

Coie, J. D., Dodge, K. A., & Coppotelli, H. (1982). Dimensions and types of social status: A cross age perspective. *Developmental Psychology, 18*, 557–570.

Cole, E., & Stewart, A. (1996). Meanings of participation among black and white women: Political identity and social responsibility. *Journal of Personality and Social Psychology, 71*(1), 130–140.

Cole, S. S., & Cole, T. M. (1993). Sexuality, disability, and reproductive issues through the lifespan. In F. P. Haseltine, S. S. Cole, & D. B. Gray (Eds.), *Reproductive issues for persons with physical disabilities* (pp. 3–21). Baltimore: Brookes.

Coles, L. S. (2004). Demography of human supercentenarians. *Journal of Gerontology: Biological Sciences, 59*(6), 579–586.

Coles, R. (1987). *The moral life of children.* Boston: Houghton/Mifflin.

Coles, R. (1997). *The moral intelligence of children.* New York: Random House.

Collins, A. L., & Smyer, M. A. (2005). The resilience of self-esteem in late adulthood. *Journal of Aging and Health, 17*(4), 471–489.

Comer, J. P. (1980). *School power: Implications of an intervention project.* New York: Free Press.

Comer, J. P. (1994). Home, school, and academic learning. In K. I. Goodland & P. Keating (Eds.), *Access to knowledge: The continuing agenda for our nation's schools.* New York: College Board.

Comprehensive School Reform Quality Center and American Institutes for Research. (2006). *CSRQ Center report on middle and high school comprehensive school reform models.* Retrieved December 30, 2006, from http://www.csrq.org/documents/MSHS2006Report_FinalFullVersion11–16–06.pdf

Condon, J. (2006). What about dad? Psychosocial and mental health issues for new fathers. *Australian Family Physician, 35*(9), 690–692.

Conger, R., Conger, K., Elder, G., Jr., Lorenz, F., Simons, R., & Whitbeck, B. (1993). Family economic stress and adjustment of early adolescent girls. *Developmental Psychology, 29*(2), 206–219.

Conger, R., Elder, G., Jr., Lorenz, F., Simons, R., & Whitbeck, L. (1992). A family process model of economic hardship and adjustment of early adolescent boys. *Child Development, 63,* 526–541.

Conn, D. K. (2001). Mental health issues in long-term care facilities. In D. Conn, N. Herrmann, A. Kaye, D. Rewilak, & B. Schogt (Eds.), *Practical psychiatry in the long-term care facility: A handbook for staff* (pp. 1–16). Seattle, WA: Hogrefe & Huber.

Connie, T. A. (1988). *Aids and adaptations for disabled parents: An illustrated manual for service providers and parents with physical or sensory disabilities* (2nd ed.). Vancouver: University of British Columbia, School of Rehabilitation Medicine.

Connor, M. E., & White, J. L. (2006). *Black fathers: An invisible presence in America.* Mahwah, NJ: Lawrence Erlbaum Associates.

Constable, R., & Walberg, H. (1996). School social work: Facilitating home-school partnerships in the 1990s. In R. Constable, J. P. Flynn, & S. McDonald (Eds.), *School social work: Practice and research perspectives* (3rd ed., pp. 182–196). Chicago: Lyceum Books.

Coohey, C. (1996). Child maltreatment: Testing the isolation hypothesis. *Child Abuse and Neglect, 20*(3), 241–254.

Coohey, C. (1998). Home alone and other inadequately supervised children. *Child Welfare, 77*(3), 291–310.

Cook, E. A., Jelen, T. G., & Wilcox, C. (1992). *Between two absolutes: Public opinion and the politics of abortion.* Boulder, CO: Westview Press.

Cooksey, E., Menaghan, E., & Jekielek, S. (1997). Life-course effects of work and family circumstances on children. *Social Forces, 76*(2), 637–665.

Cooper, P. G. (2000). Ectopic pregnancy. *Clinical Reference Systems, Annual, 2000,* 565.

Copeland, V. (1996). Immunization among African American children: Implications for social work. *Health and Social Work, 21*(2), 105–114.

Corbin, J. M. (1987). Women's perceptions and management of pregnancy complicated by chronic illness. *Health Care Women International, 8*(5–6), 317–337.

Corcoran, M., Danziger, S. K., Kalil, A., & Seefeldt, K. S. (2000). How welfare reform is affecting women's work. *Annual Review of Sociology, 26,* 241–269.

Cordero, L., Hines, S., Shibley, K. A., & Landon, M. B. (1992). Perinatal outcome for women in prison. *Journal of Perinatology, 12,* 205–209.

Corsaro, W. (2005). *The sociology of childhood* (2nd ed.). Thousand Oaks, CA: Pine Forge.

Costa, F. M., Jessor, R., Donovan, J. E., & Fortenberry, J. D. (1995). Early initiation of sexual intercourse: The influence of psychosocial unconventionality. *Journal of Research on Adolescents, 5,* 93–121.

Costa, P., & McCrae, R. (1994). Set like plaster? Evidence for stability of adult personality. In T. F. Heatherton & S. L. Weinberger (Eds.), *Can personality change?* (pp. 21–40). Washington, DC: American Psychological Association.

Costa, P., Terracciano, A., & McCrae, R. (2001). Gender differences in personality traits across cultures: Robust and surprising findings. *Journal of Personality and Social Psychology, 81*(2), 322.

Cota-Robles, S., Neiss, M., & Rowe, D. C. (2002). The role of puberty in violent and nonviolent delinquency among Anglo American, Mexican American, and African American boys. *Journal of Adolescent Research, 17,* 364–376.

Cotter, A., & O'Sullivan, M. (2004). Update on managing HIV in pregnancy: It's imperative to identify more HIV-infected women earlier in pregnancy through HIV testing and to reduce mother-to-child transmission of the virus that causes AIDS. *Contemporary OB/GYN, 49*(11), 57–66.

Counts, D. R., & Counts, D. A. (1991). *Coping with the final tragedy: Cultural variation in dying and grieving.* Amityville, NY: Baywood.

Cousins, E. (2000). *Roots: From outward bound to expeditionary learning.* Dubuque, IA: Kendall Hunt Publishing.

Cowan, P. A. (1991). Individual and family life transitions: A proposal for a new definition. In P. A. Cowan & M. Hetherington (Eds.), *Family transitions* (pp. 3–30). Hillsdale, NJ: Lawrence Erlbaum.

Cowles, K. V. (1996). Cultural perspectives of grief: An expanded concept analysis. *Journal of Advanced Nursing, 23,* 287–294.

Cowley, C., & Farley, T. (2001). Adolescent girls' attitudes toward pregnancy. *Journal of Family Practice, 50*(7), 603–617.

Cox, S. J., Glazebrook, C., Sheard, C., Ndukwe, G., & Oates, M. (2006). Maternal self-esteem after successful treatment for infertility. *Fertility and Sterility, 85*(1), 84–89.

Craig, G. J, &. Baucum, D. (2002). *Human development* (9th ed.). Upper Saddle River, NJ: Prentice Hall.

Crain, R. (1996). The influences of age, race, and gender on child and adolescent multidimensional self-concept. In B. Bracken (Ed.), *Handbook of self-concept* (pp. 395–420). New York: Wiley.

Crawford, J. J., Nobles, W. W., & Leary, J. D. (2003). Reparations and healthcare for African Americas: Repairing the damage from the legacy of slavery. In R. Winbush (Ed.), *Should America pay? Slavery and the raging debate on reparations* (pp. 251–281). New York: Harper Collins Publishing.

Crawley, L., Payne, R., Bolden, J., Payne, T., Washington, P., & Williams, S. (2000). Palliative and end-of-life care in the African American community. *Journal of the American Medical Association, 284*(19), 2518–2521.

Cristafalo, V., Tresini, M., Francis, M., & Volker, C. (1999). Biological theories of senescence. In V. L. Bengston & K. W. Schaie (Eds.), *Handbook of theories of aging* (pp. 98–112). New York: Springer.

Critchley, H. O., & Wallace, W. H. (2005). Impact of cancer treatment on uterine function. *Journal of the National Cancer Institute, 34,* 64–68.

Croxatto, H. B., Brache, V., Massai, R., Ivarez, F., Forcelledo, M. L., Pavez, M., et al. (2005). Feasibility study of Nestorone-ethinylestradiol vaginal contraceptive ring for emergency contraception. *Contraception, 73*(1), 46–52.

Croteau, D., & Hoynes, W. (2006). *The business of media: Corporate media and the public interest* (2nd ed.). Thousand Oaks, CA: Pine Forge Press.

Csikszentmihalyi, M., & Larson, R. (1984). *Being adolescent: Conflict and growth in the teenage years.* New York: Basic Books.

Csikszentmihalyi, M., & Schneider, B. (2000). *Becoming adult: How teenagers prepare for the world of work.* New York: Basic Books.

Culp, R., McDonald Culp, A., Dengler, B., & Maisano, P. (1999). First-time young mothers living in rural communities use of corporal punishment with their toddlers. *Journal of Community Psychology, 27*(4), 503–509.

Cumming, E., & Henry, W. (1961). *Growing old.* New York: Basic Books.

Cwikel, J., Gidron, Y., & Sheiner, E. (2004). Psychological interactions with infertility among women. *European Journal of Obstetrics and Gynecology and Reproductive Biology, 117,* 126–131.

Dalby, P. (2006). Is there a process of spiritual change or development associated with ageing? A critical review of research. *Aging and Mental Health, 10*(1), 4–12.

Damon, W. (1977). *The social world of the child.* San Francisco: Jossey-Bass.

Dannefer, D. (2003a). Whose life course is it, anyway? Diversity and "linked lives" in global perspective. In R. Settersten, Jr. (Ed.), *Invitation to the life course: Toward new understandings of later life* (pp. 259–268). Amityville, NY: Baywood Publishing Co., Inc.

Dannefer, D. (2003b). Toward a global geography of the life course: Challenges of late modernity for life course theory. In J. Mortimer & M. Shanahan (Eds.), *Handbook of the life course* (pp. 647–659). New York: Kluwer Academic/Plenum Publishers.

Dannefer, D., & Perlmutter, M. (1990). Development as a multidimensional process: Individuals and social constituents. *Human Development, 33,* 108–137.

David, H. P. (1996). Induced abortion: Psychosocial aspects. In J. J. Sciarra (Ed.), *Gynecology and obstetrics* (Vol. 6, pp. 1–8). Philadelphia: Lippincott-Raven.

Davidson, J., & Smith, R. (1990). Traumatic experiences in psychiatric outpatients. *Journal of Traumatic Stress Studies, 3,* 459–475.

Davidson, J., Moore, N., & Ullstrup, L. (2004). Religiosity and sexual responsibilities: Relationships of choice. *Journal of Health Behavior, 28*(4), 335–346.

Davies, D. (2004) *Child development: A practitioner's guide* (2nd ed.). New York: Guilford Press.

Davis, M., & Vander Stoep, A. (1997). The transition to adulthood for youth who have serious emotional disturbance: Developmental transition and young adult outcomes. *Journal of Mental Health Administration, 24*(4), 400–427.

Davis, R. (2001). The postpartum experience for southeastern Asian women in United States. *MCN: The American Journal of Maternal/Child Nursing, 26*(4), 208–213.

Dean, R. G. (1993). Teaching a constructivist approach to clinical practice. In J. Laird (Ed.), *Revisioning social work education: A social constructionist approach* (pp. 55–75). New York: Haworth Press.

De Casper, A., & Fifer, W. (1980). Of human bonding: Newborns prefer their mothers' voices. *Science, 208,* 1174–1176.

Dee, T. S. (2005). *Teachers and the gender gaps in student achievement* (NBER Working Paper No. 116600). Cambridge, MA: National Bureau of Economic Research.

Deeg, D. (2005). The development of physical and mental health from late midlife to early old age. In S. Willis & M. Martin (Eds.), *Middle adulthood: A lifespan perspective* (pp. 209–241). Thousand Oaks, CA: Sage.

de Escobar, G. M. (2004). Maternal thyroid hormones early in pregnancy and fetal brain. *Clinical Endocrinology and Metabolism, 18*(2), 225–248.

DeHart, G. B., Sroufe, L. A., & Cooper, R. G. (2000). *Child development: Its nature and course* (4th ed.). Boston: McGraw-Hill.

DeJong, W. (1993). Obesity as a characterological stigma: The issue of responsibility and judgments of task performance. *Psychological Reports, 73,* 963–970.

De La Cancela, V., & Martinez, I. (1983). An analysis of culturalism in Latino mental health: Folk medicine as a case in point. *Hispanic Journal of Behavioral Sciences, 5*(3), 251–274.

Delany, S., & Delany, E., with Hearth, A. (1993). *Having our say: The Delany sisters' first 100 years.* New York: Kodansha International.

Delany, S., with Hearth, A. (1997). *On my own at 107: Reflections on life without Bessie.* New York: HarperCollins.

Dellmann, T. (2004). "The best moments of my life." A literature review of fathers' experience of childbirth. *Australian Midwifery, 17*(3), 20–26.

Dellmann-Jenkins, M., Blankemeyer, M., & Pinkard, O. (2001). Incorporating the elder caregiving role into the developmental tasks of young adulthood. *International Journal of Aging and Human Development, 52*(1), 1.

Del Rio, N. (2004). A framework for multicultural end-of-life care: Enhancing social work practice. In J. Berzoff & P. R. Silverman (Eds.), *Living with dying: A handbook for end-of-life healthcare practitioners* (pp. 439–461). New York: Columbia University Press.

Dennis, C., & Chung-Lee, L. (2006). Postpartum depression help-seeking barriers and maternal treatment preferences: A qualitative systematic review. *Birth, 33*(4), 323–331.

Dennison, B., & Edmunds, & Stratton, H. (2006). Rapid infant weight gain predicts childhood overweight. *Obesity, 14*(3), 491–499.

Department of Health and Human Services. (2006a). *Drug Abuse Warning Network, 2004: National estimates of drug-related emergency department visits* (DAWN Series D-28, DHHS Publication No. (SMA) 06-4143). Rockville, MD: Author.

Department of Health and Human Services. (2006b). *Fertility, contraception, and fatherhood: Data on men and women from cycle 6 of the 2002 National Survey of Family Growth* (DHHS Publication No. (PHS) 2006–1978). Hyattsville, MD: Author.

DeRosier, M. E., Kupersmidt, J. B., & Patterson, C. J. (1994). Children's academic and behavioral adjustment as a function of the chronicity and proximity of peer rejection. *Child Development, 65,* 1799–1813.

DeSpelder, L. A., & Strickland, A. L. (2005). *The last dance: Encountering death and dying* (7th ed.). Boston: McGraw-Hill.

Devitt, N. (1977). The transition from home to hospital births in the United States. *Birth and Family Journal, 4,* 47–58.

Devore, W., & Schlesinger, E. (1999). *Ethnic sensitive social work practice* (5th ed.). Boston: Allyn & Bacon.

de Vries, B. (Ed.). (1999). *End of life issues: Interdisciplinary and multidimensional perspectives.* New York: Springer Publishing Company.

de Vries, B., & Watt, D. (1996). A lifetime of events: Age and gender variations in the life story. *International Journal of Aging and Human Development, 42*(2), 81–102.

de Vries, M., & Sameroff, A. (1984). Culture and temperament: Influences on infant temperament in three East African societies. *American Journal of Orthopsychiatry, 54,* 83–96.

Diamond, L. (2000). Passionate friendships among adolescent sexual-minority women. *Journal of Research on Adolescence, 10,* 191–209.

Diamond, L. M., & Savin-Williams, R. C. (2003). Gender and sexual identity. In R. M. Lerner, F. Jacobs, & D. Wertlieb (Eds.), *Handbook of applied developmental science Vol. 1* (pp. 101–121). Thousand Oaks, CA: Sage.

Dickason, E. J., Schult, M., & Silverman, B. L. (1990). *Maternal-infant nursing care*. St. Louis, MO: Mosby.

Dickason, E., Silverman, B., & Kaplan, J. (1998). *Maternal-infant nursing care* (3rd ed.). St. Louis, MO: Mosby.

Dick-Read, G. (1944). *Childbirth without fear: Principles and practices of natural childbirth*. New York: Harper & Row.

Direnfeld, D., & Roberts, J. (2006). Mood congruent memory in dysphoria: The roles of state affect and cognitive style. *Behavior Research and Therapy, 44*(9), 1275–1285.

Dirubbo, N. E. (2006). Counsel your patients about contraceptive options. *The Nurse Practitioner, 31*(4), 40–44.

Dittmann-Kohli, F. (2005). Middle age and identity in a cultural and lifespan perspective. In S. Willis & M. Martin (Eds.), *Middle adulthood: A lifespan perspective* (pp. 319–353). Thousand Oaks, CA: Sage.

Dodge, D. T. (1995). The importance of curriculum on achieving quality child care programs. *Child Welfare, 74,* 1171–1188.

Dolinsky, A. L., & Rosenwaike, I. (1988). The role of demographic factors in the institutionalization of the elderly. *Research on Aging, 10,* 235–257.

Dollahite, D., Slife, B., & Hawkins, A. (1998). Family generativity and generative counseling: Helping families keep faith with the next generation. In D. McAdams & E. de St. Aubin (Eds.), *Generativity and adult development: How and why we care for the next generation* (pp. 449–481). Washington, DC: American Psychological Association.

Domina, T. (2005). Leveling the home advantage: Assessing the effectiveness of parental involvement in elementary school. *Sociology of Education, 78*(3), 233–249.

Donahue, M. J., & Benson, P. L. (1995). Religion and the well-being of adolescents. *Journal of Social Issues, 51*(2), 145–161.

Donovan, J., Jessor, R., & Costa, F. (1999). Adolescent problem drinking: Stability of psychosocial and behavioral correlates across a generation. *Journal of Studies on Alcohol, 60*(3), 352–361.

Dorner, J., Mickler, C., & Studinger, U. (2005). Self-development at midlife: Lifespan perspectives on adjustment and growth. In S. Willis & M. Martin (Eds.), *Middle adulthood: A lifespan perspective* (pp. 277–317). Thousand Oaks, CA: Sage.

Douglas, D. (2006, July 11). Normal delivery can be OK after multiple cesareans. *Reuters Health Information*. Retrieved July 29, 2006, from http://www.nlm.nih.gov.eres.regent.edu:2048/medlineplus/print/news/fullstory_35899.html

Dowling, C. (1996). *Red hot mamas: Coming into our own at fifty*. New York: Bantam.

Downs, A. C., & Langlois, J. H. (1988). Sex typing: Construct and measurement issues. *Sex Roles, 18*(1–2), 87–100.

Downs, S. W., Moore, E., McFadden, E. J., Michaud, S. M., & Costin, L. B. (2004). *Child welfare and family services: Policies and practice* (7th ed.). Boston: Pearson.

Draut, T. (2005). *Strapped: Why America's 20- and 30-somethings can't get ahead*. New York: Doubleday.

Drisko, J. (1992). Intimidation and projective identification in group therapy of physically abused early adolescent boys. *Journal of Child and Adolescent Group Therapy, 2*(1), 17–30.

Dryfoos, J. G. (1990). *Adolescents at risk*. New York: Oxford University Press.

Dryfoos, J. G. (1994). *Full-service schools: A revolution in health and social services for children, youth, and families.* San Francisco: Jossey-Bass.

Duarte, A., Ranganath, C., Trujillo, C., & Knight, R. T. (2006). Intact recollection memory in high-performing older-adults: RP and behavioral evidence. *Journal of Cognitive Neuroscience, 18*(1), 33–47.

Dubrow, N., & Garbarino, J. (1989). Living in the war zone: Mothers and young children in a public housing development. *Child Welfare, 68,* 3–20.

Ducharme, S. (2001). Aging and sexuality (results of the Association for Advancement of Retired Persons survey). *Paraplegia News, 55*(2), 18–20.

Dunbar, H. T., Mueller, C. W., Medina, C., & Wolf, T. (1998). Psychological and spiritual growth in women living with HIV. *Social Work, 43,* 144–154.

Dundas, S., & Kaufman, M. (2000). The Toronto Lesbian Family Study. *Journal of Homosexuality, 34*(2), 65–79.

Dunkle, R., Roberts, B., & Haug, M. (2001). *The oldest old in everyday life: Self perception, coping with change, and stress.* New York: Springer.

DuPlessis, H. M., Bell, R., & Richards, T. (1997). Adolescent pregnancy: Understanding the impact of age and race on outcomes. *Journal of Adolescent Health, 20*(3), 187–197.

Dupper, D. R., & Poertner, J. (1997). Public schools and the revitalization of impoverished communities: School-linked, family resource centers. *Social Work, 42,* 415–422.

Durkin, K. (1995). *Developmental social psychology.* Malden, MA: Blackwell.

Dychtwald, K. (1999). *Age power: How the 21st century will be ruled by the new old.* New York: Jeremy P. Tarcher/Putnam.

Dyson, J. (1989). Family violence and its effects on academic underachievement and behavior problems in school. *Journal of the National Medical Association, 82,* 17–22.

East, P. L. (1996). The younger sisters of childbearing adolescents: Their attitudes, expectations, and behaviors. *Child Development, 67,* 267–282.

East, P. L., & Shi, C. R. (1997). Pregnant and parenting adolescents and their younger sisters: The influence of relationship qualities and younger sister outcomes. *Journal of Developmental and Behavioral Pediatrics, 18*(2), 84–90.

Easterlin, R., Schaeffer, C., & Macunovich, D. (1993). Will the baby boomers be less well off than their parents? Income, wealth, and family circumstances over the life cycle in the United States. *Population and Development Review, 19,* 497–522.

Edin, K., & Lein, L. (1997). *Making ends meet.* New York: Russell Sage Foundation.

Edlich, R. F., Winters, K. L., Long, W. B., III, & Gubler, K. D. (2005). Rubella and congenital rubella. *Journal of Long-Term Effects of Medical Implants, 15*(3), 319–328.

Education Trust. (2006). *Yes we can: Telling truths and dispelling myths about race and education in America.* Retrieved November 7, 2006, from http://www2.edutrust.org/edtrust

Edwards, C. (1992). Normal development in the preschool years. In E. V. Nuttall, I. Romero, & J. Kalesnik (Eds.), *Assessing and screening preschoolers* (pp. 9–22). Boston: Allyn & Bacon.

Edwards, E., Eiden, R., & Leonard, K. (2006). Behavior problems in 18–36-month-old children of alcoholic fathers: Secure mother-father attachment as a protective factor. *Developmental and Psychopathology, 18*(2), 395–407.

Egeland, B., Carlson, E., & Sroufe, L. A. (1993). Resilience as process. *Development and Psychopathology, 5,* 517–528.

Egley, A., Jr. (2002). *National youth gang survey trends from 1996–2000* (Volume 3 Fact Sheet, February 2002). Washington, DC: U.S. Department of Justice, Office of Justice Programs, Office of Juvenile Justice and Delinquency Programs.

Ego, A. (2001). Survival analysis of fertility after ectopic pregnancy. *JAMA, The Journal of the American Medical Association, 285*(23), 2955.

Eisenberg, N. (2000). Emotion, regulation, and moral development. *Annual Review of Psychology, 51,* 665–697.

Eisenberg, M., & Resnick, M. (2006). Suicidality among gay, lesbian and bisexual youth: The role of protective factors. *Journal of Adolescent Health, 39,* 662–668.

Eisenberg, N. Guthrie, I., Murphy, B., Shepard, S., Cumberland, A., & Carlo, G. (1999). Consistency and development of prosocial dispositions: A longitudinal study. *Child Development, 70,* 1360–1372.

Elder, G., Jr. (1974). *Children of the Great Depression.* Chicago: University of Chicago Press.

Elder, G., Jr. (1986). Military times and turning points in men's lives. *Developmental Psychology, 22,* 233–245.

Elder, G., Jr. (1992). Life course. In E. Borgatta & M. Borgatta (Eds.), *Encyclopedia of sociology* (pp. 1120–1130). New York: Macmillan.

Elder, G., Jr. (1994). Time, human agency, and social change: Perspectives on the life course. *Social Psychology Quarterly, 57*(1), 4–15.

Elder, G., Jr. (1998). The life course as developmental theory. *Child Development, 69*(1), 1–12.

Elder, G., Jr., & Kirkpatrick Johnson, M. (2003). The life course and aging: Challenges, lessons, and new directions. In R. Settersten, Jr. (Ed.), *Invitation to the life course: Toward new understandings of later life* (pp. 49–81). Amityville, NY: Baywood Publishing Co., Inc.

Elkind, D. (1981). *The hurried child: Growing up too fast too soon.* Reading, MA: Addison-Wesley.

Elley, N. (2001). Early birds, too early: Prematurity may mean poor performance. *Psychology Today, 34*(15), 28.

Elliott, M. (1996). Impact of work, family, and welfare receipt on women's self-esteem in young adulthood. *Social Psychology Quarterly, 59*(1), 80–95.

Ellis, B. J., & Garber, J. (2000). Psychosocial antecedents of pubertal maturation in girls: Parental psychopathology, stepfather presence, and family and marital stress. *Child Development, 71,* 485–501.

Ellison, C. G. (1992). Are religious people nice? Evidence from a national survey of Black Americans. *Social Forces, 71*(2), 411–430.

Ellison, C. G. (1993). Religious involvement and self-perception among Black Americans. *Social Forces, 71*(4), 1027–1055.

Ellor, J. W., Netting, F. E., & Thibault, J. M. (1999). *Understanding religious and spiritual aspects of human service practice.* Columbia, SC: University of South Carolina Press.

Elman, C., & O'Rand, C. (1998). Midlife work pathways and educational entry. *Research on Aging, 20*(4), 475–505.

Elster, N. R. (2006). Art for the masses? Racial and ethnic inequality in assisted reproductive technologies. *DePaul Journal of Health Care Law, 9*(1), 719–33.

Emde, R., Biringen, Z., Clyman, R., & Oppenheim, D. (1991). The moral self of infancy: Affective core and procedural knowledge. *Developmental Review, 11,* 51–270.

Emmons, P. G. (2005). *Understanding sensory dysfunction: Learning, development and sensory dysfunction in autism spectrum disorders, ADHD, learning disabilities and bipolar disorder.* London: Jessica Kingsley Publishers.

Epps, S., & Jackson, B. J. (2000). *Empowered families, successful children: Early intervention programs that work.* Washington, DC: American Psychological Association.

Epstein, J. L., & Lee, S. (1995). National patterns of school and family connections in the middle grades. In B. A. Ryan, G. R. Adams, T. P. Gullotta, R. P. Weissberg, & R. L. Hampton

(Eds.), *The family-school connection: Theory, research, and practice* (pp. 108–154). Thousand Oaks, CA: Sage.

Epstein, N., Bishop, D., Ruan, C., Miller, I., & Keitner, G. (1993). The McMaster model: View of healthy functioning. In F. Walsh (Ed.), *Normal family processes* (pp. 138–160). New York: Guilford.

Epstein, S. (1973). The self-concept revisited: Or, a theory of a theory. *American Psychologist, 28,* 404–416.

Epstein, S. (1991). Cognitive-experiential self-theory: An integrative theory of personality. In R. Cutis (Ed.), *The self with others: Convergences in psychoanalytic, social, and personality psychology* (pp. 111–137). New York: Guilford.

Epstein, S. (1998). Cognitive-experiential self-theory. In D. Barone & M. Hersen (Eds.), *Advanced personality* (pp. 211–238). New York: Plenum Press.

Epstein, S., Lipson, A., Holstein, C., & Huh, E. (1993). Irrational reactions to negative outcomes: Evidence for two conceptual systems. *Journal of Personality and Social Psychology, 62,* 328–339.

Erikson, E. H. (1950). *Childhood and society.* New York: Norton.

Erikson, E. H. (1959b). The problem of ego identity. *Psychological Issues, 1,* 101–164.

Erikson, E. H. (1963). *Childhood and society* (2nd ed.). New York: Norton.

Erikson, E. H. (1968). *Identity: Youth and crisis.* New York: Norton.

Erikson, E. H. (Ed.). (1978). *Adulthood.* New York: Norton.

Erikson, E. H. (1982). *The life cycle completed.* New York: Norton.

Escobar, J., Hoyos-Nervi, C., & Gara, M. (2000). Immigration and mental health: Mexican Americans in the United States. *Harvard Review of Psychology, 8*(2), 64–72.

Espelage, D. L., & Swearer, S. M. (2003). (Ed.). *Bullying in American schools: A social-ecological perspective on prevention and intervention.* Mahwah, NJ: Lawrence Erlbaum Associates.

Fabelo-Alcover, H. (2001). *Black beans and chopsticks: A refugee Latino social worker collaborates with Vietnamese survivors of reeducation camps.* Unpublished manuscript, Virginia Commonwealth University.

Fabes, R., Eisenberg, N., Nyman, M., & Michealieu, Q. (1991). Young children's appraisals of others' spontaneous emotional reactions. *Developmental Psychology, 27,* 858–866.

Fagan, J., Barnett, M., Bernd, E., & Whiteman, V. (2003). Prenatal involvement of adolescent unmarried fathers. *Fathering, 1*(3), 283–302.

Fahy, T. (1991). Fasting disorders in pregnancy. *Psychological Medicine, 21,* 577–580.

Falicov, C. (2005). The Latino family life cycle. In B. Carter & M. McGoldrick (Eds.), *The expanded family life cycle: Individual, family, and social perspectives* (3rd ed., pp. 141–152). Boston: Allyn & Bacon.

Family Health International (2006). *FHI research briefs on the female condom. No. 2: Effectiveness for preventing pregnancy and sexually transmitted infections.* Retrieved November 12, 2006, from http://www.fhi.org/en/RH/Pubs/Briefs/fcbriefs/EffectiveSTIs.htm

Fan, X. (2001). Parental involvement and students' academic achievement: A growth modeling analysis. *Journal of Experimental Education, 70,* 27–61.

Fan, X., & Chen, M. (2001). Parental involvement and students' academic achievement: A meta-analysis. *Educational Psychology Review, 13*(1), 1–22.

Fantuzzo, J. W., Mohr, W. K., & Noone, M. J. (2000). Making the invisible victims of violence against women visible through university/community partnerships. In R. A. Geffner, P. G. Jaffe, & M. Suderman (Eds.), *Children exposed to domestic violence: Current issues in research, intervention, prevention, and policy development* (pp. 9–24). New York: Haworth Press.

Farber, S., Egnew, T., & Farber, A. (2004). What is a respectful death? In J. Berzoff & P. R. Silverman (Eds.), *Living with dying: A handbook for end-of-life healthcare profession-als* (pp. 102–127). New York: Columbia University Press.

Fass, S., & Cauthen, N. K. (2005). *Who are American's poor children?* National Center for Children in Poverty. Retrieved November 13, 2006, from http://www.nccp.org/pub_cpt05b.html

Fass, P., & Mason, M. (Eds.). (2000). *Childhood in America.* New York: New York University Press.

Federal Interagency Forum on Aging-Related Statistics. (2004). *Older Americans 2004: Key indicators of well-being.* Washington, DC: U.S. Printing Office.

Feijoo, A. (2001). Adolescent pregnancy, birth, and abortion rates in Western Europe far out-shine U.S. rates. *Transitions, 14*(2), 4–5.

Felson, R. B. (2002). Pubertal development, social factors, and delinquency among adoles-cent boys. *Criminology, 40*(4), 967–988.

Fergusson, D. M., Horwood, L. J., & Woodward, L. J. (2001). Unemployment and psychosocial adjustment in young adults: Causation or selection? *Social Science & Medicine, 53*(3), 305.

Ferlin, A., Arredi, B., & Foresta, C. (2006). Genetic causes of male infertility. *Reproductive Technology, 22*(2), 133–141.

Fertility Plus. (n.d.). *Frequently asked questions about intrauterine insemination (IUI).* Retrieved November 6, 2002, from http://www.fertilityplus.org/faq/iui.html

Field, D., & Gueldner, S. H. (2001). The oldest-old: How do they differ from the old-old? *Journal of Gerontological Nursing, 27*(8), 20–27.

Field, T., Woodson, R., Greenberg, R., & Cohen, C. (1982). Discrimination and imitation of facial expressions by neonates. *Science, 218,* 179–181.

Fields, J. (2003). *Children's living arrangements and characteristics: March 2002. Current Population Reports.* Retrieved January 14, 2007, from http://www.census.gov/prod/2003 pubs/p20-547.pdf

Fields, J. (2004). *America's families and living arrangements: 2003. U.S. Census Bureau Current Population Reports.* Retrieved December 3, 2006, from http://www.census.gov/prod/2004pubs/p20-553.pdf

Figa-Talamanca, I., Cini, C., Varricchio, G. C., Dondero, F., Gandini, L., Lenzi, A., et al. (1996). Effects of prolonged auto vehicle driving on male reproduction: A study among taxi drivers. *American Journal of Industrial Medicine, 30*(6), 750–758.

Figueira-McDonough, J. (1990). Abortion: Ambiguous criteria and confusing policies. *Affilia, 5*(4), 27–54.

Fiksenbaum, L. M., Greenglass, E. R., & Eaton, J. (2006). Perceived social support, hassles, and coping among the elderly. *Journal of Applied Gerontology, 25*(1), 17–30.

Finch, C. (2001). Toward a biology of middle age. In M. Lachman (Ed.), *Handbook of midlife development* (pp. 77–108). New York: Wiley.

Findlay, L., Girardi, A., Coplan, R. (2006). Links between empathy, social behavior, and social understanding in early childhood. *Early Childhood Research Quarterly, 21*(3), 347–359.

Finer, L., & Henshaw, S. (2006). Disparities in rates of unintended pregnancy in the United States, 1994 and 2001. *Perspectives on Sexual and Reproductive Health, 38*(2), 90–96.

Finn, J. D. (1989). Withdrawing from school. *Review of Educational Research, 59,* 117–142.

Fischer, C., & Phillips, S. (1982). Who is alone? Social characteristics of people with small networks. In L. A. Peplau & D. Perlman (Eds.), *Loneliness: A sourcebook of current theory, research and therapy* (pp. 21–39). New York: Wiley Interscience.

Fischer, K. (1993). Aging. In M. Downey (Ed.), *The new dictionary of Catholic spirituality* (pp. 31–33). Collegeville, MN: Liturgical Press.

Fitzpatrick, K. M., & Boldizar, J. P. (1993). The prevalence and consequences of exposure to violence among African American youth. *Journal of the American Academy of Child and Adolescent Psychiatry, 56*, 22–34.

Flammer, A., & Schaffner, B. (2003). Adolescent leisure across European nations. In S. Verma & R. Larson (Eds.), *Examining adolescent leisure time across culture: New directions for child and adolescent development, No. 99* (pp. 65–77). San Francisco: Jossey-Bass.

Flanagan, C. A. (1990). Change in family work status: Effects on parent-adolescent decision making. *Child Development, 61*, 163–177.

Fleming, A. R. (2000). Welcoming the stork later in life. *Insight on the News, 16*(46), 32.

Flint, M. (1975). The menopause: Reward or punishment? *Psychosomatics, 15*, 161–163.

Floyd, F., Stein, T., Harter, K., Allison, A., & Nye, C. (1999). Gay, lesbian, and bisexual youths: Separation-individuation, parental attitudes, identity consolidation, and well-being. *Journal of Youth and Adolescence, 28*, 719–739.

Foley, K. M. (Ed.). (2005). *When the focus is on care: Palliative care and cancer.* Atlanta: American Cancer Society.

Foner, A. (1995). Social stratification. In G. L. Maddox (Ed.), *The encyclopedia of aging: A comprehensive resource in gerontology and geriatrics* (2nd ed., pp. 887–890). New York: Springer.

Foner, A. (1996). Age norms and the structure of consciousness: Some final comments. *The Gerontologist, 36*(2), 221–223.

Fong, R. (Ed.). (2003). *Culturally competent practice with immigrant and refugee children and families.* New York: Guilford Press.

Food and Drug Administration (FDA). (2006, June 8). *FDA licenses new vaccine for prevention of cervical cancer and other diseases in females caused by human papillomavirus* (FDA News P06-7). Retrieved November 29, 2006, from http://www.fda/gov/bb/topics/NEWS/2006/NEW01385.html

Fost, N. (1981). Counseling families who have a child with severe congenital anomaly. *Pediatrics, 67*, 321–323.

Foster, D. G., Landau, S.C., Monastersky, N., Chung, F., Kim, N., Melton, M., et al. (2006). Pharmacy access to emergency contraception in California. *Perspectives on Sexual and Reproductive Health, 38*(1), 46–52.

Fowler, J. (1981). *Stages of faith: The psychology of human development and the quest for meaning.* San Francisco: Harper.

Fracasso, M., Busch-Rossnagel, N., & Fisher, C. (1994). The relationship of maternal behavior and acculturation to the quality of attachment in Hispanic infants living in New York City. *Hispanic Journal of Behavioral Sciences, 16*, 143–154.

Franklin, C., & Corcoran, J. (2000). Preventing adolescent pregnancy: A review of programs and practices. *Social Work, 45*(1), 40–48.

Fraser, M. (2004). *Risk and resilience in childhood: An ecological perspective* (2nd ed.). Washington, DC: NASW Press.

Fraser, M., Kirby, L., & Smokowski, P. (2004). Risk and resilience in childhood. In M. Fraser (Ed.), *Risk and resilience in childhood: An ecological perspective* (2nd ed., pp. 13–66). Washington, DC: NASW Press.

Freeman, E., & Dyer, L. (1993). High risk children and adolescents: Family and community environments. *Families in Society, 74*, 422–431.

Freeman, L., Shaffer, D., & Smith, H. (1996). Neglected victims of homicide: The needs of young siblings of murder victims. *American Journal of Orthopsychiatry, 66,* 337–345.

Freeman, S. (2004). Nondaily hormonal contraception: Considerations in contraceptive choice and patient counseling. *Journal of the American Academy of Nurse Practitioners, 16*(6), 226–238.

Freud, S. (1905/1953). Three essays on the theory of sexuality. In J. Strachey (Ed. & Trans.), *The standard edition of the complete works of Sigmund Freud* (Vol. 7, pp. 135–245). London: Hogarth.

Freud, S. (1917/1957). Mourning and melancholia. In J. Strachey (Ed. & Trans.), *The standard edition of the complete psychological works of Sigmund Freud* (Vol. 14, pp. 237–258). London: Hogarth.

Freud, S. (1927). Some psychological consequences of the anatomical distinction between the sexes. *International Journal of Psycho-Analysis, 8,* 133–142.

Freud, S. (1938/1973). *An outline of psychoanalysis.* London: Hogarth Press.

Friedmann, E., & Havighurst, R. (1954). *The meaning of work and retirement.* Chicago: University of Chicago Press.

Fry, C. (2003). The life course as a cultural construct. In R. Settersten, Jr. (Ed.), *Invitation to the life course: Toward new understandings of later life* (pp. 269–294). Amityville, NY: Baywood Publishing Co., Inc.

Fry, D. (1995). Kinship and individuation: Cross-cultural perspectives on intergenerational relations. In V. Bengtson, K. Schaie, & L. Burton (Eds.), *Adult intergenerational relations: Effects of social change* (pp. 126–156). New York: Springer.

Frye, C. A. (2006). Efficacy of hormonal contraceptives. *Neurology, 66*(6), S29–S36.

Fu, H., Darroch, J., Haas, T., & Ranjit, N. (1999). Contraceptive failure rates: New estimates from the 1995 National Survey of Family Growth. *Family Planning Perspectives, 31*(2), 52–58.

Fuligni, A. (1997). The academic achievement of adolescents from immigrant families: The roles of family background, attitudes, and behavior. *Child Development, 68*(2), 351–363.

Fuligni, A., & Stevenson, H. (1995). Time use and mathematics achievement among American, Chinese and Japanese high school students. *Child Development, 66*(3), 830–842.

Furstenberg, F., Jr., Cook, T., Eccles, J., Elder, G., Jr., & Sameroff, A. (1999). *Managing to make it: Urban families and adolescent success.* Chicago: University of Chicago Press.

Gabel, K., & Johnston, D. (Eds.). (1995). *Children of incarcerated parents.* New York: Lexington Books.

Gagnon, A., Dougherty, G., Platt, R., Wohoush, O., Stewart, D., George, A., et al. (2004). Needs of refugee mothers after pregnancy–early response services (normap-ers): An example of scientific challenges in studies of migration. *Journal of Epidemiology & Community Health, 58*(1), A23–A24.

Galambos, N. L., & Almeida, D. M. (1992). Does parent-adolescent conflict increase in early adolescence? *Journal of Marriage and the Family, 54,* 737–747.

Gallagher, J. J. (1993). The future of professional/family relations in families with children with disabilities. In J. L. Paul & R. J. Simeonsson (Eds.), *Children with special needs: Family, culture, and society* (2nd ed., pp. 295–310). Fort Worth, TX: Harcourt Brace Jovanovich.

Gallup, G., Jr., & Lindsay, D. M. (1999). *Surveying the religious landscape: Trends in U.S. beliefs.* Harrisburg, PA: Morehouse.

Gamoran, A., & Himmelfarb, H. (1994). *The quality of vocational education.* Washington, DC: U.S. Department of Education.

Gandelman, R. (1992). *Psychobiology of behavioral development.* New York: Oxford University Press.

Garbarino, J. (1992). The meaning of poverty to children. *American Behavioral Scientist, 35,* 220–237.

Garbarino, J. (1995). *Raising children in a socially toxic environment.* San Francisco: Jossey-Bass.

Garbarino, J. (1999). *Lost boys: Why our sons turn violent and how we can save them.* New York: Free Press.

Garbarino, J. (2006). *See Jane hit: Why girls are growing more violent and what we can do about it.* New York: Penguin.

Garcia, E. (2001). Parenting in Mexican American families. In N. Boyd Webb (Ed.), *Culturally diverse parent-child and family relationships: A guide for social workers and other practitioners* (pp. 157–179). New York: Columbia University Press.

Gardner, H. E. (1993). *Multiple intelligences: The theory in practice.* New York: Basic Books.

Gargiulo, R. M. (2005). *Young children with special needs.* Albany, NY: Thomson/Delmar Learning.

Garmezy, N. (1993). Vulnerability and resilience. In D. C. Funder, R. D. Parke, C. Tomlinson-Keasey, & K. Widaman (Eds.), *Studying lives through time* (pp. 377–398). Washington, DC: American Psychological Association.

Garmezy, N. (1994). Reflections and commentary on risk, resilience, and development. In R. J. Haggerty, L. R. Sherrod, N. Garmezy, & M. Rutter (Eds.), *Stress, risk, and resilience in children and adolescents: Processes, mechanisms, and interventions* (pp. 1–18). New York: Cambridge University Press.

Garrett, J. L. (2006). Educating the whole child. *Kappa Delta Pi Record, 42*(4), 154–155.

Garrett, M. W. (1995). Between two worlds: Cultural discontinuity in the dropout of Native American youth. *The School Counselor, 10,* 199–208.

Garton, A. F., & Pratt, C. (1991). Leisure activities of adolescent school students: Predictors of participation and interest. *Journal of Adolescence, 14,* 305–321.

Gartrell, N., Hamilton, J., Banks, A., Mosbacher, D., Reed, N., Sparks, C., & Bishop, H. (1996). The national lesbian family study: 1. Interviews with prospective mothers. *American Journal of Orthopsychiatry, 66,* 272–281.

Garver, K. L. (1995). Genetic counseling. In G. B. Reed, A. E. Claireaux, & F. Cockburn (Eds.), *Diseases of the fetus and newborn* (2nd ed., pp. 1007–1012). London: Chapman & Hall.

Garvey, C. (1984). *Children's talk.* Cambridge, MA: Harvard University Press.

Garvin, V., Kalter, N., & Hansell, J. (1993). Divorced women: Factors contributing to resiliency and vulnerability. *Journal of Divorce and Remarriage, 21*(1/2), 21–39.

Ge, X., Conger, R. D., & Elder, G. H., Jr. (1996). Coming of age too early: Pubertal influences on girls' vulnerability to psychological distress. *Child Development, 67,* 3386–3401.

Ge, X. Conger, R. D., & Elder, G. H., Jr. (2001). The relation between puberty and psychological distress in adolescent boys. *Journal of Research on Adolescence, 11,* 49–70.

Gee, J. P. (1996). *Social linguistics and literacies: Ideology in discourses* (2nd ed.). London: Falmer.

Geiger, B. (1996). *Fathers as primary caregivers.* Westport, CT: Greenwood Publishing.

Gelles, R. (1989). Child abuse and violence in single-parent families: Parent absence and economic deprivation. *American Journal of Orthopsychiatry, 59,* 492–501.

Gelles, R., & Hargreaves, E. (1981). Maternal employment and violence toward children. *Journal of Family Issues, 2,* 509–530.

Generations. (2002, Summer), *25*(2).

Gennetian, L., Duncan, G., Knox, V., Vargas, W., Clark-Kauffman, E., & London, A. (2002). *How welfare and work policies for parents affect adolescents: A synthesis of research.* New York: Manpower Demonstration Research Corporation.

Gent, P. J., & Mulhauser, M. B. (1993). Public integration of students with handicaps: Where it's been, where it's going, and how it's getting there. In M. Nagler (Ed.), *Perspectives on disability* (2nd ed., pp. 397–409). Palo Alto, CA: Health Markets Research.

George, L. (1993). Sociological perspectives on life transitions. *Annual Review of Sociology, 19,* 353–373.

George, L. (1996). Missing links: The case for a social psychology of the life course. *The Gerontologist, 36*(2), 248–255.

George, L. (2003). What life-course perspective offers the study of aging and health. In R. Settersten, Jr. (Ed.), *Invitation to the life course: Toward new understandings of later life* (pp. 161–188). Amityville, NY: Baywood Publishing Co., Inc.

George, L. K. (2005). Socioeconomic status and health across the life course: Progress and prospects. *The Journal of Gerontology: Series B Psychological Sciences and Social Sciences, 60B,* 135–139.

George, L., & Gold, D. (1991). Life course perspectives on intergenerational and generational connections. *Marriage & Family Review, 16*(1–2), 67–88.

George, L. K., Larson, D. B., Koenig, H. G., & McCullough, M. E. (2000). Spirituality and health: What we know, what we need to know. *Journal of Social & Clinical Psychology, 19,* 102–116.

Georgiades, S. D. (2005). Emancipated young adults' perspectives on independent living programs. *Families in Society, 86*(4), 503–510.

Gerhardt, S. (2004). *Why love matters: How affection shapes a baby's brain.* New York: Brunner-Routledge.

Gerstel, N., & Gallagher, S. (1993). Kinkeeping and distress: Gender, recipients of care, and work-family conflict. *Journal of Marriage and the Family, 55,* 598–607.

Gibbs, J. T., & Huang, L. N. (1989). A conceptual framework for assessing and treating minority youth. In J. T. Gibbs & L. N. Huang (Eds.), *Children of color: Psychological interventions with minority youth* (pp. 1–29). San Francisco: Jossey-Bass.

Gielen, U., & Markoulis, D. (2001). Preference for principled moral reasoning: A developmental and cross-cultural perspective. In L. Adler & U. Gielen (Eds.), *Cross-cultural topics in psychology* (2nd ed., pp. 81–101). Westport, CT: Praeger/Greenwood.

Gilbert, W. M., Nesbitt, T., & Danielsen, B. (2003). The cost of prematurity: Quantification by gestational age and birth weight. *Obstetrics and Gynecology, 102,* 488–492.

Gilligan, C. (1982). *In a different voice: Psychological theory and women's development.* Cambridge, MA: Harvard University Press.

Gilman, S. E., Kawachi, I., & Fitzmaurice, G. M. (2003). Family disruption in childhood and risk of adult depression. *American Journal of Psychiatry, 160*(5), 939–946.

Giudice, L. C. (2006). Infertility and the environment: The medical context. *Seminars in Reproductive Medicine, 24*(5), 1039–1048.

Glaser, D. (2000). Child abuse and neglect and the brain—A review. *Journal of Child Psychology and Psychiatry, 41*(1), 97–116.

Glass, C. S., & Wegar, K. (2000). Teacher perceptions of the incidence and management of Attention Deficit Hyperactivity Disorder. *Education, 121*(2), 412–420.

Glover, R. (1996). Religiosity in adolescence and young adulthood: Implications for identity formation. *Psychological Reports, 78,* 427–431.

Gogtay, N., Giedd, J., Lusk, L., Hyashi, K., Greenstein, D., Vaituzis, A. C., et al. (2004). Dynamic mapping of human cortical development during childhood through early adulthood. *The Proceedings of the National Academy of Science, 101*(21), 8174–8179.

Goldberg, A. B., Cohen, A., & Lieberman, E. (1999). Nulliparas' preference for Epidural analgesia: Their effects on actual use in labor. *Birth: Issues In Perinatal Care, 26*(3), 139–143.

Goldberg, W., Clarke-Stewart, K., Rice, J., & Dellis, E. (2002). Emotional energy as an explanatory construct for fathers' engagement with their infants. *Parenting: Science & Practice, 2,* 379–408.

Goldenberg, R. L., & Jobe, A. H. (2001). Prospects for research in reproductive health and birth outcomes. *Journal of the American Medical Association, 285*(5), 633–642.

Goldenberg, R. L., Hauth, J. C., & Andrews, W. W. (2000). Intrauterine infection and premature delivery. *New England Journal of Medicine, 342*(20), 1500–1508.

Goldscheider, F. (1997). Recent changes in U.S. young adult living arrangements in comparative perspective. *Journal of Family Issues, 18,* 708–724.

Goldscheider, F., & Lawton, L. (1998). Family experiences and the erosion of support for intergenerational coresidence. *Journal of Marriage and the Family, 60,* 623–632.

Goldstein, H., Kaczmarek, L. A., & English, K. M. (2002). *Promoting social communication: Children with developmental disabilities from birth to adolescence.* Baltimore, MD: Paul H. Brookes Publishing Co.

Goldstein, J., & Kenney, C. (2001). Marriage delayed or marriage forgone? New cohort forecasts of first marriage for U.S. women. *American Sociological Review, 66*(4), 506–519.

Goldstein, S., & Brooks, R. B. (2005). Why study resilience? In S. Goldstein & R. B. Brooks (Eds.), *Handbook of resilience in children* (pp. 3–15). New York: Kluwer Academic/Plenum Publishers.

Goleman, D. (1995). *Emotional intelligence.* New York: Bantam.

Goleman, D. (2006). *Social intelligence: The new science of human relationships.* New York: Bantam.

Golembiewski, R. (1994). Is organizational membership bad for your health? Phases of burnout as covariants of mental and physical well-being. In A. Farazmand (Ed.), *Modern organizations: Administrative theory in contemporary society* (pp. 211–227). Westport, CT: Praeger.

Gomes, J. S., Cimo, S., & Cook, T. (2001). Baby-friendly hospital initiative improves breast-feeding initiation rates in a U.S. hospital setting. *Pediatrics, 108*(3), 677.

Gomez, N. (2001). EEG during different emotions in 10 month old infants of depressed mothers. *Journal of Reproductive and Infant Psychology, 19*(4), 295–313.

Gonyea, J. G. (1987). The family and dependency: Factors associated with institutional decision-making. *Journal of Gerontological Social Work, 10,* 61–77.

Gonzalez-Quintero, V., Tolaymat, L., Luke, B., Gonzalez-Garcia, A. Duthely, L., & O'Sullivan, M. (2006). Outcomes of pregnancies among Hispanics: Revisiting the epidemiologic paradox. *Journal of Reproductive Medicine, 51*(1), 10–14.

Good, T., & Nichols, S. (2001). Expectancy effects in the classroom: A special focus on improving the reading performance of minority students in first-grade classrooms. *Educational Psychologist, 36,* 113–126.

Googins, B. (1991). *Work/family conflicts: Private lives public responses.* New York: Auburn House.

Gopaul-McNicol, S. (1988). Racial identification and racial preference of Black preschool children in New York and Trinidad. *Journal of Black Psychology, 14*(2), 65–68.

Gottman, J. M. (1994, May/June). Why marriages fail. *Family Therapy Networker,* 41–48.

Gowen, A. (2001, December 6). School is new world for child immigrants. *Washington Post,* p. GZ14.

Graff, H. (1995). *Conflicting paths: Growing up in America.* Cambridge, MA: Harvard University Press.

Grainger, D. A., Frazier, L. M., & Rowland, C. A. (2006). Preconception care and treatment with assisted reproductive technologies. *Maternal and Child Health Journal,10* (Suppl 7), 161–164.

Green, J. (2006, May 10). *U.S. has second worst newborn death rate in modern world. Report says.* Retrieved November 5, 2006, from CNN Health Web site: http://www.cnn.com/ 2006/HEALTH/parenting/05/08/mothers.index/

Green, M. (1994). *Bright futures: Guidelines for health supervision of infants, children, and adolescents.* Arlington, VA: National Center for Education in Maternal and Child Health.

Greene, C. (1991). Clinical considerations: Midlife daughters and their aging parents. *Journal of Gerontological Nursing, 17,* 6–12.

Greenfield, P., & Zheng, Y. (2006). Children, adolescents, and the Internet: A new field of inquiry in developmental psychology. *Developmental Psychology, 42*(3), 391–394.

Greve, W., & Staudinger, U. M. (2006). Resilience in later adulthood and old age: Resources and potentials for successful aging. In Cicchetti, D. & Cohen D. J. (Eds.), *Developmental psychopathology, Vol. 3: Risk, disorder and adaptation* (pp. 796–840). Hoboken, NJ: John Wiley & Sons.

Griffith, S. (1996). *Amending attachment theory: Ambiguities among maternal care, day care peer group experience, general security and altruistic prosocial proclivities in 3, 4 & 5 year old children.* Unpublished doctoral dissertation, Adelphi University, New York.

Grimes, D. A., Lopez, L., Raymond, E. G., Halpern, V., Nanda, K., & Schulz, K. F. (2006). *Spermicide used alone for contraception.* Retrieved October 18, 2006, from EBSCO database.

Gromley, W., Gayer, T., Phillips, D., & Dawson, B. (2004). *The effects of universal pre-k on cognitive development.* Retrieved May 3, 2007, from http://www.crocus.georgetown/edu/ reports/CROCUSworkingpaper4.pdf

Gross, E. (2004). Adolescent Internet use: What we expect, what teens report. *Applied Developmental Psychology, 25,* 633-649.

Grossman, L., Fitzsimmons, S., Larsen-Alexander, J., Sachs, L., & Harter, C. (1990). The infant feeding decision in low- and upper-income women. *Clinical Pediatrics, 29*(1), 30–37.

Groves, B. M. (1997). Growing up in a violent world: The impact of family and community violence on young children and their families. *Topics in Early Childhood Special Education, 17*(1), 74–102.

Guarnaccia, P., & Lopez, S. (1998). The mental health and adjustment of immigrant and refugee children. *Child and Adolescent Psychiatric Clinic of North America, 7*(3), 537–553.

Guillemard, A., & van Gunsteren, H. (1991). Pathways and prospects: A comparative interpretation of the meaning of early exit. In M. Kohli, M. Rein, A. M. Guillemard, & H. van Gunsteren (Eds.), *Time for retirement* (362–389). Cambridge, UK: Cambridge University Press.

Guisbond, L., & Neill, M. (Sept/Oct 2004). Failing our children: No Child Left Behind undermines quality and equity in education. *Clearing House, 78*(1), 12.

Gullete, M. (1998). Midlife discourses in the twentieth-century United States: An essay on the sexuality, ideology, and politics of middle-ageism. In R. Shweder (Ed.), *Welcome to middle age (and other cultural fictions)* (pp. 3–44). Chicago: University of Chicago Press.

Gurian, M. (2001). *Boys and girls learn differently! A guide for teachers and parents.* San Francisco: Jossey-Bass.

Guterman, N. B., & Cameron, M. (1997). Assessing the impact of community violence on children and youths. *Social Work, 42,* 495–505.

Guterman, N., & Embry, R. (2004). Prevention and treatment strategies targeting physical child abuse and neglect. In P. Allen-Meares & M. Fraser (Eds.), *Intervention with children and adolescents: An interdisciplinary perspective* (pp. 130–158). Boston: Allyn & Bacon.

Gutierrez, R. A. (2004). Internal colonialism: An American theory of race. *Social Science Research on Race, 1*(2), 281–295.

Gutman, H. (1976). *The Black family in slavery and freedom, 1750–1925.* New York: Pantheon.

Gutterman, N. B., & Embry, R. A. (2004). Prevention and treatment strategies targeting physical child abuse and neglect. In P. Allen-Meares & M. W. Fraser (Eds.), *Intervention with children and adolescents: An interdisciplinary perspective* (pp. 130–158). Boston: Allyn & Bacon.

Guvendag, E. S. (2006). Serum biochemistry correlates with the size of tubal ectopic pregnancy on sonography. *Ultrasound in Obstetrics and Gynecology, 28*(6), 826–891.

Guzzetti, B. J., Young, J. P., Gritsavage, M. M., Fyfe, L. M., & Hardenbrook, M. (2002). *Reading, writing, and talking gender in literacy learning.* Newark, DE: International Reading Association and National Reading Conference.

Gyllstrom, M. E., Schreiner, P., & Harlow, B. (2007). Perimenopause and depression: Strength of association, causal mechanisms and treatment recommendations. *Best Practice & Research Clinical Obstetrics & Gynaecology, 21*(2), 275–292.

Haan, N., Millsap, R., & Hartka, E. (1986). As time goes by: Change and stability in personality over fifty years. *Psychology and Aging, 1,* 220–232.

Haden, C., Haine, R., & Fivush, R. (1997). Developing narrative structure in parent-child reminiscing across the preschool years. *Developmental Psychology, 33,* 295–307.

Hagestad, G. (1991). Trends and dilemmas in life course research: An international perspective. In W. Heinz (Ed.), *Theoretical advances in life course research* (pp. 23–57). Weinheim, Germany: Deutscher Studien Verlag.

Hagestad, G. (2003). Interdependent lives and relationships in changing times: A life-course view of families and aging. In R. Settersten, Jr. (Ed.), *Invitation to the life course: Toward new understandings of later life* (pp. 135–159). Amityville, NY: Baywood Publishing Co., Inc.

Hahn, S., Haselhorst, U., Quadbeck, B., Tan, S., Kimming, R., Mann, K., et al. (2006). Decreased soluble leptin receptor levels in women with polycystic ovarian syndrome. *European Journal of Endocrinology, 154*(2), 287–294.

Hair, E., Ling, T., & Cochran, S. W. (2003). *Youth development programs and educationally disadvantaged older youths: A synthesis.* Washington, DC: Child Trends.

Hakin, R. B., Gray, R. H., & Zacur H. (1998). Alcohol and caffeine consumption and decreased fertility. *Fertility and Sterility, 70*(4), 632–637.

Hakuta, K., Ferdman, B. M., & Diaz, R. M. (1987). Bilingualism and cognitive development: Three perspectives. In S. Rosenberg (Ed.), *Advances in applied psycholinguistics: Vol. 2. Reading, writing, and language learning* (pp. 284–319). New York: Cambridge University Press.

Hall, D. (2005). *Getting honest about grad rates: How states play the numbers and students lose.* Retrieved November 7, 2006, from http://www2.edtrust.org/edtrust

Hall, G. (1904). *Adolescence: Its psychology and its relations to physiology, anthropology, sociology, sex, crime, religion, and education.* New York: Appleton.

Halle, T. (2002). *Charting parenthood: A statistical portrait of fathers and mothers in America.* Washington, DC: Child Trends.

Halpern, A. (1996). Transition: A look at foundations. *Exceptional Children, 51,* 479–486.

Halpern, R. (1993). Neighborhood based initiative to address poverty: Lessons from experience. *Journal of Sociology and Social Welfare, 20*(4), 111–135.

Hamblen, J. (2002). *Terrorism and children.* Retrieved January 23, 2002, from http://www .ncptsd.org/facts/disasters/fs_children_disaster.html

Hamilton, B. E., Martin, J. A., Ventura, S. J., Sutton, P. D., & Menacker, P. D. (2006). Final data for 2004. *National Vital Statistics Reports, 55*(1), 1–101.

Hammarberg, K., & Clarke, V. E. (2005). Reasons for delaying childbearing—a survey of women aged 35 years seeking assisted reproductive technology. *Australian Family Physician, 34*(3), 187–188.

Hammer, T., & Vaglum, P. (1990). Use of alcohol and drugs in the transitional phase from adolescence to young adulthood. *Journal of Adolescence, 13,* 129–142.

Han, S., & Moen, P. (1999). Clocking out: Temporal patterning of retirement. *American Journal of Sociology, 105,* 191–236.

Hankins, G. D., Clark, S. M., & Munn, M. B. (2006). Cesarean section on request at 39 weeks: Impact on shoulder dystocia, fetal trauma, neonatal encephalopathy, and intrauterine fetal demise. *Seminars in Perinatology, 30*(5), 276–287.

Hanley, R. J., Alecxih, L. M., Wiener, J. M., & Kennell, D. L. (1990). Predicting elderly nursing home admissions: Results from the 1982–1984 National Long-Term Care Survey. *Research on Aging, 12,* 199–227.

Hao, L., & Cherlin, A. J. (2004). Welfare reform and teenage pregnancy, childbirth, and school dropout. *Journal of Marriage and Family, 66,* 179–184.

Hareven, T. (Ed.). (1978). *Transitions: The family and the life course in historical perspective.* New York: Academic Press.

Hareven, T. (1982a). American families in transition: Historical perspectives on change. In F. Walsh (Ed.), *Normal family processes* (pp. 446–466). New York: Guilford.

Hareven, T. (1982b). *Family time and industrial time: The relationship between the family and work in a New England industrial community.* New York: Cambridge University Press.

Hareven, T. (Ed.). (1996). *Aging and generation relations over the life course: A historical and cross-cultural perspective.* New York: Walter de Gruyter.

Hareven, T. (2000). *Families, history, and social change.* Boulder, CO: Westview.

Harkness, S. (1990). A cultural model for the acquisition of language: Implications for the innateness debate. *Developmental Psychobiology, 23,* 727–739.

Harps, S. N. (2005). Race-related stress, racial socialization, and African American adolescent adjustment: Examining the mediating role of racial identity. *Dissertation Abstracts International: The Humanities and Social Sciences, 66*(5), November 1975-A.

Harrell, S. P. (2000). A multidimensional conceptualization of racism-related stress: Implications for the well-being of people of color. *American Journal of Orthopsychiatry, 70*(1), 42–57.

Harrigan, M. P., & Farmer, R. L. (2000). The myths and facts of aging. In R. L. Schneider, N. P. Kropf, & A. J. Kisor (Eds.), *Gerontological social work: Knowledge, service settings, and special populations* (2nd ed., pp. 26–64). Belmont, CA: Wadsworth.

Harrigan, M. P., & Koerin, B. B. (in press). Long distance caregiving: Personal realities and practice implications. *Reflections: Narratives of Professional Helping.*

Harris, J. (2005). Lesbian motherhood and access to reproductive technology. *Canadian Women Studies, 24*(2–3), 43–50.

Harry, B. (2006). *Why are so many minority students in special education?: Understanding race & disability in schools.* New York: Teachers College Press.

Hart, B., & Risley, T. (1995). *Meaningful differences in the everyday experiences of young American children.* Baltimore: Brookes.

Hart, D. A. (1992). *Becoming men: The development of aspirations, values, & adaptational styles.* New York: Plenum.

Hart, H., McAdams, D., Hirsch, B., & Bauer, J. (2001). Generativity and social involvements among African-American and among Euro-American adults. *Journal of Research in Personality, 3*(2), 208–230.

Hart, V. A. (2002). Infertility and the role of psychotherapy. *Issues in Mental Health Nursing, 23*(1), 31–41.

Hatecher, R. A., Trussel, J., Stewart, F., Stewart, G. K., Kowal, D., Guest, F., Cates, W., & Policar, M. S. (1994). *Contraception technology, 16th edition.* New York: Irvington.

Harter, S. (1988). Developmental processes in the construction of self. In T. D. Yawkey & J. E. Johnson (Eds.), *Integrative processes and socialization: Early to middle childhood* (pp. 45–78). Hillsdale, NJ: Lawrence Erlbaum.

Harter, S. (1998). The development of self-representations. In W. Damon & N. Eisenberg (Eds.), *Handbook of social development: Vol. 3. Social, emotional and personality development* (pp. 553–618). New York: Wiley.

Hartup, W. W. (1983). Peer relations. In E. M. Hetherington (Ed.), *Handbook of child psychology: Vol. 4. Socialization, personality, and social development* (4th ed., pp. 103–196). New York: Wiley.

Harvey, S. M., Carr, C., & Bernheime, S. (1989). Lesbian mothers' health care experiences. *Journal of Nurse-Midwives, 34*(3), 115–119.

Harvey, S. M., Beckman, L. J., Sherman, C., & Petitti, D. (1999). Women's experience and satisfaction with emergency contraception. *Family Planning Perspectives, 31,* 237–240, 260.

Harwood, R. (1992). The influence of culturally derived values on Anglo and Puerto Rican mothers' perceptions of attachment behavior. *Child Development, 63,* 822–839.

Hass, A. (1990). *In the shadow of the Holocaust: The second generation.* Ithaca, NY: Cornell University Press.

Hassan, M. A., & Killick, S. R. (2004). Negative lifestyle is associated with a significant reduction in fecundity. *Fertility and Sterility, 81,* 384–392.

Hatch, S. L. (2005). Conceptualizing and identifying: Cumulative adversity and protective resources: Implications for understanding health inequalities. *The Journal of Gerontology: Series B Psychological Sciences and Social Sciences, 60B,* 130–135.

Hatchett, S., & Jackson, J. (1993). African American extended kin systems: An assessment. In H. McAdoo (Ed.), *Family ethnicity: Strength in diversity* (pp. 90–108). Newbury Park, CA: Sage.

Haugaard, J. J., Reppucci, N. D., & Feerick, M. M. (1997). Children's coping with maltreatment. In S. A. Wolchick & I. N. Sandler (Eds.), *Handbook of children's coping: Linking theory and intervention* (pp. 73–100). New York: Plenum Press.

Hauser-Cram, P., & Howell, A. (2003). The development of young children with disabilities and their families: Implications for policies and programs. In R. M. Lerner, F. Jacobs, & D. Wertlieb (Eds.), *Handbook of Applied Developmental Science, Vol. 1* (pp. 259–279). Thousand Oaks, CA: Sage.

Havighurst, R. J. (1968). Personality and patterns of aging. *The Gerontologist, 8,* 20–23.

Havighurst, R. J. (1972). *Developmental tasks and education* (3rd ed.). New York: David McKay.

Havighurst, R., Neugarten, B., & Tobin, S. (1968). Personality and patterns of aging. In B. L. Neugarten (Ed.), *Middle age and aging* (pp. 173–177). Chicago: University of Chicago Press.

Hawley, D. R., & DeHaan, L. (1996). Toward a definition of family resilience: Integrating life-span and family perspectives. *Family Process, 35,* 283–298.

Haycock, K. (2006). Promise abandoned: How policy choices and institutional practices restrict college opportunities. Retrieved November 3, 2006, from http://www2.edtrust .org/EdTrust/Promise+Abondoned+Report.htm

Hayes, C., Palmer, J., & Zaslow, M. (Eds.). (1990). *Who cares for America's children? Child care policy for the 1990s.* Washington, DC: National Academy Press.

Hayflick, L. (1994). *How and why we age.* New York: Ballantine Books.

Hayward, C., Killen, J. D., Wilson, D. M., Hammer, L. D., Litt, I. F., Kraemer, H. C., et al. (1997). Psychiatric risk associated with early puberty in adolescent girls. *Journal of the American Academy of Child and Adolescent Psychiatry, 36,* 255–263.

Healthy People 2010. (2000). Retrieved April 6, 2002, from http://www.health.gov/healthy people/default.htm

Heck, K. E., Schoendorf, K. C., & Chavez, G. F. (2002). The influence of proximity of prena-tal services on small-for-gestational age birth. *Journal of Community Health, 27*(1), 15–27.

Heckhausen, J. (2001). Adaptation and resilience in midlife. In M. Lachman (Ed.), *Handbook of midlife development* (pp. 345–394). New York: Wiley.

Hedley, A. A., Ogden, C. L., Johnson, C. L., Carroll, M. D., Curtin, L. R., & Flegal, K. M. (2004). Overweight and obesity among U.S. children, adolescents, and adults, 1999–2002. *Journal of American Medical Association, 291,* 2847–2850.

Hehir, T. (2003). Beyond inclusion. *School Administrator, 60*(3), 36–40.

Heimpel, S., Wood, J., Marshall, J., & Brown, J. (2002). Do people with low self-esteem really feel better? Self-esteem differences in motivation to repair negative moods. *Journal of Personality and Social Psychology, 82,* 128–147.

Heinz, W. (2003). From work trajectories to negotiated careers: The contingent work life course. In J. Mortimer & M. Shanahan (Eds.), *Handbook of the life course* (pp. 185–204). New York: Kluwer Academic/Plenum Publishers.

Helburn, S., & Bergmann, B. (2002). *America's child care problem: The way out.* New York: Palgrave Macmillan.

Helson, R., & Wink, P. (1992). Personality change in women from the early 40s to the early 50s. *Psychology and Aging, 7,* 46–55.

Hemenway, D., Solnick, S., & Carter, J. (1994). Child-rearing violence. *Child Abuse and Neglect, 18,* 1011–1020.

Henderson, K., Goldsmith, R., & Flynn, L. (1995). Demographic characteristics of subjective age. *Journal of Social Psychology, 135*(4), 447–457.

Hendricks, J. (1987). Exchange theory in aging. In G. L. Maddox (Ed.), *The encyclopedia of aging* (pp. 238–239). New York: Springer.

Hendricks, J., & Hatch, L. R. (2006). Lifestyle and aging. In R. H. Binstock & L. K. George (Eds.) *Handbook of aging and the social sciences* (pp. 301–319). Amsterdam, Netherlands: Elsevier.

Hepp, S. M., & Meuleman, E. J. (2006). Vasectomy: Indications and implementation in his-toric perspective. *Nederlands Tijdschrift Voor Geneeskunde, 150*(11), 611–614.

Herdiman, J., Nakash, A., & Beedham, T. (2006). Male contraception: Past, present and future. *Journal of Obstetrics and Gynaecology, 26*(8), 721–727.

Herdt, G., & Boxer, A. (1996). *Children of horizons: How gay and lesbian teens are leading a new way out of the closet.* Boston: Beacon Press.

Hernandez, M., & McGoldrick, M. (2005). Migration and the family life cycle. In B. Carter & M. McGoldrick (Eds.), *The expanded family life cycle: Individual, family, and social perspectives* (3rd ed., pp. 169–184). Boston: Allyn & Bacon.

Herrenkohl, T. I., Mason, W. A., Kosterman, R., Lengua, L. J., Hawkins, J. D., & Abbott, R. D. (2004). Pathways from physical childhood abuse to partner violence in young adulthood. *Violence and Victims, 19*(2), 123–145.

Herring, R. D. (1995). Developing biracial ethnic identity: A review of the increasing dilemma. *Journal of Multicultural Counseling and Development, 23*(1), 29–38.

Hessol, N., & Fuentes-Afflick, E. (2005). Ethnic differences in neonatal and postneonatal mortality. *Pediatrics, 115*(1), 164.

Hetherington, E. M., & Clingempeel, W. G. (1992). Coping with marital transitions: A family systems perspective. *Monographs of the Society for Research in Child Development, 57*(2–3, Serial No. 227).

Hetherington, E. M., & Jodl, K. M. (1994). Stepfamilies as settings for child development. In A. Booth & J. Dunn (Eds.), *Stepfamilies: Who benefits? Who does not?* (pp. 55–79). Hillsdale, NJ: Lawrence Erlbaum.

Hetherington, E. M., & Kelly, J. (2002). *For better or for worse: Divorce reconsidered.* New York: Norton.

Heyman, R. E., & Smith Slep, A. M. (2002). Do child abuse and interparental violence lead to adulthood violence. *Journal of Marriage and Family, 64*(4), 864–871.

Hill, R. B. (1972). *The strengths of black families.* New York: National Urban League.

Hillis, S. D., & Wasserheit, J. N. (1996). Screening for Chlamydia: A key to the prevention of Pelvic Inflammatory Disease. *New England Journal of Medicine, 334*(21), 1399–1401.

Hillson, J. M. C., & Kuiper, N. A. (1994). A stress and coping model of child maltreatment. *Clinical Psychology Review, 14*(4), 261–285.

Himelein, M. (1995). Risk factors for sexual victimization in dating: A longitudinal study of college women. *Psychology of Women Quarterly, 19*(1), 31–48.

Himes, C. (2001). Social demography of contemporary families and aging. In A. Walker, M. Manoogian-O'Dell, L. McGraw, & D. L. White (Eds.), *Families in later life: Connections and transitions* (pp. 47–50). Thousand Oaks, CA: Pine Forge Press.

Hines, P. M. (2005). The family life cycle of African American families living in poverty. In B. Carter & M. McGoldrick (Eds.), *The expanded family life cycle: Individual, family and social perspectives* (3rd ed., pp. 327–345). Boston: Allyn & Bacon.

Hines, P., Preto, N., McGoldrick, M., Almeida, R., & Weltman, S. (2005). Culture and the family life cycle. In B. Carter & M. McGoldrick (Eds.), *The expanded family life cycle: Individual, family, and social perspectives* (3rd ed., pp. 69–87). Boston: Allyn & Bacon.

Hinrichsen, G. A., & Clougherty, K. F. (2006). Role transitions. In *Interpersonal psychotherapy for depressed older adults* (pp. 133–152). Washington, DC: American Psychological Association.

Hinshaw, S. P. (1992). Academic underachievement, attention deficits, and aggression: Comorbidity and implications for intervention. *Journal of Consulting and Clinical Psychology, 60*(6), 893–903.

Hlatky, M., Boothrody, D., Vittinghoff, E., Sharp, P., & Whooley, M. (2002). Quality-of-life and depressive symptoms in postmenopausal women after receiving hormone therapy: Results from heart and estrogen/progestin replacement study (HERS) trial. *JAMA, The Journal of the American Medical Association, 287*(5), 591–597.

Hobbs, F., & Damon, B. (1997, April 25). *Sixty-five plus in the United States: Statistical brief.* Retrieved from http://www.census.gov/socdemo/www/agebrief

Hodge, D. R. (2001). Spiritual assessment: A review of major qualitative methods and a new framework for assessing spirituality. *Social Work, 46*(3), 203–214.

Hodge, D., Johnson, B., & Luidens, D. (1993). Determinants of church involvement of young adults who grew up in Presbyterian churches. *Journal for the Scientific Study of Religion, 32*(3), 242–255.

Hodnett, E. D, Downe, S., Edwards, N., & Walsh, D. (2005, January 25). Home-like versus conventional institutional settings for birth (Cochrane Review). *The Cochrane Database of Systematic Reviews,* Issue 1, CD000012.

Hoek, H. (2006). Incidence, prevalence and mortality of anorexia nervosa and other eating disorders. *Current Opinion in Psychiatry, 19,* 389–394.

Hogan, D. (1978). The variable order of events in the life course. *American Sociological Review, 43,* 573–586.

Hogan, D. (1981). *Transitions and social change: The early lives of American men.* New York: Academic Press.

Hogan, D. P., & Msall, M. E. (2002). Family structure and resources and the parenting of children with disabilities and functional limitations. In J. G. Borkowski, S. Landesman Ramey, & M. Bristol-Power (Eds.), *Parenting and the child's world* (pp. 311–344). Mahwah, NJ: Lawrence Erlbaum.

Hoge, C. W., Auchterlonie, J. L., & Milliken, C. S. (2006). Mental health problems, use of mental health services, and attrition from military service after returning from deployment to Iraq or Afghanistan. *Journal of the American Medical Association, 295*(9), 1023–1032.

Hogoel, L., Van-Raalte, R., Kalekin-Fishman, D., & Shlfroni, G. (1995). Psychosocial and medical factors in pregnancy outcome: A case study of Israeli women. *Social Science & Medicine, 40,* 567–571.

Hogstel, M. (2001). *Gerontology: Nursing care of the older adult.* Albany, NY: Delma-Thompson Learning.

Holmes, M. M., Resnick, H. S., Kilpatrick, D. G., & Best, C. L. (1996). Rape-related pregnancy: Estimates and descriptive characteristics from a national sample of women. *American Journal of Obstetrics and Gynecology, 175,* 320–324.

Holmes, T. (1978). Life situations, emotions, and disease. *Psychosomatic Medicine, 19,* 747–754.

Holmes, T., & Rahe, R. (1967). The social readjustment rating scale. *Journal of Psychosomatic Research, 11,* 213–218.

Holter, M. C. (2004). Autistic spectrum disorders: Assessment and intervention. In P. Allen-Meares & M. W. Fraser (Eds.), *Intervention with children and adolescents: An interdisciplinary perspective* (pp. 205–228). Boston: Allyn & Bacon.

Homans, G. C. (1961). *Social behavior: Its elementary forms.* New York: Harcourt Brace Jovanovich.

Homer, L. (2001). Home birth: Alternative medicine in obstetrics. *Clinical Obstetrics and Gynecology, 44*(4), 671–680.

Hong-zheng, L., Zue-rong, L., & Mei-ying, L. (2004). Development of Life Events Inventory for Compulsory Servicemen of Land Army. *Chinese Journal of Clinical Psychology, 12*(3), 234–236.

Hood, L. (2003). *Immigrant students, urban high schools: The challenge continues.* Retrieved November 7, 2006, from http://www.carnegie.org/pdf/immigrantstudents.pdf

Hooyman, N., & Kiyak, H. A. (2005). *Social gerontology: A multidisciplinary perspective* (7th ed.). Boston: Allyn & Bacon.

Hope, R. M., & Hodge, D. M. (2006). Factors affecting children's adjustment to the death of a parent: The social work professional's point of view. *Child and Adolescent Social Work Journal, 23*(1), 107–126.

Horn, A. W., & Alexander, C. I. (2005). Recurrent miscarriage. *Journal of Family Planning and Reproductive Health Care, 31*(2), 103–107.

Horn, J. L. (1982). The theory of fluid and crystallized intelligence in relation to concepts of cognitive psychology and aging in adulthood. In F. I. M. Craik & S. Trehub (Eds.), *Aging and cognitive processes* (pp. 237–278). New York: Plenum.

Hosmer, L. (2001). Home birth, alternative medicine, and obstetrics. *Clinical Obstetrics and Gynecology, 44*(4), 671–680.

Hosp, J. L., & Reschly, D. J. (2003). Referral rates for intervention or assessment: A meta-analysis of racial differences. *Journal of Special Education, 37*(2), 67–80.

House, J. S., Lantz, P. M., & Herd, P. (2005). Continuity and change in the social stratification of aging and health over the life course: Evidence from a nationally representative longitudinal study from 1986 to 2001/2002 (Americans' Changing Lives Study). *The Journal of Gerontology: Series B Psychological Sciences and Social Sciences, 60B,* 15–26.

Hoybert, D. L., Friedman, M. A., Strobino, D. M., & Guyer, B. (2001). Annual summary of vital statistics: 2000. *Pediatrics, 108*(16), 1241–1346.

Hoyert, D. L., Matthews, T. J., Menacker, F., Strobino, D. M., & Guyer, B. (2006). Annual summary of vital statistics: 2004. *Pediatrics, 117*(10), 168–183.

Huang, L. Z., & Winzer-Serhan, U. H. (2006). Chronic neonatal upregulates heteromeric nicotinic acetylcholine receptor binding without change in subunit mRNA expression. *Brain Research, 1113* (1), 94–109.

Huberman, B. (2001). The lessons learned: A model to improve adolescent sexual health in the United States. *Transitions, 14*(2), 6.

Huff, C. (Ed.). (1996). *Gangs in America* (2nd ed.). Thousand Oaks, CA: Sage.

Hughes, H. (1988). Psychological and behavioral correlates of family violence in child witnesses and victims. *American Journal of Orthopsychiatry, 58,* 77–90.

Human Genome Project. (2002). *Human genome project information.* Retrieved September 9, 2002, from http://www.ornl.gov/hgmis

Human Rights Watch. (2006). *Child labor.* Retrieved January 13, 2007, from http://hrw .org/children/labor.htm

Humphreys, N. A., & Quam, J. K. (1998). Middle-aged and old gay, lesbian, and bisexual adults. In G. A. Appleby & J. W. Anastas (Eds.), *Not just a passing phase: Social work with gay, lesbian, bisexual people* (pp. 243–267). New York: Columbia University Press.

Hussein, I. (2004). Prolongation of pregnancy in a woman who has sustained brain death at 26 weeks gestation. *British Journal of Obstetrics and Gynaecology: An International Journal of Obstetrics and Gynaecology, 113*(1), 120–122.

Hussein, I., Govenden, V., Grant, J., & Said, M. (2006). Prolongation of pregnancy in a woman who sustained brain death at 26 weeks of gestation. *BJOG: An International Journal of Obstetrics and Gynaecology, 113*(1), 130–133.

Hutchison, E. (2007). Community violence. In E. Hutchison, H. Matto, M. Harrigan, L. Charlesworth, & P. Viggiani (Eds.), *Challenges of living: A multidimensional working model for social workers* (pp. 71–104). Thousand Oaks, CA: Sage.

Hutchison, E., & Kovacs, P. (2007). HIV/AIDS. In E. Hutchison, H. Matto, M. Harrigan, L. Charlesworth, & P. Viggiani (Eds.), *Challenges of living: A multidimensional working model for social workers* (pp. 233–266). Thousand Oaks, CA: Sage.

Huttenlocher, P., & Kabholkar, A. (1997). Regional differences in synaptogenesis in human cerebral cortex. *Journal of Comparative Neurology, 387,* 167–178.

Huyck, M. H. (2001). Romantic relationships in later life. *Generations, 25*(2), 9–17.

Hyson, M. (2004). *The emotional development of young children: Building an emotion-centered curriculum.* New York: Teachers College Press.

Iannotti, R. (1985). Naturalistic and structured assessments of prosocial behavior in preschool children: The influence of empathy and perspective taking. *Developmental Psychology, 21,* 46–55.

Illinois Maternal and Child Health Project. (2003). *Prematurity project.* Retrieved November 5, 2006, from http://www.ilmaternal.org/Prematurity/InfoRacialDisparities.htm

Infant mortality and low birth weight among Black and White infants: United States. (1980–2000). (2001). *Morbidity and Mortality Weekly Report, 51*(27), 589–592. Retrieved November 6, 2002, from http://www.cdc.gov/mmwr/preview/mmwrhtml/mm5127al.htm

Institute for the Study of Aging. (2001). *Achieving and maintaining cognitive vitality with aging.* (International Longevity Center Workshop Report). New York: Author.

International Longevity Center-USA. (2002). *Is there an "anti-aging" medicine?* (Workshop Report D17692). New York: Author.

Irish, D., Lundquist, K., & Nelsen, V. (1993). *Ethnic variations in dying, death, and grief: Diversity in universality.* Washington, DC: Taylor & Francis.

Ironson, G. (1992). Work, job stress, and health. In S. Zedeck (Ed.), *Work, families, and organizations* (pp. 33–69). San Francisco: Jossey-Bass.

Irvine, M. (2006, November). *For kids, is 10 the new 15?* Retrieved November 26, 2006, from http://www.msnbc.msn.com/id/15905527/

Isenberg, S. (1992). Aging in Judaism. In T. Cole, D. van Tassel, & R. Kastenbaum (Eds.), *Handbook of the humanities and aging* (pp. 147–174). New York: Springer.

Iso-Ahola, S. E., & Crowley, E. D. (1991). Adolescent substance abuse and leisure boredom. *Journal of Leisure Research, 23,* 260–271.

Ito, M., & Sharts-Hopko, C. (2002). The Japanese women's experience of childbirth in the United States. *Health Care for Women International, 23*(6–7), 666–677.

Jackson, J. (1993). Multiple caregiving among African Americans and infant attachment: The need for an emic approach. *Human Development, 36,* 87–102.

Jackson, K. M., & Nazar, A. M. (2006). Breastfeeding, the immune response, and long-term health. *Journal of the American Osteopathic Association, 106,* 203–207.

Jain, T. (2006). Socioeconomic and racial disparities among infertility patients seeking care. *Fertility and Sterility, 85*(4), 876–881.

James, W. P. T. (2006). The challenge of childhood obesity. *The International Journal of Pediatric Obesity, 1*(1), 7–10.

Jang, K., Liveseley, J., Riemann, R., Vernon, P., Hu, S., Angleirner, A., et al. (2001). Covariance structure of neuroticism and agreeableness: A twin and molecular genetic analysis of the role of the serotonin transporter gene. *Journal of Personality and Social Psychology, 81*(2), 295.

Jang, Y., Borenstein, A. R., Chiriboga, D. A., & Mortimer, J. A. (2005). Depressive symptoms among African American and white older adults. *Journals of Gerontology: Series B Psychological Sciences and Social Sciences, 6*(6), 313–319.

Jans, L., & Stoddard, S. (1999). *Chartbook on woman and disability in the United States. An InfoUse Report.* Washington, DC: US Department of Education. National Institute on Disability and Rehabilitation Research.

Jarrell, A. (2000, April 2). The face of teenage sex grows younger. *The New York Times*, Section 9, p. 1, Column 1.

Jasso, G. (2003). Migration, human development, and the life course. In J. Mortimer & M. Shanahan (Eds.), *Handbook of the life course* (pp. 331–364). New York: Kluwer Academic/Plenum Publishers.

Jendrek, M. (1993). Grandparents who parent their grandchildren: Effects on lifestyle. *Journal of Marriage & Family, 55*(3), 609–622.

Jenkins, E., & Bell, C. (1997). Exposure and response to community violence among children and adolescents. In J. Osofsky (Ed.), *Children in a violent society* (pp. 9–31). New York: Guilford.

Jessor, R. (1987). Problem-behavior theory, psychosocial development, and adolescent problem drinking. *British Journal of Addiction, 82*, 331–342.

Johanson, R., Newburn, M., & Macfarlane, A. (2002). Has the medicalisation of childbirth gone too far? *British Medical Journal, 324*(7342), 892–895.

Johnson, A. (2005). *Privilege, power and difference.* New York: McGraw-Hill.

Johnson, C. L., & Barer, B. M. (1997). *Life beyond 85 years: The aura of survivorship.* New York: Springer Publishing Company, Inc.

Johnson, C., Ironsmith, M., Snow C., & Poteat, M. (2000). Peer acceptance and social adjustment in preschool and kindergarten. *Early Childhood Education Journal, 27*(4), 207–212.

Johnson, K. (2006). The SERM of my dream. *The Journal of Clinical Endocrinology & Metabolism, 91*(10), 3754–3756.

Johnson, K. C., & Davis, B. (2005). Outcomes of planned home-births with certified professional midwives: Large prospective study in North America. *British Medical Journal, 330*(7505), 1416.

Johnson, M. P. (2002). An exploration of men's experience and role at childbirth. *The Journal of Men's Studies, 10*(12), 165–183.

Johnson, M. P., & Baker, S. R. (2004). Implications of coping repertoire as predictors of men's stress, anxiety, and depression following pregnancy, childbirth, and miscarriage: A longitudinal study. *Journal of Psychosomatic Obstetrics and Gynecology, 25*(2), 87–98.

Johnson, R., Browne, K., & Hamilton-Giachritsis, C. (2006). Young children in institutional care at risk of harm. *Trauma, Violence & Abuse, 7*(1), 34–60.

Johnson, R. S., & Tripp-Reimer, T. (2001). Aging, ethnicity, and social support: A review. *Journal of Gerontological Nursing, 27*(6), 15–21.

Johnson, T., & Colucci, P. (2005). Lesbians, gay men, and the family life cycle. In B. Carter & M. McGoldrick (Eds.), *The expanded family life cycle: Individual, family, and social perspectives* (3rd ed., pp. 346–361). Boston: Allyn & Bacon.

Johnston, L., O'Malley, P., Bachman, J., & Schulenberg, J. (2004). *Monitoring the future national results on adolescent drug use: Overview of key findings, 2003* (NIH Publication No. 04-5506). Bethesda, MD: National Institute of Drug Abuse.

Johnston, L., O'Malley, P., Bachman, J., & Schulenberg, J. (2005). *Monitoring the future national results on adolescent drug use: Overview of key findings, 2004* (NIH Publication No. 04-5506). Bethesda, MD: National Institute of Drug Abuse.

Johnston, L., O'Malley, P., Bachman, J., & Schulenberg, J. (2006). *Monitoring the future national results on drug use: Overview of key findings, 2005* (NIH Publication No. 06-5882). Bethesda, MD: National Institute on Drug Abuse.

Jones, A. (1992). Self-esteem and identity in psychotherapy with adolescents from upwardly mobile middle-class African American families. In L. Vargas & J. Koss-Chioino (Eds.), *Working with culture: Psychotherapeutic interventions with ethnic minority children and adolescents.* San Francisco: Jossey-Bass Publishers.

Jones, H. P., Guildea, S. E. S., Stewart, J. H., & Cartlidge, P. H. H. (2002). The health status questionnaire: Achieving concordance of public health and disability criteria. *Archives of Disease in Childhood, 86*(11), 15–16.

Jones, R. (2001). How parents can support learning: Not all parent involvement programs are equal, but research shows what works. *American School Board Journal, 188*(9), 18–22.

Jordon, C. B., & Ferguson, R. J. (2006). Infertility-related concerns in two family practice sites. *Family, Systems, and Health, 24*(1), 28–32.

Jordan, J. V. (2005). Relational resilience in girls. In S. Goldstein & R. B. Brooks (Eds.), *Handbook of resilience in children* (pp. 79–90). New York: Kluwer Academic/Plenum Publishers.

Joshi, S., & Morley, J. (2006). Cognitive impairment. *Medical Clinics of North America, 90*(5), 769–787.

Judge, T., Higgins, C., Thoresen, C., & Barrick, M. (1999). The big five personality traits, general mental ability, and career success across the life span. *Personnel Psychology, 52*(3), 621–652.

Julian, T. (1992). Components of men's well-being at mid-life. *Issues in Mental Health Nursing, 13,* 285–299.

Jung, C. (1971). *The portable Jung.* New York: Viking Press.

Kagan, S., & Kagan, M. (1998). *Multiple intelligences: The complete multiple intelligences book.* San Clemente, CA: Kagan Cooperative Learning.

Kahn, R., & Antonucci, T. (1980). Convoys over the life course: Attachment, roles, and social support. In P. Baltes & O. Brim (Eds.), *Life-span development and behavior* (Vol. 3, pp. 253–286). New York: Academic Press.

Kakouros, E., Maniadaki, K., & Papaeliou, C. (2004). How Greek teachers perceive functioning of pupils with ADHD. *Emotional and Behavioural Difficulties, 9*(1), 41–53.

Kaltiala-Heino, R., Kosunen, E., & Rimpela, M. (2003). Pubertal timing, sexual behaviour and self-reported depression in middle adolescence. *Journal of Adolescence, 26*(5), 531–454.

Kamerman, S. (1996). Child and family policies: An international overview. In E. Zigler, S. Kagan, & N. Hall (Eds.), *Children, families, & government: Preparing for the twenty-first century* (pp. 31–48). New York: Cambridge University Press.

Kamerman, S., & Kahn, A. (1995). Innovations in toddler day care and family support services: An international overview. *Child Welfare, 74*(6), 1281–1300.

Kanabus, A. (2006, September 5). *HIV AIDS & pregnancy.* Retrieved October 1, 2006, from http://www.avert.org/pregnancy.htm

Kandel, D. B., & Logan, J. A. (1984). Patterns of drug use from adolescence to young adulthood: Periods of risk for initiation, stabilization and decline in use. *American Journal of Public Health, 74,* 660–666.

Kandel, D. B., & Logan, J. A. (1991). Cocaine use in a national sample of U.S. youth: Ethnic patterns, progression and predictors. *NIDA Monographs, 110,* 151–188.

Kandel, D. B., Davies, M., Karus, D., & Yamaguchi, K. (1986). The consequences in young adulthood of adolescent drug involvement: An overview. *Archives of General Psychiatry, 43,* 746–754.

Kao, R. S., & Lam, M. L. (1997). Asian American elderly. In E. Lee (Ed.), *Working with Asian Americans: A guide for clinicians* (pp. 208–223). New York: Guilford.

Kaplan, B., Nahum, R., Yairi, Y., Hirsch, M., Pardo, J., & Orvieto, R. (2005). Use of various contraceptive methods and time of contraception in a community-based population. *European Journal of Obstetrics, Gynecology, and Reproductive Biology, 123*(1), 72–76.

Kaplan, D. W., Feinstein, R. A., Fisher, M. M., Klein, J., Olmedo, L. F., Rome, E. S., et al. (2001). Condom use by adolescents. *Pediatrics, 107*(6), 1463–1469.

Kaplan, H., & Sadock, B. (1998). *Synopsis of psychiatry* (8th ed.). Baltimore: Williams & Wilkins.

Kaplan, M. S., & Sasser, J. E. (1996). Women behind bars: Trends and policy issues. *Journal of Sociology and Social Welfare, 23*(4), 43–56.

Kaplowitz, P. (2006). Pubertal development in girls: Secular trends. *Current Opinions in Obstetrics and Gynecology, 18,* 487–491.

Karpa, K. D. (2006). Pharmacist critique was ill-informed. *The Annals of Pharmacotherapy, 40*(7–8), 1441–1444.

Karson, M. (2001). *Patterns of child abuse: How dysfunctional transactions are replicated in individuals, families, and the child welfare system.* Binghamton, NY: Haworth Press.

Kaslow, F., & Robison, J. A. (1996). Long-term satisfying marriages: Perceptions contributing factors. *The American Journal of Family Therapy, 24*(2), 153–170.

Katz, L., Kling, J., & Liebman, J. (1999). *Moving to opportunity in Boston: Early impacts of a housing mobility program.* Working paper. Industrial Relations Section, Princeton University.

Katz, P. (1976). *Toward the elimination of racism.* New York: Pergamon Press.

Kayne, M., Greulich, M., & Albers, L. (2001). Doulas: An alternative yet complementary addition to care during childbirth. *Clinical Obstetrics and Gynecology, 44*(4), 692–703.

Kdous, M. (2006). Nonsurgical management of ectopic pregnancy. *Tunis Medicale, 84*(6), 331–339.

Keating, D. (2004). Cognitive and brain development. In R. M. Learner & L. Steinberg (Eds.), *Handbook of adolescent psychology* (2nd ed., pp. 45–84). New York: Wiley.

Keating, P. (1994). Striving for sex equity in schools. In K. I. Goodland & P. Keating (Eds.), *Access to knowledge: The continuing agenda for our nation's schools* (pp. 91–106). New York: The College Board.

Kellaghan, T., Sloane, K., Alvarez, B., & Bloom, B. S. (1993). *The home environment and school learning: Promoting parental involvement in the education of children.* San Francisco: Jossey-Bass.

Kellam, S., & Van Horn, Y. (1997). Life course development, community epidemiology, and preventive trials: A scientific structure for prevention research. *American Journal of Community Psychology, 25*(2), 177–188.

Kelly-Weeder, S., & O'Connor, A. (2006). Modifiable risk factors for impaired fertility in women: What nurse practitioners need to know. *Journal of the American Academy of Nurse Practitioners, 18,* 268–276.

Kempe, C., & Kempe, R. (1976). Assessing family pathology. In R. E. Helfer & C. H. Kempe (Eds.), *Child abuse and neglect:. The family and the community.* Cambridge, MA: Ballinger.

Keniston, K. (1966). *The uncommitted: Alienated youth in American society.* New York: Harcourt, Brace, & World.

Kenney, J. W., Reinholtz, C., & Angelini, P. J. (1997). Ethnic differences in childhood and adolescent sexual abuse and teenage pregnancy. *Journal of Adolescent Health, 21*(1), 3–10.

Kent, G. (2002). Breastfeeding vs formula-feeding among HIV-infected women in resource-poor areas. *Journal of the American Medical Association, 287*(9), 1110–1114.

Keogh, B. K., Bernheimer, L. P., & Guthrie, D. (2004). Children with developmental delays twenty years later: Where are they? How are they? *American Journal on Mental Retardation, 109*(3), 219–230.

Kertzer, D. (1989). Age structuring in comparative and historical perspective. In D. Kertzer & K. W. Schaie (Eds.), *Age structuring in comparative perspective* (pp. 3–20). Hillsdale, NJ: Lawrence Erlbaum.

Kesmodel, U., Wisborg, K., Olsen, J., Hendriksen, T., & Secher, N. (2002). Moderate alcohol intake in pregnancy and the risk of spontaneous abortion. *Alcohol and Alcoholism, 37*(1), 87–92.

Kessenich, M. (2003). Developmental outcomes of premature, low birth weight, and medically fragile infants. *Newborn and Infant Nursing Review, 3*(3), 80–87.

Keyes, C., & Ryff, C. (1998). Generativity in adult lives: Social structural contours and quality of life consequences. In D. McAdams & E. de St. Aubin (Eds.), *Generativity and adult development: How and why we care for the next generation* (pp. 227–263). Washington, DC: American Psychological Association.

Kikuzawa, S. (2006). Multiple roles and mental health in cross-cultural perspective; The elderly in the United States and Japan. *Journal of Health and Social Behavior, 47*(1), 62–76.

Kim, J., & Moen, P. (2001). Moving into retirement: Preparation and transitions in late midlife. In M. Lachman (Ed.), *Handbook of midlife development* (pp. 487–527). New York: Wiley.

Kimmel, D. (1990). *Adulthood and aging* (3rd ed.). New York: Wiley.

Kimmel, D., & Sang, B. (1995). Lesbians and gay men in midlife. In A. R. D'Augelli & C. Patterson (Eds.), *Lesbian, gay, and bisexual identities over the lifespan: Psychological perspectives* (pp. 190–214). New York: Oxford University Press.

Kindlon, D. J. (2003). *Too much of a good thing: Raising children of character in an indulgent age.* New York: Miramax Books.

Kindlon, D., & Thompson, M. (1999). *Raising Cain: Protecting the emotional life of boys.* New York: Random House.

King, B. R. (2001). Ranking of stigmatization toward lesbians and their children and the influence of perceptions of controllability of homosexuality. *Journal of Homosexuality, 41*(2), 77–97.

Kingson, E. R., & Berkowitz, E. D. (1993). *Social Security and Medicare: A policy primer.* Westport, CT: Auburn House.

Kiwi, R. (2006). Recurrent pregnancy loss: Evaluation and discussion of the causes and their management. *Cleveland Clinic Journal of Medicine, 73*(10), 913–991.

Klaczynski, P. (2000). Motivated scientific reasoning biases, epistemological beliefs, and theory polarization: A two-process approach to adolescent cognition. *Child Development, 71*(5).

Klaczynski, P., & Fauth, J. (1997). Developmental differences in memory-based intrusions and self-serving statistical reasoning biases. *Merrill-Palmer Quarterly, 43*, 539–566.

Klaus, M. H., Kennel, J. H., & Klaus, P. H. (1993). *Mothering the mother.* New York: Addison-Wesley.

Klebanov, P., Brooks-Gunn, J., Gordon, R., & Chase-Lansdale, P. (1997). The intersection of the neighborhood and home environment and its influence on young children. In J. Brooks-Gunn, G. Duncanc, & J. Aber (Eds.), *Neighborhood poverty: Context and consequences for children* (pp. 79–118). New York: Russell Sage.

Klein, M. (1995). *The American street gang: Its nature, prevalence, and control.* New York: Oxford University Press.

Kliman, J., & Madsen, W. (2005). Social class and the family life cycle. In B. Carter & M. McGoldrick (Eds.), *The expanded family life cycle: Individual, family, and social perspectives* (3rd ed., pp. 88–105). Boston: Allyn & Bacon.

Klonoff-Cohen, H. S., Natarajan, L., & Chen, R. (2006). A prospective study of the effects of female and male marijuana use on an in vitro (IVF) and gamete intrafallopian transfer (GIFT). *American Journal of Obstetrics and Gynecology, 194*(2), 369–376.

Klotter, J. (2002). Pregnancy and older women. *Townsend Letter for Doctors and Patients* (Jan 2002), 17–19.

Knapp, M. S. (1995). *Teaching for meaning in high-poverty classrooms.* New York: Teachers College Press.

Knight, M., & Plugge, E. (2005).The outcomes of pregnancy among imprisoned women: A systematic review. *An International Journal of Obstetrics & Gynaecology, 112,* 1467–1474.

Koball, H., & Douglas-Hall, A. (2006). *The new poor: Regional trends in child poverty since 2000.* Retrieved November 13, 2006, from http://www.nccp.org/pub_npr06.html

Kochanska, G. (1997). Multiple pathways to conscience for children with different temperaments: From toddlerhood to age 5. *Developmental Psychology, 33,* 228–240.

Koelling, K. (2004). *Classic connections: Turning teens on to great literature.* Westport, CT: Libraries Unlimited.

Koenig, H. G., & Brooks, R. G. (2002). Religion, health, and aging: Implications for practice and public policy. *Public Policy and Aging Report, 12,* 13–19.

Koeske, G., & Koeske, R. (1992). Parenting locus of control: Measurement, construct validation, and a proposed conceptual model. *Social Work Research and Abstracts, 28*(3), 37–45.

Kohlberg, L. (1969). Stage and sequence: The cognitive developmental approach to socialization. In D. A. Goslin (Ed.), *Handbook of socialization theory and research* (pp. 347–480). Chicago: Rand McNally.

Kohlberg, L. (1976). Moral stages and moralization: The cognitive-developmental approach. In T. Lickona (Ed.), *Moral development and behavior: Theory, research, and social issues* (pp. 31–53). New York: Holt.

Kohlberg, L. (1984). *Essays on moral development: Vol. 2. The psychology of moral development.* San Francisco: Harper & Row.

Kohli, M., & Künemund, H. (2005). The midlife generation in the family: Patterns of exchange and support. In S. Willis & M. Martin (Eds.), *Middle adulthood: A lifespan perspective* (pp. 35–61). Thousand Oaks, CA: Sage.

Kohut, H. (1971). *The analysis of the self.* New York: International Universities Press.

Kopola, M., Esquivel, G., & Baptiste, L. (1994). Counseling approaches for immigrant children: Facilitating the acculturative process. *The School Counselor, 41,* 352–359.

Korbin, J. (Ed.). (1981). *Child abuse and neglect: Cross-cultural perspective.* Berkeley and Los Angeles: University of California Press.

Kornelsen, J. (2005). Essences and imperatives: An investigation of technology in childbirth. *Social Science & Medicine, 61*(7), 1495–1504.

Koshar, J. H. (2001). Teen pregnancy 2001—Still no easy answers. *Pediatric Nursing, 25*(5), 505–512.

Koss, M. P., Gidycz, C. A., & Wisniewski, N. (1987). The scope of rape: Incidence and prevalence of sexual aggression and victimization in a national sample of higher education students. *Journal of Consulting and Clinical Psychology, 55,* 162–170.

Kotch, J., Browne, D., Ringwalt, C., Dufort, V., Ruina, E., Stewart, P., et al. (1997). Stress, social support, and substantiated maltreatment in the second and third years of life. *Child Abuse and Neglect, 21*(11), 1026–1037.

Kovacs, P. J., & Cagle, J. G. (2005, February). *Education: A complex and empowering social work intervention at the end of life.* Paper presented at the National Gerontological Social Work Conference. New York.

Kowalski, K. (1996). The emergence of ethnic/racial attitudes in preschool-age children. *Dissertation Abstracts International: Section B: The Sciences & Engineering, 56*(8-B), 4604.

Kozol, J. (1991). *Savage inequalities: Children in America's schools.* New York: HarperPerennial.

Kozol, J. (2005). *The shame of the nation: The restoration of apartheid schooling in America.* New York: Crown.

Krug, E., Dahlberg, L., Mercy, J., Zwi, A., & Lozano, R. (2002). *World report on violence and health.* Geneva, Switzerland: World Health Organization.

Kuh, D., & Ben-Sholomo, Y. (2004). *A life course approach to chronic disease epidemiology* (2nd ed.). New York: Oxford University Press.

Kübler-Ross, E. (1969). *On death and dying.* New York: Macmillan.

Kuhl, P. (1987). Perception of speech and sound in early infancy. In P. Salapatek & L. Cohen (Eds.), *Handbook of infant perception* (Vol. 1). Orlando, FL: Academic Press.

Kurdek, L. (2004). Are gay and lesbian cohabiting couples *really* different from heterosexual married couples? *Journal of Marriage and the Family, 66,* 880–900.

Kurtz, L. (1995). The relationship between parental coping strategies and children's adaptive processes in divorced and intact families. *Journal of Divorce and Remarriage, 24*(3/4), 89–110.

Kurtz, P. D. (1988). Social work services to parents: Essential to pupils at risk. *Urban Education, 22,* 444–457.

Kurtz, P. D., & Barth, R. P. (1989). Parent involvement: Cornerstone of school social work practice. *Social Work, 34,* 407–413.

Kusuda, S., Fujimura, M., Sakuma, I., Aotani, H., Kabe, K., Itani, Y., et al. (2006). Morbidity and mortality of infants with very low birth weight in Japan: Center variation. *Pediatrics, 118*(4), 1130–1138.

Kwok, O., Haine, R. A., Sandler, I. N., Ayers, T. S., Wolchik, S. A., & Tein, J. Y. (2005). Positive parenting as a mediator of the relations between parental psychological distress and mental health problems of parentally bereaved children. *Journal of Clinical Child and Adolescent Psychology, 34*(2), 260–271.

Labouvie-Vief, G. (1986). Modes of knowing and the organization of development. In M. L. Commons, L. Kohlberg, F. Richards, & J. Sinnott (Eds.), *Beyond formal operations 3: Models and methods in the study of adult and adolescent thought.* New York: Praeger.

Lachman, M. (2001a). Preface. In M. Lachman (Ed.), *Handbook of midlife development.* New York: Wiley.

Lachman, M. (Ed.). (2001b). *Handbook of midlife development.* New York: Wiley.

Lachman, M. (2004). Development in midlife. *Annual Review of Psychology, 55,* 305–331.

Lachman, M., & Bertrand, R. (2001). Personality and the self in midlife. In M. Lachman (Ed.), *Handbook of midlife development* (pp. 279–309). New York: Wiley.

LaDue, R. A. (2001). Fetal alcohol syndrome. In R. Carson (Ed.), *Encyclopedia of drugs, alcohol and addictive behavior* (Vol. 2, 2nd ed., pp. 533–537). New York: Macmillian.

Laflamme, D., Pomerleau, A., & Malcuit, G. (2002). A comparison of fathers' and mothers' involvement in childcare and stimulation behaviors during free play with their infants at 9 and 15 months. *Sex Roles, 47,* 507–518.

Laird, J. (1998). Theorizing culture. In M. McGoldrick (Ed.), *Re-visioning family therapy. Race, culture and gender in clinical practice* (pp. 20–36). New York: Guildford Press.

Laird, J., & Green, R. (Eds.). (1996). *Lesbian and gays in couples and families: A handbook for therapists.* San Francisco: Jossey-Bass.

Lamaze, F. (1958). *Painless childbirth: Psychoprophylactic method* (L. R. Celestin, Trans.). London: Burke.

Lane, A., Westbrook, A., Grady, D., O'Connor, R., Counihan, T. J., Marsh, B., et al. (2004). Maternal brain death: Medical, ethical, and legal issues. *Intensive Care Medicine, 30*(7), 1484–1486.

Lang, A. J., Stein, M. B., Kennedy, C. M., & Foy, D. W. (2004). Adult psychopathology and intimate partner violence among survivors of childhood maltreatment. *Journal of Interpersonal Violence, 19*(10), 1102–1118.

Langford, P. E. (1995). *Approaches to the development of moral reasoning.* Hillsdale: Lawrence Erlbaum.

Langle, A., & Probst, C. (2004). Existential questions of the elderly. *Archives of Psychiatry and Psychotherapy, 6*(2), 15–20.

Larson, E. J. (1995). The effects of maternal substance abuse on the placenta and fetus. In G. B. Reed, A. E. Claireaux, & F. Cockburn (Eds.), *Diseases of the fetus and newborn* (2nd ed., pp. 353–361). London: Chapman & Hall.

Larson, R., & Seepersad, S. (2003). Adolescents' leisure time in the United States: Partying, sports, and the American experiment. In S. Verma & R. Larson (Eds.), *Examining adolescent leisure time across culture: New directions for child and adolescent development, No. 99* (pp. 53–64). San Francisco: Jossey-Bass.

Larson, R. W., Wilson, S., & Mortimer, J. T. (2002). Adolescence in the 21st century: An international perspective—Adolescents' preparation for the future. *Journal of Research on Adolescence, 12*(1), 159–166.

LaSala, M. C. (2001). The importance of partners to lesbians' intergenerational relationships. *Social Work Research, 25*(1), 27–40.

Laseter, R. (1997). The labor force participation of young black men: A qualitative examination. *Social Service Review, 71,* 72–88.

Lattanzi-Licht, M., Mahoney, J. J., & Miller, G. W. (1998). *The hospice choice: In pursuit of a peaceful death.* New York: Fireside.

Laumann, E., Paik, A., & Rosen, R. (1999). Sexual dysfunction in the United States: Prevalence and predictors. *Journal of the American Medical Association, 279,* 537–544.

Laurino, M. Y., Bennett, R. L., Sariya, D. S., Baumeister, L., Doyle, D. L., Leppig, K., et al. (2005). Genetic evaluation and counseling of couples with recurrent miscarriage: Recommendations of the National Society of Genetic Counselors. *Journal of Genetic Counseling, 14*(3), 165–181.

Lazear, D. (1994). *Multiple intelligence approach to assessment: Solving the assessment conundrum.* Tucson, AZ: Zephyr Press.

Lederberg, J. (2001). The meaning of epigenetics. *The Scientist, 15*(18), 6.

Lee, B., & George, R. (1999). Poverty, early childbearing and child maltreatment: A multinomial analysis. *Children & Youth Services Review, 21*(9–10), 755–780.

Lee, E., Menkart, D., & Okazawa-Rae, M. (1998). *Beyond holidays and heroes: A practical guide to K–12 anti-racist multicultural education and staff development.* Washington, DC: Network of Educators in the Americas.

Lee, M. (2003). Korean adolescents' "examination hell" and their use of free time. In S. Verma & R. Larson (Eds.), *Examining adolescent leisure time across culture: New directions for child and adolescent development, No. 99* (pp. 9–21). San Francisco: Jossey-Bass.

Leeder, E. (2004). *The family in global perspective: A gendered journey.* Thousand Oaks, CA: Sage.

LeFever, G. B., Villers, M. S., Morrow, A. L., & Vaughn, E. S. (2002). Parental perceptions of adverse educational outcomes among children diagnosed and treated for ADHD: A call for improved school/provider collaboration. *Psychology in the Schools, 39*(1), 63–71.

Leisering, L. (2003). Government and the life course. In J. Mortimer & M. Shanahan (Eds.), *Handbook of the life course* (pp. 205–225). New York: Kluwer Academic/Plenum Publishers.

Leitenberg, H., Detzer, M. J., & Srebnik, D. (1993). Gender differences in masturbation and the relationship of masturbation experience in preadolescence and/or early adolescence and sexual behavior and sexual adjustment in young adulthood. *Archives of Sexual Behavior, 22,* 299–313.

Leonard, R. (2006). Turning points in the lives of midlife and older women: Five-year follow-up. *Australian Psychologist, 41*(1), 28–36.

Lerner, J. V., Castellino, D. R., Lolli, E., & Wan, S. (2003). Children, families, and work: Research findings and implications for policies and programs. In R. M. Lerner, F. Jacobs, and D. Wertlieb (Eds.), *Handbook of applied developmental science, Vol. 1* (pp. 281–304). Thousand Oaks, CA: Sage.

Lerner, R., & Galambos, N. (1998). Adolescent development: Challenges and opportunities for research. *Annual Review of Psychology, 49,* 413–446.

Levin, D. E. (2005). So sexy, so soon: The sexualization of childhood. In S. Olfman (Ed.), *Childhood lost: How American culture is failing our kids* (pp. 137–154). Westport, CT: Praeger.

Levine, E., & Sallee, A. (1999). *Child welfare: Clinical theory and practice.* Dubuque, IA: Eddie Bowers Publishing.

Levinson, D. (1977). The mid-life transition. *Psychiatry,* 40, *99–112.*

Levinson, D. (1978). *The seasons of a man's life.* New York: Knopf.

Levinson, D. (1980). Toward a conception of the adult life course. In N. J. Smelser & E. H. Erikson (Eds.), *Themes of work and love in adulthood* (pp. 265–290). Cambridge, MA: Harvard University Press.

Levinson, D. (1986). A conception of adult development. *American Psychologist, 41*(1), 3–13.

Levinson, D. (1990). A theory of life structure development in adulthood. In C. N. Alexander & E. J. Langer (Eds.), *Higher stages of human development* (pp. 35–54). New York: Oxford University Press.

Levinson, D., & Levinson, J. (1996). *The seasons of a woman's life.* New York: Ballantine Books.

Levinson, D., Darrow, C., Klein, E., Levinson, M., & McKee, B. (1978). *The seasons of a man's life.* New York: Knopf.

Levy, B. (1991). *Dating violence: Young women in danger.* Seattle, WA: Seal Press.

Levy, G. D., Taylor, M. G., & Gelman, S. A. (1995). Traditional and evaluative aspects of flexibility in gender roles, social conventions, moral rules and physical laws. *Child Development, 66,* 515–531.

Levy, L., Martinkowski, K., & Derby, J. (1994). Differences in patterns of adaptation in conjugal bereavement: Their sources and potential significance. *Omega, 29,* 71–87.

Levy, S. (2000). Still confused after all these years. *Fieldwork, 13*(2). Retrieved December 30, 2006, from http://www.elschools.org/publications/webarchive/vol8no2.html

Lewis, T. (1994). A comparative analysis of the effects of social skills training and teacher directed contingencies on social behavior of preschool children with disabilities. *Journal of Behavioral Education, 4,* 267–281.

Lichtenstein, S. (1993). Transition from school to adulthood: Case studies of adults with learning disabilities who dropped out of school. *Exceptional Children, 59*(4), 336–347.

Lidow, M., Goldman-Rakic, P., & Rakic, P. (1991). Synchronized overproduction of neurotransmitter receptors in diverse regions of the primate cerebral cortex. *Proceedings of the National Academy of Sciences,* 88, 10218–10221.

Light, J., Irvine, K., & Kjerulf, L. (1996). Estimating genetic and environmental effects of alcohol use and dependence from a national survey: A "quasi adoption" study. *Journal of Studies on Alcohol, 57,* 507–520.

Limber, S. P., & Small, M. A. (2003). State laws and policies to address bullying in schools. *School Psychology Review, 32*(3), 445–455.

Lindemann, E. (1944). Symptomatology and management of acute grief. *American Journal of Psychiatry, 101,* 141–148.

Linver, M. R., Fuligni, A. S., Hernandez, M., & Brooks-Gunn, J. (2004). Poverty and child development. In P. Allen-Meares and M. W. Fraser (Eds.), *Intervention with children and adolescents: An interdisciplinary perspective* (pp. 106–129). Boston: Allyn & Bacon.

Lipsky, D., & Abrams, A. (1994). *Late bloomers.* New York: Times Books.

Little, S. E., Ratcliffe, J., & Caughey, A. B. (2006). Cost of transferring one through five embryos per in vitro fertilization cycle from various payer prospectives. *Obstetrics and Gynecology, 108*(3 Pt 1), 593–601.

Liu, P. Y., Swerdloff, R. S., Christenson, P. D., Handelsman, D., & Wang, C. (2006). Rate, extent, and modifiers of spermatogenic recovery after hormonal male contraception: An integrated analysis. *The Lancet, 367*(9520), 1412–1420.

Lloyd, C. B., Behrman, J. R., Stromquist, N. P., & Cohen, B. (2006). *The changing transitions to adulthood in developing countries: Selected studies.* Washington, DC: National Research Council.

Lochman, J. E., Coie, J. D., Underwood, M. K., & Terry, R. (1993). Effectiveness of a social relationship intervention program for aggressive and nonaggressive, rejected children. *Journal of Consulting and Clinical Psychology, 61,* 1053–1058.

Locke, A., Ginsborg, J., & Peers, I. (2002). Development and disadvantage: Implications for the early years and beyond. *International Journal of Language & Communication Disorders, 37*(1), 3–15.

Lodhi, F., Fattah, A., Abozaid, T., Murphy, J., Formantini, E., Sasy, M., et al. (2004). Gamete intra-fallopian transfer or intrauterine insemination after controlled ovarian hyperstimulation for treatment of infertility due to endometriosis. *Gynecological Endocrinology, 152*(8), 152–160.

Logan, S. L., Freeman, E. M., & McRoy, R. G. (Eds.). (1990). *Social work practice with black families: A culturally specific perspective.* New York: Longman.

Lonzano, H., & Ballesteros, F. (2006). A study on breakfast and school performance in a group of adolescents. *Nutrition Hospital, 21*(3), 346–352.

Loveless, T. (1999). *The tracking wars: State reform meets school policy.* Washington, DC: Brookings Institution Press.

Lowenthal, M., Thurnher, M., & Chiriboga, D. (1975). *Four stages of life: A comparative study of women and men facing transition.* San Francisco: Jossey-Bass.

Lowry, R., Holtzman, D., Truman, B. I., Kann, L., Collins, J. L., & Kolbe, L. J. (1994). Substance use and HIV-related sexual behaviors among U.S. high school students: Are they related? *American Journal of Public Health, 84,* 1116–1120.

Lui, M., Robles, B., Leondar-Wright, B., Brewer, R., & Adamson, R. (2006). *The color of wealth.* New York: The New Press.

Lum, D. (2003a). *Social work practice and people of color: A process state approach* (5th ed.). Belmont, CA: Wadsworth Publishing.

Lum, D. (2003b). *Culturally competent practice: A framework for understanding diverse groups and justice issues* (2nd ed). Belmont, CA: Brooks/Cole.

Luna, B., Thulborn, K., Munoz, D., Merriam, E., Garver, K., Minshew, N., et al. (2001). Maturation of widely distributed brain function subserves cognitive development. *Neuroimage, 13,* 786–793.

Luthar, S. (2003). *Resilience and vulnerability: Adaptation in the context of childhood adversities.* New York: Cambridge University Press.

Lux, M., Reyes, V., Morgentaler, A., & Levine, L. (2007). Outcomes and satisfaction rates for the redesigned 2-piece penile prosthesis. *Journal of Urology, 177*(1), 262–266.

Lydon-Rochelle, M., Holt, V., Martin, D., & Easterling, T. (2000). Association between method of delivery and maternal rehospitalization. *Journal of the American Medical Association, 283*(18), 2411–2416.

Lynch, R. (2000). *New directions for high school career and technical education in the 21st century.* Washington, DC: U.S. Department of Education.

Lynch, T. R., Cheavens, J. S., Morse, J. Q., & Rosenthal, M. Z. (2004). A model predicting suicidal ideation and hopelessness in depressed older adults: The impact of emotion inhibition and affect intensity. *Aging and Mental Health, 8*(6), 486–497.

Maccoby, E. (1980). *Social development: Psychological growth and the parent-child relationship.* San Diego: Harcourt Brace Jovanovich.

Maccoby, E. (1992). The role of parents in the socialization of children: An historical overview. *Developmental Psychology, 28,* 1006–1017.

Maccoby, E. E. (2002). Parenting effects: Issues and controversies. In J. G. Borkowski, S. Landesman Ramey, & M. Bristol-Power (Eds.), *Parenting and the child's world* (pp. 35–45). Mahwah, NJ: Lawrence Erlbaum.

Mack, R., Pike, M., Henderson, M., Pfeffer, R., Gerkins, V., Arthur, M., et al. (1976). Estrogens and endometrial cancer in a retirement community. *The New England Journal of Medicine, 294,* 1262–1267.

Mackey, W. C. (2001). Support for the existence of an independent man-(to)-child afiiliative bond. *Psychology of Men and Masculinity, 2,* 51–66.

MacLennan, B. (1994). Groups for poorly socialized children in the elementary school. *Journal of Child and Adolescent Group Therapy, 4,* 243–250.

Magill-Cuerden, J. (2006). Nurturing and supporting mothers: A hidden skill in midwifery. *British Journal of Midwifery, 14*(6), 374.

Magwaza, A., Kilian, B., Peterson, I., & Pillay, Y. (1993). The effects of chronic violence on preschool children living in South African townships. *Child Abuse and Neglect, 17,* 795–803.

Main, M., & Hesse, E. (1990). Parents' unresolved traumatic experiences are related to infant disorganized attachment status: Is frightened and/or frightening parental behavior the linking mechanism? In M. Greenberg, D. Cicchetti, & E. M. Cumming (Eds.), *Attachment in the preschool years: Theory, research and intervention* (pp. 161–182). Chicago: University of Chicago Press.

Malinger, G., Lev, D., & Lerman-Sagie, T. (2006). Normal and abnormal fetal brain development during the third trimester as demonstrated by neurosonography. *European Journal of Radiology, 57*(22), 226–32.

Mallampalli, A., & Guy, E. (2005). Cardiac arrest in pregnancy and somatic support after brain death. *Critical Care Medicine, 33*(10 Suppl.), S325–S331.

Maloney, M. J., & Klykylo, W. M. (1983). An overview of anorexia nervosa, bulimia and obesity in children and adolescents. *Journal of the American Academy of Child Psychiatry, 22,* 99–107.

Maluccio, A. N. (2006). The nature and scope of the problem. In N. B. Webb (Ed.), *Working with traumatized youth in child welfare* (pp. 3–12). New York: Guilford Press.

Manly, J. J., Schupf, N., Tang, M., & Stern, Y. (2005). Cognitive decline and literacy among ethnically diverse elders. *Journal of Geriatric Psychiatry and Neurology, 18*(4), 213–217.

Manton, K. G., & Liu, K. (1984). *The future growth of the long-term care population: Projections based on the 1977 national nursing home survey and the 1981 long-term care survey.* Washington, DC: Health Care Financing Administration.

March of Dimes. (2004). *Racial and ethnic disparities in prematurity: Data and trends: Medical perspectives on prematurity.* Retrieved November 5, 2006, from http://www.marchofdimes.com/files/Racial_EthnicPremDataTrends071404.pdf#search='prematurity%20rates'

March of Dimes. (2006a). *Pregnancy after 35.* Retrieved October 22, 2006, from http://www.marchofdimes.com/professionals/681_1155.asp

March of Dimes. (2006b). *Drinking alcohol during pregnancy.* Retrieved July 19, 2006, from http://www.marchofdimes.com/professionals/681_1170.asp

Marcia, J. E. (1966). Development and validation of ego-identity status. *Journal of Personality and Social Psychology, 3,* 551–558.

Marcia, J. E. (1980). Identity in adolescence. In J. Adelson (Ed.), *Handbook of adolescent psychology* (pp. 159–187). New York: Wiley.

Marcia, J. E. (1993). The ego identity status approach to ego identity. In J. E. Marcia, A. S. Waterman, D. R. Mattesson, S. L. Arcjer, & J. L. Orlofksy (Eds.), *Ego identity: A handbook for psychosocial research.* New York: Springer.

Marini, M. M. (1989). Socioeconomic consequences of the process of transition to adulthood. *Social Science Research, 18,* 89–135.

Marino, R., Weinman, M., & Soudelier, K. (2001). Social work intervention and failure to thrive in infants and children. *Health & Social Work, 26*(2), 90–98.

Markides, K., & Boldt, J. (1983). Change in subjective age among the elderly: A longitudinal analysis. *The Gerontologist, 23*(24), 422–427.

Marks, A., & Rothbart, B. (2003). *Healthy teens, body and soul: A parent's complete guide.* New York: Simon & Schuster.

Marks, N. (1998). Does it hurt to care? Caregiving, work-family conflict, and midlife well-being. *Journal of Marriage and the Family, 60,* 951–966.

Marks, N., Bumpass, L., & Jun, H. (2004). Family roles and well-being during the middle life course. In O. Brim, C. Ryff, & R. Kessler (Eds.), *How healthy are we? A national study of well-being at midlife* (pp. 514–549). Chicago: University of Chicago Press.

Marks, N., & Lambert, J. (1998). Marital status continuity and change among young and midlife adults. *Journal of Family Issues, 19,* 652–686.

Markstrom, C., & Mullis, R. (1986). Ethnic differences in the imaginary audience. *Journal of Adolescent Research, 1*(3), 289–301.

Markstrom-Adams, C., & Adams, G. R. (1995). Gender, ethnic group, and grade differences in psychosocial functioning during middle adolescence. *Journal of Youth and Adolescence, 24,* 397–417.

Marmot, M., & Fuhrer, R. (2004). Socioeconomic position and health across midlife. In O. Brim, C. Ryff, & R. Kessler (Eds.), *How healthy are we? A national study of well-being at midlife* (pp. 64–89). Chicago: University of Chicago Press.

Marshall, N. L., Noonan, A. E., McCartney, K., Marx, F., & Keefe, N. (2001). It takes an urban village: Parenting networks of urban families. *Journal of Family Issues, 22*(2), 163.

Marshall, V., & Mueller, M. (2003). Theoretical roots of the life-course perspective. In W. Heinz & V. Marshall (Eds.), *Social dynamics of the life course: Transitions, institutions, and interrelations* (pp. 3–32). New York: Aldine de Gruyter.

Marsiglio, W. (1986). Teenage fatherhood: High school accreditation and educational attainment. In A. B. Elster & M. E. Lamb (Eds.), *Adolescent fatherhood.* Hillside, NJ: Lawrence Erlbaum.

Martikainen, P., & Valkonen, T. (1996). Mortality after the death of a spouse: Rates and causes of death in a large Finnish cohort. *American Journal of Public Health, 86,* 1087–1093.

Martin, J., Hamilton, B., Ventura, J., Menacker, F., & Park, M. (2002). Births: Final data for 2000. *National Vital Statistics Reports, 50*(5). Hyattsville, MD: National Center for Health Statistics.

Martin, J. A., Hamilton, B. E., Sutton, P. D., Ventura, S. J., Menacker, F., & Munson, M. L. (2003). Births: Final data for 2002. *National Vital Statistics Reports, 52*(10).

Martin, M., & Zimprich, D. (2005). Cognitive development in midlife. In S. Willis & M. Martin (Eds.), *Middle adulthood: A lifespan perspective* (pp. 179–206). Thousand Oaks, CA: Sage.

Martin, K. A. (1996). *Puberty, sexuality, and the self: Boys and girls at adolescence.* New York: Routledge.

Martin, S. L., Clark, K. A., Lynch, S. R., Kupper, L. L. & Cilenti, D. (1999). Violence in the lives of pregnant teenage women: Associations with multiple substance abuse. *American Journal of Drug and Alcohol Use, 25*(3), 425–431.

Martin, S. L., Kim, H., Kupper, L. L., Meyer, R. E., & Hays, M. (1997). Is incarceration during pregnancy associated with infant birthweight? *American Journal of Public Health, 87,* 1526–1531.

Masciadrelli, B. P., Pleck, J. H., & Stueve, J. L. (2006). Fathers' role model perceptions: Themes and linkages with involvement. *Men and Masculinities, 9*(1), 23–34.

Masse, L., & Barnett, W. S. (2002). *A benefit cost analysis of the Abecedarian Early Childhood Intervention.* Retrieved May 3, 2007, from http://niecr.org/resources/research/Abecedarian Study.pdf

Masten, A. S., Burt, K. B., Roisman, G. I., Obradovic, J., Long, J. D., & Tellegen, A. (2004). Resources and resilience in the transition to adulthood: Continuity and change. *Development and Psychopathology, 16,* 1071–1094.

Mathews, T., MacDoman, M., & Menacker, F. (2002). Infant mortality statistics from the 1999 period linked birth/infant death data set. *National Vital Statistics, 50*(4), 1–27.

Mathews, T., Menacker, F., & MacDoman, M. (2004). Infant mortality statistics for the 2002 period linked birth/infant death data set. *National Vital Statistics Report, 53*(1), 1–30.

Matsumoto-Grah, K. (1992). Diversity in the classroom: A checklist. In D. Byrnes & G. Kiger (Eds.), *Common bonds: Anti-bias teaching in a diverse society* (pp. 105–108). Olney, MD: Association for Childhood Education International.

Matute-Bianchi, M. E. (1986). Ethnic identities and patterns of school success and failure among Mexican-descent and Japanese-American students in a California school: An ethnographic analysis. *American Journal of Education, 95,* 233–255.

Mbori-Ngacha, D., Nduati, R., John, G., Reilly, M., Richardson, B., Mwatha, A., et al. (2001). Morbidity and mortality in breastfed and formula-fed infants of HIV-1-infected women: A randomized clinical trial. *Journal of American Medical Association, 286*(19), 2413–2420.

McAdams, D. (2001). Generativity in midlife. In M. Lachman (Ed.), *Handbook of midlife development* (pp. 395–443). New York: Wiley.

McAdams, D., & de St. Aubin, E. (1992). A theory of generativity and its assessment through self-report, behavioral acts, and narrative themes in autobiography. *Journal of Personality and Social Psychology, 62,* 1003–1015.

McAdams, D., & de St. Aubin, E. (Eds.). (1998). *Generativity and adult development: How and why we care for the next generation.* Washington, DC: American Psychological Association.

McAdams, D., de St. Aubin, E., & Logan, R. (1993). Generativity among young, midlife, and older adults. *Psychology and Aging, 8,* 221–230.

McAdams, D., Hart, H., & Maruna, S. (1998). The anatomy of generativity. In D. McAdams & E. de St. Aubin (Eds.), *Generativity and adult development: How and why we care for the next generation* (pp. 7–43). Washington, DC: American Psychological Association.

McAdoo, H. (1986). Societal stress: The black family. In J. Cole (Ed.), *All American women: Lines that divide, ties that bind* (pp. 187–197). New York: Free Press.

McAdoo, H. P. (2001). Parent and child relationships in African American families. In N. B. Webb (Ed.), *Culturally diverse parent-child and family relationships: A guide for social workers and other practitioners* (pp. 89–106). New York: Columbia University Press.

McArdle, J. J., Small, B. J., Backman, L., & Fratiglioni, L. (2005). Longitudinal models of growth and survival applied to the early detection of Alzheimer's disease. *Journal of Geriatric Psychiatry and Neurology, 18*(4), 234–241.

McAuley, E., Konopack, J. F., Motl, R. W., Morris, S., Doerksen, S., & Rosengren, K. (2006). Physical activity and quality of life in older adults: Influence of health status and self-efficacy. *Annuals of Behavioral Medicine, 31*(1), 99–103.

McCabe, M. P., & Ricciardelli, L. A. (2003). Sociocultural influences on body image and body changes among adolescent boys and girls. *Journal of Social Psychology, 143*(1), 5–26.

McCaig, L. F., & Burt, C. W. (2005). *National Hospital Ambulatory Medical Care Survey: 2003 Emergency Department Summary.* (Advance data from the vital and health statistics, no. 358). Hyattsville, MD: National Center for Health Statistics.

McCarter, S. (1997). *Understanding the overrepresentation of minorities in Virginia's juvenile justice system.* Unpublished doctoral dissertation, Virginia Commonwealth University, Richmond.

McCarter, S. (1998). *Interviews with adolescents regarding health topics.* Work in progress, Virginia Commonwealth University, School of Social Work.

McCloskey, L. A., Figueredo, A. J., & Koss, M. P. (1995). The effects of systemic family violence on children's mental health. *Child Development, 66,* 1239–1261.

McClure, E. M., Nalubamba-Phiri, M., & Goldenberg, R. L. (2006). Stillbirth in developing countries. *International Journal of Gynaecology and Obstetrics: The Official Organ of the International Federation of Gynaecology and Obstetrics, 94*(2), 82–90.

McCluskey, U., & Duerden, S. (1993). Pre-verbal communication: The role of play in establishing rhythms of communication between self and others. *Journal of Social Work Practice, 7*(1), 17–27.

McCrae, R., & Costa, P., Jr. (1990). *Personality in adulthood.* New York: Guilford Press.

McCrae, R., Costa, P., Jr., Ostendorf, F., Angleitner, A., Caprara, G., Barbaranelli, C., et al. (1999). Age differences in personality across the adult life span: Parallels in five cultures. *Developmental Psychology, 35*(2), 466.

McDermid, S., Heilbrun, G., & DeHaan, L. (1997). The generativity of employed mothers in multiple roles: 1979 and 1991. In M. Lachman & J. James (Eds.), *Multiple paths of midlife development* (pp. 207–240). Chicago: University of Chicago Press.

McDonnell, J., Thorson, N., Disher, S., Mathot-Buckner, C., Mendel, J., & Ray, L. (2003). The achievement of students with developmental disabilities and their peers without disabilities in inclusive settings: An exploratory study. *Education and Treatment of Children, 26*(3), 224–236.

McElhatton, P. R. (2000). Fetal effects of substances of abuse. *Journal of Toxicology: Clinical Toxicology, 38*(2), 194–195.

McFalls, J., Jr. (1998). Population composition. *Population Bulletin, 53*(3), 26–34.

McGill, D., & Pearce, J. (1996). American families with English ancestors from the colonial era: Anglo Americans. In M. McGoldrick, J. Giordanao, & J. Pearce (Eds.), *Ethnicity and family therapy* (pp. 451–466). New York: Guilford Press.

McGlade, M., Saha, S., & Dahlstrom, M. (2004). The Latina paradox: An opportunity for restructuring prenatal care delivery. *American Journal of Public Health, 94*(12), 2062–2065.

McGoldrick, M. (2004). Legacies of loss: Multigenerational ripple effects. In F. Walsh & M. McGoldrick (Eds.), *Living beyond loss: Death in the family* (2nd ed., pp. 61–84). New York: W.W. Norton & Company, Inc.

McGoldrick, M. (2005). Becoming a couple. In B. Carter & M. McGoldrick (Eds.), *The expanded family life cycle: Individual, family, and social perspectives* (3rd ed., pp. 231–248). Boston: Allyn & Bacon.

McGoldrick, M., Broken Nose, M., & Potenza, M. (1999). Violence and the family life cycle. In B. Carter & M. McGoldrick (Eds.), *The expanded family life cycle: Individual, family, and social perspectives* (3rd ed., pp. 470–491). Boston: Allyn & Bacon.

McGoldrick, M., Giordano, J., & Pearce, J. (1996). *Ethnicity and family therapy* (2nd ed.). New York: Guilford.

McGroder, S. M., Zaslow, M. J., Moore, K. A., Hair, E. C., & Ahluwalia, S. K. (2002). The role of parenting in shaping the impacts of welfare-to-work programs on children. In J. G. Borkowski, S. Landesman Ramey, & M. Bristol-Power (Eds.), *Parenting and the child's world* (pp. 383–410). Mahwah, NJ: Lawrence Erlbaum.

McHale, S., Crouter, A., & Whiteman, S. (2003). The family contexts of gender development in childhood and adolescence. *Social Development, 12,* 125–148.

McInnis-Dittrich, K. (2005). *Social work with elders: A biopsychosocial approach to assessment and intervention* (2nd ed.). Boston: Allyn & Bacon.

McIntosh, P. (1988). *White privilege: Unpacking the invisible knapsack.* (Available from Peggy McIntosh, Wellesley College Center for Research on Women, Wellesley, MA 02181.)

McIntyre, J., & Gray, G. (2002). What can we do to reduce mother to child transmission of HIV? (Education and debate). *British Medical Journal, 324*(7331), 218–222.

Mckee, K. J., Wilson, F., Chung, C. M., Hinchliff, S., Goudie, F., Elford, H., et al. (2005). Reminiscence, regrets and activity in older people in residential care: Associations with psychological health. *British Journal of Clinical Psychology, 44*(4), 543–561.

McKeering, H., & Pakenham, K. (2000). Gender and generativity issues in parenting: Do fathers benefit more than mothers from involvement in child care activities? *Sex Roles, 43*(7–8), 459–480.

McKinlay, S., Brambilla, D., & Posner, J. (1992). The normal menopause transition. *Journal of Human Biology, 4,* 37–46.

McLeod, J., & Almazan, E. (2003). Connections between childhood and adulthood. In J. Mortimer & M. Shanahan (Eds.), *Handbook of the life course* (pp. 391–411). New York: Kluwer.

McLeskey, J., Hoppey, D., Williamson, P., & Rentz, T. (2004). Is inclusion an illusion? An examination of national and state trends toward the education of students with learning disabilities in general education classrooms. *Learning Disabilities Research & Practice, 19*(2), 109–115.

McLoyd, V. (1990). The impact of economic hardship on black families and children: Psychological distress, parenting, and socioemotional development. *Child Development, 61,* 311–346.

McLoyd, V., & Wilson, L. (1991). The strain of living poor: Parenting, social support and mental health. In A. C. Huston (Ed.), *Children and Poverty* (pp. 105–136). New York: Cambridge University Press.

McLoyd, V. C. (1998). Socioeconomic disadvantage and child development. *American Psychologist, 53*(2), 185–204.

McMichael, P. (2004). *Development and social change: A global perspective* (3rd ed.). Thousand Oaks, CA: Pine Forge.

McKnight, J. (1995). *The careless society.* New York: Basic Books.

McQuaide, S. (1998). Women at midlife. *Social Work, 43*(1), 21–31.

McWhirter, J. J., McWhirter, B. T., McWhirter, A. M., & McWhirter, E. H. (1993). *At-risk youth: A comprehensive response.* Pacific Grove, CA: Brooks/Cole.

Mead, G. H. (1934). *Mind, self and society.* Chicago: University of Chicago Press.

Mechcatie, E. (2002). Patch, vaginal ring offer steady hormone levels. *OB GYN News, 37*(4), 18–20.

Mechelli, A., Crinion, J., Noppeney, U., O'Doherty, J., Ashburner, J., Frackowiak, R. S., et al. (2004). Structural plasticity in the bilingual brain. *Science, 431*(7010), 757.

Medicare Advocacy. (2007). *Calculating costs to and through the Part D doughnut hole.* Retrieved January 19, 2007, from http://www.medicareadvocacy.org/PartD_Calculating CostsThroughDonutHole.htm

Meek, M. (2000). Foreword. In K. Roskos & J. Christie (Ed.), *Play and literacy in early childhood: Research from multiple perspectives* (pp. vii–xiii). Mahwah, NJ: Lawrence Erlbaum.

Meng, M. V., Greene, K. L., & Turek, P. J. (2005). Surgery or assisted reproduction? A decision analysis of treatment costs in male infertility. *The Journal of Urology, 174*(5), 1926–1931.

Menon, U. (2001). Middle adulthood in cultural perspective: The imagined and the experienced in three cultures. In M. Lachman (Ed.), *Handbook of midlife development* (pp. 40–74). New York: Wiley.

Merriam Webster, Inc. (1998). *Merriam-Webster's collegiate dictionary* (10th ed.). Springfield, MA: Author.

Merrill, S., & Verbrugge, L. (1999). Health and disease in midlife. In S. Willis & J. Reid (Eds.), *Life in the middle: Psychological and social development in middle age* (pp. 78–103). San Diego, CA: Academic Press.

Merton, R. (1968). The Matthew Effect in science: The reward and communications systems of science. *Science, 199,* 55–63.

MetLife/National Alliance for Caregiving. (2004). *Miles away: The MetLife study of long-distance caregiving.* West Point, CT: MetLife.

Meyer, D. R., & Garasky, S. (1993). Custodial fathers: Myths, realities, and child support policy. *Journal of Marriage and the Family, 55,* 73–89.

Meyer, J. (1986). The institutionalization of the life course and its effects on the self. In A. Sorensen, F. Weinert, & L. Sherrod (Eds.), *Human development and the life course: Multidisciplinary perspectives* (pp. 199–216). Hillsdale, NJ: Lawrence Erlbaum.

Meyers, A., Sampson, A., Weitzman, M., Rogers, B., & Kayne, H. (1989). School breakfast program and school performance. *American Journal of Diseases of Children, 143*(10), 1234–1239.

Miller, B. (1992). Adolescent parenthood, economic issues, and social policies. *Journal of Family and Economic Issues, 13*(4), 467–475.

Miller, J., & Holman, J. R. (2006). Contraception: The state of the art. *Consultant, 46*(4), 28.

Miller, K. E., & Rasco, L. M. (2004). *The mental health of refugees: Ecological approaches to healing and adaptation.* Mahwah, NJ: Lawrence Erlbaum.

Minkler, M. (1985). Social support and health in the elderly. In S. Cohen & S. L. Syme (Eds.), *Social support and health* (pp. 199–216). Orlando, FL: Academic Press.

Minino, A., Heron, M., & Smith, B. (2006, June 28). Deaths: Preliminary data for 2004. *National Vital Statistics Reports, 54*(19). Retrieved December 19, 2006, from http://www.cdc.gov/nchs/data/nvsr/nvsr54/nvsr54_19.pdf

Miyake, K., Campos, J., Kagan, J., & Bradshaw, D. (1986). Issues in socioemotional development in Japan. In H. Azuma, I. Hakuta, & H. Stevenson (Eds.), *Dodoma: Child development and education in Japan* (pp. 239–261). New York: W. H. Freeman.

Mize, J., & Ladd, G. W. (1990). A cognitive-social learning approach to social skill training with low status preschool children. *Developmental Psychology, 26,* 388–397.

Modell, J., Furstenberg, F., Jr., & Hershberg, T. (1976). Social change and transitions to adulthood in historical perspective. *Journal of Family History, 1,* 7–32.

Moen, P. (1997). Women's roles and resilience: Trajectories of advantage or turning points? In I. H. Gotlib & B. Wheaton (Eds.), *Stress and adversity over the life course: Trajectories and turning points* (pp. 133–156). New York: Cambridge University Press.

Moen, P. (2003). Midcourse: Navigating retirement and a new life stage. In J. Mortimer & M. Shanahan (Eds.), *Handbook of the life course* (pp. 269–291). New York: Kluwer Academic/Plenum Publishers.

Moen, P., & Wethington, E. (1999). Midlife development in a life course context. In S. Willis & J. Reid (Eds.), *Life in the middle* (pp. 3–24). San Diego, CA: Academic Press.

Mofenson, L. (2006, June 2). Achievements in public health: Reduction in perinatal transmission of HIV infection—United States 1985–2005. *Morbidity and Mortality Weekly*

Report, 55(21), 592–597. Retrieved on January 13, 2007, from http://www.cdc.gov/mmwr/preview/,mwrhtml./mm5521a3.htm

Moffitt, T. E., Caspi, A. Belsky, J., & Silva, P. A. (1992). Childhood experience and the onset of menarche: A test of a sociobiological model. *Child Development, 63,* 47–58.

Monaghan, J., Robinson, J., & Dodge, J. (1979). The children's life events inventory. *Journal of Psychosomatic Research, 23*(1), 63–68.

Monahon, C. (1997). *Children and trauma: A guide for parents and professionals.* San Francisco: Jossey-Bass.

Montgomery, R. J. V., & Kosloski, K. (1994). A longitudinal analysis of nursing home placement for dependent elders cared for by spouses vs. adult children. *Journal of Gerontology: Social Science, 49,* S62–S74.

Moore, D. (1987). Parent-adolescent separation: The construction of adulthood by late adolescents. *Developmental Psychology, 23,* 298–307.

Moore, K. L., & Persaud, T. V. N. (1993). *Before we are born* (4th ed.). Philadelphia: Saunders.

Morales, A. (1992). Therapy with Latino gang members. In L. Vargas & J. Koss-Chioino (Eds.), *Working with culture: Psychotherapeutic interventions with ethnic minority children and adolescents.* San Francisco: Jossey-Bass.

Moremen, R. D. (2004–2005). What is the meaning of life? Women's spirituality at the end of the life span. *Omega: Journal of Death and Dying, 50*(4), 309–330.

Morgan, A. (2000). *What is narrative therapy?* Adelaide, South Australia: Dulwich Centre Publications.

Morgan, L., & Kunkel, S. (1996). *Aging: The social context.* Thousand Oaks, CA: Pine Forge.

Morris, J. C. (2006). Mild cognitive impairment is early-stage Alzheimer disease. *Archives of Neurology, 63*(1), 15–16.

Morrison, J. W., & Bordere, T. (2001). Supporting biracial children's identity development. *Childhood Education, 77*(3), 134–138.

Mortimer, J. T., & Almazan, E. (2003). Connections between childhood and adulthood. In J. Mortimer & M. Shanahan (Eds.), *Handbook of the life course* (pp. 391–411). New York: Kluwer Academic/Plenum Publishers.

Mortimer, J. T., & Finch, M. D. (1996). *Adolescents, work, and family: An intergenerational developmental analysis.* Thousand Oaks, CA: Sage.

Mosher, W., Chandra, A., & Jones, J. (2005, September 15). Sexual behavior and selected measures. Men and women 15–44 years of age, United States, 2002. *Vital and Health Statistics,* (362). Retrieved November 20, 2006, from http://www.cdc.gov/nchs/data/ad/ad362.pdf

Moshman, D. (1998). Cognitive development beyond childhood. In D. Kuhn & R. Siegler (Eds.), *Handbook of child psychology: Vol. 2. Cognition, perception, and language* (5th ed., pp. 947–978). New York: Wiley.

Moss, N. E. (1987). Effects of father-daughter contact on use of pregnancy services by Mexican, Mexican-American, and Anglo adolescents. *Journal of Adolescent Health Care, 8,* 419–425.

Moss, R. H., Mortens, M. A., & Brennan, P. L. (1993). Patterns of diagnosis and treatment among late-middle-aged and older substance abuse patients. *Journal of Studies in Alcohol, 54,* 479–487.

Most ELBW infants make up ground by young adulthood (extremely low birth weight) (Brief article). (2006). *Nursing Standard* (Clinical report), *19,* 1.

Motamedi, G. K., & Meador, K. J. (2006). Antiepileptic drugs and neurodevelopment. *Current neurology and neuroscience reports, 6*(4), 341–346.

Mowrer, R., & Klein, S. (Eds.). (2001). *Handbook of contemporary learning theories.* Mahwah, NJ: Lawrence Erlbaum.

Moyer, K. (1974). Discipline. In K. Moyer, *You and your child: A primer for parents* (pp. 40–61). Chicago: Nelson Hall.

Moyers, B. (1993). *Healing and the mind.* New York: Doubleday.

Mueller, M., Wilhelm, B., & Elder, G. (2002). Variations in grandparenting. *Research on Aging, 24*(3), 360–388.

Muir, D., & Lee, K. (2003). The still face effect: Methodological issues and new applications. *Infancy, 4,* 483–491.

Munakata, Y., McClelland, J., Johnson, M., & Siegler, R. (1997). Rethinking infant knowledge: Toward an adaptive process account of successes and failures in object permanence tasks. *Psychological Review, 104*(4), 618–713.

Murphy, J., Jellinek, M., Quinn, D., Smith, G., Poitrast, F., & Goshko, M. (1991). Substance abuse and serious child maltreatment: Prevalence, risk, and outcome in a court sample. *Child Abuse & Neglect, 15*(3), 197–211.

Murray, J. A. (2001). Loss as a universal concept: A review of the literature to identify common aspects of loss in diverse situations. *Journal of Loss and Trauma, 6,* 219–241.

Must, A., & Strauss, R. S. (1999). Risks and consequences of childhood and adolescent obesity. *International Journal of Obesity, 23*(2), 2–11.

Mynatt, C. R., & Algeier, E. R. (1990). Risk factors, self-attributions and adjustment problems among victims of sexual coercion. *Journal of Applied Social Psychology, 20,* 130–153.

Nabukera, S., Wingate, M. S., Alexander, G. R., & Salihu, H. M., (2006). First-time births among women 30 years and older in the United Sates: Patterns and risk of adverse outcomes. *Journal of Reproductive Medicine, 51*(9), 676–682.

Nakamoto, J. M. (2000). Myths and variations in normal pubertal development. *The Western Journal of Medicine, 172*(3), 182–185.

Naleppa, M. J. (1996). Families and the institutionalized elderly: A review. *Journal of Gerontological Social Work, 27,* 87–111.

National Association of Child Care Resource and Referral Agencies. (2006). *Piggy bank: Parents and the high price of child care.* Retrieved December 30, 2006, from http://www.naccrra.org/docs/policy/breaking_the_piggy_bank.pdf

National Campaign to End Teen Pregnancy. (2002). *General facts and stats.* Retrieved August 26, 2002, from http://www.teenpregnancy.org/resources/data/genlfact.asp

National Cancer Institute. (2002). *Statistics.* Retrieved September 7, 2002, from http://www.nci.nih.gov

National Center for Child Abuse and Neglect. (1995). *Child maltreatment 1995: Reports of the states to the National Child Abuse Neglect Data Systems.* Retrieved from http://www/calib.com/nccanch/services/stats.htm#NIS-3

National Center for Children in Poverty. (2006a). *Basic facts about low-income children: Birth to age 3.* Retrieved December 3, 2006, from http://www.nccp.org/pub_ecp06b.html

National Center for Children in Poverty. (2006b). *Basic facts about low-income children: Birth to age 6.* Retrieved December 3, 2006, from http://www.nccp.org/pub_ecp06b.html

National Center for Children in Poverty (2006c). *Low-income children in the United States: National and state trend data 1995–2005.* Retrieved December 30, 2006, from http://nccp.org/media/nst06a_text.pdf

National Center for Children in Poverty. (2006d). *Who are America's poor children? The official story.* Retrieved January 15, 2007, from http://www.nccp.org/media/cpt06a_text.pdf

National Center for Children in Poverty. (n.d.). *Demographics of poor children.* Retrieved January 15, 2007, from http://nccp.org/state_detail_demographic_poor_US.html

National Center for Clinical Infant Programs. (1992). How community violence affects children, parents, and practitioners. *Public Welfare, 50*(4), 25–35.

National Center for Health Statistics. (2001a). *Trends in deaths caused by infectious diseases in the United States, 1900–1994.* Retrieved September 4, 2001, from http://www.cdc.gov/ncidod/emergplan/box01.htm

National Center for Health Statistics (2001b). *Health, United States, 2001.* Hyattsville, MD: Author.

National Center for Health Statistics (NCHS). (2004, October 6). *Obesity still a major problem, New data show: Prevalence of overweight and obesity among children and adolescents: United States, 1999–2002.* Atlanta: Author.

National Committee for Quality Assurance (NCQA). (2003). Prenatal and postpartum care (Timelinesss of prenatal care, checkups after delivery). *State of Health Care Quality Report, 2003.* Retrieved November 5, 2006, from http://www.ncqa.org/sohc2003/prenatal_and_postpartum_care.htm

National Council on the Aging. (2000, March). *Myths and realities 2000 survey results.* Washington, DC: Author.

National Council on the Aging. (n.d.). *Facts about older Americans.* Retrieved June 29, 2002, from http://www.ncoa.org/press/facts.html

National Eating Disorders Association. (2005). *Eating disorders & pregnancy: Some facts about the risks.* Retrieved October 9, 2006, from http://www.NationaEatingDisorders.org

National Geographic Society. (1998). *Eyewitness to the 20th century.* Washington, DC: Author.

National Health Statistics. (2005). *Health United States 2005 with chartbook on trends in the health of Americans.* Hyattsville, MD: U.S. Centers for Disease Control and Prevention.

National Hospice and Palliative Care Organization. (2006). *NHPCO facts and figures.* Retrieved August 1, 2006, from http://www.nhpco.org

National Institute of Alcohol Abuse and Alcoholism. (2005, March). *Social work curriculum on alcohol disorders.* Retrieved June 2006 from http://pubs.niaa.hih.gov/publications/Social.main/html

National Institute of Mental Health. (2000). *Depression in children and adolescents.* Retrieved August 27, 2002, from http://www.nimh.nih.gov/publicat/depchildresfact.cfm

National Institute on Drug Abuse. (2006). *Monitoring the Future Survey: Overview of findings 2006.* Retrieved January 14, 2007, from http://www.drugabuse.govnewsroom/06MTF06overview.html

National Institutes of Health. (1997). *Working group report on problem sleepiness.* Retrieved November 15, 2006, from http://www.nhlbi.nih.gov/health/prof/sleep/pslp_wg.pdf

National Institutes of Health. (2001). *Vital connections: Science of mind-body interactions: A report on the interdisciplinary conference held at NIH March 26–28, 2001.* Bethesda, MD: Author.

National Institutes of Health. (2002). *NHLBI stops trial of estrogen plus progestin due to increased cancer risk, lack of overall benefit.* Retrieved September 3, 2002, from http://www.nhlbi.nih.gov/new/press/02-07-09.htm

National Institutes of Health—National Institute of Allergy and Infectious Diseases. (1996, August). *An introduction to sexually transmitted diseases.* Bethesda, MD: U.S. Department of Health and Human Services, Public Health Service.

National Institutes of Health—National Institute of Allergy and Infectious Diseases. (2002). *Basic information about AIDS and HIV.* Retrieved July 2, 2002, from http://www.niaid.nih.gov/aidsvaccine/basicinfo.htm

National Institutes of Health—National Institute on Drug Abuse. (2001). *Monitoring the future study.* Bethesda, MD: U.S. Department of Health and Human Services, National Institutes of Health, National Institute on Drug Abuse.

National Research Council. (1990). *Who cares for America's children?* Washington, DC: Author.

National Research Council. (1993). *Understanding child abuse & neglect.* Washington, DC: National Academy Press.

National Sleep Foundation. (2005). *Drowsy driving: Facts and stats.* Retrieved November 15, 2006, from http://www.sleepfoundation.org

National Sleep Foundation. (2006). *2006 sleep in America poll: Highlights and key findings.* Retrieved November 15, 2006, from http:www.sleepfoundation.org

National Vaccine Information Center. (n.d.). *History of NVIC.* Retrieved June 7, 2002, from http://www.909shot.comnvichistory.htm

National Vital Statistics Report. (2002, January 30), *50*(4). Retrieved from www.cdc.gov/nchs/data/ibid/nvsr50_04-+2.pdf.

Nelson, R. (2004). Premature births on the rise. *American Journal of Nursing, 104*(5), 23–25.

Nepomnaschy, P., Welch, K., McConnell, D., Low, B., Strassmann, B., & England, B. (2006). Cortisol levels and very early pregnancy loss in humans. *Proceedings of National Academy of Science USA, 103*(10), 3938–3942.

Nettles, S., Mucherah, W., & Jones, D. (2000). Understanding resilience: The role of social resources. *Journal of Education for Students Placed at Risk, 5*(1&2), 47–60.

Neugarten, B. L., & Weinstein, K. K. (1964). The changing American grandparent. *Journal of Marriage and the Family, 26,* 199–204.

Neugarten, B., & Gutmann, D. (1968). Age-sex roles and personality in middle age: A thematic apperception study. In B. L. Neugarten (Ed.), *Middle age and aging* (pp. 58–71). Chicago: University of Chicago Press.

Neugarten, B., & Hagestad, G. (1976). Age and the life course. In R. Binstock & E. Shanas (Eds.), *Handbook of aging and the social sciences* (pp. 35–55). New York: VanNostrand Reinhold.

Neugarten, B. L., Havighurst, R. J., & Tobin, S. S. (1968). Personality and patterns of aging. In B. L. Neugarten (Ed.), *Middle age and aging.* Chicago: University of Chicago Press.

Neugebauer, R., Kline, J., Markowitz, J. C., Blelerg, K. L., Baxi, L., Rosing, M. A., et al. (2006). Pilot randomized controlled trial of interpersonal counseling for sybsyndromal depression following miscarriage. *The Journal of Clinical Psychiatry, 67*(8), 1299–1304.

New concepts on the causes of recurrent miscarriages. (2006). *Reproductive Biomedicine Online, 12*(3), 291–291. Retrieved November 4, 2006, from http://find.galegroup.com/itx/infomark.do?&contentSet=INGENTA&type=retrieve&tabID=T002&prodId=EAIM&docId=CA14389140&source=gale&srcprod=EAIM&userGroupName=vic_regent&version=1.0

Newcomb, A. F., Bukowski, W. M., & Pattee, L. (1993). Children's peer relations: A meta-analytic review of popular, rejected, neglected, controversial, and average sociometric status. *Psychological Bulletin, 113,* 99–128.

Newcomb, N., & Dubas, J. S. (1992). A longitudinal study of predictors of spatial ability in adolescent females. *Child Development, 63,* 37–46.

Newman, B., & Newman, P. (2006). *Development through life: A psychosocial approach* (9th ed.). Belmont, CA: Thomson.

Newman, D. (2006). *Sociology: Exploring the architecture of everyday life* (6th ed.). Thousand Oaks, CA: Pine Forge.

Newman, P., & Newman, B. (1997). *Childhood and adolescence.* Pacific Grove, CA: Brooks/Cole.

Newman, R. B. (2005). *Calm birth: New method for conscious childbirth.* Berkeley, CA: North Atlantic Books.

Newton, C., Sherrard, W., & Glavac, I. (1999). The Fertility Problem Inventory: Measuring perceived infertility-related stress. *Fertility and Sterility, 72,* 54–62.

Nhu, T. N., Merialdi, M., Abdel-Aleem, H., Carroli, G., Purwar, M., Zavaleta, N., et al. (2006). Causes of stillbirth and early neonatal deaths: Data from 7993 pregnancies in six developing countries. *Bulletin of the World Health Organization, 84,* 699–705.

Nishino, H., & Larson, R. (2003). Japanese adolescents' free time: Juku, Bakatsu, and government efforts to create more meaningful leisure. In S. Verma & R. Larson (Eds.), *Examining adolescent leisure time across culture: New directions for child and adolescent development, No. 99* (pp. 23–35). San Francisco: Jossey-Bass.

Noddings, N. (1984). *Caring: A feminine approach to ethics and moral education.* Berkeley: University of California Press.

Nojomi, M., Akbarian, A., & Ashory-Moghadam, S. (2006). Burden of abortion: Induced or spontaneous. *Archives of Iranian Medicine, 9*(10), 39–45.

Norton, D. (1993). Diversity, early socialization, and temporal development: The dual perspective revisited. *Social Work, 38*(1), 82–90.

Nosek, M. (1995). Findings on reproductive health and access to health care. *National study of women with physical disabilities.* Houston, TX: Baylor College of Medicine, Department of Physical Medicine and Rehabilitation.

Nosek, M. A., Howland, C. A., Rintal, D. H., Young, M. E., & Chanpong, G. F. (1997). *National study of women with physical disabilities: Final report.* Houston, TX: Center for Research on Women with Disabilities.

Nourhashemi, F., Sinclair, A., & Vellas, B. (2006). *Clinical aspects of Alzheimer's disease: Principles and practice of geriatric medicine* (4th ed.). Sussex, UK: John Wiley and Sons Ltd.

Novak, G., & Pelaez, M. (2004). *Child and adolescent development: A behavioral system approach.* Thousand Oaks, CA: Sage.

Novak, J. C., & Broom, B. (1995). *Maternal and child health nursing.* St. Louis, MO: Mosby.

Novins, D., Beals, J., Shore, J., & Manson, S. (1996). Substance abuse treatment of American Indian adolescents: Comorbid symptomatology, gender differences, and treatment patterns. *Child & Adolescent Psychiatry, 35*(12), 1593–1601.

Novins, D., Fleming, C., Beals, J., & Manson, S. (2000). Commentary: Quality of alcohol, drug, and mental health services for American Indian children and adolescents. *American Journal of Medicine Quarterly, 15*(4), 148–156.

Oakes, J. (1985). *Keeping track of tracking: How schools structure inequality.* New Haven, CT: Yale University Press.

Oakes, J., & Lipton, M. (1992). Detracking schools: Early lessons from the field. *Phi Delta Kappan, 73,* 448–454.

Oakley, A., Hickey, D., Rojan, L., & Rigby, A. S. (1996). Social support in pregnancy: Does it have long-term effects? *Journal of Reproductive and Infant Psychology, 14*(1), 7–22.

Oberklaid, F., Sanson, A., Pedlow, R., & Prior, M. (1993). Predicting preschool behavior problems from temperament and other variables in infancy. *Pediatrics, 91,* 113–120.

O'Brien, M. (1992). Gender identity and sex roles. In V. B. Van Hasselt & M. Hersen (Eds.), *Handbook of social development: A lifespan perspective* (pp. 325–345). New York: Plenum.

O'Conor, A. (1994). Who gets called queer in school? Lesbian, gay and bisexual teenagers, homophobia and high school. *High School Journal, 77*(1–2), 7–12.

Odent, M. (1998). *Men's role in the labour room.* Conference presentation at the Royal Society of Medicine, London.

Odent, M. (1999). *The scientification of love.* London: Free Association Books.

Odent, M. (1999). Is the participation of the father at birth dangerous? *Midwifery Today, 51,* 23–24.

Of meat, Mexicans and social mobility. (2006, June 17). *The Economist, 379*(8482), 31–32.

Office on Smoking and Health. (2000). *Youth tobacco surveillance—United States, 1998–1999.* Washington, DC: Author.

Ogbu, J. U. (1994). Overcoming racial barriers to equal access. In K. I. Goodland & P. Keating (Eds.), *Access to knowledge: The continuing agenda for our nation's schools* (pp. 59–90). New York: The College Board.

Ogden C. L., Flegal, K. M., Carroll, M. D., & Johnson, C. L. (2002). Prevalence and trends in overweight among US children and adolescents, 1999–2000. *Journal of American Medical Association, 288,* 1728–1732.

O'Keefe, M. (1994). Adjustment of children from maritally violent homes. *Families in Society, 75,* 403–415.

O'Keefe, M. (1997). Adolescents' exposure to community and school violence: Prevalence and behavioral correlates. *Journal of Adolescent Health, 20,* 368–376.

Oken, E., Wright, R. O., Kleinman, K. P., Bellinger, D., Amarasiriwardena, H. H., Rich-Edwards, J. W., et al. (2005). Maternal fish consumption, hair mercury, and infant cognition in a U.S. Cohort. *Environmental Health Perspectives, 113*(10), 1376–1381.

Okie, S. (2002, February 6). Hormone therapy no panacea: Study tracks menopause treatments' effect on well-being. *Washington Post,* p. A7.

O'Leary, V. E., & Bhaju, J. (2006). Resilience and empowerment. In J. Worell & C. D. Goodheart (Eds.), *Handbook of girl's and women's psychological health: Gender and well-being across the life span* (pp. 157–165). New York: Oxford Press.

Olds, D., Eckenrode, J., Henderson, C., Kitzman, H., Powers, J., Cole, R., et al. (1997). Long-term effects of home visitation on maternal life course and child abuse and neglect: Fifteen-year follow-up of a randomized trial. *JAMA, 278*(8), 637–643.

Oliver, R. (2005). Birth: Hospital or home: That is the question. *Journal of Prenatal and Perinatal Psychology and Health, 19*(4), 341–348.

Ollendick, T. H., Weist, M. D., Borden, M. C., & Greene, R. W. (1992). Sociometric status and academic, behavioral, and psychological adjustment: A five year longitudinal study. *Journal of Consulting and Clinical Psychology, 60,* 80–87.

O'Malley, P. L., Johnston, L., & Bachman, J. (1991). Quantitative and qualitative changes in cocaine use among American high school seniors, college students, and young adults. *NIDA Monographs, 110,* 19–43.

Opitz, J. M. (1996). Origins of birth defects. In J. J. Sciarra (Ed.), *Gynecology and obstetrics* (rev. ed., pp. 23–30). Philadelphia: Lippincott-Raven.

O-Prasetsawat, P., & Petchum, S. (2004). Sexual behavior of secondary school students in Bangkok metropolis. *Journal of the Medical Association of Thailand, 87*(7), 755–759.

O'Rand, A. (1996). The precious and the precocious: Understanding cumulative disadvantage and cumulative advantage over the life course. *The Gerontologist, 36*(2), 230–238.

O'Rand, A. (2003). The future of the life course: Late modernity and life course risks. In J. Mortimer & M. Shanahan (Eds.), *Handbook of the life course* (pp. 693–701). New York: Kluwer Academic/Plenum Publishers.

Orenstein, P. (1994). *Schoolgirls: Young women, self-esteem, and the confidence gap.* New York: Doubleday.

Orfield, G., Losen, D., Wald, J., & Swanson, C. (2004). *How minority youth are being left behind by the graduation rate crisis.* Cambridge, MA: The Civil Rights Project at Harvard University. Contributors: Advocates for Children of New York, The Civil Society Institute.

Ornoy, A. (2006). Neuroteratogens in man: An overview with special emphasis on the teratogenicity of antiepileptic drugs in pregnancy. *Reproductive Technology, 22*(2), 214–226.

Osofsky, J. D., Hann, D., & Peebles, C. (1993). Adolescent parenthood: Risks and opportunities for mothers and infants. In C. Zeanah, Jr. (Ed.), *Handbook of infant mental health* (pp. 106–119). New York: Guilford.

Ostir, G., & Goodwin, J. (2006). High anxiety is associated with an increased risk of death in an older tri-ethnic population. *Journal of Clinical Epidemiology, 59*(5), 534–540.

Ostrov, J., Crick, N., & Stauffacher, K. (2006). Relational aggression in sibling and peer relationships during early childhood. *Journal of Developmental Psychology, 27*(3), 241–253.

Overpeck, M., Hediger, M., Ruan, W., Davis, W., Maurer, K., Troendle, J., et al. (2000). Stature, weight, and body mass among U.S. children born with appropriate birth weights. *The Journal of Pediatrics, 137*(2), 205–213.

Owens, D. (1985). *None of the above.* New York: Houghton Mifflin.

Oyserman, D., Bybee, D., Mowbray, C., & MacFarlane, P. (2002). Positive parenting among African American mothers with a serious mental illness. *Journal of Marriage and Family, 65,* 65–77.

Padilla, Y. C., & Jordan, M. W. (1997). Determinants of Hispanic poverty in the course of the transition to adulthood. *Hispanic Journal of Behavioral Sciences, 19*(4), 416–433.

Pallas, A. (2003). Educational transitions, trajectories, and pathways. In J. Mortimer & M. Shanahan (Eds.), *Handbook of the life course* (pp. 165–184). New York: Kluwer Academic/Plenum Publishers.

Palmore, E. B., Burchett, B. M., Fillenbaum, C. G., George, L. K., & Wallman, L. M. (1985). *Retirement: Causes and consequences.* New York: Springer.

Palsson, S., Johansson, B., Berg, B., & Skoog, I. (2000). A population study on the influence of depression on neuropsychological functions in 85-year-olds. *Acta Psychiatrica Scandinavica, 101*(3), 185–193.

Panksepp, J. (1986). The psychobiology of prosocial behaviors: Separation distress, play, and altruism. In C. Zahn-Waxler, E. M. Cummings, & R. Iannotti (Eds.), *Altruism and aggression: Biological and social origin* (pp. 465–492). Cambridge, UK: Cambridge University Press.

Papachristou, F., Lialiaris, T., Touloupidis, S., Kalaitzis, C., Simopoulos, C., & Sofiktitis, N. (2006). Evidence of increased chromosomal instability in infertile males after exposure to mitomycin C and caffeine. *Asian Journal of Andrology, 8*(2), 199–204.

Papachristou Ornoy, A. (2006). Neuroteratogens in man: An overview with special emphasis on the teratogenicity of antiepileptic drugs in pregnancy. *Reproductive Technology, 22*(2), 214–226.

Pardington, S. (2002, January 13). Multilingual pupils pose a challenge to educators. *Contra Costa Times.* Retrieved January 17, 2002, from http://www.uniontrib.com/news/union trib/sun/news/news_0n13lingos.html

Parkes, C. M. (2002). Grief: Lessons from the past, visions, for the future. *Death Studies, 26,* 367–385.

Parents, Family and Friends of Lesbians and Gays [PFLAG]. (2001). *Read this before coming out to your parents.* Washington, DC: Sauerman.

Parette, H. (1995, November). *Culturally sensitive family-focused assistive technology assessment strategies.* Paper presented at the DEC Early Childhood Conference on Children with Special Needs, Orlando, FL.

Parke, M. (2003). Are married parents really better for children? What research says about the effects of family structure on well-being, *CLASP Couples and Marriage Series, Brief #2.* Retrieved January 15, 2007, from http://www.clasp.org/publications/marriage_brief3_annotated.pdf

Parrenas, R. (2001). *Servants of globalization: Women, migration, and domestic work.* Stanford, CA: Stanford University Press.

Pascoe, J., Pletta, K., Beasley, J., & Schellpfeffer, M. (2002). Best start breastfeeding promotion campaign. *Pediatrics, 109*(1), 170.

Pasquali, R. (2006). Obesity, fat distribution, and infertility. *Maturitas, 54*(4), 363–371.

Pasquali, R., Gambineri, A., & Pagotto, U. (2006). The impact of obesity on reproduction in women with polycystic ovary syndrome. *British Journal of Gynaecology: An International Journal of Obstetrics and Gynaecology, 113*(10), 1148–1159.

Pasqualotto, F. F., Sobreiro, B. F., Hallak, J., Pasqualotto, E. B., & Lucon, A. M. (2006). Cigarette smoking is related to a decrease in semen volume in a population of fertile men. *British Journal of Urology International, 97*(2), 324–326.

Patrikakou, E. N., Weisberg, R. P., Redding, S., & Walberg, H. J. (2005). (Eds.). *School-family partnerships for children's success.* New York: Teachers College Press.

Paul, E. (1997). A longitudinal analysis of midlife interpersonal relationships and well-being. In M. Lachman & J. James (Eds.), *Multiple paths of midlife development* (pp. 171–206). Chicago: University of Chicago Press.

Pauw, M. (1991). The social worker's role with fetal demise and stillbirth. *Health and Social Work, 16*(4), 291–298.

Payer, L. (1991). The menopause in various cultures. In H. Burger & M. Boulet (Eds.), *A portrait of the menopause.* Park Ridge, NJ: Parthenon.

Payne, R. K. (2005). *A framework for understanding poverty* (2nd ed.). Highlands, TX: aha! Process, Inc.

Paz, J. (1993). Support of Hispanic elderly. In H. McAdoo (Ed.), *Family ethnicity: Strength in diversity* (pp. 177–183). Newbury Park, CA: Sage.

Pearlin, L., & Skaff, M. (1996). Stress and the life course: A paradigmatic alliance. *The Gerontologist, 36*(2), 239–247.

Peart, N. A., Pungello, E. P., Campbell, F. A., & Richey, T. G. (2006). Faces of fatherhood: African-American young adults view the paternal role. *Families in Society, 87*(1), 71–83.

Peck, P. (1997). Study shows puberty hits girls at a young age. *Family Practice News, 27*(16), 61.

Pelligrini, A., & Galda, L. (2000). Cognitive development, play, and literacy: Issues of definition and developmental function. In K. Roskos & J. Christie (Eds.), *Play and literacy in early childhood: Research from multiple perspectives* (pp. 63–76). Mahwah, NJ: Lawrence Erlbaum.

Pena, R., & Wall, S. (2000). Effects of poverty, social inequality and maternal education on infant mortality in Nicaragua, 1988–1993. *American Journal of Public Health, 90*(1), 64–69.

Pennekamp, M. (1995). Response to violence. *Social Work in Education, 17,* 199–200.

Perlman, D., & Fehr, B. (1987). The development of intimate relationships. In D. Perlman & S. Duck (Eds.), *Intimate relationships: Development, dynamics, & deterioration* (pp. 13–42). Newbury Park, CA: Sage.

Perlman, J. M. (2001). Neurobehavioral deficits in premature graduates of intensive care—potential medical and neonatal environmental risk factors. *Pediatrics, 108*(16), 1339–1449.

Perloff, J., & Buckner, J. (1996). Fathers of children on welfare: Their impact on child well being. *American Journal of Orthopsychiatry, 66,* 557–571.

Perls, T. T., & Wood, E. R. (1996). Acute care costs of the oldest old. *Archives of Internal Medicine, 156,* 754–760.

Pernice, R., & Brook, J. (1996). Refugees' and immigrants' mental health: Association of demographic and post-immigration factors. *Journal of Social Psychology, 136*(4), 511–519.

Perrone, B., Stockel, H., & Krueger, V. (1989). *Medicine women, curanderas, and women doctors.* Norman: University of Oklahoma.

Perry, B. (1997). Incubated in terror: Neurodevelopmental factors in the "cycle of violence." In J. Osofsky (Ed.), *Children in a violent society* (pp. 124–149). New York: Guilford.

Perry, B. (2002). Childhood experience and the expression of genetic potential: What childhood neglect tells us about nature and nurture. *Brain & Mind, 3*(1), 79–100.

Perry, H. (1993). Mourning and funeral customs of African Americans. In D. Irish, K. Lundquist, & V. Nelsen (Eds.), *Ethnic variations in dying, death, and grief: Diversity in universality* (pp. 51–65). Washington, DC: Taylor & Francis.

Perry, J. (2006). Applying principles of neurodevelopment to clinical work with maltreated and traumatized children: The neurosequential model of therapeutics. In N. B. Webb (Ed.), *Working with traumatized youth in child welfare* (pp. 27–52). New York: Guilford Press.

Perry, W. G. (1994). Forms of intellectual and ethical development in the college years: A scheme. In B. Puka (Ed.), *Defining perspectives in moral development. Moral development: A compendium* (pp. 231–248). New York: Garland.

Pettit, G. S., Bakshi, A., Dodge, K. A., & Coie, J. D. (1990). The emergence of social dominance in young boy's play groups: Developmental differences and behavioral correlates. *Developmental Psychology, 26,* 1017–1025.

Phinney, J. S. (1989). Stages of ethnic identity development in minority group adolescents. *Journal of Early Adolescence, 9,* 34–49.

Piaget, J. (1936/1952). *The origins of intelligence in children.* New York: International Universities Press.

Piaget, J. (1932/1965). *The moral judgment of the child.* New York: Free Press.

Piaget, J. (1972). Intellectual evolution from adolescence to adulthood. *Human Development, 15,* 1–12.

Pipher, M. (1994). *Reviving Ophelia: Saving the selves of adolescent girls.* New York: Ballantine Books.

Pipher, M. (1999). *Another country: Navigating the emotional terrain of our elders.* New York: Riverhead Books.

Pirog-Good, M. (1996). The education and labor market outcomes of adolescent fathers. *Youth & Society, 28,* 236–262.

Piwoz, E., Ross, J., & Humphrey, J. (2004). Human immunodeficiency virus transmission during breastfeeding: Knowledge, gaps, and challenges for the future. *Advances in Experimental Medical Biology, 554,* 195–210.

Plaford, G. (2006). *Bullying and the brain: Using cognitive and emotional intelligence to help kids cope.* Lanham, MD: Rowman & Littlefield Education.

Plante, M. (2000). Fertility preservation in the management of gynecological cancers. *Current Opinion in Oncology, 12*(5), 497–507.

Plante, M. (2006). Fertility-preserving options for cervical cancer. *Oncology, 20*(6), 479.

Plath, D. (1980). *Long engagements.* Stanford, CA: Stanford University Press.

Platt, R., Rice, P., & McCormack, W. (1983). Risk of acquiring gonorrhea and prevalence of abnormal adnexal findings among women recently exposed to gonorrhea. *Journal of the American Medical Association, 250,* 3205–3209.

Poehlmann, J., & Fiese, B. (1994). The effects of divorce, maternal employment, and maternal social support on toddlers' home environments. *Journal of Divorce and Remarriage, 22*(1/2), 121–135.

Pollack, W. (1999). *Real boys: Rescuing our sons from the myths of boyhood.* New York: Henry Holt & Co.

PollingReport.com. (2006). *Abortion and birth control.* Retrieved January 11, 2006, from http://www.pollingreport.com/abortion.htm

Pollock, L. (2005). Benefits of birth centres. *RCM Midwives, 8*(6), 248.

Ponton, L., & Judice, S. (2004). Typical adolescent sexual development. *Child and Adolescent Psychiatric Clinics of North America, 13*(3), 497–511.

Poon, L. W., Clayton, G. M., Martin, P., Johnson, M. A., Courtenay, B. C., Sweaney, A. L., et al. (1992). The Georgia centenarian study. *International Journal of Aging and Human Development, 34*(1), 1–17.

Population Council, Inc. (1999). CDC on infant and maternal mortality in the United States: 1900–1999. *Population and Development Review, 25*(25), 821–824.

Portes, A., & Rumbaut, R. G. (2001). *Legacies.* Berkeley: University of California Press.

Posmontier, B., & Horowitz, J. (2004). Postpartum practices and depression prevalences: Technocentric and ethnokinship cultural perspectives. *Journal of Transcultural Nursing, 15,* 34–43.

Post, S. (1992). Aging and meaning: The Christian tradition. In T. Cole, D. van Tassel, & R. Kastenbaum (Eds.), *Handbook of the humanities and aging* (pp. 127–146). New York: Springer.

Pothoff, S., Bearinger, L., Skay, C., Cassuto, N., Blum, R., & Resnick, M. (1998). Dimensions of risk behaviors among American Indian youth. *Archives of Pediatric & Adolescent Medicine, 152,* 157–163.

Potter, C. C. (2004). Gender differences in childhood and adolescence. In P. Allen-Meares & M. W. Fraser (Eds.), *Intervention with children and adolescents: An interdisciplinary perspective* (pp. 54–79). Allyn & Bacon.

Powlishta, K. K., Serbin, L. A., Doyle, A., & White, D. R. (1994). Gender, ethnic, and body type biases: The generality of prejudice in childhood. *Developmental Psychology, 30,* 526–536.

Preto, N. (2005). Transformation of the family system during adolescence. In B. Carter & M. McGoldrick (Eds.), *The expanded family life cycle: Individual, family, and social perspectives* (3rd ed., pp. 274–286). Boston: Allyn & Bacon.

Price, S. K. (2006). Prevalence and correlates of pregnancy loss history in a national sample of children and families. *Maternal and Child Health Journal, 10*(6), 489–500.

Pridham, K., & Chang, A. (1992). Transition to being the mother of a new infant in the first 3 months: Maternal problem solving and self-appraisals. *Journal of Advanced Nursing, 17,* 204.

Proot, I. M., Abu-Saad, H. H., ter Meulen, R. H. J., Goldsteen, M., Spreeuwenberg, C., & Widdershoven, G. A. M. (2004). The needs of terminally ill patients at home: Directing one's life, health and things related to beloved others. *Palliative Medicine, 18,* 53–61.

Providers examine teen contraceptive use. (2001, September). *Contraceptive technology update.* Electronic Collection A77711625.

Pulkkinen, L., & Kokko, K. (2000). Identity development in adulthood: A longitudinal study. *Journal of Research in Personality, 34,* 445–470.

Putney, N., & Bengtson, V. (2001). Families, intergenerational relationships, and kinkeeping in midlife. In M. Lachmann (Ed.), *Handbook of midlife development* (pp. 528–570). New York: Wiley.

Putney, N., & Bengtson, V. (2003). Intergenerational relations in changing times. In J. Mortimer & M. Shanahan (Eds.), *Handbook of the life course* (pp. 149–164). New York: Kluwer Academic/Plenum Publishers.

Pyke, D., & Bengtson, V. (1996). Caring more or less: Individualistic and collectivist systems of family eldercare. *Journal of Marriage and the Family, 58,* 379–392.

Rabkin, J., Balassone, M., & Bell, M. (1995). The role of social workers in providing comprehensive health care to pregnant women. *Social Work in Health Care, 20*(3), 83–97.

Rando, T. (1993). *Treatment of complicated mourning.* Champaign, IL: Research Press.

Rank, M. R. (2005). One nation, underprivileged: Why American poverty affects us all. New York: Oxford University Press.

Rapoport, J. L., Giedd, J. N., Blumenthal J., Hamburger, S., Jeffries, N., Fernandez, T., et al. (1999). Progressive cortical change during adolescence in childhood-onset schizophrenia: A longitudinal magnetic resonance imaging study. *Archives of General Psychiatry, 56*(7), 649–654.

Rauch, J. (1988). Social work and the genetics revolution: Genetic services. *Social Work, 9/10,* 389–395.

Reed, G. B. (1996). Introduction to genetic screening and prenatal diagnoses. In J. J. Sciarra (Ed.), *Gynecology and obstetrics* (Rev. ed., pp. 999–1003). Philadelphia: Lippincott-Raven.

Reed, R. K. (2005). *Birthing fathers: The transformation of men in American rites of birth.* New Brunswick. NJ: Rutgers University Press.

Reid, T. R. (2004). *The United States of Europe: The new superpower and the end of American supremacy.* New York: Penguin.

Remafedi, G., Farrow, J. A., & Deisher, R. W. (1991). Risk factors for attempted suicide in gay and bisexual youth. *Pediatrics, 87,* 869–875.

Remez, L. (2000). Oral sex among adolescents: Is it sex or is it abstinence? *Family Planning Perspectives, 32*(6), 298–304.

Rennison, C. M., & Welchans, S. (2000). *Intimate partner violence* (Special Report). Washington, DC: U.S. Bureau of Justice Statistics, National Institute of Justice. (NCJ 178247).

Rew, L. (2005). *Adolescent health: A multidisciplinary approach to theory, research, and intervention.* Thousand Oaks, CA: Sage.

Rexrode, K., & Manson, J. (2002) Postmenopausal hormone therapy and quality of life: No cause for celebration. *JAMA, The Journal of the American Medical Association, 287*(5), 591–597.

Riberio, S. C., Tormena, R. A., Giribela, C. G., Izzo, C. R., Santos, N. C., & Pinotti, J. A. (2004). Laparoscopic tubal anastomosis. *International Journal of Gynaecology and Obstretics, 84*(2), 142–148.

Richards, M. H., & Larson, R. (1993). Pubertal development and the daily subjective states of young adolescents. *Journal of Research on Adolescence, 3,* 145–169.

Richmond, M. (1917). *Social diagnosis.* New York: Russell Sage.

Riedmann, G. (1996). Preparation for parenthood. In J. J. Sciarra (Ed.), *Gynecology and obstetrics* (Vol. 2, 2nd ed., pp. 1–8). Philadelphia: Lippincott-Raven.

Rieker, P. R., & Bird, C. E. (2005). Rethinking gender differences in health: Why we need to integrate social and biological perspectives. *The Journal of Gerontology: Series B Psychological Sciences and Social Sciences, 60B,* 40–47.

Rieser-Danner, L. (2003). Individual differences in infant fearfulness and cognitive performance: A testing, performance, or competence effect? *Genetic, Social, and General Psychology Monographs, 129*(1), 41–71.

Rifas-Shiman, S. L., Rich-Edwards, J. W., Willett, W. C., Kleinman, K. P., Oken, E., & Gillman, M. W. (2006). Changes in dietary intake from first to second trimester of pregnancy. *Perinatal Epidemiology, 20*(1), 35–42.

Riley, M. (1996). Discussion: What does it all mean? *The Gerontologist, 36*(2), 256–258.

Riley, M. W. (1971). Social gerontology and the age stratification of society. *The Gerontologist, 11,* 79–87.

Rimm, S. (1999). *See Jane win.* New York: Three Rivers Press.

Rindfuss, R. R., Cooksey, E. C., & Sutterlin, R. L. (1999). Young adult occupational achievement: Early expectations versus behavioral reality. *Work & Occupations, 26*(2), 220–263.

Rindfuss, R., Swicegood, G., & Rosenfeld, R. (1987). Disorder in the life course: How common and does it matter? *American Sociological Review, 52,* 785–801.

Riordan, J., & Auerbach, K. (1999). *Breastfeeding and human lactation* (2nd ed.). Sudbury, MA: Jones & Bartlett.

Roberts, B., Helson, R., & Klohnen, E. (2002). Personality development and growth in women across 30 years: Three perspectives. *Journal of Personality, 70,* 79–102.

Roberts, B., Robins, R., Trzesniewski, K., & Caspi, A. (2003). Personality trait development in adulthood. In J. Mortimer & M. Shanahan (Eds.), *Handbook of the life course* (pp. 579–595). New York: Kluwer Academic/Plenum Publishers.

Roberts, E., Burchinal, M., & Bailey, D. (1994). Communication among preschoolers with and without disabilities in same-age and mixed-age classes. *American Journal on Mental Retardation, 99,* 231–249.

Roberts, R. E. L., & Bengston, V. L. (1993). Relationship with parents, self-esteem, & psychological well-being in young adulthood. *Social Psychology Quarterly, 56*(4), 263–278.

Roberts, R. E., Roberts, C. R., & Chen, Y. R. (1997). Ethnocultural differences in prevalence of adolescent depression. *American Journal of Community Psychology, 25*(1), 95–111.

Robinson, J. A. (1998). The impact of race and ethnicity on children's peer relations. In P. T. Slee & K. Rigby (Eds.), *Children's peer relations* (pp. 76–88). New York: Routledge.

Robinson, L. C. (2000). Interpersonal relationship quality in young adulthood: A gender analysis. *Adolescence, 35*(140), 775–785.

Rock, P. (1996). Eugenics and euthanasia: A cause for concern for disabled people, particularly disabled women. *Disability & Society, 11*(1), 121–127.

Roe, K., & Minkler, M. (1998/99). Grandparents raising grandchildren: Challenges and responses. *Generations, 22*(4), 28–33.

Roebers, C., & Schneider, W. (1999). Self-concept and anxiety in immigrant children. *International Journal of Behavioral Development, 23*(1), 125–147.

Roehrs, T., Beare, D., Zorick, F., & Roth, T. (1994). Sleepiness and ethanol effects on simulated driving. *Alcoholism: Clinical and Experimental Research, 18*(1), 154–158.

Roggman, L. (2004). Do fathers just want to have fun? *Human Development, 47,* 228–236.

Rogoff, B. (2003). *The cultural nature of human development.* New York: Oxford University Press.

Ronka, A., & Pulkkinen, L. (1995). Accumulation of problems in social functioning in young adulthood: A developmental approach. *Journal of Personality and Social Psychology, 69*(2), 381–391.

Roof, W. (1993). *A generation of seekers: The spiritual journeys of the baby boom generation.* San Francisco: HarperCollins.

Roof, W. (1999). *Spiritual marketplace: Baby boomers and the remaking of American religion.* Princeton, NJ: Princeton University Press.

Roopnarine, J., Shin, M., Donovan, B., & Suppal, P. (2000). Sociocultural contexts of dramatic play: Implications for early education. In K. Roskos & J. Christie (Eds.), *Play and literacy in early childhood: Research from multiple perspectives* (pp. 205–220). Mahwah, NJ: Lawrence Erlbaum.

Rose, S., & Zand, D. (2000). Lesbian dating and courtship from young adulthood to midlife. *Journal of Gay & Lesbian Social Services, 11*(2/3), 77–104.

Rosenbaum, J. (1991). Black pioneers: Do their moves to the suburbs increase economic opportunity for mothers and children? *Housing Policy Debate, 2*(4), 1179–1213.

Rosenberg, M. (1986). *Conceiving the self.* Malabar, FL: Robert E. Krieger.

Rosenthal, C. (1985). Kinkeeping in the familial division of labor. *Journal of Marriage and the Family, 47,* 965–974.

Roskos, K., & Christie, J. (2000). *Play and literacy in early childhood: Research from multiple perspectives.* Mahwah, NJ: Lawrence Erlbaum.

Ross, L. E., Steele, L. S., & Epstein, R. (2006). Lesbian and bisexual women's recommendations for improving the provision of assisted reproductive technology services. *Fertility and Sterility, 86*(3), 735–738.

Ross, L. J. (1992). African-American women and abortion: A neglected history. *Journal of Health Care for the Poor and Underserved, 3,* 274–284.

Ross, M., & Holmberg, D. (1992). Are wives' memories for events in relationships more vivid than their husband's memories? *Journal of Social and Personal Relationships, 9,* 585–604.

Rossi, A. (2004a). The menopausal transition and aging processes. In O. Brim, C. Ryff, & R. Kessler (Eds.), *How healthy are we? A national study of well-being at midlife* (pp. 153–201). Chicago: University of Chicago Press.

Rossi, A. (2004b). Social responsibility to family and community. In O. Brim, C. Ryff, & R. Kessler (Eds.), *How healthy are we? A national study of well-being at midlife* (pp. 550–585). Chicago: University of Chicago Press.

Rossi, A., & Rossi, P. (1990). *Of human bonding: Parent-child relations across the life course.* New York: Aldine de Gruyter.

Rotenberg, K., McDougall, P., Boulton, M., Vaillancourt, T., Fox, C., & Hymel, S. (2004). Cross-sectional and longitudinal relations among peer-reported trustworthiness, social relationships, and psychological adjustment in children and early adolescents from the United Kingdom and Canada. *Journal of Experimental Child Psychology, 88,* 46–67.

Rotheram-Borus, M. J. (1993). Biculturalism among adolescents. In M. Bernal & G. Knight (Eds.), *Ethnic identity* (pp. 81–102). Albany: State University of New York Press.

Rothman, B. K. (1991). *In labor: Women and power in the birthplace* (2nd ed.). New York: W. W. Norton.

Roueche, J. E., & Baker, G. A., III. (1986). *Profiling excellence in America's schools.* Arlington, VA: American Association of School Administrators.

Roumen, F. J., Op Ten Berg, M. M., & Hoomans, E. H. (2006). The combined contraceptive vaginal ring (NuvaRign®): First experience in daily clinical practice in the Netherlands. *The European Journal of Contraception and Reproductive Health: The Official Journal of the European Society of Contraception, 11*(1), 14–22.

Rovee-Collier, C. (1999). The development of infant memory. *Current Directions in Psychological Science, 8*(3), 80–85.

Rowan, L., Knobel, M., Bigum, C., & Lankshear, C. (2002). *Boys, literacies, and schooling: The dangerous territories of gender-based literacy reform.* Buckingham, UK: Open University Press.

Roy, K. K., Baruah, J., Kumar, S., Malhotra, N., Deorari, A. K., & Sharma, J. B. (2006). Maternal antenatal profile and immediate neonatal outcome in VLBW and ELBW babies. *Indian Journal of Pediatrics, 73*(8), 669–673.

Rubia, K., Overmeyer, S., Taylor, E., Brammer, M., Williams, S. C., Simmons, A., et al. (2000). Functional frontalisation with age: Mapping neurodevelopmental trajectories with fMRI. *Neuroscience & Biobehavioral Review, 24,* 13–19.

Rubin, K. (1986). Play, peer interaction, and social development. In A. Gottfried & C. Brown (Eds.), *Play interactions: The contribution of play materials and parental involvement to children's development* (pp. 163–174). Lexington, MA: Heath.

Rubin, K., Fein, G., & Vandenberg, B. (1983). Play. In E. M. Hetherington (Ed.), *Handbook of child psychology: Vol. 4. Socialization, personality, and social development* (4th ed., pp. 693–744). New York: Wiley.

Rubin, R. (1995). *Maternal identity and the maternal experience: Childbirth educator.* New York: Springer.

Rudacille, D. (2005). *The riddle of gender: Science, activism, and transgender rights.* New York: Pantheon.

Rue, V., Coleman, P., Rue, J., & Reardon, D. (2004). Induced abortion and traumatic stress: A preliminary comparison of American and Russian women. *Medical Science Monitor, 10*(10), SR5–SR16.

Rueda, R., Monzo, L., Shapiro, J., Gomez, J., & Blacher, J. (2005). Cultural models of transition: Latina mothers of young adults with developmental disabilities. *Exceptional Children, 71*(4), 401–414.

Rutter, M. (1996). Transitions and turning points in developmental psychopathology: As applied to the age span between childhood and mid-adulthood. *International Journal of Behavioral Development, 19*(3), 603–636.

Ryan, B. A., & Adams, G. R. (1995). The family-school relationships model. In B. A. Ryan, G. R. Adams, T. P. Gullotta, R. P. Weissberg, & R. L. Hampton (Eds.), *The family-school connection: Theory, research, and practice* (pp. 3–28). Thousand Oaks, CA: Sage.

Ryan, C., & Futterman, D. (1998). *Lesbian and gay youth: Care and counseling.* New York: Columbia University Press.

Ryan, S., Franzetta, K., & Manlove, J. (2005). Hispanic teen pregnancy and birth rates: Looking behind the numbers. *Child Trends* (Publication #2005-01). Retrieved December 12, 2006, from http://childtrends.org

Sabbagh, M., & Baldwin, D. (2001). Learning words from knowledgeable versus ignorant speakers: Links between preschoolers' theory of mind and semantic development. *Child Development, 72,* 1054–1070.

Sacchetti, A. D., Gerardi, M., Sawchuck, P., & Bihl, I. (1997). Boomerang babies: Emergency department utilization at early discharge neonates. *Pediatric Emergency Care, 13,* 365–368.

Sadker, M., & Sadker, D. (1994). *Failing at fairness: How our schools cheat girls.* New York: Touchstone.

Sadovsky, R. (2002). Evaluation and management of male infertility. *American Family Physician, 66*(77), 1299.

Safren, S., & Heimberg, R. (1999). Depression, hopelessness, suicidality, and related factors in sexual minority and heterosexual adolescents. *Journal of Consulting and Clinical Psychology, 67*(6), 859–866.

Sagara, J. (2000). Development of attitudes toward gender roles in children: Stereotypes and flexibility. *Japanese Journal of Educational Psychology, 48*(2), 174–181.

Saghir, M. T., & Robins, E. (1973). *Male and female homosexuality: A comprehensive examination.* Baltimore, MD: Williams & Wilkins.

Saldinger, M. A., Cain, A., Kalter, N., & Lohnes, K. (1999). Anticipating parental death in families with young children. *American Journal of Orthopsychiatry, 69*(1), 39–48.

Saleeby, D. (1996). The strengths perspective in social work practice: Extensions and cautions. *Social Work, 41*(3), 296–304.

Sallmen, M., Sandler, D. P., Hoppin, J. A., Blair, A., & Baird, D. D. (2006). Reduced fertility among overweight and obese men. *Epidemology, 17*(5), 520–523.

Sameroff, A., Bartko, W., Baldwin, A., Baldwin, C., & Seifer, R. (1998). Family and social influences on the development of child competence. In M. Lewis & C. Feiring (Eds.), *Families, risk, and competence* (pp. 161–186). Mahwah, NJ: Lawrence Erlbaum.

Sampson, R. J., & Laub, J. H. (1990). Crime and deviance over the life course: The salience of adult social bonds. *American Sociological Review, 55,* 609–627.

Sands, R., & Goldberg, G. (2000). Factors associated with stress among grandparents raising their grandchildren. *Family Relations, 49*(1), 97–105.

Santrock, J. W. (1995). *Life-span development* (5th ed.). Madison, WI: Brown & Benchmark.

Sapolsky, R. (1998). *Why zebras don't get ulcers: An updated guide to stress, stress-related diseases, and coping.* New York: W. H. Freeman.

Savin-Williams, R. C. (1979). Dominance hierarchies in groups of early adolescents. *Child Development, 50,* 923–935.

Savin-Williams, R., & Diamond, L. (2004). Sex. In R. Lerner & L. Steinberg (Eds.), *Handbook of adolescent psychology* (2nd ed., pp. 189–231). New York: Wiley.

Sawin, K. S. (1998). Health care concerns for women with physical disability and chronic illness. In E. Q. Youngkin & M. S. Davis (Eds.), *Women's health: A primary care clinical guide* (2nd ed., pp. 905–941). Stamford, CT: Appleton & Lange.

Sax, L. (2005). *Why gender matters: What parents and teachers need to know about the emerging science of sex differences.* New York: Random House.

Scarlett, A. G., Naudeau, S., Salonius-Pasternak, D., & Ponte, I. (2005). *Children's play.* Thousand Oaks, CA: Sage.

Schachere, K. (1990). Attachment between working mothers and their infants: The influence of family processes. *American Journal of Orthopsychiatry, 60,* 19–34.

Schafer, J. E., Osborne, L. M., Davis, A. R., & Westhoff, C. (2006). Acceptability and satisfaction using Quick Start with the contraceptive vaginal ring versus an oral contraceptive. *Contraception, 73*(5), 488–492.

Schaie, K. W. (1982). Toward a stage theory of adult cognitive development. In K. W. Schaie & J. Geiwitz (Eds.), *Readings in adult development and aging.* Boston: Little, Brown.

Schaie, K. W. (1984). The Seattle Longitudinal Study: A 21-year exploration of psychometric intelligence in adulthood. In K. W. Schaie (Ed.), *Longitudinal studies of adult psychological development* (pp. 64–135). New York: Guilford.

Schild, S., & Black, R. (1984). *Social work and genetics: A guide for practice.* New York: Haworth.

Schmitt, B. (1988). Failure to thrive: The medical evaluation. In D. Bross, R. Krigman, M. Lenherr, D. Rosenberg, & B. Schmitt (Eds.), *The new child protection team handbook* (pp. 82–101). New York: Garland.

Schmitz, C., & Hilton, A. (1996). Combining mental health treatment with education for preschool children with severe emotional and behavioral problems. *Social Work in Education, 18,* 237–249.

Schneider, H., & Eisenberg, D. (2006). Who receives a diagnosis of Attention Deficit/ Hyperactivity Disorder in the United States elementary school population. *Pediatrics, 117*(4), 601–609.

Schoeni, R. F., Martin, L. G., Andreski, P. A., & Freedman, V. A. (2005). Persistent and growing socioeconomic disparities in disability among the elderly: 1982–2002. *American Journal of Public Health, 95*(11), 2065–2072.

Schubot, D. (2001). Date rape prevalence among female high school students in a rural Midwestern state during 1993, 1995, and 1997. *Journal of Interpersonal Violence, 16*(4), 291–296.

Schuetze, P., Lewis, A., & DiMartino, D. (1999). Relation between time spent in daycare and exploratory behavior. *Infant Behavior & Development Special Issue, 22*(2), 267–276.

Schulenberg, J., Maggs, J., & O'Malley, P. (2003). How and why the understanding of developmental continuity and discontinuity is important: The sample case of long-term consequences of adolescent substance use. In J. Mortimer & M. Shanahan (Eds.), *Handbook of the life course* (pp. 413–436). New York: Kluwer Academic/Plenum Publishers.

Schumm, W. R., Bell, D. B., & Knott, B. (2000). Characteristics of families of soldiers who return prematurely from overseas deployments: An assessment from Operation Restore Hope (Somalia). *Psychological Reports, 86*(3 pt 2), 1267–1272.

Schupf, N., Tang, M., Albert, S., Costa, A. R., Andrews, H., Lee, J., et al. (2005). Decline in cognitive and functional skills increases mortality risk in nondemented elderly. *Neurology, 65*(8), 1218–1226.

Schwartz, S., Cote, J., & Arnett, J. (2005). Identity and agency in emerging adulthood: Two developmental routes in the individualization process. *Youth and Society, 37*(2), 201–229.

Schweinhart, L., Montie, J., Xiang, Z., Barnett, W., Belfield, C., & Nores, M. (2005). *Lifetime effects: The High/Scope Perry preschool study through age 40.* Ypsilanti, MI: High/Scope Educational Research Foundation.

Sclowitz, I. K., & Santos, I. S. (2006). Risk factors for repetition of low birth weight, intrauterine growth retardation, and prematurity in subsequent pregnancies: A systematic review. *Cadernos De Saude Publica, 22*(6), 1129–1136.

Scott, J. (1997). Family relationships of midlife and older women. In J. Coyle (Ed.), *Handbook on women and aging* (pp. 367–384). Westport, CT: Greenwood Press.

Scott, K. D., Berkowitz, G., & Klaus, M. H. (1999). A comparison of intermittent and continuous support during labor: A meta-analysis. *American Journal of Obstetrics and Gynecology, 180*(5), 1054.

Sedikides, C., Gaertner, L., & Toguchi, Y. (2003). Pancultural self-enhancement. *Journal of Personality and Social Psychology, 84,* 60–69.

Sedlak, A., & Broadhurst, D. (1996). *Third National Incidence Study of Child Abuse and Neglect: Final report.* Washington, DC: U.S. Department of Human Services.

Seefeldt, C. (1993). Educating yourself about diverse cultural groups in our country by reading. *Young Children, 48,* 13–16.

Seeman, P. (1999). Images in neuroscience. Brain development, X: Pruning during development. *American Journal of Psychiatry, 156,* 168.

Segal, B. M., & Stewart, J. C. (1996). Substance use and abuse in adolescence: An overview. *Child Psychiatry and Human Development, 26*(4), 193–210.

Sehgal, A., Telang, S., Passah, S. M., & Jyothi, M. C. (2004). Maternal and neonatal profile and immediate outcome in extremely low birth weight babies in Delhi. *Tropical Doctor, 34*(3), 165–168.

Seifer, R., & Dickstein, S. (2000). Paternal mental illness and infant development. In C. Zeanah (Ed.), *Handbook of infant mental health* (2nd ed., pp. 145–160). New York: Guilford.

Seifert, K. L., Hoffnung, R. J., & Hoffnung, M. (1997). *Lifespan development.* New York: Houghton Mifflin.

Seligman, M. E. P., Reivich, K., Jaycox, L., & Gillham, J. (1995). *The optimistic child.* New York: Houghton Mifflin.

Selman, R. L. (1976). Social-cognitive understanding: A guide to educational and clinical practice. In T. Lickona (Ed.), *Moral development and behavior: Theory, research, and social issues* (pp. 219–316). New York: Holt, Rinehart, & Winston.

Sen, A., Partelow, L., & Miller, D. (2005). *Comparative indicators of education in the United States and other G8 countries: 2004* (NCES 2005-021). U.S. Department of Education, National Center for Education Statistics. Washington, DC: U.S. Government Printing Office.

Sepaniak, S., Forges, T., Gerald, H., Foliquet, B., Bene, M. C., & Monnier-Barbarino, P. (2006). The influence of cigarette smoking on human sperm quality and DNA fragmentation. *Toxicology, 223*(1–2), 54–60.

Serbin, L. A., Powlishta, K. K., & Gulko, J. (1993). The development of sex typing in middle childhood. *Monographs of the Society for Research in Child Development, 58*(2), Serial No. 232.

Sethi, V. (2004). Iodine deficiency and development of brain. *Indian Journal of Pediatrics, 71*(4), 325–329.

Settersten, R., Jr. (1998). A time to leave home and a time never to return? Age constraints on the living arrangements of young adults. *Social Forces, 76*(4), 1373–1400.

Settersten, R., Jr. (2003a). Introduction: Invitation to the life course: The promise. In R. Settersten, Jr. (Ed.), *Invitation to the life course: Toward new understandings of later life* (pp. 1–12). Amityville, NY: Baywood Publishing Co., Inc.

Settersten, R., Jr. (2003b). Age structuring and the rhythm of the life course. In J. Mortimer & M. Shanhan (Eds.), *Handbook of the life course* (pp. 81–98). New York: Kluwer Academic/Plenum Publishers.

Settersten, R. A., Furstenberg, F. F., & Rumbaut, R. G. (2005). *On the frontier of adulthood: Theory, research, & public policy.* Chicago: University of Chicago Press.

Settersten, R., Jr., & Lovegreen, L. (1998). Educational experiences throughout adult life: New hopes or no hope for life-course flexibility? *Research on Aging, 20*(4), 506–538.

Settersten, R. A., & Mayer, L. U. (1997). The measurement of age, age structuring, and the life course. *Annual Review of Sociology, 23,* 233–261.

Severy, L.J., & Spieler, J. (2000). New methods of family planning: Implications for intimate behavior. *Journal of Sex Research, 37*(3), 258–265.

Sex bias cited in vocational ed. (2002, June 6). *Washington Post,* pp. 18–19.

Shanahan, M. (2000). Pathways to adulthood in changing societies: Variability and mechanisms in life course perspective. *Annual Review of Sociology, 27,* 667–692.

Shanahan, M., & Flaherty, B. (2001). Dynamic patterns of time use in adolescence. *Child Development, 72*(2), 385–401.

Shanahan, M., Miech, R., & Elder, G., Jr. (1998). Changing pathways to attainment in men's lives: Historical patterns of school, work, and social class. *Social Forces, 77*(1), 231–266.

Shapiro, P. (1996). *My turn: Women's search for self after the children leave.* Princeton, NJ: Peterson's.

Shapiro, T. (2004). *The hidden cost of being African-American: How wealth perpetuates inequality.* New York: Oxford University Press.

Shaver, J., Giblin, E., Lentz, M., & Lee, K. (1988). Sleep patterns and stability in perimenopausal women. *Sleep, 11,* 556–561.

Shaw, S., Kleiber, D., & Caldwell, L. (1995). Leisure and identity formation in male and female adolescents: A preliminary examination. *Journal of Leisure Research, 27,* 245–263.

Shedler, J., & Block, J. (1990). Adolescent drug use and psychological health. *American Psychologist, 45,* 612–630.

Sheehy, G. (1995). *New passages.* New York: Random House.

Sheiner, E. K., Sheiner, E., Hammei, R. D., Potashnik, G., & Carel, R. (2003). Effect of occupational exposures on male fertility: Literature review. *Industrial Health, 41*(2), 55–62.

Sheldon, K. (2006). Getting older, getting better? Recent psychological evidence. In M. Csikszentmihalyi & I. Csiksezentmihali (Eds.), *A life worth living: Contributions to positive psychology* (pp. 215–229). New York: Oxford Press.

Sheldon, K., & Kasser, T. (2001). Getting older, getting better? Personal striving and psychological maturity aross the life span. *Developmental Psychology, 37,* 491–501.

Shepard, M. (1992). Child visiting and domestic abuse. *Child Welfare, 71,* 357–367.

Sheridan, M. (2008). The spiritual person. In E. Hutchison (Ed.), *Dimensions of human behavior: Person and environment* (3rd ed.). Thousand Oaks, CA: Sage.

Sherman, A., de Vries, B., & Lansford, J. (2000). Friendship in childhood and adulthood: Lessons across the life span. *International Journal of Aging and Human Development, 51*(1), 31–51.

Sherman, E. (1991). *Reminiscence and the self in old age.* New York: Springer.

Shin, H. B., & Bruno, R. (2003). *Language use and English speaking ability: 2000.* Washington, DC: U.S. Census Bureau. Retrieved November 6, 2006, from http://www.census.gov/prod/2003pubs/c2kbr-29.pdf

Shonkoff, J., & Phillips, D. (Eds.). (2000). *From neurons to neighborhoods: The science of early childhood development.* Washington, DC: National Academy Press.

Shonkoff, J., Hauser-Cram, P., Krauss, M., & Upshur, C. (1992). Development of infants with disabilities and their families: Implications for theory and service delivery. *Monographs of the Society for Research in Child Development, 57*(6), 230–239.

Shrier, L. A., Emans, S. J., Woods, E. R., & DuRant, R. H. (1996). The association of sexual risk behaviors and problem drug behaviors in high school students. *Journal of Adolescent Health, 20,* 377–383.

Shweder, R. (Ed.). (1998). *Welcome to middle age (and other cultural fictions).* Chicago: University of Chicago Press.

Siefert, K., & Pimlott, S. (2001). Improving pregnancy outcome during imprisonment: A model residental care program. *Social Work, 46*(2), 125–134.

Siegel, D. (1999). *The developing mind: Toward a neurobiology of interpersonal experience.* New York: Guilford Press.

Silbereisen, R. (2003). Contextual constraints on adolescents' leisure. In S. Verma & R. Larson (Eds.), *Examining adolescent leisure time across cultures: New directions for child and adolescent development, No. 99* (pp. 95–102). San Francisco: Jossey-Bass.

Silverman, P. R. (2004). Bereavement: A time of transition and changing relationships. In J. Berzoff & P. R. Silverman (Eds.), *Living with dying: A handbook for end-of-life healthcare practitioners* (pp. 226–241). New York: Columbia University Press.

Silverman, J., Raj, A., Mucci, L., & Hathaway, J. (2001). Dating violence against adolescent girls and associated substance use, unhealthy weight control, sexual risk behavior, pregnancy, and suicidality. *Journal of American Medical Association, 286*(5), 572–579.

Silvern, L., & Kaersvang, L. (1989). The traumatized children of violent marriages. *Child Welfare, 68*, 421–436.

Silverstein, M., & Bengtson, V. (1997). Intergenerational solidarity and the structure of adult child-parent relationships in American families. *American Journal of Sociology, 103*, 429–460.

Silverstein, M., & Bengtson, V. (2001). Intergenerational solidarity and the structure of adult child-parent relationships in American families. In A. Walker, M. Manoogian-O'Dell, L. McGraw, & D. L. White (Eds.), *Families in later life: Connections and transitions* (pp. 53–61). Thousand Oaks, CA: Pine Forge.

Silverstein, M., & Long, J. (1998). Trajectories of grandparents' perceived solidarity with adult grandchildren: A growth curve analysis over 23 years. *Journal of Marriage and the Family, 60*, 912–923.

Simeonsson, R., Edmondson, R., Smith, T., Carnahan, S., & Bucy, J. (1995). Family involvement in multidisciplinary team evaluation: Professional and parent perspectives. *Child: Care, Health, and Development, 21*(3), 199–215.

Simmons, H. C. (2005). Religion, spirituality and aging for "The Aging" themselves. *Journal of Gerontological Social Work, 45*(1–2), 41–49.

Simmons, R. (2003). *Odd girl out: The hidden culture of aggression in girls.* Orlando, FL: Harcourt Trade Publishing.

Singer, M. I., Anglin, T. M., Song, L.Y., & Lunghofer, L. (1995). Adolescents' exposure to violence and associated symptoms of psychological trauma. *Journal of American Medical Association, 273*(6), 477–482.

Singh, L., Morgan, J., & Best, C. (2002). Infants' listening preferences: Baby talk or happy talk? *Infancy, 3*, 365–394.

Sitzer, A. R. (1998). Early discharge and the neonate. *Clinical Pediatrics, 37*(10), 617–620.

Skaalvik, S., & Skaalvik, E. (2004). Frames of reference for self-evaluation of ability in mathematics. *Psychological Reports, 94*, 619–632.

Skinner, B. F. (1957). *Verbal behavior.* Englewood Cliffs, NJ: Prentice-Hall.

Skolnick, A., & Skolnick, J. (1996). *The family in transition* (9th ed.). Reading, MA: Addison-Wesley.

Sleeter, C. (1995). White pre-service students and multicultural education coursework. In J. M. Larkin & C. E. Sleeter (Eds.), *Developing multicultural teacher education curricula* (pp. 17–30). Albany, NY: State University of New York Press.

Sloter, E., Schmid, T. E., Marchetti, F., Eskenzai, B., Nath, J., & Wyrobek, A. J. (2006). Quantitative effects of male age on sperm motion. *Human Reproduction, 21*(11), 2868–2875.

Small, S., Silverberg, S., & Kerns, D. (1993). Adolescents' perceptions of the costs and benefits of engaging in health-compromising behaviors. *Journal of Youth and Adolescence, 22*, 73–87.

Smetana, J. G., Killen, M., & Turiel, E. (1991). Children's reasoning about interpersonal and moral conflicts. *Child Development, 62,* 629–644.

Smith, A., Dannison L., & Vach-Hasse, T. (1998). When grandma is mom. *Childhood Education, 75*(1), 12–16.

Smith, C., & Denton, M. L. (2005). *Soul searching: The religious and spiritual lives of American teenagers.* Oxford: Oxford University Press.

Smith, C., Denton, M. L., Faris, R., & Regnerus, M. (2002). Mapping American adolescent religious participation. *Journal for the Scientific Study of Religion, 41*(4), 597–612.

Smith, D., Prentice, R., Thompson, D., & Hermann, W. (1975). Association of extrogenous estrogen and endometrial carcinoma. *New England Journal of Medicine, 293*(23), 1164–1167.

Smith, D., Stormshak, E., Chamberlain, P., & Whaley, R. (2001). Placement disruption in foster care. *Journal of Emotional and Behavioral Disorders, 9,* 200–211.

Smith, J. D., & Polloway, E. A. (1993). Institutionalization, involuntary sterilization, and mental retardation: Profiles from the history of the practice. *Mental Retardation, 314,* 208–214.

Smith, J., O'Connor, I., & Berthelsen, D. (1996). The effects of witnessing domestic violence on young children's psycho-social adjustment. *Australian Social Work, 49*(4), 3–10.

Smith, M. A., Acheson, L. S., Byrd, J. E., Curtis, P., Day, T. W., Frank, S. H., et al. (1991). A critical review of labor and birth care. *Journal of Family Practice, 33*(3), 281–293.

Smyer, M. A., Gatz, M., Simi, N. L., & Pedersen, N. L. (1998). Childhood adoption: Long-term effects in adulthood. *Psychiatry: Interpersonal and Biological Processes, 61*(3), 191.

Snarey, J. (1993). *How fathers care for the next generation: A four-decade study.* Cambridge, MA: Harvard University Press.

Snyder, H., & Sickmund, M. (2006). *Juvenile offenders and victims: 2006 national report.* U.S. Department of Justice, Office of Justice Programs, Office of Juvenile Justice and Delinquency Prevention.

Social Security Administration. (n.d.). *Full retirement age goes from 65 to . . . 66 . . . 67.* Retrieved June 25, 2002, from http://www.ssa.gov/pub/retirechart.htm

Solomon, R. C. (1988). *About love: Reinventing romance for modern times.* New York: Simon & Schuster.

Solomon, Z., & Mikulincer, M. (2006). Trajectories of PTSD: A 20-year longitudinal study. *American Journal of Psychiatry, 163*(4), 659–666.

Sommers, C. H. (2000). *The war against boys: How misguided feminism is harming our young men.* New York: Simon & Schuster.

Song, Y., & Lu, H. (2002). *Early childhood poverty: A statistical profile (March 2002).* New York: National Center for Children in Poverty. Retrieved August 21, 2002, from http://cpmcnet.columbia.edu/dept/nccp/ecp302.html

Sonfield, A. (2003). Preventing unintended pregnancy: The need and the means. *The Guttmacher Report on Public Policy, 6*(5), 7–10.

Soto, O. (2001, June 3). Drug-assisted date rapes on rise, hard to prosecute. *San Diego Union Tribune.* Retrieved August 26, 2002, from http://www.vachss.com/help_text/archive/drug_assisted.html

Souza, J. P., Oliveria-Neto, A., Surita, F. G., Cecatti, J. G., Arnaral, E., & Pinto e Silva, J. L. (2006). The prolongation of somatic support in a pregnant woman with brain-death: A case report. *Reproductive Health, 3,* 3.

Speare, A., Jr., & Avery, R. (1993). Who helps whom in older parent-child families? *Journal of Gerontology, 48,* S64–S73.

Spector-Mersel, G. (2006). Never-aging stories: Western hegemonic masculinity scripts. *Journal of Gender Studies, 15*(1), 67–82.

Spencer, M. (1985). Black children's race awareness, racial attitudes and self concept: A reinterpretation. *Annual Progress in Child Psychiatry & Child Development,* 616–630.

Spencer, M. B., Harpalani, V., Fegley, S., Dell'Angelo, T., & Seaton, G. (2003). Identity, self, and peers in context: A culturally sensitive, developmental framework for analysis. In R. M. Lerner, F. Jacobs, and D. Wertlieb (Eds.), *Handbook of applied developmental science, Vol. 1* (pp. 123–142). Thousand Oaks, CA: Sage.

Spencer, N., & Logan, S. (2002). Social influences on birth weight: Risk factors for low birth weight are strongly influenced by the social environment. *Archives of Disease in Childhood: Fetal and Neonatal Edition, 86*(1), 6–8.

Sperling, D. (2004). The maternal brain death. *American Journal of Law and Medicine, 30*(4), 453–500.

Spieker, S., Nelson, D., & Petras, A. (2003). Joint influence of child care and infant attachment security for cognitive and language outcomes of low-income toddlers. *Infant Behavior & Development, 26*(3), 326–344.

Spillman, B. (2003). Changes in elderly disability rates and the implications for health care utilization and cost. Washington, DC: Urban Institute.

Spiro, A. (2001). Health in midlife: Toward a life-span view. In M. Lachmann (Ed.), *Handbook of midlife development* (pp. 156–187). New York: Wiley.

Spitz, I. M., Bardin, C. W., Benton, L., & Robbins, A. (1998). Early pregnancy termination with mifepristone and misoprostol in the United States. *The New England Journal of Medicine, 338*(18), 983–987.

Spitze, G., Logan, J., Joseph, G., & Lee, E. (1994). Middle generations and the well-being of men and women. *Journal of Gerontology: Social Sciences, 49,* S107–S116.

Splete, J. (2002). New tool assesses ectopic pregnancy (Microculdoscopy). *OB GYN News, 37*(3), 1–2.

Spring, J. (2004). *Deculturalization and the struggle for educational equality.* New York: McGraw-Hill.

Stacey, J. (1996). *In the name of the family: Rethinking family values in the postmodern age.* Boston: Beacon.

Stack, C. (1974). *All our kin.* New York: Harper & Row.

Stamler, J., Stamler, R., Neaton, J., Wentworth, D., Daviglus, M., Garside, D., et al. (1999). Low risk-factor profile and long-term cardiovascular and noncardiovascular mortality and life expectancy: Findings for 5 large cohorts of young adult and middle-aged men and women. *Journal of the American Medical Association, 282,* 2012–2018.

Staudinger, U., & Bluck, S. (2001). A view on midlife development from life-span theory. In M. Lachman (Ed.), *Handbook of midlife development* (pp. 3–39). New York: Wiley.

Stefankiewicz, J., Kurzawa, R., & Drozdzik, M. (2006). Environmental factors disturbing fertility in men. *Ginekologia Polska, 77*(2), 163–169.

Stein, L. D. (2004) Human genome: End of the beginning. *Nature, 431,* 915–916.

Steinhauer, J. (1995, April 10). Big benefits in marriage, studies say. *New York Times,* p. A10.

Stepp, L. S. (1999, July 8). Parents are alarmed by an unsettling new fad in middle schools: Oral sex. *The Washington Post,* p. A1.

Sternberg, K. J., Lamb, M. E., Greenbaum, C., Cicchetti, D., Dawut, S., Cortes, R. M., et al. (1993). Effects of domestic violence on children's behavior problems and depression. *Developmental Psychology, 29,* 44–52.

Sternberg, S., Wolfson, C., & Baumgarten, M. (2000). Undetected dementia in community-dwelling older people. *Journal of the American Geriatrics Society, 48*(11), 1430–1434.

Sterns, H., & Huyck, M. (2001). The role of work in midlife. In M. Lachman (Ed.), *Handbook of midlife development* (pp. 447–486). New York: Wiley.

Stevens, S. J., & Patton, T. (1998). Residential treatment for drug addicted women and their children: Effective treatment strategies. *Drugs and Society, 13,* 235–249.

Stewart, A., & Vandewater, E. (1998). The course of generativity. In D. McAdams & E. de St. Aubin (Eds.), *Generativity and adult development: How and why we care for the next generation* (pp. 75–100). Washington, DC: American Psychological Association.

Stockard, J., & O'Brien, R. (2002). Cohort effects on suicide rates: International variation. *American Sociological Review, 67,* 854–872.

Stokes, J., & Greenstone, J. (1981). Helping black grandparents and older parents cope with child rearing: A group method. *Child Welfare, 60*(10), 691–701.

Stolzenberg, R. M., Blair-Loy, M., & Waite, L. J. (1995). Religious participation in early adulthood: Age and family life cycle effects on church membership. *American Sociological Review, 60*(1), 84–104.

Stouthamer-Loeber, M., & Wei, E. H. (1998). The precursors of young fatherhood and its effect on delinquency of teenage males. *Journal of Adolescent Health, 22,* 56–65.

Stovall, K., & Dozier, M. (1998). Infants in foster care: An attachment theory perspective. *Adoption Quarterly, 2*(1), 55–88.

Strathearn, L., Gary, P., & O'Callaghan, M. (2001). Childhood neglect and cognitive development in extremely low birth weight infants: A prospective study. *Pediatrics, 108*(1), 142–152.

Strauss, L. T., Herndon, J., Chang, J., Parker, W. Y., Bowens, S. V., & Berg, C. J. (2002). *Centers for Disease Control and Prevention. Abortion Surveillance—United States, 2002.* Retrieved November 15, 2006, from http://www.cdc.gov/mmwr/preview/mmwrhtml/ss5407a1.htm

Stroberg, P., Hedelin, H., & Ljunggren, C. (2006). Prescribing all phosphodiesterase 5 inhibitors to a patient with erectile dysfunction—a realistic and feasible option in everyday clinical practice—outcome of a simple treatment regime. *European Urology, 49*(5), 900–907.

Strock, M. (2004). *Autism Spectrum Disorders (Pervasive Developmental Disorders)* (NIH Publication No. NIH-04-5511). Bethesda, MD: National Institute of Mental Health. Retrieved January 15, 2007, from http://www.nimh.nih.gov/publicat/autism.cfm

Strock, M. (2006). *Attention Deficit Hyperactivity Disorder.* Bethesda, MD: National Institute of Mental Health. Retrieved December 5, 2006, from http://www.nimh.nih.gov/publicat/NIMHadhdpub.pdf

Stroebe, M., Stroebe, W., & Hansson, R. (1993). *Handbook on bereavement: Theory, research and intervention.* New York: Cambridge University Press.

Subramanian, S. V., Kubzansky, L., Berman, L., Fay, M., & Kawachi, I. (2006) Neighborhood effects on the self-rated health of elders: Uncovering the relative importance of structural and service-related neighborhood environments. *The Journals of Gerontology: Series B; Psychological Sciences and Social Sciences, 61B*(3), 153–161.

Substance Abuse and Mental Health Services Administration. (2000). *Uniform Facility Data Set (UFDS)* (DHHS: Publication No. (SMA) 00-3463). Rockville, MD: Author.

Substance Abuse and Mental Health Services Administration. (2005). *Overview of findings from the 2004 National Survey on Drug Use and Health* (Office of Applied Studies, NSDUH Series H-27, DHHS Publication No. SMA 05-4061). Rockville, MD: Author.

Sue, D. W., & McGoldrick, M. (2005). *Multicultural social work practice*. Hoboken, NJ: Wiley.

Suh, E., & Abel, E. (1990). The impact of violence on the children of the abused. *Journal of Independent Social Work, 4*(4), 27–43.

Sum, A., Fogg, N., & Mangum, G. (2000). *Confronting the youth demographic challenge: The labor market prospects of out-of-school young adults*. Baltimore, MD: Sar Levitan Center for Social Policy Studies.

Summer, L., O'Neill, G., & Shirey, L. (1999). *Chronic conditions: A challenge for the 21st century*. Washington, DC: National Academy on an Aging Society.

Sun, A., Shillington, A., Hohman, M., & Jones, L. (2001). Caregiver AOD use, case substantiation, and AOD treatment: Studies based on two southwestern counties. *Child Welfare, 80*(2), 151–177.

Sun, S. S., Schubert, C. M., Chumlea, W. C., Roche, A. F., Kulin, H. E., Lee, P. A., et al. (2002). National estimates of the timing of sexual maturation and racial differences among U.S. children. *Pediatrics, 110*(5), 911–919.

Swap, S. M. (1993). *Developing home-school partnerships: From concepts to practice*. New York: Teachers College Press.

Sweet, J., & Bumpass, L. (1996). *The national survey of families and households—Waves 1 and 2*. Madison, WI: Center for Demography and Ecology, University of Wisconsin-Madison.

Sword, W., Watt, S., & Krueger, P. (2006). Postpartum health, service needs, and access to care experiences of immigrant and Canadian-born women. *Journal of Obstetric Gynecological and Neonatal Nurses, 35*(6), 717–727.

Szinovacz, M. (1998). Grandparents today. A demographic profile. *The Gerontologist, 38,* 37–52.

Taddio, A., Shah, V., Gilbert-Macleod, C., & Katz, J. (2002). Conditioning and hyperalgesia in newborns exposed to repeated heel lances. *Journal of American Medical Association, 288*(7), 857–861.

Taffett, G. (1996). Age-related physiologic changes. In D. Reuben, T. Yoshikawa, & R. Besdine, R. (Eds.), *Geriatric review syllabus* (3rd ed., pp. 11–15). Dubuque, IA: Kendall/Hunt.

Takahashi, E. A., & Turnbull, J. E. (1994). New findings in psychiatric genetics: Implications for social work practice. *Social Work in Health Care, 20*(2), 1–21.

Takahashi, K. (1990). Are the key assumptions of the "strange situation" procedure universal? A view from Japanese research. *Human Development, 33,* 23–30.

Tate, A., Dezateux, C., Cole, T., and the Millennium Cohort Study Child Health Group. (2006). Is infant growth changing? *International Journal of Obesity, 30,* 1094–1096.

Tatum, B. D. (1992). Talking about race, learning about racism: The application of racial identity development in the classroom. *Harvard Educational Review, 62*(1), 1–24.

Tatum, B. D. (1999). *Why are all the Black kids sitting together in the cafeteria? And other conversations about race* (rev. ed.). New York: Basic Books.

Tay, J. I., Moore, J., & Walker, J. J. (2000). Ectopic pregnancy. *British Medical Journal, 320*(7239), 916–922.

Taylor, H. (2000). Meeting the needs of lesbian and gay young adolescents. *Clearing House, 73*(4), 221–224.

Taylor, J. M., Gilligan, C., & Sullivan, A. M. (1995). *Between voice and silence: Women and girls, race and relationship*. Cambridge, MA: Harvard University Press.

Taylor, M. Y., Wyatt-Asmead, J. W., Gray, J., Bofill, J. A., Martin, R., & Morrison, J. C. (2006). Pregnancy loss after first-trimester viability in women with sickle cell trait: Time for a reappraisal? *American Journal of Obstetrics and Gynecology, 194*(6), 1604–1609.

Taylor, W., Blair, S., Cummings, S., Wun, C., & Malina, R. (1999). Childhood and adolescent physical activity patterns and adult physical activity. *Medicine and Science in Sports and Exercise, 31,* 118–123.

Teicher, M. (2002). Scars that won't heal: The neurobiology of child abuse. *Scientific American, 286*(3), 68–75.

Teitelman, J. L. (1995). Homosexuality. In G. L. Maddox (Ed.), *The encyclopedia of aging: A comprehensive resource in gerontology and geriatrics* (2nd ed., p. 270). New York: Springer.

Thomas, A., & Chess, S. (1986). The New York longitudinal study: From infancy to early adult life. In R. Plomin & J. Dunn (Eds.), *The study of temperament: Changes, continuities, and challenges* (pp. 39–52). Hillside, NJ: Lawrence Erlbaum.

Thomas, A., Chess, S., & Birch, H. G. (1968). *Temperament and behavior disorders in children.* New York: New York University Press.

Thomas, A., Chess, S., & Birch, H. G. (1970). The origin of personality. *Scientific American, 223,* 102–109.

Thomlison, B. (2004). Child maltreatment: A risk and protective factor perspective. In M. F. (Ed.), *Risk and resilience in childhood: An ecological perspective* (2nd ed., pp. 89–131). Washington, DC: NASW.

Thompson, P. M., Giedd, J. N., Woods, R. P., MacDonald, D., Evans, A. C., & Toga, A. W. (2000). Growth patterns in the developing brain detected by using continuum mechanical tensor maps. *Nature, 404*(6774), 190–193.

Thompson, R., & Nelson, C. (2001). Developmental science and the media: Early brain development. *American Psychologist, 56*(1), 5–15.

Thornberry, T. P., Smith, C. A., & Howard, G. J. (1997). Risk factors for teenage fatherhood. *Journal of Marriage & Family, 59,* 505–523.

Thursby, G. (1992). Islamic, Hindu and Buddhist conceptions of aging. In T. Cole, D. van Tassel, & R. Kastenbaum (Eds.), *Handbook of humanities and aging* (pp. 175–196). New York: Springer.

Tiedje, L. B. (2001). Fathers' coping style, antenatal preparation, and experiences of labor and postpartum. *MCN, The American Journal of Maternal and Child Nursing, 26*(2), 108.

Tiet, A., Bird, H., Hoven, C., Wu, P., Moore, R., & Davies, M. (2001). Resilience in the face of maternal psychopathology and adverse life events. *Journal of Child and Family Studies, 10*(3), 347–365.

Tiran, D., & Chummun, H. (2004*).* Complementary therapies to reduce physiologic stress in pregnancy. *Complementary Therapy for Nursing Midwifery, 10*(3), 162–167.

Tobin, S. (1988). Preservation of the self in old age. *Social Casework: The Journal of Contemporary Social Work, 66* (9), 550–555.

Tolstrup, J. Kjaer, S., Munk, C., Madsen, L., Ottesen, B., Bergholt, T., et al. (2003). Does caffeine and alcohol intake before pregnancy predict the occurrence of spontaneous abortion? *Human Reproduction, 18*(12), 2704–2710.

Tomal, A. (1999). Determinants of teenage birth rates as an unpooled sample: Age matters for socioeconomic predictors. *American Journal of Economics and Sociology, 58*(1), 57.

Tout, K., & Zaslow, M. (2003). Public investments in child care quality: Needs, challenges, and opportunities. In R. M. Lerner, F. Jacobs, and D. Wertlieb (Eds.), *Handbook of applied developmental science, Vol. 1* (pp. 339–366). Thousand Oaks, CA: Sage.

Trattner, W. I. (1994). *From poor law to welfare state: A history of social welfare in America* (5th ed.). New York: Free Press.

Trifiletti, R. (2001). Febrile seizures following childhood vaccinations: A risk worth taking. *Neurology Alert, 20*(2), 15.

Trimble, J., Gay, H., & Docherty, J. (1986). Characterization of the tumor-associated 38-kd protein of herpes simples virus Type II. *Journal of Reproductive Medicine, 31*(5), 399–409.

Tueth, M. J. (1993). Anxiety in the older patient: Differential diagnosis and treatment. *Geriatrics, 48*, 51–54.

Turner, H., Finkelhor, D., & Ormord, R. (2006). The effect of lifetime victimization on the mental health of children and adolescents. *Social Science & Medicine, 62*(1), 13–27.

Tutty, L., & Wagar, J. (1994). The evolution of a group for young children who have witnessed family violence. *Social Work With Groups, 17*(1/2), 89–104.

Udry, J. R. (1993). The politics of sex research. *Journal of Sex Research, 30*(2), 103–110.

Uhlenberg, P. (1996). Mutual attraction: Demography and life-course analysis. *The Gerontologist, 36*(2), 226–229.

Ulizzi, L., & Zonta, L. (1994). Sex ratio and selection by early mortality in humans: Fifty year analysis in different ethnic groups. *Human Biology, 66*(6), 1037–1048.

UNAID. (2005). *Global summary of the HIV and AIDS epidemic in 2004.* Retrieved April 24, 2005, from http://www.unaids.org/en/resources/epidemiology

UNAID. (2006). *06 report on the global AIDS epidemic: Executive summary.* Retrieved January 13, 2007, from http://data.unaids.org/pub/GlobalReport/2006/2006_GR-Executive Summary_en.pdf

UNICEF. (2005). *The state of the world's children 2006: Excluded and invisible.* New York: Author.

Underwood, M. K. (2003). *Social aggression among girls.* New York: Guilford Press.

UNICEF Innocenti Research Centre. (2005). *Child poverty in rich countries 2005* (Innocenti Report Card No. 6). Florence, Italy: Author.

United Nations Children's Fund. (2000a). A league table of child poverty in rich nations. *Innocenti Report Card (1).* Retrieved December 3, 2006, from http://www.unicef-icdc.org/publications/pdf/repcard1e.pdf

United Nations Children's Fund. (2000b). *Poverty reduction begins with children.* New York: Author. Retrieved January 15, 2007, from http://www.unicef.org/publications/index_5616.html

United Nations Development Program. (2005). *Human development report 2005: International cooperation at the crossroads: Aid, trade, and security in an unequal world.* New York: Oxford University Press.

Uotinen, V. (1998). Age identification: A comparison between Finnish and North-American cultures. *International Journal of Aging & Human Development, 46*(2), 109–125.

Update: Interim recommendations for antimicrobial prophylaxis for children and breast-feeding mothers and treatment for children with anthrax. (2001, November 16). *Morbidity and Mortality Weekly Report.* Electronic collection: A80485416.

U.S. Bureau of Labor Statistics. (1997). Developments in women's labor force participation. *Monthly Labor Review, September 1977* (pp. 41–46). Washington, DC: U.S. Government Printing Office.

U.S. Bureau of the Census. (1999). *Statistical abstract of the United States.* Washington, DC: U.S. Government Printing Office.

U.S. Bureau of the Census. (2001a). *Children of "baby boomers" and immigrants boost school enrollment to equal all-time high.* Retrieved February 22, 2002, from http//:www.census.gov/pressrelease/www/2001/cb01–52.html

U.S. Bureau of the Census. (2001b). *Age: 2000.* Washington, DC: U.S. Government Printing Office.

U.S. Bureau of the Census. (2001c). *The 65 years and over population: 2000* (C2KBR/01-10). Washington, DC: U.S. Department of Commerce.

U.S. Bureau of the Census. (2004). *We the people: Aging in the United States* (Census 2000 Special reports). Washington, DC: U.S. Department of Commerce.

U.S. Bureau of the Census. (2005*). 2005 American community survey.* Retrieved January 14, 2007, from http://www.census.gov/hhes/www/disability/2005acs.html

U.S. Bureau of the Census. (n.d.). *The living arrangements of children in 2003. Population profile of the United States: Dynamic version.* Washington, DC: Author. Retrieved November 15, 2006, from http://www.census.gov/population/pop-profile/dynamic/LivArrChildren.pdf

U.S. Department of Energy Human Genome Program. (2001, October*). Genomics and its impact on medicine and society: A 2001 primer.* Washington, DC: U.S. Department of Energy.

U.S. Department of Health and Human Services. (1995). *A nation's shame: Fatal child abuse and neglect in the United States* (Report of the U.S. Advisory Board on Child Abuse and Neglect). Washington, DC: U.S. Government Printing Office.

U.S. Department of Health and Human Services. (2000). *Trends in the well-being of America's children and youth.* Washington, DC: U.S. Government Printing Office.

U.S. Department of Health and Human Services. (2001a). New CDC report shows teen birth rate hits record low. *HHS News.* Retrieved April 7, 2002, from http//:www.cdc.gov/nchs/releases/01news/newbirth.html

U.S. Department of Health and Human Services. (2001b). *Child maltreatment 1999: Reports from the states to the National Child Abuse and Neglect Data System.* Washington, DC: U.S. Government Printing Office.

U.S. Department of Health and Human Services. (2001c). *Youth violence: A report of the surgeon general.* Rockville, MD: U.S. Department of Health and Human Services, Substance Abuse and Mental Health Services Administration, Center for Mental Health Services.

U.S. Department of Health and Human Services. (2006). Center for Medicare and Medicaid Services: *Coordination of benefits Part D: Overview.* Retrieved December 10, 2006, from http://www.cms.hhs.gov/COBPartD/

U.S. Department of Health and Human Services, Administration on Children, Youth, and Families. (2005). *Child maltreatment 2003.* Washington, DC: U.S. Government Printing Office.

U.S. Department of Health and Human Services, Centers for Disease Control and Prevention. National Center for Injury Prevention and Control. (2001). *Injury fact book 2001–2002.* Atlanta, GA: Centers for Disease Control and Prevention. Retrieved October 9, 2006, from http://www.cdc.gov/ncipc/fact_book/factbook.htm

U.S. Department of Health and Human Services, Health Resources and Services. Administration, Maternal and Child Health Bureau. (1995). *Adolescent health fact sheet.* Washington, DC: U.S. Government Printing Office.

U.S. Department of Health and Human Services, Public Health Service. (1991). *Healthy people 2000.* Washington, DC: U.S. Government Printing Office.

U.S. Department of Health and Human Services/U.S. Department of Agriculture. (2005). *Dietary guidelines for Americans 2005.* Retrieved November 15, 2006, from http://www.healthierus.gov/dietaryguidelines

U.S. Department of Justice Bureau of Justice Statistics. (2000). *Women ages 16 to 24 experience the highest rates of violence by current or form partners.* Washington, DC: Author.

U.S. Federal Bureau of Prisons. (1998). *A profile of female offenders.* Washington, DC: Author.

U.S. Food and Drug Administration. (2005). *FDA updates labeling for the Ortho Evra contraceptive patch.* Retrieved December 12, 2006, from http://www.fda.gov/bbs/topics/news/2005/NEW01262.html

U.S. Food and Drug Administration. (2006). *CDER drug and biologic approvals for calendar year updated through November 30, 2006.* Retrieved December 12, 2006, from http://www.fda/gov/cder/rdmt/InternetNDA06.htm

Vahtera, J., Kivimaki, M., Vaananen, A., Linna, A., Pentti, JL., Helenius, H., et al. (2006). Sex differences in health effects of family death or illness: Are women more vulnerable than men? *Psychosomatic Medicine, 68*(2), 283–289.

Vaillant, G. (1977). *Adaptation to life.* Boston: Little, Brown.

Vaillant, G. (1993). *The wisdom of the ego.* Cambridge, MA: Harvard University Press.

Vaillant, G. (1998). Are social supports in late midlife a cause or a result of successful physical aging? *Psychological Medicine, 28,* 1159–1168.

Vaillant, G. (2002). *Aging well: Surprising guideposts to a happier life from the Landmark Harvard Study of Adult Development.* Boston: Little, Brown.

Vallacher, R., & Nowak, A. (1998). *Dynamical social psychology.* New York: Guilford.

Valsiner, J. (1989a). *Human development and culture: The social nature of personality and its study.* Lexington, MA: Lexington Books.

Valsiner, J. (1989b). Social development in infancy and toddlerhood. In *Human development and culture: The social nature of personality and its study* (pp. 163–253). Lexington, MA: Lexington Books.

Valsiner, J. (2000). *Culture and human development.* Thousand Oaks, CA: Sage.

van de Beek, C., Thijssen J. H., Cohen-Kettenis, P. T., van Goozen, S. H., & Buitelaar, J. K. (2004). Relationships between sex hormones assessed in amniotic fluid, and maternal and umbilical cord serum: What is the best source of information to investigate the effects of fetal hormonal exposure? *Hormones and Behavior, 46*(5), 663–669.

Vandell, D. L., & Wolfe, B. (2000). *Child care quality: Does it matter and does it need to be improved?* (Special Report #78). Madison, WI: Institute for Research on Poverty.

van den Akker, O. B. (2005). Coping, quality of life, and psychological symptoms in three groups of sub-fertile women. *Patient Education and Counseling, 57*(2), 183–189.

van der Hulst, L. A., van Teijlengen, E. R., & Bonsel, G. J. (2004). Does a pregnant woman's intended place of birth influence her attitudes toward and occurrence of obstetric interventions? *Birth: Issues in Perinatal Care, 31*(1), 28–33.

van der Spuy, Z. M., & Dyer, S. J. (2004). The pathogenesis of infertility and early pregnancy loss in polycystic ovary syndrome. *Best Practice and Research: Clinical Obstetrics and Gynaecology, 18*(5), 755–771.

Van der Vegt, G., Eman, B., & Van De Vliert, E. (2001). Patterns of interdependence in work teams: A two-level investigation of the relations with job and team satisfaction. *Personnel Psychology, 54,* 51–69.

Van der Wijden, C., Keijnen, J., & Van den Berk, T. (2003). Lactational amenorrhea for family planning. *Cochrane Database Systematic Review,* Issue 3, CD001329.

Vandivere, S., Moore, K. A., & Brown, B. (2000). Child well-being at the outset of welfare reform: An overview of the nation and 13 states. *New Federalism, National Survey of American Families,* Series B, No. B-23. Washington, DC: The Urban Institute.

Van Naarden Braun, K., Yeargin-Allsopp, M., & Lollar, D. (2006). Factors associated with leisure activity among young adults with developmental disabilities. *Research in Developmental Disabilities, 27,* 567–583.

Van Riper, M. (2001). Family-provider relationships and well-being in families with preterm infants in the NICU. *Heart and Lung: The Journal of Acute and Critical Care, 30*(1), 74–84.

Vatuk, S. (1992). Sexuality and the middle-aged woman in South Asia. In V. Kerns & J. K. Brown (Eds.), *In her prime: New views of middle-aged women.* Urbana: University of Illinois Press.

Vaughn, B., & Bost, K. (1999). Attachment and temperament. In J. Cassidy & P. Shaver (Eds.), *Handbook of attachment: Theory, research, and clinical applications* (pp. 198–225). New York: Guilford Press.

Vekemans, M. (1996). Cytogenetics. In J. J. Sciarra (Ed.), *Gynecology and obstetrics* (rev. ed., pp. 57–66). Philadelphia: Lippincott-Raven.

Vellery-Rodot, R. T. (1926). *The life of Pasteur.* Garden City, NY: Doubleday.

Veltman, L., & Miller, T. (1994). *Clinical handbook of child abuse and neglect.* Madison, CT: International Universities Press.

Veltman, M., & Browne, K. (2001). Three decades of child maltreatment research: Implications for the school years. *Trauma Violence & Abuse, 2*(3), 215–239.

Ventura, S. J., Martin, J. A., Curtin, S. C., & Mathews, T. J. (1998). Report of final natality statistics: 1996. *Monthly Vital Statistics Report, 46*(225), 1–99.

Verhaak, C., Smeenk, J., Evers, A., van Minnen, A., Kremer, J., & Kraaimaat, F. (2005). Predicting emotional response to unsuccessful fertility treatment: A prospective study. *Journal of Behavioral Medicine, 28*(2), 181–190.

Verkuyten, M. (2005). Ethnic group identification and group evaluation among minority and majority groups: Testing the multiculturalism hypothesis. *Journal of Personality and Social Psychology, 88*(1), 121–138.

Verma, S., & Larson, R. (Eds.). (2003). *Examining adolescent leisure time across cultures. New directions for child and adolescent development, No. 99.* San Francisco: Jossey-Bass.

Vicary, J. R., Klingaman, L. R., & Harkness, W. L. (1995). Risk factors associated with date rape and sexual assault of adolescents. *Journal of Adolescence, 18*, 289–307.

Vissing, Y., Straus, M., Gelles, R., & Harrop, J. (1991). Verbal aggression by parents and psychosocial problems of children. *Child Abuse & Neglect, 15*(3), 223–238.

Vita, A., Terry, R., Hubert, H., & Fries, J. (1998). Aging, health risks, and cumulative disability. *New England Journal of Medicine, 338*, 1035–1041.

Vohr, B. R., Wright, L. L., Dusick, A. S., Mele, L., Verter, J., Steicher, J. J., et al. (2000). Neurodevelopmental and functional outcomes of extremely low birth weight infants: National Institute of Child Health and Human Development Neonatal Research Network 1994. *Pediatrics, 105*(6), 1216–1227.

Volgt, M., Hermanussen, M., Wittwer-Backofen, U., Fusch, C., & Hesse, V. (2006). Sex-specific differences in birth weight due to maternal smoking during pregnancy. *European Journal of Pediatrics, 165*(110), 757–761.

Volker, D. L. (2005). Control and end-of-life care: Does ethnicity matter? *American Journal of Hospice & Palliative Care, 22*(6), 442–446.

Volling, B., Blandon, A., & Kolak, A. (2006). Marriage, parenting, and the emergence of early self-regulation in the family system. *Journal of Child and Family Studies, 15*(4), 493–506.

Volkmar, F. R., Paul, R., Klin, A., & Cohen, D. J. (2005). *Handbook of autism and pervasive developmental disorders.* Hoboken, NJ: John Wiley.

von Salisch, M. (2001). Children's emotional development: Challenges in their relationships to parents, peers, and friends. *International Journal of Behavioral Development, 25*, 310–319.

Vuorenkoski, L., Kuure, O., Moilanen, I., Penninkilampi, V., & Myhrman, A. (2000). Bilingualism, school achievement, and mental wellbeing: A follow-up study of return migrant children. *Journal of Child Psychology and Psychiatry and Allied Disciplines, 41*(2), 261–266.

Vygotsky, L. (1986). *Thought and language.* Cambridge, MA: MIT Press.

Wachs, T. D. (2000). *Necessary but not sufficient: The respective roles of single and multiple influences on individual development.* Washington, DC: American Psychological Association.

Wacker, R. R., Roberto, K. A., & Piper, L. E. (1997). *Community resources for older adults: Programs and services in an era of change.* Thousand Oaks, CA: Pine Forge.

Wadensten, B. (2005). Introducing older people to the theory of gerotranscendence. *Journal of Advanced Nursing, 52*(4), 381–388.

Wahl, H., & Kruse, A. (2005). Historical perspectives of middle age within the life span. In S. Willis & M. Martin (Eds.), *Middle adulthood: A lifespan perspective* (pp. 3–34). Thousand Oaks, CA: Sage.

Waldenstrom, U., Hildingsson, I, Rubertsson, C., & Radestad, I. (2004). A negative birth experience: Prevalence and risk factors in a national sample. *Birth: Issues in Prenatal Care, 31*(4), 17–27.

Waldner, L., & Magruder, B. (1999). Coming out to parents: Perceptions of family relations, perceived resources, and identity expression as predictors of identity disclosure for gay and lesbian adolescents. *Journal of Homosexuality, 37*(2), 83–84.

Walker, A., Manoogian-O'Dell, M., McGraw, L., & White, D. (2001). *Families in later life: Connections and transitions.* Thousand Oaks, CA: Pine Forge.

Walker, L. (1989). A longitudinal study of moral reasoning. *Child Development, 5,* 33–78.

Walker, L., & Taylor, J. (1991). Family interactions and the development of moral reasoning. *Child Development, 62,* 262–283.

Walker, S., Berthelsen, D., & Irving, K. (2001). Temperament and peer acceptance in early childhood: Sex and social status differences. *Child Study Journal, 31*(3), 177–192.

Wallerstein, I. (1974). *The modern world system: Capitalist agriculture and the origins of the European world economy in the 16th century.* New York: Academic Press.

Wallerstein, I. (1979). *The capitalist world economy.* London: Cambridge University Press.

Wallerstein, J. S. (1983). Children of divorce: The psychological task of the child. *American Journal of Orthopsychiatry, 53,* 230–243.

Wallerstein, J. S., & Blakeslee, S. (1989). *Second chances: Men, women and children a decade after divorce.* New York: Ticknor & Fields.

Wallerstein, J. S., & Corbin, S. (1991). The child and the vicissitudes of divorce. In M. Lewis (Ed.), *Child and adolescent psychiatry: A comprehensive textbook* (pp. 1108–1118). Baltimore, MD: Williams & Wilkins.

Wallerstein, J. S., Corbin, S., & Lewis, J. (1988). Children of divorce: A ten year study. In E. Hetherington & J. Arasteh (Eds.), *Impact of divorce, single-parenting and step-parenting on children* (pp. 198–214). Hillsdale, NJ: Lawrence Erlbaum.

Walling, A. D. (2001). What is optimal strategy in diagnosing ectopic pregnancy? *American Family Physician, 64*(18), 1420–1421.

Walsh, F. (2005). Families in later life: Challenges and opportunities. In B. Carter & M. McGoldrick (Eds.), *The expanded family life style: Individual, family, and social perspectives* (3rd ed., pp. 307–326). Boston: Allyn & Bacon.

Walsh, F. (1998). *Strengthening family resilience.* New York: Guilford.

Wang, D., & Lin, R. S. (1999). Perinatal mortality in Taiwan. *Public Health, 113*(1), 27–33.

Wang, M., Walberg, H., & Reynolds, A. (2004). *Can unlike students learn together? Grade retention, tracking, and grouping.* Charlotte, NC: Information Age Publishing.

Wang, H., Parry, S., Macones, G., Sammel, M. D., Kuivaniemi, H., Tromp, G., et al. (2006). A functional SNP in the promoter of the *SERPINH1* gene increases risk of preterm premature rupture of membranes in African Americans. *Proceedings of the National Academy of Sciences of the United States of America (PNMS), 103*(36), 13463–13467.

Wang, R., Needham, L., & Barr, D. (2005). Effects of environmental agents on attainment of puberty: Considerations when assessing exposure to environmental chemicals in the National Children's Study. *Environmental Health Perspectives, 113*(8), 1100–1107.

Wang, Y., & Zhang, Q. (2006). Are American children and adolescents of low socioeconomic status at increased risk of obesity? Changes in the association between overweight and family income between 1971 and 2002. *American Journal of Clinical Nutrition, 84*(4), 707–716.

Ward, R. R., Logan, J., & Spitze, G. (1992). The influence of parent and child needs on coresidence in middle and later life. *Journal of Marriage and the Family, 54,* 209–221.

Ware, L. (1995). The aftermath of the articulate debate: The invention of inclusive education. In C. Clark, A. Dyson, & A. Millward (Eds.), *Towards inclusive schools?* (pp. 127–146). New York: Teachers College Press.

Waterstone, M., Bewley, S., Wolfe, C., & Murphy, D. J. (2001). Incidence and predictors of severe obstetric morbidity: Case-control study. *British Medical Journal, 322*(7294), 1089–1092.

Watkins, D. R. (2001). Spirituality in social work practice with older persons. In D. O. Moberg (Ed.), *Aging and spirituality: Spiritual dimensions of aging theory, research, practice, and policy* (pp. 133–146). New York: Haworth Pastoral.

Watson, J., & Crick, F. (1953). Molecular structure of nucleic acids. *Nature, 171,* 737–738.

Waxman, B. F. (1994). Up against eugenics: Disabled women's challenge to receive reproductive health services. *Sexuality and Disability, 12*(2), 155–171.

Weaver-Hightower, M. (2003). The "boy turn" in research on gender and education. *Review of Educational Research, 73*(4), 471–498.

Webb. N., & Dumpson, J. (2006). *Working with traumatized youth in child welfare.* New York: Guilford.

Wechselberger, G., Wolfram, D., Pulzl, P., Soelder, E., & Schoeller, T. (2006). Nerve injury caused by removal of an impantable hormonal contraceptive. *American Journal of Obstetrics and Gynecology, 195*(1), 323–326.

Weibel-Orlando, J. (2001). Grandparenting styles: Native American perspectives. In A. Walker, M. Manoogian-O'Dell, L. McGraw, & D. White (Eds.), *Families in later life: Connections and transitions* (pp. 139–145). Thousand Oaks, CA: Pine Forge.

Weinman, M. L., Buzi, R. S., & Smith, P. B. (2005). Addressing risk behaviors, service needs, and mental health issues in programs for young fathers. *Families in Society, 86*(2), 261–266.

Weinstock, H., Berman, S., & Cates, W. (2004). Sexually transmitted diseases among American youth: Incidence and prevalence estimates, 2000. *Perspectives on Sexual and Reproductive Health, 36*(1), 6–10.

Welsh, R. (1985). Spanking: A grand old American tradition? *Children Today, 14*(1), 25–29.

Wen, W., Shu, X., Jacobs, D., & Brown, J. (2001). The associations of maternal caffeine consumption and nausea with spontaneous abortions. *Epidemiology, 12*(10), 38–42.

Werner, E. (2000). Protective factors and individual resilience. In J. Shonkoff & S. Meisels (Eds.), *Handbook of early childhood intervention* (2nd ed., pp. 115–132). New York: Cambridge University Press.

Werner, E. E., & Smith, R. S. (1992). *Overcoming the odds: High risk children from birth to adulthood.* Ithaca, NY: Cornell University Press.

Werner, E. E., & Smith, R. S. (2001). *Journeys from childhood to midlife.* Ithaca, NY: Cornell University Press.

Wertheimer, R. (2003). *Poor families in 2001: Parents working less and children continue to lag behind.* Washington, DC: Child Trends. Retrieved January 15, 2007, from http://www.childtrends.org/Files/PoorFamiliesRB.pdf

Wertsch, J. V., del Rio, P., & Alvarez, A. (Eds.). (1995). *Sociocultural studies of the mind.* New York: Cambridge University Press.

West, J. (Ed.). (1991). *The Americans with Disabilities Act.* New York: Millbank Fund.

Weston, K. (1991). *Families we choose: Lesbians, gays, kinship.* New York: Columbia University Press.

Wethington, E., Kessler, R., & Pixley, J. (2004). Turning points in adulthood. In O. Brim, C. Ryff, & R. Kessler (Eds.), *How healthy are we? A national study of well-being at midlife* (pp. 586–613). Chicago: University of Chicago Press.

Weyermann, M., Beermann, C., Brenner, H., & Rothenbacher, D. (2006). Adponectin and leptin in maternal serum, cord blood, and breast milk. *Clinical Chemistry, 52*(11), 2095–2102.

Wheaton, B., & Gotlib, I. (1997). Trajectories and turning points over the life course: concepts and themes. In I. Gotlib & B. Wheaton (Eds.), *Stress and adversity over the life course: Trajectories and turning points* (pp. 1–25). Cambridge, UK: Cambridge University Press.

Whitbourne, S. (1986). *The me I know: A study of adult identity.* New York: Springer Verlag.

Whitbourne, S. (2001). The physical aging process in midlife: Interactions with psychological and sociocultural factors. In M. Lachman (Ed.), *Handbook of midlife development* (pp. 109–155). New York: Wiley.

Whitbourne, S., & Connolly, L. (1999). The developing self in midlife. In S. Willis & J. Reid (Eds.), *Life in the middle: Psychological and social development in middle age* (pp. 25–45). San Diego, CA: Academic Press.

White, L., & Edwards, J. (1993). Emptying the nest and parental well-being: An analysis of national panel data. *American Sociological Review, 55,* 235–242.

White, L., & Rogers, S. (1997). Strong support but uneasy relationships: Coresidence and adult children's relationships with their parents. *Journal of Marriage and the Family, 59,* 62–76.

White, L., Small, B. J., Petrovitch, H., Ross, G. W., Masaki, K., Abbott, R., et al. (2005). Recent clinical-pathologic research on the causes of dementia in late life: Update from the Honolulu-Asia aging study. *Journal of Geriatric Psychiatry and Neurology, 18*(4), 224–227.

White, N. R. (2003). Changing conceptions: Young people's views of partnering & parenting. *Journal of Sociology, 39*(2), 149–164.

Whiting, B. B., & Whiting, J. W. (1975). *Children of six cultures: A psycho-cultural analysis.* Cambridge, MA: Harvard University Press.

Wichstrom, L. (2001). The impact of pubertal timing on adolescents' alcohol use. *Journal of Research on Adolescence, 11,* 130–150.

Wickrama, K. A. S., Conger, R. D., & Abraham, W. T. (2005). Early adversity and later health: The intergenerational transmission of adversity through mental disorder and physical illness. *The Journal of Gerontology: Series B Psychological Sciences and Social Sciences, 60B,* 125–129.

Widmayer, S., Peterson, L., & Larner, M. (1990). Predictors of Haitian-American infant development at twelve months. *Child Development, 61,* 410–415.

Widmer, M. A., Ellis, G. D., & Trunnell, E. P. (1996). Measurement of ethical behavior in leisure among high- and low-risk adolescents. *Adolescence, 31,* 397–408.

Wigert, H., Johannson, R., Berg, M., & Hellstrom, A. L. (2006). Mothers' experiences of having their children in a neonatal intensive care unit. *Scandinavian Journal of Caring Sciences, 20*(10), 35–41.

Wilber, K. (1977). *The spectrum of consciousness.* Wheaton, IL: Quest.

Wilber, K. (1995). *Sex, ecology, spirituality: The spirit of evolution.* Boston: Shambhala.

William T. Grant Foundation, Commission on Work, Family, and Citizenship. (1988). *The forgotten half: Pathways to success for America's youth and young families.* New York: Author.

Williams, D. R. (2005). The health of U.S. racial and ethnic populations. *The Journal of Gerontology: Series B Psychological Sciences and Social Sciences, 60B,* 53–63.

Willis, S., & Martin, M. (Eds.). (2005). *Middle adulthood: A lifespan perspective.* Thousand Oaks, CA: Sage.

Willis, S., & Schaie, K. (1999). Intellectual functioning in midlife. In S. Willis & J. Reid (Eds.), *Life in the middle: Psychological and social development in middle age* (pp. 234–247). San Diego, CA: Academic Press.

Willis, S., & Schaie, K. W. (2005). Cognitive trajectories in midlife and cognitive functioning in old age. In S. Willis & M. Martin (Eds.), *Middle adulthood: A lifespan perspective* (pp. 243–275). Thousand Oaks, CA: Sage.

Wilmoth, J. M., & Longino, C. F. (2006). Demographic trends that will shape U.S. policy in the twenty-first century. *Research on Aging, 28*(3), 269–288.

Wilson, R. (1966). *Feminine forever.* New York: M. Evans.

Winkler, I., & Cowan, N. (2005). From sensory to long-term memory: Evidence from auditory memory reactivation studies. *Experimental Psychology, 52*(1), 3–20.

Winters, W. G. (1993). *African American mothers and urban schools: The power of participation.* New York: Lexington Books.

Wiseman, R. (2002). *Queen bees and wannabes: Helping your daughter survive cliques, gossip, boyfriends, and other realities of adolescence.* New York: Crown Publishers.

Wisner, K., Chambers, C., & Sit, D. (2006). Postpartum depression: A major public health problem. *Journal of American Medical Association, 296*(21), 2616–2618.

Wolfner, G., & Gelles, R. (1993). A profile of violence toward children: A national study. *Child Abuse and Neglect, 17,* 197–212.

Wolak, J., Mitchell, K. J., & Finkelhor, D. (2003). Escaping or connecting? Characteristics of youth who form close online relationships. *Journal of Adolescence, 26,* 105–119.

Wolak, J., Mitchell, K. J., & Finkelhor, D. (2006). *Online victimization of youth: Five years later.* Retrieved November 15, 2006, from http://www.unh.edu/ccrc/pdf/CV138.pdf

Woodward, L. J., Anderson, J., Austin, N. C., Howard, K., & Inder, T. E. (2006). Neonatal MRI to predict neurodevelopmental outcomes in preterm infants. *The New England Journal of Medicine, 355*(7), 685–694.

Woody, D. J., & Green, R. (2001). The influence of race/ ethnicity and gender on psychological and social well-being. *Journal of Ethnic & Cultural Diversity in Social Work, 9*(3/4), 151–166.

Wooldredge, J. D., & Masters, K. (1993). Confronting problems faced by pregnant inmates in state prisons. *Crime and Delinquency, 39*(2), 195–203.

Woollett, A., Dosanjh-Matwala, N., Nicolson, P., Marshall, H., Djhanbakhch, O., & Hadlow, J. (1995). The ideas and experiences of pregnancy and childbirth of Asian and non-Asian women in East London. *British Journal of Medical Psychology, 68*, 65–84.

Worden, J. W. (2001). *Grief counseling and grief therapy: A handbook for the mental health practitioner* (3rd ed.). New York: Springer.

World Health Organization. (2003a). *Causes of death.* Retreived December 20, 2006, from http://www.who.int/mip/2003/other_documents/en/causesofdeath.pdf

World Health Organization Multicentre Growth Reference Study Group. (2006a). Assessment of differences in linear growth among populations in the WHO Multicentre Growth Reference Study. *Acta Paediatrica, Supplement, 450*, 56–65.

World Health Organization Multicentre Growth Reference Study Group. (2006b). WHO motor development study: Windows of achievement for six gross motor developmental milestones. *Acta Paediatrica, Supplement, 450*, 86–95.

World Health Organization Multicentre Growth Reference Study Group. (2006c). Assessment of sex differences and heterogeneity in motor milestone attainment among populations in the WHO Multicentre Growth Reference Study. *Acta Paediatrica, Supplement, 450*, 66–75.

World Health Organization. (2003b). *The world health report 2003.* Geneva, Switzerland: Author.

World Health Organization. (2004). *Unsafe abortion: Global and regional estimates of unsafe abortion and associated mortality in 2000.* Retrieved January 14, 2006, from http://www.who.int/reproductive-ealth/publications/unsafe_aboriton_estimates_04/estimates.pdf

World Health Organization Scientific Group. (1996). *Research on the menopause in the 1990s* (World Health Organization Technical Services Report Series No. 886). Geneva: World Health Organization.

Wortman, C., & Silver, R. (1989). The myths of coping with loss. *Journal of Consulting and Clinical Psychology, 57*, 349–357.

Wortman, C., & Silver, R. (1990). Successful mastery of bereavement and widowhood. A life course perspective. In P. Baltes & M. Baltes (Eds.), *Successful aging: Perspectives from the behavioral sciences* (pp. 225–264). Cambridge, UK: Cambridge University Press.

Wright, W. C., Chang, J., Jeng, G., & Masaluso, M. (2006). Assisted reproductive technology surveillance—United States, 2003. *MMWR: Surveillance Summaries: Morbidity and Mortality Weekly Report, 55*(4), 1–22.

Wrigley, E. (1966). Family limitation in pre-industrial England. *Economic History Review, 19*, 82–109.

Wu, F. C. (2006). Hormonal approaches to male contraception: Approaching reality. *Molecular and Cellular Endocrinology, 250*(1–2), 2–7.

Wyman, P. A., Cross, W., & Barry, J. (2004). Applying research on resilience to enhance school-based prevention: The promoting resilient children initiative. In C. S. Clauss-Ehlers & M. D. Weist (Eds.), *Community planning to foster resilience in children* (pp. 249–266). New York: Kluwer Academic/Plenum Publishers.

Xie, H., Cairns, B. D., & Cairns, R. B. (2001). Predicting teen motherhood and teen fatherhood: Individual characteristics and peer affiliations. *Social Development, 10*, 488–511.

Yeo, S., & Maeda, Y. (2000). Japanese couples' childbirth experiences in Michigan: Implications for care. *Birth: Issues in Prenatal Care, 27*(3), 191–195.

Young, D. S. (1996). Contributing factors to poor health among incarcerated women: A conceptual model. *Affilia: Journal of Women and Social Work, 11*(4), 440–461.

Young, K. R., Marchant, M., & Wilder, L. K. (2004). School-based interventions for students with emotional and behavioral disorders. In P. Allen-Meares & M. W. Fraser (Eds.), *Intervention with children and adolescents: An interdisciplinary perspective* (pp. 175–204). Boston: Allyn & Bacon.

Younoszai, B. (1993). Mexican American perspectives related to death. In D. Irish, K. Lundquist, & V. Nelsen (Eds.), *Ethnic variations in dying, death, and grief: Diversity in universality* (pp. 67–78). Washington, DC: Taylor & Francis.

Yu, C. K., Teoh, T. G., & Robinson, S. (2006). Obesity in pregnancy. *British Journal and Obstetrics and Gynaecology: An International Journal of Obstetrics and Gynaecology, 113*(10), 1117–1125.

Yu, V. Y. H., Jamieson, J., & Asbury, J. (1981). Parents' reactions to unrestricted parental contact in the intensive care unit nursery. *Medical Journal of Australia, 1*, 294–296.

Zaslow, M. J., & Emig, C. A. (1997). When low-income mothers go to work: Implications for children. *Future of Children, 7*(1), 110–115.

Zea, M. C., Diehl, V. A., & Porterfield, K. S. (1997). Central American youth exposed to war violence. In J. Garcia & M. C. Zea (Eds), *Psychological interventions and research with Latino populations* (pp. 39–55). Needham Heights, MA: Allyn & Bacon.

Zeisel, J. (2006). *Inquiry by design: Environment/behavior/neuroscience in architecture, interiors, landscape, and planning* (revised ed.). New York: W.W. Norton & Company.

Zeiss, A. M., & Kasl-Godley, J. (2001). Sexuality in older adults' relationships. *Generations, 25*(2), 18–25.

Zellman, G. L., & Waterman, J. M. (1998). Understanding the impact of parent school involvement on children's educational outcomes. *Journal of Educational Research, 91*(6), 370–380.

Ziel, H., & Finkle, W. (1975). Increased risk of endometrial carcinoma among users of conjugated estrogens. *New England Journal of Medicine, 293*(23), 1167–1170.

Zigler, E., Finn-Stevenson, M., & Hall, N. (2002). *The first three years and beyond: Brain development and social policy.* Chicago: R. R. Donnelly & Sons.

Ziolko, M. E. (1993). Counseling parents of children with disabilities: A review of the literature and implications for practice. In M. Nagler (Ed.), *Perspectives on disability* (2nd ed., pp. 185–193). Palo Alto, CA: Health Markets Research.

Zipper, I., & Simeonsson, R. (1997). Developmental vulnerability in young children with disabilities. In M. Fraser (Ed.), *Risk and resilience in childhood: An ecological perspective* (pp. 161–181). Washington, DC: NASW.

Zucker, K. (1985). The infant's construction of his parents in the first six months of life. In T. Field & N. Fox (Eds.), *Social perception in infants.* Norwood, NJ: Ablex.

Zuckerman, B., & Kahn, R. (2000). Pathways to early child health and development. In S. Danziger & J. Waldfogel (Eds.), *Securing the future: Investing in children from birth to college* (pp. 87–121). New York: Russell Sage.

Zuniga, M. (1992). Families with Latino roots. In E. Lynch & M. Hanson (Eds.), *Developing cross-cultural competence: A guide for working with young children and their families* (pp. 151–179). Baltimore, MD: Paul H. Brookes.

Zuravin, S., & DiBlasio, F. (1996). The correlates of child physical abuse and neglect by adolescent mothers. *Journal of Family Violence, 11*(2), 149–166.

Zutlevics, T. (2006). Should ART be offered to HIV-serodiscordant and HIV-seroconcordant couples: An ethical discussion. *Human Reproduction, 21*(8), 1956–1960.

INDEX/GLOSSARY

AAMI (age-associated memory impairment), 394

Abdel-Latif, M. E., 80

Abel, E., 168

Abel, E. L., 87

Abortion
  abortion rates, 62
  amnioinfusion, 63
  chemical abortion, 63
  curettage abortion, 63
  instrumental evacuation, 63
  medical abortion, 61–63
  religious beliefs and, 63
  social class and, 63
  spontaneous abortion, 79
  teenage pregnancy and, 264
  vacuum curettage, 63

Abraham, K., 255

Abraham, W. T., 382, 392

Accommodation (identity) Process in which an individual changes some aspect of identity in response to new experiences, 349, 350

Acculturation Process by which two or more cultures remain distinct but exchange cultural features (such as foods, music, clothing), 204

Achievements in Public Health, 50

Acquaintance rape Forced, manipulated, or coerced sexual contact by someone you know, 274–275

Acquired immunodeficiency syndrome (AIDS), 90–91, 267–268

Activities of daily living (ADLs) Basic self-care activities, such as bathing, dressing, walking a short distance, shifting from a bed to a chair, using the toilet, and eating, 429

Activity theory, 383

Adair, L. S., 185

Adam, E. K., 220

Adams, G. R., 192, 198, 205, 242, 245, 255

Adams, R., 361

Adamson, R., 291

ADHD (attention deficit hyperactivity disorder), 85, 182, 188, 215, 216

ADL (activities of daily living), 429

Adler, L., 208

Adlercreutz, H., 339

Administration on Aging, 375, 376, 377, 378, 379, 396, 397, 399, 405, 406, 424

Adolescence
  active learning exercises, 280
  biological aspects of, 233–238
  brain and, 237–238
  challenges during, 258–259
  childbearing and, 264–265
  cluster analysis and, 252
  cognition changes and, 240–241
  cultural construction of, 255–256
  curanderismo and, 258
  dating violence during, 274–275
  David's coming-out process case study, 230
  depression and, 239, 251, 252, 261, 274, 278
  dispositions and, 243
  eating disorders and, 276–277
  educational attainment and, 275–276
  exercise and, 233, 235–236
  family relationships and, 247–248
  gender differences and, 246–247
  generalized other and, 245–246
  gonads and, 236
  homosexuality and, 260–261, 278
  identity formation and, 245–246
  immigration experience and, 255–256
  individuation and, 247
  institution relationships and, 249–255

Internet relationships and, 253–255
juvenile delinquency and, 271–273
leisure relationships and, 251–253
lesbianism and, 260–261, 278
mastery and, 242
masturbation and, 259
menarche and, 237
mental health threats and, 273–278
minority culture and, 255–256
Monica's quest for mastery case study, 231
moral development and, 240, 243
nutrition and, 233, 235
obesity and, 276–277
oral sex and, 263–264
peer relations and, 248–249
physical characteristics and, 243
physical health threats and, 273–278
postconventional moral reasoning and, 243
poverty issues and, 275–276
pregnancy and, 264–265
primary sex characteristics and, 237
problems during, 258–259
psychological aspects of, 238–245
psychological reactions to biological changes
    and, 238–239
puberty and, 236–237
rape and, 274–275
resilience and, 279
risk/preventive factors and, 278–279
rites of passage and, 233
school relationships and, 249–251
secondary sex characteristics and, 237
self-efficacy and, 251
self/identity theories and, 242–245
sex hormones and, 236
sexual decision making and, 261–263
sexual orientation and, 259–261
sexuality issues and, 259–268
sexually transmitted diseases (STDs)
    and, 265–268
sleep and, 233, 235–236
social aspects of, 247–256
social construction of, 232
social identity and, 243
social work practice and, 279–280
spermarche and, 237
spirituality and, 256–258
status offenses and, 272
substance use/abuse and, 239, 268–271
suicide and, 261, 278

teenage pregnancy and, 73–74
transition from childhood to, 232–233
violence and, 273–275
web resources, 280–281
work relationships and, 251
See also Middle childhood
Adult day care, 410
Adult homes, 410
Adulthood. *See* Late adulthood; Middle
    adulthood; Very late adulthood;
    Young adulthood
Advance directive Document that gives
    instructions about desired health care if, in
    the future, an individual cannot speak for
    herself or himself, 439–440
Advanced maternal age (AMA), 75, 78, 80, 81
Advocates for Youth, 263
Age dimensions
    psychological age, 21
    social age, 22
    spiritual age, 22
    See also Biological age
Age norm The behaviors expected of people of
    a specific age in a given society at a
    particular point in time, 22
Age stratification perspective Theory of social
    gerontology proposed by Riley (1971) and
    Foner (1995). Similar to the way society is
    structured by socioeconomic class, it is
    also stratified by age. Roles and rights of
    individuals are assigned based on their
    membership in an age group or cohort.
    Individuals proceed through their life
    course as part of that cohort. Theory falls
    into the tradition of the life course
    perspective, 385–386
Age structuring The standardizing of the ages
    at which social role transitions occur, by
    developing policies and laws that regulate
    the timing of these transitions, 23
disengagement theory (of aging), 383
    Age-associated memory impairment
    (AAMI), 394
Agency, human, 26–27
Agency for Healthcare Research and Quality,
    388, 406
Aggression, 150
Ahluwalia, S. K., 311
Ahrons, C., 25
Ai, A. L., 436

AIDS, 90–91, 267–268

Ainsworth, M., 118, 119

Ainsworth's theory of attachment, 119–122

Akbarian, A., 79

Akiyama, H., 353, 357, 358, 359

Alan Guttmacher Institute, 59, 262, 263, 264, 265

Albers, L., 51

Aldwin, C., 375, 386, 389, 390, 394

Alecxih, L. M., 40

Alexander, C. I., 79

Alexander, G. R., 75, 81

Algeier, E. R., 275

Alink, L., 150

Allan, G., 361

Allen, E. K., 182

Allen, K., 359, 408

Allen-Meares, P., 181, 187

Allison, A., 261

Almeida, D. M., 248

Almeida, R., 127, 247

Alsaker, F. D., 239

Altken, R. J., 64

Alvardo, B., 397

Alvarez, A., 200

Alvarez, B., 205

Alwin, D., 11, 20

Aly, H., 80

AMA (advanced maternal age), 75, 78, 80, 81

Amato, P. R., 209, 220

American Academy of Child & Adolescent Psychiatry, 54

American Academy of Family Physicians, 59

American Academy of Pediatrics, 60, 107

American Academy of Pediatrics-Committee on Adolescence, 61

American Association of Retired Persons, 375

American Association of University Women, 186, 189

American College of Nurse-Midwives, 50

American Medical Association, 61

American Psychiatric Association (APA), 215, 216, 217

American Psychiatric Association Work Group on Eating Disorders, 277

American Society for Reproductive Medicine, 91

Ameta, E. S., 205

Amett's "emerging adulthood" theory, 292–296

Amniocentesis, 85

Amnioinfusion, 64

Anderson, C., 165

Anderson, D. A., 50, 260

Anderson, J., 59, 82

Anderson, M., 273

Anderson, R., 341

Anderson, R. E., 50

Anderson, R. N., 278

Andreski, P. A., 378

Andrews, L. B., 57

Andrews, W. W., 81

Angelini, P. J., 72

Anglin, T. M., 274

Ankum, W. M., 78

Anorexia nervosa An eating disorder characterized by a dysfunctional body image and voluntary starvation in the pursuit of weight loss, 88, 253, 277

Anthony Bryant's impending assessment case study, 177–178

Antonucci, T., 353, 354, 357, 358, 359, 361, 362

APA (American Psychiatric Association), 215, 216, 217

Apgar score, 71

Api, O., 78

Applegate, J. S., 187

Aquilino, W., 359

Arber, S., 358

Archer, J., 199

Ardelt, M., 311

Argetsinger, A., 12

Armatowski, J., 436

Armstrong, E. M., 52, 53

Arnett, J., 293

Arnett, J. J., 288, 289, 292, 293, 299

Aroian, K., 344

Aronson, J., 356

Arredi, B., 64

Arrendondo, P. M., 255

ART (assisted reproductive technologies), 65–67

Asante, O., 254

Asbury, J., 83

Asher, S., 199

Ashford, J. B., 51, 288, 296

Ashory-Moghadam, S., 79

Ashton, D., 80

Assimilation (culture) Process by which the minority culture must adapt and become incorporated into the majority culture, 192, 204

Assimilation (identity) Process by which individuals incorporate new experiences into their existing identity, 349–350

Assisted reproductive technologies (ART) A range of techniques to help women who are infertile to conceive and give birth, 65–67

in vitro fertilization (IVF) 64–66, 75, 78

gamete intrafallopian tube transfer (GIFT), 66

intrauterine insemination, 66

preservation and gestational surrogacy, 67–68, 93

Astone, N. M., 295, 317

Astor, R. A., 196

Atkinson, T., 193

At-risk newborns

congenital anomalies and, 83–86

ethical issues and, 82

low birth rate and, 80–82

newborn intensive care, 82–83

pregnancy and, 80

prematurity and, 80–82

See also Special parent populations

Attachment An enduring emotional bond between two people who are important to each other. Provides affection and a sense of security

Ainsworth's theory of, 119–122

anxious attachment, 119

avoidant attachment, 119

Bowlby's theory of, 118–119

definition of, 118

early childhood and, 150, 157–158

fathers, and play as vehicle for, 157–158

infants'/toddlers' brain development and, 122–123

insecure disorganized/disoriented attachment

secure attachment, 119

Attention deficit hyperactivity disorder (ADHD), 85, 182, 188, 215, 216

Auchterlonie, J. L., 317

Auerbach, J., 366

Austin, N. C., 82

Australian Government: Department of Family and Community Services: Office for Women, 125

Authoritarian parenting A parenting style, identified by Baumrind, that involves unresponsive, inflexible, harsh, and controlling interactions with the child, 163

Authoritative parenting A parenting style, identified by Baumrind, that involves responsive and supportive interactions with the child while also setting firm limits. Thought to be the most effective parenting style, 163

Autonomy v. shame and doubt,

Avery, R., 398

Avis, N., 338, 339

Awsare, N. S., 60

Ayers, T. S., 221

Bachman, J., 268, 269

Backman, L., 394

Bada, H. S., 81

Bahr, H., 359

Bailey, D., 158

Bailey, J., 153

Bailey, S. M., 189

Baillargeon, R., 112, 113

Bain, M. D., 51

Baird, D. D., 65

Baker, A., 167

Baker, G. A., III, 203

Baker, S. R., 52

Bakhru, A., 61

Bakshi, A., 197

Balassone, M., 52

Baldwin, A., 158

Baldwin, C., 158

Baldwin, D., 113

Baltes, P., 335

Bandura, A., 27, 147

Baptiste, L., 192

Barak, B., 21

Baranowski, T., 128

Barbarin, O., 193

Bardin, C. W., 63

Bardwell, J. R., 201

Barer, B. M., 430, 432

Barker, K. K., 52

Barnett, M., 52, 74

Barnett, W. S., 160

Baron, J., 241

Barr, 185

Barr, R. D., 202, 203

Barranti, C., 398

Barrick, M., 347

Barrs, M., 189

Barry, J., 198

Barry, T. D., 215
Barth, R., 132
Barth, R. P., 206
Bartko, W., 158
Bartko, W. T., 251, 252
Bartley, M., 21, 30, 31
Barton, L., 82
Bassali, R., 131
Baucum, D., 182, 183
Bauer, J., 334
Baum, K., 274
Baumeister, R. F., 245
Baumgarten, M., 394
Baumrind, D., 163, 164
Bausch, R. S., 67
Bautista de Domanico, Y., 192
Beals, J., 270, 271
Beasley, J., 128
Beatson, J., 143
Beaudoin, M., 196
Beckman, D., 87
Beckman, L. J., 61
Beedham, T., 57
Beermann, C., 128
Behrman, J., 294
Behrman, J. R., 288
Beland, F., 397
Beliefs. *See* Religious beliefs
Bell, C., 214
Bell, D. B., 47
Bell, M., 52
Bell, R., 73
Bell, S., 339
Bellamy, C., 129, 210
Belsky, J., 119, 120, 185, 213
Bem, S. L., 152, 200
Benbenishty, R., 196
Benefice, E., 185
Benenson, J., 157
Bengston, V. L., 304
Bengtson, V., 355, 356, 357, 358, 359,
      360, 396, 397
Benjamin, J., 131
Benjamin, K., 383
Ben's new environment case study, 286–287
Ben-Sholomo, Y., 31
Benson, P. L., 222, 257
Benton, L., 63
Bereavement The state of having suffered
      a loss, 444–449

Berg, B., 393
Berg, M., 82
Bergen, D., 187, 188
Bergmann, B., 209
Bergquist, W., 361
Berk, L. E., 59, 113, 182, 184, 195
Berkeley children, 30
Berkeley Guidance Study, 348
Berkeley Planning Associates, 90
Berkowitz, E. D., 409
Berkowitz, G., 51
Berliner, K., 362
Berman, L., 379
Berman, S., 265
Bernd, E., 52, 74
Berndt, T. J., 199
Berne, L., 262, 265
Bernheime, S., 89
Bernheimer, L. P., 304
Bern-Klug, M., 438
Berry, E. M., 88
Berryman, J. C., 75
Berthelsen, D., 151, 168
Bertrand, J., 87
Bertrand, R., 330, 349
Best, C., 113
Best, C. L., 72
Best, K., 58
Betts, S., 108, 109
Bewley, S., 75
Bhaju, J., 407
Bharti, V. K., 383
Bhathena, R. K., 60
Bhattacharya, G., 204
Bianchi, S., 220
Bicultural or multicultural competence, 191
Biculturalism, 29, 191, 255
Biernat, M., 201
Big Five personality traits, 347-348
Biggs, S., 350, 351
Bigler, R. S., 192
Bigum, C., 189
Bihl, I., 54
Billingsley, A., 26
Bina Patel outlives her son case study, 421
Bioethical issues, 57
Biological age A person's level of biological
      development and physical health, as
      measured by the functioning of the
      various organ systems, *See also* Age issues

genetic theories of aging, 386
life course perspective and, 21, 386
molecular/cellular theories of aging and, 386
system level theories of aging, 386–387
theories of aging, 386–387
Birch, H. G., 117
Bird, C. E., 375, 382, 385
Biringen, Z., 147
Birth control options, 58–61
Barrier methods, and, 59, 89,
Breastfeeding, and, 59
Coitus interruptus, and, 59
Contraceptive patch, and, 61
Emergency contraception, and, 60–61
Intrauterine devices, and, 60
Intramuscular injections, and, 59–60
Male contraception, and, 57, 61
New contraceptive methods, and, 61
Oral contraceptives, and, 59-61, 89
Periodic abstinence, and, 58–59
Voluntary surgical sterilization, and, 60, 89
Birth rates, 58, 80–82, 264
Birth weight issues
extremely low birth weight (ELBW), 81
low birth weight (LBW), 80–81
very low birth weight (VLBW), 80–81
Birthing center, 50
Bishop, D., 164
Bishop, K., 57
Bitzan, J. E., 406
Black, R., 57
Blacker, L., 357, 359
Blair, A., 65
Blair, S., 199
Blair-Loy, M., 300
Blakeslee, S., 165
Blandford, J. M., 78
Blandon, A., 120
Blane, D., 21
Blankemeyer, M., 296
Blass, E., 104
Blau, P. M., 385
Blazer, D. G., 395
Blehar, M., 118
Blewitt, P., 182
Bliatot, B., 448
Blieszner, R., 408, 433
Blinn, C., 90
Block, J., 269
Bloom, B., 90

Bloom, B. S., 205
Bloom, L., 146
Blooming A period of overproduction of brain
synapses during infancy, followed by a
period of synapse pruning, 107
Bluck, S., 330, 335
Blume, J., 239
Blyth, D. A., 222
Boldizar, J. P., 200, 274
Boldt, J., 21
Bon Secours Hospice, 442, 443
Bonanno, G., 447
Bonding issues
infancy/toddlerhood and, 54, 82, 122
young adults and, 300
Bonne, O. B., 88
Bonsel, G. J., 51
Boothrody, D., 340
Borden, M. C., 198
Bordere, T., 191, 192
Borenstein, A. R., 395
Borke, H., 148
Bortz, W. M., 433
Borysenko, J., 190, 349, 352
Borzekowski, D., 254
Bos, H., 47, 64
Bost, K., 117
Bowlby, J., 118, 119, 439
Bowlby's theory of attachment, 118–119
Bowles, S., 206
Boxer, A., 260
Bradley, L. A., 52, 132, 150
Bradshaw, D., 117
Brain death, maternal, 79–80
Brain development
adolescence and, 237–238
attachment and, 122–123
infancy/toddlerhood and, 107–108, 122–123
Brain plasticity The ability of the brain to
change in response to stimuli, 187, 393
Brambilla, D., 338, 339
Brandtstadter, J., 384, 388
Brantlinger, E., 90
Braungart, J., 118
Braungart, J. M., 120
Braxton-Hicks contractions, 70
Brazelton, T. B., 107
Breastfeeding practices, 59, 127–128
Bredekamp, S., 126
Brennan, P. L., 396

Brenner, H., 128
Brent, R., 87
Brewer, R., 291
Brianna Shaw's new self-image case study, 178–179
Bright Futures, 142
Brim, O., 330
Brinch, M., 88
Broadhurst, D., 170
Broderick, P. C., 182
Brody, E., 356
Broken Nose, M., 131
Brokenleg, M., 449
Bromberger, J., 338
Bronfenbrenner, U., 222
Brook, J., 204
Brooks, R. B., 194
Brooks, R. G., 436
Brooks-Gunn, J., 26, 163, 210, 239, 271
Broom, B., 52, 68
Brown, B., 210
Brown, B. B., 248
Brown, J., 64, 151, 152
Brown v. Board of Education, 206
Browne, K., 121, 131
Brown-Guttovz, H., 78
Brubaker, E., 405
Brumberg, J., 277
Brunner, E., 31
Bruno, R., 191
Bryson, K., 399
Buchmann, M., 23
Buckner, J., 168
Bucy, J., 124
Buekens, P., 48
Buitelaar, J. K., 70
Buitendijk, S. E., 50
Bukowski, W. M., 198
Bulimia nervosa An eating disorder characterized by a cycle of binge eating; feelings of guilt, depression, or self-disgust; and purging, 277
Bullis, R. K., 49, 436
Bullying, 196
Bumpass, L., 334, 355
Bunting, L., 264
Burchinal, M., 158
Burchinal, M. R., 210
Bureau of Labor Statistics, 251, 359
Bureau of the Census, 13, 204, 209, 215, 329, 330, 375, 378, 379, 399, 401, 424, 429

Burnette, D., 399
Burt, C. W., 297
Burton, L., 396
Busch-Rossnagel, N., 121
Buss, L., 79
Bustan, N. M., 78
Butler, R. N., 407
Buzi, R. S., 310
Bybee, D., 170
Byock, R., 439

Cagle, J. G., 442
Cain, A., 221
Cain, A. C., 221
Cairns, B. D., 310
Cairns, R. B., 310
Caius, N., 185
Caldwell, L., 252
Call, J., 123
Calman, L., 159
Cameron, L., 270
Cameron, M., 212, 214
Campbell, B., 203
Campbell, F. A., 310
Campbell, L., 203
Campbell, R., 50, 191, 359
Campbell, S., 119, 151
Campos, J., 117
Canda, E., 22
Canda, E. R., 436
Capital A term used in different ways by different disciplines, but generally refers to having the potential, capacity, and resources to function, produce, or succeed; in the social sciences, refers to possession of attributes associated with civic engagement and economic success, 195–196
Capital, human, 312
Carel, R., 64
Carey, T. A., 163
Carla's transition to parenthood case study, 287–288
Carl's struggle for identity case study, 230–231
Carlson, E., 222
Carmen Ruiz is institutionalized case study, 420
Carnahan, S., 124
Carney, J., 361
Carr, C., 89
Carrasco, D., 258

Carroll, M. D., 276

Carskadon, M. A., 236

Carstensen, L., 361, 431

Carter, B., 15, 25, 30, 47, 48, 127, 182, 357

Carter, D. B., 201

Carter, J., 163

Carter, S., 209

Cartlidge, P. H. H., 82

Cartlidge, P. H. J, 79

CASA, 269, 270, 271

Casale-Giannola, D., 295

Case, R., 241

Case studies
   coming-out process, 230
   environmental issues, 286–287
   family disruptions in middle
      childhood, 179–181
   grandparenthood, 141
   identity issues, 140–141, 230–231
   late-life pregnancy, 45–46
   life course perspectives, 4–9
   middle child development, 177–178
   overprotecting infants, 99–100
   pregnancy in adolescence, 42
   premature birth, 43–44, 98
   self-identity, 178–179
   status in adolescence, 231
   teenage parenthood, 99
   temperment in early childhood, 140
   transition to parenthood, 287–288

Casey, B., 238

Casper, L., 399

Caspi, A., 185, 347, 348

Castellino, D. R., 209

Cates, W., 265

Caughey, A. B., 66

Cauthen, N. K., 210

Cavanaugh, J., 21

Centers for Disease Control and Prevention
   (CDC), 62, 66 128, 268

Cerebral cortex The outer layer of gray matter
   in the human brain thought to be
   responsible for complex, high level
   intellectual functions such as memory,
   language, and reasoning, 188

Cervantes, J., 257, 258

Chadiha, L., 47

Chadwick, R., 57

Chamberlain, P., 121

Chambers, C., 128

Champion, J. D., 64

Chandra, A., 264

Chang, A., 76

Chang, G., 87

Chang, J., 65

Chang, L., 154

Chang, S. H., 65

Chanpong, G. F., 89

Chapman, M. V., 256, 305, 311

Chapman, P., 256

Character education The direct teaching and
   curriculum inclusions of mainstream
   values thought to be universal by a
   community (e.g., kindness, respect,
   tolerance, and honesty), 196

Charlesworth, L., 213

Charter school education, 196

Chase-Lansdale, L. P., 220

Chase-Lansdale, P., 26

Chase-Lansdale, P. L., 210

Chasnoff, I., 132

Chatfield, J. E., 61

Chatters, L., 362

Chavez, G. F., 81

Cheap IVF needed: Editorial, 66

Cheavens, J. S., 392

Chen, C., 354, 356

Chen, M., 206

Chen, R., 66

Chen, Y. R., 278

Cherlin, A. J., 264

Chess, S., 117

Chestang, L., 191

Chethik, M., 156

Cheung, G., 392

Child abuse, 131–132, 170

Child behavior, 25, 152, 159
   See also Early childhood; Middle childhood

Child maltreatment Physical, emotional, and
   sexual abuse and neglect of children, most
   often by adult caregivers. Definitions vary
   by culture and professional discipline but
   typically entail harm, or threatened harm,
   to the child, 131–132, 170. *See also* Early
   childhood; Middle childhood

Child Trends study, 303, 304

Child Welfare League of America, 221

Childbearing
   active learning exercises, 92–93
   advanced maternal age (AMA), 75, 78, 80, 81

Braxton-Hicks contractions and, 70
congenital anomalies and, 83–86
family diversity and, 46–47
gender roles and, 47
hospital stay and, 53–54
immigration experience and, 47–48
intrauterine fetal death (IUFD), 79
lesbian mothers and, 88–89
lightening movement and, 70
newborn intensive care and, 82–83
parents with disabilities and, 89–90
postpartum depression and, 128–129
prematurity and, 80–81
quickening experience and, 70
risk/preventive factors and, 76–77
sensitive period and, 85
small for gestational age (SGA) and, 88
social work practice and, 77, 97
sociocultural organization of, 46–54
special parent populations and, 86–91
web resources, 93–94
See also At-risk newborns; Conception;
   Pregnancy; Reproductive genetics
Childbirth
birth rates, 58, 80–82, 264
birthing center and, 50
cultural construction of, 50–54
education about, 51–52
extremely low birth weight (ELBW)
   and, 81
labor and delivery of neonate and, 70–71
low birth weight (LBW) and, 80–81
maternal brain death and, 79–80
places of, 51–52
premature births and, 43–44, 80
stillbirth and, 79
Thompsons' premature birth case
   study, 43–44
very low birth weight (VLBW) and, 80–81
See also Childbearing; Conception;
   Pregnancy; Reproductive genetics
ChildbirthSolutions, Inc, 59
Childcare issues, 124–126
Children of Immigrants Longitudinal
   Study (CILS), 313
Children's Defense Fund, 121, 162,
   165, 170, 210, 212
Chiriboga, D., 349
Chiriboga, D. A., 395
Chlamydia, 365–266

Chodorow, N., 200
Choice-making, 26–27
Chomsky, N., 146
Chorion villi testing (CVT), 86
Chowdhury, F., 28
Christenson, P. D., 61
Christiansen, O. B., 79
Christie, J., 156
Chromosomes Threadlike structures
   composed of DNA and proteins that carry
   genes and are found within each body cell
   nucleus, 55–56
Chromosomal aberration, 84-85
Chudacolff, H., 22
Chugani, H., 122
Chumlea, W. C., 185
Chummun, H., 80
Chung-Lee, L., 128
Ciaramitaro, V., 104
Cicirelli, V., 398, 431
Cilenti, D., 73
Clare, R., 159
Clark, H., 132
Clark, K., 153
Clark, K. A., 72
Clark, M., 153
Clark, M. K., 60
Clark, S. M., 79
Clarke, J., 13
Clarke, V. E., 67, 75
Clarke-Stewart, K., 158
Clarke-Stewart, K. A., 120, 121
Clearinghouse on International Developments
   in Child, Youth and Family Policies at
   Columbia University, 125
Clingempeel, W. G., 221
Clougherty, K. F., 396
Cluster analysis, 252
Clyman, R., 147
Cochran, S. W., 201, 295
Cockey, C. D., 80
Cognition Ability to process and store
   information and solve problems.
   Commonly called thinking, 109
adolescence, and changes in, 240–241
definition of, 109
disease in late adults and, 394
gender and, 200
school education and, 202–204
spirituality in young adults and, 300

Cognitive development
early childhood and, 143–146, 156
infancy/toddlerhood and, 109–113
middle childhood and, 186–191, 202–204
mild cognitive impairment (MCI) and, 394
Piaget's stages of, 110–113, 144–145
play and, 156
young adulthood and, 298–299
Cohen, A., 52
Cohen, B., 288
Cohen, C., 103
Cohen, D. J., 215
Cohen, H., 398
Cohen-Kettenis, P. T., 70
Cohler, B., 361
Cohn, J., 119
Cohort Group of persons who are born in the same time period and who are of the same age group at the time of specific historical events and social changes, 11
Cohort effects The effects of social change on a specific cohort, 20
Coid, J., 214
Coie, J. D., 197, 198
Cole, E., 334, 362
Cole, S. S., 89
Cole, T., 102
Cole, T. M., 89
Coleman, C., 193
Coleman, P., 63
Coles, L. S., 427
Coles, R., 189, 196
Collaborative classroom, 207
Collins, A. L., 388
Colucci, P., 362
Comer, J. P., 205, 206
Coming-out process, 230, 260–261, 308
Community assets Community resources such as public infrastructure (e.g., adequate transportation to get to work), community networks, and educational opportunities, 312
Community Epidemiology, 31
Community violence, 166–167
Comprehensive School Reform Quality Center and American Institutes for Research, 209
Conception, 48–50
assisted reproductive technologies (ART) and, 65–67
contraception and, 58–62
cultural construction of, 48–50
fetal viability and, 63
gamete intrafallopian tube transfer (GIFT) and, 67
intrauterine insemination (IUI) and, 67
medical abortion and, 62–64
preservation/gestational surrogacy and, 67
sperm donors and, 65
in vitro fertilization (IVF) and, 66
See also Abortion; Childbearing; Childbirth; Pregnancy; Reproductive genetics
Concrete operations stage The third stage in Piaget's theory of cognitive development. School-age children (ages 7 to 11) begin to use logical reasoning but their thinking is not yet abstract, 110
Condon, J., 129
Conflict perspective, 35
Conger, R., 25
Conger, R. D., 239, 382, 392
Conjunctive faith The fifth faith stage in James Fowler's theory of faith development, a stage when individuals look for balance among competing moral systems, recognize that there are many truths, and open themselves in service to others, 351
Conn, D. K., 394
Connections, 4–5
Connie, T. A., 89
Connolly, L., 349, 350
Connor, M. E., 310
Constable, R., 206
Contemporary cultural construction of very late adulthood, 422–423
Contextual model Avshalom Caspi's model of personality, which proposes that personality is stable across the life course because individuals choose environments that reinforce their personal styles, 347
Continuity theory Theory of social gerontology initially proposed by Neugarten, Havighurst, and Tobin (1968) in response to critiques of the disengagement and activity theories. Individuals adapt to changes by using the same coping styles they have used throughout the life course, with new roles serving as substitutes for roles lost due to age, 383
Contraception options, 58–62
Conventional moral reasoning, 147, 243

Convoy A person's network of social relationships that protects, defends, aids, and socializes, 353, 362

Coohey, C., 132, 133

Cook, E. A., 63

Cook, K., 151

Cook, T., 26

Cooksey, E., 15, 20, 25

Cooksey, E. C., 293

Cooper, P. G., 78, 81

Cooper, R. G., 52

Copeland, V., 162

Coping mechanism Strategy used to master the demands of life, 347

immature mechanisms, 347

mature mechanisms, 347, 392

Coplan, R., 150

Coppotelli, H., 198

Corbin, J. M., 89

Corbin, S., 165

Corcoran, J., 74

Corcoran, M., 315

Corsaro, W., 123, 151, 156, 157

Coscia, J., 187, 188

Costa, F., 270

Costa, F. M., 263

Costa, P., 348, 349

Costa, P., Jr., 392

Costin, L. B., 221

Cota-Robles, S., 239

Cote, J., 293

Counts, D. A., 443, 444

Counts, D. R., 443, 444

Cousins, E., 209

Cowan, N., 393

Cowan, P. A., 309

Cowles, K. V., 448

Cowley, C., 74

Cox, S. J., 66

Craig, G. J., 182, 183

Crain, R., 154

Crane, P., 198

Craven, A., 13

Crawford, I., 192

Crawford, J. J., 183

Crawley, L., 441

Crick, F., 54

Crick, N., 150

Cristafalo, V., 386

Critchley, H. O., 79

Criterion-referenced testing, 204

Cross, W., 198

Cross-sectional research, 333, 351, 391, 408, 422

Crouter, A., 153

Crowley, E. D., 253

Croxatto, H. B., 61

Crystallized intelligence The ability to use knowledge from accumulated learning, 392

Csikszentmihalyi, M., 250

Culp, R., 164

Cultural construction

adolescence and, 255–256

childbirth and, 50–54

conception and, 48–50

contemporary cultural construction of very late adulthood, 422–423

dying process and, 437–439

historic cultural construction of very late adulthood, 423–427

late adulthood and, 379–382

middle adulthood and, 331–332

young adulthood and, 294–295

Culture issues

acculturation, 204

adolescence, and relationship with culture, 255–256

assimilation (cultural), 192, 204

biculturalism, 29, 191, 255

cultural identity, 191–193

deculturalizing, 181

minority culture, 29, 255–256

sociocultural organization of childbearing, 46–54

Cumming, E., 383

Cummings, S., 199

Cumulative advantage The accumulation of increasing advantage as early advantage positions an individual for later advantage, 30–31, 382

Cumulative disadvantage The accumulation of increasing disadvantage as early disadvantage positions an individual for later disadvantage, 30–31, 382

Curanderismo A holistic folk medicine philosophy followed by many Latino families, 258

Curettage abortion, 63

CVT (chorion villi testing), 86

Cwikel, J., 64

Dahlberg, L., 166
Dahlstrom, M., 130
Dalby, P., 436
Damon, B., 379
Damon, W., 199
Danielsen, B., 83
Dannefer, D., 21, 22, 26, 27, 29, 33, 34, 384
Dannison L., 162
Danziger, S., 47
Danziger, S. K., 315
Darroch, J., 58
Darrow, C., 334
Dating violence, 274–275
David, H. P., 63
David Sanchez's search for connections
    case study, 4–5
David's coming-out process case study, 230
Davidson, J., 214, 259
Davies, D., 102, 114, 115, 116, 119, 123,
    144, 145, 150, 151, 153, 156, 182, 190,
    191, 193, 223
Davies, M., 302
Davis, A. R., 61
Davis, B., 50
Davis, M., 304, 305
Davis, R., 47
Dawson, B., 160
Day care issues, 124–126
De Casper, A., 103
De Escobar, G. M., 68
De Iullis, G. N., 64
De La Cancela, V., 258
De St. Aubin, E., 333, 334
De Vries, B., 361
Dean, R. G., 384
Death rates. *See* Mortality rates
Dechaux, J., 359
Deculturalizing The intentional or
    unintentional process that results in the
    destruction, or severe limitation, of a
    culture's ability to sustain itself (language,
    customs, rituals, and so forth), 181
Dee, T. S., 189
Deeg, D., 343
Default individualization One possible
    pathway in young adulthood, which
    involves making transitions defined by
    circumstance and situation, 293
DeFries, J. C., 118
DeHaan, L., 77, 362

DeHart, G. B., 52
DeJong, W., 277
Del Rio, P., 200
Del Ser, T., 397
Delany, E., 423, 446
Delany, S., 423, 446
Delirium Syndrome characterized by an
    impairment of consciousness. It has a
    sudden onset (a few hours or days),
    follows a brief and fluctuating course that
    includes impairment of consciousness, and
    has the potential for improvement when
    causes are treated. Prevalence of delirium
    is high among hospitalized elderly persons;
    toxicity from prescribed medications is a
    common cause, 395
Dell,Angelo, T., 198
Dellis, E., 158
Dellmann, T., 51
Dellmann-Jenkins, M., 296
Dementia Impairment or loss of cognitive
    functioning caused by damage in the brain
    tissue. Dementia is not part of the brain's
    normal aging process, but its prevalence
    increases with age, 394
Dengler, B., 164
Dennis, C., 128
Dennison, B., 102, 142
Denton, M. L., 256, 257
Department of Health and Human Services,
    131, 235, 273
Dependency ratio A demographic indicator
    expressing the degree of demand placed
    on society by the dependent young and the
    dependent elderly combined, 376
Depression
    adolescence and, 239, 251, 252, 261, 274, 278
    early childhood and, 163, 167, 169
    genetics and, 84
    infertility and, 64, 66
    late adulthood and, 392, 395, 407
    middle adulthood and, 343–344, 361–362
    middle childhood and, 182, 194, 214
    parental, 130, 131, 132
    postpartum depression, 128–129
    race and, 278
    stages of accepting impending death and, 438
    stages of grief and, 446
    suicide and, 278
    very late adulthood and, 433, 434

Derby, J., 447

DeRosier, M. E., 198

DeSpelder, L. A., 438

Detzer, M. J., 259

Developmental delays Delays in developing skills and abilities in infants and preschoolers, 124, 158

Developmental Disabilities Assistance and Bill of Rights Act, 124

Developmental individualization One possible pathway in young adulthood, which involves making transitions defined by personal agency and deliberately charted growth opportunities in intellectual, occupational, and psychosocial domains, 293

Developmental perspective, 35

Developmental psychology, 11, 31

Developmental risks/protective factors
adolescence and, 278–279
childbearing and, 76–77
late adulthood and, 411–412
life course perspective and, 30–32
middle adulthood and, 365–366
middle childhood and, 221–223
young adulthood and, 316–317

Devitt, N., 50

Devore, W., 30

DeVries, B., 433

DeWolfe, A., 192

Dezateux, C., 102

Diamond, L., 200, 201, 260

Diamond, L. M., 199, 200, 201, 260

Diaz, R. M., 191

DiBlasio, F., 132

Dickason, E., 52, 128

Dickinson, D., 203

Dick-Read, G., 51

Dickstein, S., 131

Diehl, V. A., 212

Dillon, J., 60

DiMartino, D., 126

Direct bullying Intentionally inflicting emotional or physical harm on another person through fairly explicit physical or verbal harassment, assault, or injury, 196

Direnfeld, D., 393

Dirubbo, N. E., 58

Disabilities, parents with, 89–90

Disability Adjusted Life Year (DALY), 343

Disability insurance, 410

Discipline Action taken by a child's caretaker to help the child correct behavioral problems 163–165

Discrimination
institutional, 192, 207
race and, 314–315

Disengaged parenting Aloof, withdrawn, and unresponsive parenting, 164

Disengagement theory Theory of social gerontology that suggests that as elderly individuals grow older, they gradually decrease their social interactions and ties and become increasingly self-preoccupied, 383

Dispositions An individual's attitudes, traits, abilities, values, personality traits, specific habits, tendencies, and likes or preferences. One element in Morris Rosenberg's model of identity, 243

Dittmann-Kohli, F., 330, 331, 363, 364

Diversity issues
childbearing and, 46–47
families and, 46–48
life course trajectories and, 27–30
school education and, 204–205

Divorce
late adulthood and, 378, 398
middle adulthood and, 355, 357, 359
middle childhood, and effects of, 220, 221
very late adulthood and, 445

Dodge, D. T., 126

Dodge, J., 18

Dodge, K. A., 197, 198

Dolinsky, A. L., 406

Dollahite, D., 351

Domestic violence, 168–169, 212–215

Domina, T., 205

Dominance hierarchy, 197

Dominant genes Genes that express themselves if present on one or both chromosomes in a pair, 57

Donahue, M. J., 257

Donovan, B., 155

Donovan, J., 270

Donovan, J. E., 263

Dorner, J., 347, 348, 349

Douglas, D., 50

Douglas-Hall, A., 210

Dowling, C., 357

Downe, S., 51
Downs, A. C., 201
Downs, S. W., 221
Down's syndrome, 45, 62, 75, 84
Doyle, A., 191
Dozier, M., 120
Draut, T., 288, 296
Drozdzik, M., 64
Dryfoos, J. G., 208, 259
Duarte, A., 393
Dubas, J. S., 200
Dubrow, N., 166, 167
Ducharme, S., 433
Duerden, S., 123
Dunbar, H. T., 298, 301, 391
Duncan, G., 163
Dundas, S., 89
Dunkle, R., 423
DuPlessis, H. M., 73
Dupper, D. R., 206
DuRant, R. H., 263
Durkin, K., 309
Dutton, K., 151
Dychtwald, K., 390, 391
Dyer, L., 158
Dyer, S. J., 79
Dying process
    advance directives and, 439
    care of people dying, 440–441
    cultural construction of, 437–439
    end-of-life signs/symptoms and, 441–443
    hospice care and, 411, 441
    living will and, 439
    palliative care and, 440
    stages of accepting impending death
        and, 438
Dyson, J., 214

Early childhood
    active learning exercises, 172
    aggression and, 150
    attachment and, 150, 157–158
    authoritarian parenting and, 163
    child abuse and, 170
    cognitive development and, 143–146, 156
    community violence and, 166–167
    depression and, 163, 167, 169
    developmental delays and, 158
    developmental disruptions and, 158–159
    discipline and, 163

disengaged parenting and, 164
domestic violence and, 168–169
education, 159-161
egocentrism and, 145
empathy and, 148
Erikson's psychosocial theory and, 149
ethnic identity and, 153–154
exploration of reality through play and, 156
fathers, and play as vehicle for
        attachment in, 157–158
fine motor skills and, 143
gaining control through play and, 156
gender identity and, 149, 151
gross motor skills and, 143
healthy development and, 142–159
hostile aggression and, 150
ineffective discipline and, 163–165
instrumental aggression and, 150
Jack's name change case study, 140–141
language development and, 143–146
lateralization and, 142–143
learning play and, 156
maltreatment and, 170
mastery and, 156, 161, 171
moral development and, 146–149
multigenerational families and, 160–162
obesity and, 128
peer relations and, 151
permissive parenting and, 163–164
personality, and emotional
        development in, 149–150
perspective taking and, 148
physical aggression and, 150
physical development and, 142–143
Piaget's stages of cognitive development and,
        144–145
play and, 154–158
poverty issues and, 162–163
preconvential level of moral
        reasoning and, 147
relational aggression and, 150
religious beliefs and, 149
risk/preventive factors and, 170–171
risks to healthy development and, 162–170
Ron and Rosiland's grandmother case study,
        new role for, 141
school education and, 159–160
self-concept and, 151–152
self-efficacy and, 171
self-esteem and, 151–152

self-theory and, 151
sexual interests and, 152–153
shared experience through play and, 156–157
social development and, 150–154
social work practice and, 171
sociodramatic play and, 157
symbolic play and, 155
Terri's terrible temper case study, 140
transductive reasoning and, 145
violence and, 166–170
web resources, 172–173
East, P. L., 74
Easterlin, R., 12
Easterling, T., 54
Eating disorders
adolescence and, 276–277
anorexia nervosa, 88, 253, 277
bulimia nervosa, 277
middle childhood and, 194
pregnancy and, 88
Eaton, J., 388, 391
Eccles, J., 26, 251, 252
Eccles, J. S., 311
Economic hardship. *See* Poverty
Ectopic pregnancy, 78
Edin, K., 290
Edlich, R. F., 79
Edmondson, R., 124
Edmunds, L, 102, 142
Education
childbirth education, 52–53
reproductive genetics and, 55
risk/prevention for infancy/toddlerhood
and, 132–133
See also Formal schooling education
Education for All Handicapped Children
Act, 219
Edwards, C., 110
Edwards, E., 120
Edwards, J., 357, 359
Edwards, N., 51
Edwards, N. C., 383
Efficacy expectation, 27
Egeland, B., 222
Egley, A., Jr., 273
Egnew, T., 439
Ego integrity versus ego despair The
psychosocial crisis of Erik Erikson's eighth
and final stage of development, which
centers on one's ability to process what has

happened in life and accept these
experiences as integral to the
meaning of life, 391
Egocentrism The assumption by children in the
preoperational stage of cognitive
development that others perceive, think,
and feel just the way they do. Inability to
recognize the possibility of other
perspectives, 145
Eichorn, D., 239
Eiden, R., 120
Eisenberg, 150
Eisenberg, D., 215
Eisenberg, N., 148
ELBW (extremely low birth weight), 81
Elder, G., 399, 400
Elder, G. Jr., 14, 15, 25
Elder, G., Jr., 11, 15, 20, 23, 25, 26, 31, 239
Elderly gravidas, 75
Elkind, D., 161
Elley, N., 82
Elliott, M., 302
Ellis, B. J., 185
Ellis, G. D., 253
Ellison, C. G., 300
Ellor, J. W., 436
Elman, C., 363, 364, 365
El-Mohandes, A. A., 80
Elster, N. R., 64
Eman, B., 199
Emans, S. J., 263
Embry, R., 132, 214
Embry, R. A., 133, 214
Embryo The stage of prenatal development
beginning in the second week and lasting
through the eighth week, 67
Emde, R., 147
Emerging adulthood A developmental phase
distinct from both adolescence and young
adulthood, occurring between the ages of
18 and 25 in industrialized societies,
292–296
Emig, C. A., 310, 311
Emmons, P. G., 215
Emotional intelligence The ability to motivate
oneself to persist in the face of frustration,
to control impulses, to delay gratification,
to regulate one's moods, and to empathize
with others; theory proposed by Daniel
Goleman, 196

Emotions. *See* Socioemotional development
Empathy Ability to understand another person's emotional condition, 148
Employment
    adolescence and, 251–252
    gender and, 363–364
    late adulthood and, 402
    life course perspective and, 20, 23, 29
    middle adulthood and, 363, 364, 365
    parenting and, 302–304
    race and, 251, 304, 314–315, 363
    retirement patterns, 401–404
    young adulthood and, 309–315
    See also Work relationships
English, K. M., 217
Ensminger, M., 295
Environmental issues, 286–287, 294–295
Environment-person transactions. *See* Life course perspective
Epigenetics The study of changes in genetic expression due to environmental influences on body chemistry that do not alter the genetic sequence, 84
Epps, S., 77
Epstein, J. L., 205
Epstein, N., 164
Epstein, R., 67
Epstein, S., 151
Erikson, E. H., 116, 290, 292, 333, 391
Erikson's psychosocial theory
    early childhood and, 149
    infancy/toddlerhood and, 114–115
    young adulthood and, 290
Erikson's theory of generativity, 333–334
Escobar, J., 204
Espelage, D. L., 196
Esquivel, G., 192
Ethical issues
    at-risk newborns and, 82
    late adulthood medical treatments and, 391
    middle childhood and, 148, 190
    special parent populations and, 67
    young adulthood and, 299
Ethics issues
    bioethics and, 57
    genetic engineering, 57
    globalization and, 47
    medical advances and, 47
    pregnancy, 63, 80
    preservation/gestational surrogacy and, 67

    social justice and, 57
    sperm donors and, 65
Ethnic identity, 153–154
    early childhood and, 153–154
    race and, 314–315
    work relationships and, 314–315
    young adulthood and, 314–315
Event history The sequence of significant events, experiences, and transitions in a person's life from birth to death, 10
Extremely low birth weight (ELBW) A newborn weight of less than 1,000 grams (2.2 pounds), 81
Extroversion Orientation to the external world, in contrast to introversion, which is orientation to the internal world, 334, 347

Fabelo-Alcover, H., 30
Fabes, 150
Fagan, J., 53, 74
Fahy, T., 88
Failure to thrive, 131
Faith development theory, 22, 300, 350–351
Falicov, C., 26
Families
    adolescence, and family relationships, 247–248
    diversity and, 46–48
    family leave for care of children and, 124–125
    family member links, 24–25
    infancy/toddlerhood issues, 124–125, 133
    late adulthood and, 396–400
    middle childhood, and disruptions in, 220–221
    social support for, 133
    See also Multigenerational families
Family Health International, 60
Family pluralism Recognition of many viable types of family structures, 47
Fan, X., 206
Fantuzzo, J. W., 212
Farber, A., 439
Farber, S., 439
Faris, R., 256
Farley, T., 74
Farmer, R. L., 436
FAS (fetal alcohol syndrome), 86–87
Fass, P., 181, 182, 232
Fass, S., 210
Fauth, J., 241

Fay, M., 379

FDA (Food and Drug Administration), 62

Federal Interagency Forum on Aging-related Statistics, 375, 378, 387, 402, 404, 406, 424, 429

Feerick, M. M., 214

Fegley, S., 198

Fehr, B., 305

Feijoo, A., 263

Fein, G., 123, 199

Felson, R. B., 186

Feminist theory (of aging) Theory of social gerontology suggesting that, because gender is a central organizing principle in our society, we can only understand aging by taking gender into account), 385

Ferdman, B. M., 191

Ferguson, R. J., 64

Fergusson, D. M., 313

Ferlin, A., 64

Fertilization The penetration of an ovum by a spermatozoon, usually occurring in the fallopian tube, 55, 65, 66

　Fertilization age The number of completed weeks of pregnancy counting from 14 days after the beginning of the last menstrual period to the birth of the neonate, 67

Fertilization of egg, 67

Fetal alcohol syndrome (FAS), 86–87

Fetal differentiation, 70

Fetal viability The capability to survive outside the womb, typically requiring at least 25, 62

Fetus The developing organism from the ninth week of pregnancy to birth, 69

Fetus development, 69

　fetal period, 69

　first trimester and, 69

　second trimester and, 70

　third trimester and, 70

　viability of, 62

Fictive kin Friends who are neither biologically nor romantically related to the family but who are adopted as family and given the same rights and responsibilities as family members, 310, 362

Field, D., 424

Field, T., 103

Fields, J., 209

Fiese, B., 165

Fifer, W., 103

Figa-Talamanca, I., 64

Figueira-McDonough, J., 47, 62

Figueredo, A. J., 213

Fiksenbaum, L. M., 388, 391

Finch, C., 337

Finch, M. D., 251

Findlay, L., 150

Fine motor skills Skills based on small muscle movements, particularly in the hands, as well as eye-hand coordination, 143

Finer, L., 62

Finkelhor, D., 168, 253, 254

Finkle, W., 339

Finn, J. D., 205

Finn-Stevenson, M., 108

First Steps, 52

Fischer, C., 362

Fischer, K., 437

Fisher, C., 121

Fitzmaurice, G. M., 220

Fitzpatrick, K. M., 274

Fivush, R., 146

Flaherty, B., 250

Flammer, A., 252

Flanagan, C. A., 248

Flegal, K. M., 276

Fleming, A. R., 75

Fleming, C., 271

Flexible grouping, 203

Flint, M., 338

Floyd, F., 261

Floyd, R. L., 87

Fluid intelligence Abstract reasoning skills, 392

Flynn, L., 21

Fobil, J., 254

Fogg, N., 288

Foley, K. M., 442, 443

Foner, A., 23, 385

Fong, R., 193

Food and Drug Administration (FDA), 62

Forbes, S., 438

Foresta, C., 65

Formal operations stage The fourth and final stage in Piaget's theory of cognitive development, generally experienced in adolescence. Involves the capacity to apply hypothetical reasoning and to use symbols to solve problems 110, 187, 298

Formal school education
  immigration experience and, 204, 207
Formal schooling education
  character education and, 196
  cognition and, 202–204
  collaborative classroom and, 207
  diversity issues and, 204–205
  early childhood and, 159–160
  full-service school and, 208
  gender and, 188, 206, 208
  heterogeneous grouping, 207–208
  mainstreaming and, 207
  middle childhood and, 202–204, 206–209
  norm-referenced testing, 203–204
  privilege and, 207
  racial segregation and, 206
  tracking and, 207
Fortenberry, J. D., 263
Fost, N., 86
Foster, D. G., 61
Fowler, J., 22, 290, 298, 300, 350
Foy, D. W., 214
Fracasso, M., 121
Francis, M., 386
Franklin, C., 74
Franzetta, K., 78
Fraser, M., 31, 132, 170, 171, 222, 223
Fratiglioni, L., 394
Frazier, L. M., 64
Freedman, V. A., 378
Freeman, E., 158
Freeman, E. M., 121
Freeman, L., 167
Freeman, S., 60
Freud, S., 147, 190, 242, 445
Friedman, M. A., 80
Friedmann, E., 363
Fries, J., 366
Fry, C., 33
Fry, D., 356
Frye, C. A., 60
Fu, H., 58, 59, 60
Fuentes-Afflick, E., 130
Fuhrer, R., 343
Fuligni, A., 192, 204, 250
Fuligni, A. S., 210
Fulker, D., 118
Full-service school, 208
Full-Spectrum Model of Consciousness, 22
Furman, L. D., 436

Furstenberg, F., 271
Furstenberg, F. F., 288
Furstenberg, F., Jr., 23, 26
Fusch, C., 81
Futterman, D., 260
Fyfe, L. M., 189

Gabel, K., 90
Gaertner, L., 152
Gagnon, A., 47
Galambos, N., 232, 279
Galambos, N. L., 248
Galda, L., 155
Gallagher, J. J., 219
Gallagher, S., 356
Gallup, G., Jr., 300, 353, 408
Gambineri, A., 64
Gamete intrafallopian tube transfer
  (GIFT), 66
Gamoran, A., 250
Gandelman, R., 155
Gara, M., 204
Garasky, S., 220
Garbarino, J., 166, 167, 196, 197, 211, 212,
  221, 246, 249, 257
Garber, J., 185
Garcia, E., 233
Gardner, H. E., 202
Gargiulo, R. M., 219
Garmezy, N., 77, 194, 222
Garnier, D., 185
Garrett, J. L., 219, 250, 255
Garton, A. F., 253
Gartrell, N., 88
Garver, K. L., 57
Garvey, C., 157
Garvin, V., 170
Gary, P., 131
Gatz, M., 295
Gau, D., 51
Gayer, T., 160
Gays. *See* Homosexuality; Lesbianism
Ge, X., 239
Gee, J. P., 204
Geiger, B., 120
Gelles, R., 168, 170
Gelman, S. A., 199
Gender
  adolescence, and differences in, 246–247
  bullying and, 196

cognition and, 200
convoy of relationships and, 353–354
eating disorders in middle childhood
and, 194
emotional development and, 194
emotional expression in very late
adulthood and, 448
employment and, 303, 363–364
feminist theory (of aging), 385
gender roles, 47, 199–201, 392
intellectual functioning and, 190
late adulthood and, 375, 378
leisure relationships and, 251–253
life course trajectory and, 21–23, 29
life expectancy and, 424
longevity and, 428
marriage status in late adulthood, 378
mental abilities and, 345–346
mortality rates and, 340, 341, 378, 387
peer relations and, 151, 197–198, 248–249
personality traits, 349
play in early childhood and, 157
poverty in very late adulthood and, 424
privilege and, 294, 385
puberty and, 236–237
puberty onset comparison and, 184–185
school education and, 188, 189, 206, 208
work relationships and, 251–253, 402
young adulthood issues and, 294, 301, 310
Gender identity, 149, 151–153, 199–201
Gender roles, 38, 153, 199–200, 294, 349
Gender schema theory, 200
Generalized other A construction that
represents how others might view and
respond to our behavior, 245–246
Generativity The ability to transcend personal
interests to provide care and concern for
generations to come, 333–334
Genes Basic units of heredity, made of DNA,
and found on chromosomes, 45. *See also*
Reproductive genetics
Genetic disorders, 84–86
Genetic engineering, 57
Genetic heterogeneity A genetic principle that a
trait, such as mental retardation, can have a
different etiology in different persons, 84
Genetic liability The state of being prone to
hereditary disorders, 84
Genetic theories of biological aging Theories
proposing that there are genetically

determined differences between species in
the maximum life span, 386
Genetics. *See* Reproductive genetics
Genital herpes, 266
Genital warts, 266
Genotype The totality of the hereditary
information present in an organism, 55
Gent, P. J., 219
George, L., 14, 15, 18, 21, 23, 25, 30, 33, 34, 132
George, L. K., 300, 375, 382, 386, 388
George, R., 131
Georgia Centenarian Study, 428
Georgiades, S. D., 311
Gerardi, M., 54
Gerekes' late-life pregnancy case study, 45–46
Gerhardt, S., 122
Germ cells The ova and spermatozoa whose
function is to reproduce the organism, 55
Gerontology, social, 382
See also Late adulthood
Gerstel, N., 356
Gessert, C., 438
Gestation The length of maturation time
from conception to birth. In humans it
averages 280 days, with a range of 259 to
287 days, 67
Gestational age The number of completed
weeks of pregnancy counting from the
first day of the last normal menstrual
cycle to the birth of the neonate, 67
small for gestational age (SGA), 88
Gibbs, J. T., 189, 192
Giblin, E., 339
Gidron, Y., 64
Gielen, U., 148
Gift, T. L., 78
GIFT (gamete intrafallopian tube transfer), 66
Gilbert, W. M., 83
Gilbert-Macleod, C., 104
Gillham, J., 195
Gilligan, C., 189, 190
Gilman, S. E., 220
Gilmer, D., 375, 386, 389, 390, 394
Ginn, J., 358
Ginsborg, J., 163
Gintis, H., 206
Giordano, J., 360
Girardi, A., 150
Giudice, L. C., 64
Glaser, D., 165, 167

Glass, C. S., 215

Glazebrook, C., 66

Global relationships and comparisons

core

developed countries

developing contries

First World

global economy

global North

global South

immigration

periphery

Second World

semiperiphery

Third World

Glover, R., 300, 310

Gogtay, N., 237, 238

Gold, D., 23

Goldberg, A. B., 52

Goldberg, G., 162

Goldberg, W., 158

Goldenberg, R. L., 58, 79, 81

Goldscheider, F., 358

Goldsmith, R., 21

Goldstein, H., 217

Goldstein, J., 307

Goldstein, S., 194

Goleman, D., 193, 194

Gomez, N., 131

Gonads Sex glands—ovaries in females and testes in males, 236

Gonorrhea, 265

Gonyea, J. G., 406

Gonzalez-Quintero, V., 130

Good, T., 202

Goodwin, J., 395

Gopaul-McNicol, S., 154

Gorback, S., 339

Gordon, R., 26

Gordon-Larsen, P., 185

Gorman, M. A., 405

Goshko, M., 132

Gotlib, I., 18, 19

Gottman, J. M., 306

Govenden, V., 80

Gowen, A., 212

Graff, H., 232

Grainger, D. A., 64

Granato, L., 241

Grandparenthood, 141, 399–401

Grant, J., 80

Gray, G., 91

Gray, R. H., 64

Great Depression, 11, 20, 24, 30, 31

Green, M., 195

Green, R., 88, 89, 315

Greenberg, E., 361

Greenberg, R., 103

Greene, C., 360

Greene, K. L., 64

Greene, R. W., 198

Greenfield, P., 254

Greenglass, E. R., 388, 391

Greenstone, J., 162

Greulich, M., 51

Greve, W., 385, 388

Grief The normal internal reaction of an individual experiencing a loss, a complex process that is highly individualized, 444–449

Wortman and Silver's patterns of grieving, 446-447

Grief work A necessary period of working to sever the attachment bond to a lost person or object

Griffith, S., 120

Grimes, D. A., 59

Gritsavage, M. M., 189

Grodin, B., 339

Gromley, W., 160

Gross, E., 254

Gross motor skills Skills based upon large muscle group movements and most easily observed during whole body movements, such as hopping, skipping, and running, 143

Group norms, 197

Groves, B. M., 212, 214, 215, 221

Guarnaccia, P., 192, 204

Gubler, K. D., 79

Gueldner, S. H., 424

Guildea, S. E. S., 82

Guillebaud, J., 61

Guillemard, A., 23

Guillemin, A., 23

Guisbond, L., 208

Gulko, J., 200

Gullete, M., 332

Gurian, M., 188

Guterman, N., 132, 214

Guterman, N. B., 212, 214

Guthrie, D., 304
Gutierrez, R. A., 192
Gutman, H., 26
Gutmann, D., 349
Gutterman, N. B., 133, 214
Guvendag, E. S., 78
Guy, E., 80
Guyer, B., 53, 80
Guzzetti, B. J., 189
Gyllstrom, M. E., 338

Haan, N., 391
Haas, T., 58
Haden, C., 146
Hagestad, G., 14, 15, 21, 23
Hahn, S., 64
Haine, R., 146
Haine, R. A., 221
Hair, E., 295
Hair, E. C., 311
Hakin, R. B., 64
Hakuta, K., 191
Hall, D., 276
Hall, G., 232
Hall, N., 108
Hallak, J., 64
Halle, T., 310
Halpern, A., 289
Hamalaiven, O., 339
Hamblen, J., 214
Hamilton, B., 58
Hamilton, B. E., 53, 58, 72
Hamilton-Giachritsis, C., 121
Hammarberg, K., 67, 75
Hammei, R. D., 64
Hammer, T., 302
Han, S., 364
Handelsman, D., 61
Hankins, G. D., 79
Hanley, R. J., 40
Hann, D., 74
Hansell, J., 170
Hansson, R., 444
Hao, L., 264
Hardenbrook, M., 189
Hareven, T., 11, 17, 19, 20, 24, 25, 26, 27, 398
Hargreaves, E., 170
Harkness, S., 146
Harkness, W. L., 275
Harlow, B., 338

Harootyan, R., 359
Harpalani, V., 198
Harps, S. N., 192
Harrell, S. P., 315
Harrigan, M., 49
Harrigan, M. P., 430, 436
Harris, J., 67
Harrop, J., 168
Harry, B., 206
Hart, B., 146
Hart, H., 333, 334
Hart, V. A., 65, 66
Harter, K., 261
Harter, S., 152, 202
Hartka, E., 391
Hartup, W. W., 197, 199
Harvey, S. M., 61, 89
Harville, E. W., 48
Harwood, R., 117
Hass, A., 183
Hassan, M. A., 64
Hatch, L. R., 383, 385, 388
Hatch, S. L., 382
Hatchett, S., 360
Hathaway, 275
Haug, M., 423
Haugaard, J. J., 214
Hauser-Cram, P., 124, 215, 219
Hauth, J. C., 81
Havighurst, R., 349, 363
Havighurst, R. J., 290, 383
Hawkins, A., 351
Hawley, D. R., 77
Hayes, C., 210
Hayflick, L., 386
Hays, M., 90
Hayward, C., 239
Health issues
    adolescence physical health threats, 273–278
    early childhood, 142–159, 162–170
    HIV-infected pregnant mothers, 90–91
    infancy/toddlerhood, 100–101, 129–132
    late adulthood and, 387–388
    middle adulthood, 336–345
    sexually transmitted diseases
        (STDs), 265–268
    teenage pregnancy and, 72–73
    See also Eating disorders; Mental health;
        specific illnesses
Health related senior facilities, 410

Healthy People 2000, 52
Healthy People 2010, 128
Hearth, A., 423, 446
Heck, K. E., 81
Heckhausen, J., 335
Hedelin, H., 340
Hedley, A. A., 276
Hehir, T., 220
Heilbrun, G., 362
Heimberg, R., 261
Heimpel, S., 151
Heinz, W., 15, 23, 29, 363
Helburn, S., 209
Helen Tyson, struggling to be a "good mother"
    at 42 case study, 326–327
Hellstrom, A. L., 82
Helson, R., 349
Hemenway, D., 163
Henderson, K., 21
Hendricks, J., 383, 385, 388
Hendriksen, T., 87
Henry, W., 383
Henry case study, overprotecting, 99–100
Henshaw, S., 62
Hepp, S. M., 60
Herd, P., 381, 382
Herdiman, J., 57, 62
Herdt, G., 260
Hermann, W., 339
Hermanussen, M., 81
Hernandez, M., 25, 30
Hernanzed, M., 210
Heron, M., 341, 342
Herrenkohl, T. I., 214
Herring, R. D., 192
Hershberg, T., 23
Hesse, E., 119
Hesse, V., 81
Hessol, N., 130
Heterogeneous grouping, 207–208
Hetherington, E. M., 165, 220, 221
Heyman, R. E., 214
Hickey, D., 75
Hiestand, M., 405
Higgins, C., 347
Hildingsson, I., 52
Hill, R. B., 121
Hillis, S. D., 266
Hillson, J. M. C., 213
Hilton, A., 158

Himes, C., 397
Himmelfarb, H., 250
Hines, P., 127, 247
Hinrichsen, G. A., 396
Hinshaw, S. P., 215
Hirsch, B., 334
Historical perspective of middle
    childhood, 181–182
Historical time, 11-12, 19-20, 22, 28, 35
HIV/AIDS, 90–91, 267–268
Hlatky, M., 340
Hobbs, F., 379
Hodge, D., 299
Hodge, D. M., 221
Hodge, D. R., 300
Hodgman, J. E., 82
Hodnett, E. D., 51
Hoek, H., 88
Hoffnung, M., 429
Hoffnung, R. J., 429
Hogan, D., 23
Hogan, D. P., 311
Hoge, C. W., 317
Hogoel, L., 75
Hogstel, M., 434, 449
Hohman, M., 132
Holden, A., 64
Holly's early arrival case study, 98
Holman, J. R., 58, 61
Holmberg, D., 17
Holmes, M. M., 72
Holmes, T., 16, 17
Holstein, C., 151
Holt, V., 54
Holter, M. C., 217
Homans, G. C., 385
Home health care services, 410
Homer, L., 76
Homosexuality
    adolescence and, 260–261, 278
    coming-out process, 230, 260–261, 308
    convoy of relationships and, 362
    gay/lesbian partnerships and,
        307–309, 357, 433
    late adulthood and, 398, 433
    special parent populations and, 248
    See also Lesbianism
Hong-zheng, L., 18
Hood, L., 276
Hoomans, E. H., 61

Hooyman, N., 424, 431, 432, 433, 435, 437

Hope, R. M., 221

Hoppey, D., 219

Hoppin, J. A., 65

Hormone replacement therapy (HRT), 339

Horn, A. W., 79

Horn, J. L., 392

Horowitz, J., 128

Horwood, L. J., 313

Hosmer, L., 50

Hosp, J. L., 207

Hospice Program that provides care to the terminally ill. Patients typically receive treatment by a team of doctors, nurses, social workers, and care staff through inpatient or outpatient care, 411, 441

Hospital Insurance Trust Fund (Medicare Part A), 409

Hostile aggression Aggression that is an attack meant to hurt another individual, 150

House, J. S., 381, 382

Howard, G. J., 310

Howard, K., 82

Howell, A., 215, 219

Howland, C. A., 89

Hoybert, D. L., 80

Hoyert, D. L., 53, 58, 80

Hoyos-Nervi, C., 204

HPV (Human Papillomavirus), 266

HRT (hormone replacement therapy), 339

Huang, L. N., 189, 192

Huang, L. Z., 70, 81

Huberman, B., 262, 263, 265

Hubert, H., 366

Huff, C., 273

Hughes, H., 168

Huh, E., 151

Human agency The use of personal power to achieve one's goals, 26–27

Human capital Individual assets such as talents, skills, intellectual capacity, social development, and emotional regulatory capacity, 291, 295, 312

Human Genome Project, 54, 56

Human Papillomavirus (HPV), 266

Human Rights Watch, 182

Humanistic perspective, 35

Humphrey, J., 128

Humphreys, N. A., 398

Hussein, I., 80

Hutchison, E., 212, 267

Huttenlocher, P., 107, 108

Huyck, M., 349, 364, 401

Huyck, M. H., 434

Hyson, M., 194

IADL (instrumental activities of daily living), 429

Iannotti, R., 148

Identity A combination of what an individual is born with and into; who the person associates with; how others see the individual; what this person has done; his or her attitudes, traits, abilities, habits, tendencies, and preferences; and what the individual looks like, 349, 350

Identify vs. role diffusion, 116, 142–143

Rosenberg's model of identity, 244–245

Identity development, 241–246

accommodation (identity) and, 349, 350

adolescence and, 230–231, 241–246, 242–245

Carl's struggle for identity case study, 230–231

cultural identity and, 191–193

early childhood and, 152–154

individuation and, 247

Marcia's theory of,

middle adulthood, 349–350

middle childhood, 191–193, 199–201

privilege and, 195, 198

self/identity theories and, 242–245

young adulthood and, 301–302

Identity groups, 27

IEP (individual education plan), 219

Illinois Maternal and Child Health Project, 81

Immigration experience

adolescence and, 255–256

childbearing and, 47

description of, 30

disruption in families and, 25

infancy/toddlerhood and, 130

late adulthood and, 378, 400

school education and, 204, 207

very late adulthood and, 445

work force of immigrants, 12

young adulthood and, 305, 312, 313–314

Immunization A method of administering microorganisms, bacteria, or viruses that have been modified or killed to stimulate the body's immune system to build a defense against a specific disease;

also known as vaccination or inoculation, 108–109

In vitro fertilization (IVF), 64, 66

Incidence, 341

Incidental memory Memory that relates to facts a person has learned without the intention to retain and recall, 393

Inder, T. E., 82

Indirect bullying Less explicit and less detectable than direct bullying, including more subtle verbal, psychological, and social or "relational" bullying tactics, 196

Individual education plan (IEP) An individualized, collaboratively developed plan that focuses on facilitating achievement and is designed to respond to the unique needs of a child with a disability in the school setting. Such plans are mandated by the Individuals with Disabilities Education Act of 1990, 219

Individuals with Disabilities Education Act, 217

Individuation The development of a self and identity that are unique and separate
default individualization
definition of, 247
developmental individualization, 293

Individuative-reflective faith The fourth stage of James Fowler's six-stage model of faith development, a stage when adults no longer rely on outside authority and look for authority within the self, 300, 351

Industry versus inferiority, 116, 190, 195

Infancy
active learning exercises, 134
Ainsworth's theory of attachment and, 119–122
attachment and brain development in, 122–123
bonding and, 54, 82, 122
Bowlby's theory of attachment and, 118–119
brain and, 107–108
breastfeeding vs. bottle feeding decision and, 127–128
child abuse and, 131–132
child care and, 124–126
cognitive development and, 109–113
concrete operations stage and, 110
development disruptions and, 124
developmental delays and, 124

education for risk/prevention and, 132–133
emotional control and, 115–117
Erikson's psychosocial theory and, 114–115
family leave for care and, 124–125
formal operations stage and, 110
healthy development and, 100–101, 129–132
Holly's early arrival case study, 98
immigration experience and, 130
immunizations for, 108–109
inadequate caregiving for, 131
mastery and, 103, 111, 114–115
mortality issues and, 130
motor skills and, 105–107
multigenerational families and, 126–129
nonorganic failure to thrive (NOFTT) and, 131
object permanence mastery and, 111
overprotecting Henry case study, 99–100
physical development and, 101–109
Piaget's stages of cognitive development and, 110–113
poverty issues and, 129–130
prelanguage skills and, 113
preoperational stage and, 110
reflexes and, 104–105
resilience and, 132
risk/preventive factors and, 132–133
risks to healthy development and, 129–132
role play and, 122–123
Sarah's teen Dad case study, 99
self-regulation, 102–103
sensorimotor stage and, 110
sensory abilities and, 103–104
sensory systems and, 103
separation anxiety and, 111–112
social support for families and, 133
social work practice and, 133–134
socioemotional development and, 114–124
stranger anxiety and, 111
sudden infant death syndrome (SIDS) and, 103
symbolic functioning and, 110
synapses and, 107
temperament and, 113, 117–118, 133
transitional objects and, 119
web resources, 134–135
See also At-risk newborns; Early childhood; Middle childhood

Infant A young child in the first year of life, 100

Infant mortality The death of a child before his or her first birthday, 130

Infertility The inability to create a viable embryo, 63–67

Infertility treatment, 47, 63–67

Inheritance, multifactorial, 84 *See also* Reproductive genetics

Initiative versus guilt, 116, 139, 149

Institute for the Study of Aging, 393, 394

Institutional discrimination The systematic denial of access to assets, economic opportunities, associations, and organizations based on minority status, 192, 207

Instrumental activities of daily living (IADL), 429

Instrumental activities of daily living (IADLs) More complex everyday tasks such as doing light housework, doing the laundry, using transportation, handling finances, using the telephone, and taking medications, 150, 429

Instrumental aggression Aggression that occurs while fighting over toys and space, etc., 150

Intelligence
  crystallized intelligence, 392
  emotional intelligence, 196
  fluid intelligence, 392
  gender, and intellectual functioning, 190
  interrelational intelligence, 190
  late adulthood and, 392–394
  middle adulthood and, 345–346
  middle childhood and, 190, 196, 203
  multiple intelligence theory, 203

Intentional memory Memory that relates to events that a person plans to remember, 393

Interactive genes Corresponding genes that give separate yet controlling messages, 57

Interdependency, 24–26, 33, 305, 433

Interlocking trajectories, 15, 36

International Longevity Center-USA, 390

Internet relationships, 253–255

Internet resources. *See* Web resources

Interrelational intelligence Based on emotional and social intelligence and similar to Howard Gardner's concept of interpersonal intelligence, 190

Intimacy Characteristic of close interpersonal relationships, includes interdependence, self-disclosure, and affection, 290

  Intimacy versus isolation Erik Erikson's description of the developmental task of young adulthood, a time when individuals move from the identity fragmentation, confusion, and exploration of adolescence into more intimate engagement with significant others or become isolated, 290

Intrauterine fetal death (IUFD), 79

Intrauterine insemination (IUI), 67

Introversion Orientation to the internal world, in contrast to extroversion, which is orientation to the external world, 334

Irish, D., 448

Ironsmith, M., 151

Irvine, K., 87

Irvine, M., 185

Irving, K., 151

Isager, T., 88

Isenberg, S., 350

Iso-Ahola, S. E., 253

Ito, M., 47

IUFD (intrauterine fetal death), 79

IUI (intrauterine insemination), 67

IVF (in vitro fertilization), 66

Jack's name change case study, 140–141

Jackson, B. J., 77

Jackson, J., 121, 360

Jackson, K. M., 128

Jacob, D., 362

Jacobs, D., 64

Jain, T., 65

James, W. P. T., 276, 277

Jamieson, J., 83

Jang, Y., 348, 395

Jans, L., 89

Jarrell, A., 263

Jasso, G., 18

Jayakody, R., 362

Jaycox, L., 195

Jekielek, S., 15, 20, 25

Jelen, T. G., 62

Jellinek, M., 132

Jendrek, M., 162

Jeng, G., 65

Jenkins, E., 214
Jerome's break from school case study, 286
Jessor, R., 263, 270
Jobe, A. H., 58
Jodl, K. M., 220
Johannson, R., 82
Johanson, R., 50
Johansson, B., 393
Johnson, A., 195
Johnson, B., 299
Johnson, C., 151
Johnson, C. L., 276, 430, 432
Johnson, K., 340
Johnson, K. C., 50
Johnson, M., 112
Johnson, M. P., 51, 53
Johnson, R., 121
Johnson, R. S., 435
Johnson, T., 362
Johnston, D., 90
Johnston, L., 268, 269
Jones, A., 246
Jones, D., 170
Jones, H. P., 82
Jones, J., 264
Jones, L., 132
Jones, R., 205, 206
Jordan, J. V., 194
Jordan, M. W., 314
Jordon, C. B., 64
Joseph, G., 358
Joshi, S., 394, 395
Judge, T., 347
Julian, T., 361
Jun, H., 334
Jung's theory of finding a balance, 334
Juvenile delinquency Acts that, if committed by
an adult, would be considered crimes, plus
status offenses such as running away from
home, skipping school, violating curfew,
and possession of tobacco or alcohol,
271–273
Jyothi, M. C., 82

Kabholkar, A., 107, 108
Kaczmarek, L. A., 217
Kaersvang, L., 168
Kagan, J., 117
Kagan, M., 203
Kagan, S., 203
Kahn, A., 125, 126
Kahn, R., 353
Kakouros, E., 215
Kalekin-Fishman, D., 75
Kalil, A., 315
Kalter, N., 170, 221
Kaltiala-Heino, R., 186
Kaltman, S., 447
Kamens, M. W., 295
Kamerman, S., 125, 126
Kanabus, A., 90, 91
Kandel, D. B., 269, 302
Kao, R. S., 379
Kaplan, B., 60
Kaplan, D. W., 72, 73
Kaplan, H., 90, 214, 278, 393, 395
Kaplan, J., 53, 128
Kaplan, M. S., 90
Kaplowitz, P., 184, 185, 186
Karpa, K. D., 61
Karson, M., 183
Karus, D., 302
Kasl-Godley, J., 434
Kaslow, F., 300
Kasser, T., 333
Katz, J., 104
Katz, L., 26
Katz, P., 153
Kaufman, M., 89
Kawachi, I., 220, 379
Kayne, 235
Kayne, M., 51
Kdous, M., 78
Keating, D., 240
Keating, P., 206
Keefe, N., 311
Keeper of the meaning A stage of psychosocial
development proposed by George Vaillant
to come between Erik Erikson's stages of
generativity and integrity, a stage when
older adults take on the task of passing on
the traditions of the past to the next
generation, 391
Keijnen, J., 59
Keitner, G., 164
Kellaghan, T., 205, 206
Kellam, S., 31, 33, 34
Kelly, J., 165
Kelly-Weeder, S., 64
Kempe, C., 132

Kempe, R., 132
Keniston, K., 307
Kennedy, C. M., 214
Kennel, J. H., 51
Kennell, D. L., 40
Kenney, C., 307
Kenney, J. W., 72
Kent, G., 91
Keogh, B. K., 304, 305
Kerns, D., 241
Kertzer, D., 22
Kesmodel, U., 87
Kessenich, M., 80, 82
Kessler, R., 330, 349
Keyes, C., 334
Kikuzawa, S., 395
Kilian, B., 167
Killen, M., 248
Killick, S. R., 65
Kilpatrick, D. G., 72
Kim, H., 90
Kim, J., 363
Kimmel, D., 21, 362
Kindlon, D., 246
Kindlon, D. J., 195
Kingson, E. R., 409
Kinkeepers Family members who work at keeping family members across the generations in touch with one another and make sure that both emotional and practical needs of family members are met, 356
Kinship ties, 27, 356, 359, 398
Kirby, L., 132, 170, 223
Kirkpatrick Johnson, M., 14, 15
Kiwi, R., 79
Kiyak, H. A., 424, 431, 432, 433, 435, 437
Kjerulf, L., 87
Klaczynski, P., 241
Klaum, G., 361
Klaus, M. H., 50
Klaus, P. H., 50
Klebanov, P., 26
Kleiber, D., 252
Klein, E., 334
Klein, M., 249
Klein, S., 189
Kliman, J., 29
Klin, A., 215
Kling, J., 26

Klingaman, L. R., 275
Klinger, L. G., 215
Klohnen, E., 349
Klonoff-Cohen, H. S., 66
Klotter, J., 75
Knapp, M. S., 204
Knight, M., 90
Knight, R. T., 393
Knobel, M., 189
Knott, B., 47
Koball, H., 210
Kochanska, G., 149
Koelling, K., 238
Koenig, H. G., 300, 436
Koerin, B. B., 430
Koeske, G., 82
Koeske, R., 82
Kohlberg, L., 147, 148, 190, 243, 299
Kohlberg's theory of moral development, 190
Kohli, M., 331, 355, 357, 358, 359
Kohut, H., 147
Kolak, A., 120
Kolte, A. M., 79
Kopola, M., 192
Koppers, A. J., 64
Korbin, J., 103
Kornelsen, J., 51
Korte, J., 64
Koshar, J. H., 72, 74
Kosloski, K., 406
Koss, M. P., 213
Kosunen, E., 186
Kotch, J., 170
Kovacs, P., 267
Kovacs, P. J., 442
Kowalski, K., 153
Kozol, J., 159, 181, 206, 207, 211
Krauss, M., 124
Krimgold, B., 366
Krueger, P., 128
Krueger, V., 258
Krug, E., 166, 167
Kruse, A., 329
Kruzich, J. M., 406
Kübler-Ross, E., 437, 438, 446
Kubzansky, L., 379
Kuh, D., 31
Kuhl, P., 103
Kuiper, N. A., 213
Künemund, H., 331, 355, 357, 358, 359

Kunkel, S., 376, 402
Kupersmidt, J. B., 198
Kupper, L. L., 73, 90
Kurdek, L., 308
Kurtz, L., 165
Kurtz, P. D., 206
Kurzawa, R., 64
Kusuda, S., 80
Kuure, O., 204
Kwok, O., 221

Labouvie-Vief, G., 298
Lachman, M., 330, 331, 349
Ladd, G. W., 198
LaDue, R. A., 87
Laflamme, D., 158
Laird, J., 88, 89, 380
Lam, M. L., 379
Lamaze, F., 52
Lambert, J., 357, 362
Lane, A., 80
Lang, A. J., 214
Langford, P. E., 189
Langle, A., 392
Langlois, J. H., 201
Language development
   early childhood and, 143–146
   infancy/toddlerhood and, 113
   language skills, 145–146
   middle childhood and, 204–205
   prelanguage skills, 113
Language register The idea that
   communication has informal as well as
   formal elements, the informal being that
   communication that originates from a
   baby's first contacts with caregiver and
   continues in family, neighborhood and
   peer communal interaction, the formal
   being that communication that is required
   by community institutions and conforms
   to accepted mainstream normative
   conventions and traditions often
   established by the prevailing academic,
   political, and social power structures,
   204–205
Lankshear, C., 189
Lansford, J., 361
Lantz, P. M., 381, 382
Larner, M., 130
Larson, D. B., 300

Larson, E. J., 87
Larson, R., 239, 252
Larson, R. W., 248, 263
LaSala, M. C., 309
Laseter, R., 314, 315
Late adulthood
   active learning exercises, 414–415
   activity theory and, 383
   age stratification perspective and, 385–386
   age-associated memory impairment (AAMI)
      and, 394
   age-related changes and physiology and,
      389–391
   biological aging theories and, 386
   biological changes and, 386–391
   brain plasticity, 393
   care receiving and, 404–405
   caregiving and, 404–405
   continuity theory and, 383
   crystallized intelligence and, 392
   cultural construction of, 379–382
   delirium and, 395
   dementia and, 394
   demographics and, 374–379
   dependency ratio and, 376
   depression and, 392, 395, 407
   disengagement theory (of aging) and, 383
   divorce and, 378, 398
   ego integrity vs. ego despair and, 391
   employment and, 402
   ethical issues, and medical treatments in, 391
   families and, 396–400
   feminist theory (of aging) and, 385
   fluid intelligence and, 392
   formal resources for meeting needs
      and, 409–411
   gender and, 375, 378
   genetic theories of biological aging and, 386
   gerontology and, social, 382
   grandparenthood and, 141, 399–401
   health issues and, 387–388
   homosexuality and, 398, 433
   immigration experience and, 378, 400
   incidental memory and, 393
   informal resources for meeting
      needs and, 408–409
   institutionalization and, 405–406
   intellectual changes and, 392–394
   intentional memory and, 393
   keeper of the meaning and, 391

learning and, 392–394
life course perspective, in, 424
life events in, 396–406
life review and, 407
longevity and, 387–388
mastery and, 383, 388, 391, 395, 407
memory and, 393–394
mental health, and disorders in, 394–396
molecular/cellular theories of biological
    aging and, 386
morbidity rates, 387
Moros' increasing needs for care
    case study, 374
mortality rates and, 387
personal meaning search and, 407–408
personality changes and, 391–392
power of attorney (POA) and, 411
programmed aging theories and, 386
psychological changes and, 391–396
psychosocial theories and, 382–386
random error theories and, 386
reminiscence and, 407
resilience and, 411–412
resources for meeting needs and, 408–410
retirement and, 372, 401–404
risk/preventive factors and, 411–412
Ruby Johnson, caretaker for three
    generations case study, 373
Search for personal meaning, 407–408
self-efficacy and, 383, 388
Smiths in early retirement case study, 372
social construction theory and, 384–385
social exchange theory and, 385
social work practice and, 413
substance use/abuse and, 393, 395–396
suicide and, 395, 396
system level theories of biological aging
    and, 386–387
transitions regarding social roles and,
    396–407
Vaillant's Study of Adult Development, 411
web resources, 414–415
widowhood and, 405
work relationships and, 401–404
Lateralization Process in which the two
    hemispheres of the brain begin to operate
    slightly differently during early childhood,
    142–143
Lattanzi-Licht, M., 441
Laub, J. H., 302

Laumann, E., 339
Laurino, M. Y., 79
Lawton, L., 358
Lazear, D., 203
LBW (low birth weight), 80–81
Learning play Play that is focused on language
    and thinking skills, 156
Leary, J. D., 183
LeCroy, C. W., 51, 288
Lederberg, J., 84
Lee, B., 131
Lee, E., 192, 358
Lee, K., 104, 339
Lee, S., 205
Leeder, E., 28
LeFever, G. B., 215
Lein, L., 290
Leisering, L., 23, 34
Leisure relationships, 251–253
Leitenberg, H., 259
Lentz, M., 339
Leonard, K., 120
Leonard, R., 19
Leondar-Wright, B., 291
Lerman-Sagie, T., 70
Lerner, J. V., 209, 210
Lerner, R., 232, 279
Lesbianism
    adolescence and, 260–261, 278
    late adulthood and, 398, 433
    long-term relationships and, 433
    middle adulthood and, 357, 362
    motherhood and, 88–89, 248
    partnerships and, 307–309, 357, 433
    very late adulthood and, 433
    young adulthood relationships and, 307–309
Lev, D., 70
Levin, D. E., 185
Levine, E., 132
Levine, L., 340
Levinson, D., 288, 291, 334, 348
Levinson, J., 334, 348
Levinson, M., 334
Levinson's theories
    finding a balance in middle adulthood
        and, 334
    life structure in young adulthood and, 291
Levitt, M., 57
Levy, B., 275
Levy, G. D., 199

Levy, L., 447
Levy, S., 209
Lewis, A., 126
Lewis, J., 165
Lewis, T., 158
Liben, L. S., 192
Lichtenstein, S., 303
Lidow, M., 238
Lieberman, E., 52
Liebman, J., 26
Life course perspective An approach to human behavior that recognizes the influence of age but also acknowledges the influences of historical time and culture active learning exercises, 36
active learning exercises, 36
age norm and, 22
age structuring and, 23
biological age and, 21, 386
cohort concept and, 11
cohort effects and, 20
completion of life course and, 449
concepts of, 11–19
cumulative advantage/disadvantage and, 30–31
David Sanchez's search for connections case study, 4–5
definition of, xviii, 9–11
dimensions of age and, 21–22
diversity and, 27–30
employment and, 20, 23, 29
event history and, 10
family member links and, 24–25
gender, 21–23, 29
human agency and, 26–27
interlocking trajectories and, 15, 36
interplay of human lives and historic time in, 19–20
life change events and, 12, 15–18
life course completion and, 449
life events and, 12
life review and, 407
life-span theory and, 334–336
linked or interdependent lives and, 24–26
Mahdi Mahdi's shared journey case study, 5–7
population pyramid and, 12
privilege and, 26, 31, 33
psychological age and, 21
resilience and, 31
risk/protection and, 30–32
self-efficacy and, 27
sex ratios and, 13
social age and, 22
social support and, 24
social work practice and, 36
spiritual age and, 22
strengths and limitations of, 33–34
Suarez family after September 11, 2001 case study, 8–9
themes of, 19–32
theoretical perspectives and, 34–35
theoretical roots of, 11
timing of lives and, 19, 20–21, 22–24
trajectories and, 12, 14–15, 27–30
transitions and, 12, 14–15, 396–407
turning points and, 12, 18–19
web resources, 37–38
wider world links and, 25–26
Life event Incident or event that is brief in scope but is influential on human behavior, 12, 396–406
Life expectancy, 424
Life review A process of evaluating and making sense of one's life. It includes a reinterpretation of past experiences and unresolved conflicts. The process of life review relates to the eighth stage of Erikson's theory of adult development (ego integrity versus ego despair), 407
Life structure, 291
Life-span theory A theory that begins with the premise that development is lifelong and is based in ongoing transactions between persons and environments; based in psychology, whereas the life course perspective has more multidisciplinary roots, 334–336
linked or interdependent lives and, 24–26
Life structure In Levinson's seasons of adulthood theory, the patterns and central components of a person's life at a particular point in time, 291
Light, J., 87
Lightening, 70
Limber, S. P., 196
Lin, R. S., 78
Lindemann, E., 445, 446
Lindenberger, U., 335
Lindsay, D. M., 300, 353, 408

Ling, T., 295

Linver, M. R., 210, 211

Lipson, A., 151

Lipton, M., 207

Little, S. E., 66

Liu, P. Y., 61

Living will A document that describes the medical procedures, drugs, and types of treatment that an individual would choose for oneself if able to do so in certain situations. It also describes the situations for which this individual would want treatment withheld, 439

Ljunggren, C., 340

Lloyd, C. B., 288, 293

Lochman, J. E., 198

Locke, A., 163

Lodhi, F., 66

Logan, J., 358, 398

Logan, J. A., 269

Logan, R., 334

Logan, S., 81

Logan, S. L., 121

Lohnes, K., 221

Lollar, D., 304

Lolli, E., 209

Long, J., 360

Long, W. B., III, 79

Longevity, 387–388, 428

Longino, C. F., 387

Longitudinal research design, 18

Lopez, S., 192, 204

Lorenz, F., 25

Lortie, K. L., 51, 288

Losen, D., 250

Loss The severing of an attachment an individual has with a loved one, a love object, or an aspect of one's self or identity, 444–449

    Erich Lindemann's common reactions to loss, 445-446

    theories and models of loss, 445-447

Lovegreen, L., 22, 23, 29, 31

Loveless, T., 207

Low birth weight (LBW) A newborn weight of less than 2,500 grams (5 pounds, 8 ounces), 80–81

Lowenthal, M., 349

Lowry, R., 271

Lozano, R., 166

Lucon, A. M., 65

Lui, M., 291

Luidens, D., 299

Lum, D., 191, 193

Luna, B., 238

Lundquist, K., 448

Lunghofer, L., 274

Luthar, S., 31, 194

Lux, M., 340

Lydon-Rochelle, M., 54

Lyman, R. D., 215

Lynch, R., 251

Lynch, S. R., 72

Lynch, T. R., 392

Maccoby, E., 147, 164, 309

MacDoman, M., 80

MacFarlane, A., 50

MacFarlane, P., 170

Mack, R., 339

Mackey, 169

MacLennan, B., 167

Macunovich, D., 12

Madsen, W., 29

Maeda, Y., 47

Maggs, J., 18

Magill-Cuerden, J., 53

Magruder, B., 261

Magwaza, A., 167

Mahdi Mahdi's shared journey case study, 5–7

Mahoney, J. J., 441

Main, M., 119

Mainstreaming, 207

Maisano, P., 164

Malcuit, G., 158

Malina, R., 199

Malinger, G., 70

Mallampalli, A., 80

Maltreatment of children, 131–132, 170

Maluccio, A. N., 212

Mangum, G., 288

Maniadaki, K., 215

Manlove, J., 78

Manly, J. J., 393

Manoogian-O'Dell, M., 375

Manson, J., 340

Manson, S., 270, 271

Manuel Vega's difficult transition case study, 179–181

March of Dimes, 75, 80, 81, 83

Marchant, M., 198, 217, 218
Marcia, J. E., 242, 301
Marini, M. M., 289, 314
Marino, R., 131
Markides, K., 21
Markoulis, D., 148
Marks, A., 235, 236
Marks, N., 334, 357, 359, 362
Markstrom, C., 255
Markstrom-Adams, C., 192, 255
Marmot, M., 343
Marotz, L. R., 182
Marshall, J., 151
Marshall, N. L., 311
Marshall, S. K., 242, 245
Marshall, V., 23
Martikainen, P., 405
Martin, D., 54
Martin, J., 59
Martin, J. A., 53, 265
Martin, K. A., 186, 240, 259
Martin, L. G., 378
Martin, M., 330, 345
Martin, S. L., 72, 90
Martinez, I., 258
Martinkowski, K., 447
Maruna, S., 333
Marx, F., 311
Masaluso, M., 65
Masciadrelli, B. P., 310
Mason, M., 181, 182, 232
Massaro, A. N., 80
Masse, L., 160
Masten, A. S., 316
Masters, K., 90
Mastery
    adolescence and, 242
    early childhood and, 156, 161, 171
    infancy/toddlerhood and, 103, 111,
        114–115
    late adulthood and, 383, 388, 391, 395, 407
    middle childhood and, 183, 184, 195
Masturbation Self-stimulation of the genitals
    for sexual pleasure, 259
Maternal brain death, 79–80
Maternity Care Access Act of 1989, 52
Mathews, T., 80
Matsumoto-Grah, K., 193
Matthews, T. J., 53
Matute-Bianchi, M. E., 192

Mayer, L. U., 11, 20, 23
Mazzucchelli, T., 159
Mbori-Ngacha, D., 128
Mc Candies, T., 193
McAdams, D., 333, 334
McAdoo, H., 26, 190
McArdle, J. J., 394
McArthur, E., 220
McAuley, C., 264
McAuley, E., 388
McCabe, M. P., 186
McCaig, L. F., 297
McCammon, R., 11, 20
McCartney, K., 311
McClelland, J., 112
McCloskey, L. A., 213
McClure, E. M., 79
McCluskey, U., 123
McCrae, R., 348, 349, 392
McCullough, M. E., 300
McDermid, S., 362
McDonald Culp, A., 164
McDonnell, J., 219
McElhatton, P. R., 86
McFadden, E. J., 221
McFalls, J. Jr, 12
McGill, D., 247
McGlade, M., 130
McGoldrick, M., 15, 25, 30, 47, 48, 127,
        131, 182, 183, 193, 247, 357, 360, 362
McGraw, L., 375
McGroder, S. M., 311
McHale, S., 153
MCI (mild cognitive impairment), 394
McInnis-Dittrich, K., 431, 437, 439, 441
McIntosh, P., 31
McIntyre, J., 91
McKee, B., 334
Mckee, K. J., 408
McKeering, H., 334
McKinlay, S., 338, 339
McKnight, J., 444, 448
McLaughlin, E. A., 65
McLeskey, J., 219
McLoyd, 163
McLoyd, V. C., 210
McMichael, P., 28, 201
McNamara, T., 87
McQuaide, S., 361
McRoy, R. G., 121

McWhirter, J. J., 163, 209
Mead, G. H., 245
Meador, K. J., 84
Mechelli, A., 191
Medicaid, 62, 410
Medicare, 409, 410
Medicare Advocacy, 410
Medina, C., 298
Meek, M., 156
Mei-ying, L., 18
Memory, 393–394
Menacker, F., 53, 58, 80
Menacker, P. D., 53
Menaghan, E., 15, 20, 25
Menarche The onset of menstruation, 237
Meng, M. V., 64
Menkart, D., 193
Menon, U., 332
Menopause Permanent cessation of
    menstruation, usually defined as 12
    consecutive months with absence of
    menstruation, 337–338
Mental health
    adolescence and, 273–278
    gender, and mental abilities, 345–346
    late adulthood and, 394–396
    middle adulthood and, 336–345
    middle childhood and, 215–220
    See also Health issues
Mercy, J., 166
Merline, A., 353
Merrill, S., 336, 337, 342
Merton, R., 30
Mesmon, J., 150
Mestizo perspective A spiritual perspective
    embraced by many Latinos; focuses on
    wholeness, harmony, and balance
MetLife/National Alliance for Caregiving, 430
Meuleman, E. J., 61
Meyer, D. R., 220
Meyer, H. A., 196
Meyer, J., 23
Meyer, R. E., 90
Meyers, 235
Michaud, S. M., 221
Michealieu, 150
Mickler, C., 347
Middle adulthood
    accommodation (identity) and, 349, 350
    active learning exercises, 367–368
    assimilation (identity) and, 349–350
    bilingual children, 191
    biological changes and, 336–345
    children, and relationships in, 358–359
    community relationships and, 362
    conjunctive faith and, 351
    contextual model for personality
        stability and, 347
    convoy of relationships and, 353
    coping mechanisms and, 347
    cultural construction of, 331–332
    definition of, 330–331
    demographics and, 329–330
    depression and, 343–344, 361–362
    divorce and, 355, 357, 359
    employment and, 363, 364, 365
    Erikson's theory of generativity and, 333–334
    extroversion and, 334, 347,
    friends' relationships and, 361–362
    gain-loss balance and, 335
    health status changes and, 340–345
    Helen Tyson, struggling to be a "good
        mother" at 42 case study, 326–327
    homosexuality and, 357, 362
    immigration experience and, 343–344
    intellectual changes and, 345–346
    introversion and, 334
    Jung's theory of finding a balance and, 334
    kinkeepers and, 356
    Levinson's theory of finding a balance and, 334
    life-span theory and, 334–336
    menopause and, 337–338
    mental health and, 336–345
    mobility changes and, 337
    multigenerational families and,
        355–361, 358–359
    organizational relationships and, 362
    parents, and relationships in, 359–360
    perimenopause and, 338
    personality changes and, 346–350
    physical appearance changes and, 336–337
    physical health and, 336–345
    premenopause and, 338
    relationships and, 353–362
    religious beliefs and, 353
    reproductive system changes and, 337–340
    resilience and, 366
    risk/preventive factors and, 365–366
    Robert Johnson, enjoying fatherhood at
        48 case study, 327–328

secondary sexual development and, 185
sexuality changes and, 337–340
social construction changes and, 328–332
social work practice and, 367
spirituality and, 350–353
spousal/partner relationships and, 357–358
substance use/abuse and, 343, 361
suicide and, 341
theories of, 332–336
trait theory and, 347
universalizing faith and, 351
Viktor Spiro, assuming new responsibilities as he turns 40 case study, 324–325
web resources, 368
Whitbourne's identity process model and, 349–350
work relationships with, 362–365
Middle childhood
acculturation and, 204
active learning exercises, 225
Anthony Bryant's impending assessment case study, 177–178
assimilation (cultural) and, 204
attention deficit hyperactivity disorder (ADHD) and, 85, 182, 188, 215, 216
autistic spectrum disorders and, 215, 217
brain plasticity and, 187
Brianna Shaw's new self-image case study, 178–179
bullying and, 196
capital and, 195–196
cerebral cortex and, 188
challenges and, 209–215
charter school education and, 196
cognitive development and, 186–191, 202–204
community link with school and, 206–209
community violence and, 212–215
cultural identity development and, 191–193
deculturalizing and, 181
depression and, 182, 194, 214
development and, 183–201
diversity issues and, 204–205
divorce, and effects on, 220, 221
eating disorders and, 194
education in, formal schooling, 201–209
emotional development and, 193–194
emotional intelligence and, 196
emotional/behavioral disorder and, 217–220
ethical issues and, 148, 190

family disruption and, 220–221
friendship and, 198–199
gender identity and, 199–201
gender roles and, 199–201
historic cultural construction of, 181–182
home link with school and, 205–206
individual education plan (IEP) and, 219
institutional discrimination and, 192, 207
interrelational intelligence and, 190
intimacy and, 198–199
language register and, 204–205
Manuel Vega's difficult transition case study, 179–181
mastery and, 183, 184, 195
mental health and, 215–220
moral development and, 189, 196, 197
multigenerational families and, 182–183
multiple intelligence theory and, 203
obesity and, 185
oppression and, 183
peer relations and, 197–198
perspective taking and, 199
physical development and, 183–186
play/leisure activities and, 182, 216
post-traumatic stress disorder (PTSD) and, 214
poverty issues and, 210–212
precociousness and, 182
prepubescence and, 184
prosocial behavior and, 148, 223
relative poverty and, 212
resilience and, 194, 222
risk/preventive factors and, 221–223
school education and, 202–204, 206–209
secondary sex characteristics and, 185
self-competence and, 194–195, 219
self-efficacy and, 195, 215
social competence and, 198
social development and, 194–199
social work practice and, 224
suicide and, 184, 221
team play and, 199
trauma and, 194, 214
web resources, 225–226
zone of proximal development and, 197
Middleton, D., 449
Midwives, 50, 128
Miech, R., 15, 23
Mikulincer, M., 344
Mild cognitive impairment (MCI), 394

Millennium Cohort Study Child Health Group, 102
Miller, 170
Miller, B., 256
Miller, D., 159, 201
Miller, G. W., 441
Miller, I., 164
Miller, J., 59, 61
Miller, K. E., 204
Milliken, C. S., 317
Millsap, R., 391
Minino, A., 341, 342
Minkler, M., 162
Minority culture, 29, 255–256
   See also Race
Miscarriage Naturally occurring loss of a fetus prior to 20 weeks' gestation; also known as spontaneous abortion, 79
Mitchell, K. J., 253, 254
Miyake, K., 117
Mize, J., 198
Modell, J., 23
Moen, P., 330, 362, 363, 364, 365
Mofenson, L., 91
Moffitt, T. E., 185
Mohr, W. K., 212
Moilanen, I., 204
Molecular/cellular theories of biological aging Theories proposing that biological aging is caused by molecular or cellular processes, 386
Monaghan, J., 18
Monahon, C., 214
Monica's quest for mastery case study, 231
Monitoring the Future Study, 269
Montgomery, R. J. V., 406
Montgomery, S., 21
Monzo, L., 295
Moore, D., 247
Moore, E., 221
Moore, G., 119
Moore, J., 78
Moore, K. A., 210, 311
Moore, N., 259
Moral behavior, 147, 189
Moral development
   cognitive developmental approaches, early childhood and, 146–149
   middle childhood and, 189, 196, 197
   psychodynamic approach, 147

psychosocial development
   dependency on, 298
   social learning approach, 147, 198
   stage theory of, 189–190, 243, 299
   young adulthood and, 298, 299
Morales, A., 278
Morbidity The incidence of disease and illness in a population group, 73, 78, 82, 387
Morbidity rates, 78, 82, 387
Moremen, R. D., 436
Morgan, A., 407
Morgan, J., 113
Morgan, L., 376, 402
Morgentaler, A., 340
Morley, J., 394, 395
Moros' increasing needs for care case study, 374
Morris, J. C., 394
Morrison, J. W., 191, 192
Morrow, A. L., 215
Morrow, B., 59
Morse, J. Q., 392
Mortality rate The incidence of death in a population group
   childbearing and, 80–82
   definition of, 387
   early adult pregnancies and, 75
   gender and, 340, 341, 378, 387
   infancy/toddlerhood, 130
   infants, 130
   late adulthood and, 387
Mortens, M. A., 396
Mortimer, J. A., 395
Mortimer, J. T., 248, 251, 263
Mosher, W., 264, 265
Moshman, D., 241
Moss, R. H., 396
Motamedi, G. K., 84
Motor skills Control over movements of body parts, 105
Mourning The external expression of grief, also a process, influenced by the customs of one's culture, 444–446, 448
   Worden's tasks of mourning, 446
Mowbray, C., 170
Mowrer, R., 189
Moyer, K., 163
Msall, M. E., 311
Mucci, 275
Mucherah, W., 170
Mueller, C. W., 298

Mueller, M., 23, 399, 400

Muir, D., 104

Mulhauser, M. B., 219

Mullis, R., 255, 256

Multicentre Growth Reference Study (MGRS), 101-102, 105-107

Multifactorial inheritance Genetic traits that are controlled by multiple genes, 84

Multigenerational families
early childhood and, 160–162
infancy/toddlerhood and, 126–129
middle adulthood and, 355–361, 358–359
middle childhood and, 182–183
young adulthood and, 295–296
See also Families

Multigravida A pregnant woman who has previously experienced pregnancy, 69

Multipara A mother who has previously given birth, 70

Multiple intelligences Howard Gardner's theory that humans have at least eight critical intelligences: verbal/linguistic, logical/mathematical, visual/spatial, musical/rhythmic, bodily kinesthetic, naturalist, interpersonal, intrapersonal, 203

Munakata, Y., 112

Munn, M. B., 79

Muraven, M., 245

Murphy, D. J., 75

Murphy, J., 132, 235

Murray, J. A., 448

Must, A., 276

Myhrman, A., 204

Mynatt, C. R., 275

Nabukera, S., 75

Nakamoto, J. M., 184

Nakash, A., 57

Naleppa, M. J., 406

Nalubamba-Phiri, M., 79

Natarajan, L., 66

National Association of Child Care Resource and Referral Agencies, 209

National Campaign to Prevent Teen Pregnancy, 74, 262

National Center for Child Abuse and Neglect, 73

National Center for Children in Poverty (NCCP), 129, 162, 211

National Center for Clinical Infant Programs, 167

National Center for Health Statistics, 21, 276, 329, 343

National Center for Injury Prevention and Control, 184

National Committee for Quality Assurance (NCQA), 80, 81

National Council on the Aging, 330, 390

National Eating Disorders Association, 88

National Geographic Society, 426

National Health Statistics, 387

National Hospice and Palliative Care Organization, 441

National Institute of Alcohol Abuse and Alcoholism, 396

National Institute of Mental Health, 278, 396

National Institute on Drug Abuse, 269

National Institutes of Health, 55, 236

National Research Council, 126, 210

National Sleep Foundation, 236

National Survey of Family Growth (NSFG), 264, 310

National Vaccine Information Center, 109

National Youth Gang Survey, 273

Naudeau, S., 123

Nazar, A. M., 128

NCCP (National Center for Children in Poverty), 129, 162, 211

Ndukwe, G., 66

Needham, 185

Neighborhood effects, 26, 166–167, 291

Neill, M., 208

Neiss, M., 239

Nelsen, V., 448

Nelson, C., 108

Nelson, D., 120

Nelson, R., 80

Neonate Infant up to 1 month of age. 71, See also *infant*

Neonatology, 83

Nepomnaschy, P., 79

Nesbitt, T., 83

Netting, F. E., 436

Nettles, S., 170

Neugarten, B., 23, 349

Neugarten, B. L., 383, 399

Neugebauer, R., 79

New concepts on the causes of recurrent miscarriages, 79

New England Centenarian Study, 428

New role for Ron and Rosiland's grandmother
    case study, 141
Newborns. *See* At-risk newborns;
    Infancy/toddlerhood
Newborns' and Mothers' Health Protection
    Act of 1996, 54
Newburn, M., 50
Newcomb, A. F., 198
Newcomb, N., 200
Newman, B., 103, 104, 124, 127, 146, 151,
    152, 153, 161, 197, 237, 291
Newman, D., 11, 13
Newman, P., 103, 104, 124, 127, 146,
    151, 152, 153, 161, 197, 237, 291
Newman, R. B., 52
Nhu, T. N., 79
Nichols, S., 60, 202
Nicole Evans' change of plans case study, 42
Nielsen, H. S., 79
Nishino, H., 252
No Child Left Behind (NCLB), 208, 276
Nobles, W. W., 183
Noddings, N., 205
NOFTT (nonorganic failure to thrive), 131
Nojomi, M., 79
Nonorganic failure to thrive (NOFTT), 131
Noonan, A. E., 311
Noone, M. J., 212
Norm-referenced testing, 203–204
Norris, A., 344
Norton, D., 191
Nosek, M., 89
Nosek, M. A., 89
Nourhashemi, F., 394
Novak, G., 103, 146, 164
Novak, J. C., 52, 68
Novice phase According to Daniel Levinson, the
    ages of 17 to 22, in which the transition
    into young adulthood occurs, including the
    tasks of leaving adolescence and making
    preliminary decisions about relationships,
    career, and belief systems, 291
Novins, D., 270, 271
Nowak, A., 77
Nutrition programs, 411
Nye, C., 261
Nyman, 150

Oakes, J., 207
Oakland children, 30

Oakley, A., 75
Oates, M., 66
Oberklaid, F., 117, 118
Obesity
    adolescence and, 128, 276–277
    contraception and, 62
    early childhood and, 128
    infertility and, 65, 66
    pregnancy and, 76
Object permanence The ability to understand
    that objects exist even when they cannot
    be seen, 111
O'Brien, M., 152
O'Brien, R., 12
O'Callaghan, M., 131
O'Connor, A., 65
O'Connor, I., 168
O'Conor, A., 260
Odent, M., 51
Of meat, Mexicans and social mobility, 314
Offerhaus, P. M., 50
Office on Smoking and Health, 269
Ogbu, J. U., 206
Ogden, C. L., 276
Okazawa-Rae, M., 193
O'Keefe, M., 168, 169, 274
Oken, E., 70
Okie, S., 340
Old-Age and Survivors Insurance (OASI), 409
Olds, D., 31
O'Leary, V. E., 407
Oliver, R., 51
Ollendick, T. H., 198
Olsen, J., 87
O'Malley, P., 18, 268
O'Malley, P. L., 269, 270
O'Neill, G., 342, 343
Op Ten Berg, M. M., 61
Opitz, J. M., 83, 84, 87
Oppenheim, D., 147
Oppression The intentional or unintentional
    act or process of placing restrictions on an
    individual, group, or institution; may
    include observable actions, but more
    typically refers to complex, covert,
    interconnected processes and practices
    (such as discriminating, devaluing, and
    exploiting a group of individuals) reflected
    in and perpetuating exclusion and
    inequalities over time, 183

O-Prasetsawat, P., 259
O'Rand, A., 30, 34, 363
O'Rand, C., 363, 364, 365
Orav, E., 87
Orenstein, P., 189
Orfield, G., 250
Ormord, R., 168
Ornoy, A., 65, 84
Osborne, L. M., 61
Osofsky, J. D., 74
Ostir, G., 395
Ostrov, J., 150
Otero, A., 397
Other, generalized, 245–246
Overpeck, M., 142
Overprotecting Henry case study, 99–100
Owens, D., 207
Oyserman, D., 170

Padilla, Y. C., 314
Pagotto, U., 65
Paik, A., 339
Pakenham, K., 334
Pallas, A., 23
Palliative care Active care of patients who have
    received a diagnosis of a serious, life-
    threatening illness; a form of care focusing
    on pain and symptom management as
    opposed to curing disease, 440
Palmer, J., 210
Palsson, S., 393
Panksepp, J., 155
Papachristou, F., 64
Papachristou-Ornoy, A., 64
Papaeliou, C., 215
Paquette, J., 199
Pardington, S., 205
Parenthood
    authoritarian parenting, 163
    depression and, 130, 131, 132
    disengaged parenting, 164
    employment and, 302–304
    fatherhood, and play as vehicle for
        attachment, 157–158
    grandparenthood, 141, 399–401
    permissive parenting, 163–164
    teenage, 99
    teenage fatherhood, 74, 99
    transitions and, 287–288
    young adulthood and, 309

Parents
    disabilities, and childbearing issues, 89–90
    middle adulthood, and relationship to,
        359–360
    multigenerational families, and relationships
        with, 359–360
    special populations of, 86–91
    young adults as, 287–288, 309–311
Parents, Family and Friends of Lesbians and
    Gays (PFLAG), 261
Parette, H., 158
Park, M., 59
Parke, M., 209
Parkes, C. M., 445
Parrenas, R., 26
Parrett, W. H., 202, 203
Partelow, L., 159, 201
Pascoe, J., 128
Pasquali, R., 64
Pasqualotto, E. B., 64
Pasqualotto, F. F., 64
Passah, S. M., 82
Patrikakou, E. N., 206
Pattee, L., 198
Patterson, C. J., 198, 201
Patton, T., 90
Paul, E., 355, 360, 361
Paul, R., 215
Pauw, M., 79
Payer, L., 338
Payne, R. K., 204, 205, 212
Paz, J., 360
Pearce, J., 247, 360
Pearlin, L., 12, 17, 21, 34
Peart, N. A., 310
Peck, P., 185
Pedersen, N. L., 295
Pedlow, R., 117
Peebles, C., 74
Peer relations
    adolescence and, 248–249
    early childhood and, 151
    middle childhood and, 197–198
Peers, I., 163
Peiotropy principle, 84
Pelaez, M., 103, 146, 164
Pelligrini, A., 155
Pelvic inflammatory disease (PID), 266
Pena, R., 132
Pennekamp, M., 166

Penninkilampi, V., 204

Perimenopause A period of time that begins immediately prior to menopause, when there are biological and clinical indicators that a woman's reproductive capacity is reaching exhaustion, and continues through the first year after the last menstrual period, 338

Perlman, D., 305

Perlman, J. M., 82

Perlmutter, M., 384

Perloff, J., 168

Perls, T. T., 428

Permissive parenting A parenting style, identified by Baumrind, that involves no limit setting on the part of the parent, 163–164

Pernice, R., 204

Perreira, K. M., 256, 305, 311

Perrone, B., 258

Perry, B., 122, 214

Perry, H., 448

Perry, J., 214

Perry, W. G., 298

Personality

contextual model for personality stability, 347

early childhood, and development of, 149–150

gender, and traits of, 349

late adulthood, and changes in, 391–392

middle adulthood, and changes in, 346–350

Person-environment transaction. *See* Life course perspective

Perspective taking The ability to see a situation from another person's point of view, 148, 199

Petchum, S., 259

Pete Mullin loses his sister's support case study, 421–422

Petersen, A. C., 239

Peterson, I., 167

Peterson, L., 130

Petitti, D., 61

Petras, A., 120

Pettit, G. S., 197

PFLAG (Parents, Family and Friends of Lesbians and Gays), 261

Phenotype The expression of genetic traits in an individual, 56

Phillips, D., 26, 102, 103, 108, 109, 113, 114, 115, 117, 120, 123, 124, 126, 160, 187, 188

Phillips, S., 362

Phinney, J. S., 192

Physical aggression Aggression against another person using physical force, 150

Physical characteristics An individual's physical traits, such as height, weight, body build, and facial features. One element in Morris Rosenberg's model of identity, 243

Physical development

early childhood and, 142–143

infancy/toddlerhood and, 101–109

middle childhood and, 183–186

self-regulation in infancy/toddlerhood of, 102–103

Physical disabilities, 89–90, 124, 410

Physical health. *See* Health issues

Piaget, J., 187, 190, 243

Piaget's stages of cognitive development, 110–113, 144–145

PID (pelvic inflammatory disease), 266

Pillay, Y., 167

Pinkard, O., 296

Piper, J., 64

Piper, L. E., 411

Pipher, M., 189, 200, 246, 422, 430, 431, 433, 435, 448

Pirog-Good, M., 310

Pitner, R. O., 196

Piwoz, E., 128

Pixley, J., 349

Plaford, G., 196

Plante, M., 66

Plasticity (brain) Susceptibility of the brain to environmental influences, 187

Plath, D., 329

Play routines

early childhood and, 154–158

exploration of reality through, 156

fathers, and attachment through, 157–158

gaining control through, 156

infancy/toddlerhood and, 122–123

learning play, 156

middle childhood and, 199

role play, 122–123

shared experience through, 156–157

sociodramatic play, 157

symbolic play, 155

team play, 199

Play/leisure activities, 182, 216

Pleck, J. H., 310

Pleiotropy principle The ability of a single gene to have many effects, 84

Pletta, K., 128

Plomin, R., 118

Plugge, E., 90

Poehlmann, J., 165

Poertner, J., 206

Poitrast, F., 132

Pollack, W., 246

PollingReport.com, 62

Pollock, L., 51

Polloway, E. A., 90

Pomerleau, A., 158

Ponte, I., 123

Poon, L. W., 427, 428

Population Council Inc., 73

Population pyramid A chart that depicts the proportion of the population in each age group, 12

Porterfield, K. S., 212

Portes, A., 312, 313, 314

Posmontier, B., 128

Posner, J., 338

Post, S., 350

Postconventional level of moral reasoning Third and final level of Lawrence Kohlberg's stage theory of moral development; morality based on moral principles that transcend societal rules, 243

Post-traumatic stress disorder (PTSD), 214

Potashnik, G., 64

Poteat, M., 151

Potenza, M., 131

Pothoff, S., 271

Potter, C. C., 194, 198, 199, 200, 201

Poverty

    adolescence and, 275–276

    early childhood and, 162–163

    education attainment and, 275–276

    infancy/toddlerhood and, 129–130

    middle childhood and, 210–212

    relative poverty, 212

    teenage pregnancy and, 73

    very late adulthood and, 424

Power of attorney (POA) A person appointed by an individual to manage his or her financial and legal affairs. A POA can be limited (for a limited time period), general (no restrictions), or durable (begins after reaching a specified level of disability), 411, 439

Powlishta, K. K., 191, 200

Pratt, C., 253

Precociousness Early development; most often refers to a rare level of intelligence at an early age, but may refer to "premature" ability or development in a number of areas, 182

Preconventional level of moral reasoning First level of moral reasoning in Lawrence Kohlberg's stage theory of moral reasoning; morality based on what gets rewarded or punished or what benefits either the child or someone the child cares about, 147

Pregnancy

    delayed pregnancies, 75–76

    early adulthood and, 74–75

    eating disorders and, 88

    ectopic, 78

    elderly gravidas and, 75

    embryonic period and, 68

    embryos and, 64

    ethics issues and, 63, 80

    fertilization age and, 68

    fertilization of egg and, 68

    fetal development and, 68–71

    fetal period and, 68–69

    fetus and, 68

    Gerekes' late-life pregnancy case study, 45–46

    gestation and, 68

    gestational age and, 68

    HIV-infected mothers and, 90–91

    incarcerated women and, 90

    late-life, 45–46

    life course perspectives and, 71–76

    miscarriage and, 79

    multigravidas and, 69

    multipara and, 70

    neonate and, 70–71

    neonatology and, 83

    Nicole Evans' change of plans case study, 42

    obesity and, 76

    primipara and, 70

    problems and, 78–80

    small for gestational age (SGA) and, 88

    substance use/abuse during, 86–88

    teratogens and, 68

ultrasonography (ultrasound) and, 86
undesired, 78
zygote and, 67
See also Childbirth; Conception;
Reproductive genetics; Teenage
pregnancy
Premature birth A fetus born anytime prior to
37 weeks of gestation, 43–44, 80
Premenopause The beginning of the
menopause process when a woman begins
to have occasional menstrual cycles
without ovulation, 338
Prentice, R., 339
Preoperational stage The second stage in
Piaget's theory of cognitive development.
Young children (ages 2 to 7) use symbols
to represent their earlier sensorimotor
experiences. Thinking is not yet logical,
110, 144
Prepubescence, 184
Preservation/gestational surrogacy, 66–67
Prevalence, 341
Preto, N., 127, 247, 248
Price, S. K., 79
Pridham, K., 76
Primary aging Changes that are a normal part
of the aging process, 429
Primary sex characteristics Physical
characteristics that are directly related to
maturation of the reproductive organs and
external genitalia, 237
Primipara A woman who has delivered only
one infant of at least 500 grams (20 weeks'
gestation), whether the child is alive or
dead at the time of birth, 70
Prior, M., 117
Privilege Unearned advantage that comes from
one's position in the social structure, 31
definition of, 31
gender and, 294, 385
identity development and, 195, 198
institutionalized, 31
school education and, 159, 188, 189, 207
Probst, C., 392
Programmed aging theories Theories of
biological aging that start from the
assumption that the aging process is
genetically determined, 386
Project on Death in America (PDIA), 437
Proot, I. M., 442

Prosocial behavior, 148, 223
Protective factors Personal and societal factors
that reduce or protect against risk
See Developmental risks/protective factors;
Resilience factor
Pruning Reduction of brain synapses to
improve the efficiency of brain
functioning; follows a period of blooming
of synapses, 107
Psychodynamic perspective, 35, 147
Psychological age The capacities that people
have and the skills they use to adapt to
changing biological and environmental
demands, including skills in memory,
learning, intelligence, motivation,
emotions; also how old people fee, 21
PTSD (post-traumatic stress disorder), 214
Puberty Stage during which individuals
become capable of reproduction, 236–237
Puberty onset comparison, 184–185
Pubescence, 184, 185
Pulkkinen, L., 303
Pulzl, P., 61
Pungello, E. P., 310
Putney, N., 355, 356, 357, 358, 359
Pyke, D., 356, 360

Quam, J. K., 398
Quickening experience, 70
Quinn, D., 132

Rabkin, J., 52
Race
adolescence, and relationship with culture,
255–256
bereavement and, 448–449
breastfeeding practices and, 128
causes of death and, 341
child maltreatment and, 170, 213
death and, 449
depression and, 278
discrimination and, 192, 207, 314–315
employment and, 251, 304, 314–315, 363
ethnic identity and, 314–315
human agency and, 293
identity and, 151, 153, 191
late adulthood living arrangements and, 397
minority culture, 29, 255–256
mortality rates and, 340
pregnancy statistics and, 264

puberty onset and, 184, 185
puberty onset comparison and, 184–185
rites of passage and, 233
school education and, 204
segregation and, 206
self-concept and, 151
socioeconomic status (SES) and,
382, 387–388
spiritual aspects of adolescence and, 258–259
suicide and, 341
work relations and, 314–315
young adulthood and, 314–315
See also Ethnic identity
Race for the Cure, 296
Racial identity, 153–154
Radestad, I., 52
Rahe, R., 16
Raj, 275
Ramirez, O., 257, 258
Rando, T., 446
Random error theories Theories of biological
aging that propose that physiological aging
occurs because of damaging processes that
become more frequent in late adulthood
but are not a part of a genetic unfolding
process, 386
Ranganath, C., 393
Ranjit, N., 58
Rank, M. R., 291, 295, 312
Rape, 274–275
Rapoport, J. L., 237, 238
Rasco, L. M., 204
Ratcliffe, J., 66
Rational choice perspective, 35
Rauch, J., 57, 84
Reardon, D., 63
Recessive genes Genes that express themselves
only if present on both chromosomes
in a pair, 56
Redding, S., 206
Reed, G. B., 51, 57, 84
Reed, R. K., 52
Reflex An involuntary response to a simple
stimulus, 104–105
Regnerus, M., 256
Reid, T. R., 352
Reinholtz, C., 72
Reivich, K., 195
Relational aggression Aggression that involves
behaviors that damage relationships without
physical force, such as threatening to leave a
relationship unless a friend complies with
demands, or using social exclusion or the
silent treatment to get one's way, 150
Relative poverty A conceptualization of poverty
that emphasizes the tendency to define
one's poverty status in relation to others
within one's social environment, 212
Religious beliefs
abortion and, 64
contraception and, 58
early childhood and, 149
middle adulthood and, 353
young adulthood and, 299, 301
Remez, L., 264
Reminiscence Recalling and recounting past
events. Reminiscing serves several
functions: it may be an enjoyable activity,
it may be directed at enhancing a person's
self-image, it may serve as a way to cope
with current or future problems, and it
may assist in the life review as a way to
achieve ego integrity, 407
Rennison, C. M., 275
Rentz, T., 219
Reppucci, N. D., 214
Reproductive genetics
chorion villi testing (CVT) and, 86
dominant genes and, 57
education and, 55
epigenetics and, 84
ethics issues and, 58
fertilization and, 54
gene replacement therapy and, 86
genes and, 54
genetic counseling and, 39, 57–58, 76, 77
genetic disorders and, 84–86
genetic heterogeneity and, 84
genetic liability and, 84
genetic mechanisms and, 54–56
genotype and, 54
germ cells and, 54
interactive genes and, 57
multifactorial inheritance and, 84
phenotype and, 56
pleiotropy principle and, 84
recessive genes and, 57
sex chromosomes and, 55–56
sex-linked traits and, 57
variable expressivity and, 83–84

Reschly, D. J., 207

Resilience Healthy development in the face of risk factors. Thought to be due to protective factors that shield the individual from the consequences of potential hazards, 31

Resilience factor
  adolescence and, 279
  infancy/toddlerhood and, 132
  late adulthood and, 411–412
  middle adulthood and, 366
  middle childhood and, 194, 222
  very late adulthood and, 429

Resnick, H. S., 72

Resources. *See* Web resources

Retirement patterns, 401–404

Rew, L., 237, 238, 249, 262

Rexrode, K., 340

Reyes, V., 340

Riberio, S. C., 60

Ricciardelli, L. A., 186

Rice, J., 158

Richards, M. H., 239

Richards, T., 73

Richey, T. G., 310

Richmond, M., 54, 56

Riedmann, G., 53, 54

Rieker, P. R., 375, 382, 385

Rieser-Danner, L., 111

Rifas-Shiman, S. L., 68

Rigby, A. S., 75

Riley, M., 20

Riley, M. W., 385

Rimm, S., 246

Rimpela, M., 186

Rindfuss, R., 20, 29

Rindfuss, R. R., 293

Rintal, D. H., 89

Risk factors Personal or social factors that increase the likelihood of a problem occurring, 31–32
  See also Developmental risks/protective factors

Risley, T., 146

Rites of passage Ceremonies that demarcate transition from one role or status to another, 233

Robbins, A., 63

Robert Johnson, enjoying fatherhood at 48 case study, 327–328

Roberto, K., 408

Roberto, K. A., 411

Roberts, B., 347, 348, 349, 423

Roberts, C. R., 278

Roberts, E., 158

Roberts, J., 393

Roberts, R. E., 278

Roberts, R. E. L., 304

Robins, E., 260

Robins, R., 347

Robinson, J., 18

Robinson, J. A., 198

Robinson, L. C., 306

Robinson, S., 79

Robison, J. A., 300

Robles, B., 291

Rock, P., 90

Roe, K., 162

Roe v. Wade, 62

Roebers, C., 192

Roehlkepartian, E. C., 222

Roehrs, T., 236

Rogers, 235

Rogers, S., 358

Roggman, L., 158

Rogoff, B., 101

Rojan, L., 75

Romantic love An intimate relationship that is sexually oriented, 306–309

Ron and Rosiland's grandmother case study, new role for, 141

Ronka, A., 303

Roof, W., 149, 352

Roopnarine, J., 155, 156

Rose, S., 307, 308

Rosen, R., 339

Rosenbaum, J., 26

Rosenberg, M., 243, 244

Rosenfeld, R., 20

Rosenthal, C., 356, 396

Rosenthal, M. Z., 392

Rosenwaike, I., 406

Roskos, K., 156

Ross, J., 128

Ross, L. E., 67

Ross, L. J., 62

Ross, M., 17

Rossi, A., 337, 338, 339, 340, 352, 356, 362

Rossi, P., 356

Rotenberg, K., 198

Rothbart, B., 235, 236
Rothenbacher, D., 128
Rotheram-Borus, M. J., 191, 192
Rothert, K., 295
Rothman, B. K., 50
Roueche, J. E., 203
Roumen, F. J., 61
Rovee-Collier, C., 111
Rowan, L., 189
Rowe, D. C., 239
Rowland, C. A., 65
Roy, K. K., 80, 82
Ruan, C., 164
Rubertsson, C., 52
Rubia, K., 238
Rubin, K., 123, 157, 199
Rubin, R., 72
Rubinoff, B., 88
Ruby Johnson, caretaker for three generations
    case study, 373
Rudacille, D., 152
Rue, J., 63
Rue, V., 63
Rueda, R., 295
Rumbaut, R. G., 288, 312, 313, 314
Rutter, M., 18, 31
Ryan, B. A., 205
Ryan, C., 260
Ryan, S., 78
Ryff, C., 330, 334

Sabbagh, M., 113
Sacchetti, A. D., 54
Sadker, D., 189
Sadker, M., 189
Sadock, B., 90, 214, 278, 393, 395
Safren, S., 261
Saghir, M. T., 260
Saha, S., 130
Said, M., 80
Sais, E., 191
Saldinger, M. A., 221
Saleeby, D., 27
Salihu, H. M., 75
Sallee, A., 132
Sallmen, M., 64
Salonius-Pasternak, D., 123
Sameroff, A., 26, 158
Sampson, 235
Sampson, R. J., 302

Sanders, M., 159
Sandler, D. P., 64
Sandler, I. N., 221
Sands, R., 162
Sang, B., 362
Sanson, A., 117
Santelli, J., 59
Santos, I. S., 81
Santrock, J. W., 389
Sapolsky, R., 341, 387
Sarah's teen Dad case study, 99
Sasser, J. E., 90
Savin-Williams, R., 200, 201, 260
Savin-Williams, R. C., 197, 199, 200, 201, 260
Sawchuck, P., 54
Sawin, K. S., 89, 90
Sax, L., 188, 189
Scarlett, A. G., 123
Schachere, K., 120
Schaeffer, C., 12
Schafer, J. E., 61
Schaffner, B., 252
Schaie, K., 345, 346
Schaie, K. W., 298, 392
Schedule of recent events, 16-17
Schellpfeffer, M., 128
Schild, S., 57
Schlesinger, E., 30
Schmitz, C., 158
Schneider, B., 250
Schneider, H., 215
Schneider, W., 192
Schoeller, T., 61
Schoen, R., 295
Schoendorf, K. C., 81
Schoeni, R. F., 378
School education. *See* Formal schooling
    education
Schreiner, P., 338
Schuetze, P., 126
Schulenberg, J., 18, 268
Schumm, W. R., 47
Schupf, 394
Schupf, N., 393
Schwartz, S., 293
Schwartzberg, N., 362
Schweinhart, L., 159
Sclowitz, I. K., 81
Scott, J., 357
Scott, K. D., 50

Seaton, G., 198

Secher, N., 87

Secondary aging Changes caused by health-compromising behaviors such as smoking or environmental factors such as pollution, 429–430

Secondary sex characteristics Physical characteristics associated with sexual maturation that are not directly related to the reproductive organs and external genitalia, 185, 237

Secondary sexual development Associated with puberty and referring to the development of secondary sex characteristics such as the growth of pubic, chest, and facial hair in males and the growth of pubic hair and breasts in females, 185

Sedikides, C., 152

Sedlak, A., 170

Seefeldt, C., 193

Seefeldt, K. S., 315

Seeman, P., 238

Seepersad, S., 252

Segal, B. M., 270, 271

Sehgal, A., 82

Seifer, R., 131, 158

Seifert, K. L., 429

Self-competence, 194–195, 219

Self-efficacy
    adolescence and, 251
    early childhood and, 171
    late adulthood and, 383, 388
    life course perspective and, 27
    middle childhood and, 195, 215
    young adulthood and, 315

Self-esteem The way one evaluates the self in relation to others, 151–152

Self/identity theories, 242–245

Self-theory An organized understanding of the self in relation to others; begins to develop in early childhood, 151

Seligman, M. E. P., 195

Selman, R. L., 190, 199

Sen, A., 159, 201

Sengupta, P., 294

Senior centers, 410

Senior housing, 410

Sensitive period A time in fetal development that is particularly sensitive to exposure to teratogens. Different organs have different sensitive periods. Also called critical period, 85

Sensorimotor stage The first stage in Piaget's theory of cognitive development. Infants (ages 0 to 2 years) learn through sensory awareness and motor activities, 110

Sensory system The system of senses: hearing, sight, taste, smell, touch, responsiveness to the body's position, and sensitivity to pain, 103–104

Sepaniak, S., 64

Separation anxiety When an infant becomes anxious at the signs of an impending separation from parents, at about 9 months of age, 111–112

September 11, 2001 case study, Suarez family after, 8–9

Serbin, L. A., 191, 200, 201

SES (socioeconomic status), 251, 314, 382, 387–388

Sethi, V., 68

Settersten, R. A., 11, 20, 23, 288

Settersten, R., Jr., 11, 20, 21, 22, 23, 28, 29, 30, 31

Severy, L. J., 59, 60

Sex Bias cited in vocational education, 251

Sex characteristics, 185, 237

Sex chromosomes Chromosome pair number 23, which determines the sex of the individual, 56–57

Sex ratio The number of males per 100 females in a population, 13

Sex-linked trait A trait that is controlled by a gene located on one of the sex chromosomes, 56

Sexual identity/sexuality
    acquaintance rape and, 274–275
    adolescence and, 236, 237
    masturbation and, 259
    middle adulthood and, 185
    oral sex and, 263–264
    pregnancy/childbearing and, 264–265
    secondary sex characteristics, 185, 237
    secondary sexual development, 185
    Sex hormones Hormones that affect the development of the gonads, functioning of the gonads, and mating and child-caring behavior; includes androgen, progestins, and estrogens, 236
    sexual decision making and, 261–262

sexual orientation and, 259–263
transition to adulthood and, 259
Sexual interests, 152–153
Sexually transmitted diseases (STDs)
Infectious diseases that are most often
contracted through oral, anal, or vaginal
sexual contact. Also called venereal
diseases, 265–268
SGA (small for gestational age), 88
Shaffer, D., 167
Shah, V., 104
Shain, R. N., 64
Shanahan, M., 15, 21, 22, 23, 30, 250
Shapiro, J., 295
Shapiro, J. R., 187
Shapiro, P., 357
Shapiro, T., 312
Sharp, P., 340
Sharts-Hopko, C., 47
Shaver, J., 339
Shaw, S., 252
Sheard, C., 66
Shedler, J., 269
Sheehy, G., 292, 293
Sheiner, E., 64
Sheiner, E. K., 64
Sheldon, K., 333, 391
Shepard, M., 168
Sheridan, M., 436
Sherman, A., 361
Sherman, C., 61
Sherman, E., 407
Sherrard, P. A., 205
Shi, C. R., 74
Shickle, D., 57
Shillington, A., 132
Shin, H. B., 191
Shin, M., 155
Shirey, L., 342, 343
Shlfroni, G., 75
Shonkoff, J., 26, 102, 103, 108, 109, 113, 114,
115, 117, 120, 123, 124, 126, 187, 188
Shore, J., 270
Shrier, L. A., 263, 271
Shu, X., 64
Shweder, R., 331
Sickmund, M., 272, 273, 274, 275
SIDS (sudden infant death syndrome), 103
Siegel, D., 115
Siegler, R., 112

Silbereisen, R., 252
Silva, P. A., 185
Silver, R., 446, 447
Silverberg, S., 241
Silverman, 275
Silverman, B., 53, 128
Silverman, P. R., 444, 447
Silvern, L., 168
Silverstein, M., 359, 360, 397
Simeonsson, R., 124, 158
Simi, N. L., 295
Simmons, H. C., 436
Simmons, R., 196, 200
Simons, R., 25
Sinclair, A., 394
Singer, M. I., 274
Singh, L., 113
Sit, D., 128
Sitzer, A. R., 54
Skaalvik, E., 202
Skaalvik, S., 202
Skaff, M., 12, 17, 21, 34
Skinner, B. F., 146
Skolnick, A., 47
Skolnick, J., 47
Skoog, I., 393
Sleeter, C., 207
Slife, B., 351
Sloane, K., 205
Sloter, E., 65
Small, B. J., 394
Small, M. A., 196
Small, S., 241
Small for gestational age (SGA) Lower than
normal birth weight, given the number
of weeks of gestation 88
Smetana, J. G., 248
Smith, A., 162
Smith, B., 341, 342
Smith, B. L., 278
Smith, C., 256, 257
Smith, C. A., 310
Smith, D., 121, 339
Smith, G., 132
Smith, H., 167
Smith, J., 168
Smith, J. D., 90
Smith, M. A., 51
Smith, P. B., 310
Smith, R., 214

Smith, R. S., 31, 133, 194, 222, 278, 316, 317

Smith, T., 124

Smith Slep, A. M., 214

Smiths in early retirement case study, 372

Smokowski, P., 132, 170, 223

Smyer, M. A., 295, 388

Snarey, J., 310

Snow, C., 151

Snyder, H., 272, 273, 274, 275

Sobreiro, B. F., 64

Social age Age measured in terms of age-graded roles and behaviors expected by society— the socially constructed meanings of various ages, 22

Social and behavior sciences, xviii

Social behavioral perspective, 35

Social capital, 291

Social class

    abortion rates and, 63

    bias, 191

    institutional discrimination and, 192, 207

    life course trajectories and, 29–30

    privilege and, 26, 31

    relative poverty and, 362

    retirement patterns and, 401

    suicide and, 341

    upward mobility and, 276

Social competence The ability to engage in sustained, positive, and mutually satisfactory peer interactions, 198

Social construction theory (of aging) A theory that attempts to understand and explain the influence of social definitions, social interactions, and social structures on the aging process, 384–385

Social exchange theory (of aging) A theory that attempts to understand the realignments of roles and values in late adulthood in light of the shifting resources that older adults bring to social exchanges, 385

Social gerontology The social science that studies human aging, 382.

    See also Late adulthood

Social identity In Morris Rosenberg's model of identity, consists of social statuses, membership groups, labels, derived statuses, social types, and personal identities, 243

Social learning, 147

Social Security Administration, 403

Social Security benefits, 403

Social support Help rendered by others that benefits an individual, 24, 133

Social work assessment, xviii

Social work practice, xvii–xviii, 36

    adolescence and, 279–280

    childbearing and, 77, 97

    early childhood and, 171

    infancy/toddlerhood and, 133–134

    late adulthood and, 413

    life course perspective and, 36

    middle adulthood and, 367

    middle childhood and, 224

    very late adulthood and, 450

Sociodramatic play Fantasy play in a group, with the group coordinating fantasies; important type of play in early childhood, 157

Socioeconomic status (SES), 251, 314, 382, 387–388

Socioemotional development

    early childhood personality and, 149–150

    emotional intelligence in middle childhood and, 196

    emotional/behavioral disorder and, 217–220

    expression of emotions in very late adulthood and, 448

    gender and, 194, 448

    infancy/toddlerhood and, 115–117

    middle childhood and, 193–194

Soelder, E., 61

Sokol, R. J., 87

Solnick, S., 163

Solomon, R. C., 306

Solomon, Z., 344

Sommers, C. H., 189

Sonfield, A., 63

Song, L. Y., 274

Soudelier, K., 131

Souza, J. P., 80

Sowers, M., 60

Speare, A., Jr., 398

Special parent populations

    childbearing and, 86–91

    eating disorders during pregnancy and, 88

    ethical issues and, 67

    HIV-infected mothers, 90–91

    homosexuals, 248

    lesbian mothers, 88–89, 248

parents with disabilities, 89–90
substance users/abusers, 86–88
Spector-Mersel, G., 385
Spencer, M., 154
Spencer, M. B., 198
Spencer, N., 81
Sperling, D., 80
Sperm donors, 65
Spermarche Onset of the ability to ejaculate
mobile sperm, 237
Spieker, S., 120
Spieler, J., 60, 61
Spillman, B., 429
Spiritual age The position of a person in the
ongoing search for meaning and fulfilling
relationships, 22
Spirituality That which gives meaning,
purpose, and direction to one's life
adolescence and, 256–258
definition of, 22, 256–258
middle adulthood and, 350–353
very late adulthood and, 435–437
young adulthood and, 299–301
Spiro, A., 366
Spitz, I. M., 63
Spitze, G., 358, 398
Splete, J., 78
Spontaneous abortion Naturally occurring loss
of a fetus prior to 20 weeks' gestation; also
known as miscarriage, 79
Spranca, M., 241
Spring, J., 181
Srebnik, D., 259
Sroufe, L. A., 52, 222
Stacey, J., 47
Stack, C., 29
Stage theory of moral development, 189–190,
243, 299
Stages of labor, 71-72
Stamler, J., 366
Stanwood, N., 61
Status offenses Behaviors that would not be
considered criminal if committed by an
adult but are considered delinquent if
committed by an adolescent—for example,
running away from home, skipping school,
violating curfew, and possessing tobacco or
alcohol, 272
Statutory rape, 274–275
Staudinger, U., 330, 335
Staudinger, U. M., 385, 388

Stauffacher, K., 150
STDs (sexually transmitted diseases), 265–268
Steele, L. S., 67
Stefankiewicz, J., 64
Stein, L. D., 67
Stein, M. B., 214
Stein, T., 261
Steinhart, D., 90
Steinhauer, J., 306
Stepp, L. S., 263
Stern, B., 21
Stern, Y., 393
Sternberg, K. J., 213
Sternberg, S., 394
Sterns, H., 349, 364, 401
Stevens, S. J., 90
Stevenson, H., 250
Stewart, A., 334, 362
Stewart, J. C., 270, 271
Stewart, J. H., 79, 82
Stiehr, K., 359
Stillbirth, 79
Stockard, J., 12
Stockel, H., 258
Stoddard, S., 89
Stokes, J., 162
Stolzenberg, R. M., 300
Stormshak, E., 121
Stouthamer-Loeber, M., 310, 317
Stovall, K., 120
Stranger anxiety When an infant reacts with
fear and withdrawal to unfamiliar persons,
at about 9 months of age, 111
Strathearn, L., 131
Stratton, H., 102, 142
Straus, M., 168
Strauss, L. T., 63
Strauss, R. S., 276
Strickland, A. L., 438
Stroberg, P., 340
Strobino, D. M., 53, 80
Strock, M., 215
Stroebe, M., 444
Stroebe, W., 444
Stromquist, N. P., 288
Studinger, U., 347
Studman, L., 159
Study of Adult Development, 381, 391, 392, 411
Stueve, J. L., 310
Suarez family after September 11, 2001 case
study, 8–9

Subramanian, S. V., 379

Substance Abuse and Mental Health Services Administration, 296

Substance use/abuse
  adolescence and, 239, 268–271
  caregivers and, 131–132
  late adulthood and, 393, 395–396
  middle adulthood and, 343, 361
  pregnancy and, 86–88
  very late adulthood and, 434
  young adulthood and, 303, 305, 313

Sudden infant death syndrome (SIDS), 103

Sue, D. W., 193

Suh, E., 168

Suicide
  adolescence and, 261, 278
  depression and, 278
  late adulthood and, 395, 396
  middle adulthood and, 341
  middle childhood and, 184, 221
  race and, 341
  social class and, 341
  statistics, 342
  very late adulthood and, 440

Sullivan, A. M., 190

Sum, A., 288

Summer, L., 342, 343

Sun, A., 132

Sun, S. S., 185

Supernutrition, 390

Suppal, P., 155

Supplementary Medical Insurance (Medicare Part B), 409

Supplementary Social Security Income (SSI), 410

Sutterlin, R. L., 293

Sutton, P. D., 53

Swanson, C., 250

Swap, S. M., 206

Swearer, S. M., 196

Sweet, J., 355

Swerdloff, R. S., 61

Swicegood, G., 20

Sword, W., 128

Symbolic functioning The ability to think using symbols to represent what is not present, 110

Symbolic play Fantasy play, begins around the age of 2, 155

Synapses Neural connections, 107

Synthetic-conventional faith The third stage of James Fowler's six-stage model of faith development; faith that is rooted in external authority, 300

Syphilis, 265

System level theories of biological aging Theories that propose that aging is caused by processes operating across biological systems, 386–387

Systems perspective, 35

Szinovacz, M., 361

Taber, S., 292

Taddio, A., 104

Taffett, G., 387

Takahashi, E. A., 57, 84

Takahashi, K., 121, 122

Tang, M., 393

Tanner, J. L., 292

Tarr-Whelan, L., 159

Taryan, S., 143

Tate, A., 102

Tatum, B. D., 195

Tay, J. I., 78

Taylor, H., 260

Taylor, J., 148

Taylor, J. M., 190

Taylor, M., 196

Taylor, M. G., 199

Taylor, M. Y., 79, 260

Taylor, W., 199

Teenage pregnancy
  abortion and, 264
  adolescence and, 73–74
  family relationships and, 74
  fatherhood and, 74, 99
  grandparenthood and, 399
  health issues and, 72–73
  poverty and, 73
  race and, 264
  statistical rate of, 59, 72
  violence and, 72, 74

Teicher, M., 108

Tein, J. Y., 221

Teitelman, J. L., 398

Telang, S., 82

Temperament A person's disposition and primary behavioral characteristics in infants and young children, 113, 117–118

Teoh, T. G., 79

Teratogen Anything present during prenatal life that adversely affects normal cellular

development in form or function in the embryo or fetus, 68
  at-risk infants' exposure to, 85
  definition of, 68
  special parent populations and, 86–87, 91
Terracciano, A., 349
Terri's terrible temper case study, 140
Terry, R., 198, 366
Teubal, E., 241
Thibault, J. M., 436
Thijssen, J. H., 70
Thomas, A., 117
Thomlison, B., 132, 170, 213
Thompson, D., 339
Thompson, M., 246
Thompson, P. M., 238
Thompson, R., 108
Thompsons' premature birth case study, 43–44
Thoresen, C., 347
Thornberry, T. P., 310
Thurnher, M., 349
Thursby, G., 350
Tiedje, L. B., 52
Tiet, A., 171
Timing of lives, 19, 20–21, 22–24
Tiran, D., 80
Tobin, S., 383
Tobin, S. S., 383
Toddler A young child from about 12 to 36 months of age, 100. *See also* Infants and toddlers
Todd-Oldehaver, C., 392
Toguchi, Y., 152
Tolstrup, J., 65
Tolstrup, K., 88
Tomal, A., 72, 73
Tout, K., 210
Tracking, 207
Trait theory A theory that proposes that personality traits are enduring characteristics rooted in early temperament and influenced by genetic and organic factors, 347
Trajectory A long-term pattern of stability and change based on unique person-environment configurations over time, 12, 14–15, 27–30
  definition of, 12
  diversity issues and, 27–30
  gender and, 21–23, 29
  interlocking trajectories, 15, 36
  social class and, 29–30

Transductive reasoning Reasoning from one particular event to another particular event rather than in a logical causal manner, 145
Transitional object Comfort objects, such as a favorite blanket or stuffed animal, that toddlers often use to help them cope with separations from parents, 119
Transitions Changes in roles and statuses that represent a distinct departure from prior roles and statuses, 12, 14–15, 396–407
  adolescence and, 232–233
  childhood and, 232–233
  definition of, 12
  life course perspective and, 14–15, 396–407
  parenthood and, 287–288
  sexual identity/sexuality and, 259
  social roles and, 396–407
Transportation services, 411
Trattner, W. I., 210
Trauma A physical or mental injury generally associated with violence, shock, or an unanticipated situation, 194, 214
Tresini, M., 386
Trichomoniasis, 266–267
Trifiletti, R., 109
Tripp-Reimer, T., 435
Trujillo, C., 393
Trunnell, E. P., 253
Trust v. mistrust, 97, 114-116
Trzesniewski, K., 347
Tueth, M. J., 395
Turek, P. J., 64
Turiel, E., 248
Turnbull, J. E., 57, 84
Turner, H., 168
Turning point A special event that produces a lasting shift in the life course trajectory, 12, 18–19
Tutty, L., 168

Udry, J. R., 47
Uhlenberg, P., 12
Ulizzi, L., 13
Ullstrup, L., 259
Ultrasonography (ultrasound), 86
UNAID, 90, 267
Underwood, M. K., 196, 198
UNICEF, 129, 130
UNICEF Innocenti Research Centre, 129
United Nations Children's Fund, 210, 211

United Nations Development Program, 130, 201, 249

Universalizing faith The final stage of James Fowler's theory of faith development; a stage in which individuals lead selfless lives based on principles of absolute love and justice, 351

Uotinen, V., 21

Upshur, C., 124

U.S. Department of Justice Bureau of Justice Statistics, 274

U.S. Federal Bureau of Prisons, 90

U.S. Food and Drug Administration, 62

Vach-Hasse, T., 162

Vacuum curettage, 63

Vaglum, P., 302

Vahtera, J., 405

Vaillant, G., 347, 348, 361, 380, 381, 388, 390, 391, 392, 394, 401, 402, 403, 408, 412, 423

Valkonen, T., 405

Vallacher, R., 77

Valliant, G., 392

Valsiner, J., 47, 50, 101, 107

Van Balan, F., 47

Van de Beek, C., 70

Van De Vliert, E., 199

Van den Akker, O. B., 66

Van den Berk, T., 58

Van der Hulst, L. A., 51

Van der Pal-de-Bruin, K. M., 50

Van der Spuy, Z. M., 79

Van der Vegt, G., 199

Van der Wijden, C., 58

Van Dommelen, P., 50

Van Goozen, S. H., 70

Van Gunsteren, H., 23

Van Horn, Y., 31, 33, 34

Van Naarden Braun, K., 304

Van Teijlengen, E. R., 51

Van Zeijl, J., 150

Vandell, D. L., 209, 210

Vandenberg, B., 123, 199

Vander Stoep, A., 304, 305

Vandewater, E., 334

Vandivere, S., 210

Van-Raalte, R., 75

Variable expressivity, 83–84

Vass, K., 339

Vatuk, S., 338

Vaughn, B., 117

Vaughn, E. S., 215

Vekemans, M., 84, 85

Vellas, B., 394

Vellery-Rodot, R. T., 50

Veltkamp, 170

Veltman, M., 131

Ventura, J., 59

Ventura, S. J., 50, 53

Verbrugge, L., 336, 337, 342

Verhaak, C., 64

Verkuyten, M., 191

Verma, S., 252

Very late adulthood
    active learning exercises, 450–451
    activities of daily living (ADL) and, 429
    bereavement issues and, 444–449
    Bina Patel outlives her son case study, 421
    Carmen Ruiz is institutionalized case study, 420
    centenarians and, 427–428
    community relationships and, 434
    cultural construction of, 422–423
    depression and, 433, 434
    divorce and, 445
    emotional expression, and gender in, 448
    end-of-life signs/symptoms and, 441–443
    ethnogerontology, 424
    functional capacity and, 429–430
    gender gap, 428
    grief issues and, 444–449
    historic cultural construction of, 423–427
    housing continuum and, 434–435
    immigration experience and, 445
    instrumental activities of daily living (IADL) and, 429
    intimacy and, 433–434
    lesbianism and, 433
    life course completion and, 449
    living will and, 439
    longevity and, 428
    loss issues and, 444–449
    mastery and, 439
    mourning and, 444–446, 448
    organizational relationships and, 434
    Pete Mullin loses his sister's support case study, 421–422
    power of attorney (POA) and, 439
    primary aging and, 429
    relationships and, 431–434
    resilience and, 429
    secondary aging and, 429–430

sexuality and, 433–434
social work practice and, 450
spirituality and, 435–437
substance use/abuse and, 434
suicide and, 440
theories and models of loss and, 445–447
web resources, 451–452
See also Dying process
Very low birth weight (VLBW) A newborn
weight of less than 1,500 grams (3 pounds,
3 ounces), 80–81
Vicary, J. R., 275
Viktor Spiro, assuming new responsibilities as
he turns 40 case study, 324–325
Villers, M. S., 215
Vinovskis, M. A., 210
Violence
adolescence and, 273–275
community violence, 166–167, 212–215
dating violence, 274–275
domestic violence, 168–169, 212–215
early childhood and, 166–170
middle childhood and, 212–215
teenage pregnancy and, 72, 74
Visser, A., 47
Vissing, Y., 168
Vita, A., 366
Vittinghoff, E., 340
VLBW (very low birth weight), 80–81
Vohr, B. R., 82
Volgt, M., 81
Volker, C., 386
Volker, D. L., 440
Volkmar, F. R., 215
Volling, B., 120
Von Salisch, M., 199
Vuorenkoski, L., 204
Vygotsky, L., 197

Wachs, T. D., 77
Wacker, R. R., 411
Wadensten, B., 385
Wagar, J., 168
Wahl, H., 329
Waite, L. J., 300
Walberg, H., 206
Walberg, H. J., 206
Wald, J., 250
Waldenstrom, U., 53
Waldner, L., 261
Walker, A., 375

Walker, J. J., 78
Walker, L., 148
Walker, S., 151, 201
Wall, S., 118, 132
Wallace, D. H., 433
Wallace, W. H., 79
Wallerstein, I., 28
Wallerstein, J. S., 165, 166
Walling, A. D., 78
Walsh, B., 181
Walsh, D., 51
Walsh, F., 77
Wan, S., 209
Wang, 62, 185
Wang, C., 61
Wang, D., 78
Wang, H., 57
Wang, Y., 142
Ward, R. R., 398
Washington, R. O., 181
Wasserheit, J. N., 266
Waterman, J. M., 206
Waters, E., 118
Waterstone, M., 75
Watkins, D. R., 436
Watson, J., 55
Watt, S., 128
Waxman, B. F., 90
Weaver-Hightower, M., 188
Web resources
adolescence, 280–281
childbearing, 93–94
early childhood, 172–173
infancy/toddlerhood, 134–135
late adulthood, 414–415
life course perspective, 37–38
middle adulthood, 368
middle childhood, 225–226
very late adulthood, 451–452
Weber, M. K., 87
Webster v. Reproductive Health Services, 62
Wechselberger, G., 61
Wegar, K., 215
Wei, E. H., 310, 317
Weibel-Orlando, J., 401
Weinman, M., 131
Weinman, M. L., 310
Weinstein, K. K., 399
Weinstock, H., 265, 266
Weisberg, R. P., 206
Weist, M. D., 198

Weitzman, 235

Welchans, S., 275

Welsh, R., 163

Weltman, S., 127, 247

Wen, W., 64

Wendridge, K., 75

Werner, E., 32, 132

Werner, E. E., 31, 133, 194, 222, 278, 316, 317

Wertheimer, R., 209

Wertsch, J. V., 200

West, J., 365

Westhoff, C., 61

Weston, K., 362

Wethington, E., 330, 349

Weyermann, M., 128

Whaley, R., 121

Wheaton, B., 18, 19

Whitbeck, L., 25

Whitbourne, S., 336, 337, 349, 350,
    366, 386, 389, 390

Whitbourne's identity process
    model, 349–350

White, D., 375

White, D. R., 191

White, J. L., 310

White, L., 357, 358, 359, 394

White, N. R., 293

Whiteman, S., 153

Whiteman, V., 52, 74

Whiting, B. B., 155

Whiting, J. W., 155

WHO (World Health Organization), 58, 62,
    338, 341, 344

WHO Multicentre Growth Reference Study
    Group, 102, 105, 106

Whooley, M., 340

Wichstrom, L., 239

Wickrama, K. A. S., 382, 392

Widmayer, S., 130

Widmer, M. A., 253

Widowhood, 405

Wiener, J. M., 40

Wigert, H., 82

Wilber, K., 22

Wilcox, C., 62

Wilder, L. K., 198, 217, 218

Wilhelm, B., 399, 400

Wilkins-Haug, L., 87

William T. Grant Foundation, Commission on
    Work, Family, and Citizenship, 250

Williams, D. R., 375, 382

Williamson, P., 219

Willis, S., 330, 345, 346

Wilmoth, J. M., 378, 387

Wilson, 163

Wilson, R., 339

Wilson, S., 248, 263

Wingate, J. K., 64

Wingate, M. S., 75

Wink, P., 349

Winkler, I., 393

Winters, K. L., 79

Winters, W. G., 207

Winzer-Serhan, U. H., 70, 81

Wisborg, K., 87

Wiseman, R., 246

Wisner, K., 128

Wittwer-Backofen, U., 81

Wolak, J., 253, 254, 255

Wolchik, S. A., 221

Wolf, T., 298

Wolfe, B., 209, 210

Wolfe, C., 75

Wolfner, G., 170

Wolfram, D., 61

Wolfson, C., 394

Women's Health Initiative (WHI), 340

Wood, E. R., 428

Wood, J., 151

Woods, E. R., 263

Woodson, R., 103

Woodward, L. J., 82, 313

Woody, D. J., 315

Wooldredge, J. D., 90

Woollett, A., 51

Worden, J. W., 446

Work relationships
    adolescence and, 251
    ethnicity issues and, 314–315
    gender and, 251–253, 402
    immigrant workers and, 313–314
    late adulthood and, 401–404
    middle adulthood and, 362–365
    race and, 304
    role changes of workers and, 314
    young adulthood and, 312–315

World Health Organization (WHO), 59, 338,
    341, 344

Wortman, C., 446, 447

Wright, W. C., 65, 66

Wrigley, E., 26

Wu, F. C., 61

Wun, C., 199
Wyman, P. A., 198

Xie, H., 310
Xiong, X., 48

Yamaguchi, K., 302
Yeargin-Allsopp, M., 304
Yeo, S., 47
Young, D. S., 90
Young, J. P., 189
Young, K. R., 198, 217, 218
Young, M. E., 89
Young adulthood
    active learning exercises, 318
    Ben's new environment case study, 286–287
    Carla's transition to parenthood case study,
        287–288
    cognitive development and, 298–299
    community assets and, 312
    cultural construction of, 294–295
    default individualization and, 293
    definition of, 288–290
    developmental individualization and, 293
    emerging adulthood and, 292–296
    employment and, 309–315
    Erikson's psychosocial theory and, 290
    ethical issues in, 299
    ethnicity issues, 314–315
    fictive kin and, 310
    gender issues and, 294, 301, 310
    homosexuality and, 307–309
    human capital and, 312
    identity development and, 301–302
    immigrant worker relationships and, 313–314
    immigration experience and, 305, 312, 313–314
    intimacy vs. isolation and, 290
    Jerome's break from school case study, 286
    Levinson's theory of life structure and, 291
    mentoring relationships and, 311
    moral development, 298–299
    multigenerational families and, 295–296
    novice phase and, 291
    physical functioning and, 296–298
    psychological self and, 298–302
    race and, 314–315
    relationship development and, 305–309
    religious beliefs and, 299, 301
    risk/preventive factors and, 316–317
    role changes of workers and, 314
    romantic love relationships and, 306–30

    self-efficacy and, 315
    sexual orientation, and, 307–308
    social development/functioning and, 302–317
    spirituality and, 299–301
    substance use/abuse and, 303, 305, 313
    synthetic-conventional faith and, 300
    transitions into parenthood and, 309–311
    vulnerable youth, making transition to
        adulthood, 303
    web resources, 318–319
    work relationships and, 312–315
    See also Adolescence
Young adults
    bonding and, 300
Younoszai, B., 449
Youth Risk Behavior Survey (YRBS),
    235, 262, 274
Yu, C. K., 79
Yu, V. Y. H., 83

Zacur, H., 64
Zand, D., 307, 308
Zaslow, M., 210
Zaslow, M. J., 310, 311
Zea, M. C., 212
Zeisel, J., 83, 108
Zeiss, A. M., 434
Zellman, G. L., 206
Zhang, Q., 142
Zheng, Y., 254
Ziel, H., 339
Zigler, E., 108, 122
Zimprich, D., 345
Ziolko, M. E., 219
Zipper, I., 124, 158
Zone of proximal development According to
    Vygotsky, the theoretical space between the
    child's current developmental level (or
    performance) and the child's potential
    level (or performance) if given access to
    appropriate models and developmental
    experiences in the social environment, 197
Zonta, L., 13
Zucker, K., 103, 153
Zue-rong, L., 18
Zuniga, M., 233
Zunzunegui, M., 397
Zuravin, S., 132
Zutlevics, T., 66
Zwi, A., 166
Zygote A fertilized ovum cell, 68

ABOUT THE AUTHOR

 **Elizabeth D. Hutchison,** MSW, PhD, received her MSW from the George Warren Brown School of Social Work and PhD from the University at Albany. She is currently an Associate Professor in the School of Social Work at Virginia Commonwealth University, Northern Virginia Program, where she teaches courses in human behavior and the social environment, social work and social justice, and child and family policy, along with serving as field practicum liaison. She has been a social worker in health, mental health, aging, and child and family welfare settings. She is committed to providing social workers with comprehensive, current, and useful frameworks for thinking about human behavior. Her other research interests focus on child and family welfare.

ABOUT THE CONTRIBUTORS

Suzanne M. Baldwin, PhD, LCSW, MSW, BSN, RN, received her PhD in social work from the School of Social Work at Virginia Commonwealth University. She works as a clinical social worker in private practice with families and spent almost two decades working as a clinical nurse specialist in newborn intensive care. Her major areas of interest are health social work and family systems. She has taught human behavior, practice, communications, and research courses at Old Dominion University and at the School of Social Work at Virginia Commonwealth University.

Leanne Charlesworth, LMSW, PhD, is Assistant Professor in the Department of Social Work at Nazareth College of Rochester. She has practiced within child welfare systems and her areas of service and research interest include poverty and child and family well-being. She has taught human behavior and research at the undergraduate and graduate levels.

Marcia P. Harrigan, MSW, PhD, is Associate Professor and Associate Dean of Student and Academic Affairs in the School of Social Work at Virginia Commonwealth University. She has practiced in child welfare, juvenile justice, and mental health. Her major areas of interest are nontraditional family structures, family assessment, multigenerational households, and long-distance family caregiving. She has taught human behavior and practice courses.

Lesley Hewitt, BSc, BsocWk (Hons), MSW, GCHE, is the undergraduate coordinator of distance education programs in the Department of Social Work, Monash University, Melbourne, Australia. Her practice experience includes working in sexual assault services and child protection. She teaches human development, group work, and aged care at both undergraduate and post graduate levels. Her research interests include family violence and sexual assault, and social work education.

Pamela J. Kovacs, MSW, PhD, is Associate Professor in the School of Social Work at Virginia Commonwealth University. Her practice experience includes work with individuals, families, and groups in oncology, hospice, and mental health settings. Her major areas of interest are HIV/AIDS, hospice and palliative care, volunteerism, caregiving, and preparing social workers for health care and other settings serving older adults. She teaches clinical practice, social work practice and health care, qualitative research, and additionally serves as a field liaison.

Peter Maramaldi, CSW, MPH, PhD, is Associate Professor at Simmons School of Social Work, Senior Social Work Scientist at the Massachusetts General Hospital in Boston, and a Hartford Faculty Scholar and National Mentor in Gerontology. His current research focuses on behavioral oncology and aging. He worked in a broad range of practice settings for more than 25 years in New York City, and has since taught courses at Simmons in practice, health policy, and research methodology in social work. At Harvard Medical School, he has taught interviewing and interdisciplinary collaboration courses.

Holly C. Matto, MSW, PhD, LCSW-C, is Assistant Professor in the School of Social Work at Virginia Commonwealth University. Her research focuses on substance abuse assessment and treatment. She has taught courses in human behavior, social work practice, art therapy in social work practice, and research methodology.

Susan Ainsley McCarter, MS, MSW, PhD, lives in Charlotte, North Carolina. She has worked as a juvenile probation officer; mental health counselor for children, adolescents, and families; AmeriCorps coordinator; mentor trainer; and mother. Her current research interest is minority overrepresentation in the juvenile justice system. She has taught human behavior, social policy, and sociology courses at both the undergraduate and graduate levels.

Michael Melendez, LICSW, MSW, PhD, is Associate Professor and Chair of the Clinical Practice Sequence at Simmons College School of Social Work, and Council on Social Work Education Gero-Institute Fellow. Prior to his appointment at Simmons College, he was senior social worker at the Judge Baker Child Guidance Center in Boston, Massachusetts. He also maintained a private practice and consulted to organizations, agencies, and individuals on culturally responsive treatment. Current research interests focus on culturally competent social work practice, addictions, HIV/AIDS, and aging.

Derek Morch, BS, QMHP, is an MSW student in the School of Social Work at Virginia Commonwealth University. He has worked in a variety of settings as a clinical case manager, providing treatment to adults with serious mental illness. His areas of interest include community-based treatment, mental health parity, and ongoing practice with multicultural populations.

Matthias J. Naleppa, MSW, PhD, is Associate Professor in the School of Social Work at Virginia Commonwealth University and a Hartford Geriatric Social Work Scholar. His research focuses on social work with elderly clients, specifically on applying the task-centered model to case management and gerontological practice. He has taught courses in human behavior, social work practice, and research methodology at the University at Albany, Marywood University, and Virginia Commonwealth University.

Pamela Viggiani, MSW, PhD, is Adjunct Professor in the Department of Social Work Department at Nazareth College of Rochester. Her research focuses on poverty and pedagogy. She has worked in schools with at-risk children and has served as the legislative liaison for the National Association of Social Workers, New York State Chapter. She also has served as an evaluator and consultant for several grants funding public child welfare professionalization. She teaches courses in social justice, social advocacy, diversity, policy, and social work methods.

Jim Wood, EdD, is a 33-year veteran in teaching and administration at all levels of public schools and is currently Associate Professor of Childhood Education at the Ralph C. Wilson, Jr. School of Education at St. John Fisher College in Rochester, New York. His areas of interest include social justice education, integrated school environments, achievement gap issues, and diverse school cultures.

David Woody, III, PhD, LCSW, is currently Director of Programs at Catholic Charities, Diocese of Ft. Worth, Inc. After several years in academia at the University of Texas at Arlington and Baylor University, Dr. Woody has returned to work in the local community, focused on economic self-sufficiency, clinical counseling for those in poverty, and establishing low-cost medical homes for those without health care insurance. In addition to issues related to poverty, Dr. Woody's major areas of interest include research exploring strengths of African American single mothers, and initiatives enhancing the significance of fatherhood in the African American community.

Debra J. Woody, PhD, LMSW, is Associate Professor in the School of Social Work at the University of Texas at Arlington. Her areas of research and practice interests focus upon child and family issues related to drug and alcohol use. She is the principal investigator for several grants that support a drug and alcohol intervention program called New Connections, providing services to mothers and their drug-exposed infants and toddlers. She currently teaches both undergraduate and graduate research and practice courses.

Maria E. Zuniga, MSW, PhD, is Professor Emeritus from the School of Social Work at San Diego State University, where she taught for 16 years, with an additional 11 years at Sacramento State University. Along with human behavior courses, Dr. Zuniga's areas of focus were direct practice, gerontological practice, and practice with multicultural populations, in particular practice with Latinos. She was also a member of the board of directors of the Council on Social Work Education (CSWE) and helped to develop a CSWE-sponsored conference on Cultural Competence held at the University of Michigan in 1999. She is a consultant on cultural competence for local, state, and national agencies and publishing houses.

PHOTO CREDITS

Chapter 1

Photo 1.1: © Kristy-Anne Glubish/Design Pics/Corbis; Photos 1.2 & 1.3: © Istockphoto.com

Chapter 2

Photo 2.1: © Istockphoto.com; Photo 2.2: © Rune Hellestad/Corbis; Photo 2.3: © Istockphoto.com

Chapter 3

Photos 3.1, 3.2, & 3.3: © Istockphoto.com

Chapter 4

Photos 4.1 & 4.2: © Istockphoto.com; Photo 4.3: © Kelly Redinger/Design Pics/Corbis; Photo 4.4: © Istockphoto.com

Chapter 5

Photos 5.1, 5.2, & 5.3: © Istockphoto.com

Chapter 6

Photo 6.1: © Don Hammond/Design Pics/Corbis; Photos 6.2, 6.3, 6.4, & 6.5: © Istockphoto.com

Chapter 7

Photo 7.1: © Istockphoto.com; Photo 7.2: © Corbis; Photo 7.3: Copyright © 1995–2006 City of Alexandria, Virginia; Photo 7.4: © Istockphoto.com

Chapter 8

Photo 8.1: © Istockphoto.com; Photo 8.2: © Istockphoto.com; Photo 8.3: © Randy Faris/Corbis; Photo 8.4: © Istockphoto.com

Chapter 9

Photo 9.1a & b, 9.2, & 9.3: © Istockphoto.com; Photo 9.4: © Stephen Beaudet/zefa/Corbis

Chapter 10

Photo 10.1: © Chris Rank/Corbis; Photo 10.2: Copyright © 2007 State of Utah; Photos 10.3, 10.4, & 10.5: © Istockphoto.com